The Handbook of

CORPORATE

Company Performance

EARNINGS

and Stock Market Valuation

ANALYSIS

Brian R. Bruce ■ **Charles B. Epstein**

PROBUS PUBLISHING COMPANY
Chicago, Illinois
Cambridge, England

ISBN 1-55738-540-8

Printed in the United States of America

BB

1 2 3 4 5 6 7 8 9 0

To Susan, Robert, and Jacqueline Bruce.
Brian R. Bruce

To my parents.
Charles B. Epstein

Contents

List of Contributors

Robert D. Arnott
Chief Executive Officer
First Quadrant

Lawrence D. Brown, Ph.D.
Samuel P. Carpen Professor of Accounting
Jacobs Management Center
State University of New York at Buffalo

Stanley C. Chamberlin
Chairman
Chamberlin and Pearson Research
   Associates, Inc.

T. Daniel Coggin, Ph.D.
Director of Research
Virginia Retirement System

John G. Cragg, Ph.D.
Professor of Economics
University of British Columbia

Wayne E. Daniel
President
Daniel Consulting

Werner F. M. De Bondt, Ph.D.
Frank Graner Professor of Investment
   Management
University of Wisconsin-Madison

Edwin J. Elton, Ph.D.
Nomura Professor of Finance
New York University

Gail E. Farrelly, Ph.D.
Associate Professor of Accounting
Faculty of Management
Rutgers University

Dov Fried, Ph.D.
Professor of Accounting
New York University

Dan Givoly, Ph.D.
Professor of Accounting Information
   Systems
J.L. Kellogg Graduate School of
   Management
Northwestern University

Paul A. Griffin, Ph.D.
Professor of Accounting and Management
University of California-Davis

David A. Goodman

Martin J. Gruber, Ph.D.
Nomura Professor of Finance
New York University

John B. Guerard, Jr.
Vice President
Daiwa Securities Trust Co.

Mustafa Gultekin, Ph.D.
Associate Professor of Finance
Kenan-Flagler Business School
University of North Carolina

Robert L. Hagerman, Ph.D.
Professor of Accounting and Finance
State University of New York at Buffalo

Eugene H. Hawkins
President
Investment Analytics

John E. Hunter, Ph.D.
Distinguished Professor of Industrial
   Psychology
Michigan State University

William E. Jacques
Partner and Chief Investment Officer
Martingale Asset Management

Edward F. Keon, Jr.
Vice President
I/B/E/S Inc.

Robert C. Klemkosky, Ph.D.
Fred T. Greene Professor of Finance
Indiana University

Josef Lakonishok, Ph.D.
William G. Karnes Professor of Finance
University of Illinois at Urbana-Champaign

Burton G. Malkiel, Ph.D.
Chemical Bank Chairman's Professor
   of Economics
Princeton University

William P. Miller
Portfolio Manager
IDS Financial Services

John W. Peavy III, Ph.D.
Chairman
Founders Trust Co.

Donald J. Peters
Vice President
T. Rowe Price Associates

Donna R. Philbrick, Ph.D.
Associate Professor of Accounting
Portland State University

William R. Reichenstein, Ph.D.
The Pat and Thomas R. Powers Chair
   in Investment Management
Baylor University

William E. Ricks, Ph.D.
Director of Accounting Research
Barr Rosenberg Investment Management

Dan Rie
Senior Vice President
Colonial Management Assoc.

Scott E. Stickel, Ph.D.
Joseph Markmann Accounting Alumni
   Endowed Chair
La Salle University

Bernell K. Stone, Ph.D.
Harold F. Silver Professor of Finance
The Marriott School of Management
Brigham Young University

Richard H. Thaler, Ph.D.
Henrietta Johnson Louis Professor of
   Economics
Cornell University

Langdon B. Wheeler, CFA
President
Numeric Investors L.P.

Leonard Zacks, Ph.D.
President
Zacks Investment Research, Inc.

Mark E. Zmijewski, Ph.D.
Professor of Accounting
Graduate School of Business
University of Chicago

Preface

The origins for this book stemmed from some of the major changes which have swept over the investment analysis business: the introduction of programs to objectively measure analyst recommendations; the increasing availability of analyst revisions via electronic media; and most importantly, the tremendous growth in the amount of investment analyst research data being produced on a daily basis.

Indeed, due to the sheer volume of readily available research, the analyst community needs to make the distinction between data and information in order to improve their corporate earnings forecasting function. This distinction is not sublime. Information is to data what statesmenship is to politics. By evaluating, selecting and including the papers in this volume, our intention was to distill the best works of academics and practitioners in a single volume.

While this is an admittedly ambitious task, we attempted to work out a system which imposed some parameters. First, we asked the following individuals to serve as judges and make their recommendations for papers to be included in this volume.

Robert D. Arnott, First Quadrant
William Reichenstein, Baylor University
Don Peters, T. Rowe Price
Ed Keon, I/B/E/S, Inc.

The criteria used in selecting these papers was straightforward: papers could be either published or unpublished over the past 25-year period. Jurors submitted a list of the papers which they felt should be included. Based on polling among the jury and ourselves, the final papers were selected for inclusion in this volume. This process resulted in 25 papers being selected. The papers are grouped into four categories. While the scope of this search process was worldwide, because the U.S. is considered to have produced the broadest and most in-depth corporate earnings analysis research, most of the papers originally appeared in U.S. journals.

We would like to thank all the jurors who participated in the selection process, and the authors and journal publishers of the selected papers who agreed that their works could be reprinted in this volume. Chuck would also like to thank Vikas Saluguti of the Investment Technology Group (ITG), Inc., New York, who provided the original encouragement to pursue this project. Brian would like to thank Ed Keon and the team at I/B/E/S for their support throughout this process.

Lastly, because of the sheer scope of this project and its inherently subjective nature, we take all responsibility for any articles in this highly critical area which may have been omitted. Our intention was to bring together the best papers to help the next generation of analysts and portfolio managers understand from whence they came. We can only hope that we have succeeded.

Section 1:
In the Beginning

Chapter 1

Twenty-Five Years of Observation

Edward F. Keon, Jr.
Vice President
I/B/E/S Inc.

Earnings expectations drive equity markets. Even a casual reader of the financial press will note the many stories each day that explain stock price movements as due to changes in respected analysts' forecasts or due to earnings reports different from analysts' expectations. The papers in this book help any investor understand earnings expectations and how to profit by using them.

In 1968, Cragg and Malkiel observed, "For years, economists have emphasized the importance of expectations . . . The price of a share (of common stock) is—or should be—determined primarily by investors' current expectations about the future values of variables that measure the relevant aspects of corporations' performance and profitability, particularly the anticipated growth rate of earnings per share . . . The extent of agreement on the significance of expectations is almost matched, however, by the paucity of data that can be considered even reasonable proxies for these forecasts . . . ."

This pioneering work leads this book because it demonstrates that researchers have wrestled with the problem of measuring and determining the role of expectations in equity prices for several decades. It is only in the past 20 years, however, that the problem of the "paucity of data" has been overcome.

In 1971, I/B/E/S Inc. (then a part of the brokerage firm, Lynch, Jones & Ryan) began collecting the earnings forecasts of institutional equity analysts and organizing this information into a database. For the first several years, this work was primarily a convenience for customers who did not want to wade through reams of printed brokerage reports to obtain earnings forecasts. In the mid 1970s, however, users noticed some interesting relationships between analysts' forecasts and stock price movements. I/B/E/S began an active program of supporting professional research (a program that continues today), and in the last 15 years or so, a remarkable set of papers has clearly established the investment value of earnings expectations data.

In 1981, Zacks Investment Research began providing another source of earnings forecasts, which later also expanded to include the recommendations made by individual analysts. By the 1990s, electronic vendors and non-U.S. firms also began to provide EPS data.

In their seminal paper "Expectations and Share Prices," Elton, Gruber, and Gultekin established two key facts:

- Analysts' earnings expectations are a more accurate forecast of corporate earnings than extrapolations of historical earnings or managements' forecasts.

- Knowing the future course of earnings expectations would be more profitable for investors than knowing actual future earnings.

Hawkins, Chamberlin, and Daniel demonstrated a practical strategy to use changes in expectations to boost portfolio returns. They found that firms with the greatest monthly increases in consensus EPS forecasts tend to significantly outperform the market for six months.

Hagin and Brown's work established earnings surprise as a practical investment strategy, a technique that repeated studies show continues to generate excess returns today.

In other papers, you'll read about the "torpedo effect," in which a negative earnings surprise sinks high P/E stock; and the "cock-roach theory," in which if you see one earnings surprise, others are likely lurking.

Peavy and Goodman show that the use of forward P/E ratios helps identify attractive low P/E stocks. Malkiel shows that the distribution of analysts forecasts may be a useful proxy for expected risk.

Perhaps the most promising area of new research is the international arena. Jacques and Rie offer an initial report from the front lines, and the results look promising.

Earnings expectations information continues to offer practical value to investors regardless of investment style. As this book demonstrates, these strategies can be used by both quants and fundamental managers, whose only other common bond may be a desire to increase portfolio returns.

Chapter 2

The Consensus and Accuracy of Some Predictions of the Growth of Corporate Earnings[*]

John G. Cragg, Ph.D.
Professor of Economics
University of British Columbia

Burton G. Malkiel, Ph.D.
Chemical Bank Chairman's Professor of Economics
Princeton University

For years, economists have emphasized the importance of expectations in a variety of problems.[1] The extent of agreement on the significance of expectations is almost matched, however, by the paucity of data that can be considered even reasonable proxies for these forecasts. One area in which expectations are highly important is the valuation of the common stock of a corporation. The price of a share is—or should be—determined primarily by investors' current expectations about the future values of variables that measure the relevant aspects of corporations' performance and profitability, particularly the anticipated growth rate of earnings per share.[2] This theoretical emphasis is matched by efforts in the financial community where security analysts spend considerable effort in forecasting the future earnings of companies they study. These forecasts are of particular interest because one can observe divergence of opinion among different individuals dealing with the same quantities. This paper is devoted to the analysis of a small sample of such predictions and certain related variables obtained from financial houses.[3]

I. Nature and Sources of Data

The principal data used in this study consisted of figures representing the expected growth of earnings per share for 185 corporations[4] as of the end of 1962 and 1963. These data were collected from five investment firms. The participants were recruited through requests to two organizations. One was a group of firms who used computers for financial analysis and who met periodically to discuss mutual problems, the other was the New York Society of Financial Analysts. As a result, eleven firms agreed to

*This research was supported by the Institute for Quantitative Research in Finance, the National Science Foundation, and the Graduate School of Business, University of Chicago. We are indebted to Paul Cootner for helpful comments.

Reprinted with permission from *The Journal of Finance*, Vol. XXIII, No. 1, March, 1968, pgs. 67-84.

participate in the proposed study. From the original eleven, however, only five were able to supply comparable sets of long-term earnings forecasts for use in this study.[5] Even among these five, there was not complete overlap in the corporations for which predictions were available. One of them had no data for 1962. For only two were data available for the full set of 185 companies.

Of the five participating firms, two are large New York City banks heavily involved in trust management, one is an investment banker and investment adviser doing mainly an institutional brokerage business, one is a mutual fund manager, and the remaining firm does a general brokerage and investment advisory business. We would not argue that these estimates give an accurate picture of general market expectations. It would, however, seem reasonable to suggest that they are representative of opinions of some of the largest professional investment institutions and that they may not be wholly unrepresentative of more general expectations. Since investors consult professional investment institutions in forming their own expectations, individuals' expectations may be strongly influenced—and so reflect—those of their advisers.[6] Also, insofar as investors follow the same sorts of procedures as those used by security analysts in forming expectations, the investors' expectations would resemble those of the analysts. It should be noted, however, that security analysts are not limited to published data in forming their expectations. They frequently visit the companies they study and discuss the corporations' prospects with their executives.

Each growth-rate figure was reported as an average annual rate of growth expected to occur in the next five years. At first thought, such a rate of growth depends on what earnings are expected to be in five years' time and on the base-year earnings figures. However, this dependence need not be very great if the growth rate is regarded more as a parameter of the process determining earnings than as

an arithmetic quantity linking the current value to the expected future value. Discussion with the suppliers of the data indicated that all firms were attempting to predict the same future figure, the long-run average (normalized) earnings level, abstracting from cyclical or special circumstances. The bases used were less clear. Some firms explicitly used their estimates of normalized earnings during the year in which the prediction was made. Others provided different figures as bases: In one case, the firm estimated actual earnings, in another a prediction of earnings four years in the future was furnished. These differences did not seem to be reflected in the growth rates, however, since attempts to adjust the rates for differences in base figures introduced rather than removed disparities among the predictions.

The growth rates were given as single numbers for each corporation. No indication was provided of the confidence with which these point estimates were held. One firm did provide an instability index of earnings, which represented a measure of the past variability of earnings (around trend) adjusted by the security analyst to indicate potential future variability. Moreover, two firms provided quality ratings, which classified companies into three or four quality categories.

Two of the firms provided estimates of past growth rates as well as predictions. The figures represented perceived growth over the past 8-10 years, the past 4-5 years, the past 6 years, and the last year. It may seem unnecessary to rely on the participating firms for estimates of historic growth rates. However, the past growth of a company's earnings is not, in any meaningful sense, a well-defined concept. Earnings—being basically a small difference between two large quantities—can exhibit large year-to-year fluctuations. They also can be negative, which creates problems for most mechanical calculations. In addition, the accounting definition of earnings is not an exact conformity with the economically relevant concept of profits or return on investors' capital. For these reasons, calculated growth rates are sensitive to the particular method employed and the period chosen for the calculation. Consequently, such calculations may be a poor reflection of what growth is generally considered to have been, and may not be useful in assessing the past performance of corporations. Furthermore, it may be supposed that in assessing security analysts' predictions of growth, their own estimates of past growth are more likely to be relevant than objectively calculated rates. The extent of agreement among the two types of measures is among the subjects considered in the next section.

Our participating firms also supplied an industrial classification. While other classifications are available, the concept of industry is not really precise enough to get a fixed, unquestionable assignment of corporations to industries. Particular problems are presented by conglomerate companies. Perceived industry may be more relevant than any other grouping when investigating anticipations. The classification we use represents a consensus about industry among our participants. Where disagreements occurred (as was often the case with conglomerates), the corporation was simply classified as "miscellaneous." The classification represented considerable aggregation over finer classifications and only eight industries were distinguished. These were:

1) Electricals and Electronics
2) Electric Utilities
3) Metals
4) Oils
5) Drugs and Specialty Chemicals
6) Foods and Stores
7) "Cyclical"—including companies such as automobile and aircraft manufacturers and meat packers
8) "Miscellaneous"

II. Agreement Among Predictors

The agreement among the growth-rate projections is described and summarized in this sec-

tion. In the course of this description, the extent of agreement about base-earnings figures and the closeness of the projections to past, perceived, and calculated growth rates are also considered.

A. Comparisons of Predictions of Future Growth Rates

The extent of agreement among the predictors about future growth rates is summarized in Exhibit 1. Of the five predictors, the correlations among predictors A, B, C, and E were all roughly of the same orders of magnitude.[7] Predictor D showed some tendency toward lower agreement. (Predictor D also had the highest average-growth forecast and standard deviation for the companies for which it and others made forecasts.) Overall agreement among the predictors is further summarized in the second and third parts of Exhibit 1, which show the values of Kendall's coefficient of concordance and the proportion of total variance of the predictions that can be accounted for by differences in the mean prediction among companies.[8] It may be remarked that the entries in Exhibit 1 are based on different numbers of observations. In each case, we used the maximum number of observations (companies) for which a comparison could be made. The impressions to be gained from Exhibit 1 would be little changed, however, by basing all calculations only on the set for which all predictors provided data.

Though Exhibit 1 suggests considerable agreement, the lack of agreement it also reveals can hardly be considered negligible. In addition to the lack of correlation, there were also some systematic differences among the predictors. For the matched set of observations, the means and the standard deviations were of roughly the same sizes. However, the differences among the central tendencies were significant according to both parametric and nonparametric tests.

Exhibit 1 Agreement Among Growth-Rate Predictions*

I. Correlation Coefficients
(Simple correlations in lower left portion, Spearman rank correlations in upper right portion)

		1962						1963		
	A	**B**	**C**	**D**		**A**	**B**	**C**	**D**	**E**
A	1.000	.768	.751	.388	**A**	1.000	.795	.717	.374	.709
B	.840	1.000	.728	.597	**B**	.832	1.000	.760	.518	.821
C	.889	.819	1.000	.690	**C**	.854	.764	1.000	.750	.746
D	.563	.621	.848	1.000	**D**	.537	.567	.898	1.000	.450
					E	.827	.835	.889	.704	1.000

II. Kendall's Coefficient of Concordance for Ranks of Companies by Different Predictors

Predictors	(A,B,C)	(A,B,D)	(A,B,C,D)	(A,B,C,D,E)
1962	.82	.73	.78	
1963	.83	.71	.81	.79

III. Proportions of Total Variance Due to Variance in Average Predictions

Predictors	(A,B,C)	(A,B,D)	(A,B,C,D)	(A,B,C,D,E)
1962	.87	.70	.79	
1963	.85	.68	.83	.87

* The numbers of observations on which this exhibit and other exhibits are based varies between cells. For the correlations, the numbers of observations are reported below:

		1962				1963		
	A	**B**	**C**		**A**	**B**	**C**	**D**
B	185			**B**	185			
C	60	60		**C**	62	62		
D	178	178	58	**D**	182	182	61	
				E	125	125	39	124

For other comparisons, the number of observations is the minimum of the numbers of observations used to compute the correlations.

B. Analysis of Predictions Within Industrial Classifications

One might suspect that the correlations among the predictors reflect little more than consensus about the industries that are expected to grow most rapidly rather than agreement about the relative rates of growth of firms within industries. This possibility was investigated by decomposing the correlation coefficients into two parts, one due to correlation within industries (r_w) and one due to correlation among the industry means (r_a).

$$r = r_w + r_a$$

where

$$r_w = \frac{\sum_{j=1}^{J} \sum_{i=1}^{N_j} (x_{ij} - \bar{x}_j)(y_{ij} - \bar{y}_j)}{\sqrt{\sum_{j=1}^{J} \sum_{i=1}^{N_j} (x_{ij} - \bar{x})^2 \sum_{j=1}^{J} \sum_{i=1}^{N_j} (y_{ij} - \bar{y})^2}}$$

and

$$r_a = \frac{\sum_{j=1}^{J} N_j (\bar{x}_j - \bar{x})(\bar{y}_j - \bar{y})}{\sqrt{\sum_{j=1}^{J} \sum_{i=1}^{N_j} (x_{ij} - \bar{x})^2 \sum_{j=1}^{J} \sum_{i=1}^{N_j} (y_{ij} - \bar{y})^2}}$$

Exhibit 2 Industrial Classification and Agreement Among Predictors

I. Values of r_a

	1962 A	1962 B	1962 C		1963 A	1963 B	1963 C	1963 D
B	.299			B	.305			
C	.285	.323		C	.230	.315		
D	.090	.184	.300	D	.057	.137	.317	
				E	.266	.348	.366	.194

II. Partial Correlations Holding Industrial Classification Constant

	1962 A	1962 B	1962 C		1963 A	1963 B	1963 C	1963 D
B	.799			B	.786			
C	.861	.760		C	.838	.690		
D	.656	.665	.887	D	.657	.650	.861	
				E	.828	.790	.897	.777

with

x_{ij}, y_{ij} being the ith observations in the jth class (industry),

N_j being the number of observations in the jth class,

J being the number of classes,

$\bar{x}_j, \bar{y}_j$ being the averages within the classes, and

$\bar{x}, \bar{y}$ being the over-all averages.

This decomposition indicated that agreement concerning industry growth rates is not the major factor accounting for the correlations among the forecasts. The first part of Exhibit 2 shows the values of r_a using the industrial classification obtained from the participating firms. As comparison with Exhibit 1 shows, only a small part of the correlations among the predictions are due to correlations among the industry means. Further light can be shed on this question by calculating the partial correlations between the predictions, holding industry classification constant. The second panel of Exhibit 2 reveals that these partial correlations tended to be only slightly less than the simple correlations and, in the case of Predictor D, the partial correlations were actually higher.

It is also interesting to examine the extent to which the correlations among predictors' forecasts varied over the different industry groups. This should indicate whether certain industry groups are more difficult to forecast in an *ex ante* sense. The correlations among forecasters tended to be lowest in the oil and cyclical industry groups, and highest for electric utility companies. These differences were significant for all pairs of predictions considered. Ranking the correlations over industries, and then comparing these ranks among pairs of predictors, showed substantial concordance over the ordering of the correlations.[9]

C. Comparisons of Predictions and Past Growth Rates

The extent of agreement among the predictors can usefully be evaluated by comparisons of the predicted growth rates with earlier predictions and with the past growth rates of earnings. The correlations of the 1963 predictions with the 1962 ones were: .94, .95, .96, and .88 for predictors A through D respectively. All of these are considerably higher than the correlations of the predictions with each other. On the other hand, changes in expected

Exhibit 3 Predictions and Past Growth Rates*
(Correlations of Predicted with Past Growth Rates)

	1962				1963				
	A	B	C	D	A	B	C	D	E
g_{p1}	.78	.68	.75	.41	.85	.73	.84	.56	.67
g_{p2}	.75	.67	.72	.51	.79	.69	.80	.58	.76
g_{p3}	.77	.71	.82	.61	.75	.72	.79	.70	.74
g_{p4}	.34	.37	.59	.44	.33	.45	.70	.75	.58
g_{c1}	.55	.46	.65	.32	.63	.52	.61	.30	.58
g_{c2}	.67	.60	.68	.18	.72	.58	.73	.20	.56
g_{c3}	.75	.63	.73	.17	.79	.66	.76	.17	.57
g_{c4}	.82	.68	.79	.24	.83	.69	.79	.29	.60

* g_{p1} is 8-10 year historic growth rate supplied by A g_{c1} is log-regression trend fitted to last 4 years
   g_{p2} is 4-5 year historic growth rate supplied by A g_{c2} is log-regression trend fitted to last 6 years
   g_{p3} is 6 year historic growth rate supplied by D g_{c3} is log-regression trend fitted to last 8 years
   g_{p4} is preceding 1 year growth rate supplied by D g_{c4} is log-regression trend fitted to last 10 years

growth rates were not highly correlated among predictors.[10]

Correlations of the predictions with eight past growth figures are shown in Exhibit 3. Four of these past growth rates were supplied by the participating firms and represent the firms' perceptions of the growth of earnings per share that had occurred in different preceding periods. The others were calculated as the coefficient in the regression of the logarithms of earnings per share on time over the past 4, 6, 8, and 10 years. These correlations generally are

not much lower than those found in comparing the predictions with each other. Among the perceived past growth rates, the correlations are apt to be lowest with the growth rates over the most recent year. With the calculated growth rates, there was a tendency for the correlations to increase with the length of period over which the calculations were made.[11]

These comparisons of past with predicted growth rates suggest that the apparent agreement among the predictors may reflect little more than use by all of them of the historic

Exhibit 4 Partial Correlations of Predictions Holding Past Growth Rates Constant

	1962				1963			
	A	B	C		A	B	C	D
B	.49			B	.49			
C	.49	.18		C	.25	.03		
D	.35	.39	.22	D	.56	.46	.40	
				E	.56	.62	−.11	.51

Numbers of Observations

	1962				1963			
	A	B	C		A	B	C	D
B	111			B	112			
C	49	49		C	50	50		
D	111	111	49	D	112	112	50	
				E	78	78	36	78

figures. In investigating this possibility, the partial correlations among the predictions, holding constant past perceived growth rates, holding constant past calculated growth rates, and holding both sets constant were calculated. The first two sets of partial correlations were not much smaller than the simple correlations. Holding both sets constant produced the partial correlations shown in Exhibit 4. These are considerably smaller than the simple correlations, though all but the four smallest entries would be significant beyond the .05 level. Thus, while a substantial part of the agreement among predictors appears to result from their use of historic growth figures, there is also evidence that security analysts tend to make similar adjustments to the past growth rates.[12]

Examination of the correlations among past growth rates helps both to evaluate the correlations among the predictions and to indicate the sensitivity of measurements of growth rates to the methods by which they were calculated. Exhibit 5 presents correlations between 13 such past growth rates for our 1962 data. The correlations between the different measures of past growth are fairly low. When exactly the same data are used in the calculations, however, the correlations among the growth rates calculated by different methods are relatively high, though probably not so high that the choice of method of calculation would be a matter of no importance. Finally, the perceived growth rates furnished by the security firms tend to be more highly correlated with the growth rates calculated over longer periods. The increase in correlation coefficients did not continue, however, when calculations over more than ten years were made and, as shown in Exhibit 5, it stopped before ten years in some cases. Correlations for other periods and for the 1963 data were of about the same magnitude as those in Exhibit 5.

D. Comparisons of Predictions with Price-Earnings Ratios

Finally, we may examine the extent of agreement among predictors by comparing their forecasts with the price-earnings ratios of the corresponding securities. By utilizing a nor-

Exhibit 5   Past Growth Correlations, 1962*

	g_{p1}	g_{p2}	g_{p3}	g_{p4}	g_{c1}	g_{c2}	g_{c3}	g_{c4}	g_{c5}	g_{c6}	g_{c7}	g_{c8}
g_{p2}	.70											
g_{p3}	.82	.87										
g_{p4}	.49	.39	.37									
g_{c1}	.34	.47	.48	.15								
g_{c2}	.68	.74	.76	.05	.62							
g_{c3}	.81	.89	.97	.15	.49	.90						
g_{c4}	.93	.80	.87	.27	.41	.75	.93					
g_{c5}	.14	.19	.25	.39	.38	.24	.16	.15				
g_{c6}	.34	.46	.47	.14	.96	.59	.45	.37	.53			
g_{c7}	.92	.67	.78	.32	.48	.67	.83	.95	.33	.46		
g_{c8}	.36	.56	.49	.23	.99	.63	.50	.43	.40	.90	.51	
g_{c9}	.87	.75	.88	.18	.46	.77	.93	.99	.17	.40	.91	.43

* g_{p1} – g_{p4}, g_{c1} – g_{c4} as defined in footnote to Exhibit 3

  g_{c5} is 1 year growth rate calculated from first differences of logarithm

  g_{c6} is 4 year growth rate calculated from average of first differences of logs

  g_{c7} is 10 year growth rate calculated from average of first differences of logs

  g_{c8} is 4 year growth rate calculated from regression of earnings on time

  g_{c9} is 10 year growth rate calculated from regression of earnings on time

mative valuation model (see e.g., [4] or [8]) it is possible to calculate an implicit growth rate from the market-determined earnings multiple of a security. Thus, comparisons of the predictions with price-earnings ratios may be interpreted as examinations of the relationship between the forecasts and market-expected growth rates. Correlations with two versions of the price-earnings ratio are shown in Exhibit 6. The prices used were the closing prices for the last day of the year. The earnings were either the actual earnings or the average of the base-earnings figures supplied by A and B for their growth rates. These latter figures represent normalized or trend-earnings figures. Specifically, they represent an attempt to estimate what earnings would be in the absence of cyclical or special factors. The correlation coefficients in the exhibit are about the same as those obtained when the forecasts were compared with each other. Since price-earnings ratios are affected by several variables other than expected growth rates, this exercise underscores the extent of disagreement among the forecasters.

III. Accuracy of Predictions

In assessing the forecasting abilities of the predictors, we encountered one major difficulty. The five years in the future for which the forecasts were made have not yet elapsed. As a result, we were forced to compare the forecasts with the realized growth of actual and normalized earnings (as estimated by

Predictors A and B) through 1965. Since the latter figures represent what earnings are thought to be on their long-run growth path, perhaps not too much violence is done to the intentions of the forecasters by making these a standard of comparison.

A. Method of Evaluation

The forecasts were evaluated by the use of simple correlations and by the inequality coefficient,[13]

$$U^2 = \frac{\Sigma (P_1 - R_1)^2}{\Sigma R_1^2}, \qquad (1)$$

where P_1 is the predicted and R_1 the realized growth rates for the ith company. It will be noticed that the inequality coefficient, in effect, gives a comparison between perfect prediction ($U^2 = 0$) and a naive prediction of zero growth for all corporations ($U^2 = 1$).

We also investigated the extent to which errors in predictions were related to 1) errors in predicting the average over-all earnings growth of the sample firms; 2) errors in predicting the average growth rate of particular industries; and 3) errors in predicting the growth rates of firms within industries. To accomplish this, we decomposed the numerator of (1) into three parts. The first comes from the average prediction for all companies not being equal to the average realization. The second part arises from differences among the average industry predictions not being equal

Exhibit 6 Correlations of Predictions with Price-Earnings Ratios*

	A	B	C	D	
			1962		
P/E	.76	.80	.86	.56	
P/NE	.82	.83	.83	.55	

	A	B	C	D	E
			1963		
P/E	.77	.74	.86	.67	.85
P/NE	.81	.76	.80	.60	.85

* P/E is the price-earnings ratio. P/NE is price/average of base (normalized) earnings of A and B.

to the corresponding differences in industry realizations. The third arises from the differences in predictions for the corporations within an industry not being the same as the differences in realization.[14] The proportions of U^2 arising from these three sources will be called U^M, U^{BI}, and U^{WI} respectively for mean errors, between-industry errors, and within-industry errors.

B. Overall Accuracy of the Forecasts

Statistics summarizing the forecasting abilities of the predictors and the success of using perceived past growth rates to predict the future are presented in Exhibit 7. By and large, the correlations of predicted and realized growth rates are low, though most of them are significantly greater than zero, and the in-

Exhibit 7 Accuracy of Predictions

I. 1962 Predictions Compared with Growth of Actual Earnings: 1962-1965

Predictor	A	B	C	D	g_{p1}	g_{p2}	g_{p3}	g_{p4}
Correlation	.07	.16	.66	.45	.22	−.01	.23	.16
U	.80	.78	.57	.67	.74	.88	.74	.78
U^M	.31	.32	.20	.24	.17	.12	.10	.20
U^{BI}	.11	.10	.08	.06	.11	.04	.04	.12
U^{WI}	.58	.58	.71	.70	.73	.84	.75	.68
Number of Obs.	185	185	60	178	168	140	140	145

II. 1962 Predictions Compared with Growth of Normalized Earnings: 1962-1965

Correlation	.26	.32	.68	.45	.23	.16	.38	.09
U	.74	.72	.57	.62	.72	.80	.67	.76
U^M	.25	.25	.08	.13	.09	.12	.09	.19
U^{BI}	.07	.06	.06	.08	.08	.07	.05	.08
U^{WI}	.68	.69	.86	.79	.83	.80	.86	.73
Number of Obs.	180	180	59	175	164	136	138	142

III. 1963 Predictions Compared with Growth of Actual Earnings: 1963-1965

Predictor	A	B	C	D	E	g_{p1}	g_{p2}	g_{p3}	g_{p4}
Correlation	.05	.16	.78	.47	.29	.20	.31	.22	.55
U	.85	.84	.59	.73	.81	.78	.75	.77	.62
U^M	.33	.34	.27	.28	.40	.20	.19	.16	.27
U^{BI}	.12	.11	.11	.07	.11	.09	.06	.06	.05
U^{WI}	.54	.55	.62	.66	.49	.70	.74	.79	.69
Number of Obs.	185	185	62	182	125	167	143	138	169

IV. 1963 Predictions Compared with Growth of Normalized Earnings: 1963-1965

Correlation	.27	.29	.70	.34	.49	.36	.52	.41	.32
U	.78	.78	.61	.70	.74	.69	.64	.67	.69
U^M	.35	.35	.22	.23	.40	.22	.33	.23	.12
U^{BI}	.07	.06	.08	.09	.09	.08	.09	.05	.06
U^{WI}	.58	.59	.70	.68	.50	.70	.57	.72	.82
Number of Obs.	180	180	61	177	123	163	139	136	165

equality coefficients are large. The major exception to this is Predictor C's forecasts. However, this apparent superiority is largely illusory since C tended to concentrate on large, relatively stable companies and, we suspect, predictions were made only when there was *a priori* reason to believe that the forecasts would be reliable. That this conjecture has some validity is borne out by the fact that the set of companies for which C made forecasts had a lower average instability index than did our whole sample. Moreover, all the other forecasts, including the perceived past growth rates, did better for this set of companies than for the larger set.[15]

Several additional points about the overall accuracy of the forecasts are worth mentioning. First, the forecasts based on perceived past growth rates, including even growth over the most recent year, do not perform much differently from the predictions. There seems to be no clear-cut forecasting advantage to the careful and involved procedures our predictors employed over their perceptions of past growth rates either in terms of correlation or of the inequality coefficient.

Second, all predictors had a better record than the no-growth forecast for each company. However, it is possible to find a single growth rate that would yield lower mean square errors than any of the predictions. This is a result of the average realized growth rates being considerably higher than the average expectation of each predictor. This may simply indicate a failure to anticipate the continuation of the expansion through the period considered, but it may also reflect the underestimation of change frequently found in investigating forecasts.[16]

Third, with the exception of the past growth rate in the year immediately preceding the forecast date, all predicted and perceived past growth rates were better at predicting the average normalized growth rates than the actual ones. However, whether this is because normalized earnings gave a better picture of the true growth of corporations or because normalized

earnings calculations are influenced by past growth-rate forecasts is open to question.

C. Analysis of the Forecasts by Industrial Categories.

Turning to the industry breakdown of the forecasts, we find that failure to forecast industry means (U^{BI}) accounted for only a very small proportion of the inequality coefficient. The main sources of inequality were the within-industry errors.

Looking at the correlations of predictions with future growth rates within industries permits us to assess which industries were most difficult to forecast in an *ex post* sense. The extent to which forecasters found the various industries difficult to predict is indicated in Exhibit 8. To calculate the exhibit, we first ranked each predictor's correlation coefficients between his forecasts and realizations over the eight industry groups. The industry for which the predictor had the most difficulty (worst correlation) was given a rank of one. In Exhibit 8, we present the sums of the ranks for each industry over the four predictors.[17] If the difficulty ranking for all predictors was identical, the rank totals would be 4 for the most difficult industry (in 1963 when there are four predictors compared), 8 for the next most difficult, etc., and the coefficient of concordance (Kendall's W) would be unity. For each of the sets presented, the values of Kendall's W are significant (beyond the .05 level) as were the differences between industries for the correlation coefficients for each predictor.[18] Correlation coefficients between forecasts and realizations tended to be highest in the following industries: (1) electricals and electronics, (8) miscellaneous, and (2) electric utilities; they were lowest in: (6) foods and stores and (4) oils. Industry (5) drugs, showed very low correlations for the 1962 predictions and high ones for the 1963 predictions. Similar patterns emerged, though more weakly, when perceptions of past growth rates over more than one year were used as forecasts. It is interesting to note that certain industries, which were difficult to forecast in an *ex ante* sense (see Section II. B) actually turned out to be difficult to predict, *ex post*. For example, there was high (low) agreement among predictors concerning the growth rates for the electric utilities (oils) and also high (low) correlation between predictions and realizations.

In general, we had little success in associating forecasting success with any industry or company characteristics. The differences between industries in forecasting success were only moderately related either to the average growth rates to be realized or to the variances of the realized growth rates. Two of the industries where the highest correlations were found, industries (1) and (2), had respectively the highest and the lowest average growth rates and variances. The third industry where success occurred, (8), fell in the middle range for both quantities. The rank-totals of the last column of Exhibit 8 had a rank correlation with the rank-totals for average growth rates of .14 and of .37 with the rank-totals for the variances.

To further investigate how forecasting ability was related to company characteristics, the corporations were classified according to the quality ratings supplied by two of the predicting firms. There was a tendency for the correlations to be lowest (and negative) in the poorest-quality grouping, but they did not get systematically higher with quality, the highest correlations tending to occur in the middle classes. Similarly, classifying by high, low, or medium values of the instability index showed no pronounced differences in performance. The forecasting performances were again worst for the lowest-quality corporations and best in the middle category. When the corporations were classified by high, medium, or low price-earnings multiple; or past growth rate of earnings; or future growth rates of earnings, sales; or assets; no pronounced or significant patterns emerged.

IV. An Appraisal of the Forecasts

The rather poor overall forecasting performances of the predictors and the fact that their past perceptions of growth rates were about as reliable forecasts as their explicit predictions raises two questions: 1) Does any naive forecasting device based on historic data yield as good forecasts as the painstaking ef-

Exhibit 8 Rank Scores of Correlations of Predictions and Realizations Summed over Predictors*

	1962-65 Growth of Actual Earnings	1962-65 Growth of Normalized Earnings	1963-65 Growth of Actual Earnings	1963-65 Growth of Normalized Earnings	Total
Industry					
1)	20	23	20	28	91
2)	18	22	14	25	79
3)	9	11	24	14	58
4)	10	10	8	7	35
5)	5	7	24	26	62
6)	8	5	5	10	28
7)	14	15	20	20	69
8)	24	15	29	14	82
Kendall's W	.76	.74	.72	.65	.32

* Entries are sums of ranks over predictors for correlations of predictions with growth rates indicated in column headings.

forts of security analysts? 2) Is it the basically volatile nature of earnings that explains our results, and would the predictions appear more accurate if they were taken to be forecasts of more stable measures of the growth of corporations?

To investigate the first of these questions, past growth rates calculated on the basis of arithmetic and logarithmic regressions and on the geometric means of first ratios, calculated over periods up to 14 years, were compared with the realized growth rates through 1965. A selection of these comparisons based on data ending in 1962 is found in Exhibit 9.[19]

It is interesting to note first that the calculated growth rates tend to be more closely correlated with the growth rates of normalized earnings than with the growth rates of actual earnings. This is an even more pronounced feature of the calculated growth

rates than of the data considered earlier. Second, while the correlations of the calculated growth rates with the realized growth rates tended to be lower than those found for the predictions and perceptions, and fewer of them differed significantly from zero, these differences are not pronounced. However, unlike the earlier data, the calculations seem to have almost no forecasting ability, a finding similar to that of I. M. D. Little (1962) for British corporations. Among the calculated rates, those for shorter periods of time tend to be somewhat better in terms of correlation than those for longer ones, a feature highlighted by the strong showing of the growth rates calculated over only one year (g_{c5}). Third, while one would have expected that extrapolations using as the last year for the calculation the same year that is used for the first year in calculation of the realization would have a

Exhibit 9 Correlations of Calculated Past Growth Rates on Realizations*

I. Correlations

	Growth of Actual Earnings 1962-65	Growth of Normalized Earnings 1962-65	Growth of Actual Earnings 1963-65	Growth of Normalized Earnings 1963-65
g_{c1}	.03	.42	.01	.26
g_{c2}	−.15	.19	−.15	.06
g_{c3}	−.13	.15	−.16	.02
g_{c4}	−.10	.09	−.11	−.02
g_{c5}	.22	.62	.18	.46
g_{c6}	.12	.51	.06	.34
g_{c7}	.01	.24	−.01	.12
g_{c8}	−.02	.37	−.03	.23
g_{c9}	−.12	.09	−.14	−.01

II. Inequality Coefficients

g_{c1}	.93	.79	.93	.85
g_{c2}	1.03	.95	1.01	.96
g_{c3}	.95	.88	.96	.91
g_{c4}	.88	.82	.90	.86
g_{c5}	1.27	1.22	1.11	1.08
g_{c6}	.89	.73	.90	.80
g_{c7}	.83	.75	.86	.80
g_{c8}	.98	.85	.96	.87
g_{c9}	.89	.83	.91	.86

* For definition of g's, see footnote to Exhibit 5.

lower correlation than extrapolations where the data ended a year earlier, in fact the reverse tendency manifested itself. Finally, among the possible ways of calculating growth rates, those based on the geometric means of the first ratios surpassed those based on regressions.

The superiority of the past perceived growth rates over the calculated ones should not be taken too seriously, however, for it was largely due to the fact that negative perceived growth rates were not reported by our participants. The survey respondents only indicated that the rates were negative. As a result, companies for which this was true had to be dropped from the sample when correlations of realized with perceived past growth rates were made. When we dropped the companies whose past calculated growth rates were negative (in order to put the calculated and pereived growth rates on a similar basis), the correlation coefficients of the calculated with the realized growth rates were raised. For example, with this change the first row of Exhibit 9 would read

.30, .53, .17, .42,

which compares favorably with the data in Exhibit 7. Similar improvements occurred using the other types of calculated growth rates.

The possibilities of obtaining useful forecasts from simple extrapolation were also examined by calculating growth rates over the four preceding years[20] for (1) earnings plus depreciation, (2) earnings before taxes, (3) sales, (4) assets, and (5) share prices. The correlations of these growth rates calculated to the end of 1962, both with 1962-1965 and 1963-1965 earnings growth and the growth rates of the same variables, are shown in the first five rows of Exhibit 10. It will be noticed that both the levels and the variation of these correlation coefficients are quite similar to

Exhibit 10 Extrapolations from Other Series as Predictors of Earnings and Own Growth Rates* (Correlation Coefficients)

	Growth of Actual Earnings 1962-65	Growth of Normalized Earnings 1962-65	Growth of Actual Earnings 1963-65	Growth of Normalized Earnings 1962-65	Growth Rate of Corresponding Variable 1962-65	Growth Rate of Corresponding Variable 1963-65
g_{e1}	.11	.39	.05	.27	.28	.20
g_{e2}	.29	.21	.42	.30	.24	.38
g_{e3}	.23	.37	.15	.29	.39	.31
g_{e4}	.29	.46	.47	.60	.63	.27
g_{e5}	.04	.34	−.03	.20	−.06	.05
P/E	.21	.25	.13	.18	—	—
P/NE	.14	.35	.08	.21	—	—

* g_{e1} is growth of earnings plus depreciation

g_{e2} is growth of earnings plus taxes

g_{e3} is growth of sales

g_{e4} is growth of assets

g_{e5} is growth of price of stock

P/E is price-earnings ratio at end of 1962

P/NE is price-normalized earnings ratio at end of 1962

The period used for the calculations of the growth rates was 1958-62 and the rates were calculated as:

$g = \sqrt[4]{V_{62} / V_{58}}$ where V_{62} and V_{58} are the values of the variables

those found for the predictions and perceptions of past growth and the equivalently calculated past growth rates of earnings. There was also no marked tendency for the extrapolations to do better at predicting their own growth rates than the growth rates of normalized earnings, but they tended to be better at predicting their own rates than the growth of actual earnings.

The last two rows of Exhibit 10 show the correlations of the price-earnings ratio and the price-to-normalized-earnings ratio with the actual future growth of earnings. As mentioned earlier, these ratios have implicit in them a forecast of the rate of growth anticipated by the market. We find that, in terms of correlation, the market-determined earnings multiples perform no differently from the other predictors we have considered.

A similar picture emerged when the predictions and perceptions of growth rates of earnings were used to predict the growth that would occur in these same variables through the end of 1965. With the exception of the growth of price, the performance of the predictions and perceptions were about the same in terms of correlation as those shown when they were used to forecast the growth of normalized earnings. The inequality coefficients were, if anything, slightly lower. For price growth, however, these forecasts had virtually no merit, with even poorer performance than they had for the growth of actual earnings.

Conclusion

In this paper, we have examined the characteristics of a small sample of security analysts' predictions of the long-run earnings growth of corporations. The extent of agreement among the different predictors was considered and their forecasting abilities assessed. Evidence has recently accumulated [7] that earnings growth in past periods is not a useful predictor of future earnings growth. The remarkable conclusion of the present study is that the careful estimates of the security analysts' participating in our survey, the bases of which are not limited to public information, perform little better than these past growth rates. Moreover, the market price-earnings ratios themselves were not better than either the analysts' forecasts or the past growth rates in forecasting future earnings growth.

We must be cautious, however, in overgeneralizing these results. We did not have data to investigate directly whether the performance of the predictions of growth in the period considered were atypical of the usual forecasting abilities of such forecasts. The question is important, however, since it can be argued that the peculiarities of the expansion that occurred after the date of the forecasts made the period especially difficult to forecast. Moreover, our work is hampered by the fact that only a few firms were able to participate in our survey. It may also be that shorter-term earnings predictions are considerably more successful relative to naive forecasting methods. Fortunately, we are presently collecting additional data that will help shed light on these conjectures and permit a study of the generation of earnings forecasts and their usefulness in security evaluation.

Endnotes

1. A number of studies of anticipations data have been collected in two National Bureau Volumes: *Short-Term Economic Forecasting: Studies in Income and Wealth* (1955) and *The Quality and Economic Significance of Anticipating Data* (1960). Some more recent work on the assessment of expectations or forecasts has been done by Zarnowitz (1967).

2. The classic theoretical statement of the anticipations view of the determination of share valuation may be found in J. B. Williams (1938). This position is also adopted in the standard textbook in the field Graham (1962). The emphasis on the importance of earnings growth may also be found in Gordon (1962), Holt (1962), and Williams (1938).

3. One of the few attempts to conduct a study of this type was made by the Continental Illinois Bank and Trust Company of Chicago in 1963.

The bank collected a sample of earnings estimates one year in advance from three investment firms. An analysis of these projections revealed that the financial firms tended to overestimate earnings and that overall quality of the estimates tended to be poor.

4. The 185 companies for which the growth-rate estimates were made tended to be the large corporations in whose securities investment interest is centered. This selection was made on the basis of availability of data and was not chosen as a random sample.

5. We are deeply grateful to the participating firms, who wish to remain anonymous. Not all volunteers were able to supply data useful to this study, either because the actual supply of data would have been too burdensome (being kept for internal records in a form that made their extraction difficult) or because the data supplied were not comparable to data used here (either being of a short-term nature or being made at different dates). Because one of our main objectives is to examine differences and similarities in predictions of the same quantities, such data were not used in the present paper.

6. That several of our participating firms find it worthwhile to publish these projections and provide them to their customers provides *prima facie* evidence that a certain segment of the market places some reliance on such information in forming its own expectations.

7. The analysis is presented mainly for the raw growth figures, but very similar impressions would be obtained from examining their logarithms.

8. The values shown in all parts of Exhibit 1 are significant well beyond the conventionally used levels of significance. We may note that Tukey's test for interaction in a two-way analysis of variance [11, pp. 129-37]—the typical model in which the breakdown of variance used in Part 3 of Exhibit 1 is employed—indicated a small but highly "significant" proportion of variance attributable to interaction. However, the usual analysis-of-variance model does not seem appropriate for this data, not only because of interactions, but also because of possible lack of homogeneity of variance.

9. The test for individual pairs of predictions was the likelihood-ratio test. Note that the ranking comparison is not based on independent observations so a statistical test of the concordance is not appropriate. This suggests that the "significance" of the overall correlations mentioned earlier should really be treated only as descriptive indications of their sizes. The hypotheis that the correlations are all zero within industries could, however, be rejected well beyond conventional significance levels. Predictor C was dropped from these tests due to paucity of data in many industries.

10. These correlations, for the participants supplying data in both years, were:

	A	B	C
B	.19		
C	.04	.04	
D	.07	.11	.29

Only the two largest of these correlations would be significant at the .05 level.

11. This effect was also found when the calculated growth rates were based on either 1) the regression of earnings per share on time; or 2) the appropriate root of the ratio of earnings per share at the end of the period to earnings at the beginning.

12. The numbers of observations on which Exhibit 4 is based are considerably smaller than those for which predictions were available. Only a small part of this loss was due to inability to calculate past growth rates due to negative earnings figures. Much more important was the fact that the predictors did not give numerical figures for past growth rates when these would be negative. One might think that the companies for which past growth rates were easily calculated would be ones with highest simple correlations among the predictors. However, the only cases for which this appeared to be true were the correlations of predictor D with A, B, and E.

13. Note that this is similar to the inequality coefficient introduced by Theil (1966).

14. Letting P_{kj} and R_{kj} be the predicted and realized growth rates for the kth company ($k = 1,..., N_j$) in the jth industry ($j = i,...,J$), we can write the numerator of (1) as:

$$\sum_{j=1}^{J} \sum_{k=1}^{N_j} (P_{kj} - R_{kj})^2 = \left[\sum_{j=1}^{J} N_j (\bar{P} - \bar{R})^2 \right]$$
$$+ \left[\sum_{j=1}^{J} N_j \{ (\bar{P}_j - \bar{P}) - (\bar{R}_j - \bar{R}) \}^2 \right]$$
$$+ \left[\sum_{j=1}^{J} \sum_{i=1}^{N_j} \{ (P_{kj} - \bar{P}_j) - (R_{kj} - \bar{R}_j) \}^2 \right],$$

when $\bar{P}_j$, $\bar{R}_j$ are the averages for the jth industry and $\bar{P}$ and $\bar{R}$ are the overall means. The three terms in square brackets are the ones referred to in the text.

15. For this smaller group of companies, the differences among predictors was far less than is suggested by Exhibit 7. It is worth noting that C had a higher correlation and lower inequality index than the others in 1962 (with D a very close second), but both D and E were slightly better on the matched set in 1963.

16. See, for example, Zarnowitz (1967). Since almost all the actual growth rates were positive, we do not know whether underestimation of change would also characterize predictions when earnings were generally declining. No forecasters predicted a negative rate of growth.

17. Predictor C could not be included in this calculation because of a lack of observations in some industries.

18. The latter, however, was tested only on the basis of the asymptotic distribution of the correlation coefficient and the assumption that the data were distributed normally.

19. The figures there are typical both of what was found when other periods were used and of the comparisons of calculations ending in 1961 and 1963 with the perceived growth after 1962 and 1963 respectively.

20. Other periods and methods of calculating growth rates were also used. The ones presented tended to be very slightly better than the others and are comparable to the most successful of the longer-term earnings extrapolations.

References

Buckman, John W. *The Reliability of Earnings Forecasts,* prepared for the Trust Investment Committee of the Continental Illinois Bank. Chicago: September 13, 1963, mimeographed.

Culbertson, John M. "The Term Structure of Interest Rates." *Quarterly Journal of Economics* (November 1957): 485-517.

Gordon, Myron J. *The Investment, Financing, and Valuation of the Corporation.* Homewood: Richard D. Irwin, 1962.

Graham, Benjamin. David L. Dodd and Sidney Cottle. *Security Analysis, Principles and Technique,* 4th ed. New York: McGraw-Hill, 1962.

Holt, C. C. "The Influence of Growth Duration on Share Prices." *Journal of Finance* (September 1962): 465-75.

Kessel, Reuben. T*he Cyclical Behavior of the Term Structure of Interest Rates.* New York: National Bureau of Economic Research, 1962.

Little, I. M. D. "Higgledy Piggledy Growth." *Oxford Institute of Statistics Bulletin* (November 1962): 387-412.

Malkiel, Burton G. "Equity Yields, Growth, and the Structure of Share Prices." *American Economic Review* (December 1963): 1004-31.

Meiselman, David. *The Term Structure of Interest Rates.* Englewood Cliffs: Prentice-Hall, 1962.

Modigliani, Franco and Richard Sutch. "Innovations in Interest Rate Policy." *American Economic Review: Papers and Proceedings.* (May 1966): 178-197.

Scheffe, Henry. *The Analysis of Variance.* New York: John Wiley & Sons, 1959.

Short-Term Economic Forecasting. Studies in Income and Wealth. Princeton: Princeton University Press for NBER, 1955.

The Quality and Economic Significance of Anticipations Data. Princeton: Princeton University Press for NBER, 1960.

Theil, Henri. *Applied Economic Forecasting.* Chicago: Rand McNally, 1966.

Williams, J. B. *The Theory of Investment Value.* Cambridge: Harvard University Press, 1938.

Zarnowitz, Victor. *An Appraisal of Short-Term Economic Forecasts.* New York: National Bureau of Economic Research, 1967.

Chapter 3

EPS Forecasts—Accuracy Is Not Enough

Leonard Zacks, Ph.D.
President
Zacks Investment Research, Inc.

Many investors select stocks on the basis of companies' earnings prospects. Since an efficient market will already have impounded these prospects in share prices, such investors will not outperform the market.

The author collected consensus forecasts of 1976 earnings per share growth for 260 of the S&P companies and found no relation between forecast EPS growth and subsequent actual price movement.

On the other hand, portfolios of companies whose consensus forecasts underestimated actual earnings growth outperformed the market on the average, while portfolios of companies whose consensus forecasts overestimated actual earnings growth underperformed the market. These results suggest that, if the objective of stock selection is abnormal portfolio returns, selection must be based on anticipating changes in the consensus, rather than changes in the earnings.

Institutions can increase the efficiency of their investment departments by using a two-stage selection process. First, analysts make preliminary forecasts of EPS growth, which are compared with consensus forecasts. Second, analysts concentrate on those companies for which the discrepancy between their forecasts and the consensus forecasts is greatest. In this way, analysts expend the bulk of their efforts on those firms most likely to offer exceptional share price performance.

If the stock market is efficient, and if price movements result from changes in expectations of earnings, payout ratios, and discount rates, then (1) current expectations should be unrelated to future price movements because the expectations are already reflected in stock prices by the time they become measurable, but (2) changes in expectations should be directly related to price movements. Furthermore, changes in the discount rate should be felt uniformly across all companies, hence correlate with the market return, whereas changes in expected earnings and payout ratios should correlate with the deviations of individual stock returns from the market return—i.e., with abnormal returns. Moreover, changes in payout expectations would correlate so highly with changes in earnings expectations, that it would be hard to distinguish the two.

Unfortunately, the paucity of good expectational data severely limits our ability to test most of these hypotheses. The cross-sectional test described below examines the limited hypothesis that excess returns are directly related to changes in earnings expectations. The results clearly confirm that an analyst able to forecast changes in expectations, rather than changes in earnings themselves, can achieve superior returns.

Consensus Forecast and Price

We began our analysis with the 320 companies of the Standard & Poor's (S&P) 500 index for which Lynch, Jones & Ryan provides consensus earnings forecasts. We excluded from our sample those companies that reported deficits for 1975 and those with fiscal years not ending on December 31st. For each of the 260 remaining companies, we identified a consensus forecast for 1976 earnings per share (EPS) made as of December 1975 and calculated the forecast growth in EPS for 1976 and the actual stock price growth during 1976.[1]

To examine the general relation between forecast EPS growth and stock price movement, we first ranked the 260 companies by forecast 1976 EPS growth and created five portfolios of approximately equal size—companies with forecast EPS growth (A) above 40 percent, (B) between 23 and 40 percent, (C) between 12 and 23 percent, (D) between zero and 12 percent, and (E) below zero. We then calculated the actual, equal-weighted price change of each of those five portfolios during 1976.[2]

As Exhibit 1 shows, we found no relation between forecast EPS growth and actual price movement: In fact, the group of companies with the lowest forecast EPS growth (Portfolio E) actually outperformed the group with the highest forecast EPS growth (Portfolio A). This finding is consistent with efficient market concepts and confirms that forecast data are fully incorporated into price by the time they become measurable.

The Effect of Changing Forecasts

In examining the relation between price movement and changes in consensus forecasts of earnings, we focused on the error in the December 1975 consensus forecast of 1976 EPS as a surrogate for changes in the forecast of 1976 EPS over the period December 1975 to December 1976.[3] Using the percentage difference between each company's 1976 EPS and the consensus forecast of its EPS made as of December 1975, we divided each portfolio, A through E, into three sub-portfolios according to whether the forecast underestimated EPS by more than 10 percent, fell on target (between −10 and +10 percent), or overestimated EPS by more than 10 percent. For example, the consensus forecasts of 1976 EPS growth for companies in Portfolio A-1 (all above 40 percent) turned out to have underestimated actual growth by at least 10 percent, while those for companies in Portfolio E-1 (all below zero) also turned out to have underestimated actual growth by at least 10 percent.

Exhibit 1 shows the relevant statistics for each of these 15 portfolios, including the equal-weighted price performance for 1976. Compare the price performance of each portfolio with the magnitude of the original EPS growth forecast and the magnitude of its error. The companies with on-target forecast errors (−10 to +10 percent) all performed about the same as the market, regardless of their EPS forecasts. For example, Portfolio E-2, comprised of companies with on-target forecasts predicting EPS growth below zero, was up 21 percent, while Portfolio A-2, comprised of companies with on-target forecasts predicting EPS growth of over 40 percent, was up 24 percent; during 1976, the S&P 500 price advance was 20 percent. Moreover, with the exception of the four companies in Portfolio B-1, the portfolios of companies with consensus forecasts that significantly underestimated EPS growth substantially outperformed the S&P, whereas the portfolios of companies

Exhibit 1 1976 Price Performance of Portfolios with Differing Consensus Forecasts and Forecast Errors

(1) Portfolio	(2) Range of Consensus Forecasts of Individual Company 1976 EPS Growth as of 12/75		(3) Actual Portfolio Performance During 1976	(4) Sub-portfolio	(5) Range of Forecast Errors		(6) Portfolio Performance During 1976	(7) Number of Securities in Portfolio
	From	To			From	To		
A	40%	335%	31.0	A-1	10%	130%	49%	14
				A-2	−10%	+10%	24%	13
				A-3	−90%	−10%	23%	20
B	23%	40%	20.4	B-1	10%	29%	25%	4
				B-2	−10%	+10%	25%	17
				B-3	−10%	−62%	14%	15
C	12%	23%	25.1	C-1	10%	95%	49%	19
				C-2	−10%	+10%	21%	38
				C-3	−40%	−10%	−2%	11
D	0%	12%	27.0	D-1	10%	90%	35%	27
				D-2	−10%	+10%	26%	42
				D-3	−82%	−10%	14%	13
E	−44%	0%	38.0	E-1	10%	55%	50%	17
				E-2	−10%	+10%	21%	7
				E-3	−33%	−10%	14%	3

with consensus forecasts that overestimated EPS growth underperformed the S&P. These results indicate strongly that *surprise earnings or equivalent changes in consensus forecasts are a key determinant of abnormal returns.*

This relation between surprise earnings and prices explains the familiar historical relation between actual EPS and price performance. Companies for which the consensus overestimated earnings would tend to have lower actual EPS growth and be found near the bottom of a ranking by actual EPS growth, while companies for which the consensus underestimated earnings would be found near the top of a ranking by actual EPS growth.

The relation between surprise earnings and price movement can also explain many cases in which prices move in a direction opposite to that of earnings—an aberration traditionally attributed to price-earnings ratio expan-sions or contractions. If, for example, a company's EPS growth were forecast to exceed 30 percent and turned out to be only 15 percent, its share price could easily drop 10 to 20 percent, thereby reducing its price-earnings ratio despite the respectable earnings growth. Conversely, if a company's actual earnings fell only 10 percent, when they were expected to fall 30 percent, share price could easily move upward, resulting in substantial price-earnings ratio expansion. This interplay between expectation and realization may be a significant determinant of changes in price-earnings ratios.

Implications for Managing the Investment Decision Process

Assuming that our results are not specific to 1976 or to the data used, but are generally valid, their implications are significant—especially for the many investment organizations that follow an investment strategy of continually ranking companies by EPS growth forecasts and shifting assets from the bottom of the list to the top. As experience has shown, and as statistics demonstrate, this strategy, when based on accurate EPS forecasts, does result in superior performance.

On the other hand, changing expectations determine price movements, and if there is a direct relation between efforts expended by analysts in forecasting EPS and the accuracy of such forecasts, an institution can increase the efficiency of its own resources by adopting a two-stage investment decision process. In the first stage, an institutional analyst would develop a preliminary independent forecast of company EPS growth, which would then be compared with the Street's consensus forecast. If the forecasts were reasonably close, the institutional analyst would expend little additional effort on the company. If the analyst's estimate fell above or below the consensus, however, he would devote considerable time to refining his forecast of the company's EPS. This approach could increase the productivity of an institutional research department by focusing analysts' time on those areas with the highest potential payoffs.

Implications for Specific Investment Decisions

These general results gloss over wide variations in the performance of individual companies. To translate them into a practical format, we show in Exhibit 2 the chances of outperforming a market index (the S&P 500), based upon a detailed statistical analysis of forecast errors involving individual companies.[4]

Column 1 of Exhibit 2 shows the probability of outperforming the S&P 500 in 1976 if an analyst had randomly selected in December 1975 a single company that had been correctly classified by the error in the consensus forecast. For example, if he had been able

Exhibit 2 Chance of Outperforming S&P 500 Based Upon Accurate Knowledge of Errors in Consensus Forecasts

| | Chance of Outperforming S&P by Selecting Portfolio with Varying Number of Issues | | | |
| | 1 | 2 | 4 | 8 |
Consensus Forecast	Issue	Issues	Issues	Issues
Underestimates EPS by 30% or more	88%	95%	99%	99%
Underestimates EPS by 10 to 30%	69	77	85	93
Within 10% of EPS	51	51	52	53
Overestimates EPS by 10 to 30%	31	24	16	7
Overestimates EPS by 30% or more	24	16	7	3

to identify a company for which the consensus EPS forecast underestimated actual EPS by 10 to 30 percent, he would have had a 69 percent chance of outperforming the S&P 500 (or odds of 2.2 to one in favor). If he had identified a company for which the consensus EPS forecast was within 10 percent of actual EPS, his chances of outperforming the S&P would have been only 51 percent.

The remaining columns of Exhibit 2 show that the chances of outperforming the S&P 500, given foreknowledge of consensus errors, increase substantially if portfolios are based on forecast error. A portfolio of eight stocks, all having consensus forecasts of EPS that underestimated actual EPS by 10 to 30 percent, would have a 93 percent chance of outperforming the market (or odds of 13 to one in favor). On the other hand, a portfolio of eight stocks selected from among those with accurate consensus forecasts would have only a 53 percent chance of outperforming the S&P index. If one accepts 1976 as a representative year, Exhibit 2 can serve as a useful guide for making portfolio decisions on the basis of consensus forecasts and internal EPS estimates.

Endnotes

1. The consensus EPS forecast for calendar-year 1976 was taken to be the mean estimate as of December 1975 for 1976 earnings; the consensus forecast growth for 1976 was the percentage difference between the consensus EPS forecast and actual 1975 earnings, while the corresponding stock price growth was the percentage difference between the price on December 31, 1976, and the price a year earlier.

2. Equal-weighted performance of a portfolio is the arithmetic average of the percentage changes in prices of the individual securities in the portfolio.

3. We implicitly assume that the 1976 EPS forecast made as of December 1976 would equal the 1976 actual EPS. This approach eliminates a number of timing and reporting problems inherent in the definition and collection of consensus forecasts.

4. The chances are based on an analysis of the data for the 260 companies with fiscal years corresponding to the calendar year.

Chapter 4

Expectations and Share Prices

Edwin J. Elton, Ph.D.
Nomura Professor of Finance
New York University

Martin J. Gruber, Ph.D.
Nomura Professor of Finance
New York University

Mustafa Gultekin, Ph.D.
Associate Professor of Finance
Kenan-Flagler Business School
University of North Carolina

It is generally believed that security prices are determined by expectations concerning firm and economic variables. Despite this belief, there is very little research examining expectational data. In this paper, we examine how expectations concerning earnings per share affect share price. We first show that knowledge concerning analysts' forecasts of earnings per share cannot by itself lead to excess returns. Any information contained in the consensus estimate of earnings per share is already included in share price. Investors or managers who buy high-growth stocks, where high growth is determined by consensus beliefs, should not earn an excess return.

This is not due to earnings having no effect upon share price, since knowledge of actual earnings leads to excess return. Much larger excess returns are earned if one is able to determine those stocks for which analysts most underestimate return. Finally, the largest returns can be earned by knowing which stocks for which analysts will make the greatest revision in their estimates. This pattern of results suggests that share price is affected by expectations about earnings per share. Given any degree of forecasting ability, managers can obtain best results by acting on the differences between their forecasts and consensus forecasts.

Reprinted by permission of Edwin J. Elton, Martin J. Gruber, and Mustafa Gultekin, "Expectations and Share Prices." *Management Sciences,* Vol. 27, No. 9, Sept. 1981, pgs. 975-987. © 1981, The Institute of Management Sciences, 290 Westminister St., Providence, RI 02903.

1. Introduction

A central theme of modern investment theory is that expectations about firm characteristics are incorporated into security prices. This theme can be found in most investment texts and is utilized in much of the current research in finance. Not only does this belief pervade academia, it is commonly held by the financial community.

Surprisingly, in light of the strength of this belief, there is very little empirical evidence to support it. Almost all research which attempts to measure the impact of expectations utilizes not expectational data but historical extrapolations of past data that the authors hope will serve as a proxy for expectational data. This is true for most tests of valuation models as well as almost all tests in the efficient markets literature.

The purpose of this article is to examine the importance of expectations concerning one variable, earnings per share, in the determination of share price. Earnings per share is considered a key variable in determining share price and has been studied extensively in the efficient markets literature. In almost all studies, expectations of future earnings per share are formulated as an extrapolation of past earnings.[1] Justification for using historical extrapolation is sometimes found in tests of the accuracy of extrapolated data in forecasting future earnings.

While tests such as those found in Brown and Rozeff (1978); Cragg and Malkiel (1968); and Elton and Gruber (1972) provide some evidence of the relative accuracy of historical extrapolation versus expectational data as forecasts of the future, they do not address the question of the role of expectations in share price formation. The purpose of this paper is to directly address this question. More specifically, we will address the question of the role of actual future changes in earnings on stock returns, the role of expected changes in earnings, and finally the role of changes in expectations.

In addition to examining the importance of expectations and earnings, we briefly explore the issue of the scale of returns that can be earned by being "more accurate" than average forecasts. If market prices reflect average expectations, then superior forecasting ability should be rewarded with excess returns. We will explore both the size of these returns and the timing of their occurrence.

2. Overview: Variables Examined and Sample Design

The testing of the impact of earnings expectations has awaited the development of a broad consistent database. Lynch, Jones, and Ryan have constructed a database, which contains one- and two-year consensus earnings estimates on all corporations followed by one or more analysts at most major brokerage firms.[2] Lynch, Jones, and Ryan define the consensus earnings estimate for any stock as a simple arithmetic average of the estimates prepared by all of the analysts following that stock. Given this database, a study can be made of the role of average expectations in price formation and, in particular, the importance of earnings expectations in determining share price.

In order to study the role of expectations, we need some measure of the excess returns that can be earned from knowledge concerning future earnings. To examine this, we analyzed the actual growth rate in earnings. The actual growth rate was defined as actual earnings for the forecast year minus actual earnings in the previous fiscal year, divided by actual earnings in the previous fiscal year. This variable is computed only for those firms for which the denominator is positive. This does not bias the results of our tests, as the denominator is known at the time this variable is formulated. However, the population of stocks to which our tests apply is restricted. Letting G_t stand for the growth rate in earnings,

$$G_t = \frac{E_t - E_{t-1}}{E_{t-1}} \text{ for } E_{t-1} > 0 \qquad (1)$$

where E_t is reported earnings per share at time t.

Anticipating our results for a moment, we will find that knowledge of actual growth will allow a significant risk-adjusted excess return to be earned. This indicates that growth in earnings is an important variable affecting share price and that expectations concerning this variable are worth studying.

If expectations determine share price, then knowledge of the average value of these expectations should already be incorporated in the share price, and buying on the basis of average expectations should not lead to excess returns. Thus, the second variable we examined was the consensus forecast of the growth rate in per-share earnings. We call this the forecasted growth rate. It is formulated as the consensus forecast of fiscal year earnings minus the actual earnings in the previous fiscal year divided by the actual earnings that occurred in the previous fiscal year. Since this measure cannot be interpreted for a negative denominator, it is computed only for those companies for which the denominator is positive. To be more explicit, let

$$FG_t = \frac{C_t - E_{t-1}}{E_{t-1}} \text{ for } E_{t-1} > 0 \qquad (2)$$

where C_t is the consensus forecasts of the earnings per share that will occur at time t, and FG_t is the consensus forecast of the growth rate in earnings per share.

If expectations are important and are incorporated in present prices, then one should observe larger excess returns by having knowledge concerning the error in the growth estimate than by knowing actual growth itself. Investment in a firm with high actual growth should not necessarily lead to excess returns unless investors were forecasting low growth. Thus, if expectations are important, knowledge concerning differences between actual growth and forecasted growth should lead to higher excess returns than knowledge concerning growth itself. Thus, the third variable we examine is actual growth minus fore-

casted growth. This differential growth can be expressed as

$$DG_t = G_t - FG_t \qquad (3)$$

Since the effect of differences between expectations and realizations is the key phenomenon that we wish to study, we have measured this phenomenon in two additional ways. The first is the error in the earnings forecast defined as the actual earnings in the forecast year minus the forecast earnings. If we denote this variable by M_t for misestimate in consensus forecast of earnings, then

$$M_t = E_t - C_t \qquad (4)$$

The second is the percentage forecast error, which is measured as the actual earnings in the forecast year minus the forecast earnings divided by the absolute value of the actual earnings. If we use $\%M_t$ to stand for the percentage, then

$$\%M_t = \frac{E_t - C_t}{|E_t|} \qquad (5)$$

While most of our analysis consists of an examination of one-year forecasts, we decided to take a brief look at the excess returns associated with errors in two-year forecasts. We duplicated the one-year measures and examined the error in earnings forecast for two years and the percentage error in earnings forecast for two years.

If consensus forecasts are more important than the actual level of future earnings in determining prices, then one should be able to do a better job of selecting stocks by knowing the change in consesus forecasts than by knowing actual earnings. To test this hypothesis, a variable measuring the percentage adjustment in forecasts over time was used. This variable is formulated as negative of the following quantity: the forecast of earnings prepared for the next (as opposed to this) fiscal year minus the forecast of earnings for the same fiscal year made one year later divided by this latter number. To better understand this variable, let $_{t-a}C_t$ stand for the consensus forecast for earnings at time t, which are produced at time $t - a$, and $_{(t-a+12)}C_t$ stands for the forecast for time t, which is produced 12 months later. Then the forecast revision denoted by FR_t can be represented as

$$FR_t = -\frac{_{(t-a)}C_1 - _{(t-a+12)}C_t}{_{(t-a+12)}C_t} \qquad (6)$$

3. The Sample

The raw data consisted of a monthly file of one- and two-year earnings forecasts prepared in the years 1973, 1974, and 1975. We limited our sample of data in several ways. First, the sample was restricted to firms having fiscal years ending on December 31. By confining our sample to firms with fiscal years ending on the same date, forecasts prepared a certain number of months (e.g., nine) in advance of the end of the fiscal year fall on the same calendar date. This procedure assures that the same general economic influences (e.g., the economy, the market, etc.) were available to all forecasters at the time forecasts were prepared. The date of December 31 was selected because more companies had fiscal years ending on that date than on any other.

Second, forecasts are restricted to two forecast dates, March and September. March was selected because it is the earliest date on which financial data for the previous fiscal year would be reported by most companies. September was selected as a month that is far enough from the first forecast and far enough into the fiscal year that significant evidence on companies' performance during the year should be available. Yet it is not so far into the year that earnings are known with certainty. Both dates are used for all variables involving one-year forecasts. However, so few two-year forecasts were available in March that only the September date could be used when examining two-year forecasts.

Finally, because we are interested in the impact of consensus forecasts, the sample was restricted to companies which were followed by three or more analysts. The consensus prepared from less than three forecasts could be idiosyncratic and not typical of broad feelings about the stock.

The final sample consisted of a total of 919 one-year forecasts of the fiscal years 1973, 1974, and 1975 and a total of 710 two-year forecasts of fiscal years 1974, 1975, and 1976. Because of negative earnings, some firms had to be eliminated over several measures. This caused the sample size to fall to as low as 913 and 696 for one- and two-year forecasts, respectively. As discussed earlier, Lynch, Jones, and Ryan survey most large brokerage firms. Since we have included all stocks followed by three or more analysts, the group of stocks in our sample can be considered a universe of all stocks with important analyst interest. Since brokerage firms are interested in providing information to their customers, our sample should include most stocks of major institutional interest.

4. Methodology

The first step in our procedure was for each time period studied (March and September) and for each year to rank all stocks on each variable and to divide the stocks into deciles by each variable. For example, we formed deciles for the forecasted growth rates made in September 1973, with the first decile containing the 10 percent of the stocks with the highest forecasted growth rate. For each decile, we calculated the average value of the variable being studied (in this case, forecasted growth).

In order to determine whether certain types of information lead to excess returns, it is necessary to have a measure of what return is expected. If we have a measure of expected return, then excess return is the difference between actual return and expected return. In order to measure expected return, we use the market model. The market model is a relationship between the return on a security and the return on a market index.

Let

1. r_{it} be the return on portfolio i in period t.
2. r_{mt} be the return on the market in period t.
3. $\alpha_{i \text{ and}} \beta_i$ be parameters for portfolio i.
4. e_{it} be deviations from the model.

The market model is:

$$r_{it} = \alpha_i + \beta_i\, r_{mt} + e_{it}$$

Using the market model leads to expected returns being determined by the security's normal relationship with the market (β_i), the market return in the period (r_m), and the security's average nonmarket return (α_i). Using the market model, excess return is

$$r_{it} - (\alpha_i + \beta_i\, r_{mt})$$

Although the market model is frequently used in finance, there are some problems with its use that can lead to biased tests. First, there is measurement error in the coefficients, and if this varies systematically with the test statistic, it can lead to an appearance of a relationship when none exists. This was guarded against in several ways.

First, we calculated the market model for the deciles discussed earlier. Using grouped data is one way of reducing the measurement error. The one variable where measurement error can be especially bothersome is beta. As Blume (1975) has shown, the error in measuring beta varies systematically with its difference from one. The use of grouped data helps. In addition, we examined the individual betas on the groups. There was no systematic pattern, nor did any group beta differ very much from one (the range was 0.93 to 1.09). Given this result, we judged that any further adjustment in beta was unnecessary. In the original CAPM tests, grouping data was common. Litzenberger and Ramaswamy (1979), and Ross and Roll (1980) have criticized this on the grounds that the CAPM is a theory of the pricing of single assets and, as such, has to be shown to explain differences in asset returns. Our purpose here is not to test CAPM but rather to examine the effect of expectations on share price. Hence grouping is a reasonable procedure for dealing with measurement error.

The second problem in the use of the market model is its difference from a capital asset pricing model. There are numerous general equilibrium models that have been derived. If one of these ultimately is shown to be correct, then better estimates of returns should be obtained by using that model rather than the market model. Brennan (1979) has shown that the use of alternative models can make some difference. However, in this study the magnitude of the results, the grouping techniques, and the spread in the β_i's should mean that there is minimal chance of this source of potential bias explaining the results.[3] For example, assuming that the beta for each group was equal to one would not change any of our conclusions.

The market model was estimated by treating each decile as an equally weighted portfolio of the stocks which composed it and estimating the market model parameters for each decile. The market index we used was the Standard & Poor's index adjusted for dividends. The parameters of the model were estimated in each case using 60 monthly observations on returns up to and including forecast month. The data dissemination procedure followed by Lynch, Jones, and Ryan means that forecasts are in the hands of the subscriber by the end of the month. The estimated parameters of the market model were then used in conjunction with actual market returns to forecast normal risk-adjusted returns for each of the deciles during each of the 24 months after the forecast month. The risk-adjusted returns in each month were close to but not exactly equal to zero. This should not be surprising to the reader. The sum of the residuals in any one month should equal zero only if they are weighted in market proportions and include all stocks in the index. Our sample meets neither of these conditions. We adjusted our residuals to have a mean (across all deciles) of zero for ease of presentation. Our primary statistical test is a *rank* correlation test; subtracting a constant from each entry cannot affect the rank. Thus our adjustment had very little effect on the numbers reported and had no effect on their statistical significance or on our conclusions.

As discussed earlier, we calculated risk-adjusted excess returns for each of the deciles for each of the variables for the 24 months after the forecast month. In the case of the March data, we calculated risk-adjusted excess returns from April on, and in the case of September, from October on. This was done for each of the three years for which we had data. We combined these years and have reported the average risk-adjusted return across the three years for each decile.

To aid in understanding the results, we report the sum of the risk-adjusted excess returns from the month after the forecast month to the month under consideration, rather than reporting the risk-adjusted excess returns in any one month.[4] Thus, for March forecasts, the entry in month 3 is the sum of the risk-adjusted excess returns earned in April, May, and June. This allows the reader to more easily determine the cumulative effect of any influence.

After examining the data, we determined that there were no further effects after month 15 for March data and month 9 for September data. Thus, we have not reported results beyond these dates.

In reporting results, we have combined the deciles in two ways. First, we report the cumulative risk-adjusted excess returns in the upper 30 percent, middle 40 percent, and lowest 30 percent of firms ranked on each variable. Second, we report the cumulative risk-adjusted excess returns in the upper 50%. Since the risk-adjusted excess returns add to zero, across all deciles the risk-adjusted excess return in the upper 50 percent is the negative of the lowest 50 percent. We chose to present the data in this way since using the ungrouped deciles increases the size of the tables substantially without providing additional insights.

The reader can judge the economic significance of the results by examining the cumulative residuals in Exhibits 1 through 4. These excess returns are reported before transaction costs. While estimates of round-trip transaction costs differ, a reasonable estimate is in the range of 2 to 4 percent. Thus, cumulative residuals in excess of 4 percent can be accepted as of economic significance.

It is also logical to examine whether the relationship between any of the variables under study and excess return is statistically significant. This was examined by computing Spearman rank order correlation coefficient between the decile and the rank order of the cumulative excess return for each decile. A statistically significant rank order correlation coefficient would indicate that there was a significant relationship between the variable under study and cumulative excess returns. Furthermore, by using a nonparametric test, this statement is free of any distributional assumptions (across deciles) about the pattern of excess returns and/or the variables under study. Note that when we compute the statistical significance of the cumulated residuals in successive periods, these tests are not independent.

Exhibit 5 presents the average values for each variable studied in this paper.

5. Results

The first question to analyze is: Can an investor earn excess returns by selecting stocks on the basis of the consensus growth rate forecasted by security analysts [Equation (2)] The answer is no. There is no discernible pattern in the cumulative excess returns. In some months, the stocks for which high growth was forecasted had positive risk-adjusted cumulative excess returns; in other months, they had negative ones. As a further check, we performed a rank order correlation test on the deciles in each month. The rank order correlation between forecasted growth and risk-adjusted cumulative excess return was never significantly different from zero at the 1 per-

Exhibit 1 Time Series of Cumulative Excess Returns Ranked by Error in the Forecast of the Growth Rate (Equation (3)) for March Data

Month	1	2	3	4	5	6	7	8	9	10	11	12	13	14	15
Upper 30%	0.0166	0.0221	0.0221	0.0321	0.0630	0.0698	0.0767	0.0782	0.0855	0.0664	0.0729	0.0775	0.0909	0.0801	0.0897
Middle 40%	−0.0069	−0.0037	+0.0037	−0.0001	−0.0139	−0.0170	−0.0038	−0.0041	−0.0063	−0.0162	−0.0107	−0.0120	−0.0144	−0.0209	−0.0126
Bottom 30%	−0.0075	−0.0169	−0.0173	−0.0320	−0.0444	−0.0470	−0.0719	−0.0726	−0.0773	−0.0448	−0.0588	−0.0731	−0.0717	−0.0523	−0.0729
Rank Correlation[a]	0.71**	0.73**	0.76**	0.83*	0.83*	0.76**	0.84*	0.87*	0.89*	0.90*	0.85*	0.87*	0.93*	0.92*	0.89*

[a]Rank Correlation coefficients

* Indicates significance at the 1% level

** Indicates significance at the 5% level

Exhibit 2 Time Series of Cumulative Excess Returns for the Error in the Forecast of Growth Rate Using September Data (Equation (3))

	1	2	3	4	5	6	7	8	9
Upper 30%	0.0187	0.0272	0.0421	0.0429	0.0466	0.0506	0.0618	0.0638	0.0680
Middle 40%	0.0100	0.0092	0.0014	−0.0035	−0.0036	−0.0045	−0.0069	−0.0065	−0.0034
Lower 30%	−0.0318	−0.0394	−0.0441	−0.0384	−0.0421	−0.0445	−0.0526	−0.0550	−0.0635
Rank Correlation[a]	0.77*	0.88*	0.84*	0.88*	0.99*	0.92*	0.95*	0.94*	0.85*

[a] Rank correlation coefficients are computed across deciles.
* Indicates significance at 1% level.
** Indicates significance at 5% level.

Exhibit 3 Excess Returns for Months 7 and 13 March Data

Time of Analysis		Forecasted Growth Equation (2)	Actual Growth Equation (1)	Error in Growth Equation (3)	Error is Forecast (One Year) Equation (4)	Percentage Error in Forecast Equation (5)
	Upper 30%	−0.0064	+0.0591	+0.0767	0.0633	+0.0711
	Middle 40%	0.0068	0.0006	−0.0033	-0.0092	−0.0033
Month 7	Lower 30%	−0.0028	−0.0597	−0.0719	−0.0754	−0.0719
	Upper 50%	−0.0080	0.0463	0.0426	0.0462	0.0426
	Rank Correlations[a]	−0.35	0.90*	0.84*	0.98*	0.90*
	Upper 30%	+0.0006	+0.0748	+0.0908	+0.0715	+0.0861
	Middle 40%	−0.0093	−0.0191	−0.0144	+0.0022	−0.0156
Month 13	Lower 30%	+0.0019	−0.0493	−0.0717	−0.0743	−0.0651
	Upper 50%	−0.0139	0.0411	0.0577	0.0571	0.0554
	Rank Correlation[a]	−0.30	0.88*	0.93*	0.96*	0.85*

[a] Rank correlation coefficients are computed across deciles.
* Indicates significance at 1% level.
** Indicates significance at 5% level.

cent level and only significantly different from zero at the 5 percent level in two months. In the months it was significant it was negative, which is opposite to what one would expect if growth estimates contained information which was not incorporated in stock prices. The lack of a pattern was even more evident in the September data. In no month was the cumulative excess return significantly different from zero at even the 5 percent level, and the average cumulative excess return varied frequently from positive to negative. The results for each individual month are not reported in the paper, but the

results for selected months can be seen by examining Exhibits 3 and 4.

This lack of risk-adjusted excess returns occurs even though the analysts were projecting some very large growth rates. In September the analysts were projecting that the average growth rate for the top decile would be over 100 percent and the growth rate in the second decile would be 33 percent. In contrast, the earnings of stocks in the last decile were expected to decline by 34 percent.

A number of financial institutions purchase growth stocks as an investment strategy. In the three years we examined, pursuing such a strat-

Exhibit 4 Excess Returns for Month 7 from September Data

	Forecasted Growth Equat. (1)	Actual Growth Equat. (2)	Error in Growth Equat. (3)	Error in Forecast (One Yr.) Equat. (4)	Error in Forecast (One Yr.) Equat. (5)	Error in Forecast (Two Yrs.) Equat. (4)	Error in Forecast (Two Yrs.) Equat. (5)	Forecast Revision Equat. (6)
Upper 30%	0.0135	0.0399	0.0618	0.0567	0.0652	0.0773	0.0792	0.0889
Middle 40%	−0.0079	−0.0161	−0.0069	−0.0053	−0.0084	−0.0023	−0.0062	−0.0141
Lower 30%	−0.0029	−0.0186	−0.0526	−0.0497	−0.0541	−0.0741	−0.0711	−0.0701
Upper 50%	0.0073	0.0245	0.0405	0.0402	0.0409	0.0496	0.0498	0.0512
Rank Cor-relation[a]	0.37	0.53	0.95*	0.95*	0.89*	0.96*	0.98*	0.83*

[a] Rank correlation coefficients are computed across deciles.
* Indicates significance at the 1% level.
** Indicates significance at the 10% level.

Exhibit 5 Mean Values for Each Variable

	Equat. (1) Forecasted Growth	Equat. (2) Actual Growth	Equat. (3) Error in Growth	Equat. (4) Forecast in Growth Error (1 yr.)	Equat. (5) Percentage Forecast Errors (1 yr.)	Equat. (4) Percentage Forecast Errors (2 yrs.)	Equat. (5) Percentage Forecast Errors (2 yrs.)	Equat. (6) Forecast Revision
March Data								
Upper 30%	56.61%	107.45%	63.62%	1.08%	26.24%			
Middle 40%	6.9	8.27	1.35	0.01	−0.32			
Lower 30%	−9.16	−34.95	−38.88	1.05	−159.24			
Sept. Data								
Upper 30%	81%	98.83%	26.36%	0.53%	14.72%	0.13%	26.74%	43.76%
Middle 40%	9.34	8.32	−0.17	−0.07	−0.23	−0.09	−3.75	1.19
Lower 30%	−15.75	−32.95	−27.02	−0.67	−94.01	−1.64	−155.29	−27.34

gy based on consensus estimates would not have led to superior returns; growth forecasts were already incorporated in the security prices. This is what one would expect if expectations are incorporated into security price.

On the other hand, our results show that growth is an important determinant of security returns. Investors with perfect forecasting ability could make risk-adjusted excess returns. The results for individual months are not reported. However, the results for selected months can be seen by examining Exhibits 3 and 4. From month 4 on, the rank order of excess returns for the deciles is significant at the 1 percent level. The excess return builds up to 7.23 percent for the upper 30 percent of all stocks by month 9. It then declines and builds up again to over 7 percent. A similar but less distinct pattern can be seen by examining the lowest 30 percent.

The risk-adjusted excess returns from possessing perfect forecasting ability in September are much lower than they were from possessing perfect forecasting ability in March. Furthermore, in most months the rank order of the deciles is insignificant at the 1 percent level (although it's still sometimes significant at the 5 percent level). This is what one would expect. By September, investors have a much better idea of actual growth than they do in March.

If prices reflect consensus forecasts, then knowing the error in the consensus estimate of growth should lead to larger profits than just knowing actual growth. How large is the mis-estimate of actual growth by the analysts? In March, the average error for the 30 percent of the companies for which earnings growth was most underestimated was 63.6 percent, while the average error for the 30 percent of the companies for which growth was most overestimated was 38.9 percent. The corresponding numbers for September forecasts are 26.4 percent and 20.3 percent. It is apparent that while there are still large size errors in the September forecasts, the size of the error has decreased markedly between March and September. Analysts can improve the accuracy of their forecasts as interim earnings reports or as other information comes out, and more information is available on company performance.

Exhibits 1 and 2 show the time series of cumulative risk-adjusted excess return for the errors in the March and September estimates [Equation (3)]. The rank order of the deciles is significant from the first month for both the September and March estimates. The risk-adjusted excess returns build up very quickly in both cases. For the March forecasts, the risk adjusted excess returns are close to 7% by month 6 (September); the major increase occurring in month 5. Once again, the risk-adjusted excess returns have a temporary peak in month 9 and then increase to a global peak in month 13. This rapid build-up is consistent with information about true earnings growth being disseminated over time and the market correctly incorporating the information.

Even in September, investors with a better estimate of growth than the consensus had an opportunity for excess profits. Notice that while knowledge of the forecast error as of September allows an excess profit to be earned, perfect forecast ability did not allow an excess profit to be earned. This suggests that, on average, forecasts are accurate enough in September that excess profits can be earned only by isolating those cases where forecasted growth is very much different than actual.

The time pattern for all variables is very similar with March forecasts producing excess returns, which level out after month 13 and September forecasts producing excess returns, which level out after month 7. Consequently, we shall only report results for these months. The cumulated excess returns in these months are reported in Exhibit 3 and Exhibit 4. In addition, in Exhibit 3 we show the risk-adjusted cumulative excess returns 7 months after the March forecasts for comparison with the effect 7 months after the September forecast.

Note that among the variables discussed so far for both March and September forecasts, the risk-adjusted excess return was highest for the error in the growth rate, next highest for actual growth, and close to zero for the forecasted growth. What an investor desirous of making excess profits should be most concerned with is finding securities where his forecasts are not only good in the sense of being right but where they are both accurate and different from the consensus.

The same conclusion can be reached by examining errors in the earnings estimates Exhibits 3 and 4 present the analysis of excess returns for the error in forecast earnings and the percentage error in earnings forecasts for one year forecasts as of March and September and two-year forecasts as of September. In each case, the excess returns appear to be sufficient to cover transaction costs and the rank order correlation coefficient is significant at the 1% level.

Furthermore, the amount of excess returns that can be earned vary with the magnitude of the forecast error. The two-year estimates made in September and the one-year estimates made in March were considerably less accurate than the one-year forecast made in September. They also produced higher risk adjusted excess returns. However, even in September, there is a considerable forecast error in year-end earnings. In September, the percentage forecast error was 26% for the top decile, 11.6% in the next decile, and 6.3% in the next. These errors, while lower, were still significant enough to lead to an excess risk-adjusted return.

We have now examined evidence that consensus forecasts are incorporated into price. Further, we have seen that the ability to forecast with more accuracy than the consensus forecast can lead to an excess risk-adjusted return. If consensus forecasts play a major role in price determination, then the ability to forecast consensus forecasts themselves should lead to a superior return. Since we have estimates of the earnings for each company made 15 months in advance (the two-year forecast as of September) and estimates of the same earnings made 12 months later (one-year forecast made in September of the following year), we can measure the impact of being able to forecast the change in the estimate [Equation (6)]. As shown in Exhibit 4, the returns from being able to estimate forecast revision are substantial. In fact, the return from forecasting future forecasts themselves is higher than the return from being able to forecast actual earnings. This is consistent with our other evidence that it is consensus forecasts which determine security prices.

All of the results presented in this section could be used to analyze the amount of accuracy necessary to earn excess returns. Assume the analysts can identify firms that are in various deciles with respect to the error in estimated earnings. For example, suppose he could identify the 10% of the firms with the largest forecast error. Column 2 of Exhibit 6 shows the cumulative excess return he would earn. Columns 3 and 4 assumes that he identifies the members of a decile with error. Column 3 assumes that 50% of the time he identifies a firm as a member of a decile he is randomly selecting from among all firms and 50% of the time he is accurate. Column 4 assumes that 90% of the time he is randomly selecting from all firms.

For example, if an analyst is attempting to select from among the 30% of the firms for which the consensus forecast most underestimate true earnings, and he is right 50% of the time, he will earn an excess risk-adjusted return of 4.54%.

As can be seen from an examination of the table, a little bit of information leads to substantial cumulative excess returns. These kinds of excess returns provide some justification for the effort undertaken by many organizations to forecast earnings.

Exhibit 6 Error in Growth* (Forecast-actual)

Percentage of firms eliminated	Excess return if completely accurate	Excess return if 50% error	Excess return if 90% error
0%	0	0	0
10%	1.56	0.78	0.16
20%	2.88	1.44	0.29
30%	3.07	1.53	0.31
40%	4.32	2.16	0.43
50%	5.77	2.88	0.58
60%	7.35	3.67	0.74
70%	9.08	4.54	0.91
80%	9.90	4.95	0.99
90%	10.42	5.21	1.04

* Forecasts of one year growth rates prepared in March. Cumulative returns calculated as of April of the following year.

6. Conclusions

In this study, we present evidence in support of the hypothesis that expectations are incorporated into security prices. In addition, we have analyzed the timing and size of returns from forecasts which are more accurate than the consensus. Since prices reflect consensus forecasts, the payoff from being accurate in forecasting is increased markedly as the consensus forecast becomes inaccurate. Finally, we have demonstrated that the payoff from being able to forecast the consensus estimate is higher than the payoff from being able to forecast earnings. The market reacts to expectational data. But despite this, or rather because of it, Lord Keynes (1964) appears to have been right when he likened professional investing to participating in a newspaper contest on a beauty contest, where ". . . each competitor has to pick, not those faces which he himself finds prettiest, but those which he thinks likeliest to catch the fancy of other competitors, all of whom are looking at the contest from the same point of view."

Endnotes

1. Malkiel and Cragg (1968) used expectational data on earnings growth in a valuation model. However, their sample of expectational data was very limited.

2. Lynch, Jones, and Ryan, a New York-based brokerage firm, have available, in computer readable form, consensus (average) earnings estimates updated monthly for the current and next fiscal year as well as forecasts of each individual analyst following each stock. They designate this as the I/B/E/S service. During the time period studied Lynch, Jones, and Ryan surveyed brokerage firms. Our sample consisted of all stocks listed on the New York Stock Exchange which were followed by three or more analysts. The average number of analysts following each of these firms was slightly above seven. Furthermore, slightly less than 70 stocks were followed by ten or more analysts. The maximum number of analysts following any stock was 18.

3. We could have used differences from Rm, rather than the market model in reporting our results. However the reader might then question to what extent our conclusions were due to differences in market risk. Alternatively, we could have followed Watts (1978) methodology to force the beta on each portfolio to be exactly one. However, since the differences in beta from one were neither large nor systematically related to any criteria across our deciles, we did not take this additional step.

4. Many authors accumulate residuals by calculating the product of one plus the residuals. The justification for this is that return over N periods is the product of the N one period returns. There is a difficulty with this procedure. The null hypothesis is that the residuals average zero. If this hypothesis is true, it is easy to show that the product of one plus the one period residuals minus one becomes negative and significantly so as N gets large. The sum of the residuals is zero under the null hypothesis and deviations from zero are indications of real effects.

References

Blume, Marshall. "Betas and their Regression Tendencies." *J. Finance* (June 1975).

Brennan, M. "The Sensitivity of the Efficient Market Hypothesis to Alternative Specifications of the Market Model." *J. Finance*. Vol. 34 (1979): 53-69.

Brown, B. and Rozeff, M. "The Superiority of Analyst Forecasts as Measures of Expectations. Evidence from Earnings." *J. Finance*, Vol. 33 (1978): 1-16.

Cragg, L. and Malkiel, B. "The Consensus and Accuracy of Some Predictions of the Growth of Corporate Earnings." *J. Finance,* Vol. 23 (1968): 67-84.

Elton, B. J. and Gruber, M. J. "Earnings Estimate and the Accuracy of Expectations Data." *Management Science,* Vol. 18 (1972): 409-424.

Keynes, M. *The General Theory of Employment Interest, and Money.* New York: Harcourt Brace and World, (1964): 156.

Litzenberger, Robert and Ramaswamy, K. "The Effects of Personal Taxes and Dividends on Capital Asset Prices: Theory and Empirical Evidence." *J. Financial Econom.* (June 1979).

Malkiel, B. and Cragg, J. "Expectations and the Structure of Share Prices." *Amer. Econom. Rev.* Vol. 60 (1970): 601-617.

Roll, Richard and Ross, Steve. "An Empirical Investigation of Arbitrage Pricing Theory." *J. Finance* (December 1980): 1073-1105.

Watts, R. L. "Systematic Abnormal Returns After Quarterly Savings Announcements." *J. Financial Econom.* (1978): 127-150.

Chapter 5

The Analyst and the Investment Process

An Overview

T. Daniel Coggin, Ph.D.
Director of Research
Virginia Retirement System

I. Introduction

This article presents an overview of a very broad topic: the role of the financial analyst in the investment process.[1] There are at least two reasons why this topic is worthy of attention. First, the analyst performs a critically important function as an instrument that translates information for the stock market. Second, the issue of the *evaluation* of analysts' job performance is also of great importance. Specifically, *can* analysts forecast earnings and returns, and (if so) are there *individual differences* in analysts' forecast ability?

In October 1982, I mailed out a questionnaire to which 41 (out of 75) large U.S. "buy-side" investment management firms (i.e. banks, insurance companies, and investment advisers responded. The term "buy-side" refers to non-brokerage investment management firms. Brokerage houses are often referred to as "sell-side" firms. Primarily because of the availability of information, the vast majority of studies to date have focused on sell-side analysts. There are four major differences between buy-side and sell-side

analysts. Sell-side analysts (1) are fewer in number and concentrated in the Northeast; (2) are generally more highly compensated; (3) follow fewer companies in typically only one industry; and (4) serve as an important source of information for buy-side analysts.

The object of the survey was to gain information about the management structure and performance evaluation of financial analysts. According to that survey, the typical (large) buy-side investment management firm employed eight or more full-time equity analysts who followed 25 or more stocks in three or more industries and were responsible for both fundamental analysis and stock selection. The typical analyst in these firms did not have portfolio management responsibility and was evaluated on his ability to forecast earnings, pick stocks, and communicate effectively. While these results are based on a relatively small sample, I believe they are representative of a general population of medium-to-large, buy-side investment management firms. This survey clearly suggests that the analyst is a key player in the equity investment game.

Reprinted with permission from F. J. Fabozzi, ed. *Managing Institutional Assets* (New York: HarperCollins 1990) 105-118. Copyright 1990 by Ballinger Publishing Co. Reprinted by permission of HaperCollins Publishing, Inc.

The remainder of this article is divided into three sections. Section II deals with analyst forecasts of company-level earnings. Contained in that section is a comparison of analyst forecasts to the forecasts of statistical models. In addition, there is a discussion of analyst error in forecasting earnings and the relationship between analyst earnings forecasts and stock returns. Section III looks at analyst forecasts of stock returns and the implications of existing research for the measurement of analyst job performance. Section IV examines the role of the analyst in the capital market. Included in that section is a discussion of the role of the analyst as an "information processor" for the stock market and the use of quantitative methods. The reader should note that the terms "earnings" and "EPS" (earnings per share) and "financial analyst" and "investment analyst" are used interchangeably in this article.

II. Analyst Earnings Forecast

Analyst Forecasts versus Statistical Models

A classic book by Paul E. Meehl [1954] compared the predictive ability of trained psychologists to statistical models of personality and behavior. Meehl's fascinating study found that the statistical models did a *better* job of classifying subjects than the psychologists. Thirty-five years and hundreds of studies later, his basic finding has been supported in a number of areas of human judgment; that is, well-formulated statistical models tend to outperform the judgment of trained professionals. This is largely attributed to the fact that human judgment introduces biases and other imperfections in information processing that well-formulated statistical models do not.[2]

A number of studies have looked at the time series properties of annual earnings. While there are some rather complicated statistical issues involved, the general finding is that (both at the firm level and most clearly at the aggregate level) the random walk statisti-

cal model provides a reasonably accurate *description* of the time series of annual earnings.[3] However, when it comes to *predicting* annual (and quarterly) earnings, the analyst emerges as the winner in comparison with a number of statistical models (including the random walk model).[4] On the other hand, the analyst generally fails to outperform company management forecasts.[5]

Brown et al. [1978a] looked at the determinants of analyst superiority relative to univariate time-series models. Their study suggests that analyst superiority is related to at least two factors. One, analysts can better utilize *existing* information relative to simple univariate time-series models (a contemporaneous advantage). Two, analysts can use information that occurs *after* the cut-off date for the time-series data but *before* the data of the analyst forecast (a timing advantage). Another study by Brown, Richardson, and Schwager [1987] found that financial analyst superiority is positively related to firm size, meaning that the larger the company, the more advantage analysts have over time-series models.

While the weight of the current evidence tends to favor analysts over statistical time-series models in predicting earnings, studies by Richards [1976], O'Brien [1988b], and Coggin and Hunter [1989] suggest that individual analysts are largely *undifferentiated* in their ability to predict EPS. This finding (discussed in more detail in the next section) suggests that the *consensus* (mean) analyst forecast is generally superior to the forecasts of individual analysts. It should be noted that some recent studies suggest that there are benefits from *combining* statistical time-series and analyst forecasts.[6] Other studies have shown that more complex statistical models that include additional variables affecting earnings growth (such as leading economic indicators) can challenge the superiority of analysts in predicting earnings.[7] Thus, it may be premature to reject the generalizability to financial analysts of Meehl's finding regarding the superiority of statistical models.

Analyst Error in Forecasting Earnings

Having established that analysts generally do a better job of forecasting earnings than relatively simple extrapolative statistical models, it now seems appropriate to examine the general characteristics of the *errors* made by analysts. Two recent studies are relevant to this question. Elton, Gruber, and Gultekin [1984] studied this issue in detail using data for the period 1976-1978. One advantage of their study relative to many previous studies in this area is that they used a large database of analyst EPS forecasts (i.e., the I/B/E/S database maintained by IBES, New York). Earlier studies typically used very small samples of analysts or the Value Line analyst group.

Elton, Gruber, and Gultekin found that (1) analyst errors in forecasting annual EPS (revised monthly) declined monotonically as the end of the fiscal year approached; (2) analysts were reasonably accurate in forecasting aggregate-level EPS for the entire economy; (3) analysts were better at forecasting industry-level EPS than company-level EPS; (4) analysts had a tendency to overestimate EPS growth for companies they believed would do well and underestimate EPS growth for companies they believed would do poorly; (5) analysts had more difficulty forecasting EPS for some companies relative to others (specifically, if analysts had large errors for a company in one year, they tended to have large errors the next year); (6) analyst divergence of opinion about EPS growth for a company tended to be at its greatest during the first four months of the year; and (7) analyst divergence of opinion about EPS growth for a company was positively related to the magnitude of the EPS growth forecast error for that company.

A recent study by Coggin and Hunter [1989] examined the errors made by analysts in forecasting year-ahead EPS and 5-year EPS growth over the period 1978-1985. Their study used both the I/B/E/S database and the ICARUS database (maintained by Zacks Investment Research, Inc., Chicago). Using a variance decomposition theorem from the analysis of variance, they derived an equation for the total mean squared error (MSE) in individual analysts' forecasts for a company:

$$E(EPS_A - EPS_j)^2 = (EPS_A - C)^2 + E(C - EPS_j)^2 \quad (1)$$

where $E(\ )$ is the standard expected value operation, EPS_A is the actual earnings for the company, EPS_j is the forecast of the jth analyst, and C is the consensus (mean) analyst forecast for the company.

In words, this equation says that the total MSE in individual analysts' forecasts has two components: the squared error in the consensus forecast and the mean squared deviation from the consensus forecast. That is, the total MSE in individual forecasts is the sum of the squared consensus error plus the mean squared idiosyncratic error. This decomposition shows that the total MSE for randomly chosen individual analysts is always greater than the squared consensus error by an amount equal to the *variance* of the individual forecasts. This result is formally derived in the appendix to their paper. Thus, only if it were possible to predict *a priori* which analyst would be more accurate than the consensus would it be possible to improve on the consensus forecast. Current research on individual differences in analyst forecasts suggests that is not possible.

The Coggin and Hunter study had three basic findings. First, for both the 1-year and the 5-year forecast data, the squared consensus error component of total MSE was much larger than the mean squared idiosyncratic error component, indicating relatively small differences among analysts' earnings forecasts for a given company. They suggested at least four reasons for the relatively low level of diversity among individual analysts' forecasts. One, there could be significant communication among analysts with respect to EPS forecasts. They noted that their experience in dealing with Wall Street and regional financial analysts led them to believe that there is minimal direct communication of EPS fore- casts among analysts. However, analysts do read many of the same industry reports and journals containing short- and long-term fore- casts of industry activity. This is a form of *indirect* communication that could stand- ardize the assumptions analysts make and thus reduce the level of idiosyncracy in indi- vidual company forecasts.

Two, they noted that analysts often talk with company management concerning the outlook for a company. This is another source of "common information" available to ana- lysts that could serve to further reduce the level of idiosyncratic error. Three, many ana- lysts use similar financial models in deriving their forecasts. The relative uniformity of generally accepted techniques of financial analysis could help lower idiosyncratic error. A discussion of the techniques of financial analysis is beyond the scope of this chapter. A good summary is given in Cohen, Zinbarg, and Zeikel [1987, Part 4]. Common factors considered by analysts in valuing a company are discussed here in a later section on the valuation process. Four, they noted that their sample of companies was somewhat skewed toward larger, more well-known companies. It is possible that analysts tend to be in greater agreement concerning the future pros- pects of these firms.

The second major finding of the Coggin and Hunter study was that positive consensus errors (analogous to "earnings surprises") were associated with higher returns for the forecast period, while negative consensus er- rors (analogous to "earnings disappoint- ments") were associated with lower returns for the forecast period. Specifically, they found that by the end of the fiscal year, the market had already begun to adjust return on a stock to the fact that actual earnings for the year were either less than or in excess of expectations. This find- ing extends previous research that used a statis- tical model to generate expected earnings[8] and supports results reported in Brown, Foster, and Noreen [1985, Chapter 4].

Finally, they found that the variance of the analysts' 5-year growth estimates (the idi- osyncratic error component) was negatively correlated with return to forecast periods of 1 through 5 years. This finding does not sup- port the use of the variance of analysts' 5- year growth estimates as a measure of sys- tematic investment risk advocated by Malkiel [1981] and others. This leads us to a more complete discussion of the general topic of the relationship between analyst earnings forecasts and stock returns.

Analyst EPS Forecasts and Stock Returns

The major reason analysts are asked to per- form fundamental analysis and forecast earn- ings is because there is an implied link be- tween EPS forecasts and stock returns. Indeed, it is a fundamental tenet of financial theory that expectations for earnings for a company be related to return to stockholders. And indeed they are. In one of the earlier studies of this relationship, Niederhoffer and Regan [1972] verified that stock prices were strongly dependent on earnings changes— both in terms of absolute change and change relative to analysts' estimates—in data for 1970. Later studies by Elton, Gruber, and Gultekin [1981]; Hawkins, Chamberlin, and Daniel [1984]; and van Dijk [1986] used larger samples of analysts' expectational data (from the I/B/E/S database) to further refine our understanding of this relationship. These studies showed that *current* expectations for earnings (as represented by the mean of the analysts' current forecasts) are incorpo- rated into *current* stock prices. Further- more, they showed that *revisions* in the consensus (i.e. mean) forecast for year- ahead earnings are *predictive* of future stock returns.

Specifically, these studies presented three key findings. First, as mentioned above, any information contained in the current consen- sus forecast by itself is largely reflected in the current stock price. Hence, a policy of buying stocks solely on the basis of large consensus growth estimates is generally unrewarded. Second, excess returns are available to those who can predict those stocks for which analysts will *underestimate* earnings, and even larger excess returns are possible if one can predict which stocks will experience the largest positive earnings estimate *revisions*. The phrase "excess returns" here refers to returns in excess of those required by the capital asset pricing model (CAPM). (Some authors use the phrase "abnormal returns.") The results reported in this section are generally robust to the substitution of raw, "unadjusted" returns.

Third, revisions in the consensus estimate for earnings tend to have *momentum;* that is, an increase in the consensus forecast in one month is often followed by another increase in the next month. The availability of excess returns on stocks that experience sizable increases in the consensus earnings forecast has been measured to last for holding periods of from 2 to 12 months. It has been argued by some that this finding in inconsistent with the existence of an "efficient market."[9] The stock market does not "instantaneously" react to changes in the consensus forecast and allows excess returns to a strategy that takes advantage of that fact. This topic will be briefly discussed in the concluding section.

In summary, as several authors have noted, Lord Keynes appears to have been correct when he compared professional investing to participating in a contest to pick which 6 contestants out of 100 in a photo-beauty contest will be chosen by the rest of the judges. In Keynes's words ". . . each competitor has to pick, not those whose faces, which he himself finds prettiest, but those which he thinks likeliest to catch the fancy of other competitors, all of whom are looking at the contest from the same point of view."[10]

III. Analyst Return Forecasts

As we have seen, a key responsibility of investment analysts is forecasting stock returns.

In most cases, the analyst forecasts company-level returns directly. However, in some cases, the analyst provides input (i.e. forecasts of earnings, dividends, and growth rates) to a valuation model (such as a dividend discount model), which, in turn, forecasts returns. In either case, the analyst is central to the process of generating expected returns. These forecasts are usually in the form of "Buy," "Hold," and "Sell" recommendations. The portfolio manager uses these recommendations, in conjunction with other quantitative and nonquantitative aspects of evaluating a company, to construct stock portfolios for clients.

The Valuation Process

In a survey of 1,000 members of the Financial Analysts Federation (170 responded), Chugh and Meador [1984] expanded and updated an earlier study by Bing [1971] and examined the process by which financial analysts evaluate common stocks. They found that analysts consistently emphasize the long term over the short term. Key variables for the long term were expected changes in EPS, expected return on equity (ROE), and industry outlook. Key variables for the short term were industry outlook, expected change in EPS, and general economic conditions. Other important factors mentioned by the analysts were quality and depth of management, market dominance, and "strategic credibility" (ability to achieve stated goals). According to their survey, expected growth in earnings and ROE appeared to be the most significant aspects of the valuation process. The primary sources of information for the analysts were presentations by top management, annual reports, and Form 10-K reports.

The Quality of Return Forecasts

Each quarter, Zacks Investment Research, Inc. tracks the performance of stocks recommended by analysts at 10 major brokerage houses and reports the results in *The Wall Street Journal*. Exhibit 1 presents a summary of the results on 12/30/88. For the 12 months ending 12/30/88, 6 of the 10 brokerage house Recommended Lists outperformed the S&P 500 stock index. For the 30 months ended 12/30/88, 5 of the 10 outperformed the S&P 500.

A number of other studies have examined the value of analysts' forecasts of stock returns. The majority of these studies have also focused on the forecasts of sell-side analysts. While there is some disagreement in this area,[11] the general finding is that there is economically valuable information in analysts' buy/sell recommendations. Specifically, recent studies of U.S., Canadian, and U.K. analysts have shown that excess returns are available to investors who follow the published recommendations of analysts employed by brokerage houses.[12]

Put in current jargon, these studies show that analysts' stock recommendations have a "positive IC" (information coefficient). The IC is defined as the correlation between predicted and actual stock returns. Some researchers have argued that analysts are "worth their keep" if and only if it can be shown that they can forecast earnings and returns. The evidence to date supports the hypotheses that they can (1) outperform simple statistical models in forecasting earnings and (2) provide economically valuable information in forecasting returns.

Evaluating Analyst Job Performance

Having now established the fact that analysts are indeed a valuable component of the investment process, it seems logical to discuss how they themselves are evaluated. My 1982 survey indicated that analysts are evaluated on their ability to forecast earnings and returns and on how well they communicate investment ideas and information.

A number of investment organizations have established quantitative rating systems to evaluate their analysts. My 1982 survey indicated that 71% had done so. Several articles have been written on the topic of evaluating financial analysts.[13] These papers have focused overwhelmingly on the ability of analysts to forecast return, while other "relatively minor" issues such as ability to communicate investment information received little or no attention. My 1982 survey found that the most common elements of an analyst rating system are: accuracy of stock performance forecasts, accuracy of estimate information (e.g., earnings, dividends, and growth rates), and ability to communicate investment information to portfolio managers. It would then seem that ability to forecast stock return is a key (if not *the* key) element of an ana-

Exhibit 1 How the Big Brokerage Houses' Favorite Stocks Performed in Periods Ending 12/30/88[a]

Brokerage House	3 Months	12 Months	30 Months
A.G. Edwards	3.4%	27.5%	19.9%
Paine Webber	3.6	22.7	19.6
Smith Barney	1.8	20.8	21.1
Shearson	0.4	20.3	25.5
Dean Witter	1.0	18.1	8.0
Prudential-Bache	3.2	17.6	14.9
Kidder Peabody	2.3	16.5	15.6
Merril Lynch	0.4	14.6	10.9
Drexel Burnham	3.2	14.3	12.4
Thomson McKinnon	1.5	6.5	24.5
Average Broker	2.1	17.9	17.2
Comparison Yardsticks			
Dow Jones 30 Index	3.6	16.2	21.5
S&P 500 Index	3.0	16.6	19.0
Average Stock[b]	−0.6	20.3	5.8

[a] Source: *The Wall Street Journal*, 2/3/89 and Zacks Investment Research, Inc. All figures are price change plus dividends. Broker portfolios are equal-weighted and rebalanced monthly (with no transaction costs) to reflect changing recommendations.

[b] Equal-weighted average of 3,000 stocks followed by the 10 brokerage houses.

lyst's job description.

Three recent studies are relevant to this issue. Coggin and Hunter [1983] examined a fundamental question: Are there individual differences in analysts' abilities to forecast stock returns? Using a statistical technique called *meta-analysis*, they analyzed the ICs for analysts at a regional trust company over the period 1979-1981, and for a larger sample of analysts nationwide in 1982. Meta-analysis showed that all apparent differences in analysts' ICs were attributable to *sampling error*. Hence, in their data, there were no real individual differences in analysts' abilities to forecast return. Dimson and Marsh [1984] replicated the Coggin and Hunter analysis on a sample of British brokers and analysts over the period 1980-1981 and got the same basic result. Elton, Gruber, and Grossman [1986] found no evidence of one U.S. brokerage firm being consistently better than another in recommending stocks over the period 1981-1983.

It was previously noted that research suggests minimal differences in analysts' abilities to forecast earnings. We now have evidence that there are no differences in analysts' abilities to forecast returns. Thus, the combined evidence suggests that rating schemes that base an individual analyst's salary and bonus on differential ability to forecast earnings and returns amount to holding a *lottery* for that award!

It is important to emphasize that the existing evidence does not suggest that analysts can't forecast return. Indeed, there is previously cited evidence that they can. The mean analyst IC is *not zero*; rather, it is about 0.10. The point here is that the existing data suggest there are no real *between-analyst differences* in ability to forecast return.

In an effort to accommodate this finding, the regional trust company mentioned above designed an analyst evaluation system that rates the analysts as a *group* on the return prediction dimension. At this firm, the analysts supply estimates of earnings, dividends, and growth rates to a three-phase dividend discount model, which then calculates expected returns for stocks followed by the group of analysts. If that IC is significantly positive, the analysts (as a group) are rated favorably on that dimension. Other specific criteria are then rated on an individual analyst basis, such as ability to communicate investment information and analyses in both verbal and written form.

IV. Analysts and the Capital Market

The Analyst as Information Processor

As O'Brien [1988a] has noted, accounting and finance researchers (and practitioners) are increasingly relying on analysts' forecasts as proxies for the "unobservable market expectation" for future earnings. The empirical evidence that financial analysts are, in general, superior to univariate time-series models in forecasting earnings and the increasing availability of analyst forecast data (from sources like IBES and Zack's Investment Research, Inc., cited above) have fostered this tendency. The idea that the information content of analysts' forecasts for earnings and returns is relevant to the theory and practice of accounting and finance is well established.

In a totally efficient capital market, analysts' forecasts for earnings and returns would not matter. Every market participant (both analysts and investors) would have exactly the same information at exactly the same time; hence, no one would have an "informational advantage" over anyone else. However, there is mounting evidence that the stock market is not totally efficient. While the weight of the evidence suggests that analysts are generally undifferentiated in their ability to predict earnings and returns, those predictions *can* be profitably employed by investors in the stock market.

This article has noted evidence that the ability to forecast changes in the consensus analyst earnings forecast for a company yields excess returns in the stock market.

Some studies have examined the *timing* and *speed* at which analyst forecast information is disseminated to stock market investors.[14] This is an important area of research that will likely yield insights into just how that information is translated into excess returns. Evidence was also discussed that supports the hypothesis that analysts' buy/sell recommendations can be used to earn excess returns in the stock market. Other research has shown that the dividend discount model of expected stock returns (driven by analyst forecast data) is an economically valuable tool in predicting actual stock returns.[15]

Quantitative Methods

Recent studies have shown that a majority of investment management firms do not use quantitative methods to value common stocks. A survey reported in *Pensions & Investment Age* (November 10, 1986) reported that only 8% of respondents use quantitative methods to manage stocks; a survey conducted by Arthur D. Little, Inc., in March 1987 reported that only 30% of respondents indicated intensive use of quantitative methods in their overall money management effort. This small minority of quantitative managers spans a continuum from using analysts to provide input to quantitative models to using *no* analysts at all, relying instead on computers and "artificial intelligence" to process information, and select and trade stocks. Hence, 20 years after the "quantitative revolution" of the late 1960s, most money managers apparently continue to rely on conventional (i.e., nonquantitative) methods of investment management. In the case of stocks, this generally means that financial analysts perform fundamental security analysis and make recommendations to portfolio managers about which stocks to buy and sell. A relatively large subjective component is then applied to the final investment decision. No doubt, this process has been successful (and will continue to be successful) for *some*

investment management firms. A discussion of the fact that most investment managers continue to *underperform* the stock market (i.e., the S&P 500 stock index) is beyond the scope of this article.[16]

The fact remains that analysts provide a valuable information processing service to the vast majority of *active* stock market investors. There is another form of stock market investing called *passive* investing, which includes the growing index fund business. Passive investment management assumes that securities are efficiently priced and does *not* involve the use of analysts' estimates in an effort to "beat the market."[17] Currently, however, the vast majority of money invested in the stock market is actively managed. As long as active stock market investing remains popular, analysts will be a vital component of the investment process.

Endnotes

1. It is difficult for a summary article to do justice to such a subject. Those desiring more detail should go directly to the references cited here, including the excellent monograph by Brown, Foster, and Noreen [1985].

2. For a good introduction to this literature, see Kahneman, Slovic, and Tversky [1982].

3. For a more detailed discussion, see Foster [1986], Appendix 7.C.

4. See, for example, Brown and Rozeff [1978], Coggin and Hunter [1982-83], Rozeff [1983], and O'Brien [1088a].

5. See Armstrong [1983], and Hassell and Jennings [1986].

6. See Conroy and Harris [1987], L.D. Brown, *et al.* [1978b] and Guerard [1989].

7. See Chant [1980], and Hunter and Coggin [1988].

8. See, for example, Ball and Brown [1968].

9. See, for example, Givoly and Lakonishok [1980].

10. Keynes [1936], p. 156.

11. See, for example, Diefenbach [1972], Bidwell [1977], and Shepard [1977].

12. See Davies and Canes [1978], Stanley, Lewellen, and Schlarbaum [1981], Bjerring, Lakonishok, and Vermaelen [1983], Dimson and Marsh [1984], and Elton, Gruber, and Grossman [1986].

13. See Gray [1966], Barnea and Logue [1973], Mastrapasqua and Bolten [1973], and Korschot [1978].

14. See Brown, Foster, and Noreen [1985], Chapter 4, and Appendix A.1 and A.2, and O'Brien [1988a].

15. See Sorensen and Williamson [1985], and Coggin [1986].

16. See Coggin [1989] for a discussion.

17. For more detail on "active" versus "passive" investment management, see Sharpe [1985], Chapter 20.

References

Armstrong, J.S. "Relative Accuracy of Judgemental and Extrapolative Methods in Forecast Annual Earnings," *Journal of Forecasting* 2 (October-December 1983): 437-447.

Ball, R., and P. Brown. "An Empirical Evaluation of Accounting Income Numbers," *Journal of Accounting Research* 6 (Autumn 1968): 159-178.

Barnea, A., and D.E. Logue. "Evaluating the Forecasts of a Security Analyst," *Financial Management* 2 (Summer 1973): 38-45

Bidwell, C.M., III. "How Good is Institutional Brokerage Research?" *Journal of Portfolio Management* 3 (Winter 1977): 26-31.

Bing, R.A. "Survey of Practitioners' Stock Evaluation Methods," *Financial Analysts Journal* 27 (May-June 1971): 55-60.

Bjerring, J.H., J. Lakonishok, and T. Vermaelen. "Stock Prices and Financial Analysts' Recommendations," *Journal of Finance* 38 (March 1983): 187-204.

Brown, L.D., R.L. Hagerman, P.A. Griffin, and M.E. Zmijewski. "Security Analyst Superiority Relative to Univariate Time-Series Models in Forecasting Quarterly Earnings," *Journal of Accounting and Economics* 9 (1987a): 61-87.

Brown, L.D., R.L. Hagerman, P.A. Griffin, and M. E. Zmijewski. "An Evaluation of Alternative Proxies for the Market's Assessment of Unexpected Earnings," *Journal of Accounting and Economics* 9 (1987b): 159-163.

Brown, L.D., G.D. Richardson, and S. J. Schwager. "An Information Interpretation of Financial Analyst Superiority in Forecasting Earnings," *Journal of Accounting Research* 25 (Spring 1987): 49-67.

Brown, L.D., and M.S. Rozeff. "The Superiority of Analyst Forecasts as Measures of Expectations" Evidence form Earnings." *Journal of Finance* 33 (March 1978): 1-16.

Brown, P., G. Foster, and E. Noreen. *Security Analyst Multi-Forecasts and the Capital Market* (Sarasota, FL: American Accounting Association, 1985).

Chant, P.D. "On the Predictability of Corporate Earnings Per Share Behavior," *Journal of Finance* 35 (March 1980): 13-21.

Chugh, L.C., and J.W. Meador. "The Stock Valuation Process: The Analysts' View," *Financial Analysts Journal* 40 (November-December 1984): 41-48.

Coggin, T.D. "The Dividend Discount Model and the Stock Selection Process." *Handbook of Modern Finance,* 1986 Update, edited by D.E. Logue (Boston: Warren, Gorham & Lamont, 1986).

Coggin, T.D. "Active Equity Management." *Portfolio & Investment Management,* edited by Frank J. Fabozzi (Chicago: Probus Publishing Company, 1989).

Coggin, T.D., and J.E. Hunter. "Analysts' EPS Forecasts Nearer Actual than Statistical Models," *Journal of Business Forecasting* 1 (Winter 1982-1983): 20-23.

Coggin, T.D., and J.E. Hunter. "Problems in Measuring the Quality of Investment Information: The Perils of the Information Coefficient," *Financial Analysts Journal* 39 (May-June 1983): 25-31.

Coggin, T.D., and J.E. Hunter. "Analyst Forecasts of EPS and EPS Growth: Decomposition of Error, Relative Accuracy and Relation to Return." Working Paper, Virginia Retirement System, Richmond, VA (1989).

Cohen, J.B., E.D. Zinbarg, and A. Zeikel. *Investment Analysis and Portfolio Management,* 5e. (Homewood, IL: Richard D. Irwin, 1987).

Conroy, R., and R. Harris. "Consensus Forecasts of Corporate Earnings: Analysts' Forecasts and Time Series Methods," *Management Science* 33 (June 1987): 725-738.

Davies, P.L., and M. Canes. "Stock Prices and the Publication of Second-Hand Information," *Journal of Business* 51 (January 1978): 43-46.

Diefenbach, R.E. "How Good is Institutional Brokerage Research," *Financial Analysts Journal* 28 (January-February 1972): 65-60.

Dimson, E., and P. Marsh. "An Analysis of Brokers' and Analysts' Unpublished Forecasts of UK Stock Returns," *Journal of Finance* 39 (December 1984): 1257-1292.

Elton, E.J., M.J. Gruber, and M. Gultekin. "Expectations and Share Prices," *Management Science* 27 (September 1981): 975-987.

Elton, E.J., M.J. Gruber, and M.N. Gultekin. "Professional Expectations: Accuracy and Diagnosis of Errors," *Journal of Financial and Quantitative Methods Analysis* 19 (December 1984): 351-363.

Elton, E.J., M.J. Gruber, and S. Grossman. "Discrete Exceptional Data and Portfolio Performance," *Journal of Finance* 41 (July 1986): 699-714.

Foster, G. *Financial Statement Analysis,* 2e. (Englewood Cliffs, NJ: Prentice-Hall, 1986).

Givoly, D., and J. Lakonishok. "Financial Analysts of Earnings: Their Value to Investors," *Journal of Banking and Finance* 4 (September 1980): 221-233.

Gray, W.S. "Measuring the Analyst's Performance," *Financial Analysts Journal* 22 (March-April 1966): 56-63.

Guerard, J.B., Jr. "Combining Time-Series Model Forecasts and Analysts' Forecasts for Superior Forecasts of Annual Earnings," *Financial Analysts Journal* 45 (January-February 1989): 69-71.

Hassell, J., and R. Jennings. "Relative Forecast Accuracy and the Timing of Earnings Forecast Announcements," *Accounting Review* 61 (January 1986): 58-75.

Hawkins, E.H., S.C. Chamberlin, and W.F. Daniel. "Earnings Expectations and Security Prices," *Financial Analysts Journal* 40 (September-October 1984): 24-38.

Hunter, J.E., and T.D. Coggin. "Analyst Judgment: The Efficient Market Hypothesis Versus a Psychological Theory of Human Judgment," *Organizational Behavior and Human Decision Processes* 42 (December 1988): 284-302.

Kahneman, D., P. Slovic, and A. Tversky. *Judgment Under Uncertainty: Heuristics and Biases* (New York: Cambridge University Press, 1982).

Keynes, J.M. *The General Theory of Employment, Interest and Money* (New York: Harcourt, Brace & Company, 1936).

Korschot, B.C. "Quantitative Evaluation of Investment Research Analysts," *Financial Analysts Journal* 34 (July-August 1978): 41-46.

Little, Arthur D., Inc. *Quantitative Methods and Information Technologies for Investment Advising,* Cambridge, MA (April 1987).

Malkiel, B.G. "Risk and Return: A New Look." Working Paper no. 700, National Bureau of Economic Research, Cambridge, MA (1981).

Mastrapasqua, F., and S. Bolten. "A Note on Financial Analyst Evaluation," *Journal of Finance* 28 (June 1973): 707-712.

Meehl, P.E. *Clinical Versus Statistical Prediction* (Minneapolis, MN: University of Minnesota Press, 1954).

Neiderhoffer, V., and P.J. Regan. "Earnings Changes, Analysts' Forecasts and Stock Prices," *Financial Analysts Journal* 28 (May-June 1972): 65-71.

O'Brien, P.C. "Analysts' Forecasts as "Earnings Expectations," *Journal of Accounting and Economics* 20 (January 1988a): 533-83.

O'Brien, P.C. "Forecast Accuracy of Individual Analysts in Nine Industries." Working Paper no. 1940-87, Sloan School of Management, MIT, Cambridge, MA (May 1988b).

Richards, F.M. "Analysts' Performance and the Accuracy of Corporate Earnings Forecasts." *Journal of Business* 49 (July 1976): 350-357.

Rozeff, M.S. "Predicting Long-Term Earnings Growth: Comparisons of Expected Return Models, Submartingales and Value Line Analysts," *Journal of Forecasting* 2 (October-December 1983): 425-435.

Sharpe, W.F. *Investments,* 3rd ed. (Englewood Cliffs, NJ: Prentice-Hall, 1985).

Shepard, L. "How Good Is Investment Advice for Individuals," *Journal of Portfolio Management* 3 (Winter 1977): 32-36.

Sorensen, E.H., and D.A. Williamson. "Some Evidence of the Value of Dividend Discount Models," *Financial Analysts Journal* 41 (November-December 1985): 60-69.

Stanley, L., W.G. Lewellen, and G.G. Schlarbaum. "Further Evidence on the Value of Professional Investment Research," *Journal of Financial Research* 4 (Spring 1981): 1-9.

van Dijk, D. *Almost Everything You Ever Wanted to Know about Consensus Earnings Revisions.* Unpublished MBA thesis, Baruch College-CUNY, New York, NY (June 1986).

Section 2:
Forecast Revisions

Chapter 6

The Use and Misuse of Consensus Earnings*

Robert D. Arnott
Chief Executive Officer
First Quadrant

The significance of earnings in stock price behavior has been demonstrated repeatedly. Elton and Gruber have demonstrated that the knowledge of true earnings is highly profitable. Furthermore, they have shown that knowledge of the future consensus for earnings is still more profitable.[1,2] Unfortunately, we cannot know in advance what future earnings or future consensus earnings estimates will be.

As a result, several questions deserve our attention. Can traditional earnings momentum based on consensus EPS forecasts help us to select superior investments? Do stocks that we expect to have sharply improved earnings offer superior performance? How much can perfect foresight of future earnings help us? If we know the answer to these questions, we will also know how much we can be helped by superior research, which yields good but not perfect foresight.

Our questions do not end here, however. How valuable is it to know where consensus earnings estimates are headed? Is it more productive for analysts to forecast future esti-mates than to forecast earnings per se? Can past trends in consensus lead to earnings estimates that are superior to consensus? Can we forecast future consensus estimates by extrapolating past trends in the consensus? If so, how much of this information is already reflected in stock prices?

To answer these questions, I use I/B/E/S[3] consensus earnings estimates covering some 700 securities[4] over 27 quarters from the second quarter of 1976 to the fourth quarter of 1982. I use several measures to evaluate the effectiveness of security selection models.

First, I group stocks by decile, to see whether the stocks falling into the top decile(s), based on some criterion, outperform those in the bottom decile(s). I refine this test by looking at the top and bottom 5% as well as the top and bottom deciles. This procedure allows us to see whether a model offers consistent results from decile to decile and whether a model is better on the "buy" side or "sell" side.

Second, I compute the correlation in each quarter between a stock selection model and

---

* The author gratefully acknowledges Lynch, Jones, & Ryan, the suppliers of I/B/E/S data, for their assistance and helpful comments in this project.

Reprinted with permission from *The Journal of Portfolio Management,* Spring 1985, pgs. 18-27.

subsequent stock performance, based on the universe of 700 issues. This is widely known as an "Information Content" (or IC) test.[5] This masks some of the subtleties of a security selection model,[6] but it is the best one-number indication of model effectiveness and has the advantage of simplicity.

Last, I examine model consistency, which is every bit as important as long-term effectiveness, by counting how many of the 27 quarterly correlations (ICs) are positive. I show the percent of the 27 quarters in which the model adds value, using asterisks to indicate whether the model is consistent enough to have statistical significance.

Consensus EPS and Returns

Exhibit 1 summarizes the results for the tests of traditional earnings momentum based on consensus earnings estimates. A detailed review of the first column of Exhibit 1 will help the reader understand this and subsequent tables.

The 700 stocks in the test universe were ranged according to the percentage change in earnings from the latest full fiscal year earnings (hereafter to be called FY0) to the consensus earnings estimate for the current fiscal year (FY1), for *each* of the 27 quarters tested. This measure is traditionally called "earnings momentum" or, more accurately, "earnings momentum for the current fiscal year."[7]

The 5% of the 700 stocks with the highest expected earnings increase from FY0 to FY1 reaped an average total return in the subsequent quarter of 5.2%. The first, second, and third deciles reaped returns of 5.9%, 4.9% and 4.0%, respectively, while the eighth, ninth, and tenth deciles reaped returns of 4.4%, 4.5% and 4.1%, respectively. The 5% of the 700 stocks with the greatest anticipated drop in earnings from FY0 to FY1 generated an average return of 3.9%.

The mean correlation (or IC), over the 27 quarters tested between anticipated earnings change and subsequent *three*-month total returns was +0.025%, although individual quarterly ICs ranged as high as 0.229 and as low as –0.168 in the 27 quarters tested. The IC was positive in only 59% of the 27 quarters

Exhibit 1 EPS Momentum (expected % change)

	Est FY1	vs.	Act FY0	Est FY2	vs.	Est FY1
	3-mo		12-mo	3-mo		12-mo
Total Returns by Decile						
Top 5%	5.2%		24.5%	3.7%		24.2%
1st decile	5.9%		23.7%	5.2%		24.4%
2nd decile	4.9%		18.3%	4.5%		20.2%
3rd decile	4.0%		17.1%	4.2%		16.5%
8th decile	4.4%		15.4%	3.3%		13.7%
9th decile	4.5%		16.5%	3.3%		13.6%
10th decile	4.1%		16.4%	3.4%		13.6%
Bottom 5%	3.9%		16.4%	3.2%		13.8%
Correlations						
Mean	– 0.025		+ 0.051	+ 0.036		– 0.090
Best Case	– 0.229		+ 0.213	+ 0.260		+ 0.294
Worst Case	– 0.168		– 0.181	– 0.351		– 0.296
% Above Zero	59%		60%	44%		60%

tested. Thus, fully 41% of the time this kind of earnings momentum model would have harmed investment performance. The *lack* of any asterisk(s) after this number indicates that this model is not consistent enough to be statistically significant.

The second column of Exhibit 1 shows similar results for *twelve*-month returns. Thus, we are comparing consensus FY1 earnings momentum (the percentage change from actual FY0 earnings to consensus FY1 estimated earnings) with subsequent 12-month stock performance. The decile with the strongest estimated FY1 earnings momentum reaps some 7% higher return over the subsequent 12 months than the tenth decile. The average IC for 12-month returns is +0.051, which is better than the three-month result; but the model still only works 60% of the time, which is not statistically significant.

Earnings momentum is also measured based on the percentage change from the estimated earnings for the current fiscal year (FY1) to the next fiscal year (FY2). The third and fourth columns of Exhibit 1 show the results for stocks ranked according to FY2 earnings momentum over a subsequent three-month and 12-month span, respectively. These results are better than the results for FY1 earnings momentum. The top decile (based on expected FY2 earnings momentum) beats the bottom decile by an average of 2% over the subsequent three months and 11% over the subsequent 12 months. The three-month IC averages +0.036 and the 12-month IC averages +0.090. On the other hand, an FY2 earnings momentum model is, if anything, *less* consistent than an FY1 earnings momentum model. The three-month IC is positive in only 44% of the 27 quarters tested, versus 59% for the FY1 model, while the 12-month IC is positive some 60% of the time.

Is Consensus Earnings Momentum Useless?

Prior studies have shown that consensus estimates of earnings momentum are not at all correlated with stock performance. This would suggest that the market efficiently prices stocks in accordance with consensus earnings estimates. This would further suggest that the ever-popular earnings momentum approach to stock selection is comparatively useless.

The results, in Exhibit 1, are *somewhat* more favorable than past studies and show that a strategy of buying stocks with strong expected earnings gains may be *somewhat* profitable. This implies that the market may be *somewhat* inefficient in discounting current consensus earnings estimates (in the form of "earnings momentum" models).

Nevertheless, an earnings momentum strategy appears to lead to underperformance almost as often as it leads to superior performance. This level of consistency is so low that the results cannot be considered statistically significant. These modestly favorable results could very well be a fluke!

A rather striking and counterintuitive result appears in Exhibit 2. If we rank stocks based on the anticipated *dollar* change in earnings, rather than on percentage changes, the results are the opposite of those in Exhibit 1. The stocks with large expected dollar gains in EPS *underperform* those with large expected dollar drops in EPS. Furthermore, this relationship is consistent enough to be statistically significant.

This paradoxical dichotomy between a dollar-momentum model and a conventional percentage-momentum model leads to an unusual idea. We can rank issues into percentiles based on both anticipated *dollar* changes of EPS and anticipated *percent* change of EPS. By taking the difference between the two percentile rankings for individual issues, we can favor issues with large positive percentage momentum and small positive dollar momentum or issues with large negative dollar momentum and modest negative percentage momentum.

Exhibit 3 shows that this approach is profitable and consistent, whether we use FY1 or

Exhibit 2   EPS Momentum (expected dollar change)

	Est FY1	vs.	Act FY0	Est FY2	vs.	Act FY1
	3-mo		12-mo	3-mo		12-mo
Total Returns by Decile						
Top 5%	3.6%		13.6%	2.5%		9.4%
1st decile	3.2%		10.6%	2.5%		8.5%
2nd decile	3.3%		11.0%	3.3%		11.1%
3rd decile	4.1%		13.3%	3.0%		10.6%
8th decile	5.8%		24.8%	4.7%		21.5%
9th decile	5.0%		20.6%	5.0%		23.3%
10th decile	3.3%		12.3%	4.1%		18.7%
Bottom 5%	2.6%		9.4%	3.8%		15.0%
Correlations						
Mean	− 0.018		− 0.055	− 0.041		− 0.114
Best Case	+ 0.127		+ 0.085	+ 0.217		+ 0.097
Worst Case	− 0.222		− 0.330	− 0.248		− 0.419
% Above Zero	41%		16%***	26%**		16%***

* 5% significance (two-tailed test)
** 1% significance (two-tailed test)
*** 0.1% significance (two-tailed test)

FY2 estimates, and whether we look at subsequent three-month or subsequent 12-month returns. It is beyond the scope of this article to speculate on the implications of this relationship, as a detailed review of this paradox would be quite lengthy, but this is clearly an area that merits further investigation. In any event, Exhibits 2 and 3 are included as "food for thought."

Perfect Foresight and Return

If the conventional use of consensus earnings momentum is not a reliable predictor of stock price behavior, then let us examine the question of how much value we can add if we possess perfect information about actual earnings. If consensus earnings momentum is not strongly related to price behavior but perfect forecasts are strongly related to price behavior, then we will have a clear indication of how much value we can add if our own forecasts are better than consensus forecasts. This will give a clear indication of the potential value of superior research.

Exhibit 4 shows the value that perfect earnings forecasts would have as a security selection tool—if they could be found. The first column of Exhibit 4 shows that the decile of stocks with the largest positive change[8] in actual FY1 earnings from FY0 earnings outperforms the decile with the poorest earnings comparison by an impressive 9.3% *per quarter.* The correlation (IC) between the actual earnings change and the quarterly stock price averages 0.198 and the relationship is positive in all but one of the quarters tested. If we look further down the road and compare the actual change in earnings from FY1 to FY2, the relationship is slightly weaker but still strong. The third column of Exhibit 4 shows that the average IC is 0.171, and the top decile outperforms the bottom decile by some 8% per quarter. As with FY1, the correlation is positive in all but one of the quarters tested.

Since we are dealing with full fiscal year earnings, it is not surprising that the relationship between EPS momentum and 12-month total returns is even stronger than three-

Exhibit 3　EPS Momentum—%/$ Divergence

	FY1 Divergence		FY2 Divergence	
	3-mo	12-mo	3-mo	12-mo
Total Returns by Decile				
Top 5%	8.4%	44.9%	8.4%	47.2%
1st decile	7.4%	37.1%	7.4%	40.0%
2nd decile	5.2%	20.7%	5.0%	22.6%
3rd decile	4.3%	15.7%	4.2%	17.1%
8th decile	4.1%	14.9%	3.1%	10.8%
9th decile	3.1%	11.4%	2.3%	9.0%
10th decile	2.8%	7.9%	2.5%	8.2%
Bottom 5%	2.9%	7.6%	2.4%	8.1%
Correlations				
Mean	0.080	0.204	0.096	0.247
Best Case	0.315	0.420	0.367	0.441
Worst Case	− 0.175	− 0.074	− 0.239	− 0.005
% Above Zero	74%**	93%***	78%***	96%***

* 5% significance (two-tailed test)
** 1% significance (two-tailed test)
*** 0.1% significance (two-tailed test)

Exhibit 4　Perfect Foresight—Actual EPS Change

	Act FY1	vs.	Act FY0		Act FY2	vs.	Act FY1
	3-mo		12-mo		3-mo		12-mo
Total Returns by Decile							
Top 5%	11.2%		48.9%		11.9%		60.8%
1st decile	9.3%		40.3%		9.7%		50.8%
2nd decile	6.8%		26.4%		6.0%		31.0%
3rd decile	4.8%		17.9%		4.5%		22.8%
8th decile	1.6%		10.1%		2.3%		8.4%
9th decile	0.5%		5.8%		1.5%		2.7%
10th decile	0.0%		4.4%		1.6%		− 0.8%
Bottom 5%	− 0.3%		5.2%		1.8%		0.3%
Correlations							
Mean	0.198		0.295		0.171		0.441
Best Case	0.360		0.505		0.308		0.540
Worst Case	− 0.045		0.058		− 0.002		0.241
% Above Zero	96%***		100%***		96%***		100%***

* 5% significance (two-tailed test)
** 1% significance (two-tailed test)
*** 0.1% significance (two-tailed test)

month returns. The second column of Exhibit 4 shows that the decile with the most favorable actual FY1 earnings momentum outperforms the decile with the least favorable EPS comparison by some 36%. The average IC is 0.295, and there are no instances in which this relationship fails. The last column of Exhibit 4 shows that the results for FY2 are even more striking with the top decile outperforming the bottom decile by over 50% in 12 months. The average IC is 0.441, and, as with the FY1 results, there is not a single case of a negative correlation between the actual FY2 EPS change and 12-month returns.

These results echo those of Elton and Gruber. They tested earnings momentum and found that issues with strong actual earnings perform well and issues with poor earnings fare badly in the months prior to the earnings announcement. Since Exhibit 4 is based on more issues and covers a longer time span than prior studies, it adds weight to the existing evidence.

Elton and Gruber also observed that the relationship was stronger for issues exhibiting favorable or unfavorable "earnings surprise." In other words, if we focus on the differences between the consensus FY1 or FY2 estimates and the subsequent actual results, we can do better than if we focus on actual results alone.

This analysis echoes these findings, as we can see by comparing Exhibit 5 with Exhibit 4. On a quarterly basis, the decile of stocks with the best *unanticipated* EPS outperformed the worst decile by some 10% using both FY1 and FY2 earnings. For both FY1 and FY2 earnings, the mean correlation exceeds 0.2, and the positive relationship between earnings surprise and quarterly stock returns *never* fails. If we look at 12-month performance, the results are even more impressive. The decile of stocks with the most favorable FY1 earnings surprise outperform the worst decile by over 30%, while the excess performance for FY2 exceeds 50%. The correlation between earnings surprise and 12-

Exhibit 5 Perfect Foresight—Actual EPS Surprise

	Act FY1	vs.	Est FY1	Act FY2	vs.	Est FY2
	3-mo		12-mo	3-mo		12-mo
Total Returns by Decile						
Top 5%	10.4%		43.5%	12.2%		60.3%
1st decile	9.2%		37.9%	10.0%		51.1%
2nd decile	7.0%		27.2%	7.8%		34.2%
3rd decile	5.9%		20.9%	4.7%		23.7%
8th decile	1.0%		7.8%	0.9%		5.4%
9th decile	− 0.1%		4.2%	0.3%		1.0%
10th decile	− 0.8%		3.7%	0.3%		− 3.2%
Bottom 5%	− 1.2%		2.7%	0.6%		− 2.0%
Correlations						
Mean	0.221		0.301	0.226		0.481
Best Case	0.359		0.434	0.362		0.621
Worst Case	0.063		0.030	0.022		0.239
% Above Zero	100%***		100%***	100%***		100%***

* 5% significance (two-tailed test).
** 1% significance (two-tailed test).
*** 0.1% significance (two-tailed test).

month returns for FY1 and FY2 earnings are 0.301 and 0.481, respectively, with no instances of a negative relationship.

Finally, we would do better if we could perfectly foresee the change in consensus earnings *forecasts* over the next three months than we would do with perfect foresight of earnings *per se* and nearly as well as with perfect foresight of earnings surprise! Exhibit 6 shows that the decile with the biggest increase in earnings expectations outperforms the decile with the worst drop in consensus earnings forecast by over 10% in a single quarter for both FY1 and FY2 earnings. The mean correlations are 0.207 and 0.212, respectively. These results are better than the results for perfect foresight of actual earnings shown in Exhibit 4 and almost match the earnings surprise model shown in Exhibit 5. Once again, this relationship virtually never fails.

Exhibit 6 Perfect Foresight—Consensus EPS Change

	3-month Concurrent FY1 Change	3-month Concurrent FY2 Change
3-Month Total Returns by Decile		
Top 5%	13.0%	12.6%
1st decile	11.2%	11.1%
2nd decile	8.6%	8.1%
3rd decile	6.5%	5.6%
8th decile	2.8%	2.5%
9th decile	1.3%	0.7%
10th decile	0.7%	0.7%
Bottom 5%	1.0%	0.6%
Correlations		
Mean	0.207	0.212
Best Case	0.391	0.449
Worst Case	0.039	− 0.118
% Above Zero	100%***	96%***

* 5% significance (two-tailed test)
** 1% significance (two-tailed test)
*** 0.1% significance (two-tailed test)

In short, we find that:

- Consensus estimates are largely reflected in stock prices. While traditional earnings momentum models may add value, the evidence is mixed. At best, such models are not consistent enough to inspire confidence.

- Earnings *do* affect stock prices in a meaningful and consistent way. Perfect foresight of earnings would add considerable value, virtually without fail. By extension, superior research will add value to the extent that superior earnings estimates result.

- Earnings surprises and changes in consensus expectations are more important than earnings per se. By extension, research targeted to anticipate surprise or changes in the consensus will be more valuable than research targeted to earnings forecasts per se.

These findings are not surprising; they match those of past studies, and they are consistent with common sense:

- Well-publicized consensus expectations should be reflected in stock prices.
- Rising (or falling) earnings affect corporate health and should affect stock prices, if they are unanticipated.
- Stock prices change in response to changes in outlook; hence, shifts in consensus estimates should affect stock prices.

These tests serve to confirm and add weight to past results, since they cover a longer time span with a larger sample.

Earnings Forecast Momentum

Thus far, we have learned little of practical investment value, since we cannot have perfect foresight of either future actual earnings or future consensus expectations. In order to reap any benefit from this work, we must be able to generate forecasts of earnings that are better than consensus or we must be able to generate forecasts of the future consensus itself.

Naturally, superior research can lead to superior earnings forecasts or even to forecasts of consensus. This is not easy to achieve; by definition, only half of all forecasts are better than consensus. It follows that roughly half of all analyses are better than average. Developing a superior research team is possible, but not easy.

Two questions that we have yet to address are: Can we forecast future earnings or consensus estimates based on past trends in the consensus? If so, how much of this information is already reflected in stock prices?

Predicting EPS

The evidence unequivocally supports a relationship between past trends in consensus earnings estimates and future earnings.

First, the latest one-month change in FY1 consensus is significantly related to the subsequent "earnings surprise," with a correlation of 0.31. In other words, the shift in FY1 consensus from last month to this month is meaningfully related to the shift from this month's FY1 consensus to the subsequent actual FY1 earnings. This relationship never failed in our 27 quarters of testing. Second, the results for FY2 are less compelling, but still significant, with a correlation of 0.18. Third, the relationship between the latest three-month shift in consensus and the subsequent "earnings surprise" is stronger than the one-month relationship for both FY1 and FY2 earnings (correlations of 0.33 and 0.20, respectively).

A superficial interpretation of this information might lead us to conclude that analysts are overly conservative in predicting changes from the latest actual earnings levels. It would lead to a tendency for consensus estimates to be steadily revised upward or downward in the direction of the actual earnings as new information becomes available.

This idea is readily discarded. If it was true, the difference between the current consensus and the latest actual earnings (FY0) would be positively related to the subsequent "earnings surprise," or the difference between the actual realized earnings and the current consensus. Yet, these are insignificantly correlated (correlations for FY1 and FY2 are 0.00 and 0.06 respectively). We can conclude that analysts do not tend to overstate or understate the difference between FY0 and FY1 earnings and between FY1 and FY2 earnings.

A more accurate appraisal of these data, coupled with an understanding of human nature, leads to a different conclusion. If an analyst's earnings estimates are based on all available information, then the next revision in an estimate would be equally likely to be followed by a continuation of this upward trend or by a reversal. Analysts are not rewarded for such reversals, however. An analyst who lowers an estimate one month and raises it the next risks a loss of credibility. Furthermore, estimates that differ sharply from consensus attract much attention. An analyst who goes out on a limb with an estimate that differs sharply from consensus loses credibility each time such an estimate is faulty. In short, analysts are encouraged to make estimates close to the consensus and to make revisions in estimates that are unlikely to require reversals. Both of these factors lead to a consensus that tends to maintain trends.

We can apply regression analysis to the correlation data to develop an optimized earnings estimate that is consistently superior to the consensus. A detailed review of Exhibit 7 will help the reader to understand this and other figures.

Let us designate actual earnings for FY1 as E, current consensus estimate for FY1 as E_t, and the consensus for the past six months as $E_{t-1}, \ldots, E_{t-6}$. The "earnings surprise" is simply $E - E_t$, and we can compute six one-month changes in consensus, from the "latest month" $(E_t - E_{t-1})$ to "five month-old data" $(E_{t-5} - E_{t-6})$. The solid line (with the scale to

Exhibit 7 FYI "Earnings Surprise" Forecasting

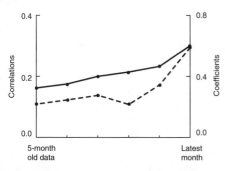

— Correlations of past one-month FY1 consensus change with subsequent "earnings surprise."

- - Coefficients of FY1 consensus changes in "optimal" estimate of subsequent "earnings surprise."

Exhibit 8 FY2 "Earnings Surprise" Forecasting

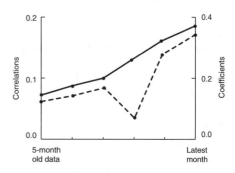

— Correlations of FY2 consensus changes with subsequent "earnings surprise."

- - Coefficients of FY2 consensus changes in "optimal" estimate of subsequent "earnings surprise."

the left) shows the correlation between these various one-month changes in consensus and "earnings surprise." The right-most point on the solid line is at 0.3 (on the left axis), meaning that the correlation between the latest one-month change $(E_t - E_{t-1})$ in consensus and the future "earnings surprise" $(E - E_t)$ is 0.3. The left-most point on the line is at 0.15, meaning that even a five-month-old change in consensus estimates $(E_{t-5} - E_{t-6})$ is correlated with "earnings surprise" relative to current consensus $(E - E_t)$. We can use a regression model with these data to design an "optimal" model for estimating "earnings surprise." The coefficients for this kind of model are shown as the dashed line in the figure. Thus, using the scale on the right, we can see that a best estimate for $E - E_t$ is:

$$(E - E_t) = 0.6 (E_t - E_{t-1}) + 0.35 (E_{t-1} - E_{t-2}) + \ldots + 0.2 (E_{t-5} - E_{t-6})$$

Exhibit 8 shows this same information for FY2 "earnings surprise" versus FY2 changes in consensus estimates.

This admittedly simple earnings model has a correlation with earnings surprise of 0.40 for FY1 and 0.25 for FY2. Since the "average" earnings estimate is (by definition) no better than consensus, and would thus be uncorrelated with "earnings surprise," these "optimized" estimates are clearly far better than the estimates of an average analyst. A progressive research department might choose to use these "optimal" estimates as a starting point for developing superior estimates. It goes without saying that a superior revised earnings estimate based on consensus would also be a superior benchmark for evaluating analyst estimates.

Naturally, the relationship between consensus change and estimation error changes as the fiscal year progresses. This, in turn, means that the framework for estimating an "optimal" earnings forecast will change as the year advances. The relationship strengthens as the actual earnings announcement approaches. Also, the weight on the most recent change in the earnings estimates rises as the fiscal year progresses. It is beyond the scope of this article to delve into the subtleties of this relationship over time.

Predicting Consensus

If past trends in consensus earnings estimates are correlated with the error in the current consensus, it is reasonable to expect a positive relationship between past changes in consensus and future changes in consensus. The one-month past change in FY1 consensus is meaningfully correlated with the change in consensus over the next month, with an average correlation of 0.41 (Exhibit 9). The FY2 relationship is weaker, but still significant with a correlation of 0.23 (Exhibit 10).

These correlations understate the true strength of the relationship. Often the consensus is unchanged in a given month; if it rises in one month, does not change in the second month, and rises again in the third month, there is zero correlation from one month to the next. For this reason, the correlation between a one-month change in consensus and the following three-month span is stronger than the correlations cited above (0.43 for FY1 and 0.25 for FY2). Finally, the correlation between the three-month change in consensus and the subsequent three-month change is similarly strong (0.44 for FY1 and 0.25 for FY2). These positive relationships never failed in the 27 quarters tested.

The consistency of these relationships across all quarters tested conclusively demonstrates the tendency for consensus estimates to maintain trends. Furthermore, it is clear that forecasting the future for consensus estimates is not only feasible, but is also actually easy.

As with forecasting "earning surprise," we can use regression analysis to develop an estimate of the change in consensus three months hence. Exhibits 9 and 10 show for FY1 and FY2, respectively, the correlations between past monthly changes in consensus and the subsequent three-month change in consensus, and the weight of these lagged consensus changes in the "optimal" forecast of the consensus estimate three months in the future.

Such a model has an excellent record for forecasting the change in consensus over the next three months. Correlations are 0.51 for FY1 and 0.30 for FY2. Unlike the forecast of earnings surprise, there is no appreciable variability over the course of a fiscal year in model effectiveness. There is no significant tendency for the model to work better or worse at different times in the fiscal year.

Predicting Returns

We can demonstrably improve earnings forecasts vis-a-vis consensus, and we can generate very good forecasts of the future consensus, merely by examining past trends in consensus. On the other hand, unless this can lead to superior investment returns, it is little more than an interesting academic exercise.

Exhibit 9 FY1 Future Consensus Change Forecasting

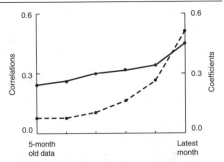

— Correlation of past one-month FY1 consensus change with subsequent three-month consensus change.

- - Coefficients of past one-month FY1 consensus change in "optimal" forecast of future three-month consensus change.

Exhibit 10 FY2 Future Consensus Change Forecasting

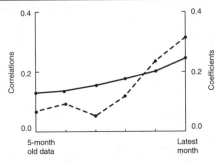

— Correlation of past one-month FY2 consensus change with subsequent three-month consensus change.

- - Coefficients of past one-month FY2 consensus change in "optimal" forecast of future three-month consensus change.

The critical question is: How much of the information in the past shift in consensus is already discounted in the current stock price?

Although the market is relatively efficient in discounting current consensus, the startling fact is that it seems to reflect essentially *none* of the information in recent *shifts* in consensus! Exhibit 11 shows that past shifts in consensus are meaningfully correlated with future stock returns:

- The latest one-month shifts in consensus FY1 and FY2 estimates have ICs of 0.090 and 0.074, respectively, with the subsequent three-month stock returns.[9] The FY1 and FY2 changes worked in 89% and 78% of the quarters tested, respectively.
- Even when we use one-month-old data for the one-month consensus change, we find correlations of 0.071 and 0.048, respectively.
- If we look at the latest three-month change

in consensus, we find virtually identical results as with the one-month consensus change.

- Even if we look at *three-month-old* data for the three-month change in consensus, we find correlations of 0.042 and 0.026 for FY1 and FY2, respectively. Thus, even after three months, the market has not yet fully discounted the change in consensus estimates.
- While 12-month ICs are generally no higher than three-month ICs, the spreads between the 12-month returns for the top and bottom deciles are approximately twice as wide as the spreads in three-month results. This suggests that trends in consensus are more valuable for security timing than for longer-term issue selection. It also suggests that past shifts in consensus are only about half discounted in the market even three months after they are public.

Exhibit 11 Value Added—Past Consensus EPS Change

	1-Month Est. FY1 Change	1-Month Est. FY2 Change	3-Month Est. FY1 Change	3-Month Est. FY2 Change	1-Month Est. FY1 Change	1-Month Est. FY2 Change	3-Month Est. FY1 Change	3-Month Est. FY2 Change
3-Month Total Return by Decile					**12-Month Total Return by Decile**			
Top 5%	9.4%	6.5%	9.7%	7.9%	31.2%	26.0%	33.7%	29.1%
1st decile	8.1%	5.9%	8.3%	6.5%	27.0%	23.7%	28.9%	26.4%
2nd decile	5.3%	5.2%	5.3%	4.2%	17.9%	18.7%	18.8%	18.2%
3rd decile	4.9%	4.0%	4.9%	4.4%	16.8%	14.6%	15.9%	15.5%
8th decile	2.8%	2.0%	3.9%	2.4%	10.8%	10.5%	14.2%	12.0%
9th decile	2.9%	2.0%	2.6%	2.3%	14.4%	12.4%	12.8%	11.9%
10th decile	3.5%	2.8%	3.7%	2.9%	16.1%	16.8%	18.6%	16.9%
Bottom 5%	4.3%	3.4%	4.7%	3.6%	20.3%	21.4%	21.5%	21.1%
Correlations					**Correlations**			
Mean	0.090	0.074	0.087	0.074	0.081	0.067	0.082	0.082
Best case	0.197	0.227	0.221	0.207	0.203	0.265	0.268	0.297
Worst case	−0.063	−0.141	−0.104	−0.191	−0.047	−0.193	−0.075	−0.175
% Above zero	89%***	78%***	92%***	78%***	89%***	80%***	85%***	84%***
Correlations for Lagged Estimate Change					**Correlations for Lagged Estimate Change**			
Mean	0.071	0.048	0.042	0.026	0.056	0.056	0.040	0.038
% Above zero	81%***	67%*	63%	59%	78%***	76%**	67%*	71%**

* 5% significance (two-tailed test)
** 1% significance (two-tailed test)
*** 0.1% significance (two-tailed test)

Lest there be some concern that these results do not allow adequate time between the availability of consensus data and measurement of subsequent return, it should be noted that I/B/E/S data are computed and made available in mid-month. This means, for example, that the one-month change in consensus is measured from mid-February to mid-March, while the subsequent three-month return is measured from March 31 through June 30. Thus, a two-week response lag is built into these tests. An investor who can respond faster is likely to achieve even better results.

These results are striking, yielding a spread in return of 3% to 5% between the top and bottom decile *each quarter* and a spread of 7% to 11% if positions are held for a full year. It is even more striking to note that these models are useful predictors of return about 85% of the time. This is a degree of consistency that not only passed statistical tests of significance, but can also inspire the confidence of investment practitioners.

As before, we can apply regression techniques to construct a model that incorporates the information included in past changes in both the FY1 and FY2 estimates. Exhibits 12 and 13 show for FY1 and FY2, respectively:

- Correlations of past monthly changes in consensus with subsequent three-month returns, and
- Coefficients in an "optimal" three-month regression model for return forecasting.

Exhibit 14 shows that this model has a 0.107 correlation with three-month return and a 0.102 correlation with 12-month return. Consistency for this model exceeds 90%, with a spread in returns between the top and bottom decile of over 5% per quarter and 12% per year.

It is easy to demonstrate that essentially none of the information in changes in consensus are discounted by the market. If the one-month FY1 change in consensus has a 0.43 correlation with the subsequent three-month change in consensus (from Exhibit 9) and if that three-month shift in consensus has a 0.207 correlation with the concurrent three-month stock return (from Exhibit 6), then a correlation of 0.089 (0.207 x 0.43) would suggest that the latest one-month consensus change is totally ignored by the market. Since the actual correlation is 0.90, this represents a significant market inefficiency. Comparable

Exhibit 12 Three-month Security Return Forecasting

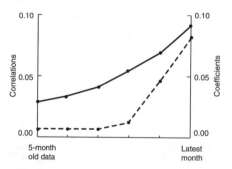

— Correlations of past one-month FY1 consensus change with subsequent three-month stock returns.

- - Coefficients of past one-month FY1 consensus change in "optimal" forecast of future three-month stock returns.

Exhibit 13 Three-month Security Return Forecasting

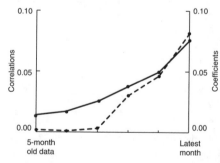

— Correlations of past one-month FY2 consensus change with subsequent three-month stock returns.

- - Coefficients of past one-month FY2 consensus change in "optimal" forecast of future three-month stock returns.

Exhibit 14 Value-Added—Consensus Change Model

3-month Total Returns by Decile	3-month Concurrent FY1 Change	3-month Concurrent FY2 Change
Top 5%	10.3%	35.7%
1st decile	8.7%	29.1%
2nd decile	5.5%	19.3%
3rd decile	5.0%	17.3%
8th decile	2.0%	9.8%
9th decile	1.8%	9.6%
10th decile	2.6%	14.2%
Bottom 5%	3.5%	18.3%
Correlations		
Mean	0.107	0.102
Best Case	0.242	0.293
Worst Case	− 0.081	− 0.092
% Above Zero	89%***	89%***

* 5% significance (two-tailed test)
** 1% significance (two-tailed test)
*** 0.1% significance (two-tailed test)

tests on the other measures of past consensus change suggest similar inefficiency.

In summary, the market is relatively efficient in discounting current consensus earnings momentum but is quite inefficient in discounting past shifts in consensus, which are in fact meaningful indicators of both the future consensus and of the future earnings surprise. The evidence suggests that falling consensus estimates are likely to continue to fall and that the stock price is not likely to rise until earnings estimates stop falling. Conversely, if consensus estimates have been rising, they are likely to continue to rise, with the result that sale of the stock may be imprudent until estimates stop rising.

Conclusions

We have demonstrated that:

- While the market may efficiently discount current consensus, it clearly does *not* efficiently discount past trends in

consensus. As a result, past trends in consensus can be moderately profitable and are a *highly* consistent security timing indicator.

- Trends in consensus have a strong tendency to persist. By looking at both current consensus earnings estimates and recent trends in consensus, we can generate superior estimates of earnings and of the future consensus itself.

- Traditional earnings momentum may be mildly useful in security selection. On the other hand, the consistency of such a model is so poor that we cannot reject the hypothesis that the market efficiently discounts current consensus earnings and momentum estimates.

- One unconventional approach to earnings momentum (%/$ divergence) may be both effective and consistent. Further research in earnings momentum is clearly indicated.

- Perfect foresight adds considerable value. Advance knowledge of true year-to-year earnings change is extremely useful in security selection. This suggests that superior research can add value.

- Coupled with readily available consensus earnings estimates, advance knowledge of earnings gives us advance knowledge of "earnings surprise." This is more valuable than advance knowledge of earnings per se.

- Advance knowledge of future consensus earnings is more valuable than advance knowledge of earnings per se. It is approximately as valuable as perfect foresight of "earnings surprise." This suggests an avenue for a more profitable application of superior research.

Endnotes

1. Edwin J. Elton, Martin J. Gruber, and Mustafa Gultekin, "Earnings Expectations and Share Prices," *Management Science.* September 1981, pp. 975-987.

2. Edwin J. Elton, Martin J. Gruber, and Sak Mo Koo, "Expectational Data: The Effect of Quarterly Reports," Working Paper, New York University.

3. Institutional Brokers Estimation Service (I/B/E/S) is a service offered by Lynch, Jones, & Ryan. I/B/E/S surveys some 50 institutional brokerage houses for current earnings estimates covering earnings for the current fiscal year (FY1), the next fiscal year (FY2), and 3-5 year future growth rates. Average (consensus) estimates for each of these are provided, along with other information, such as standard deviation of estimates, highest and lowest estimates, and past trends in estimates.

4. The stocks used for these tests included the current membership of the S&P 500 combined with the current membership of the Boston Company stock monitor. Certain of these tests were repeated on the Boston Company full database of 4000 securities for confirmation purposes, with similar results.

5. The "Information Content" is a correlation, or a rank correlation, between an ex-ante attractiveness measure for a stock and the subsequent performance. I prefer a raw correlation, which is what I used in this article, since more weight is given to stocks on the extremes, both in ex-ante return forecasts and in subsequent performance. I also truncate results that deviate from the mean by more than 3.0 standard deviations, so that no single stock is likely to dominate the results. The specific algorithm for computing ICs typically has only a modest effect on the resulting correlation numbers.

6. An IC does not reveal nonlinear relationships between a model and subsequent performance. It also understates the effectiveness of any model that is useful only on one tail (i.e., which is useful for isolating "buy" or "sell" candidates, but not both).

7. To allow for negative earnings, I actually compute the percentage earnings momentum for FY1 as follows:

$$\% \text{ Change} = 100 \times \frac{(FY1 - FY0)}{\max(FY0, FY1)}$$

This also eliminates extreme percentage change numbers (the results will always be between -200% and $+200\%$). As a result, individual cases need not distort the results. For most stocks, this measure of percentage change is almost identical to an ordinary percentage measure.

8. For Exhibits 4, 5, 6 and 11, changes in earnings, consensus, or earnings surprise are normalized by dividing an earnings uncertainty measure, which is constructed as follows. The standard deviation of the past five years' earnings is computed, the standard deviation of current FY1 and FY2 earnings estimates is computed, and earnings uncertainty is defined to equal the geometric mean of these past and future earnings risk measures. In so doing, a 10c/share change in consensus (or in earnings) for Chrysler (with its highly unstable earnings stream) is deemed to be far less significant than a 10c/share shift for IBM (with its relatively stable, predictable earnings stream).

9. Some of these results were crosschecked against a measure of alpha with virtually identical results. Also, some results were crosschecked on a larger database of some 200 stocks, once again with virtually identical results.

Chapter 7

Changes in Consensus Earnings Estimates and Their Impact on Stock Returns

Langdon B. Wheeler, CFA
President
Numeric Investors L.P.

This study updates and expands upon previous research into the impact of changes in earnings estimates on U.S. stock returns. This study examines the ability of a wide variety of estimate revision measures to predict relative returns within a broad universe of stocks (and subsets of this universe) over a nine-year period from 1981 through 1989.

Summary

This study has five major parts. In the first part, the impact of earnings estimate revisions on contemporaneous stock returns is investigated to verify that revisions continue to be important determinants of returns. Estimate revisions are found to have had a powerful influence on relative stock returns in each of the last nine years. Of all nine years, they had their greatest impact on stock returns in 1989.

The second part of the study reviews what is known from previous research and industry lore about the interaction of earnings surprise, estimate revisions, and analyst behavior, all over the dimension of time. Behavioral explanations for these interactions are postulated.

In the study's third section, simple measures of the trend in estimates over the recent past are evaluated as predictors of estimate revisions and relative stock returns in the future. Changes in the mean estimate, the high and low estimates, and the number of estimates being raised or lowered over the last few months are used to rank stocks at the start of each month from 1981 through 1989. The spread between top and bottom quintiles of stocks ranked with these measures averages 1 to 1 1/2% in the following month.

Part Four of the study tests a proprietary multifactor estimate revisions model (Estrend™) that incorporates several of the simple measures tested in part three. The mean spread between the top and bottom quintiles ranked by Estrend widens to 1.68% in the following month. At the same time, there was a less than proportionate increase in the standard deviation of these spreads, suggesting that higher predictive power, with greater consistency, is achieved by combining simple measures.

The final part of the study partitions the universe along several dimensions to determine whether estimate trend prediction models like Estrend are more or less effective in specific segments of the market or in specific time periods.

Over the dimension of time, Estrend provided substantial return prediction power in each of the nine years tested, but some years were notably more robust than others.

Preliminary evidence was found that there is some seasonality to Estrend's effectiveness, specifically that January and August were notably weak months for the strategy during the nine years of this study.

Finally, Estrend's rankings were found to have some return-predicting ability even five months after their creation, though this ability diminished at the rate of about 20% per month.

Over the dimension of market sectors, Estrend was found to provide higher return spreads with greater consistency when used across all economic sectors rather than just within sectors.

Estrend was found to be more powerful with stocks that were smaller, had fewer estimates, and had higher estimate uncertainty.

Methodology and Backtest Environment

This study was conducted in early 1990 using the computers, strategy simulation software, and databases of the DAIS Group, formerly of Drexel Burnham Lambert.

The study endeavored to test the impact of estimate revisions on all stocks of institutional interest that were available during the study's test period, from December 31, 1980, through December 29, 1989. Accordingly, the study included all stocks in the I/B/E/S database with at least three fiscal year one estimates and an unadjusted share price of $7.00 or higher at the start of each month during the test. The number of stocks in the universe grew from about 1,100 stocks at the beginning of the test period to almost 1,900 by the end of the period. Efforts were made to minimize survivorship bias by screening stocks for the test from a comprehensive CUSIP list for the period. Nonetheless, some stocks were excluded because of lack of price histories, so the study does contain a limited amount of survivorship bias. The author believes that

such bias would have minimal impact on the findings, however.

A separate stock universe was created for each of the 108 months in the test period. Each month's universe contained all stocks meeting both criteria at the start of that month. Then the I/B/E/S data for all of the stocks within each month's universe was analyzed to develop scores or rankings for each stock using the various calculations to be described subsequently. Ticker files containing each stock's raw ranking were then submitted to the strategy-simulation software.

The simulation software sorted the stocks into quintiles based on their raw rankings. Returns for each quintile, containing equal weighted positions in each stock, were calculated for each month or each quarter of the test period. Returns for each year were calculated by linking shorter period returns. Cumulative and annualized returns were calculated for the total nine-year period. To compare the power and stability of the various measures being tested, a mean relative return for each quintile (and the standard deviation of these relative returns) was calculated for the 108 months or 36 quarters tested. The mean and standard deviation of the rank-order information coefficients was also calculated.

1. Back to the Future: Measuring the Impact of Earnings Estimate Revisions on Contemporaneous Stock Returns

The impact of earnings estimate revisions on contemporaneous stock returns can be measured by ranking stocks by the changes that occur to their earnings estimates during a particular period and then comparing these rankings to their returns earned during this same period. Although it demonstrates great return forecasting power, such a process would be impossible to implement in a real-world investment strategy because it requires perfect foreknowledge of estimate changes. It does however, provide a good measure of the importance of earnings estimate revisions to contemporaneous stock returns.

As a first and simplest measure of change in consensus estimates, the change in the mean estimate (expressed in dollars and cents) can be divided by the price of each stock.

rate of change =
change in mean estimate ($) / price ($)

This calculation creates a standardized measure of change that equates a five-cent change in the estimate for a ten-dollar stock to a fifty-cent change in the estimate for a hundred dollar stock. The change in the mean divided by the price is superior to a simple rate of change for the mean itself, because discontinuities are eliminated when the estimates are close to zero (producing very high rates of change in the mean) or negative (producing nonsensical results).

Exhibit 1 shows the impact of perfect foreknowledge of estimate revisions on stock returns. Stocks were sorted into quintiles at the start of each of the 36 quarters of the test period based on the change in their estimates (mean divided by price) during that quarter. The best quintile's return averaged almost 12% per quarter higher than the worst quintiles. When quarterly quintile returns were linked, annual spreads between the best and worst quintiles averaged (geometrically) almost 50% per year. In the weakest year, the spread was "only" 33%; in the best year it was twice as large. In every year, the quintile returns increased monotonically from the least attractive to the most attractive quintile. Exhibit 2 shows that in every quarter of the test period, the information coefficient was positive and the top quintile's returns exceeded the bottom quintile's returns. Clearly, estimate revisions have a powerful and persistent impact on contemporaneous stock returns. It follows then that if such revisions can be predicted, it should be possible to earn superior investment returns by owning stocks of the companies enjoying the most favorable revisions relative to the market as a whole.

2. Relating Estimate Revisions, Earnings Surprise, and the Analyst's Revision Process

There are at least two ways to predict future consensus estimate revisions. The first method (the hard way) is to perform superior fundamental research on all companies in the investable universe, and then to compare the superior estimate for each company with the consensus estimate for that company, seeking to identify the companies where the consensus estimate is furthest from the superior estimate. The problem with this method of predicting estimate revisions is that it requires extensive (and expensive) fundamental research capabilities. Superior fundamental research requires many analysts to follow many companies. The more analysts one employs, the more money is spent, and the greater the probability that some of the analysts will not provide superior estimates.

The second method to predict future revisions to consensus earnings estimates is to closely measure the recent trend in these revisions and to bet that such trends will continue in the near future. Why such trends exist is the subject of part two of this study.

Why Do Revisions Form Trends?

Revisions form trends because of the way analysts work and because there are many analysts following most companies.

Analysts create trends to their estimates because they tend to make frequent small revisions, each in the same direction as their last revision, rather than making a single large revision. There are at least two behavioral or sociological reasons why this occurs.

First, individual analysts make estimates for the companies they follow in the context of an economic scenario that unfolds gradually over time. As the economy evolves, estimates must be changed to reflect an economic environment different than previously expected.

Exhibit 1 Perfect Forecast of Estimate Revisions

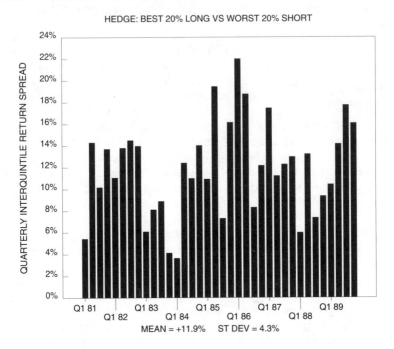

HEDGE: BEST 20% LONG VS WORST 20% SHORT

MEAN = +11.9%   ST DEV = 4.3%

Second, most analysts have more to lose personally by being different from the consensus and wrong than they have to gain by being different and right, so they have a strong motivation to keep their estimates close to the consensus unless they are certain their research is correct. This occurs because an analyst that makes a different and wrong estimate loses credibility with his customers (portfolio managers), hurting his ability to generate commissions for his firm, and thus damaging his career. One different and wrong estimate may take several different and correct estimates to repair. Analysts resolve this conflict by moving their estimates gradually toward what they perceive as the new reality.

It is instructive to compare the investor's interests with those of the analysts. Treynor has shown that in an efficient market, investors will only earn excess returns to the extent that their information is better than and differ-

ent from the consensus, because consensus information is already priced into the stock. Even information that is different and wrong will not hurt the investor (aside from transaction costs), because the misinformation will not be priced into the stock. Investors seeking to beat the market need better and different information, but analysts are motivated, on average, not to be different.

Most stocks of institutional interest are followed by many analysts. Because most analysts follow several stocks (at least), they must shift their focus among the several companies they follow. Collectively then, the several analysts following a particular company will revise their estimates at different times (except when a major event such as an earnings surprise occurs). Multiple analysts making multiple revisions, each on their own time schedules, causes the revisions to occur in trends, spread over time.

Exhibit 2 Contemporaneous Quarterly Stock Returns Sorted into Quintiles on the Basis of Actual Changes in Consensus Earnings Expectations:1981–1989 (First Quintile containing most negative estimate revisions)

From:	12/31/80	03/31/81	06/30/81	09/30/81	12/31/81	03/31/82	06/30/82	09/30/82	12/31/82	03/31/83	06/30/83	09/30/83
To:	03/31/81	06/30/81	09/30/81	12/31/81	03/31/82	06/30/82	09/30/82	12/31/82	03/31/83	06/30/83	09/30/83	12/30/83
Absolute Returns												
Quintile 1	6.29	−5.08	−21.73	0.53	−11.76	−8.09	3.13	19.84	13.13	13.77	−7.39	−3.68
Quintile 2	7.20	0.11	−14.69	4.83	−10.60	−3.30	11.83	21.61	15.04	14.37	−3.42	−3.81
Quintile 3	9.08	4.41	−12.70	9.94	−7.04	−0.33	13.60	21.68	14.04	12.53	−0.33	−1.52
Quintile 4	8.16	6.17	−9.70	12.98	−4.37	3.48	17.25	25.73	15.67	18.88	−0.22	−0.82
Quintile 5	11.72	9.24	−11.55	14.24	−0.70	5.70	17.64	33.83	19.21	21.89	1.55	0.44
Universe	8.49	2.98	−14.07	8.50	−6.89	−0.51	12.70	24.54	15.42	16.30	−1.95	−1.88
S&P 500	1.31	−2.31	−10.24	6.97	−7.32	−0.58	11.57	18.27	10.08	11.11	−0.13	0.39
Rank Corr	0.10	0.36	0.32	0.42	0.30	0.39	0.34	0.19	0.11	0.17	0.22	0.12
Rank T-sta	3.53	12.96	11.39	16.08	11.12	14.68	12.88	7.18	4.21	6.36	8.65	4.87

From:	12/30/83	03/30/84	06/29/84	09/28/84	12/31/84	03/29/85	06/28/85	09/30/85	12/31/85	03/31/86	06/30/86	09/30/86
To:	03/30/84	06/29/84	09/28/84	12/31/84	03/29/85	06/28/85	09/30/85	12/31/85	03/31/86	06/30/86	09/30/86	12/31/86
Absolute Returns												
Quintile 1	−9.16	−11.45	1.82	−6.99	6.60	−3.39	−8.63	8.37	3.11	−6.31	−13.89	−3.48
Quintile 2	−6.63	−4.16	5.06	−1.16	10.19	2.97	−5.36	14.54	12.29	1.24	−9.59	1.82
Quintile 3	−6.63	−0.38	8.47	1.82	12.26	8.02	−3.90	17.60	17.83	7.01	−8.31	4.14
Quintile 4	−5.22	3.11	10.41	4.25	14.15	12.52	−2.51	20.01	21.32	13.09	−8.36	6.32
Quintile 5	−5.52	0.96	12.82	7.04	17.52	14.96	−1.34	24.52	25.12	12.45	−5.57	8.69
Universe	−6.63	−2.38	7.72	1.00	12.14	7.02	−4.35	17.01	15.94	5.50	−9.14	3.50
S&P 500	−2.41	−2.66	9.29	1.97	9.19	7.22	−4.01	17.11	14.26	5.90	−6.90	5.69
Rank Corr	0.10	0.36	0.32	0.42	0.30	0.39	0.34	0.19	0.11	0.17	0.22	0.12
Rank T-sta	3.53	12.96	11.39	16.08	11.12	14.68	12.88	7.18	4.21	6.36	8.65	4.87

Continued on next page

Exhibit 2 Contemporaneous Quarterly Stock Returns Sorted into Quintiles on the Basis of Actual Changes in Consensus Earnings Expectations:1981–1989 (continued)

From:	12/31/86	03/31/87	06/30/87	09/30/87	12/31/87	03/31/88	06/30/88	09/30/88	12/30/88	03/31/89	06/30/89	09/29/89
To:	03/31/87	06/30/87	09/30/87	12/31/87	03/31/88	06/30/88	09/30/88	12/31/88	03/31/89	06/30/89	09/29/89	12/29/89
Absolute Returns												
Quintile 1	14.89	−5.52	−1.46	−33.25	13.70	1.67	−5.39	−3.90	3.85	1.07	0.73	−13.64
Quintile 2	17.84	−0.55	4.52	−26.29	15.19	6.39	−0.28	1.07	7.76	7.04	7.73	−4.45
Quintile 3	23.71	1.59	4.87	−21.64	17.45	7.00	0.58	0.94	6.91	10.01	11.43	−0.15
Quintile 4	26.35	3.56	8.56	−18.81	14.70	8.88	2.30	3.93	10.01	11.64	12.18	3.31
Quintile 5	32.35	5.70	10.81	−20.29	19.69	14.89	1.98	5.45	14.28	15.23	18.45	2.43
Universe	23.03	0.95	5.46	−24.05	16.15	7.77	−0.16	1.50	8.57	9.00	10.10	−2.50
S&P 500	21.29	5.08	6.62	−22.54	5.69	6.66	0.38	3.01	7.08	8.83	10.71	2.04
Rank Corr	0.30	0.27	0.26	0.38	0.08	0.28	0.16	0.28	0.23	0.32	0.35	0.38
Rank T-sta	13.66	12.42	11.33	16.50	3.53	12.02	6.95	12.55	10.29	14.53	16.55	17.97

The Interaction Between Earnings Surprise and Estimate Revisions

Earnings surprises cause estimate revisions and estimate revisions anticipate earnings surprises, so the interaction between the two and between the resultant price behavior is complex.

In its simplest form, an earnings surprise should cause estimate revisions. Whether the revisions have an impact on the price of the stock depends on the nature of the revision however. Foster has shown that revisions to the long-term earnings power of a company (measured by changes to the mean of the fiscal year two estimates) have an impact on a stock's price, while revisions to the current year's earnings estimate merely to make it include one-time events and conform to Generally Accepted Accounting Principles have no lasting impact on price.

Several researchers have shown that earnings surprises tend to repeat themselves (the cockroach effect) and that most of the price impact of an earnings surprise occurs before the actual announcement. In particular, Rendelman has shown that the excess returns that accrue to portfolios of stocks with favorable surprises is actually just from those stocks that produce another favorable surprise in the next quarter. Those stocks in the portfolio that do not repeat their previous quarter's surprise earn no excess returns in the following quarter.

Some managers claim to have created successful investment strategies by buying stocks with favorable earnings surprises. Their process works because their portfolios contain more than a proportionate share of stocks that will repeat their favorable surprises in the subsequent quarter(s), because surprise is serially correlated. A more direct strategy would be to concentrate the portfolio holdings in stocks where the estimates themselves are rising, because estimate revisions are more directly connected to price action than earnings surprises are.

Most analysts try to respond quickly to significant earnings surprises to provide timely investment recommendations to their clients.

Thus there is a tendency for revisions to the consensus data to cluster in the few weeks immediately after the earnings announcement. Then comparatively few estimates are changed in the remaining month or two until the next quarter's earnings announcements confirm the changes made previously. This cycle perpetuates itself each quarter.

Indeed, the author has found while managing portfolios using an estimate revisions model that the portfolio's relative returns are noticeably more robust during and immediately after each quarterly reporting season. This is the period when earnings surprises occur and when portfolios selected on the basis of rising estimates enjoy a disproportionate share of favorable surprises.

3. Analyzing the Recent Trend in Estimate Revisions to Predict Future Revisions and Relative Stock Returns

There are several different ways to measure the recent trend in estimate revisions using consensus estimate data. This section discusses three of these techniques and documents their ability to select stocks that will earn excess returns.

Change in the Mean Divided by the Price

The concept of the change in the mean estimate divided by the price of the stock as a useful measure of estimate revisions was introduced in part one. This technique measures changes to the central tendency of the estimates and contains whatever new information is present in all of the available estimates. Changes in the mean divided by the price should be directly related to price action because such changes represent an unexpected change in the earnings yield for the consensus investor who bought the stock previously on the basis of consensus earnings expectations that have since been revised.

Because it includes all of the estimates however, any measure using the mean of the estimates is fraught with special problems. A single outlying estimate distorts the mean, whether it contains information or just dirty data. Corrections to erroneous outliers create large spurious changes to the mean, so using the mean requires testing for unusually high or low estimates and rejecting them when they are found. This study used mean estimates that were recalculated if the low estimate was several times further from the median estimate than the high estimate or vice versa.

A related problem with the mean estimate is that it contains old estimates as well as new. New estimates have been shown to be more accurate than old estimates, so the mean contains some obsolete data. No adjustments were made in the testing of this study to correct for this.

The period over which changes to the mean are measured must also be considered; both one-month and three-month periods were tested in this study. One month has the advantage of containing just the most current changes, and so detects inflections in the trend of the revisions quickly. However, one month creates a noisy ranking, because of the quarterly cycle of estimate revisions in response to large earnings surprises. In the month following the surprise, when most of the estimate revisions occur, stocks with surprises will move to the tails of the ranking (a desirable outcome). However, in subsequent months these stocks will tend to move toward the middle of the rankings as other stocks that have reported more recently push their way to the tails. By ranking stocks on the basis of a three-month change in the mean, the quarterly cycle is minimized. However, a three-month change takes longer to adjust to recent inflections in the trend.

Ranking stocks by changes in their mean estimate divided by the current price shows predictive ability in forecasting next month's returns, as shown in Exhibit 3. Exhibit 3 also shows that three-month changes in the mean produce higher average return spreads and information coefficients, but at the price of higher volatility in the results.

Changes to the High and/or Low Estimates

Changes to the high or low estimates are different in character than changes to the mean because they contain changed information only at the extremes, rather than changed information for all of the estimates. As explained in part two, extreme estimates can contain a disproportionate share of information because the analyst making such estimates is incurring personal risk by differentiating his opinion from the consensus. For just this reason, an analyst making a higher high estimate or a lower low estimate is making a stronger statement than one who is moving his estimate closer to the consensus.

Alternatively, an extreme estimate may contain old or dirty data.

This study examined changes in the high estimate singly, changes in the low estimate singly, and changes in both estimates jointly.

Exhibit 3 Mean Monthly Returns Relative to an Equal Weighted Universe of Stocks Sorted into Quintiles on the Basis of Changes in the Mean Estimate Divided by the Price: 1981–1989

	Measured Over the Previous	
	One Month	Three Months
Quintile 1	−0.74%	−0.82%
Quintile 2	−0.23	−0.23%
Quintile 3	+0.04	+0.02%
Quintile 4	+0.24	+0.25%
Quintile 5	+0.68	+0.78%
Q1 to Q5 Spread	+1.42%	+1.60%
Std. Dev. of Spread	1.80%	2.01%
Mean Rank Order IC	0.06	0.07
Stand. Dev. of IC	0.07	0.08

In each case, changes (expressed in cents per share) were divided by the current price to achieve comparability between stocks. All changes were measured over just the most recent one month, and estimates were used as given, without any attempt to identify dirty data.

As Exhibit 4 shows, changes to the outlying estimates have predictive power for the next month's stock returns, though less power than changes to the mean. Both quintile spreads and information coefficients are lower with changes to the extreme estimates than with changes to the mean.

Exhibit 4 appears to confirm the expectation that lower low estimates have more investment significance than higher low estimates. Also, the table appears not to demonstrate that higher highs have more significance than lower highs. This may be a premature conclusion however, because the general trend in the estimates for most of the nine-year period of this study was down. Thus in almost every month, all of the stocks in Quintile 1 had lower estimates, while only a portion of the stocks in Quintile 5 had rising estimates, thus diluting whatever impact the rising estimates would have had.

Exhibit 4 Mean Monthly Returns Relative to an Equal Weighted Universe of Stocks Sorted into Quintiles on the Basis of Changes in the Outlying Estimate(s) Divided by the Price: 1981–1989

| | One Month Changes in the | | |
	High Est.	Low Est	Both
Quintile 1	–0.49%	–0.57%	–0.64%
Quintile 2	–0.07%	–0.01%	–0.16%
Quintile 3	+0.05%	+0.11%	+0.11%
Quintile 4	+0.03%	+0.08%	+0.07%
Quintile 5	+0.49%	+0.39%	+0.60%
Q1 to Q5 Spread	+0.98%	+0.96%	+1.24%
Stand Dev. of Spread	1.20%	1.28%	1.49%
Mean Rank Order IC	0.03	0.03	0.05
Stand. Dev. of IC	0.04	0.04	0.05

Exhibit 4 shows that simply combining changes to the high and low estimates is a surprisingly robust measure. This measure produced investment returns and information coefficients similar in magnitude to those produced with the mean of all of the estimates by using just the two most extreme estimates in the database. The median company in this study had six to eight estimates, so changes to the two extreme estimates appear to contain more than their proportional share of the total information.

The Diffusion Index: Using the Number of Estimates Rising or Falling

The third measure tested by this study was the diffusion index, calculated as the net number of estimates up versus down, divided by the total number of estimates.

$$(\text{\# estimates up} - \text{\# estimates down}) / \text{total \# estimates}$$

This measure is similar in construction to diffusion indices constructed by economists, where the number of components changing in an economic index (like the Index of Leading Economic Indicators) is calculated to assess the breadth of change underlying the percentage change in the Index itelf.

A diffusion index with estimate revisions indicates what fraction of the analyst community following the stock has just revised their estimates. Whereas this measure should be closely correlated to changes in the mean estimate, it is easy to imagine situations where the two could give different signals.

Consider two hypothetical stocks. Stock one has highly unpredictable earnings and a low price-to-earnings ratio. Stock two has highly predictable earnings and a price-to-earnings ratio twice as large as stock one. Both sell at the same price and have equal numbers of analysts following them. Both send a signal to the market prompting analysts to revise their estimates by identical dollar amounts, causing identical changes in the mean estimates and identical results from the mean divided by the price calculation. However, two-thirds of the analysts must change their estimates for stock two, because their estimates were so close to each other that almost everyone had to adjust to the new information. Conversely, only one-third of the analysts had to change their estimates for stock one, because the estimates had a wider range in the first place. *Ceteris paribus,* if twice as many analysts had new stories to tell their customers for stock two as did for stock one, shouldn't the second stock have a stronger price reaction than the first? The diffusion index measures this effect.

Exhibit 5 confirms that the diffusion index for estimates changed over the last one month is as powerful and consistent in predicting next month's returns as the one-month change in the mean divided by the price.

Part three has demonstrated that several different measures are available to rank stocks on the basis of recent revisions to their earnings estimates, and that such rankings can identify stocks that will (on average) experience a predictable return relative to the universe of all stocks over the next month. Other analysts have developed related meas-

ures like changes to the median estimate and changes to the mean estimate divided by the standard deviation of the estimates as productive tools. The measures examined in part three were selected for this study because they offer diverse perspectives on rates of change for each stock's earnings estimates.

4. Combining Several Measures of Change into a Single Ranking of Estimate Revision Pressure

Because the several measures discussed in part three evaluate changes to the estimates from different perspectives, the rankings they produce will be imperfectly correlated. Thus it should be possible to combine these simple measures into a single multifactor ranking that should be both more powerful and more consistent over time than any of the single measures described in part three.

Part four examines the performance of one such multifactor ranking—Estrend^{TM}. The construction of Estrend is proprietary to Numeric Investors L.P.; it includes all of the measures and ideas discussed in part three and then employs calculus to provide timely identification of inflections in the trends of the estimates. The performance of Estrend is examined in this study as an example of the returns that can be earned by a multifactor estimate trend model.

Exhibit 6 contains monthly performance statistics for Estrend. As Exhibit 6 shows, Estrend produced higher average monthly spreads than any of the simple measures achieved. Similarly, the mean monthly rank order information coefficient is higher with Estrend than with any of its components.

As a further test of the predictive power of Estrend, the returns of the top and bottom quintiles were further decomposed to see if stocks with progressively more extreme estimate revision trends produced progressively more extreme returns in subsequent months. Exhibit 7 shows the mean monthly returns of the top and bottom quintiles broken down

Exhibit 5 Mean Monthly Returns Relative to an Equal Weighted Universe of Stocks Sorted into Quintiles on the Basis of a Diffusion Index of the Number of Estimates Being Revised Up or Down, as a Percent of the Total Number of Estimates:1981–1989

	Return
Quintile 1	−0.71%
Quintile 2	−0.25%
Quintile 3	+0.05%
Quintile 4	+0.16%
Quintile 5	+0.74%
Q1 to Q5 Spread	1.44%
Stand. Dev. of Spread	1.72%
Mean Rank Corr. IC	0.06
Stand. Dev. of IC	0.07

Exhibit 6 Mean Monthly Returns Relative to an Equal Weighted Universe of Stocks Sorted into Quintiles on the Basis of a Multifactor Estimate Revisions Model (Estrend): 1981-1989

	Return
Quintile 1	−0.82%
Quintile 2	−0.34%
Quintile 3	−0.05%
Quintile 4	+0.34%
Quintile 5	+0.86%
Q1 to Q5 Spread	1.68%
Stand. Dev. of Spread	1.97%
Mean Rank Corr. IC	0.07
Stand. Dev. of IC	0.08

Exhibit 7 Mean Monthly Returns Relative to an Equal Weighted Universe of Stocks Sorted into 4% Fractiles on the Basis of a Multifactor Estimate Revisions Model (Estrend): 1981–1989

	Return
Worst Quintile	
Worst 4%	−1.60%
Next 4%	−0.91%
Next 4%	−0.55%
Next 4%	−0.55%
Best 4%	−0.51%
Total Worst Quintile	−0.82%
Best Quintile	
Worst 4%	+0.60%
Next 4%	+0.58%
Next 4%	+0.78%
Next 4%	+1.01%
Best 4%	+1.31%
Total Best Quintile	+0.86%
Q1 to Q5 Spread	1.68%
Stand. Dev. of Spread	1.97%
Top 4% to Bottom 4% Spread	2.91%
Stand. Dev. of Spread	3.13%

into further quintile segments, each containing only 4% of the total universe. As Exhibit 7 shows, relative returns do become more extreme in the stocks with the most rapidly changing estimates.

Not only is Estrend more powerful, it is more consistent than any of its individual components. Exhibit 8 shows the ratio of the mean return of the spreads to their standard deviation for Estrend and for all of the simple measures discussed in part three. Estrend has the highest ratio, as well as the highest mean spread. Estrend's spreads become larger and more consistent as the fraction of the universe included is extended.

Exhibit 9 provides a graphic presentation of the monthly return spreads between top and bottom 4% portfolios (40 to 70 stocks each) with Estrend over the nine years of the study.

Because only 22 of the 108 months had negative returns, Estrend would seem to be an ideal stock selection tool for a hedged portfolio, in which attractive stocks are held long and unattractive are sold short, with a total portfolio market exposure close to zero. Assuming monthly returns in a hypothetical Estrend hedge portfolio equal to the top to bottom 4% spreads shown in Exhibit 9, less transaction costs of 1% per month and ignoring any short interest rebates, a hedged Estrend portfolio would have produced much higher returns (with less variance) than the S&P 500 over this nine-year period. Exhibit 11 provides a graphic comparison of the cumulative returns of this hypothetical hedged strategy to the returns on the S&P 500.

5. Examining the Effectiveness of an Estimate Trend Model in Different Market Segments and Across Time

Assuming that relative price performance occurs contemporaneously with estimate revisions, then the information from an estimate revisions trend model only has investment significance for the finite period of time during which the trend in the estimates visible in past months' revisions continues into the future. When the trend shifts, information from the previous trend becomes useless.

Exhibit 8 A Comparison of the Consistency of Fractile Spreads of Estrend Versus Simple Measures of Estimate Revisions

| | Monthly Returns | | |
	Mean	Std. Dev.	Ratio
Measure			
Estrend			
Quintile 1 to 5	1.68%	1.97%	.85
Top to Bottom 4%	2.91%	3.13%	.93
1 Mo. Chg. Mean/Price	1.42%	1.80%	.79
3 Mo. Chg. Mean/Price	1.60%	2.01%	.80
1 Mo. Diffusion Index	1.44%	1.72%	.84
1 Mo. Chg. High Est.	0.98%	1.20%	.82
1 Mo. Chg. Low Est.	0.95%	1.28%	.74
1 Mo. Chg. High + Low	1.24%	1.49%	.83

The Effectiveness of Estrend When Implemented with Delays

As a first measure of the time sensitivity of Estrend, tests were run using rankings that were one to five months old. As Exhibit 10 shows, Estrend is able to predict investment returns as much as five months later, but the predictive power, as measured by the monthly first to fifth quintile return spread and the average monthly information coefficient, decays at the rate of about 20% per month.

The Effectiveness of Estrend in Different Market Environments

Exhibit 2 in part one of this study showed that perfect foreknowledge of estimate revisions had positive information content in every

Exhibit 9 Estrend Simulated Monthly Return Spread

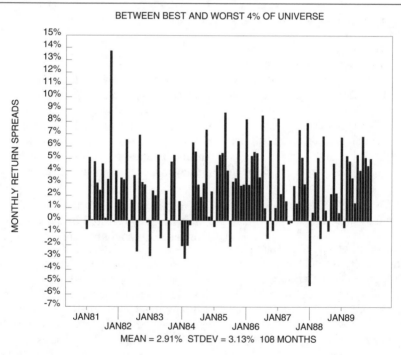

BETWEEN BEST AND WORST 4% OF UNIVERSE

MONTHLY RETURN SPREADS

MEAN = 2.91% STDEV = 3.13% 108 MONTHS

one of the 36 quarters from 1981 through 1989, but the information content (and ability to predict relative returns) varied substantially from quarter to quarter. This suggests that the market frequently responds to other stimuli in addition to estimate revisions.

Because Estrend seeks to add value by predicting future estimate revisions, Estrend's ability to predict future stock returns will be determined in part by the extent to which the market responds to the actual revisions when they occur. Exhibit 12 plots the quarterly information coefficients of Estrend versus the quarterly information coefficients of perfect foreknowledge, revealing visually a striking correlation.

Of particular interest are the three observations high on the y axis, where the market responded to estimate revisions that occurred but Estrend did not predict these revisions. These three quarters may have been inflection points for the economy and the market as a whole, where the macroeconomic background suddenly shifted leaving behind any model based on past trends.

Exhibit 13 plots the cumulative returns of each quintile of stocks rebalanced monthly on Estrend for each of the nine years of the study. 1983 and 1988 were notably weak years for Estrend, 1989 was notably better. Exhibit 13 almost suggests a five-year cycle.

Seasonality in the Effectiveness of Estrend

Exhibit 14 graphs the mean and standard deviation of the spreads between first and fifth quintile monthly returns of the Estrend model for each month in the calendar year. Because the study encompassed only nine years, however, there are relatively few observations from which to draw statistical conclusions.

As Exhibit 14 shows, the power of the Estrend model appears to vary substantially month to month, at least over this nine-year period. For instance, both January and August appear to be difficult months for Estrend to add value, based on the low average and high standard deviation of the return spreads for both months. In contrast, Estrend was consistently robust in the months of March, April, and October for these years, as can be seen by the high average and low standard deviation of return spreads for these three months.

One can only conjecture why some months appear productive or unproductive for the Estrend model. For January, Estrend may work poorly because the tax loss selling during the prior December may set up a rebound in oversold stocks that experienced poor estimate revisions patterns during the prior year. March, April, and October are all months prior to or during quarterly earnings reports, so the good performance of Estrend in these three months is probably caused by the market's attention to earnings announcements during these months. The poor performance in August is difficult to explain, unless one assumes that all of Wall Street is on summer vacation together, leaving no one to react to earnings revisions.

The Effectiveness of Estrend in Securities with Differing Information Characteristics

The universe of stocks examined in this study was also divided into halves based on each

Exhibit 10 The Decay in the Predictive Power of Estrend Over Time

| Delay Before Implementing | Mean Monthly | |
	Q1 to Q5 Spread	IC
None	1.65%	0.07
1 Month	1.41%	0.05
2 Months	1.03%	0.04
3 Months	0.99%	0.04
4 Months	0.77%	0.03
5 Months	0.50%	0.03

Exhibit 11   Estrend Hedge vs S&P 500

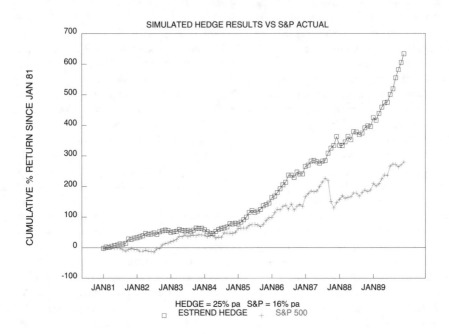

SIMULATED HEDGE RESULTS VS S&P ACTUAL

HEDGE = 25% pa   S&P = 16% pa
□   ESTREND HEDGE   +   S&P 500

Exhibit 12   Correlation of Quarterly ICs

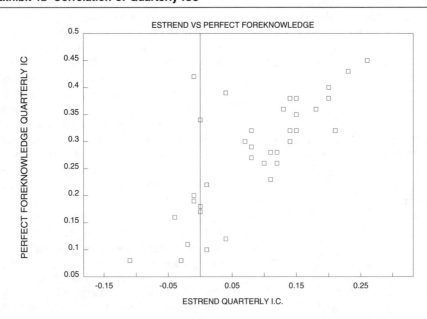

ESTREND VS PERFECT FOREKNOWLEDGE

Exhibit 13 Simulated Performance of Estrend (on Full Test Universe)

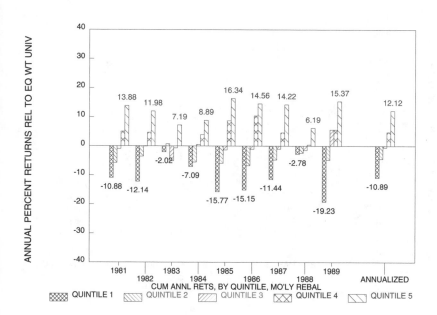

tock's market capitalization, the number of analysts following each company, and the uncertainty of each company's estimates measured by the standard deviation of the iscal year one estimates divided by the tock's price).

Small Capitalization vs. Large

Over the seven-year period from 1983 to 1989 (no capitalization data was available before 1983), Estrend was more than twice as effective in predicting returns for small capitalization stocks than it was for large cap tocks. This is shown in Exhibit 15.

Exhibits 16 and 17 show the linked monthly returns for each quintile in each year from 1983 to 1989. Estrend was so much weaker in large cap stocks that it added almost no value in 1983 and 1988. Nor were the quintile returns in proper sequence.

Stocks with Fewer or More Analysts

Estrend was almost 50% more effective for stocks with fewer analysts than for stocks with more analysts. Exhibit 18 compares the two halves of the test universe sorted on the basis of number of analysts with the universe as a whole. In most periods the median stock had six to eight analysts.

Exhibits 19 and 20 show a similar pattern to that shown in Exhibits 16 and 17. Again, Estrend was so much weaker in one-half of the universe (the half with more estimates) that it added essentially no value in 1983 or 1988.

Stocks with More or Less Earnings Uncertainty

Earnings uncertainty, measured as the standard deviation of the fiscal year one estimates (in dollars and cents) divided by the price, appears to be a variable that has a modest

Exhibit 14   Seasonality of Estrend (Interquintile Spread per Calendar Month)

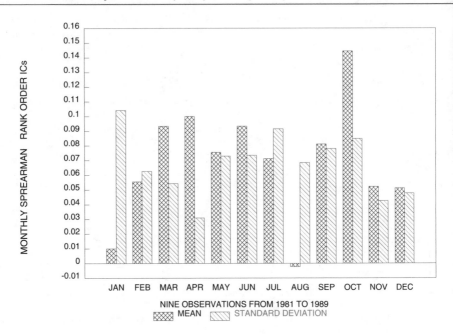

influence on the performance of Estrend. As Exhibit 21 shows, both halves of the test universe sorted on this measure produced only modestly different results.

Exhibit 15   Mean Monthly Returns Relative to an Equal Weighted Universe of Large and Small Capitalization Stocks Sorted into Quintiles with Estrend: 1983–1989

	Small Cap	Large Cap	Whole Universe
Quintile 1	−1.00%	−0.49%	−0.82%
Quintile 2	−0.44%	−0.27%	−0.34%
Quintile 3	−0.09%	−0.06%	−0.05%
Quintile 4	+0.32%	+0.27%	+0.34%
Quintile 5	+1.22%	+0.53%	+0.86%
Q1 to Q5 Spread	+2.22%	+1.02%	+1.68%
Stand. Dev. of Spread	2.06%	2.15%	1.97%
Mean Rank Order IC	0.08	0.05	0.07
Stand Dev. of IC	0.07	0.10	0.08

The findings above are consistent with the notion of information deficiency proposed by Arbel and others. Because more attention is paid to larger capitalization stocks with more brokerage research and broader institutional ownership, information is more rapidly disseminated through this half of the market, giving these stocks a more rapid price response to revised earnings expectations. In contrast, smaller stocks that are less followed by the major brokerage firms and less owned by institutional investors (who may utilize their own estimate revisions trend models) should have a slower price response to estimate revisions because new information for these companies is disseminated more slowly.

The Effectiveness of Estrend Within and Across Economic Sectors

The entire stock universe in this study was divided into eight economic sectors with each

Exhibit 16 Simulated Performance of Estrend (on Small Cap Half of Universe)

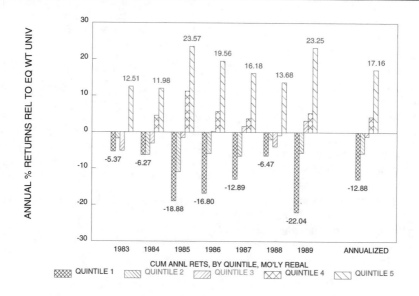

CUM ANNL RETS, BY QUINTILE, MO'LY REBAL

QUINTILE 1   QUINTILE 2   QUINTILE 3   QUINTILE 4   QUINTILE 5

Exhibit 17 Simulated Performance of Estrend (on Large Cap Half of Universe)

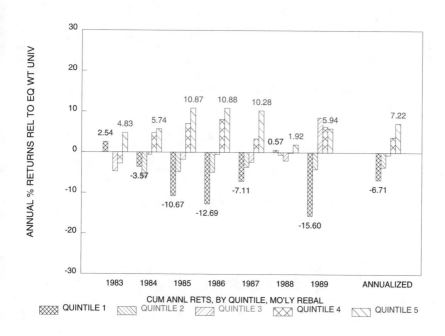

CUM ANNL RETS, BY QUINTILE, MO'LY REBAL

QUINTILE 1   QUINTILE 2   QUINTILE 3   QUINTILE 4   QUINTILE 5

company being assigned to its principal economic sector. The eight sectors were:

Basic Industries
Consumer Noncyclicals
Finance
Technology
Consumer Cyclicals
Energy
Industrial
Utilities

These sectors were designed to have fairly unique combinations of exposures to macroeconomic variables such as inflation, interest rates, risk premia, the economy, etc. These sectors have the additional advantage of being easy to monitor, because they conform closely to the eight principal sectors (excluding conglomerates) used in the new Dow Jones Equity Market Index.

Exhibit 18 Mean Monthly Returns Relative to Equal Weighted Universes of Stocks with More or Fewer Analysts Sorted into Quintiles with Estrend: 1981–1989

	Fewer	More	Whole Universe
Quintile 1	–0.97%	–0.68%	–0.82%
Quintile 2	–0.36%	–0.28%	–0.34%
Quintile 3	–0.07%	–0.06%	–0.05%
Quintile 4	+0.35%	+0.32%	+0.34%
Quintile 5	+1.04%	+0.71%	+0.86%
Q1 to Q5 Spread	+2.01%	+1.39%	+1.68%
Stand. Dev. of Spread	1.95%	2.15%	1.97%
Mean Rank Order IC	0.08	0.06	0.07
Stand Dev. of IC	0.07	0.11	0.08

Exhibit 19 Simulated Performance of Estrend (in 1/2 Universe with Fewest Estimates)

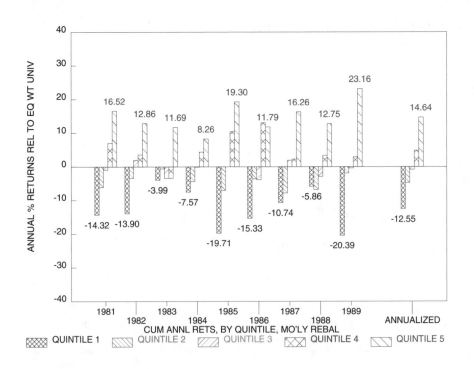

Estrend was used to rank stocks into quin-tiles for each of these sectors to determine if Estrend would produce higher and more sta-ble returns within sectors than it would if al-lowed to rotate among sectors. By constrain-ing the sector concentrations that Estrend would otherwise like to make, it was hoped that *ex-ante* portfolio risk could be reduced by insulating the portfolio from the inevitable and unforeseen economic shocks that cause whole sectors of the market to earn returns different from the market. Also, if Estrend was found to be less effective in certain sec-tors, it would be possible to eliminate these sectors from certain investment strategies.

As Exhibit 22 shows, Estrend works in every sector, but it produces higher and more consistent quintile return spreads and infor-mation coefficients if applied across the entire universe rather than just within individual sectors. *Ex-post*, Estrend returns have less volatility per unit of return when applied across the entire stock universe, despite the fact that the portfolios are allowed to concen-trate in sectors that would appear to add to risk, *ex-ante*.

Some explanation for Estrend's relative performance within sectors can be offered. Utilities has a low mean result because earn-ings are so predictable for most companies in this sector that estimates are seldom revised so powerfully that a trend is created from which excess returns can be earned.

Three other sectors, Basic Industries, En-ergy, and Technology have much more vola-tile responses to Estrend than the other sec-

Exhibit 20 Simulated Performance of Estrend (in 1/2 Universe with Most Estimates)

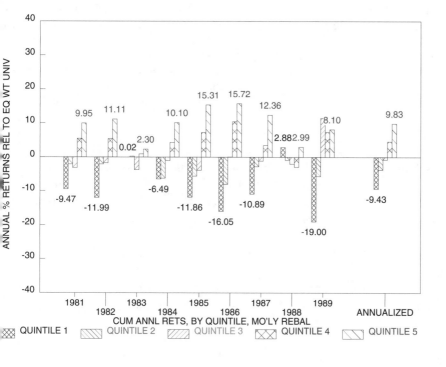

**Exhibit 21   Mean Monthly Returns
Relative to Equal Weighted Universes
of Stocks with Higher or Lower Earnings
Uncertainty Sorted into Quintiles with
Estrend: 1981–1989**

	Lower	Higher	Whole Universe
Quintile 1	–0.55%	–0.95%	–0.82%
Quintile 2	–0.38%	–0.23%	–0.34%
Quintile 3	–0.03%	–0.05%	–0.05%
Quintile 4	+0.20%	+0.29%	+0.34%
Quintile 5	+0.75%	+0.95%	+0.86%
Q1 to Q5 Spread	+1.30%	+1.90%	+1.68%
Stand. Dev. of Spread	+1.75%	2.30%	1.97%
Mean Rank Order IC	0.06	0.07	0.07
Stand Dev. of IC	0.07	0.09	0.08

tors, as evidenced by their high standard deviations. Basic Industries and Energy stocks tend to trade on the basis of changes in very visible commodity prices. Technology stocks tend to trade on book-to-bill ratios and end user surveys. Waiting for the estimates to change in these sectors may cause such a delay that most of the price action will have already occurred before the buy or sell signal is received. Thus Estrend as a stock selection tool may often be late and so produce negative results.

6. Conclusions

This study has reconfirmed that revisions to consensus earnings estimates continue to have a substantial impact on stock returns in the U.S. market. The study has also found that several simple measures of the recent trend in estimate revisions are effective tools to rank stocks for returns over the next few months.

This study has demonstrated that a more comprehensive measure of estimate revision trends can be created by assembling several of the simple measures into a combined ranking. Such a combined ranking shows sufficient power and consistency to be of use to managers of long or hedged portfolios of U.S. stocks.

Finally, this study has examined the effectiveness of such a combined ranking in predicting stock returns in different market environments and across different market sectors. The measure is most effective when used across all economic sectors and when applied to a universe of smaller capitalization stocks with less analyst coverage and greater earnings uncertainty. Trends in estimate revisions appear most amenable to exploitation in areas of the market where there is information deficiency.

**Exhibit 22   The Mean and Standard Deviation of Monthly Returns and Monthly ICs of
Stocks Sorted by Economic Sectors and then into Quintiles with Estrend:1981–1989**

	Monthly Q1–Q5 Returns		Information Coefficient	
	Mean	Std. Dev.	Mean	Std. Dev.
Basic Indus.	1.35%	4.26%	0.06	0.17
Consumer Cyc.	1.98%	2.80%	0.08	0.11
Consumer Noncyc.	1.04%	2.93%	0.06	0.11
Energy	1.07%	3.80%	0.05	0.16
Financial	1.27%	2.77%	0.06	0.11
Industrial	1.32%	2.32%	0.06	0.10
Technology	1.63%	3.80%	0.07	0.13
Utilities	0.81%	1.89%	0.06	0.12
All 8 Sectors	1.68%	1.97%	0.07	0.08

The effect of estimate revisions on stock returns has been noted by researchers for almost a decade now, but still it persists as a fruitful inefficiency from which excess returns can be earned. Perhaps this is because the explanation for this inefficiency is behavioral. Most research in the securities industry is either fundamental or quantitative, so there is no natural constituency to research and fully exploit this inefficiency.

Chapter 8

The Information Content of Financial Analysts' Forecasts of Earnings

Some Evidence on Semi-Strong Inefficiency

Dan Givoly, Ph.D.
Professor of Accounting Information Systems
J.L. Kellogg Graduate School of Management
Northwestern University

Josef Lakonishok, Ph.D.
William G. Karnes Professor of Finance
University of Illinois at Urbana-Champaign

The paper assesses the information content of revisions in financial analysts' forecasts of earnings by analyzing the relation between the direction of these revisions and stock price behavior. Abnormal returns during the months surrounding the revisions in analysts' forecasts are computed and evaluated. The results strongly indicate that information on revisions in forecasts of earnings per share is valuable to investors. It is also suggested that market reaction to the disclosure of analysts forecasts is relatively slow and gives rise to potential abnormal returns to investors who act upon this type of publicly available information.

1. Introduction

An extensive body of literature has examined the information content of earnings and the efficiency of the market with respect to their disclosure. The evidence shows that earnings possess information value: a knowledge of the contents of the forthcoming earnings announcement yields an abnormal return [see for example Ball and Brown (1968). Brown and Kennelly (1972), and Foster (1977)]. In addition, the observed stock price reaction to an earnings announcement continues over several weeks or months after the announcement [see, for example, Beaver (1968,

Reprinted with permission from *Journal of Accounting and Economics,* Volume 1, 1979, pgs. 165-185.
© North-Holland Publishing Company.

1975), Jones and Litzenberger (1970), Foster (1977), Latane and Jones (1977) and Watts (1978)]. This finding casts some doubt on the validity of the hypothesis of the semi-strong efficiency of the market.

Recently, however, Ball (1978) has suggested that the observed "inefficiency" might be due to omitted variables or to other specification errors in formulating the equilibrium model of returns. Ball has also recommended procedures which might mitigate the effect of these weaknesses. These procedures were utilized in a later research by Watts (1978) who still found statistically significant abnormal returns after the public release of quarterly reports.

The observed association between stock price movements and the content of earnings announcement might reflect, in part, the continuous efforts by investors to correctly forecast future earnings. The keen interest of investors in future earnings and the weight they assign to them is manifested by among other things, the number of brokerage houses that produce earnings forecasts on a regular basis and by the attention devoted by the financial community to the issue of the disclosure of management earnings forecasts.

Financial analysts' forecasts (FAF) have recently received an increased attention in accounting literature: Barefield and Comiskey (1975), Basi, Carey and Twark (1976) and Crichfield, Dyckman and Lakonishok (1978) evaluated the accuracy and some other statistical properties of these forecasts. Gonedes, Dopuch and Penman (1976) used them as a proxy for management forecasts in an attempt to evaluate empirically the desirability of mandatory disclosure of the latter.

The purpose of this study is to measure the information content of revisions in FAF. The pattern by which the market changes its expectations in the periods following the revisions in FAF will also be examined and some tentative conclusions concerning the efficiency of the market to revisions in FAF will be drawn.

The methodology of the study incorporates the steps suggested by Ball (1978), thus minimizes the biases in measuring the abnormal returns.

2. Research Design

The methodology of the study involves the examination of the association between revisions in financial analysts' forecast of earnings per share (EPS) and stock price movements.

The response of stock prices to changes (revisions) in financial analysts' forecasts is measured by the abnormal return in the months surrounding the revision month. Existence of abnormal returns during that period is consistent with the hypothesis that revisions in FAF have information content to investors. Furthermore, if the market is efficient with respect to the release of revisions in FAF, stock price changes associated with that information would coincide with the revisions, i.e., no abnormal returns would be expected after the public release of the revisions.

It should be noted, however, that observed abnormal returns could be due to shortcomings of the equilibrium model used to estimate them. Ball (1978) points to two possible causes for the failure of the model to properly describe the process by which equilibrium expected returns are determined. One is the fact that the variable whose information content is being tested acts as a proxy for variables which determine equilibrium expected returns and which are not included in the equilibrium model. The second cause is errors in measuring the market portfolio. Since abnormal returns are observed in the periods following the release of FAF revisions, reference is also made to the question of whether those abnormal returns are indicative of market inefficiency or are due to deficiencies in the equilibrium model.

Another potential problem in interpreting the results is the fact that stock price movements observed in the period of revisions of FAF might be caused by events other than the release of the revisions. In particular, stock price movements in that period might be triggered by the announcement of quarterly reports. In fact, the data reveal some concentration of revisions in months in which quarterly reports are customarily announced. To assess the bias that could be introduced by attributing the effect of quarterly report announcements to FAF revisions, further analysis was conducted under which revisions which occur during actual announcements months were excluded.

The abnormal returns in the study are computed separately for upward and downward revisions. Numerous variations of this measure are employed, each pertaining to a different set of two parameters: one is the period over which the abnormal returns are compounded (the holding period), and the other is the magnitude of the revision.

Denoting the month the FAF is revised as month 0 and the surrounding months according to their position relative to the revision month (i.e., by −1, +1, etc.), the following holding periods were used:

(1) Months −1, 0, 1, and 2; [−1,2] in notation form.
(2) Months 0, 1, and 2; [0,2] in notation form.
(3) Months 1 and 2; [1,2] in notation form.
(4) to (7) are holding periods of one month each, corresponding to −1, 0, 1, and 2 respectively; [−1], [0], [1], and [2] in notation form.

If there is any market response to the revisions in earnings forecasts, it is likely to be more pronounced in the months immediately surrounding the revision (i.e., over the above holding periods). Nevertheless, months which are farther away from the revision were also examined and the findings are reported with the rest of the results.

Eleven size groups of revisions are defined ranging in increments of 1% from "greater than 0%" to "greater than 10%."

Clearly, the abnormal returns during periods [−1,2] and [−1] can be achieved only by investors who know the direction of the forthcoming revision. Strictly speaking, the same is true also for periods [0,2] and [0] since the exact date of the revision is some time during the revision month.

Any abnormal returns observed at the post revision period (holding periods [1,2], [1], and [2]) indicate a gradual and slow dissemination of information contained in FAF revisions and imply that investors might (depending on their transaction costs) profitably act upon this information.

To compute the abnormal return, the normal rate of return is defined according to the familiar market model,

$$E(\tilde{R}_{it} \mid \tilde{R}_{mt}) = \alpha_i + \beta_i R_{mt}$$

where $\tilde{R}_{it}$ denotes the rate of return of security i for period t, α_i and β_i are parameters and R_{mt} is the actual market rate of return for period t.

This study uses monthly rates of return (adjusted for capitalization) and employs monthly compounding. The market rate of return is represented by the equally weighted Fisher Index (composed of all securities listed on the New York Stock Exchange). Since the test perod (the period during which abnormal returns are being measured) should be completely divorced from the estimation period, $\hat{\alpha}_i$ and $\hat{\beta}_i$ used for month t are estimated by data of prior years. Specifically, the parameters for a given year are estimated from the four years (48 months) preceding that year. The monthly abnormal returns are measured by the difference

$$\hat{\varepsilon}_{it} = R_{it} - (\hat{\alpha}_i + \hat{\beta}_i R_{mt})$$

where R_{it} and R_{mt} are the observed values of the respective rates of return and $\hat{\alpha}_i$ and $\hat{\beta}_i$ are estimated from a regression equation.

The total abnormal return for each of the seven types of holding periods is computed for each revision. The results are presented in terms of the abnormal return produced, on average, during any type of holding period over all revisions. The statistical significance of the observed abnormal returns is tested and the test statistics are provided. Breakdown of the results into years and industries is also shown.

To illustrate, the computations relating to holding period [−1,2] are as follows:

Let us denote

r as the revision index for a given security,

t as the chronological month index,

$t(r)$ as the month of revision r,

i as the security index,

N as the number of revisions in the sample, and

$\hat{\varepsilon}_{it}$ as the abnormal return for security i in month t.

Let $A_{i,r}[-1,2]$ be the abnormal return of security i during holding period [−1,2] around revision r,

$$A_{i,r}[-1,2] = \prod_{t=t(r)-1}^{t(r)+2} (1 + \hat{\varepsilon}_{it}) - 1$$

Let $A[-1,2]$ be the abnormal return produced, on average, during holding period [−1,2],

$$A[-1,2] = \frac{1}{N} \sum_{i} \sum_{r \varepsilon i} A_{i,r}[-1,2]$$

As explained, the results are presented in terms of cross-sectional averages of abnormal returns over revisions. The abnormal returns are computed in two ways. One is according to the procedure described above; the other involves a standardization of the abnormal returns which might help the analysis and ease the interpretation of the results. The following discussion clarifies the nature of this standardization.

It is expected that for a random sample the average abnormal returns will not be signifi-

cantly different from zero. However, in non-random samples cross-section average abnormal returns might be observed. Whenever the information content of a set of signals is investigated, as is done by this study, there is a potential danger of misinterpretation: the abnormal returns could be unduly attributed to the signals. Since this study's sample is not large compared to the number of firms in the population and as well is not representative of all industries (for a description of the sample, see Section 3. Sample and Data), some periods might yield abnormal returns that are significantly different from zero without implying anything regarding the value of the information that was produced during those periods. To circumvent this potential distortion, the residuals from the market line, $\hat{\varepsilon}_{it}$, were also standardized with respect to their contemporaneous cross-sectional average, as follows:

$$\hat{\varepsilon}_{it}^{s} = \hat{\varepsilon}_{it} - \bar{\hat{\varepsilon}}_{t} ,$$

where $\hat{\varepsilon}_{it}^{s}$ is the standardized abnormal return of stock i at month t, and

$$\bar{\hat{\varepsilon}} = \frac{1}{n} \sum_{i=1}^{n} \hat{\varepsilon}_{it}$$

(n is the number of firms in the sample).

By performing this transformation, the cross-sectional average abnormal return in each month becomes zero, thus making easier the interpretation of the results in the following sense: $\hat{\varepsilon}_{it}^{s}$ becomes a measure of the excess return, during t, of holding share i over a buy-and-hold strategy for the sample.

The abnormal return obtained through this transformation for a given holding period surrounding the revision could be interpreted as the average rate of return over that period from a strategy under which a certain dollar amount of all the shares in the sample is sold short and an equal dollar amount of shares with revisions is bought.[1] If the cash proceeds from the short sale are collected at the time of the transaction, no investment outlay is required. The resulting portfolio will practically have no systematic risk.[2]

The standardization procedure might potentially remove industry effects contained in the residual returns. However, as is evident from the results, the differences between the standardized and the unstandardized abnormal returns are minor.

3. Sample and Data

The need to collect and process manually a large portion of the data posed a limitation on the sample size. In order to enable some inter-industry comprisons, the sample consists of three industries (Standard Industrial Two-Digit Classification): Chemicals and Allied Products (Industry 28), Petroleum Refining and Related Industries (Industry 29), and Transportation Equipment (Industry 37). These industries were chosen since they include a relatively large number of firms which could potentially satisfy the following criteria:

(1) Availability of earnings forecasts for all years in the survey period.
(2) New York Stock Exchange listing. This criterion was introduced since stock price data were derived from the monthly CRSP tape, which contains only NYSE stocks.
(3) Fiscal year ending December 31.

The final sample consisted of 49 companies. For each company, actual earnings, EPS forecasts, and monthly stock returns were collected for the eight years 1967 to 1974.

Forecasts of EPS were collected from Standard and Poor's Earnings Forecaster. A weekly publication which first appeared in 1967, the Earnings Forecaster lists in each issue the outstanding EPS forecasts for about 1500 companies. The forecasts are those made by S&P and by about fifty other secu-

rity analysts and brokerage houses who agreed to submit their forecasts, upon release, for publication.

Typically, three to five forecasters are actively engaged in forecasting the earnings of a given company. As many as fifteen different forecasts might simultaneously be available for companies with a widely traded stock. This situation poses a difficulty in identifying the forecast of next year's EPS. One solution is to regard the average or the median forecast as the relevant forecast. This approach has some weaknesses: First, changes in the value of this forecast might occur whenever a new forecaster joins or an old forecaster drops from the initial group of forecasters. Secondly, contemporaneous revisions by separate analysts make it difficult to identify the information content of the change in this measure as "good" or "bad news."

Finally, changes in expectations under the above definition will invariably be gradual: The data reveal that revisions of various forecasters do generally move together but that there is also some lag between the first revision and the "followers," which makes the average revision change slowly and gradually over time.[3] Yet, if the market is efficient, stock prices might be primarily affected by the release of the first revision. Thus, the observed relationship between the average forecast and stock price movements will only partially reflect the true association between the content of FAF revisions and stock prices.

The above shortcomings of the average forecast measure led to the selection of the revisions produced by the most active forecaster for each company (the one with the greatest number of revisions) as the representative of the group of forecasters. The most active forecaster is likely to be the first to respond to new information. At the same time, he is probably the one who specializes in the stock and as such, the most watched and followed by investors; if this is not the case, the selection of the most active forecasters might bias downward the association between stock prices and revisions in earnings. The most active forecaster was chosen based on publicly available information at the time the forecast was issued. The forecaster selected each year was the one who was most active in the previous year. The most active forecaster for 1967, the first year for which data is available, was selected based on the experience of the first two months which were excluded from the computation of abnormal returns. For companies with no forecast during the first two months, the first forecaster to make a forecast was selected as the most active.

To ascertain that the EPS forecast figures and the actual figures were compatible in terms of the dilution definition and the treatment of extraordinary items, actual EPS figures were collected from the Earnings Forecaster. (To assure accuracy, the earnings figures were compared with those recorded in the Compustat tape.) Adjustments were occasionally called for.[4]

The dates of the actual announcement of the annual and the quarterly reports were collected from *The Wall Street Journal*. The annual announcement date is the date of the announcement of the audited statements or of the release of the preliminary earnings, whichever is earlier.

4. Empirical Results

Exhibits 1 and 2 describe some general characteristics of FAF. Note that only revisions produced by the most active forecasters are presented and analyzed. Exhibit 1 presents the number of revisions by year, size, and direction. The number of revisions above 10% is 234, of those above 5% is 584 and the number of all (above 0%) revisions is 1,420.

The revisions are quite evenly distributed over the years. The average number of all revisions (above 0%) per year is 178 with a standard deviation of 29.3. There is almost an equal number of upward and downward revisions (693 against 727 for all revisions).

The average βs presented in the last column of Exhibit 1 were computed across revisions. The β for a given revision was that applicable, at the time of the revision, to the share for which the revision was made. The results indicate that the βs for large revisions are somewhat greater than those for small revisions. There is practically no difference between βs of upward revisions and βs of downward revisions.

Exhibit 2 shows the frequency of revisions by months. The distribution apparently reflects the pattern of information arrival. An-

Exhibit 1 Cumulative Distribution of the Number of Financial Analysts' Earnings Forecast Revisions and Average β by Size of Revision, Direction (Up/Down) and Year

Size (%)	Direction[a]	Year								All years	Average β
		67	68	69	70	71	72	73	74		
	T	13	18	19	22	27	17	41	77	234	1.01
Above 10	U	2	8	3	7	13	1	36	67	137	1.02
	D	11	10	16	15	14	16	5	10	97	0.99
	T	42	59	55	76	61	49	95	147	584	0.97
Above 5	U	7	27	9	15	27	16	84	124	309	0.98
	D	35	32	46	61	34	33	11	23	275	0.96
Above 0	T	160	195	201	155	146	150	185	228	1,420	0.95
(all	U	55	97	47	39	55	70	150	180	693	0.94
revisions)	D	105	98	154	116	91	80	35	48	727	0.95

[a]"T" denotes total revisions, "U" denotes upward revisions, and "D" denotes downward revisions.

Exhibit 2 Relative Frequency of Revisions in Financial Analysts' Forecasts of Earnings by Month of Release.[a]

	Jan.	Feb.	Mar.	Apr.	May	June	July	Aug.	Sept.	Oct.	Nov.	Dec.
Percentage of all revisions	10.4	8.6	8.9	7.9	10.7	5.7	9.9	7.0	4.7	8.8	10.8	6.6

[a]All companies in the sample have fiscal years ending December 31.

nual and quarterly earnings are undoubtedly a prominent input for FAF; indeed, there is some concentration of revisions in the months in which the annual and quarterly reports are usually released. Still, a significant number of revisions are made in other months. These revisions presumably reflect the arrival of non-accounting information such as GNP, interest rate and inflation rate information, and events specific to the firm.

The main results of the study are presented in the form of abnormal returns in months surrounding the revision month. As pointed out by Ball (1978), an experimental pitfall exists if the variables used to estimate the information content of earnings are highly auto-correlated across time, and are therefore more likely to be associated with variables which explain abnormal return. In such cases the result might well be an overstatement of abnormal returns leading to erroneous conclusions. The earnings variable in this study is the sign (direction) of the revision in the earnings forecast. Therefore, serial dependence between consecutive revisions could be tested by using the run test.

For samples in which the number of positive signs or of negative signs exceeds 20, the number of runs is well approximated by the normal distribution [see Siegel (1956, p. 57)]. Since this condition does not hold for all firms in the sample, sole reliance on the firms' Z values would be inappropriate as a test for randomness in the sample. The distribution of the Z values across firms presented in Exhibit 3, indicates the extent of dependence in the sign of the revision. The median Z value in the sample is -0.58 for all revisions and –0.26 for revisions of over 5%, indicating a positive dependence. However, this dependence is small. The last column of Exhibit 3 provides the frequency with which the hypothesis of independence is rejected at the 5% significance level. The computations show that the null hypothesis of independence cannot be rejected for most firms at the 5% significance level (for cases with less than 20 observations the computations are based on the exact sampling distributions). The rejection rate is 13.5% when all revisions are considered and 5.8% when only revisions of over 5% are considered. It seems reasonable to

Exhibit 3 Distribution of the Z Values of Runs in the Sign of Financial Analysts' Earnings Forecast Revisions (upward=positive, downward=negative) and Frequency of Rejection of the Hypothesis of Serial Independence Between the Sign of Consecutive Revisions

Revision size	Mean	Percentile					Percentage of rejection of the hypothesis of independence at the 5% level
		0.10	0.25	0.50	0.75	0.90	
Revisions above 0%	−0.75	−2.02	−1.57	−0.58	1.15	1.42	13.5
Revisions above 5%	−0.56	−1.55	−1.28	−0.26	0.82	1.09	5.8

conclude, therefore, that the sign of the revision is not highly autocorrelated across time.[5] This implies that the earnings variable used here (the sign of the revision) does not proxy for possible omitted variables in the market model and that therefore the reported returns in the periods surrounding the revisions in FAF are not likely to be overstated by the proxy-effect described by Ball. (A possibility still exists, however, that the returns are overstated due to a more complex proxy-effect.)

Exhibits 4, 5, and 6 present results for revisions over 5%. (The results for other revision-size groups portray basically the same phenomena and will be commented upon later.)

The main results are summarized in Exhibit 4. The table presents the abnormal returns which are generated over each of the seven alternative holding periods described above. During each of the periods around upward and downward revisions, average abnormal returns are recorded for the entire sample.

The table is divided into three panels. The first panel presents the standardized abnormal returns for *all* revisions (over 5%). The second panel shows these abnormal returns only for revisions which were released in months with no quarterly earnings announcements. The third panel presents the unstandardized abnormal returns for all revisions. Panels 1 and 3 are based on 584 revisions, while Panel 2 is based on 385 revisions.

If the generating process of the returns is correctly specified, then the existence of abnormal returns in the period surrounding the release of FAF revision might serve as an indication that this event has information content or reflects, at least in part, contemporaneous information conveyed to the market by other sources. If the market is efficient, abnormal returns should be zero in the months after the release of the revision in FAF.

Two main findings emerge from Exhibit 4: One is the existence of abnormal returns in the months surrounding FAF revisions. In particular, positive abnormal returns are observed in periods surrounding upward revisions, and negative abnormal returns are recorded in periods surrounding downward revisions. This finding suggests that FAF revisions convey or reflect information.

The second finding is that abnormal returns prevail well after the release of FAF revisions—indicating inefficiency of the market with respect to these revisions.

To test whether each of the average abnormal returns presented in Exhibit 4 is significantly different from zero, a *t*-test was conducted. To compute the mean abnormal returns a cross-section, as well as time-series pooling of observations, was performed. Since the *t*-test employed assumes that the observations are independent, the validity of this assumption should be considered. In the present sample, dependence between the ob-

Exhibit 4   Average Abnormal Returns per Holding Period by Direction of Financial Analysts' Earnings Forecast Revisions, for Revisions over 5%[a] (Percentage)

Panel	Direction (upward/ downward)	[−1,2]	[0,2]	[1,2]	[−1]	[0]	[1]	[2]	Monthly return on buy-and-hold
				Monthly Holding Periods					Monthly
1) All Revisions (standardized)	U	4.7	3.1	2.7	1.1	0.9	1.7	1.0	
	D	−3.8	−1.9	−1.0	−1.6	−1.2	−0.4	−0.6	0.6
2) No Earnings Announcements (standardized)	U	5.3	4.1	3.4	1.4	0.7	2.5	0.9	
	D	−3.2	−2.6	−1.1	−1.1	−0.9	−0.9	−0.5	0.6
3) All Revisions (unstandardized)	U	4.9	3.3	2.8	1.1	0.9	1.7	1.0	
	D	−3.9	−2.0	−1.0	−1.6	−1.2	−0.4	−0.6	0.6

[a]All values are different from zero for a two-tailed test at the 5% significance level.

servations could take different forms. The most common type of dependence which might exist in the data is perhaps the one created by pooling across firms. Concentration of revisions of a particular industry in a given period might reflect a common underlying industry factor that triggered the revisions and hence might indicate possible dependence of the abnormal returns. To assess the extent of this form of dependence, the distribution of revisions between industries was examined for each month. Using the binomial test it was found that in only 6 out of 81 months with revisions, the number of revisions produced by any one industry was significantly above or below the number of revisions expected for that industry given its relative frequency of revisions over all months (at the 5% significance level). It should be further noted that the total number of revisions in these 6 months was small (28 revisions out of 584). The danger of revision clustering is considerably reduced when only large (over 10%) revisions are considered. Yet, as will be reported below, the main results for the large revisions are similar to those for the other revisions.

Clearly, cross-sectional dependence for an industry could still exist even in the absence of clustering of revisions of that industry in certain periods. The potential dependence exists whenever more than one revision of the same industry is made during one period. Although about 50% of the revisions of every industry occur in months with a single revision of that industry, some cross-sectional dependence of this type could still be present.

Pooling abnormal returns across years might raise a question on the validity of another assumption necessary for the use of the *t*-test—that concerning the stationarity of this variable's distribution over time. To test whether this assumption holds, the eight-year period (1967-1974) was divided into two subperiods of four years each (1967-1970, 1971-1974). The equality of the means of the first and the second subperiods was tested under the assumption of equal variances (the *t*-test).

Then, assuming that the mean abnormal returns in the two subperiods are equal, the equality of the variances of the first and the second subperiod was tested (the *F*-test). The hypothesis that the variances of the abnormal return are equal in the two subperiods could not be rejected for all holding periods for both upward and downward revisions, at the 5% significance level. The hypothesis of equal means could not be rejected for revisions in both directions and for all holding periods, at the 5% significance level, except for holding period [1] of downward revisions.

The null hypothesis that the average abnormal return is equal to zero was rejected for all values reported in Exhibit 4 (at the 5% significance level, two-tail test). Given the potential dependence between observations, the *t*-tests' results may be biased and should therefore be regarded with some caution. (It should be noted, however, that a substantial bias must be present for the results to become insignificant: The *t*-values for most holding periods are above 3.0.)

Computed, but not presented, are the abnormal returns for holding periods during months farther from the revision month. The abnormal return for months preceding month −1 and following month +2 are small and insignificant. (Their absolute values do not exceed 0.2%.)

The last column of Exhibit 4 shows the (geometric) average of the monthly return yielded by a buy-and-hold policy for the entire sample over the eight-year period. The buy-and-hold policy assumes that at the beginning of the period, an equal investment is made in the 49 stocks and retained until the end of the period. The comparison between these "normal" returns and the monthly abnormal returns produced during months −1, 0, 1, and 2, underlines the materiality of the abnormal returns in the months surrounding the public release of FAF. For instance, an investor who acts upon publicly available information can obtain over a two-month period, [1,2], an abnormal return of 2.7% to 3.4%, which represents an increase of at least 225% over his "normal" monthly return (return of 2.7% against the "normal" return over the two-month period which is 1.2%).

The magnitude of the abnormal returns compared with the normal monthly returns rules out the possibility that the results are due to nonstationarity of the securities' betas or to errors in their measurements. Even a deviation of 100% of the calculated beta from the true beta would not produce abnormal returns of such magnitude.

As explained, Panel 2 presents the results only for revisions which did not occur during months of quarterly announcements. The motivation behind this separate analysis was the possibility that the abnormal returns could be due in part to the effect of quarterly earnings announcements. The comparison between Panels 1 and 2 shows that in most cases, the abnormal returns tend to be somewhat higher for revisions which occur in months without earnings announcements. This suggests that actual earnings announcement may not be more powerful than other news signals in inducing analysts to change their future valuation of the company, which implies, in turn, that analysts are quite capable of predicting future earnings. Nonetheless, the difference between the two Panels appears to be statistically insignificant. The null hypothesis that revisions which occur in the months of earnings announcements produce the same abnormal returns as the remaining revisions was tested. For the purpose of the test, the mean abnormal returns relating to revisions which occur in the months of quarterly announcements and the mean abnormal returns relating to revisions which occur in the other months were computed for each holding period. The t-test for the difference between the means was used. The null hypothesis could not be rejected for any of the holding periods at the 5% significance level.[6]

Panel 3 exhibits the results for all revisions in terms of the unstandardized abnormal returns. As is evident from the comparison between this Panel and Panel 1, the effect of the standardization of the returns on the results is relatively small.

Since the results in the three panels are basically similar, the rest of the description of the findings and their analysis will be done in terms of the standardized returns, which appear in Panel 1.

Exhibits 5 and 6 present results which reinforce the main thrust of the findings reported above. Exhibit 5 presents the abnormal returns which are generated over the seven alternative holding periods for each industry. The results for each industry are similar to the results for the total sample. Most of the abnormal returns are significantly different from zero at the 5% significance level. (Note that

Exhibit 5 Average Abnormal Returns per Holding Period by Industry and Direction of Financial Analysts' Earnings Forecast Revisions, for Revisions Over 5% (percentage)

	Direction (upward/ downward)	Holding Periods							Monthly return on buy-and-hold
		[−1,2]	[0,2]	[1,2]	[−1]	[0]	[1]	[2]	
Chemicals and Allied Products	U	5.0	2.9	2.1	2.2	0.9	1.0	1.1	
	D	−3.4	−1.6[a]	−1.2	−1.9[a]	−0.4	−0.7	−0.4	0.7
Petroleum Refining and Related Industries	U	2.3	2.3	2.4	0.1[a]	0.1[a]	1.8	0.8	
	D	−4.5	−3.2	−1.9	−1.9	−1.0	−0.7	−1.1	0.8
Transportation Equipment	U	12.7	10.3	4.9	2.2	5.4	3.1	1.7	
	D	−3.1	−2.3	1.2[a]	−0.6	−3.2	0.8[a]	0.3[a]	−0.3

[a]All values except those marked by superscript 'a' are different from zero under a two-tailed test at the 5% significance level.

Exhibit 6   **Average Abnormal Returns per Holding Period by Year and Direction of Financial Analysts' Earnings Forecast Revisions, All Revisions Over 5% (percentage)**

Year	Direction (upward/ downward)	Holding Periods						
		[−1,2]	[0,2]	[1,2]	[−1]	[0]	[1]	[2]
1967	U	−3.5	−2.0	0.6	−1.4	−2.3	−2.5	3.1
	D	−3.7	−1.1	1.5	−2.3	−2.5	−0.6	2.2
1968	U	3.6	1.7	0.1	1.9	1.7	−0.4	0.5
	D	0.5	−0.3	0.9	0.7	−1.1	2.4	−1.5
1969	U	8.1	4.2	3.7	3.1	0.4	2.9	0.9
	D	−4.7	−3.2	−2.3	−1.6	−1.0	−1.0	−1.2
1970	U	9.4	8.0	6.1	1.9	2.1	2.0	3.8
	D	−2.3	−0.8	−0.2	−1.4	−0.5	0.3	−0.5
1971	U	1.8	2.9	2.6	−1.0	0.3	1.1	1.3
	D	−0.9	−0.8	−0.1	−0.3	−1.0	−0.1	−0.1
1972	U	3.3	2.2	2.1	1.0	0.3	2.4	−0.2
	D	−7.8	−5.8	−3.7	−2.3	−2.0	−1.5	−2.4
1973	U	5.2	3.8	3.0	1.3	0.8	1.8	1.3
	D	−5.4	−3.4	−4.5	−2.1	−0.6	−2.3	−1.6
1974	U	5.1	4.0	2.9	1.1	1.1	2.3	0.6
	D	−10.4	5.0	−2.6	−5.0	−1.5	−2.7	0.2
Simple yearly average	Upward	4.1	3.1	2.6	1.0	0.6	1.2	1.4
Standard deviation	Only	1.4	1.0	0.7	0.5	0.5	0.6	0.5
t-value		2.9	3.1	3.7	2.0	1.2	2.0	2.8

the potential bias in the *t*-test, which was discussed earlier might be present also in the results of Exhibit 5.)

Exhibit 6 provides a breakdown of the results by years. For most years, and during each of the holding periods, the "correct" sign of the abnormal return is recorded, i.e., positive abnormal returns are observed for upward revisions and negative abnormal returns are observed for downward revisions. For instance, abnormal returns during holding period [1,2] following upward revisions are positive in all eight years. A null hypothesis that the probability of positive abnormal return is 0.5% can therefore be rejected (using a binomial test) for this combination of holding period and direction of revisions, at the 0.4% significance level [(1/2)[8]]. Fourteen combinations of holding period and direction of revision (7 × 2) exist. Therefore, fourteen such tests could be conducted. For all fourteen combinations a "correct" sign of the abnor-

mal return is recorded in at least six out the eight years, and for nine of these combinations, a correct sign of the abnormal return is found in at least seven years. This means that the above null hypothesis can be rejected (using a binomial test) for all fourteen combinations at the 15% significance level, (which is the probability of obtaining at least six successes out of eight trials under the null hypothesis) and for nine out of fourteen combinations at the 3.5% significance level (the probability of obtaining at least seven successes).

A parametric test (*t*-test) could also be applied to test the hypothesis that the average annual abnormal return is zero. The *t* values for the upward revisions are presented in the Exhibit. For six of the seven holding periods, the *t* values are 2 or above. Furthermore, as evident from the table, the elimination of one year, 1967, from the sample, would increase the average abnormal return considerably.

Recall that 1967 was the first publication year of the Earnings Forecaster and the general quality of the data could possibly be inferior to that of later years.

The two tests for Exhibit 6 yield results similar to those of Exhibits 4 and 5. Since these tests are less subject to cross-sectional dependence, they allow to draw more affirmative conclusions. The results reported for the total sample, for each of the three industries, for revisions of both directions and for all eight years, are very similar. This makes it possible to generalize the conclusions beyond the framework of a 49-company sample.

All the results reported so far relate to revisions over 5%. Exhibit 7 provides a breakdown of the main findings by revision size. Presented are the average abnormal returns for all revisions (i.e., those exceeding 0%) and for those exceeding 5% and 10%. For all size groups, positive (negative) abnormal returns are observed for upward (downward) revisions. In addition, there is an increase in the absolute magnitude of the abnormal returns as the size of the revision increases. This finding seems consistent with expectations. The reason that the reported results are for 5% rather than for 10% is that for some years there are only a few revisions which exceed 10%.

Exhibit 7 Average Abnormal Returns for Selected Holding Periods by Size and Direction of Financial Analysts' Earnings Forecast Revisions (percentage)

Size of Revision	Direction (upward/downward)	Holding Period		
		[-1,2]	[0,2]	[1,2]
0%	U	3.9	2.5	1.9
	D	-3.0	-1.8	-1.1[a]
5%	U	4.7	3.6	2.7
	D	-3.8	-2.2	-1.0
10%	U	5.6	4.6	3.4
	D	-6.1	-4.3	-2.7

[a]All values except those marked by superscript 'a' are different from zero under a two-tailed test at the 5% significance level.

5. Implications for Investment Policy

The existence of abnormal returns in periods [1] and [2] can be utilized by investors. An investor might hold a portfolio which consists of companies that have recently had an upward revision of their earnings. To implement this policy, the investor would, at the end of each month, search and add to his portfolio stocks which have just had an upward revision. These stocks will be held for two consecutive months and then sold.

The large number of securities for which earnings forecasts are made and the high frequency of (upward) revisions reasonably assure the investor that at almost any given time a well-diversified portfolio could be constructed from stocks with recent upward revisions.[7]

The trading policy described above, when applied to over–5% revisions, produces in this sample a portfolio with a β of 0.95 which yields an abnormal return of 2.7% over a two-month period, or 17.3% on annual basis (compounded). In comparison, the average annual return from a buy-and-hold policy, representing a β of 0.94 is only 7.4%. However, most investors incur transaction costs and cannot enjoy the full benefit offered by this trading policy. Still, an investor subject to 1% transaction cost in each direction, could achieve an abnormal return of 0.7% over a two-month period, or 4.3% annually. This abnormal return represents a 58% improvement over the performance of a buy-and-hold policy. Similarly, an investor acting upon upward revision of 10% or more could earn an annual abnormal return of 8.7% after transaction costs, which represents a 118% improvement over the return from a buy-and-hold policy.

There are reasons to believe that the trading policy described above might not fully exploit the opportunity faced by investors to gain from the (publicly available) information on FAF. First, the data consist of monthly rates of return. As a result month 0 was excluded from the holding period: incorporation of daily returns would have further increased the abnormal returns, reflecting the opportunities that exist within month 0.

Second, no use was made of the information on downward revisions. The results indicate that such revisions are (preceded and) followed by periods with negative abnormal return. One way to utilize this information is to go short during these periods. However, the profitability of such a policy is doubtful since its yield must outperform the expected positive return on the market. Another way to use information on downward revisions is to buy shares with upward revisions and to sell short an equal dollar amount of shares with downward revisions. As explained in the Research Design section, such a portfolio could be designed to have a β of 0. If, in addition, the cash proceeds from the short sale are received upon transaction, the strategy does not involve an investment outlay. Acting upon revisions of over 5% for holding period [1,2] would yield, under this strategy, an excess return of about 3.7% (the combined abnormal return from the short and long positions, in Exhibit 7). Given the similarity between the β's of upward and downward revisions, the β of the portfolio produced by this strategy would be very close to zero. For most investors, who incur the full transaction cost, such a strategy (which involves two 'round-trips', or at least 4% transaction cost) is unprofitable. However, when applied to revisions of over 10%, the strategy yields an excess return of 6.1% which probably more than offsets the cost of transaction for many investors.

Third, as was shown, concentrating on revisions in months without earnings announcements could increase the abnormal returns even further.

Finally, the *incremental* transaction costs of the proposed trading policies are probably lower than the level implied above. Due to lack of synchronization between income and consumption, many investors find it necessary to temporarily reduce or increase their portfolio size. Transaction costs are therefore incurred anyway in the frequent process of expanding or contracting a portfolio. Selection of the stocks to be added or eliminated guided by the recent occurrence of upward or downward revision could improve the yield performance without incurring additional transaction costs.

6. Discussion and Conclusions

The results of the study indicate that FAF revisions convey information to the stock market or reflect variables which determine stock prices. Significant abnormal returns begin to form as early as two months prior to the release of the revision. In an efficient market, no abnormal returns should be observed in the periods following the revision. Yet, the findings show that the market does not respond instantaneously to FAF revisions: significant abnormal returns are observed during the two months following the month of the revision.

Not only are the reported abnormal returns significant, but they are of a considerable magnitude as well. Holding a stock during four months surrounding an upward revision of over 5% results, on average, in an abnormal return of 4.7%, representing a 195% improvement over a buy-and-hold policy. Furthermore, a substantial portion of this abnormal return, 2.7%, is observed in the two months following the revision month. This implies that an investor acting on publicly available information and incurring the full transaction cost could still earn an abnormal return of 0.7% during this two-month period (outperforming a buy-and-hold policy by 58%).

The observed abnormal returns reported in the study might have been the result of a failure of the underlying equilibrium model to properly specify the process which determines equilibrium returns. Ball, who has analyzed this possibility, outlined conditions which reduce the likelihood that the earnings variable is a proxy for omitted variables and under which therefore the bias toward overestimating abnormal returns is minimized. The experimental design of this study meets these conditions. In particular, the variable under investigation (the sign of the revision) is not highly autocorrelated across time and the experiment to test market efficiency is predictive. That is, abnormal returns are measured over periods commencing some time after the revision became public to investors. Furthermore, the fact that abnormal returns tend to disappear two or three months after the revision (for both upward and downward revisions) and the persistence of the findings in each of the three industries and in almost every year) reduce the likelihood that the abnormal returns are due to the "proxy-effect" described by Ball.

Acknowledgement

The authors are extremely grateful to the referee and to Ross Watts and Jerold Zimmerman for their constructive criticism and helpful suggestions. This research was supported by the Israel Institute of Business Research, Tel-Aviv University.

Endnotes

1. This interpretation is offered by Watts (1978, p. 131).

2. This statement assumes that the β of the sample and the β of the securities with forecast revisions are equal. Since separate portfolios are constructed for securities with upward revisions and for securities with downward revisions, the statement must further assume that the β of the shares with upward revisions is equal to the β of the shares with downward revisions. For these assumptions to hold it is necessary that (1) the frequency of the number of revisions per company is independent of its β and that (2) the sign of the revision over time is not autocorrelated. No significant correlation was found between the β of a security and the number of its revisions. The validity of the second condition has also been confirmed and the re-

sults of the statistical tests are presented in the next section. Moreover as is evident from Exhibit 1 below, there is practically no difference between the β of the shares with upward revisions and the β of the shares with downward revisions.

3. The significance of the observed gradual movement was tested. For each company the average forecast was computed each month and the signs of the changes in the average forecast between consecutive months was tested for serial dependence using runs test [see Siegel (1956, p. 57)]. In over 90% of the firms a significant positive serial dependence (5% significance level) was found.

4. In many instances the published forecasts changed not because of a revision but as a result of a change in the definition of EPS (e.g., from fully diluted to primary EPS). In those instances all EPS figures (forecasted and actual) were adjusted to conform with one definition.

5. A bias due to model misspecification could still arise: suppose that the sign of the revisions of a particular firm over time is indeed generated by a random process but that the probability of a positive sign to a given revision is 0.99. In this case the sign of the revision might very likely act as a proxy for omitted variables (which are presumably related to the firms characteristics). To ascertain that our data are free of this potential bias, the null hypothesis of an equal probability for a positive and negative sign was tested for each firm using the binomial test. The null hypothesis was rejected (at the 5% significance level) only in 7.7% of the firms for all revisions (above 0%) and in 9.6% of the firms for revisions exceeding 5%.

6. Here, again, a bias could be introduced due to a potential cross-sectional dependence. However, since such dependence would result in a downward bias in the estimate of the standard deviation (assuming positive cross-sectional dependence), the conclusion of no difference is still correct.

7. Consider the following rough estimates: Assume that the frequency of upward revisions for about 1500 companies followed by the Earnings Forecaster is similar to the frequency of upward revisions for the companies in this sample (309 upward revisions during 8 years, or 0.06 revisions per company per month). An investor would have a monthly selection of 90 companies, on average (0.06 x 1500). Assuming a binomial distribution, the probability that this selection be reduced in a

given month to, say, 70 companies is slim (less than 5%). This wide selection reasonably guarantees the possibility of constructing a well-diversified portfolio at any given time.

References

Ball, R., 1978, Anomalies in relationships between securities yields and yield-surrogates, *Journal of Financial Economics,* Sept., 103-126.

Ball, R. and P. Brown, 1968, An empirical evaluation of accounting income numbers, *Journal of Accounting Research,* Autumn, 159-178.

Barefield, R. and E. Comiskey, 1975, The accuracy of analysts forecasts of earnings per share, *Journal of Business Research,* July, 241-252.

Basi, B., K. Carey and R. Twark, 1976, A comparison of the accuracy of corporate and security analysts' forecasts of earnings, *The Accounting Review,* April, 244-254.

Basu, S., 1977, Investment performance of common stocks in relation to their price-earnings ratios: A test of the efficient market hypothesis, *Journal of Finance,* June, 663-683.

Beaver, W.H., 1968, The information content of annual earnings announcements, Empirical research in accounting: Selected studies, 1968, *Supplement to the Journal of Accounting Research,* 67-92.

Beaver, W.H., 1975, The information content of the magnitude of unexpected earnings, Unpublished manuscript (Stanford University, Stanford, CA).

Brown, P. and J.W. Kennelly, 1972, The informational content of quarterly earnings: An extension and some further evidence, *Journal of Business:* July, 403-415.

Crichfield, T., T. Dyckman and J. Lakonishok, 1978, An evaluation of security analysts' forecasts, *The Accounting Review,* July, 651-668.

Foster, G., 1977, Quarterly accounting data: Time series properties and predictive ability results, *The Accounting Review,* Jan., 1-21.

Gonedes, N.J., N. Dopuch and S.M. Penman, 1976, Disclosure rules, information production, and capital market equilibrium: The case of forecast disclosure rules, *Journal of Accounting Research,* Spring, 89-137.

Jones, C. and R. Litzenberger, 1970, Quarterly earnings reports and intermediate stock price trends, *Journal of Finance,* March, 143-148.

Latané, H. and C. Jones, 1977, Standardized unexpected earnings - A progress report, *Journal of Finance,* Dec., 1457-1465.

Siegel, S., 1956, Nonparametric statistics (McGraw-Hill, New York).

Watts, R.L., 1978, Systematic 'abnormal' returns after quarterly earnings announcements, *Journal of Financial Economics,* June-Sept., 127-150.

Chapter 9

Composite Forecasting of Annual Corporate Earnings

John B. Guerard, Jr.
Vice President
Daiwa Securities Trust Company

Bernell K. Stone, Ph.D.
Harold F. Silver Professor of Finance
The Marriott School of Management
Brigham Young University

Abstract

Recent studies have shown that composite forecasting produces superior forecasts when compared to individual forecasts. This paper extends the existing literature by employing latent root regression and robust-weighting techniques in composite model building of corporate earnings per share series. Security analysts' forecasts may be improved when combined with time series forecasts for a diversified sample of 648 year-end firms with a 1981–1985 postsample estimation period. The mean square error of analysts' forecasts may be reduced by combining analyst and univariate time series model forecasts in an ordinary least squares regression model. This reduction is very interesting when one finds that the univariate time series model forecasts are produced by ARIMA(0,1,1) random walk with drift processes. Latent root regression and robust weighting reduce forecasting errors relative to the ordinary least squares weighting scheme. Multicollinearity exists between analysts' and time series model forecasts, and latent root regression techniques are used to estimate composite earnings models. Composite earnings models produce statistically significant excess returns.

I. Introduction

The majority of the literature supports the conclusion that earnings per share (eps) forecasts prepared by security analysts are more accurate than time series model forecasts (Brown and Rozeff, 1978; Fried and Givoly, 1982; Armstrong, 1983); however, not all of the economic studies have supported the forecasting efficiency of analysts (Cragg and Malkiel, 1968; Elton and Gruber, 1972; Guerard, 1987). The purpose of this study is to

Reprinted with permission from *Research in Finance,* Vol. 10, 1992, pgs. 205-230. © 1992 by JAI Press Inc.

develop models combining analysts' and time series forecasts to more effectively forecast corporate earnings. Preliminary support for composite earnings models combining analyst and extrapolative methods can be found in Conroy and Harris (1987) and Guerard (1987). The univariate time series model forecasts follow an ARIMA(0,1,1) process (Watts and Leftwich, 1977; Ball and Watts, 1979). The majority of researchers have analyzed the annual earnings generating process and found that a random walk with a first-order moving-average operator best describes the series (Albrecht, Lookabill, and McKeown, 1977; Watts and Leftwich, 1977). Analyst forecasts will be combined with univariate time series model forecasts in order to produce superior models for estimating earnings. The problem of multicollinearity between time series model forecasts and analysts' forecasts is examined using latent root regression (LRR). Furthermore, robust-weighting (ROB) schemes are analyzed in this study to examine the problem of outliers in the composite models.

The purpose of this study is to develop composite models by estimating ordinary least squares (OLS) and biased regression models. Granger and Ramanathan (1984) propose a method of combining forecasts with no restrictions on the weights. Moreover, a constant term is estimated. The unrestricted weighting scheme of combining forecasts with a constant term produces an unbiased forecast and will produce the lowest estimated mean square error. LRR is used to address the problem of multicollinearity between analyst and time series forecasts (Gunst, Webster, and Mason, 1976). ROB of the regression lines also is used in estimating composite models (Guerard, 1987). We examine the use of transforming composite variables prior to applying regression techniques, finding Box-Cox transformations useful in developing forecasting models with lowest mean square forecasting errors.

II. Earnings Forecast Issues and Past Research

Future earnings expectations are central to security price formation. There is a massive institutional commitment to earnings forecasting. Thus, the nature of earnings time series, the impact of earnings on security pricing, the ability or lack of ability of both security analysts and statistical models to predict earnings, and the value of earnings forecasts in portfolio selection/revision have been a central focus of considerable financial research. There has been extensive research on earnings time series and the ability to forecast earnings. Reviews of much of this research are in the monographs by Foster (1981) and Brown, Foster, and Noreen (1985). Readers concerned with more extensive reviews of the early literature are referred to these works.

For the purposes of this study, the relevant research can be placed in five major categories: (1) statistical models of earnings time series, (2) security analysts' forecasts, (3) composite forecasts, (4) the value of earnings forecasts for portfolio selection/revision, and (5) implications for weak-form market efficiency.

A. Statistical Models of Earnings Time Series

The consensus conclusion of past research is that standard statistical tools for modeling and predicting times series provide very little value in forecasting annual earnings beyond a simple random walk with drift or comparable extrapolative models such as first-order exponential smoothing. See Foster (1972) for a review of this research. Moreover, even at the level of forecasting the annual earnings of individual firms, no value to time series modeling has been found (Albrecht et al, 1977; Watts and Leftwich, 1977). Chant (1980) reports some value to incorporating additional time series data related to earnings. However, except for Chant's work, this line of research has received very little attention in the literature on earnings forecasting.

For quarterly earnings forecasts, there is value to both a seasonality term and a quarter-to-quarter autocorrelation term. Moreover, while an annual autocorrelation has no value in predicting future annual earnings for the population of large companies studied by past researchers, there is some evidence that recent quarterly earnings information can improve an annual forecast (Hopwood, McKeown, and Newbold, 1984) as well as a quarterly forecast.

To many, the most surprising results of statistical forecasting research is the conclusion that there is no significant value to sophisticated statistical modeling and that very simple extrapolative techniques such as random walk with drift or first-order exponential smoothing provide the best statistical models aside from possibly including a quarterly update term or an autocorrelation/autoregressive term.

B. The Earnings Forecasts of Professional Security Analysts

Research generally supports the view that security analysts outperform both naive predictions of no earnings change and statistical models (e.g., Brown and Rozeff, 1978; Collins and Hopwood, 1980; Fried and Givoly, 1982; Elton, Gruber, and Gultekin, 1984). This result is not surprising given that (1) security analysts can use statistical models in forming their forecasts, and (2) research indicates that the only univariate statistical models that contribute significant value to annual earnings forecasts are the very simple extrapolative techniques such as a random walk with drift or a first-order exponential smoothing model.

The primary basis for the conclusion of the superiority of security analysts forecasts over univariate time series models is two generic evaluative approaches: (1) comparative predictive accuracy, and (2) the apparent inability to use univariate statistical models to improve security analysts' forecasts. Most of the research evaluating the predictive accuracy of analysts' versus statistical models has focused on their comparative predictive accuracy, with the exception of some composite model testing, namely, Fried and Givoly (1982) and, more recently, Conroy and Harris (1987) and Guerard (1987). Given the apparent ability in the latter two studies to improve analysts' forecasts with composite models, the issue of whether statistical models can improve or add to the predictive accuracy of the security analysts has become the focus of current earnings forecast research.

C. Composite Forecasts

Here the term *composite forecast* refers to combining two or more forecasts to produce another forecast. The most common method for combining the primitive forecasts is either a simple equally weighted average or a weighted average (Winkler and Makridakis, 1983; Clemen and Winkler, 1986). Composite forecasting has been the subject of considerable forecast research in recent years (see Clemen [1990] for an annotated bibliography on composite forecasting).

Within the area of earnings forecasting, there are two primary uses of composite forecasts: (1) the combination of expert (analyst) forecasts, and (2) the combination of analysts' and statistical forecasts. Both of these composite forecast formation techniques have been the subject of recent research.

In the case of combining expert predictions, the experts are professional security analysts. The question is whether combinations of two or more analysts produce earnings forecasts that are superior to those of a single analyst. The evidence to date, primarily Conroy and Harris (1987), indicates that combinations of analysts are better than individual analysts in the sense of greater predictive accuracy and superior across-time consistency.

The combination of analysts' and statistical predictions is also a subject of recent research. The hypothesis of improvement from including a statistical forecast would be validated if and only if security analysts did not fully impound all available information from past earnings time series in their forecasts. Thus, the issue of the ability to improve earnings predictions by incorporating statistical models in an analyst–statistical composite forecast provides an indication of (1) the informational efficiency of security analysts, and (2) the ability to use past earnings data to improve portfolio selection/revision.

The research to date on composite earnings forecasting is limited and in some areas reaches conflicting conclusions. Fried and Givoly (1982) use a linear correction technique to assess the incremental value of adding a time series forecast to analyst predictions. They conclude that there is no significant improvement. In contrast, Guerard (1987) and Conroy and Harris (1987) both find significant value to adding a statistical prediction to analysts' forecasts.

In forming a composite of analysts' and statistical predictions, several factors are pertinent. First, there is the choice of the analysts and the statistical model(s). Second, there is the method of forming the composite. Third, there is the issue of how one determines whether there has been significant improvement.

The most thorough study to date is that of Conroy and Harris (1987). They evaluate several statistical combinations and several weighting schemes for producing the composite. Interestingly, they find that a naive equal weighting of the analysts' forecast and the statistical model generally does better than empirically estimated weighting obtained from the performance of past time series of annual earnings. Conroy and Harris also evaluate the value of statistical models as a function of the number of security analysts

involved in producing a composite analyst estimate. They find the value to the statistical model decreases as the number of security analysts included in the analyst component of the composite increases.

D. The Value of Earnings Forecasts for Portfolio Selection

To evaluate whether earnings forecasts can improve portfolio selection, it is necessary to have (1) a prediction of earnings over time, (2) portfolio building rules, (3) a measure of portfolio performance such as excess return in the capital asset pricing model (CAPM), and (4) a criterion for deciding whether the earnings forecast produces superior performance, e.g., comparison with a naive buy-and-hold strategy or mechanical rebalancing rules and tests of whether the across-time performance of the earnings forecast-based selection/revision is economically and/or statistically superior.

Given that the primary purpose of earnings forecasting is security selection (portfolio selection/revision), one would expect extensive tests of the ability to use earnings forecasts to improve portfolio performance, especially the ability to use security analyst-based forecasts to produce superior investment performance. In contrast to this expectation, the research is quite limited. The primary work in this area is Elton et al (1984; hereafter EGG). Using portfolio-building rules based on the maximum implied earnings growth, EGG find no significant value to using the annual earnings forecasts produced by individual security analysts. However, the EGG results are not all negative. They find potential value if one could obtain sufficiently accurate earnings forecasts. In particular, EGG use actual ex post growth rates and show the potential for superior investment performance if one has a perfect forecast of earnings growth.

The EGG results and evidence that composite earnings forecasts improve on the results of individual analysts suggest two inter-dependent questions: Can a less-than-perfect forecast that improves over individual-analyst forecasts produce superior results? If so, how can such forecasts be created? In particular, given current evidence for earnings forecasting improvement via composite forecasting, can a combination of analysts' and statistical forecasts produce enough improvement to generate superior investment performance with a high degree of statistical confidence?

E. Implications for Weak-Form Market Efficiency and Earnings Surprise Models

Weak-form market efficiency asserts that it is impossible to produce superior investment returns using only publicly available information. Since the published earnings forecasts of professional security analysts are public information, the EGG result of no value in using published analysts' forecasts is consistent with weak-form market efficiency. Since both analysts' earnings forecasts and the past earnings required to estimate univariate statistical predictions are also publicly available data, the question of whether it is possible to produce superior investment performance from composites of analysts' forecasts and statistical predictions is also a test of the weak-form efficient-market hypothesis, but with a nominally broader information set than just the earnings predictions of professional analysts.

Research on earnings forecasts is also pertinent to another class of market efficiency tests: earnings surprise models. These tests include the extensive literature on the impact of earnings announcements on stock value as an assessment of the information content of accounting data. Central to this research is the need to define an earnings announcement surprise. Since the primary pioneering work of Latane and Jones (1977) and of Ball and Brown (1968), the criterion for defining an earnings surprise is to determine the difference between a predictive model of expected earnings and the actually reported earnings.

The predictive model used to define earnings surprise has ranged from the naive model of no change (random walk with zero drift) through statistical models and on to the earnings expectations based on the prevailing consensus of earnings forecasts of professional security analysts. Before consideration of predictions based on composite earnings models, research such as Brown and Rozeff (1978), Collins and Hopwood (1980), Fried and Givoly (1982), and Elton et al (1984) indicated that analysts' forecasts of annual earnings are better than any statistical model, with the possible exception of possible improvements from using within-a-year quarterly earnings data to revise annual forecasts as the quarterly data became available. Therefore, this research indicated that strong tests of earnings announcement effects should use consensus earnings forecasts of professional security analysts as the best available model for defining market expectations of future earnings. However, if it were possible to produce superior forecasts of future earnings from a composite of analysts' and statistical predictions, then weak-form market efficiency would imply that the best model for defining earnings surprise would be such a composite. Thus, the emerging research on composite forecasting of earnings is very pertinent to earnings surprise tests and the associated accounting information research.

F. Synthesis: Past Work and Research Issues

Knowledge of earnings time series and earnings forecasting is important for many areas of financial research. There is a strong interdependency in using earnings forecasts for obtaining superior portfolio selection/revision, for testing weak-form market efficiency, for models of earning announcement surprises, and for the associated tests of earnings announcement effects on security prices. Composite forecasting is clearly pertinent to strong tests in all of these areas. In addition, composite forecasting provides insight to earnings prediction methods used by professional security analysts and can contribute to assessing the informational value of analysts' earnings forecasts.

III. Security Analysts' Forecasts

The one- and two-year-ahead mean (consensus) security analysts' forecasts used in this study are those published in the I/B/E/S (IBES) survey, produced by Lynch, Jones, and Ryan, a New York-based brokerage firm that surveys brokerage firms. Analysts' forecasts are collected and published in the monthly periodical. A complete discussion of the IBES database can be found in Brown et al (1985).

A. Sample and Data Sources

This study uses earnings time series and security analysts' earnings forecast data for a sample of 648 firms. The sample firms were determined by the following selection criteria: (1) fiscal year end on December 31, (2) the IBES database provides estimates of earnings for 1981-1985, and (3) the Compustat database provides annual earnings for 1968-1985.

The companies in this sample tend to be the larger, more stable NYSE-listed companies. Most were followed by a number of professional security analysts. The average number of analysts providing forecasts for these companies was 5.5 in the 1981-1985 time period.

The IBES database provides the following information for every company: (1) average earnings forecast of reporting analysts, updated monthly, (2) the number of analysts reporting an annual earnings forecast, (3) the standard deviation of earnings forecasts among the reporting analysts, that is, the standard deviation of the analysts' estimates from the average earnings forecast. The IBES database does not provide the individual earnings estimates, nor does it identify either the individual security analysts or their brokerage firms.

Since the IBES earnings forecast is the average of individual security analysts, this forecast is already a composite of expert estimates. The question addressed here is the ability to improve on this composite of expert forecasts by adding statistically based forecasts. Improvement will be possible only if the analysts do not fully use all of the information in the time series of past earnings. Elton, Gruber, and Gultekin (1981) have shown that analysts' forecasts are immediately incorporated into the share prices such that one cannot earn an excess return by purchasing the securities forecasted to have the highest growth prospects; one can only profit by purchasing securities actually achieving a higher than expected earnings growth.

The purpose of this study is to develop composite earnings models. Better forecasting models may identify potentially high-growth securities overlooked by analysts, or may produce more accurate forecasts of growth rates than those produced by analysts alone. The identification of such securities could produce high portfolio yields for the investor. The mid-April forecasts are used because the annual earnings of the previous year are generally known by the beginning of April. Elton, Gruber, and Gultekin (1988) found that analysts' forecasts of year-end firms were no more accurate (no statistically significant differences) in April than in February.

IV. Univariate Time Series Model Building and Forecasting

Univariate time series models are estimated for 648 December year-end selected firms, during the period from 1968 to 1985. The use of only 17 observations may seem quite short for time series modeling (Newbold and Granger, 1974); however, the Ljung-Box statistics and residual plots indicate that the models are adequately fitted and the first-difference models are stationary (empirical support for using as few as 15 observations for modeling annual EPS series can be found in

Guerard [1989]). Moreover, the accounting literature is rich with many time series studies using only 25 annual observations (Albrecht et al, 1977) and Hopwood and McKeown (1986).

Annual data on EPS are taken from the COMPUSTAT tapes for the 648 firms. The form of the models is that of an ARIMA (0,1,1) process, a random walk with drift series. Most economic time series can be modeled with the ARIMA(0,1,1) process [Jenkins (1979) and Granger and Newbold (1986)]. The Little (1962) hypothesis of random earnings changes is substantiated in our analysis, as the Ljung-Box statistics indicate that only 33 of 648 firm EPS models are not adequately fitted. The simple random walk with drift models account for approximately 50 percent of the series variances.

V. Composite Earnings Estimations

The use of OLS in estimating composite earnings models as developed by Granger and Ramanathan (1984) reduces the average estimated mean square regression error relative to the analysts' forecasts of the 648 firms for the 1981-1985 post-sample period. The use of a large sample of firms produced an interesting result for relative estimating efficiency: The average five-year analyst (IBES) mean square forecasting error of 4.583 is not statistically different from the univariate time series (BJU) mean square forecasting error of 3.799 shown in Exhibit 1. This result supports the early work of Cragg and Malkiel (1968), Elton and Gruber (1972), and Guerard (1987), previously mentioned in analyzing analysts forecasting efficiency.

If one is concerned with the accuracy of the analysts' forecasts, one can examine the relationship between the actual earnings per share and analysts' forecasts. One would expect the correlation coefficient between these two variables to be approximately unity (Fried and Givoly, 1982). An examination of Exhibit 2 reveals that only in 1983 and 1985 can one not reject the null hypotheses that the correlation between the two variables is unity; however, the very high correlation coefficients indicate that analysts are not unreasonable in EPS forecasting. The large and statistically significant negative intercept terms during the 1982-1985 period show that analysts are overly optimistic in earnings forecasting.

The departure from perfect correlation suggests potential value for including univariate time series predictions with analysts' forecasts in a composite model. The term *suggests potential* is used intentionally here. If analysts used univariate time series models in forming their forecasts and departed from them only on the basis of overriding information of a departure from the time series, then regularly recurring correct departures from the time series forecast would give less than perfect correlation but would also mean no value to a composite model that includes univariate time series forecasts. However, if the information in the univariate time series model was not fully impounded in the analysts' forecasts or was rejected incorrectly, then there is potential value to a composite of the analysts' and time series forecasts. Resolving the question of value requires: (1) building statistically based composite models,

Exhibit 1   Mean Absolute Percentage Forecasting Errors (MAPE)

	1982		1983		1984		1985	
Source	$\bar{\chi}$	σ	$\bar{\chi}$	σ	$\bar{\chi}$	σ	$\bar{\chi}$	σ
BJU	1.038	4.659	0.888	4.435	0.734	3.271	1.139	6.879
IBES	1.160	4.655	0.815	4.204	0.880	4.663	1.728	9.949
EQUAL	1.064	4.612	0.603	2.673	0.554	1.935	1.453	8.252

Exhibit 2 Univariate Regression Reports[a]

Year	Method	Variable	Constant	IBES	R²
1981	OLS	EPS	−0.077	0.909	0.653
			(−0.80)	(33.92)	
	ROB	WEPS	−0.021	0.903	0.775
			(−0.31)	(45.89)	
1982	OLS	EPS	−0.605	0.818	0.250
			(−3.00)	(14.37)	
	ROB	WEPS	−0.312	0.846	0.683
			(−4.00)	(36.49)	
1983	OLS	EPS	−0.529	1.028	0.603
			(−4.77)	(30.51)	
	ROB	WEPS	−0.389	1.026	0.777
			(−5.53)	(46.24)	
1984	OLS	EPS	−0.920	1.109	0.465
			(−5.11)	(23.08)	
	ROB	WEPS	−0.402	1.018	0.723
			(−4.47)	(40.00)	
1985	OLS	EPS	−1.123	0.997	0.396
			(−5.70)	(20.05)	
	ROB	WEPS	−0.700	1.010	0.765
			(−8.24)	(44.65)	

[a]t-values in parentheses

(2) using them to generate future forecasts, (3) testing to see if the composite model significantly outperforms the analysts' forecasts.

In forming a composite model, the question arises as to what month of the IBES forecast should be used in combining with the time series forecast. To be realistic, the composite should reflect the actual availability of the annual earnings data from the prior year rather than the end of the fiscal year. In particular, the availability of the univariate time series forecast should reflect the actual information release of earnings to the public. For a December 31 company, the annual earnings are generally available to the public before the end of February and are virtually always available by the end of March. Moreover, even before the end of the fiscal year, three quarters of earnings have been announced and consequently provide a basis for a fairly accurate estimate of the fiscal year earnings.

In this study we address the issue of the appropriate month to combine with the analysts' and univariate time series forecast by forming the combinations for a series of months. Assessing how the value of a statistical-analyst composite varies over the course of the year indicates how quickly the information in last year's earnings (the last quarter's earnings) is reflected in the earnings estimates of the security analysts providing the forecasts incorporated in the IBES database. The work of Granger and Ramanathan (1984), Bopp (1985), Clemen (1986), and Guerard (1987) leads to using OLS analysis to estimate composite earnings models. The cross-sectional composite earnings model is of the form

$$EPS_t = a + b_1 BJU_t + b_2 IBES_t + e_t , \qquad (1)$$

where EPS is actual earnings per share, BJU the univariate time series model forecast

3ES the consensus IBES forecast, and e_t the indomly distributed error term.

Exhibit 3 shows that the OLS composite irnings model estimated mean absolute percentage error, MAPE (using the analyst and nivariate time series forecast) is 4.074, some 1.1 percent less than the analysts' forecast. Ioreover, we find no (statistically) meaningi differences between the unconstrained estimated equation (1) and constrained-estimated forms of Equation (1). Equation (1) is stimated using linear constraints and intercepts in OLS and ROB regression schemes lee Guerard, 1987). The estimation of conrained and intercepts in the OLS and ROB lodels is summarized in the following eight ersions of Equation (1), where X refers to ie year of estimation:

Equation	Method	Variables	Linear Contraints
X.1	OLS	Constant, SEC, BJU	No
X.2		SEC,BJU	No
X.3		Constant, SEC	Yes
X.4		SEC,BJU	Yes
X.5	ROB	Constant, SEC, BJU	No
X.6		SEC, BJU	No
X.7		Constant, SEC	Yes
X.8		SEC, BJU	Yes

The mean absolute percentage forecasting errors shown in Exhibit 3 reveal that ROB (no constraints) produces the smallest forecast errors in the transformed data. Guerard (1987) found little benefit to imposing constraints on composite modeling equations. The composite model forecasts are less optimistic than using only analysts' forecasts. The OLS-estimated composite earnings models are summarized in Exhibit 4 and the 1982-1985 average mean square estimation errors are shown in Exhibit 5.

The relatively poor (nondominant) analysts' forecasting performance was due to the 1982 and 1985 analysts' forecasts. The regression coefficients on the univariate time series forecast variable in 1981-1985 are such that the variable could not be omitted from the regression equation, Equation (1). In contrast to these results, Fried and Givoly (1982) did not find support for the construction of composite earnings models using time series and analysts' forecasts. The principal difference between the Fried and Givoly study and this study is that Fried and Givoly used a linear correction technique to examine the incremental value of the time series forecast, whereas this study examines the estimation of OLS and biased regression models, such as LRR, and avoids the inappropriate application of the incremental value technique inher-

Exhibit 3 Robust, Linear-Constrained Estimations of a Composite Model

	1982		1983		1984		1985		
Source	$\bar{\chi}$	σ	$\bar{\chi}$	σ	$\bar{\chi}$	σ	$\bar{\chi}$	σ	Overall
Eq. (1.1)	1.002	4.397	1.172	6.602	0.582	1.963	1.318	6.668	4.074
Eq. (1.2)	0.069	4.612	0.963	4.557	0.550	1.827	1.397	7.681	3.979
Eq. (1.3)	0.000	4.423	1.316	8.127	0.582	1.958	1.437	7.736	4.335
Eq. (1.4)	0.058	4.613	1.087	5.981	0.549	1.774	1.376	7.420	4.070
Eq. (1.5)	0.017	4.373	0.691	2.637	0.582	1.958	1.422	7.853	3.712
Eq. (1.6)	0.081	4.614	0.602	2.670	0.551	1.906	1.412	7.866	3.646
Eq. (1.7)	0.010	4.428	0.717	3.211	0.550	1.819	1.995	10.993	4.272
Eq. (1.8)	0.066	4.612	0.838	3.997	0.564	1.822	1.411	7.858	3.879

Exhibit 4 Composite Modeling Results[a]

Year	Method	Variable	Constant	BJU	IBES	R^2
1981	OLS	EPS	−0.86	0.458	0.520	0.685
			(−0.93)	(7.86)	(9.33)	
	LRR	EPS	0.274	0.333	0.409	0.684
				(34.30)	(38.54)	
1982	OLS	EPS	−0.536	0.921	−0.021	0.321
			(−2.78)	(8.01)	(−0.18)	
	LRR	EPS	0.196	0.201	0.183	0.324
				(16.85)	(17.49)	
1983	OLS	EPS	−0.217	0.548	0.453	0.670
			(−2.06)	(11.10)	(7.51)	
	LRR	EPS	0.114	0.296	0.394	0.658
				(28.16)	(40.14)	
1984	OLS	EPS	−0.471	0.791	0.355	0.594
			(−2.95)	(13.97)	(5.20)	
	LRR	EPS	0.178	0.047	0.440	0.484
			(5.29)	(38.54)		
1985	OLS	EPS	−0.325	1.083	−0.119	0.557
			(−1.83)	(14.91)	(−1.38)	
	LRR	EPS	−0.120	0.112	0.362	0.444
				(11.05)	(32.68)	

[a] t-values in parentheses

Exhibit 5 Mean Absolute Percentage Forecasting Error

Source	1982		1983		1984		1985		Overall
	$\bar{\chi}$	σ	$\bar{\chi}$	σ	$\bar{\chi}$	σ	$\bar{\chi}$	σ	
BJU	1.038	4.659	0.888	4.435	0.734	3.271	1.139	6.879	3.799
IBES	1.160	4.655	0.815	4.204	0.880	4.663	1.728	9.949	4.583
EQUAL	1.064	4.612	0.603	2.673	0.554	1.935	1.453	8.252	3.674
OLS	1.002	4.397	1.172	6.602	0.582	1.963	1.318	6.668	4.074
LRR	0.942	3.805	0.756	1.646	0.643	1.869	1.230	5.650	3.571
WLRR	1.016	4.317	0.681	2.495	DNC[a]	DNC	1.507	8.251	NR[b]
ROB	1.017	4.373	0.691	2.637	0.582	1.958	1.422	7.853	3.712

[a] DNC denotes did not change
[b] NR denotes not relevant (Complete)

ent in OLS analysis (see Gunst et al, [1976], Gunst and Mason [1980], and Guerard and Clemen [1989] for a complete presentation of LRR).[1] Thus, analysts do not use all available information in forming annual earnings forecasts. Also, analysts could immediately revise their forecasts with the use of the composit models. Furthermore, the OLS composit forecasting error reduction might well b translated into portfolio excess returns.

Near-multicollinearity exists between ana lysts' forecasts and univariate time serie forecasts in the sample period (1968-1980) and postsample periods (1981-1985) and leads one to question the appropriateness of OLS; near-multicollinearity inflates the estimated standard error of the regression coefficients and *t*-values are biased downward. The high levels of correlation between IBES and time series forecasts, exceeding 0.85, and the corresponding variance-decomposition proportions, also exceeding 0.85, indicate multicollinearity (Belsley et al, 1980; Belsley, 1984) (see Exhibit 6).

The relevance of LRR can be seen in the latent roots and vectors of the correlation matrices shown in Exhibit 6 (the very high correlations between IBES and Box-Jenkins forecasts). An example is shown below for the (unweighted) data for 1981. One notices the presence of a very small root (0.111) and an extremely small latent vector (−0.035). Thus, LRR is an appropriate tool to use in developing composite earnings models (with the exception of the Beaton-Tukey-weighted data of 1983).

One notices that the time series forecasts and the analysts' forecasts are highly significant in the LRR analyses (see Exhibit 4). The LRR composite models have superior forecasting performance relative to the OLS composite models in every year but 1984. The LRR composite models produce the lowest average mean square error, 3.6571. Furthermore, the unweighted data analyses indicate the appropriateness of an equally weighted scheme in 1981-1983. Analysts' forecasts have the larger weights in 1984 and 1985, despite the poor forecasting performance of analysts in 1985 (the time series had the larger weight in the OLS analysis).

One would expect that analysts use some variation of a first-order exponential smoothing model [which, of course, approximately equals the ARIMA(0,1,1)]. Thus, one would expect multicollinearity given that the forecasts are not truly derived from independent sources of information. Fried and Givoly (1982), as noted earlier, found little support

Exhibit 6 Correlation Matrix

	Actual EPS	IBES	BJU
Actual EPS	1.000	0.800	0.808
IBES	0.800	1.000	0.889
BJU	0.808	0.889	1.000
Latent Roots and Vectors, 1981			
Latent Roots	2.665	0.224	0.111
Latent Vectors	0.564	−0.825	−0.035
	0.584	0.428	−0.691
	0.585	0.369	0.722

for composite model building with time series and analysts' forecasts; however, they used a linear correction technique rather than biased regression to reduce multicollinearity. The regression coefficients on analysts' and time series forecasts tend to equality in the 1981, 1982, and 1983 OLS and LRR regressions, as one would have expected given the approximately equal standard deviations of the variables (Bates and Granger, 1969).

The OLS regressions produced white noise error terms: There are 20 to 25 outliers in the regression models (observations not within two standard deviations of the regression lines); however, given a normal distribution of 648 observations, one would have expected at least 30 observations to lie outside the confidence intervals. Thus, the error terms are not statistically different from being normally distributed. Furthermore, the calculation of the "hat matrix" and covariance deleting the *i*th row, the COVRATIO, reveals 33-45 possibly influential observations [see Belsley et al (1980) for a complete discussion of regression diagnostics]. An ROB scheme proposed by Beaton and Tukey (1974) is used and forecasting improvement is found relative to the OLS regression results (with an average mean absolute percentage error of 3.712).[2] The average mean square error is 3.674 using equal weighting, a lower mean square forecasting error than the OLS and ROB estimations. The differences between the OLS-estimated and equal weighting

Exhibit 7 Outlier-Adjusted Composite Modeling Results[a]

Year	Method	Variable	Constant	BJU	IBES	R^2
1981	ROB	WEPS	−0.022	0.371	0.583	0.796
			(−0.33)	(7.94)	(13.10)	
	WLRR	WEPS	0.266	0.606	0.250	0.779
			(30.40)	(59.45)		
1982	ROB	WEPS	−0.291	0.431	0.455	0.716
			(−3.95)	(8.50)	(8.91)	
	WLRR	WEPS	−0.234	0.435	0.414	0.715
			(39.91)	(38.69)		
1983	ROB	WEPS	−1.25	0.512	0.490	0.839
			(−2.00)	(15.26)	(12.29)	
	WLRR	WEPS	DNC[b]			
1984	ROB	WEPS	−0.062	0.651	0.388	0.849
			(−0.90)	(22.59)	(11.54)	
	WLRR	WEPS	0.319	0.801	0.106	0.835
			(77.38)	(19.75)		
1985	ROB	WEPS	−0.364	0.769	0.250	0.834
			(−4.88)	(16.00)	(4.88)	
	WLRR	WEPS	−0.333	0.148	0.655	0.798
			(21.12)	(67.25)		

[a] *t*-values in parentheses
[b] DNC denotes did not converge

scheme estimated MSE are not statistically different from zero. Thus, initial support is found for the Clemen and Winkler (1986) equal weighting scheme. The superiority of the estimated weighting scheme has been advanced by Winkler and Makridakis (1983) and Guerard (1987).

The Beaton-Tukey-weighted latent root regression (WLRR)-estimated weights tend to give larger weights to the time series models in 1981 and 1984 (see Exhibit 7). Analysts' forecasts again have the larger weight in 1985. The WLRR procedure improves upon the unweighted LRR forecasting results only in 1983. Thus, the vast forecasting superiority of weighted regression reported in Guerard (1987) is not found in the larger sample (using raw data, not log-transformed data as did Guerard), although the robust regression improves upon the OLS forecasting results.

VI. Variable Transformation And Forecasting

The composite analysis examined in the previous section used (raw) untransformed data in the regressions. It is often useful to analyze regression equations using the square root or log of the variables (using Box-Cox [1964] transformations). The logarithmic transformation is particularly useful in estimating com-

Exhibit 8 Error Reductions Relative to Analysts' Forecasts

Source	Error Reduction %
Equal-Weight Composite (raw data)	13.2
Square Root-Weighted Regression	28.0
Log-Weighted Regression	29.3
ROB-Weighted, Log Regression	28.2

Exhibit 9 Composite Modeling Results ($\lambda = 0.50$)[a]

Year	Method	Variable	Constant	BJU	IBES	R^2
1981	OLS	EPS	0.072	0.441	0.499	0.742
			(1.80)	(8.12)	(9.30)	
	ROB	WEPS	0.069	0.442	0.500	0.747
			(1.75)	(8.22)	(9.41)	
1982	OLS	EPS	0.124	0.408	0.412	0.530
			(2.13)	(5.43)	(5.43)	
	ROB	WEPS	0.079	0.424	0.424	0.560
			(1.41)	(5.80)	(5.73)	
1983	OLS	EPS	0.166	0.124	0.754	0.737
			(4.25)	(2.59)	(14.97)	
	ROB	WEPS	0.158	0.132	0.751	0.744
			(4.11)	(2.80)	(15.05)	
1984	OLS	EPS	−0.028	0.348	0.659	0.738
			(−0.60)	(7.38)	(13.30)	
	ROB	WEPS	−0.041	0.345	0.669	0.748
			(−0.88)	(7.46)	(13.74)	
1985	OLS	EPS	−0.164	0.637	0.394	0.704
			(−2.92)	(8.60)	(5.22)	
	ROB	WEPS	−0.185	0.624	0.418	0.720
			(−3.39)	(8.58)	(5.63)	

[a]t-values in parentheses

posite model weights. If one eliminates the observations (negative EPS values) that cannot be examined using a square root or logarithmic procedure, one finds statistically significant reduction in forecasting errors relative to analysts' forecasts, supporting the findings of Guerard 1987) (see Exhibit 8). See Exhibits 9 and 10 or Box-Cox regression analyses. See Clemen 1989) for an excellent survey of composite modeling and the development of the applications of statistical and econometric techniques n composite forecasting.

VII. The Market Model and Security Returns

Security returns should be positively and linearly related to an intercept (approximately the risk-free rate) and the security betas. In an efficient market, analysts' forecasts should be ncorporated into the share price such that se-

curity returns are not statistically associated with analysts' forecasts (Elton et al, 1981). However, Brown et al (1985) found that IBES one- and two-year forecasts were not fully incorporated into share prices. Brown et al used a linear-correction factor regression model to examine the relationships among security returns, betas, and analysts' forecasts. The Brown et al regression analysis does not impose a specific structural (time-specific) relationship between security returns and betas (indeed, their security returns were negatively associated with security betas with the exception of 1980).

In this study, the security return regression methodology of Brown et al (1985) is employed, although we use LRR in lieu of a linear-correction technique to produce orthogonal variables. The regression results for the 1981-1985 period are shown in Exhibit 11. LRR is warranted because the variance

Exhibit 10 Composite Modeling Results (λ = 0.00)[a]

Year	Method	Variable	Constant	BJU	IBES	R^2
1981	OLS	EPS	0.006	0.316	0.617	0.692
			(0.19)	(7.18)	(11.35)	
	ROB	WEPS	0.004	0.321	0.617	0.716
			(0.14)	(7.48)	(11.76)	
1982	OLS	EPS	−0.164	0.400	0.530	0.511
			(−3.56)	(5.50)	(6.67)	
	ROB	WEPS	−0.190	0.407	0.561	0.585
			(−4.65)	(6.18)	(7.83)	
1983	OLS	EPS	0.118	0.142	0.678	0.575
			(3.39)	(3.27)	(12.87)	
	ROB	WEPS	0.107	0.137	0.700	0.635
			(3.42)	(3.47)	(14.54)	
1984	OLS	EPS	−0.111	0.330	0.731	0.662
			(−2.64)	(8.09)	(13.84)	
	ROB	WEPS	−0.110	0.315	0.747	0.685
			(−2.78)	(8.07)	(14.84)	
1985	OLS	EPS	−0.319	0.492	0.635	0.593
			(−5.65)	(6.48)	(7.22)	
	ROB	WEPS	−0.337	0.414	0.732	0.666
			(−6.95)	(6.23)	(9.51)	

[a] t-values in parentheses

inflation factors of the OLS regression often exceed 20.0 and the variance decomposition proportions (exceeding 0.90) reveal multicollinearity between the intercept and beta and the IBES (IRESID) and composite model (CRESID) forecast errors. Security returns are associated with both IBES and composite forecast errors in the annual LRR regressions. Excess returns are found in the range of 1.3-3.9 percent using both forecasts. Thus, analysts produce value in their forecasts, the IBES variable produces additional returns of 1.3-3.5 percent during the 1981-1985 period; however, the composite model forecast errors are statistically significant, generating additional returns of 1.5-3.9%, respectively, during the 1981-1985 period, implying that analysts do not completely incorporate all information into their forecasts.

Brown et al (1985) found that the two-year IBES (IRESID2) forecasts produced larger returns (and t-statistics) than the one-year IBES forecasts. We do not find such a result, with the exception of 1985. The one and two-year composite model errors are significantly associated with returns during the 1981-1984 period, whereas the two-year IBES forecast error is not positively significantly associated with security returns (the two-year forecast actually is significantly negatively associated with security returns in 1981 and 1982).

In this study, we have used only April IBES forecasts of December year-end firms in modeling the composite earnings process as was in the case in Givoly and Lakonishok (1979); however, one would expect that as the year nears completion, December year-end firms would produce earnings more in line with analysts' expectations. That is, analysts get better as the year progresses (Elton et al, 1981). This is indeed the case with our

Exhibit 11 Return Generation Regression Results[a]

Year	Dependent Variable	Method	Constant	Beta	IRESID	CRESID	IRESID^2	R^2
1981	Return	OLS	0.287	−0.204	0.079	−0.012		0.293
			(11.82)	(−9.19)	(3.45)	(−0.49)		
	Return	LRR	0.300	−0.224	0.035	0.039		0.287
				(−10.32)	(8.83)	(9.08)		
	Return	OLS	0.333	−0.056	0.034	0.106	−0.042	0.140
			(6.50)	(−1.13)	(0.66)	(1.92)	(−2.12)	
	Return	LRR	0.346	−0.059	0.072	0.081	−0.062	0.135
				(−1.36)	(6.54)	(6.74)	(−3.17)	
1982	Return	OLS	0.386	−0.049	0.065	−0.014		0.152
			(9.91)	(−1.35)	(1.74)	(−0.36)		
	Return	LRR	0.384	−0.052	0.025	0.028		0.142
				(−1.44)	(8.23)	(8.71)		
	Return	OLS	0.739	−0.399	0.074	0.084	−0.112	0.266
			(9.62)	(−5.32)	(0.87)	(0.97)	(−4.62)	
	Return	LRR	0.764	−0.418	0.090	0.114	−0.140	0.256
				(−5.93)	(7.16)	(7.36)	(−5.69)	
1983	Return	OLS	0.238	0.074	0.066	−0.024		0.061
			(7.15)	(2.36)	(2.92)	(−0.98)		
	Return	LRR	0.305	−0.004	0.017	0.026		0.044
				(−0.10)	(3.98)	(5.40)		
	Return	OLS	0.489	0.134	−0.080	0.212	−0.029	0.091
			(5.33)	(1.46)	(−0.84)	(2.31)	(−1.09)	
	Return	LRR	0.534	0.074	0.064	0.090	−0.054	0.089
				(0.84)	(4.55)	(4.01)	(−2.15)	
1984	Return	OLS	0.239	−0.177	0.084	−0.055		0.306
			(10.76)	(−8.21)	(6.74)	(−3.99)		
	Return	LRR	0.140	−0.099	0.013	0.024		0.258
				(−9.30)	(6.48)	(10.48)		
	Return	OLS	0.445	−0.078	0.113	−0.063	−0.000	0.141
			(7.51)	(−1.28)	(2.65)	(−1.41)	(−0.73)	
	Return	LRR	0.505	−0.155	0.024	0.030	0.000	0.131
				(−2.58)	(4.54)	(5.21)	(0.85)	
1985	Return	OLS	0.435	−0.090	0.067	−0.038		0.141
			(14.89)	(−3.28)	(3.20)	(−1.66)		
	Return	LRR	0.435	−0.110	0.019	0.015		0.130
				(−3.81)	(7.21)	(6.41)		
	Return	OLS	0.823	−0.413	0.009	0.049	0.003	0.252
			(13.48)	(−6.73)	(0.13)	(0.84)	(0.10)	
	Return	LRR	0.796	−0.335	0.019	0.013	0.046	0.190
				(−4.57)	(3.41)	(2.03)	(9.38)	

[a] *t*-values in parentheses

Exhibit 12 Correlation Matrix, 1981

	ARIMA		IBES			
	Actual	(0,1,1)	March	April	July	October
Actual	1.000	0.811	0.795	0.814	0.878	0.919
ARIMA	0.811	1.000	0.879	0.886	0.887	0.871
March	0.795	0.879	1.000	0.997	0.964	0.909
April	0.814	0.886	0.997	1.000	0.975	0.925
July	0.878	0.887	0.964	0.975	1.000	0.974
October	0.919	0.871	0.909	0.925	0.974	1.000

sample of 648 firms (see Exhibit 12). We find that, on average, analysts become more accurate than the random walk with drift model around July of each year during the 1981-1985 period. Little evidence is found to substantiate the predictive power of analysts relative to a very naive ARIMA(0,1,1) process.

One notes that although analysts' forecasts are more highly correlated with actual EPS as the year progresses, the progression is not (generally) statistically significant. As one would expect in an efficient market, the excess returns to analysts' expectations of growth tend to decline in the latter months of the 1981-1985 period. The monthly information coefficients are positive and statistically significant during the April-October months of 1981-1985 and are not generally significant in the November and December months. Furthermore, if one measures the earnings surprise content of quarterly made annual earnings forecasts (April, July, October) for 1984 and 1985, one finds that the IBES error is about the size of the composite error and declines during the year. See Exhibit 12 for the results of 1981. The IBES and composite earnings surprise variables are statistically significant in the April, July, and October forecasts for 1984-1985, respectively. The excess returns fall from around 2-3 percent (for each) in the first quarter to only about 0.3-0.5 percent by the third quarter, as one would expect in a reasonably efficient market (see Exhibit 13). Thus, analysts do not use all available information in forecasting annual earnings, and the value of analysts' forecasts declines during the year.

VIII. Are Better Earnings Forecasts Enough?

The presence of highly significant excess returns suggests a less than efficient market with respect to earnings forecasts. One should now ask the question as to whether composite modeling or earnings is complementary to more traditional fundamental research such as using PE, price-to-book (PB), price-to-cash flow (PC), return on equity (RE), five-year historical growth (GH), the forecast risk factor (FRF), and the Columbine alpha (price momentum) decile (CO2) variable.[3] The total return regression equation (using LRR) can easily be expanded to incorporate these variables. The expanded total return regression equation is shown in Exhibit 14. The composite and IBES earnings forecasts add value throughout the 1981-1985 period, as does the Columbine variable. The negative coefficient on the Columbine variable occurs because one shorts securities in Columbine deciles 8-10 and the lower deciled securities should produce the highest returns. The PB ratio is highly associated with returns; the lower the PB, the higher the excess return on the securities. There is a (low) PE effect in 1984-1985, and FRF is highly significant in 1984-1985. RE is statistically significant in 1984-1985, "wrong" sign and significantly negative in 1982-1983. In summary, excess returns are produced by better earnings forecasts, IBES, and the Columbine system. The PB, FRF, and PE variables produce significant returns in several years with much lower regression coefficients than the more complex financial variables.

X. Policy and Financial Implications

The primary use of the regression results in this study is to aid analysts in revising earnings forecasts. That is, analysts can forecast annual (December end) earnings for the current year, once the previous year's earnings are known in April of the current year. It appears that analysts can substantially reduce forecasting errors by revising their forecasts using univariate time series and consensus analyst forecasts in proportions produced by the OLS or LRR analysis with Box-Cox transformations.

X. Summary and Conclusions

Composite earnings per share may be modeled combining analysts' forecasts and univariate time series forecasts. The equally weighted composite earnings models reduce the mean square forecasting error present in the analysts' forecasts by approximately 13.2 percent, despite the fact that the univariate time series models are from random walks with drift formulations. LRR produces composite models generating smaller forecasting errors than the equal-weighting scheme. Substantial forecasting improvement can be

Exhibit 13 Quarterly Forecast of Annual Earnings Surprise Efficiency[a]

Year	Method	Constant	Beta	IRESID	CRESID	R^2	F
84.1	OLS	0.208	−0.165	0.026	0.019	0.327	72.27
		(7.53)	(−7.82)	(3.18)	(3.91)		
	LRR		−0.051	0.017	0.012	0.321	105.50
			(−7.89)	(8.63)	(10.77)		
84.2	OLS	0.177	−0.051	0.017	0.012	0.144	24.97
		(7.90)	(−2.93)	(2.41)	(3.08)		
	LRR		−0.138	0.023	0.021	0.140	36.42
			(−9.42)	(6.72)	(7.06)		
84.3	OLS	0.035	−0.038	−0.002	0.0008	0.109	18.03
		(2.94)	(−4.04)	(−0.55)	(3.94)		
	LRR		−0.045	0.011	0.002	0.080	19.40
			(−4.86)	(5.78)	(1.36)		
85.1	OLS	0.301	−0.087	0.022	0.012	0.147	25.18
		(8.74)	(−3.86)	(3.12)	(1.53)		
	LRR		−0.098	0.013	0.023	0.143	36.52
			(−3.60)	(4.69)	(8.28)		
85.2	OLS	0.179	−0.087	0.009	0.009	0.192	34.62
		(9.41)	(−5.86)	(1.87)	(2.79)		
	LRR		−0.089	0.010	0.012	0.189	51.08
			(−5.94)	(5.46)	(7.25)		
85.3	OLS	0.123	−0.003	−0.002	0.002	0.013	1.91
		(8.67)	(−0.30)	(0.57)	(1.08)		
	LRR		−0.005	0.003	0.003	0.013	2.84
			(−0.46)	(2.20)	(2.07)		

t-values in parentheses

Exhibit 14 Total Return LRR Analysis; Dependent Variable: Total Return[a]

Year	Beta	COMP	IBES	RE	PE	PB	PC	FRF	CO2	GH
1981	−0.230	0.032	0.025	−0.001	0.000	−0.031	0.003	0.000	−0.042	−0.001
	(−10.63)	(7.74)	(6.46)	(−0.9)	(0.02)	(−3.05)	(1.62)	(0.7)	(−11.0)	(0.7)
1982	−0.208	0.025	0.022	−0.011	−0.001	0.053	0.001	0.003	−0.052	−0.002
	(−0.61)	(6.75)	(6.11)	(−3.8)	(−1.3)	(1.76)	(0.42)	(3.9)	(−6.0)	(1.35)
1983	0.018	0.038	0.005	−0.008	0.000	−0.032	0.001	0.001	−0.035	0.004
	(0.48)	(6.82)	(1.0)	(−5.2)	(1.2)	(−2.36)	(1.63)	(1.5)	(−5.8)	(2.47)
1984	−0.156	0.018	0.013	0.004	−0.001	−0.015	−0.000	0.000	−0.011	0.002
	(−6.54)	(6.96)	(5.82)	(4.5)	(−1.79)	(−3.2)	(−0.3)	(−2.4)	(2.8)	(1.27)
1985	−0.039	0.009	0.014	0.003	−0.001	−0.005	0.005	−0.002	−0.014	−0.003
	(−1.04)	(2.7)	(3.68)	(2.17)	(−1.65)	(−1.4)	(2.9)	(−2.9)	(−1.7)	(−1.8)

[a] t-values in parentheses

achieved by use of transformed variables in the estimated composite models. Error reductions of 28-29 percent (relative to analysts) are found by variable transformation in composite modeling. The estimation of composite earnings models may be an avenue of potential profit; univariate time series models complemented the analysts' forecasts in this study. Furthermore, the results of this study indicate that analysts may not necessarily use all information available at the time of their forecasts. The composite model errors and IBES errors are significantly associated with security returns.

Acknowledgments

Steven R. Thorley and Glen A. Hansen provided valuable research and computational assistance throughout this project. This research was supported by the Institute for Quantitative Research in Finance (the Q-group). Lynch, Jones, Ryan provided access to their IBES (Institutional Brokerage Estimate System) database. We thank Robert Hagin for having his firm, Miller, Andersen and Sherrerd, be the institutional sponsor for the use of the IBES database. Finally, the Harold F. Silver Fund at Brigham Young University provided the CRSP and COMPUSTAT databases and other financial support.

Authors' Update

Conroy and Harris (1993) and Guerard, Takano, and Yamane (1993) applied forecasting techniques to Japanese earnings series. Conroy and Harris found that IBES forecasts rarely improved upon random walk forecasts in Japan and were less accurate than the Toyo Keizai forecasts. Guerard, Takano, and Yamane found that a composite model incorporating the Toyo Keizai operating earnings forecasts as well as book value, cash flow, and sales factors and the weighted latent root regression techniques substantially outperformed the Japanese market in basetest and real-time performance.

Endnotes

1. We assume that at time t-1 we have access to k forecasts, $f_t = (f_{1t},...,f_{kt})$, for Θ_t. We can write Θ_t stochastically in terms of the (possibly biased) forecasts f_{it}:

$$\Theta_t = a_i + b_i f_{it} + u_{it}$$

$$= \beta_0 + \beta_1 f_{1t} + ... + \beta_k f_{kt} + \varepsilon_t$$

$$= f_t^* \beta + \varepsilon_t,$$

where each $u_t = (u_{1t},...,u_{kt})'$ is an independent realization from a normal process with mean vector $(0_i,...,0_i)'$ and covariance matrix Σ. We include the vector ones because, in general, we will be estimating regression coefficients including a constant term. The OLS estimator of β is given by the familiar expression

$$\beta = (F' F)^{-1m} F' \Theta .$$

As usual, β^* is the best linear unbiased estimator of β, and, assuming stationarity of the process through time, the forecast $\Theta_t^* = f_t^* \beta^*$ is the best linear unbiased predictor of Θ_t.

In the event of multicollinearity in the F matrix, β^* (and hence Θ_t^*) can be inefficient. LRR seeks to identify near-singularities in the explanatory variables and to determine their predictive value. The procedure uses this information to estimate the regression parameters β by adjusting for nonpredictive near-singularities. Define the matrix A to be an $nx(k + 1)$ data matrix containing standardized dependent and independent variables. The correlation matrix $(A'A)$ has latent roots λ_i and corresponding latent vectors α_i defined by

$$|A'A - \lambda_i I| = 0, \quad \text{and} \quad (A'A - \lambda_i I)\alpha_i = 0 .$$

Denote the elements of α_i by

$$\alpha_i' = (\alpha_{0i}, \alpha_{1i}, \ldots, \alpha_{ki}), \text{ and } \alpha_i^{0'} = (\alpha_{1i}, \ldots, \alpha_{ki})$$

That is, α_{0i} contains all of the elements of α_i except the first one. Also, define

$$\eta^2 = \Sigma (\Theta_i - \Theta)^2 ,$$

The OLS estimator β^* can be written as

$$\beta^* = -\eta \Sigma c_i \alpha_i^0 ,$$

where

$$c_i = \alpha_{0i} \lambda_i^{-1} (\Sigma \alpha_{oj}^2 / \lambda_j)^{-1}$$

Values of λ_i and α_{0i} close to zero indicate a nonpredictive near-singularity. As α_{0i} becomes close to zero, c_i should also be close to zero. However, since λ is also small, c_i may be quite large, and may have a dominant effect in the estimate β^*. Gunst et al (1976) suggest setting $c_i = 0$ for $|\lambda_i| \leq 0.3$ and $|\alpha_{0i}| \leq 0.1$, thus obtaining the LRR estimate of the parameter β. Webster et al (1974) and Gunst et al (1976) provide detailed geometrical interpretations and discussion of this technique.

2. In the Beaton-Tukey procedure, observation weights w_t are inversely related to the OLS residual values:

$$w_t = \begin{cases} (1 - (r_t/B)^2)^2 & \text{if } r_t < B , \\ 0, & \text{otherwise} . \end{cases}$$

where $r_t = \text{abs}(\text{residual}_t/\sigma_{\text{residual}})$ and $B = 4.685$. The Beaton-Tukey is one of many possible outlier adjustment procedures (Rousseeuw and Leroy, 1987).

3. The forecast risk factor, a Drexel Burnham Lambert proprietary variable, incorporates monthly mean (consensus) IBES revisions and quarterly earnings surprises into a percentage variable. Securities having lower FRF scores are preferred and generally offer higher subsequent total returns than higher FRF securities. See Douglas and Guerard (1989).

References

Albrecht, W.S., L.L. Lookabill, and J.C. McKeown. 1977. "The Time-Series Properties of Annual Earnings." *Journal of Accounting Research* 15, 226-244.

Armstrong, J.S. 1983. "Relative Accuracy of Judgemental and Extrapolative Methods in Forecasting Annual Earnings." *Journal of Forecasting* 2, 437-447.

Ball, R., and P. Brown. 1968. "An Empirical Evaluation of Accounting Income Numbers." *Journal of Accounting Research*, 159-178.

Ball, R., and R.L. Watts. 1972. "Some Time Series Properties of Accounting Income Numbers." *Journal of Finance* 27, 663-681.

Ball, R., and R.L. Watts. 1979. "Some Additional Evidence on Survival Biases." *Journal of Finance* 34, 197-206.

Bao, D.-H., M.T. Lewis, W.T. Lin, and J.G. Manegold. 1983. "Applications of Time-Series Analysis in Accounting: A Review." *Journal of Forecasting* (October-December), 405-423.

Bates, J.M., and C.W.J. Granger. 1969. "The Combination of Forecasts." *Operational Research Quarterly* 20, 451-468.

Beaton, A.E., and J.W. Tukey. 1974. "The Fitting of Power Series, Meaning Polynomials, Illustrated on Band-Spectroscopic Data." *Technometrics* 16, 147-185.

Belsley, D.A. 984. "Collinearity and Forecasting." *Journal of Forecasting* 2.

Belsley, D.A., E. Kuh, and R.E. Welsch. 1980. *Regression Diagnostics*. New York: Wiley.

Bopp, A.E. 1985. "On Combining Forecasts: Some Extensions and Results." *Management Science* 31, 1492-1498.

Box, G.E.P., and D.R. Cox. 1964. "An Analysis of Transformations." *Journal of the Royal Statistical Society* B26, 211-243.

Box, G.E.P., and G.M. Jenkins. 1970. *Time Series Analysis: Forecasting and Control.* San Francisco: Holden Day.

Box, G.E.P., and G.C. Tiao. 1975. "Intervention Analysis with Applications to Economic and Environmental Problems." *Journal of the American Statistical Association* 70, 70-79.

Brown, L.D., and M.S. Rozeff. 1978. "The Superiority of Analyst Forecasts as Measures of Expectations: Evidence From Earnings." *Journal of Finance* 33, 1-16.

Brown, L.D., and M.S. Rozeff. 1979. "Univariate Time Series Models of Quarterly Earnings per Share Behavior." *Journal of Finance* 34, 13-21.

Brown, P., G. Foster, and E. Noreen. 1985. *Security Analyst Multi-Year Earnings Forecasts and the Capital Market.* New York: American Accounting Association.

Brush, J. 1986. "Eight Relative Strength Models Compared." *Journal of Portfolio Management.*

Carbone, R., and S. Makridakis. 1986. "Forecasting When Pattern Changes Occur Beyond the Historical Data." *Management Science* 32, pp. 257-271.

Clemen, R.T., 1986. "Linear Constraints and the Efficiency of Combined Forecasts." *Journal of Forecasting* 5, 31-38.

Clemen, R.T., 1990. "Combining Forecasts: A Review and Annotated Bibliography." *International Journal of Forecasting.*

Clemen, R.T., and R.L. Winkler. 1986. "Combining Economic Forecasts." *Journal of Economic and Business Statistics* 4, 39-46.

Cleveland, W.S., and S.J. Devlin. 1980. "Calendar Effects in Monthly Time Series: Detection by Spectrum Analysis and Graphic Methods." *Journal of the American Statistical Association* 75, 487-496.

Collins, W.A., and W.S. Hopwood. 1980. "A Multivariate Analysis of Annual Earnings Forecasts Generated from Quarterly Forecasts of Financial Analysts and Univariate Time Series Models." *Journal of Accounting Research* (Fall).

Conroy, R., and R. Harris. 1987. "Consensus Forecasts of Corporate Earnings: Analysts' Forecasts and Time Series Models," *Management Science* 33, 725-738.

Conroy, R., R. Harris, and Y. Park. 1993. "Published Analysts' Earnings Forecasts: How Accurate Are They?" *Pacific-Basin Finance Journal* 1, 127-137.

Cragg, J.G., and B. Malkiel. 1968. "The Consensus and Accuracy of Some Predictions of the Growth of Corporate Earnings." *Journal of Finance* 23, 67-84.

Douglas, G.D., and J.B. Guerard. 1989. "A Summary of a Risk-Controlled Backtest Results Modeling the Forecast Risk Factor." Paper presented at the IBES Earnings Formation Research Symposium, New York City, March.

Elton, E.J., and M.J. Gruber. 1972. "Earnings Estimation and the Accuracy of Expectational Data." *Management Science* 18, 409-424.

Elton, E.J., M.J. Gruber, and M. Gultekin. 1981. "Expectations and Share Prices." *Management Science* 27, pp. 875-987.

Elton, E.J., M.J. Gruber, and M. Gultekin. 1984. "Professional Expectations: Accuracy and Diagnosis of Errors." *Journal of Financial and Quantitative Analysis* 19, 351-363.

Elton, E.J., M.J. Gruber, and M. Gultekin. 1988. "Security Analysts' Forecasting Accuracy." Paper presented at ORSA/TIMS meeting, Washington, D.C.

Farrell, J. 1983. *Guide to Portfolio Management.* New York: McGraw-Hill.

Foster, G. 1977. "Quarterly Accounting Data: Times Series Properties and Predictive Ability Results." *Accounting Review* (January), 1-21.

Foster, G. 1981. *Financial Statement Analysis.* New York: Prentice-Hall.

Fried, D., and D. Givolly. 1982. "Financial Analysts Forecasts of Earnings: A Better Surrogate for Market Expectations." *Journal of Accounting and Economics* 4, 85-107.

Givoly, D., and J. Lakonishok. 1979. "The Information Content of Financial Analysts Forecasts of Earnings." *Journal of Accounting and Economics,* 165-185.

Granger, C.W.J., and P. Newbold. 1986. *Forecasting Economic Time Series,* 2d ed. New York: Academic Press.

Granger, C.W.J. and R. Ramanathan. 1984. "Improved Methods of Combining Forecasts." *Journal of Forecasting* 3, 197-204.

Griffin, P.A. 1977. "The Time Series Behavior of Quarterly Earnings: Preliminary Evidence." *Journal of Accounting Research* 15, 71-83.

Guerard, J.B., Jr. 1987. "Linear Constraints Robust-Weighting and Efficient Composite Modeling." *Journal of Forecasting* 6, 193-199.

Guerard, J.B. 1989. "An Investigation into Adequate Data for Estimation of Annual Time Series Earnings Models." *European Journal of Operational Research* 39, 243-253.

Guerard, J.B., ad R.T. Clemen. 1989. "Collinearity and Latent Root Regression in GNP Forecasting." *Journal of Forecasting* 8, 231-238.

Guerard, J.B., Jr., M. Takano, and Y. Yamane. 1993. "The Development of Efficient Portfolios in Japan with Particular Emphasis on Sales and Earnings Forecasting." *Annals of Operations Research* 45, 91-109.

Gunst, R.F. 1984. "Toward a Balanced Assessment of Collinearity Diagnostics." *American Statistician* 38, 79-82.

Gunst, R.F., and R.L. Mason. 1980. *Regression Analysis and Its Applications.* New York: Marcel Dekker.

Gunst, R.F., J.T. Webster, and R.L. Mason. 1976. "A Comparison of Least Squares and Latent Root Regression Estimators." *Technometrics* 18, 75-83.

Hawkins, E.H., S.C. Chamberlin, and W.E. Daniel. 1984. "Earnings Expectations and Security Prices." *Financial Analysts Journal* (September/October), 24-39.

Hoerl, A.E., and R.W. Kennard. 1970. "Ridge Regression: Biased Estimation for Nonorthogonal Problems." *Technometrics* 12, 55-67, 69-82.

Hoerl, A.E., R.W. Kennard, and K.F. Baldwin. 1975. "Ridge Regression: Some Simulations." *Communications in Statistics* 4, 105-123.

Hopwood, W.S. 1980. "On the Automation of the Box-Jenkins Modeling Procedures: An Algorithm with an Empirical Test." *Journal of Accounting Research,* 289-296.

Hopwood, W.S., and P. Newbold. 1981. "Power Transformations in Time Series Models of Quarterly Earnings per Share." *Accounting Review* (October), 927-933.

Hopwood, W.S., and J.C. McKeown. 1986. *Univariate Time-Series Analysis of Quarterly Earnings: Some Unresolved Issues.* New York: American Accounting Association.

Hopwood, W.S., J.C. McKeown, and P. Newbold. 1984. "Time Series Forecasting Models Involving Power Transformations." *Journal of Forecasting* 3, 57-61.

Jenkins, G.M. 1979. "Practical Experiences with Modelling and Forecasting Time Series." In *Forecasting,* O. Anderson, ed. Amsterdam: North-Holland.

Jones, C.P., R.J. Rendleman, and H. Latane. "Stock Returns and SUEs during the 1970s." *Journal of Portfolio Management* (Winter) 18-22.

King, B.F. 1966. "Market and Industry Factors in Stock Price Behavior." *Journal of Business* 39, 139-159.

Latane, H., and C.P. Jones. 1977. "Standardized Unexpected Earnings: A Progress Report." *Journal of Finance* 32, 1457-1465.

Little, I.M.D. 1962. "Higgledy Piggledy Growth." *Oxford University Institute of Statistics* 24, 387-412.

Liu, Lon-Mu. 1980. "Analysis of Time Series and Calendar Effects." *Management Science* 26, 106-112.

Liu, Lon-Mu. 1986. "Identification of Time Series Models in Presence of Calendar Variation." *International Journal of Forecasting* 2, 357-372.

Lorek, L.S. 1979. "Predicting Annual Net Earnings with Quarterly Earnings Time-Series Models." *Journal of Accounting Research* (Spring), 190-204.

Malkiel, B. 1981. *A Random Walk Down Wall Street,* 2d ed. New York: W.W. Norton.

Mason, R.L., R.F. Gunst, and J.T. Webster. 1975. "Regression Analysis and Problems of Multicollinearity." *Communications in Statistics* 4, 277-292.

Montgomery, D.C., and E.A. Peck. 1982. *Introduction to Linear Regression Analysis.* New York: Wiley.

Newbold, P., and C.W.J. Granger. 1974. "Experience with Forecasting Univariate Time Series and the Combination of Forecasts." *Journal of the Royal Statistical Society* 137, 131-146.

Niederhoffer, V., and P.J. Regan. 1972. "Earnings Changes, Analysts' Forecasts and Stock Prices." *Financial Analysts Journal* (May-June), 65-71.

Reilly, D.P. 1980. "Experiences with an Automatic Box-Jenkins Modelling Algorithm." In *Time Series Analysis,* O. Anderson, ed. Amsterdam: North-Holland.

Rousseeuw, P.J., and A.M. Leroy. 1987. *Robust Regression & Outlier Detection.* New York: Wiley.

Salamon, G.L., and E.D. Smith. 1977. "Additional Evidence on the Time Series Properties of Reported Earnings per Share." *Journal of Finance* 32, 1795-1801.

Theil, H. 1971. *Principles of Econometrics.* New York: Wiley.

Vinod, H.D. 1978. "A Survey of Ridge Regression and Related Techniques for Improvements over Ordinary Least Squares." *Review of Economics and Statistics* 58, 121-131.

Vinod, H.D., and A. Ullah. 1981. *Recent Advances in Regression Methods*. New York: Marcel Dekker.

Watts, R.L., and R.W. Leftwich. 1971. "The Time Series of Annual Accounting Earnings." *Journal of Accounting Research* 15, 254-271.

Webster, J.T., R.F. Gunst, and R.L. Mason. 1974. "Latent Root Regression Analysis." *Technometrics* 16, 513-522.

Winkler, R.L., and S. Makridakis. 1983. "The Combination of Forecasts." *Journal of the Royal Statistical Society* 146, 150-157.

Chapter 10

Common Stock Returns Surrounding Earnings Forecast Revisions: More Puzzling Evidence[*]

Scott E. Stickel, Ph.D.
Joseph Markmann Accounting Alumni Endowed Chair
La Salle University

Synopsis

The relation between changing expectations of earnings and changing security prices is a central issue in accounting and finance. In this article, I reexamine common stock returns surrounding earnings forecast revisions, using a large database of individual analyst forecasts, and provide new evidence on market expectations of revisions, on cross-sectional differences in price effects, and on the influence of confounding events.

In summary, my findings are that revisions affect prices, but prices do not immediately assimilate the information. Price reaction is greater when the percentage change in forecast is in the top or bottom five percent of the distribution of all forecast revisions. This price effect is not simply due to an association between revisions and earnings, dividend, or stock-split announcements. Surprisingly, prices continue to drift in the direction of the revision for about six months after the revision.

Another surprise is that price reaction does not incorporate some publicly available information. Stock returns immediately after individual analyst forecast revisions suggest that an analysts' current outstanding forecast is a better measure of the market expectations of the analyst's next forecast than an updated version (i.e., the analyst's current forecast updated for information revealed after the date of the current forecast, but before the date of the next forecast).

I use this curious price reaction result to create an aggressive trading strategy that predicts changes in outstanding forecasts, in other words, a strategy that predicts price reactions. The difference in abnormal returns between securities predicted to perform best and worst is more than 13 percent every six months. Changes in beta do not explain these abnormal returns.

Key Words: Earnings forecasts, Expectations, Information content, Trading strategy.

Data Availability: All data must be obtained from the sources identified in the text.

* I wish to express my gratitude to the following: Larry Brown, Bob Holthausen, Don Lewin, Craig MacKinlay, Jerry Zimmerman, and two anonymous referees for helpful comments; the KPMG Peat Marwick Foundation, Deloitte Haskins & Sells, and the Institute for Quantitative Research in Finance for financial support and Zacks Investment Research, Inc. for supplying the analyst forecasts.

Reprinted with permission from *The Accounting Review*, Vol. 66, No. 2, April 1991, pgs. 402-416.

The relation between changing earnings expectations and changing security prices is a central issue in accounting and finance. In this article, I reexamine common stock returns surrounding earnings forecast revisions, using a large database of individual analyst forecasts, and provide new evidence on market expectations of revisions, on cross-sectional differences in price effects, and on the influence of confounding events.

Abdel-khalik and Ajinkya (1982) examine the effect of revisions on stock prices, using 288 mean forecast revisions by Merrill Lynch analysts in 1977-1978, and find significant abnormal returns during the publication week of the revisions, which is the week after the forecasts are released to employees and customers.[1] More recently, Lys and Sohn (1989), in a contemporaneous study, also examine the association between abnormal returns and revisions and find that revisions incorporate some, but not all, of the information in past prices and that revisions affect prices. My study offers a comprehensive analysis that uses 173,620 revisions for 1,465 firms by 1,869 analysts from 83 brokerage houses.

Subsequent stock price behavior warrants scrutiny because Givoly and Lakonishok (1979, 1980) and Hawkins et al. (1984) find abnormal returns long after large upward revisions. Givoly and Lakonishok, using the most active analyst reporting to Standard & Poor's *Earnings Forecaster* during 1967-1974, find abnormal returns of 2.7 percent during the *two months* following the revision month for 584 firms experiencing positive revisions of more than five percent of forecasted earnings. Hawkins et al. (1984) use a strategy that purchases the 20 stocks with the largest monthly increase in I/B/E/S mean consensus forecast and find abnormal returns of 14.2 percent in the year subsequent to revisions from 1975 to 1980. Brown et al. (1985) use about 20,000 I/B/E/S consensus revisions from 1976 to 1980 and find significant abnormal returns of -3.8 percent over the 11 months following negative revisions, but no

significant abnormal returns following positive revisions. Abdel-khalik and Ajinkya (1982) find no abnormal returns during the four weeks following the publication week, but use a relatively small sample of 288 revisions. In sum, evidence on price behavior after revisions is conflicting. Because of this and because of the magnitude of the returns reported by Givoly and Lakonishok (1979, 1980) and Hawkins et al. (1984), price behavior after revisions warrants reexamination with independent data, alternative methodologies, and different time frames.

In summary, my findings are that revisions affect prices, but prices do not immediately assimilate the information. Price reaction is greater when the percentage change in forecast is in the top or bottom five percent of the distribution of all forecast revisions. This price effect is not simply due to an association between revisions and earnings, dividend, or stock-split announcements. Surprisingly, prices continue to drift in the direction of the revision for about six months after the revision.

Another surprise is that price reaction does not incorporate some publicly available information. Stock returns immediately after individual analyst forecast revisions suggest that an analyst's current outstanding forecast is a better measure of market expectations of the analyst's next forecast than is the analyst's current forecast updated for information revealed since the date of the current forecast but before the date of the next forecast.

I use this curious price reaction result to create an aggressive trading strategy that predicts changes in outstanding forecasts, in other words, a strategy that *predicts price reactions*. The difference in abnormal returns between securities predicted to perform best and worst is more than 13 percent every *six months*. Changes in beta do not explain these abnormal returns.

Although analysts have an effect on price that is independent of earnings announcements, my findings are analogous to studies that find abnormal returns after earnings announcements (see, e.g., Bernard and Thomas 1989; Foster et al. 1984; Freeman and Tse 1989; Watts 1978). That is, changes in security prices appear to lag behind changes in earnings expectations as well as changes in earnings.

Section I describes the data and the sample. Section II presents the proxies used to measure the information content of analyst forecast revisions. Section III describes the method of detecting abnormal performance. Section IV reports the main results and section V examines the sensitivity of the main results. Conclusions are in section VI.

I. Databases and Sample Description

Individual analyst forecasts of annual earnings per share (EPS) are obtained from Zacks Investment Research, Inc. for firms with fiscal years ending in 1980-1985. Returns for firms listed on the New York Stock Exchange or American Stock Exchange are provided by the Center for Research in Security Prices (CRSP).

The forecast revisions included in the abnormal returns analysis meet the following criteria: (1) the revision date and the fiscal year-end of the firm are within 1981-1985; (2) stock returns are available on the CRSP daily returns file; (3) the revision date is within 200 trading days of the date of the analyst's prior forecast and within the current fiscal year of the firm; and (4) there are at least two analysts with an outstanding forecast for the firm on the dates of the original forecast and the revision. Of the approximately 3,600 firms on the Zacks database for fiscal year-ends within 1981-1985, 1,465 have revisions that meet the selection criteria. For these firms, 173,620 individual analyst forecast revisions and 66,306 consensus forecast revisions are subjected to empirical tests.

Brokerage houses notify Zacks of analyst revisions via reports that may not have the actual dates of less newsworthy revisions. If a brokerage house does not supply the actual revision date, Zacks uses the date of the bro-

kerage house report. These report dates are always coincidental with or later than the actual revision dates. Zacks does not identify forecasts as having either an actual date or a brokerage house report date.

For the individual analyst revisions, the date on the Zacks database is defined as event day 0. Thus, revisions with brokerage house report dates are actually revised on or prior to day 0. Any immediate abnormal price reaction caused by these revisions will appear on or prior to event day 0. Thus, the use of brokerage house report dates is not an explanation for any abnormal performance after event day 0.

Note that Zacks did not supply the dates that revisions became available to subscribers. Thus, although the revisions are publicly available on or prior to event day 0, any trading strategy must consider the (unknown) cost of gathering revisions.

II. Measures of the Information Content of Forecast Revisions

Individual Analyst Forecast Revisions

A "traditional" measure of information content is:

$$\text{Traditional Individual } SUF_{i,a,t} =$$
$$(FRCST_{i,a,t} - FRCST_{i,a,t-v}) / FRCST_{i,a,t} \quad (1)$$

where $SUF_{i,a,t}$ is defined as the scaled unexpected forecast for firm i by analyst a on day t, $FRCST_{i,a,t}$ is analyst a's EPS forecast for company i on day t, a day on which the forecast is revised, and $FRCST_{i,a,t-v}$ is analyst a's prior forecast, which is dated v days prior to day t.[2]

Traditional SUF, which is used by Givoly and Lakonishok (1979, 1980), assumes that $FRCST_{i,a,t-v}$ is the market's expectation of $FRCST_{i,a,t}$ on day $t-1$. However, an efficient market would react to $FRCST_{i,a,t}$ on the basis of expectations on day $t-1$. An "updated" measure that conditions expectations on information available on day $t-1$ is:

Updated Individual $SUF_{i,a,t} =$
$$(FRCST_{i,a,t} - E_{t-1}(FRCST_{i,a,t}))/FRCST_{i,a,t} \quad (2)$$

where $E_{t-1}(FRCST_{i,a,t})$, the expected forecast for day t as of day t-1, is estimated as:

$$E_{t-1}(FRCST_{i,a,t}) = FRCST_{i,a,t-v} + \hat{\beta}_0 \hat{\beta}_1(CONSX_{i,t-1} - CONSX_{i,t-v}) + \hat{\beta}_2(CONSX_{i,t-v} - FRCST_{i,a,t-v}) , \quad (3)$$

and $CONSX_{i,t-1}$ is the consensus forecast, excluding analyst a, for company i on day t-1.

Details of this model for estimating $E_{t-1}(FRCST_{i,a,t})$ are in Stickel (1990). Briefly, an individual analyst's next forecast is predicted by updating the analyst's current forecast. The consensus forecast revision between days t-v and t-1 proxies for new information released after the date of analyst a's current forecast. The difference between the consensus forecast and analyst a's forecast on day t-v proxies for pressure on analysts to issue forecasts closer to the consensus. Stickel finds a positive relation between each of these two variables and the change in analyst a's forecast between days t-v and t and reports that these two variables explain about 38 percent of forecast revision variability.[3]

Parameters are estimated by first segregating revisions into semimonthly subsamples on the basis of day t. Cross-sectional regressions are performed for each subsample, and parameters are averaged across subsamples (see Fama and MacBeth 1973). Parameters are estimated with forecast data from the prior year. Thus, 1980 data is used to estimate parameters for updated 1981 forecasts, and so on.

Consensus Analyst Forecast Revisions

The following measures of the information content of consensus revisions are computed on the fifteenth and last business day of each month (semimonthly).

Traditional Consensus $SUF_{i,t} =$
$$(CONS_{i,t} - CONS_{i,t-p})/CONS_{i,t} ; \quad (4)$$

Updated Consensus $SUF_{i,t} =$
$$(UCONS_{i,t} - UCONS_{i,t-p})/UCONS_{i,t} . \quad (5)$$

$CONS_{i,t}$ is the mean consensus of all outstanding forecasts on day t, with forecasts dated on or prior to day t. This is the same definition of consensus used in prior studies. $UCONS_{i,t}$ is the mean consensus with updated forecasts. Subscript t-p refers to the prior semimonthly period. Traditional $SUF_{i,t}$ is a popular measure of information content (see, e.g., Imhoff and Lobo 1984). Although it measures changing expectations of earnings, it does not use updated forecasts and thus is expected to be a noisier measure.

III. Method of Detecting Abnormal Performance

Measurement of Abnormal Returns

Expected returns are estimated from the market model (see, e.g., Fama 1976). For individual analyst revisions, event day 0 is defined as the Zacks date for a revision. For consensus revisions, day 0 is defined as the end of the semimonthly period over which change in consensus is measured. Equally weighted CRSP market returns and firm returns from event days +251 to +350 are used to estimate ordinary least squares parameters. A minimum of 30 returns are required for model estimation.[4] The period preceding the event is rejected as the estimation period because analysts are likely to respond to the information in past returns when making a revision (see Copeland and Mayers, 1982).

Event Periods

Isolating the impact of forecast revisions is difficult because forecasts are *sequentially* disseminated to market participants by sales personnel in the brokerage house rather than immediately disseminated by major news services, such as the Broad Tape. Sequential dissemination may result in a prolonged price response after event day 0 (see, e.g., Stickel 1985). As reported below, abnormal returns are positively associated with revisions from at least two months prior to revisions until approximately six months after revisions. Statistical significance is reported for the following four cumulation periods:

Subperiod (–42,0): Day –42 through day 0. Day –42 about two calendar months before day 0.

Subperiod (+1,+11): Day 11 is, on average, the end of one semimonthly period. Subperiod (+1,+11) is assumed to be the period within which revisions directly affect security prices. Day 0 is excluded because any price movement on day 0 could be caused by other events (such as earnings announcements) that cause the analyst forecast revision.

Subperiod (+12,+125): Day 125 is about the end of a six-month holding period.

Subperiod (+126,+250): Day 250 is about the end of a one-year holding period.

Tests of Statistical Significance

The sample is segregated into subsamples on the basis of the semimonthly period in which day t falls, and mean cumulative abnormal returns are calculated by semimonthly subsample. For 1981-1985, there are 120 subsamples (five years × 24 semimonthly periods). This design subsumes cross-sectional temporal dependence within subsamples and minimizes dependence between subsamples (see Jaffe 1974 and Mandelker 1974).[5] Subsample means are averaged as:

$$MCAR_{a,b} = \sum_{s=1}^{P} MCAR_{s,(a,b)} / P , \quad (6)$$

where $MCAR_{s,(a,b)}$ is the mean cumulative abnormal return from event day a to b for semimonthly period s, and P is the number of semimonthly periods. The significance of this overall mean is tested by:

$$t_{(a,b)} = MCAR_{(a,b)} / [\hat{\sigma}_{MCARs} / \sqrt{P}] , \quad (7)$$

where $\hat{\sigma}_{MCARs}$ is the estimated standard deviation of the semimonthly $MCAR$. This test

statistic is assumed to be *Student–t* distributed with P—1 degrees of freedom.

IV. Empirical Results

Abnormal Returns Surrounding Individual Analyst Revisions

Exhibit 1 reports the mean abnormal returns surrounding individual analyst revisions segregated by magnitude, and separates revisions that are in the top or bottom five percent of the semimonthly distribution of scaled unexpected forecast.[6] This filter is similar to those used by Givoly and Lakonishok (1979, 1980) and Hawkins et al. (1984).

There is evidence that individual analyst revisions, as measured by traditional SUF, affect security prices. Exhibit 1 reports that $MCAR_{(+1,+11)}$ is 0.67 percent for the top five percent and –0.64 percent for the bottom five percent. These abnormal returns are significant at less than the 0.01 level.[7] $MCAR_{(+12,+125)}$ suggests that the market slowly assimilates the information in revisions.[8]

Exhibit 1 also reports mean abnormal returns surrounding individual analyst updated SUF. Surprisingly, the magnitude of $MCAR_{(+1,+11)}$ is smaller when updated SUF is used. With paired comparisons t-tests, where mean differences are computed by semimonthly period, the difference between $MCAR_{(+1,+11)}$ for traditional and updated SUF is significant at about the 0.01 level for the top five percent (t-statistic = 2.56), but insignificant at conventional levels for the bottom five percent (t-statistic = –1.15). At least for large upward revisions, investors do not incorporate some publicly available information when reacting to revisions.

Abnormal Returns Surrounding Consensus Analyst Revisions

Exhibit 2 reports results segregated by the magnitude of traditional and updated consen-

Exhibit 1 Abnormal Returns Surrounding Individual Analyst Forecast Revisions with Traditional and Updated Measures of Market Expectations of Forecasts

Individual Analyst Revisions

	Percentile in the Distribution of Traditional and Updated Individual SUF							
	SUF<5th (Top 5%)		5th<SUF<50th		50th<SUF<95th		95th<SUF. (Bottom 5%)	
	Traditional	Updated	Traditional	Updated	Traditional	Updated	Traditional	Updated
MCAR$_{(-42,0)}$	4.60%[a]	0.73%[c]	1.17%[a]	0.88%[b]	-3.43%[a]	-2.69%[a]	-6.33%[a]	-6.10%[a]
t-statistic	(11.88)	(1.77)	(2.86)	(2.32)	(-9.27)	(-6.94)	(-11.39)	(-11.86)
MCAR$_{(+1,+11)}$	0.67%[a]	0.35%[b]	0.19%	0.20%[c]	-0.35%[a]	-0.33%[a]	-0.64%[a]	-0.54%[b]
t-statistic	(4.08)	(2.18)	(1.46)	(1.67)	(-3.03)	(-2.79)	(-2.85)	(-2.55)
MCAR$_{(+12,+125)}$	2.16%[b]	0.56%	1.13%	0.93%	-0.31%	-0.43%	-2.89%[b]	-2.91%[b]
t-statistic	(2.18)	(0.46)	(1.37)	(1.16)	(-0.99)	(-0.55)	(-2.03)	(-2.24)
MCAR$_{(+126,+250)}$	0.13%	-0.92%	0.84%	0.91%	0.31%	0.35%	-1.73%	-1.27%
t-statistic	(0.14)	(-0.85)	(1.08)	(1.20)	(0.40)	(0.45)	(-1.28)	(-1.05)
MCAR$_{(+1,+125)}$	2.83%[a]	0.91%	1.32%	1.13%	-1.16%	-0.76%	-3.53%[b]	-3.45%[b]
t-statistic	(2.66)	(0.71)	(1.48)	(1.30)	(-1.33)	(-0.91)	(-2.33)	(-2.50)
Number of Revisions	9,074	8,978	77,843	77,921	77,540	77,589	9,163	9,132

Total Number of Individual Analyst Revisions = 173,620

Revisions are segregated by magnitude and are dated within the current fiscal years of the firms. Fiscal year-ends are within 1981-1985. The t-statistics are calculated by using the mean and standard deviation of 120 semimonthly means.

Traditional Individual $SUF_{i,a,t} = (FRCST_{i,a,t} - FRCST_{i,a,t-v}) / FRCST_{i,a,t}$;

Updated Individual $SUF_{i,a,t} = (FRCST_{i,a,t} - E_{t-1}(FRCST_{i,a,t}))/FRCST_{i,a,t}$; and

$MCAR_{(a,b)}$ = Mean cumulative abnormal returns from event day a to b.

[a] Significantly different from zero at less than the 0.01 level.
[b] Significantly different from zero at less than the 0.05 level.
[c] Significantly different from zero at less than the 0.10 level.

Exhibit 2 Abnormal Returns Surrounding Consensus Analyst Forecast Revisions with Traditional and Updated Measures of the Updated Measures of the Mean Consensus Forecasts

Consensus Analyst Revisions

	Percentile in the Distribution of Traditional and Updated Individual SUF							
	SUF<5th (Top 5%)		5th<SUF<50th		50th<SUF<95th		95th<SUF (Bottom 5%)	
	Traditional	Updated	Traditional	Updated	Traditional	Updated	Traditional	Updated
MCAR $_{(-42,0)}$	4.58%[a]	3.58%[a]	1.50%[a]	1.54%[a]	−2.48%[a]	−2.38%[a]	−5.63%[a]	−6.26%[a]
t-statistic	(13.17)	(9.98)	(4.10)	(4.48)	(−8.50)	(−7.54)	(−11.07)	(−13.47)
MCAR $_{(+1,+11)}$	0.72%[a]	0.80%[a]	0.14%	0.32%[a]	−0.26%[b]	−0.40%[a]	−0.56%[b]	−0.93%[a]
t-statistic	(3.94)	(4.80)	(1.12)	(2.64)	(−2.56)	(−3.81)	(−2.38)	(−4.15)
MCAR $_{(+12,+125)}$	2.27%[a]	3.28%[a]	1.22%[c]	1.72%[b]	−0.69%	−1.21%[c]	−2.23%	−3.32%[b]
t-statistic	(2.76)	(3.83)	(1.68)	(2.43)	(−1.08)	(−1.91)	(−1.63)	(−2.54)
MCAR $_{(+126,+250)}$	0.20%	−1.31%	0.68%	0.91%	0.53%	0.38%	−1.07%	−0.66%
t-statistic	(0.26)	(−1.61)	(0.95)	(1.33)	(0.83)	(0.56)	(−0.89)	(−0.54)
MCAR $_{(+1,+125)}$	2.99%[a]	4.08%[a]	1.36%[c]	2.03%[a]	−0.95%	−1.62%[b]	−2.80%[c]	−4.25%[a]
t-statistic	(3.47)	(4.56)	(1.74)	(2.66)	(−1.38)	(−2.34)	(−1.93)	(−3.07)
Number of Revisions	3,259	3,259	29,897	30,118	29,890	29,665	3,260	3,264
Total Number of Consensus Analyst Revisions = 66,306								

Revisions are segregated by magnitude and are dated within the current fiscal year of the firm. Fiscal year-ends are within 1981-1985. The t-statistics are calculated by using the mean and standard deviation of 120 semimonthly means.

Traditional Consensus $SUF_{i,t} = (CONS_{i,t} - CONS_{i,t-p}) / CONS_{i,t}$;

Updated Consensus $SUF_{i,t} = (UCONS_{i,t} - UCONS_{i,t-p}) / UCONS_{i,t-p}$; and

$MCAR_{a,b}$ = Mean cumulative abnormal returns from event day a to b.

[a] Significantly different from zero at less than the 0.01 level.
[b] Significantly different from zero at less than the 0.05 level.
[c] Significantly different from zero at less than the 0.10 level.

sus *SUF*. Again, there is significant abnormal performance after revisions.[9] The subsequent abnormal returns are larger with updated consensus *SUF*. With paired comparisons *t*-tests, the difference between $MCAR_{(+1,+11)}$ for updated and traditional *SUF* is significant at less than the 0.01 level for the bottom five percent (*t*-statistic = –2.65), but not significant for the top five percent (*t*-statistic = 0.57). At least for negative revisions, changes in a consensus of updated forecasts are a less noisy predictor of changing prices.

It is important to note the absence of significant abnormal returns over event days +126 to +250. These results suggest that event days +251 to +350 are an unbiased benchmark period and add support for the conclusion that the abnormal returns over event days +1 to +125 are not attributable to a biased estimate of expected return.

Results for an Aggressive Trading Strategy

The individual analyst results are curious because price reaction is more closely associated with the traditional measure of unexpected forecast. A trading strategy based on this finding is to invest in securities with large deviations between the updated and current outstanding forecasts. That is, invest in securities that are predicted to have large forecast revisions, as measured by traditional individual *SUF*. This strategy is operationalized with consensus forecasts as follows:

Aggressive Consensus SUF$_{i,t}$ =

$(UCONS_{i,t} - CONS_{i,t}) / UCONS_{i,t}$.   (8)

Aggressive *SUF* uses updated forecasts to predict the direction of future revisions in current outstanding forecasts. Consensus forecasts are used because the abnormal returns are slightly larger after consensus revisions than after individual analyst revisions.

Exhibit 3 reports abnormal returns after aggressive consensus *SUF*, and Exhibit 4 plots $MCAR_{(+1,+250)}$, restated in terms of ap-

proximate semimonthly periods, for securities experiencing a consensus revision in the top and bottom five percent of the semimonthly distributions of traditional, updated, and aggressive consensus *SUF*.[10] Using paired comparisons *t*-tests with mean differences computed semimonthly, I find that $MCAR_{(+1,+125)}$ for the top five percent aggressive SUF is significantly greater than that for traditional and for updated consensus *SUF* (t-statistics of 5.53 and 4.59, respectively). For the bottom five percent, the difference between aggressive and traditional *SUF* is significant (t-statistic = –3.19) and the difference between aggressive and updated *SUF* is insignificant (*t*-statistic = –1.47).

For comparison purposes, Exhibit 3 also reports results when the difference in consensus forecasts is scaled by price per share and the standard deviation of forecasts on day *t*–1. Subsequent abnormal returns are greatest when the difference is scaled by the dispersion in forecasts (see Imhoff and Lobo 1984 for related evidence). For the bottom five percent, there are no significant differences in $MCAR_{(+1,+125)}$ with different divisors. For the top five percent, the scaling factors of forecast and standard deviation of forecasts result in significantly greater $MCAR_{(+1,+125)}$ than scaling by price (*t*-statistics of 2.10 and 2.33, respectively). The difference between using forecast and the standard deviation of forecasts is insignificant at conventional levels.

V. Sensitivity Analyses

Concurrent Earnings, Dividend, and Stock-Split Announcements

Stickel (1989) finds that earnings announcements trigger revisions, which confounds a test of the effect of revisions on prices and further suggests that analysts could be responding to other cues, such as dividend or stock-split announcements, when timing their revisions. From Foster et al. (1984, 588), a large portion (but not all) of the post-

Exhibit 3　Abnormal Returns for a Trading Strategy that Predicts Changes in Current Outstanding Forecasts

Consensus Analyst Revisions

	Top 5%			Bottom 5%		
		Other Scaling Factors			Other Scaling Factors	
	Agressive SUF	Price	σ forecasts	Agressive SUF	Price	σ forecasts
$MCAR_{(-42,0)}$	5.66%[a]	4.73%[a]	5.82%[a]	−5.56%[a]	−8.04%[a]	−4.17%[a]
t-statistic	(11.74)	(10.52)	(−12.61)	(−10.79)	(−16.45)	(−11.50)
$MCAR_{(+1,+11)}$	1.32%[a]	1.37%a	1.49%[a]	−0.95%[a]	−1.00%[a]	−1.34%[a]
t-statistic	(6.95)	(7.25)	(7.80)	(−3.92)	(−3.90)	(−7.99)
$MCAR_{(+12,+125)}$	6.91%[a]	6.20%[a]	7.87%[a]	−4.48%[a]	−5.04%[a]	−5.31%[a]
t-statistic	(7.21)	(6.75)	(9.19)	(−3.06)	(−3.95)	(−7.44)
$MCAR_{(+126,+250)}$	−0.23%	−0.25%	1.11%	−2.04%	−2.15%	0.50%
t-statistic	(−0.32)	(−0.31)	(1.41)	(−1.40)	(−1.69)	(0.74)
$MCAR_{(+1,+125)}$	8.22%[a]	7.57%[a]	9.36%[a]	−5.54[a]	−6.04%[a]	−6.65%[a]
t-statistic	(8.14)	(7.75)	(10.25)	(−3.54)	(−4.44)	(−8.64)
Total Number of Revisions	3,264	3,263	3.252	3,273	3,261	3.276

Revisions are dated within 1981-1985 and are in the top or bottom five percent of the semimonthly distributions of scaled unexpected forecast (*SUF*). The *t*-statistics are calculated by using the mean and standard deviation of 120 semimonthly means.

Aggressive Consensus $SUF_{i,t} = (UCONS_{i,t} - CONS_{i,t}) / UCONS_{i,t}$; and

　　　$MCAR_{a,b} = $ Mean cumulative abnormal returns from event day a to b.

[a] Significantly different from zero at less than the 0.01 level.

earnings-announcement drift in abnormal returns occurs within 11 days after the earnings announcement date. Studies of the effect of dividend and stock-split declarations on stock prices generally find price reaction restricted to event days −1 through +2 relative to the declaration. For example, Asquith and Mullins (1983) find reaction on days −1 and 0, and Grinblatt et al. (1984) find reaction on days 0, +1, and +2.

Exhibit 5 reports $MCAR_{(+1,+11)}$ for samples segregated by whether or not the revision occurs within 11 days of an earnings announcement or within two days of the declaration date of a dividend or stock-split. If revisions affect prices independently of earnings, dividend, and stock-split announcements, the $MCAR_{(+1,+11)}$s should be approximately equal. Again, the analysis is performed for traditional individual *SUF* and updated consensus *SUF*.[11]

There is no significant difference between the abnormal returns following revisions that are confounded and those not confounded. This suggests that there is information in revisions beyond that in earnings, dividend, and stock-split announcements.

Risk Changes

An implication of Ball et al. (1988) is that beta shifts could explain the abnormal returns subsequent to forecast revisions. Estimating betas for a 60-day period on each side of event day 0 for firms in the top and bottom five percent of the semimonthly distributions of traditional individual SUF yields a slight increase in mean beta, from 1.37 to 1.39, after positive revisions. After negative revisions, the mean beta decreases from 1.38 to 1.37.[12] As in Bernard and Thomas (1989), these beta shifts are too

Exhibit 4 Mean Cumulative Abnormal Returns After Consensus Forecast Revisions

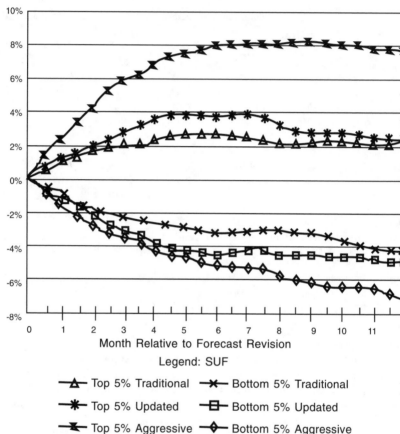

Percentage Cumulative
Abnormal Returns

Month Relative to Forecast Revision

Legend: SUF

—△— Top 5% Traditional   —✕— Bottom 5% Traditional

—✳— Top 5% Updated   —☐— Bottom 5% Updated

—✦— Top 5% Aggressive   —◇— Bottom 5% Aggressive

small to explain subsequent abnormal performance.

Conclusions

Earnings forecast revisions affect stock prices, and this price effect is a function of the magnitude of the revision. Nevertheless, prices are slow to assimilate the information. These results cannot be explained by changes in beta risk or by an association between forecast revisions and the post-earnings-announcement drift.[13] Surprisingly, abnormal returns following revisions continue to drift in the direction of the revision for about six months.

Stickel (1990) finds that updated forecasts are less biased and more accurate predictors of future forecasts than current outstanding forecasts. Surprisingly, stock returns immediately after individual-analyst revisions suggest that the current outstanding forecast is a better measure of market expectations. This finding suggests an aggressive trading strategy that uses updated forecasts to predict large revisions of current outstanding forecasts. The abnormal returns for securities pre-

Exhibit 5   Abnormal Returns Following Revisions with Segregation of Revisions Confounded by Earnings, Dividend, or Stock-Split Announcements

	Traditional Individual SUF			Updated Consensus SUF		
	Confounded	Not Confounded	**Difference**	**Confounded**	**Not Confounded**	Difference
Top 5% SUF:						
$MCAR_{(+1, +11)}$	1.05%[a]	0.85%a	0.20%	1.05%a	0.84%a	0.21%
t-statistic	(4.06)	(3.02)	(0.51)	(2.68)	(2.74)	(0.43)
Number of Revisions	3,793	2,794		974	1,086	
Bottom 5% SUF:						
$MCAR_{(+1, +11)}$	−0.55%	−0.67%[b]	0.12%	−1.32%a	−0.81%b	−0.51%
t-statistic	(−1.54)	(−1.93)	(0.23)	(−3.24)	(−1.74)	(−0.82)
Number of Revisions	3,503	3,088		1,004	1,048	

Confounded revisions occur within 11 trading days of an earnings announcement or within two days of a dividend or stock-split declaration. Revisions are in the top or bottom five percent of the semimonthly distributions of *SUF*. The t-statistics for *MCAR* following confounded and not confounded revisions are calculated by using the mean and standard deviation of 120 semimonthly means. The t-statistics for the difference in *MCAR* are for a test of difference in mean that uses semimonthly means and assumes unequal variances.

   $MCAR_{(+1,+11)}$ = Mean cumulative abnormal returns from event day +1 to +11.
[a] Significantly different from zero at less than the 0.01 level.
[b] Significantly different from zero at less than the 0.10 level.

dicted to perform best and worst average 8.22 and −5.44 percent, respectively, every six months.

The process by which changing expectations of earnings are assimilated into prices is odd. The inconsistency of these results with an efficient capital market may be attributable to trading costs and the costs of gathering and processing analyst forecasts. Thus, although prices appear inefficient because they do not immediately assimilate the information in forecasts, no claim is made that an investor could earn positive abnormal returns after these costs. Although reasonable estimates of transaction costs are available, the costs of gathering and processing forecasts are much more difficult to approximate.

Endnotes

   1. Other studies report abnormal returns during the month of the revision (e.g., Givoly and Lakonishok 1979, 1980). However, because analysts quickly respond to earnings announcements (see Stickel 1989), this evidence is confounded. Imhoff and Lobo (1984) use I/B/E/S monthly consensus revisions and eliminate revisions that are confounded by the release of other earnings information. However, the month 0 abnormal returns they report could be attributable to nonearnings information, released earlier within month 0, that triggers revisions included in the month 0 consensus revisions.

   2. A divisor of less than $.20, including any negative number, is arbitrarily set equal to $.20 to mitigate small denominators. The change in forecast is scaled by the new forecast to have the same denominator as updated *SUF*, which is defined below. Nevertheless, the results are generally insensitive to using the old forecast, the stock price, or the cross-sectional standard deviation of analyst forecasts at day t−1 as the scaling factor.

   3. Stickel (1990) also finds a significantly positive relation between the change in the analyst forecast and stock return between days $t–v$ and $t–1$. However, the marginal explanatory power of stock return is negligible.

   4. For the two percent of the sample that did not meet the minimum of 30 returns, market-adjusted returns $(R_{it} – R_{mt})$ are used. The conclusions do not change if these observations are excluded. The results are also robust to estimating market model parameters over days −400 to −301 and estimating

abnormal returns as $(R_{it} - R_{mt}) - MMAR$, where $MMAR$ is the mean market-adjusted return over days +251 to +350 (see Penman 1987).

5. As the cumulation period (a,b) lengthens, the calendar overlap across semimonthly periods increases. However, Brown and Warner (1985) find that tests with market model residuals are well-specified in the presence of extreme calendar clustering. Eliminating every other semimonthly period changes no conclusions.

6. For individual analyst revisions, the magnitude of the revision is compared to the top five percent, bottom five percent, and median cutoffs of the most recently ended semimonthly period. This avoids using distributional information not available at the date of the revision (see Holthausen 1983). Consensus analyst revisions are measured semimonthly, and cutoffs are determined at the end of those semimonthly periods.

7. A large sample size can increase the power of a test to the point where the null is rejected for trivial amounts. The abnormal returns documented in this study are large relative to other capital markets studies and are economically, as well as statistically, significant

8. The significant abnormal returns over event days –42 to 0 could be attributable to analysts, responding to the information in price changes, analysts, trading on information prior to issuing the forecast, or, as noted earlier, Zacks, using dates of brokerage house reports.

9. My traditional SUF results help reconcile Givoly and Lakonishok (1979) with Brown et al. (1985). Givoly and Lakonishok (1979) examine the top five percent SUF, finding a two-month abnormal return of 2.7 percent. Brown et al. (1985) examine all positive SUF, finding an 11-month abnormal return of less than one percent. In Exhibit 2, I report a six-month abnormal return of 2.99 for the top five percent SUF and 1.36 percent when SUF is between the fifth and fiftieth percentiles. My results are inconsistent with those in Hawkins et al. (1984), which uses the change in the traditional consensus and reports a 12-month abnormal return of 14.2 percent.

10. The abnormal returns for the top five percent aggressive SUF exceed those for the bottom five percent in 85 percent of the calendar months within 1981-1985, which indicates that the results are not driven by a few unusual months. $MCAR_{(+1,+125)}$ for securities in the top and bottom

five to ten percent of aggressive SUF are 5.29 percent (t-statistic = 5.06) and –0.60 percent (t-statistic = –0.47), respectively. Thus, the upward revisions are robust to the filter rule, but not the downward revisions.

11. Dates of earnings announcements are taken from the 1987 COMPUSTAT Quarterly Industrial and Full Coverage Files. Announcement dates for the interim or annual earnings announcement that occurs immediately before and after the forecast revision date are available on COMPUSTAT for approximately 70 percent of the revisions used in the abnormal returns analysis (e.g., for revisions in the top five percent of traditional SUF, (3,793 + 2,794)/9,074 = 73 percent of the Exhibit 1 revisions are included in Exhibit 5).

12. Finding a mean beta greater than 1.0 is expected because firms in the top and bottom five percent of SUF are, on average, smaller firms. Betas are also calculated by cumulating individual security returns and cumulating market returns for each 60-day period, which produces a single observation for a cross-sectional regression analogous to Ibbotson (1975). These beta estimates are closer to 1.0, which is unexpected and unexplained. Nevertheless, the changes in these betas are again incapable of explaining the abnormal returns after forecast revisions.

13. Atiase (1985) finds that smaller firms have a larger price reaction to earnings announcements. An interesting question for future research is whether price reaction to forecast revisions is a function of firm size.

References

Abdel-khalik, A. R., and B. Ajinkya. 1982. Returns to informational advantages: The case of analysts' forecast revisions. *The Accounting Review* 57 (October): 661-80.

Asquith, P., and D. W. Mullins. 1983. The impact of initiating dividend payments on shareholders' wealth. *Journal of Business* 56 (January): 77-96.

Atiase, R. K. 1985. Predisclosure information, firm capitalization, and security price behavior around earnings announcements. *Journal of Accounting Research* 23 (Spring): 21-36.

Ball, R., S. P. Kothari, and R. L. Watts. 1988. The economics of the relation between earnings changes and stock returns. Working paper, University of Rochester.

Bernard, V. L., and J. K. Thomas. 1989. Post-earnings-announcement drift: Delayed price response, or risk premium? *Journal of Accounting Research* 27 (Supplement): 1-36.

Brown, P., G. Foster, and E. Noreen. 1985. *Security Analyst Multi-Year Earnings Forecasts and the Capital Market.* Sarasota, FL: American Accounting Association.

Brown, S. J., and J. B. Warner. 1985. Using daily stock returns: The case of event studies. *Journal of Financial Economics* 14 (March): 3-31.

Copeland, T. E., and D. Mayers. 1982. The value line enigma (1965-1978): A case study of performance evaluation issues. *Journal of Financial Economics* 10 (November): 289-321.

Fama, E. F. 1976. *Foundations of Finance.* New York: Basic Books.,

⎯⎯ and J. D. MacBeth. 1973. Risk, return, and equilibrium: Empirical tests. *Journal of Political Economy* 81 (May/June): 607-36.

Foster, G., C. Olsen, and T. Shelvin. 1984. Earnings releases, anomalies, and the behavior of security returns. *The Accounting Review* 59 (October): 574-603.

Freeman, R. N., and S. Tse. 1989. The multiperiod information content of earnings announcements: Rational delayed reactions to earnings news. *Journal of Accounting Research* 27 (Supplement): 49-79.

Givoly, D., and J. Lakonishok. 1979. The information content of financial analysts' forecasts of earnings: Some evidence on semi-strong inefficiency. *Journal of Accounting & Economics* 1 (March): 165-85.

⎯⎯, and ⎯⎯. 1980. Financial analysts' forecasts of earnings: Their value to investors. *Journal of Banking and Finance* 4 (September): 221-34.

Grinblatt, M. S., R. W. Masulis, and S. Titman. 1984. The valuation effects of stock splits and stock dividends. *Journal of Financial Economics* 13 (December): 461-90.

Hawkins, E. H., S. C. Chamberlain, and W. E. Daniel. 1984. Earnings expectations and security prices. *Financial Analysts* Journal 40 (September/October): 24-27; 30-38; 74.

Holthausen, R. 1983. Abnormal returns following quarterly earnings announcements. *Proceedings of the Seminar on the Analysis of Security Prices,* University of Chicago: 37-59.

Ibbotson, R. G. 1975. Price performance of common stock new issues. *Journal of Financial Economics* 2 (September): 235-72.

Imhoff, E. A., and G. J. Lobo. 1984. Information content of analysts' composite forecast revisions. *Journal of Accounting Research* 22 (Autumn): 541-54.

Jaffe, J. 1974. The effect of regulation changes on insider trading. *Bell Journal of Economics and Management Science* 5 (Spring): 92-121.

Lys, T., and S. Sohn. 1989. The association between revisions of financial analysts' earnings forecasts and security prices. Working paper, Northwestern University.

Mandelker, G. 1974. Risk and return: The case of merging firms. *Journal of Financial Economics* 1 (December): 303-35.

Penman, S. H. 1987. The distribution of earnings news over time and seasonalities in aggregate stock returns. *Journal of Financial Economics* 18 (June): 199-228.

Stickel, S. E. 1985. The effect of value line investment survey rank changes on common stock prices. *Journal of Financial Economics* 14 (March): 121-43.

⎯⎯. 1989. The timing of and incentives for annual earnings forecasts near interim earnings announcements. *Journal of Accounting & Economics* 11 (July): 275-92.

⎯⎯. 1990. Predicting individual analyst earnings forecasts. *Journal of Accounting Research* 28 (Autumn): 409-17.

Watts, R. L. 1978. Systematic abnormal returns after quarterly earnings announcements. *Journal of Financial Economics* 6 (June/September): 127-50.

Chapter 11

Using Value Line and IBES Analyst Forecasts in Accounting Research[*]

Donna R. Philbrick, Ph.D.
Associate Professor of Accounting
Portland State University

William E. Ricks, Ph.D.
Director of Accounting Research
Barr Rosenberg Investment Management

1. Introduction

This paper provides descriptive data on standard sources of analyst forecasts used in accounting research: the *Value Line Investment Survey,* the Institutional Brokers Estimate System (*IBES*), and, to a lesser extent, the *Standard & Poor's Earnings Forecaster* and Zacks Investment Research. We examine the relative accuracy of seven forecast error metrics, using various combinations of *Value Line* and *IBES* forecasts of quarterly earnings per share (*EPS*) and actual earnings as reported by *Value Line, IBES,* and *Compustat.* (Appendix A reports the relative accuracy of a forecast error metric based on a smaller sample of Standard and Poor's forecasts of annual *EPS*). We find the forecast error metric that pairs the *Value Line* forecast *EPS* with the

Value Line actual *EPS* produces the smallest absolute forecast errors.

We also test the association of these forecast error metrics with three-day excess returns centered on the data of a quarterly earnings announcement. The strongest associations are obtained with the use of *Value Line* actual earnings and either *Value Line or IBES* forecast data. This suggests that the choice of actual *EPS* data is more crucial than the source of forecast *EPS* data. Our overall conclusion is that *Value Line* and *IBES* are comparable in terms of their forecast data, but *Value Line* is a better source of actual *EPS* data for the purpose of measuring earnings surprise.

In section 2, we discuss data considerations and the sample selection procedure. Section 3 explains the methodological design and presents the test results for the investiga-

* We appreciate comments from Jennifer Francis, John Elliott, the accounting workshop at Duke University, and the reviewer of an earlier draft, Lane Daley. Our thanks to Jim Bridges, Dave Fitzgerald, Rob Goodwin, Michael Guiry, Dan Gutschenritter, Jim Kacergis, and Kristina Kling for endless hours of data collection. We are particularly grateful to Meg Trauner for her assistance.

Reprinted with permission from *Journal of Accounting Research,* Vol. 29, No. 2, Autumn 1991, pgs. 397-417. © 1991 Journal of Accounting Research.

tion of forecast accuracy. Section 4 discusses the association of forecast error metrics and announcement-period excess returns; section 5 concludes the paper.

2. Data Considerations and Sample Selection

2.1 Data Sources

The *Value Line Investment Survey,* published by Arnold Bernhard and Co., covers about 91 industries and 1,700 stocks traded on various exchanges and over-the-counter. The stocks represented are those deemed by *Value Line* to be of substantial institutional interest. Typically, one or two professional analysts follow a given firm.

We obtained *Value Line* quarterly earnings forecast data and actual earnings data from the *Value Line Investment Survey,* published every Friday. Each week, about 130 stocks in seven or eight industries are examined on a predetermined schedule. Thus, all 1,700 stocks are analyzed once every 13 weeks, and their *Value Line* earnings predictions are updated four times a year. Although we use only the *EPS* forecasts and actuals, *Value Line* provides various historical and projected measures of firm performance and Safety, Timeliness, Price Stability, and Earnings Predictability ratings. The relative infrequency of *Value Line's* forecast revision is partly offset by its extensive coverage.

Since the early 1970s, *Value Line* has created and maintained commercial machine-readable databases. *Data Base-II* contains over 400 items of historical "actual" annual data from 1955 and "actual" quarterly data beginning in 1963. *Value Line's Estimates and Projections File* reports estimates and projections of over 70 items, including the Timeliness and Safety Rankings, the Earnings Predictability Index, and the Growth Persistence Index. The data in this file correspond to the estimates in the most recently published paper copy of the *Value Line Investment Survey.* Because a given file contains only the current projections, this file is not well suited for academic research requiring past forecasts.

The *IBES* database developed by Lynch Jones, and Ryan provides earnings forecasts and consensus earnings expectations derived from the forecasts, beginning in 1971. More than 2,500 analysts provide annual and quarterly earnings and long-term growth forecasts for over 3,400 stocks trading on all major U.S. and Canadian exchanges. More than 1,600 additional companies are covered only in historical files.

IBES data are available in hard copy and in a variety of computer-readable formats. *IBES* typically allows academic researchers to use their summary or consensus data with no charge. The data items reported by *IBES* in this summary include, but are not limited to, the high, low, mean, and median forecasts; the standard deviation of forecasts; the number of analysts following the firm; the number of analysts revising up and the number revising down; and actual *EPS*. The *Summary Data Tape* of *quarterly* data begins with the third quarter of 1984 and reflects monthly updating. *Annual* summary data are available on tape beginning in 1976. Reporting lags in the collection and publication system represent one limitation of the *IBES* data (see Brown Foster, and Noreen [1985] and O'Brien [1988]). Another limitation, discussed later in this paper, is the unreliability of the *IBES* reported actual quarterly earnings data.

From 1967 to April 1987, the *Standard & Poor's Earnings Forecaster* published a weekly listing of actual annual *EPS* for the prior year and forecasts of annual *EPS* for the current year and the following year, when available.[1] The forecasts were made by S&P analysts and about 65 other analysts and brokerage houses. Approximately 1,600 firms were covered in 1986/87. The number of contemporaneous forecasts available for a company was a function of the size and investor following of the company and the proximity to the fiscal year-end. Our analysis of S&P forecasts is limited by the termination of the service and the absence of quarterly data. We report a limited analysis in Appendix A.

Since 1978, Zacks Investment Research has summarized and analyzed, on a biweekly basis, annual earnings estimates of over 4,000 public companies using forecasts made by more than 2,500 security analysts at 185 brokerage houses. *Changes* in individual analysts' annual earnings forecasts for the current and next fiscal year are reported in the Zacks Investment Research biweekly *Earnings Forecaster.* The date of each revised estimate is given along with the name of the analyst. Zacks also provides consensus estimates of annual earnings for the current and next fiscal years and consensus estimates of quarterly earnings of the current quarter.

Zacks distributes four different machine-readable data bases, of which two are analogous to the *Value Line, IBES,* and *S&P* databases: the *Current Summary Tape* and the *Historical Summary Tape.* The former includes a six-month history of annual and quarterly earnings information such as the mean, most current, high, and low estimates; the standard deviation of forecasts; the number of estimates; and reported *EPS.* The *Historical Summary Tape* is a ten-year monthly history of the data items on the *Current Summary Tape.*[2] Since the Zacks database has been used infrequently in accounting research and the computer-readable data are costly relative to the *IBES* and *Value Line* databases, this study does not use Zacks forecast data.

In addition to the actual *EPS* numbers reported by *Value Line, IBES,* and *Standard & Poor's,* we use the following *Compustat* data: primary and fully diluted actual quarterly *EPS* (both before and after extraordinary items and discontinued operations) and above-the-line, nonrecurring, special items.

2.2 Sample Selection

The sample used for tests of forecast accuracy includes 4,770 firm-quarter observations representing 522 December 31 year-end firms.[3] The sample firms were required to have (1) *IBES* forecast data during the period covering the third quarter of 1984 through the fourth

quarter of 1986, (2) actual quarterly *EPS* and quarterly announcement date available on *Compustat,* and (3) forecast and actual quarterly *EPS* available from *Value Line.*[4] For tests of association with excess returns, we required that daily excess returns around the quarterly earnings announcement date be available on the *CRSP Excess Returns Tape* ($t = -105$ to $t = +2$, where $t = 0$ is the announcement date), which reduced the sample to 4,249 observations.

2.3 Data Considerations in Computing Forecast Error Metrics

The general form of the security analyst forecast error is:

$$\frac{Actual\ Quarterly\ EPS - Forecast\ Quarterly\ EPS}{Deflator} \quad (1)$$

We use two different deflators: share price, drawn from the *CRSP* tape for three days prior to the earnings announcement, and absolute value of forecast quarterly *EPS.* The latter produces a metric that can be interpreted as the percentage forecast error. Although most of the results reported are based on share price, the inferences drawn are virtually identical for both deflators.

Inconsistencies between the composition of the forecast *EPS* and the actual *EPS* used in computing the forecast error include (1) primary versus fully diluted *EPS,* (2) treatment of extraordinary items and discontinued operations, (3) treatment of above-the-line, nonrecurring, or "special" items, and (4) timing of stock splits and stock dividends. We consider each of these below.

Compustat provides both primary and fully diluted actual *EPS.* Analysts reporting to *IBES* indicate which of these their forecasts represent. The *IBES* staff decides what to report in the summary statistics and restates all forecasts to a consistent basis. In our sample, *IBES* classified 93.2% of the earnings forecasts as primary. The discussion that accompanies the *Value Line* forecast often indicates which components of earnings are included in the forecast and states whether the reported

EPS is primary or fully diluted. Examination of *Value Line* documentation indicated that 90.5% of the *Value Line EPS* used in our study are primary. In computing each forecast error metric, we state actual and forecast *EPS* for a given firm-quarter on a consistent basis, either both primary or both fully diluted.

The *Compustat* definitions of "extraordinary" and "discontinued" are based on *GAAP* guidelines and actual *EPS* both before and after these items are reported. In contrast, *IBES* provides no specific instructions to individual analysts about the treatment of extraordinary items.[5] While analysts typically forecast *EPS* before extraordinary items, "extraordinary" is undefined. In a January 1987 article, *IBES* refers to extraordinary items as "write downs which are at the discretion of management," while according to *GAAP*, not all discretionary write-downs qualify as extraordinary items. Therefore, the earnings components included in an *IBES* forecast may not be the same as those in the corresponding *Compustat* actuals. *IBES* obtains actual *EPS* from an external data service and does not assume responsibility for their accuracy. Both the actual and forecast *EPS* reported by *Value Line* generally exclude discontinued operations and extraordinary items. In *Business Week,* a senior *Value Line* analyst (Zigas [1988]) reports that *Value Line* removes such items as gains or losses from discontinued operations and other special items from earnings. We treat all *Value Line* forecasts and actuals as representing *EPS* before extraordinary items and discontinued operations unless otherwise noted.

"Special" items are above-the-line, nonrecurring gains and losses that *Compustat* includes in pretax *EPS* before extraordinary items and discontinued operations. *Value Line* forecasts and actuals generally exclude these special items.[6] On average, *IBES* forecasts appear to exclude special items, while *IBES* actuals are inconsistent in the treatment of such items. We investigate the effect of such items on the forecast error metrics.

In the *Value Line* database, if a stock split or dividend occurs between the forecast date and the earnings announcement date, the forecast (presplit) and subsequent actual (postsplit) are based on different numbers of shares. *Value Line* documentation reveals that the dividend or split and the previously reported forecast can be adjusted to postsplit terms.[7] *IBES* provides an adjustment factor to correct for the effects of stock dividends and splits. Our investigation suggests that appropriate application of this adjustment factor generally results in consistent *IBES* forecasts and *IBES* actuals even when the split occurs between the last forecast and the announcement of actual earnings. Consistency within a given database is easier to achieve than consistency across databases. Care must be taken when *Value Line* or *IBES* forecasts are paired with *Compustat* actuals to ensure that both the forecast and the actual *EPS* are stated either pre- or postsplit.

The tests that follow compare *IBES* and *Value Line* forecasts to *Compustat* actuals, where the *Compustat* actual is stated before discontinued operations, extraordinary items, and cumulative effects of accounting changes unless stated otherwise. The *IBES* or *Value Line* forecast determines the choice of primary or fully diluted *Compustat* actuals. When *Value Line* and *IBES* forecasts are paired with *Compustat* actuals, the forecast errors are denoted as (*COMP actual-VL forecast*) and (*COMP actual-IB forecast*), respectively. Since the *Value Line* and *IBES* forecasts typically exclude nonrecurring special items, we adjust the *Compustat* actual by adding back the after-tax effects of items identified by *Compustat* as special.[8] When *Value Line* and *IBES* forecasts are paired with these adjusted Compustat actuals, the forecast errors are denoted (*Adj.COMP actual-VL forecast*) and (*Adj.COMP actual-IB forecast*). We also compute forecast errors using (1) *Value Line* actuals and forecasts (*VL actual-VL forecast*), (2) *Value Line* actuals and *IBES* foreasts *(VL actual-IB forecast)*, and (3) *IBES* actuals and forecasts *(IB actual-IB forecast)*.[9]

Some insight into the choice of metrics reported in this paper is warranted. Initially, we did not include the *(VL actual-IB forecast)* metric. However, we became concerned about the reliability of the *IBES* actual data. For the 4,770 firm-quarter observations in our sample, *IBES* does not report a single negative actual *EPS,* while 6.5% of the *Value Line* actuals and 8.5% of the *Compustat* actuals are negative. In addition, we identified numerous cases where the actual *IBES EPS* for quarter *t* was, in fact, the actual *EPS* for quarter *(t - 1)*. Once this misalignment arose for a particular firm, it persisted through all remaining quarters.[10]

To determine the significance of the problem, we compared the *Value Line* and *IBES* actual *EPS* to the *Compustat* and Adjusted *Compustat* (excluding special items) actual *EPS*. The *Value Line* actual *EPS* agreed with the *Compustat* (Adjusted *Compustat EPS)* in 9% (65%) of the firm-quarter observations, while the *IBES* actual *EPS* and the *Compustat* (Adjusted *Compustat)* actual *EPS* agreed in only 33% (31%) of the cases. Consistent with this result, the Spearman correlation of *Value Line* actual *EPS* with *EPS* from *Compustat* (Adjusted *Compustat)* is 93% (94%), while Spearman correlations of *IBES* actual *EPS* with *Compustat* and Adjusted *Compustat EPS* are 68% and 69% respectively. Pearson correlations offer similar conclusions. Our uncertainty about the *IBES* actual data prompted the inclusion of the metric that compares *IBES* forecasts with *Value Line* actuals.[11]

The *IBES* forecast used is the final median forecast of *EPS* prior to an earnings announcement.[12] The *Value Line* forecast used is the final forecast made prior to the earnings announcement. Given the *Value Line* reporting system, this forecast could be made from one week to as much as three months prior to the announcement date. Previous research (Brown, Foster, and Noreen [1985], Elton, Gruber, and Gultekin [1984], and Brown et al. [1987]) indi-

cates that forecast accuracy improves as the announcement date nears. This result holds in our sample as well. We make no attempt to control for the difference in accuracy due to timing of forecasts. Although such a control would be possible for *Value Line* forecasts, it is not possible for *IBES* forecasts because we do not know when they were made.

3. Forecast Accuracy

Panels A and B of Exhibit 1 provide descriptive statistics for each of the forecast error metrics with share price as the deflator.[13] Panel A indicates that the mean signed forecast error is negative for all error metrics except *(IB actual-IB forecast)*.[14] A two-sided *t*-test rejects the null hypothesis that the mean signed forecast error is zero for all error metrics except *(VL actual-IB forecast)* and *(Adj.COMP actual-IB forecast)* *(α<.05)*. A nonparametric signed-rank test of central tendency rejects the null hypothesis for all error metrics at *α<.05*.

Panel B reports absolute forecast errors. The mean values range from .0077 to .0153 across the six metrics, with *(VL actual-VL forecast)* having the smallest mean. Median absolute forecast errors range from .0026 to .0056. Panels C and D provide results for forecast errors deflated by the absolute value of forecast *EPS*. In panel C the large mean forecast errors are due to extremely small values of forecast *EPS* in the denominator of some observations. When forecast errors are truncated to ±100%, the mean of *(IB actual–IB forecast)* is .03 and the means of the other error metrics decrease to the −.03 to −.09 range.

We compute the difference between the *(VL actual–VL forecast)* absolute forecast error and the absolute forecast error based on a *Value Line* forecast and a *Compustat*-based actual *EPS* for each firm. The design of this test implicitly uses the *(VL actual–VL forecast)* error metric as the standard for evaluating the other error metrics because it has the

Exhibit 1 Descriptive Statistics of Earnings Forecast Error Metrics[a]

($n = 4,770$)						
	VL/VL	COMP/VL	Adj.COMP/VL	IB/IB	COMP/IB	Adj.COMP/IB	VL/IB
Panel A: Signed Forecast Error (deflator is share price)							
Mean	−.0037*	−.0079*	−.006*	.0034*	−.0046*	−.0028	−.0005
Std. Dev.	.0756	.1206	.1033	.0508	.1126	.1024	.0528
Median	−.0004**	−.0004**	−.0004**	.0000**	.0006**	.0006**	.0004**
Panel B: Absolute Forecast Error (deflator is share price)							
Mean	.0077	.0130	.0110	.0087	.0153	.0133	.0102
Std. Dev.	.0753	.1201	.1029	.0501	.1116	.1016	.0519
Median	.0026	.0029	.0029	.0024	.0056	.0054	.0049
Panel C: Signed Forecast Error (deflator is | forecast *EPS* |)							
Mean	−.2865*	−.4644*	−.5383*	.3386*	−.1854*	−.2381*	−.2538*
Std. Dev.	3.9526	5.7547	5.8634	4.4085	5.9500	5.9810	4.7563
Median	−.0204*	−.0204**	−.0256**	.0000**	.0300**	.0222**	.0227**
Panel D: Absolute Forecast Error (deflator is | forecast *EPS* |)							
Mean	.5568	.8742	.8899	.5799	1.1035	1.1032	.7133
Std. Dev.	3.9237	5.7069	5.8204	4.3832	5.8497	5.8832	4.7094
Median	.1176	.1333	.1333	.1333	.3102	.3095	.2471

[a]The specific forecast error metrics used in this study are:

Metric:	Source of Actual:	Source of Forecast:
VL/VL	Value Line	Value Line
COMP/VL	Compustat Including special items	Value Line
Adj.COMP/VL	Compustat Excluding special items	Value Line
IB/IB	IBES	IBES
COMP/IB	Compustat Including special items	IBES
Adj.COMP/IB	Compustat Excluding special items	IBES
VL/IB	Value Line	IBES

* Significantly different from zero ($\alpha \leq .05$) using a two-sided parametric *t*-test.

** Significantly different from zero ($\alpha \leq .05$) using a two-sided nonparametric signed-rank test.

smallest mean absolute forecast error and has been used most frequently in previous research using *Value Line* forecasts. A negative difference indicates that the absolute forecast error using the *Compustat* actual is larger than that using the *Value Line* actual. By testing the firm-by-firm differences, we employ a matched-pairs research design, which is appropriate since the forecast error metrics for a given firm-quarter are not independent. For each comparison, we compute the mean and median differences and the significance levels of a matched-pairs *t*-test and its nonparametric analogue, a Wilcoxon matched-pairs signed-rank test.

For the full sample of 4,770 observation we compare the (*VL actual-VL forecast*) ab solute error with the error based on the *Valu Line* forecast and *Compustat's* actual *EPS* be fore extraordinary items. Since *Value Lin* generally excludes nonrecurring items from both forecast and actual *EPS,* and the *Com pustat* actual in this comparison includes th effects of special items, we expect the mea difference to be negative, indicating a smalle absolute forecast error when the *Value Lin* actual is used. The mean difference is −.004 (−.0367 when absolute forecast *EPS* is the de flator) and is significant at $\alpha \leq .0001$.

We also compare the absolute forecast error using *Value Line* as the source of both the forecast and the actual with the error based on a *Value Line* forecast and a *Compustat* actual, after removing the after-tax effects of special items. The mean difference of −.0027 (−.0357) is significantly different from zero at α ≤ .0001 and, as expected, is smaller than the mean difference when unadjusted *Compustat* actuals are used.

For the 4,294 observations where *Compustat* reports no special items, we expect a smaller mean difference than reported for the full sample because there is no disparity between *Value Line* and *Compustat* actuals resulting from special items. The mean difference of −.0023 (−.0229) is smaller than in the two previously reported tests but still significantly different from zero at α ≤ .0001. Thus the increased accuracy of forecast errors based on the use of *Value Line* actuals is not due solely to the treatment of special items.

The next two comparisons focus on the 476 observations where *Compustat* reported a special item. As expected, the mean difference of −.0221 (−.1609) is larger than the mean difference for the full data set. When the *Compustat* actual is adjusted for special items in the final comparison, the mean difference decreases to −.0062 (−.1502), a larger percentage reduction than observed for all 4,770 observations. In all comparisons, the median difference is zero and all nonparametric tests are significant at α ≤ .0001.

If forecast accuracy is the primary concern and *Value Line* forecast data are used, *Value Line* actual *EPS* produces the smallest forecast error. However, if *Compustat* is the source of reported *EPS*, an adjustment for the effects of nonrecurring special items brings the *Compustat* actual more in line with *Value Line* forecasts. One implication is that of the three measures of reported earnings examined (*Value Line, Compustat,* and Adjusted *Compustat*), the *Value Line* forecast is a better predictor of the *Value Line* earnings measure than

of either of the *Compustat*-based earnings measures. Also *Value Line* forecasts offer better predictions of *Compustat EPS* before special items than of *Compustat EPS* after special items.

Absolute forecast errors based on *IBES* forecasts and actuals are compared to forecast errors using *IBES* forecasts and the two *Compustat* actuals (adjusted and unadjusted for special items) as well as the error metric that uses *IBES* forecasts and *Value Line* actuals. A negative mean difference implies that the (*IB actual-IB forecast*) absolute forecast error is the smaller of the two forecasts being compared. The first three sets of comparisons involve all 4,770 firm-quarter observations. Because *IBES* forecasts generally exclude special items, we expect a mean difference closer to zero after the effects of special items have been removed from the *Compustat* actual. The mean difference changes from −.0053 to −.0037 (−.1829 to −.1813 using absolute forecast *EPS* as the deflator) after the adjustment for special items. When the comparison is between the (*IB actual–IB forecast*) and (*VL actual–IB forecast*) error metrics, the mean difference declines even further to −.0013 (−.0727), suggesting that *Value Line* actuals provide a better basis for evaluation of *IBES* forecasts than do *Compustat*-based actuals. In each of these comparisons, the differences are significant at α ≤ .0001 using both a parametric *t*-test and a Wilcoxon matched-pair signed-rank test.

We find a similar pattern when we examine only the 4,294 observations for which *Compustat* reports no special items. When *Compustat* is used as the actual, the mean difference is −.0038 (−.176), while use of the *Value Line* actual reduces the mean difference to −.0018 (−.0752). In both comparisons the mean and median differences are significant at the .0001 level.

The final set of comparisons involves only the 476 observations where *Compustat* indicates the presence of special items. The mean difference decreases from −.0185 to −.0028 after adjusting *Compustat* for special items with corresponding significance levels of $\alpha \leq .0001$ and $\alpha = .35$. If one compares the absolute forecast errors for *IBES* forecasts and actuals to those for *IBES* forecasts and *Value Line* actuals, the mean difference is .0027 ($\alpha = .45$) when share price is the deflator, indicating the *(IB actual–IB forecast)* absolute error is larger than the *(VL actual–IB forecast)* absolute error. The median difference is significant at $\alpha = .0003$ in the nonparametric comparison. When the absolute value of forecast *EPS* is used as the deflator, the mean and median differences are $-.0513$ ($\alpha = .0019$) and 0 ($\alpha = .0002$) respectively.

We conclude that if forecast accuracy is the primary concern and *IBES* forecast data are used, *IBES* actual *EPS* results in the smallest forecast errors. Of the four measures of reported earnings investigated (*IBES, Compustat,* Adjusted *Compustat,* and *Value Line*), the *IBES* forecast most accurately predicts the *IBES* actual earnings.

We compare the accuracy of the two forecast error metrics which pair *Value Line* actuals with each of the two forecast sources. In each comparison, the absolute forecast error based on *Value Line* actual and forecast data (*VL actual–VL forecast*) is significantly smaller ($\alpha \leq .001$) than the absolute forecast error which pairs the *Value Line* actual with an *IBES* forecast (*VL actual–IB forecast*). The full sample of 4,770 observations has a mean difference of $-.0028$ ($-.1027$ when absolute forecast *EPS* is the deflator). For the 4,294 observations with no special items and the 476 firms with special items, the mean differences are $-.0029$ ($-.1080$) and $-.0018$ ($-.0548$) respectively. The median differences are also significantly different from zero at $\alpha \leq .0001$.

Finally, we compare the *(VL actual–VL forecast)* error metric to the *(IB actual–IB forecast)* metric. For all three subsets of the data, *Value Line* absolute forecast errors are smaller than *IBES* absolute forecast errors, although the significance levels vary. These re-

sults, combined with the results reported previously, indicate that the use of *Value Line* actuals and *Value Line* forecasts results in the smallest absolute forecast error of the metrics examined in this study.

Tests of comparative accuracy and other tests not reported indicate that firms with special items have a larger average absolute forecast error than firms without. For all error metrics, the mean and median absolute forecast error of firms with special items exceeds that for firms without at less than .005 using both a two-sided *t*-test and a Wilcoxon rank-sum test. This result is consistent with (1) difficulty forecasting the earnings effect of special items, (2) discrepancies between what is included in the forecast and the actual *EPS,* or (3) other systematic differences between the two subsamples being compared.

We find that firms with extraordinary items, discontinued operations, and cumulative effects of changes in accounting method have larger mean and median absolute forecast errors than firms without such items. In 12 of the 14 statistical tests (seven error metrics; two-sided *t*-test and two-sided Wilcoxon rank-sum test), the difference is significant at $\alpha \leq .02$. These results are somewhat surprising since we would not expect forecast accuracy to be affected by below-the-line items that are typically excluded from both *Value Line* and *IBES* forecasts and actuals. However, as discussed in the following section, we observe cases where *Value Line* included such "unusual" items in their actual *EPS* values.

4. Association of Forecast Error Metrics with Excess Returns

Our "event window" for tests of association is the three-day period centered on the *Compustat* earnings announcement date. Returns are taken from the *CRSP* daily excess returns file, using the "beta-matching" approach. The reported results are based on three-day cumulative excess returns; results based on returns

tandardized by the firm's daily standard de-
iation of excess returns over the 100 prean-
ouncement trading days are similar to those
eported.

We computed ten correlations for each of
he forecast error metrics with three-day ex-
ess returns (one per quarter). Comparison of
Pearson (Spearman) correlations uses a
matched-pair *t*-test (nonparametric Wilcoxon
matched-pair signed-rank test). The statistical
ests are based on the ten *differences* in corre-
ation coefficients between any two forecast
rror metrics.

The average (over ten quarters) Pearson
and Spearman correlations of the error met-
ics with announcement-period returns are
ummarized in Exhibit 2. Reported values
epresent the mean correlations over ten quar-
ers.[15] The Spearman correlation coefficients
re consistently higher than their Pearson
ounterparts, possibly reflecting the impact of

"large" forecast errors for the Pearson correlations. The Pearson correlations increase
when we adjust *Compustat* actuals for special
items. For both *Value Line* and *IBES* forecast
data and for both types of correlations, the
highest correlations are obtained using *Value
Line* actuals.

Exhibit 2 also displays the number of significant (at α = .05 and α = .01) quarterly
correlations (out of a possible ten) for each
forecast error metric. The Spearman correlations are always at least as significant as the
corresponding Pearson correlations.

We compare correlations of excess returns
with the (*VL actual–VL forecast*) metric to
correlations of excess returns with the
(*COMP actual–VL forecast*) and (*Adj.COMP
actual–VL forecast*) metrics. Given two sets
of ten correlation coefficients, one set for
each of two forecasts error metrics, we use a
matched-pair design to compare the two fore-

Exhibit 2 Average Correlations Between Announcement-Period Excess Returns and Various Earnings Forecast Error Metrics[a] (*n* = 4,249)

		Pearson Correlations			Spearman Correlations		
			Frequency of One-Sided Test[c]			Frequency of One-Sided Test[c]	
Source of Forecast	Source of Actual[b]	Mean for Ten Qtrs.	at 1%	at 5%	Mean for Ten Qtrs.	at 1%	at 5%
Value Line	Value Line	.192	9	9	.235	10	10
Value Line	Compustat	.101	5	7	.208	10	10
Value Line	Adj. COMP	.141	8	8	.211	10	10
IBES	IBES	.134	8	8	.167	8	10
IBES	Compustat	.127	8	9	.211	9	9
IBES	Adj. COMP	.168	9	9	.207	9	9
IBES	Value Line	.198	10	10	.229	9	9

Announcement-period excess returns are excess returns for the three-day period centered on the earnings announcement date as provided in *Compustat*. Excess returns are taken from the *CRSP Excess Returns Tape* using the "beta-matched" portfolio approach. The 4,249 observations which generated the ten quarterly correlations were roughly equally distributed over the ten quarters from the third quarter of 1984 through the fourth quarter of 1986.

The *Compustat* source refers to earnings per share before extraordinary items on the *Compustat Quarterly Tapes*. *Adj. COMP* refers to estimated earnings per share before special items and extraordinary items. This item is estimated by adjusting for the after-tax impact of special items using an estimated 40% tax rate.

Those frequencies represent the number of times (out of a maximum of ten) that the indicated forecast error metric resulted in a significant association with excess returns at the indicated significance level.

cast error metrics in terms of their association with announcement-period returns. When comparing Pearson (Spearman) correlations we compute the mean (median) differences in the ten pairs of quarterly correlations using matched-pair t-tests (Wilcoxon matched-pair signed-rank tests).

The correlations based on *Value Line* actuals are significantly higher ($\alpha = .009$ t-test; $\alpha = .036$ Wilcoxon) than correlations based on *Compustat's* earnings before extraordinary items unadjusted for special items. When we remove the effects of special items from *Compustat*, the resulting forecast errors are more like the *Value Line*-based forecast errors because *Value Line* generally excludes nonrecurring items from both their forecasts and reported *EPS*. Forecast errors based on these adjusted *Compustat* data result in higher levels of association with returns. The resulting Spearman correlations are still significantly lower than those based on *Value Line* actuals ($\alpha = .058$), while the differences in Pearson correlations are not significant at conventional levels ($\alpha = .178$)

The final comparison is restricted to the 3,871 observations where *Compustat* reports no special item for the firm-quarter. We expect smaller differences between the correlations based on *Value Line* actuals and those based on *Compustat* data. While the magnitudes of the differences are slightly less, the *Value Line*-based correlations remain higher than those based on *Compustat* data. Thus the use of *Value Line* actuals results in a higher association with excess returns than the use of *Compustat* data, even when there are no special items. Although the differences in association are statistically significant, in most quarters each of the error metrics using *Value Line* forecasts is positively and significantly correlated with excess returns regardless of the actual *EPS* measure being used.

We conclude that when *Value Line* forecast data are used, "actual" *Value Line* *EPS* data result in a higher association with excess

returns than a forecast error metric using *Compustat* earnings. When *Compustat* is the source of actual *EPS* data, use of *EPS* before special items seems reasonable.

We also compare the use of *IBES* actuals with the two *Compustat*-based actuals for all 4,249 firm-quarter observations. Pearson correlations are not significantly different at conventional levels, but Spearman correlations are significantly higher when *Compustat EPS* data are used. For 3,871 observations with no *Compustat* special items, *Compustat* actual data results in Spearman and Pearson correlations which are significantly higher ($\alpha = .067$ and $\alpha = .029$) than those based on *IBES* actual *EPS* data.

When we compare the correlations based on *IBES* actuals to those based on *Value Line* actuals, *Value Line* data produce significantly higher correlations in all four statistical comparisons (Spearman and Pearson correlations all 4,249 observations and 3,871 observations with no special items). When *EPS* forecast data are taken from *IBES*, the source of actual *EPS* data resulting in the poorest performance is the *IBES* database. The highest associations with returns are obtained when *Value Line* actual *EPS* data are used in conjunction with the *IBES* forecast.

When the metric based on *Value Line* forecast and actual data is compared to the (*VL actual–IB forecast*) metric, results show no significant differences in the correlations with announcement-period returns. The use of *Value Line* actual *EPS* data produces higher associations with announcement-period returns than the use of *IBES* or *Compustat* actual earnings, regardless of the source of forecast data. These conclusions are largely unaffected by the extensions and sensitivity analyses reported below.

We assessed the robustness of these results to the presence of outliers. Forecast error and three-day excess returns in excess of 25% were truncated to 25% and the analyses were repeated. Truncation was also performed at

50%. As expected, the results of the Wilcoxon comparisons based on Spearman correlations were virtually unchanged, while the Pearson correlation coefficients increased. While the qualitative conclusions based on the matched-pair *t*-tests are unchanged, the significance levels are uniformly lower, thereby strengthening the conclusion that *Value Line* actuals result in higher levels of association.

We repeated the association tests using the absolute value of the forecast as the deflator and truncating forecast errors at ± 100%, deleting observations with a forecast equal to zero. The results based on Spearman correlations were virtually identical to those previously reported; Pearson correlation coefficients increased, but the conclusions based on these parametric comparisons were generally unchanged. *Value Line* is even more dominant as a source of actual *EPS* when absolute forecast *EPS* is the deflator. Use of *Value Line* forecasts and *Value Line* actuals now results in a significantly higher (α = .06) association with returns when compared to the use of *IBES* forecasts and *Value Line* actuals. These results strengthen the conclusion that the earnings number measured by *Value Line* actual *EPS* is closest to what is being forecast.

As an alternative comparison of the forecast metrics, we pool all 4,249 firm-quarter observations, regress three-day excess returns on the various forecast errors, and compute the absolute residuals from the regressions. We then compare the resulting absolute residuals from these regressions using the same two statistical tests previously discussed. At consistently lower significance levels, we reach the same conclusions: (1) using *Value Line* forecasts, *Value Line* actuals dominate the use of *Compustat* data; (2) using *IBES* forecasts, *Value Line* dominates both *IBES* and *Compustat* as a source of actuals; (3) using *Value Line* actuals, no significant difference exists between *Value Line* and *IBES* as a source of forecast data.

4.1 Explanation of Differences in Actuals from Various Sources

Given the goal of explaining announcement-period returns, a component of earnings "should be" included in the computation of unexpected earnings if that component is both unexpected (at the time of the earnings announcement) and "priced" by the market. While theory and prior research (e.g., Lipe [1986]) suggest that some components of earnings may be less price-relevant than others, most types of earnings components could affect stock prices. Earnings components that are both price-relevant and unexpected, even if they are "transitory," should be included in the computation of unexpected earnings (although preferably as a separate variable to allow for a differential market response).

We examine the treatment of "unusual," "transitory," or "nonrecurring" earnings components.[16] While *Value Line's* stated policy is to exclude any nonrecurring item from the forecast and actual *EPS*, identifying these nonrecurring items involves judgment. We found isolated examples where the *Value Line* analyst *included* an obvious nonrecurring item, such as the results of a discontinued segment.

Most prior research using *Compustat* as the source of actual *EPS* for computation of "earnings surprise" or "unexpected earnings" has focused on *EPS* before extraordinary items, discontinued operations, and the cumulative effects of changes in accounting method. This is appropriate in cases where the below-the-line items are either known in advance and excluded from the forecast or have little or no pricing implications.

Any problems or misclassifications resulting from these below-the-line items are likely to be less significant than the problems created by nonrecurring items that are reported above-the-line. Many of these above-the-line items are disclosed prior to the earnings announcement and do not cause a market reaction at the earnings announcement date. However, these items are included in unexpected earnings, via the use of *Compustat's EPS* before extraordinary items. The mistreatment of these above-the-line items represents a source of measurement error in a much-used explanatory variable—unexpected earnings. This may explain why the use of *unadjusted Compustat EPS* produced significantly lower correlations with excess returns as reported in Exhibit 2 and why improved correlations were obtained when *Compustat* data were adjusted for special items. The benefit of using *Value Line* actuals or adjusted *Compustat* actuals is their removal of nonrecurring, special items from the computation of unexpected earnings.

Above-the-line, special items are a major cause of differences between *Value Line* actuals and unadjusted *Compustat's EPS* before extraordinary items. However, even after we adjust the *Compustat* data to remove special items, differences remain. We investigate these differences by analyzing a subsample of firm-quarters that had *no* Compustat special items but did have large differences between *Value Line* actuals and *Compustat EPS*. We identified the 60 observations with the largest percentage differences between *Value Line* actuals and *Compustat EPS* before extraordinary items.[17] In 57 of 60 cases, *Value Line* excluded a nonrecurring item not designated as a special nonrecurring item by *Compustat*. Sixteen of these 57 cases represented industries for which *Compustat* does not provide special item designation. In the three remaining cases, *Value Line* had included a below-the-line item that was correctly excluded from *Compustat's EPS* figure.

Our conclusion that *Value Line* is the most appropriate single source of actual *EPS* data in the computation of unexpected earnings is subject to two important caveats. First, while *Value Line's* advantage largely stems from *excluding* most nonrecurring items, in our opinion cases do exist in which an unexpected nonrecurring item has pricing implications and therefore should be *included.* It would require substantial effort to determine whether a given item was known to the market prior to the earnings announcement. Second, *Value Line* occasionally includes a nonrecurring item in its actuals; a careful reading is required to identify these cases.

5. Summary and Conclusions

Using various combinations of *Value Line* IBES, and *Compustat* actual and forecast quarterly *EPS* data, we compare the forecast error metrics in terms of accuracy and level of association with announcement-period excess returns. We conclude that when forecasts are taken from *Value Line (IBES)*, the smallest forecast errors result from the use of *Value Line (IBES)* actual *EPS*. In comparison, the use of *Compustat* reported data (with forecasts from either forecast service) produces significantly larger absolute forecast errors. If *Compustat* actual *EPS* data are used, adjusting *Compustat* data for the effects of above-the-line special items produces greater accuracy. Comparing *Value Line* forecasts and actuals to *IBES* forecasts and actuals, the former produce smaller absolute forecast errors.

Analysts' forecast errors are often used as a proxy for the surprise content of an earnings announcement. Due to the frequency of their use in this capacity in past research and the continued interest in questions requiring a proxy of this nature, we consider the association of forecast errors with announcement-period excess returns to be the more important of the two issues examined in this study. Although many of the differences in relative forecast accuracy are statistically significant, the economic meaningfulness of these differences is difficult to determine. The fact that association and accuracy test results are consistent helps establish the legitimacy and economic significance of the documented differences in accuracy.

For forecasts from both *Value Line* and *IBES, Value Line* actual *EPS* data produce significantly higher levels of association with announcement-period returns (compared to sing actual *EPS* data from *Compustat* or *BES*). This result may be due to the *Value ine* reporting process. Forecasts reflect ana-*rsts'* expectations of earnings, including *dgments* about whether certain items should *e* regarded as recurring or nonrecurring. The *ctual* earnings the company reports may or *ay* not conform to analysts' expectations. *lue Line* actuals appear to be adjusted to match" the components of earnings included *t* the forecasts. The judgment exercised by *lue Line* in reporting actual *EPS* appears to *xplain* the high level of association when *lue Line* actuals are used. In summary, our *sults* suggest that (1) the source of analysts' *recast* data is not as important as the selec-*on* of actual *EPS* data, and (2) *Value Line* *ppears* to represent the most appropriate *ource* of actual *EPS* data.

ppendix A

xamination of Standard & Poor's Forecast rror Metrics

f the 4,770 firm-quarter observations identified in *e* preceding analysis, 1,431 observations are from *e* fourth quarters of 1984, 1985, and 1986. Only *ourth*-quarter observations can be used to compare *tandard & Poor's* data with *Value Line* and *IBES*, *ecause* the *Standard & Poor's* (hereafter, *S&P*) *recasts* and reported actuals are annual only. We *ssume* that any difference between the *S&P* an-*ual* forecasts made near year-end and the actual *nnual EPS* subsequently reported by *S&P* is due *o* error in forecasting fourth-quarter earnings. *herefore*, in the analyses reported in this appen-*ix*, the *S&P* forecast error is defined as:

$$\frac{\text{\textit{ctual} Annual EPS} - \text{Fourth Quarter Forecast of Annual EPS}}{\text{Deflator}}$$

he Value Line and *IBES* forecast error metrics *ontinue* to be defined as:

$$\frac{\text{\textit{ctual} Quarterly EPS} - \text{ForecastQuarterly EPS}}{\text{Deflator}}$$

We were unable to search all issues of the *S&P arnings Forecaster* to identify the forecast made *mmediately* prior to the announcement of annual *arnings* or the first reporting (by *S&P*) of actual

annual earnings. Forecasts of *EPS* were drawn from the *Earnings Forecaster Cumulative Master Lists* dated December 28, 1984; January 25, 1985; December 27, 1985; January 24, 1986; December 26, 1986; and January 23, 1987. Actual annual *EPS* as reported by *S&P* were drawn from the *Earnings Forecaster Cumulative Master Lists* dated May 31, 1985; May 30, 1986; and April 3, 1987. After dropping observations not covered by *S&P*, we had 1,118 firm-quarter observations, evenly distributed across the fourth quarters of 1984, 1985, and 1986.

S&P reports forecasts made by both *S&P* analysts and others, so any given issue of the *Earnings Forecaster* can report several forecasts. An *S&P* forecast was used when available (934 firm-quarter observations or 83.5% of the sample). Although arguments can be made for other measures (mean or median forecast), the *S&P* forecast is typically more timely and may include knowledge of other forecasts. Eighty-six (7.7%) of our observations reported a single forecast made by a forecaster other than *S&P*. In the remaining 98 cases, we used the mean of the non-*S&P* forecasts reported. The number of analysts comprising this mean ranged from two to eight.

We desire consistency between the *S&P* forecast and actual annual *EPS* with regard to (1) primary versus fully diluted *EPS*, (2) the treatment of extraordinary items and discontinued operations, (3) the treatment of above-the-line, nonrecurring, or "special" items, and (4) the timing of stock splits and stock dividends. *S&P* specifies that *EPS* are generally on a primary basis, including discontinued operations but excluding extraordinary items. If potential dilution exceeds 3%, *S&P* also reports fully diluted earnings per share. The *Earnings Forecaster* indicates whether extraordinary items are included or excluded from the *EPS* given but typically does not disclose the dollar amounts involved. *S&P* does not have an explicit policy regarding the treatment of above-the-line nonrecurring items. Appropriate adjustments were made for stock splits and dividends.

We assume that the undeflated forecast error computed using *S&P* actual annual *EPS* and *S&P* fourth-quarter annual forecasts represents error in forecasting fourth-quarter earnings. Therefore, this *S&P*-based error would be comparable in magnitude to undeflated error metrics based on *Value Line* and *IBES* quarterly *EPS*. In performing tests of deflated metrics, we use only share price as the deflator. The use of absolute forecast *EPS* as the deflator is not appropriate due to the unavailability of *S&P* quarterly forecasts.

Descriptive Statistics

The 1,118 untruncated *S&P* signed forecast error metrics have a mean of –.0077 ($\alpha \leq .05$, two-sided parametric *t*-test), a median of –.0003 ($\alpha \leq .05$, two-sided nonparametric signed-rank test), and a standard deviation of .0516. Distribution statistics were also computed for the other seven error metrics used in the body of the paper; *S&P*'s error metric had the largest negative mean and median error and the largest standard deviation. The 1,118 *S&P* absolute forecast errors have a mean of .0166 ($\alpha \leq .05$), a median of .0037 ($\alpha \leq .05$), and a standard deviation of .0495. Compared to the distribution statistics for the other metrics ($n = 1,118$), *S&P*'s metric has the largest mean and standard deviation, while the median ranks fourth out of eight.

Tests of Accuracy and Association

We test the accuracy and the association with announcement-period excess returns of the forecast error metric based on *S&P*'s annual forecast and reported *EPS (SP actual-SP forecast)* relative to the metric based on *Value Line* actuals and forecasts (*VL actual-VL forecast*) and the metric based on *IBES* data (*IB actual-IB forecast*). The tests of accuracy are performed on the total sample of 1,118 firm observations, on the subsample of 964 firms without special items, and on the 154 firms with

special items. For all three subsets of the data, *Value Line* absolute forecast errors are significantl smaller ($\alpha \leq .0001$) than *S&P* absolute foreca errors. The *IBES* absolute forecast errors ar smaller than the *S&P* forecast errors at $\alpha \leq .000$ for all three subsets.

Our association tests are based on 1,028 firm quarter observations. The procedures employed ar identical to those described in section 4 of the tex Because we are only able to focus on the fourt quarter for tests using *S&P*'s data, our results ar based on three sets of correlations.

Exhibit 3 reports the Pearson and Spearma correlations of the three forecast error metrics wit three-day excess returns. The reported values ar the mean correlations over the three fourth quarter in the sample. The Spearman correlation coeff cients are consistently higher than the correspond ing Pearson coefficients. For both types of correla tions, the highest correlations are obtained for th *Value Line*-based forecast error metric. Exhibit also reports the number of significant quarterl correlations (out of a possible three) for each err metric.

Because only three quarters of data are avai able, the statistical tests of the quarterly correla tions used in section 4 are not performed. To ana lyze the significance of differences among the thre metrics, we perform the same regression-base analysis described in the text. We pool all 1,02 firm-quarter observations, regress three-day exces returns on the various forecast errors, and compar the absolute residuals from the three regression using the same two statistical tests used in sectio

Exhibit 3 Average Correlations Between Announcement-Period Excess Returns and Select Forecast Error Metrics[a] ($n = 1,028$)

		Pearson Correlations			Spearman Correlations		
			Frequency of One-Sided Test[b]			Frequency of One-Sided Test[b]	
Source of Forecast	Source of Actual	Mean of Three Qtrs.	at 1%	at 5%	Mean of Three Qtrs.	at 1%	at 5%
Value Line	Value Line	.144	2	2	.243	3	3
IBES	IBES	.109	1	2	.148	2	2
S&P	S&P	.062	0	1	.175	3	3

[a] Announcement-period excess returns are excess returns for the three-day period centered on the earning announcement date as provided in *Compustat*. Excess returns are taken from the *CRSP Excess Returns Tap* using the "beta-matched" portfolio approach. The 1,028 observations which generated the three quarterl correlations were roughly equally distributed over the three fourth quarters of 1984, 1985, and 1986.

[b] These frequencies represent the number of times (out of a maximum of three) that the indicated forecast erro metric resulted in a significant association with excess returns at the indicated significance level.

4. The absolute residuals from the regression using (*VL actual-VL forecast*) have a smaller mean and median than the absolute residuals from either the *S&P*'s regression or the *IBES* regression. The difference is significant at $\alpha \leq .04$ when *Value Line*-based residuals are compared to *S&P*-based residuals. The *IBES*-based forecast errors are not significantly different (at conventional levels) than the *S&P*-based forecast errors.

Our experience with *S&P* data suggests that the actual annual earnings number reported often includes the effects of above-the-line nonrecurring items, while the forecasts do not. This difference in forecast and actual *EPS* may be responsible for *S&P*'s poorer performance in the tests of accuracy and association with excess returns.

Endnotes

1. Several university libraries maintain historical files of the *S&P Earnings Forecaster. S&P* currently sells paper copies for $3 per page. Zacks purchased the *S&P Earnings Forecaster* in 1986 and expanded it in 1988 to include more brokers and the Zacks consensus estimate.

2. The *Historical Summary Tape* is available to academic institutions for about $5,000. The *Current Summary Tape* costs about $3,000 annually. Zacks also sells a *Current Detail Tape* which includes the name, forecast, and recommendation of individual analysts and a *Historical Detail Tape* which includes every forecast revision since 1978.

3. Fifty-three percent of the 552 firms in our final sample have ten quarters of forecast data; 17% have nine quarters of data; 11% have forecasts for five or fewer quarters. Since the number of firms covered by *IBES* has increased over time, many of the firms with fewer than ten quarterly observations were added to the database after the third quarter of 1984. In addition, mergers, acquisitions, and bankruptcies result in firms "disappearing" from the database. The firm-quarter observations are about equally distributed over the ten quarters.

4. Quarterly earnings announcement dates are also available from the *Wall Street Journal Index* or the *Dow Jones Broad Tape*. Brown, Clinch, and Foster [1987] report that the earnings announcement appears on the *Broad Tape* (1) on the day of or the day before the announcement of earnings in the *Wall Street Journal* in 95.8% of the 553

cases examined and (2) on the day of or the day before the *Compustat* date in 91.9% of the cases examined. According to Hughes and Ricks [1987] the *Compustat* announcement date corresponds to the *Wall Street Journal* date in only 75% of the cases. We expect that our three-day event period (centered on the *Compustat* announcement date) will include the actual announcement date in most cases.

5. Brown, Foster, and Noreen [1985] report that *IBES* analysts typically forecast *EPS* before extraordinary items. This is consistent with the *IBES* January 1987 "Monthly Comments," which state, "the consensus of the analysts' expectations, as represented by the *IBES* mean, is usually based on earnings before extraordinary items."

6. *Value Line* sometimes includes special items and sometimes excludes other nonrecurring items that are not given special item designation by *Compustat*. The *Compustat* special item designation is not available for banks, utilities, life insurance, or property and casualty companies so we cannot identify special items for those firms. In section 4, we investigate a sample of observations where *Compustat* and *Value Line* report large differences in actual *EPS*.

7. While collecting the *Value Line* data, we noted that *Value Line* may restate actual quarterly *EPS* months and even years after the actual is first reported. Many of these adjustments are not the result of stock dividends or splits. This raises some question about the interpretation of the *Value Line* actuals that are subsequently restated.

8. Special items are data item 32 on the quarterly *Compustat* tapes. We incorporate them into the actual *EPS* by adjusting for an assumed 40% tax rate and translating that after-tax number into per-share terms. Results assuming a 50% tax rate were virtually identical. As pointed out by the reviewer, the use of a flat cross-sectional tax rate may introduce measurement error that could bias against the *Compustat* actuals if forecasters use firm-specific marginal tax rates. This bias could affect the 10% of our sample for which an adjustment for special items is necessary. The impact of this bias will be mitigated to the extent that our firms pay taxes at the maximum marginal rate or if forecasters use cross-sectionally constant tax rates in making their forecasts.

9. In Appendix A, we examine a seventh forecast error metric that compares *Standard & Poor's*

annual *EPS* forecasts to *Standard & Poor's* reported annual *EPS*. Tests of *Standard & Poor's* error metrics are based on a subsample of the data and therefore are not directly comparable to the results in Exhibits 1 and 2.

10. The misalignment is easily spotted when the actual reported by *IBES* for quarter (*t*) is consistently identical to the *Compustat* actual for quarter (*t* − 1). Adjustment could have been made for these cases. However, in the majority of cases, *IBES* actual and *Compustat* actual differ in any given quarter, so it is impossible to ascertain whether there is an alignment problem within *IBES* or an ongoing disparity between the two actuals. Discussions with *IBES* personnel suggest that the problems with actual *EPS* have been mitigated recently.

11. Although it is unlikely that this metric would be used in a research environment, one of our goals is to assist researchers in the selection of data sources. We conclude that the choice of forecast (*Value Line* versus *IBES*) is not as critical as whether the actual *EPS* used in the comparison is carefully constructed. The metric comparing *Value Line* and *IBES* supports our conclusion.

12. In 5% of our sample observations (compared to 19% of the sample observations in Brown, Foster, and Noreen [1985]), the final median forecast appeared on the *IBES* tape during the month after the actual earnings number was released. We treat these "late" forecasts as timely because a number of institutional features suggest that processing delays and the regularity of the *IBES* publication process cause their late inclusion on the tape. O'Brien [1988] reports that the time between the analysts' forecast date and the date of the forecast's first appearance on the *IBES* averages 34 trading days.

13. These statistics were also computed for each of the sample years individually, with no substantial differences noted. The descriptive statistics reported in Exhibit 1 are based on untruncated forecast errors. In subsequent tests the forecast errors were truncated to ±100%.

14. The positive sign of *IB/IB* may be due to the fact that *IBES* reported no negative actual *EPS,* as indicated in the text.

15. Correlation coefficients resulting from a pooling of all 4,249 observations (not reported) were very similar to the mean values shown in Exhibit 2.

16. Given the described problems with *IBES* actuals, this discussion is limited to *Value Line* and *Compustat*. Actual earnings per share are also reported in the *Wall Street Journal*. However, the level of *WSJ* disclosure of the components of earnings differs across firms. In some cases the disclosure is complete and separately indicates income from continuing operations, nonrecurring items, discontinued operations, extraordinary items, etc. In other cases, only bottom-line earnings are reported.

17. It is worth noting that half of these 60 cases occurred in the fourth quarter. Thus, consistent with prior research, "unusual" earnings components are overly represented in the fourth quarter. This suggests the need for special attention in the construction of fourth-quarter forecast errors.

References

Brown, L.D.; R.L. Hagerman; P.A. Griffin; and M.E. Zmijewski. "Security Analyst Superiority Relative to Univariate Time-Series Models in Forecasting Quarterly Earnings." *Journal of Accounting and Economics* (1987): 61–87.

Brown, P.; G. Clinch; and G. Foster. "Research Issues with Intra-Day Capital Market Data." Working paper, July 1987.

Brown, P.; G. Foster; and E. Noreen. *Security Analysts Multi-Year Earnings Forecasts and the Capital Market.* Studies in Accounting Research, no. 21. Sarasota, Fla.: American Accounting Assn., 1985.

Elton, E.; M. Gruber; and M. Gultekin, "Professional Expectations: Accuracy and Diagnosis of Errors." *Journal of Financial and Quantitative Analysis* (December 1984):351–63.

Hughes, J.S., and W.E. Ricks. "Associations Between Forecast Errors and Excess Returns Near to Earnings Announcements." *The Accounting Review* (January 1987): 158–75.

Institutional Brokers Estimate System. *Ordinary and Extraordinary Accuracy.* New York: IBES, 1987.

Lipe, R. "The Information Contained in the Components of Earnings." *Journal of Accounting Research* (Supplement 1986): 37–64.

O'Brien, P. "Analysts' Forecasts as Earnings Expectations." *Journal of Accounting and Economics* (January 1988): 53–83.

Zigas, D. "The Many Ways of Figuring Financial Results." *Business Week* (April 11, 1988): 131.

Chapter 12

Financial Analysts' Forecasts of Earnings[*]

A Better Surrogate for Market Expectations

Dov Fried, Ph.D.
Professor of Accounting
New York University

Dan Givoly, Ph.D.
Professor of Accounting Information Systems
J.L. Kellogg Graduate School of Management
Northwestern University

The specification of the market expectation of accounting numbers is a common feature of many empirical studies in accounting and finance. Givoly and Lakonishok (1979) found that financial analysts' forecasts have information content. This study evaluates the quality of analysts' forecasts as surrogates for the market expectation of earnings and compares it with that of prediction models commonly used in research. Results indicate that prediction errors of analysts are more closely associated with security price movements, suggesting that analysts' forecasts provide a better surrogate for market expectations than forecasts generated by time-series models. The study also identifies factors that might contribute to the performance of the financial analysts' forecasts. The broadness of the information set employed by analysts and, to a lesser extent, their reliance on information released after the end of the fiscal year appear to be important contributors to their performance.

1. Introduction

The specification of market expectations of stock returns and of accounting numbers is a common feature of empirical studies in accounting and finance. While expected returns in these studies have been derived customarily by the theoretically founded and empirically supported market model, no such underlying theory exists for the specification of a

* The authors wish to thank Robert Kaplan, Ross Watts, Jerold Zimmerman, and an anonymous referee for their helpful comments. The financial support of the Deloitte Haskins and Sells Foundation is gratefully acknowledged.

Reprinted with permission from *Journal of Accounting and Economics,* Vol 4, 1982, pgs. 85-107.

surrogate for market expectation of earnings. To a great extent, the expectation models selected by researchers relied exclusively on past time-series behavior of the variable.[1] Since no established theory could guide the selection of the earnings expectations models, many researchers used a wide set of time-series models so that some assessment of the robustness of the results to model selection could be made.

The selection of a time-series model as a surrogate for market expectations is further impaired by the underlying assumptions that the earnings generating processes are stationary with stable parameters and that the model characteristics are applicable to all firms. There is evidence suggesting that models applicable to one period are not necessarily relevant for other periods. Brooks and Buckmaster (1976), for example, showed that while the martingale process might describe the earnings changes in normal years, earnings behavior in periods following unusual fluctuations in earnings may best be described by a mean-reverting process. The use of such models as a proxy for market expectations of earnings thus may limit the validity and the scope of any conclusions.[2]

The purpose of this paper is to examine the performance of an alternative surrogate for market expectations, earnings forecasts made by financial analysts. These forecasts were obtained from the *Earnings Forecaster,* a weekly publication by Standard and Poor that first appeared in 1967. The *Earnings Forecaster* lists the outstanding EPS forecasts for about 1500 companies. The forecasts are those made by S & P and by about 70 other security analysts and brokerage houses who agreed to submit their forecasts, upon release, to the publication.

Givoly and Lakonishok (1979) showed that financial analysts' forecasts of earnings (FAF) have information content. Their study found a significant price reaction to the disclosure of revisions in FAF. The wide dissemination of FAF in the financial community[3] further reinforces the notion that FAF might proxy for market expectations.

Given the above evidence, tests on the information content of earnings that use FAF as a surrogate for market expectations are likely to be better specified than those based on time-series models. The first objective of this study is to evaluate FAF as a surrogate for market expectation of earnings, and to compare them with prediction models widely used in the literature. The findings show that FAF are a better surrogate for market expectation of earnings and suggest that the use of other prediction models may have weakened the tests employed by previous research.

The tests of the association between the *API* and the prediction errors, to be described later, follow those employed by Ball and Brown (1968) and Beaver et al. (1979) and rely on the correlation between *API* and forecasts made about a year before the release of the earnings report. Tests on the information content of earnings, however, are best carried out by examining the association between prediction errors from forecasts based on the most up-to-date accounting information available, and *API* calculated on a daily basis in the immediate period surrounding the earnings release date. Nonetheless, the results herein are useful in that they suggest that FAF may serve as a better proxy if used in such studies.

The finding that FAF are a better surrogate for earnings expectation of the market is important for other reasons. Stock valuation models as well as P/E studies often rely on expected earnings or derivation thereof, as a basic parameter. The results of this study would thus offer valuable input to these studies in providing better identification of earnings expectations used by investors.

The existence of an empirical surrogate for earnings expectations will enable researchers to examine more thoroughly the formation of earnings expectations. Questions concerning the rationality of earnings expectations, the extent to which they employ accounting information and their consistency with the observed time-series behavior of earnings might be addressed. Some interesting work on the time-series behavior of FAF has been done by Abdel-Khalik and Espejo (1978) and by Brown et al. (1978, 1979, 1980). Establishing that FAF provide a satisfactory surrogate for market expectations would underscore the relevance of these studies and provides a motivation for further research.

The second objective of this study is to analyze the factors that contribute to FAF having information content. While forecasts of earnings based solely on past accounting data are revisable only in certain time intervals (annual or quarter), FAF incorporate presumably all publicly available (firm-specific, industry, and market) information, and can be continuously updated with the arrival of any new information. These characteristics suggest two factors which explain FAF superiority, and which will come under examination in this study: one is the broadness of the information set available to them, and the other is their timing advantage, in that they employ information that becomes available only after the last accounting report.

The paper is organized as follows. Section 2 describes the data and discusses the statistical tests concerning identification of the best surrogate for market expectations. Section 3 explores the broadness of information and timing issues and provides evidence on their effect on the performance of FAF. Concluding remarks are made and implications for future research are suggested in the final section.

2. FAF vs. Time-series Models as Surrogates for Market Expectations

The model evaluation methodology follows the one used by Beaver and Dukes (1972), Collins (1975) and Patell (1976), and which was articulated by Patell (1979). The presumption is made that accounting earnings possess information content. Alternative mod-

els are then evaluated by their ability to correctly classify the signal produced by the accounting number and hence by their usefulness in developing profitable trading strategies for which the buy/sell decisions are determined by this signal classification.

The association between the signals (e.g., the prediction error) produced by each expectation model (time-series or FAF) and abnormal stock return is analyzed. The expectation model whose signals (concerning future earnings) are the most strongly associated with stock price behavior is considered the best surrogate for the true, unobservable, market expectation.

This section is divided into four subsections. In the first we describe our data and the forecasting models, and present some results on the forecasting accuracy of the models. The next subsection describes the measure used to gauge stock market reaction. The third subsection discusses the tests to be used for the evaluation of the models; results of these tests are presented and discussed in the fourth subsection.

2.1 Data and Forecasting Models

Financial analysts' forecasts of earnings of a sample of companies listed in the *Earnings Forecaster* were evaluated in each of the eleven years 1969 to 1979. Considered each year were the FAF of that year's earnings outstanding at the beginning of April. These forecasts were first issued to the public typically in early March. The time of the forecast is between the release of the annual report for the previous year [which is made on average, in February—see Givoly and Palmon (1981)] and the release of the first quarterly report (typically late April).

Included in the sample each year were companies which satisfied these criteria:

1) fiscal year ending December 31,
2) N.Y.S.E. listing,
3) existence of at least four forecasts (by dif-

ferent forecasters) of the current year's earnings,

4) availability of monthly return data for the forecast year, the following year and the preceding four years,

5) availability of actual earnings numbers for the forecast year and the preceding nine years.

The third criterion was introduced to allow the derivation of a reliable measure for the average or "consensus" forecast.

All the contemporaneous company forecasts were for primary EPS before extraordinary items. To ensure that the comparison between the forecast and the actual EPS was not unduly affected by changes in capitalization not incorporated in the forecasts, we adjusted any earnings forecasts announced prior to the disclosure of the change in capitalization.

The final sample consists of 1247 cases (company-years) with a total of 6020 forecasts. The number of cases in each year differs and varies from 95 (1972) to 173 (1969). This sample represents 424 distinct companies. The FAF for each company-year are represented by their simple average.

Two alternative models of earnings expectation were employed to define the news content of earnings announcements:

$$P_t = f(A_{t-1}, A_{t-2}, \ldots) \;,\qquad\qquad \text{(a)}$$

$$P_t = A_{t-1} + \gamma_t + \delta_t E\,(\Delta A_{mt}) \;,\qquad\qquad \text{(b)}$$

where A_t is the realized earnings. The earnings variable was the primary earnings per share before extraordinary items (EPS) of year t adjusted for capitalization, P_t is the expected (predicted) value of A_t, γ_t and δ_t and are regression parameters,[4] and $E(\Delta A_{mt})$ is the expected change in market earnings. A_m is represented by the average EPS of the S&P's Composite 500. The expected change in market earnings is derived from a submartingale model using the (arithmetic) average growth over years $t-6$ to $t-1$ as an estimate of the drift term.[5] The regression parameters are re-

estimated each year from the available past annual EPS data (the first available year is 1958).

The first model is a univariate time-series model derived from the results of Brooks and Buckmaster (1976). For most of our observations, the submartingale model of the form

$$P_t = A_{t-1} + C_t$$

was used, where C_t is the (arithmetic) average growth in EPS computed over the years $t-6$ to $t-1$.

This model was found by recent studies to represent quite adequately the time-series behavior of earnings [see Albrecht et al. (1977) and Watts and Leftwich (1977)]. Furthermore, as a general representative firm model, the martingale with drift was found to perform as well as the firm-specific Box-Jenkins models in describing the time-series characteristics of annual earnings (see also Albrecht et al.). However, periods that follow extreme earnings fluctuations were found by Brooks and Buckmaster (B & B) (1976) to behave in a way more consistent with a mean reverting process. To provide better specification of the earnings time-series, the sample was stratified each year according to the size of the deviation of previous year's earnings from some "norm." The model used for the extreme strata was, in accordance with B & B's findings, an exponential smoothing rather than the martingale with trend.[6] About 23% of the cases (company-years) in our sample fell in these extreme strata. For the stratification procedure and the specification of the exponential smoothing models, see the appendix. We shall refer to the univariate time-series model used as the modified submartingale (MSM).

The use of Model b, the index model (IM), is supported by the relationship that was found between the first differences in individual company earnings and an economy-wide index of earnings such as the differences in earnings across all firms [see Ball and Brown (1968) and Gonedes (1973)].

The relative prediction error was defined as

$$e_{it}^k = (A_{it} - P_{it}^k) / |A_{it}| , \qquad (1)$$

where k denotes the expectation model, i the observation index ($i = 1, ..., N$), and t the year.

In the few cases (3-4% of the cases, depending on the model) where $|e_{it}^k| > 1.00$, the error measure was equated to ± 1.0. This truncation of the distribution of e_{it} was introduced to avoid the distortive effect of a small denominator and to suppress the effect of possible data and measurement errors.

One measure of accuracy of model k in period t is the mean absolute relative error,

$$\left| e_t^k \right| = (1/N) \sum_i \left| e_{it}^k \right| . \qquad (2)$$

The corresponding measure of bias in model k in period t is the mean relative error,

$$e_t^k = (1/N) \sum_i e_{it}^k . \qquad (3)$$

The relative accuracy of the forecasts is presented in Exhibit 1. The table reveals that in almost all years the accuracy of FAF measured by the mean relative error is greater than that of the competing models both for cases of positive prediction error (i.e., actual earnings are above expectation) and for cases of negative prediction error. The average prediction error of FAF is significantly lower than that of the other models for both types of cases. For the positive errors, the t-values (computed from the 11 observations) are 5.27 and 6.57 for the comparison with MSM and IM, respectively. For the negative errors, the values are 5.02 and 3.04, and for all cases 3.14 and 3.37. The critical t-value for a one-tail test with 10 degrees of freedom and 1% significance level is 2.76.

The bias of each model is provided by the fourth (bottom) panel in the table which shows the mean relative error measured over all cases. The results indicate some tendency for FAF to overestimate next year's earnings.[7] Yet, the bias of FAF is present only in 6 of the 11

years and, except for the first three years, appears to be quite small. The finding of some bias conforms to the persistent optimism of FAF reported by previous studies [Barefield and Comiskey (1971) and McDonald (1973)].[8]

Any comparison between the performance of the models is, however, incomplete if it ignores the potential for improvement inherent in each. The existence of a systematic behavior of the model's errors may allow forecast users to improve upon (increase accuracy and eliminate the bias of) the original forecast. To the extent that stationarity of the prediction and realization processes is assumed, forecast users will rely for that improvement on all available past information.[9]

To examine the potential improvement of each model, we employed the linear correction procedure suggested by Mincer and Zarnowitz [see Mincer (1969)] and Theil (1966). The results reveal that all three models offer very little in terms of potential reduction in error through a linear correction of the forecasts. The tests conducted for the corrected forecasts yielded results similar to those obtained for the raw forecasts; therefore, we report only the latter.

The accuracy of FAF is not necessarily related to the adequacy of their use as a surrogate for market expectations. It is conceivable that FAF are superior to other prediction models in terms of ex-post accuracy tests, but inferior in terms of association with stock price movements. In the next subsection, we describe the metric to be used to measure stock price movements.

2.2 Market Reaction Measure

Stock price movements are measured in this study by the abnormal return where the expected return was defined according to the familiar market model,

$$E (R_{it}) = \alpha_i + \beta_i R_{mt} , \qquad (4)$$

where R_{it} denotes the return of security i for

Exhibit 1 Mean Relative Earnings Prediction Errors—Annual Models (Percentages)[a]

	All Years[b]	1969	1970	1971	1972	1973	1974	1975	1976	1977	1978	1979
Cases of positive errors												
FAF (608)	10.4	4.8	5.2	7.5	8.9	14.5	19.4	8.9	10.2	10.1	10.9	14.2
MSM (767)	13.8	8.1	8.2	10.9	14.6	20.1	19.7	9.7	17.5	11.5	14.7	16.9
IM (801)	16.3	9.8	3.6	16.8	15.1	18.8	20.6	17.0	22.0	16.4	16.3	17.9
Cases of negative errors												
FAF (639)	−20.4	−18.5	−31.1	−23.8	−12.3	−17.1	−26.0	−25.0	−11.3	−22.0	−19.2	−17.9
MSM (480)	−24.2	−17.8	−34.1	−29.3	−13.4	−17.5	−36.4	−37.5	−13.9	−24.1	−24.9	−17.0
IM (446)	−24.3	−17.7	−35.6	−26.3	−15.3	−23.5	−33.4	−39.4	−15.8	−19.1	−23.4	−17.4
All cases (accuracy results)[c]												
FAF (1247)	16.4	14.0	25.9	17.6	10.4	15.4	22.0	18.6	10.7	17.1	13.7	15.0
MSM (1247)	19.3	13.1	26.2	18.3	14.4	19.6	24.9	28.0	16.8	16.7	17.4	16.9
IM (1247)	20.3	13.6	26.0	20.3	15.1	19.4	24.5	30.1	20.9	17.6	18.1	17.7
All cases (bias results)[d]												
FAF (1247)	−5.3	−10.9	−23.9	−11.8	−0.5	4.3	1.6	−11.6	1.2	−8.7	0.6	1.4
MSM (1247)	−1.2	−5.2	−21.5	−5.2	8.1	12.5	2.4	−21.3	11.2	−3.2	4.2	4.9
IM (1247)	1.4	−3.2	−19.8	1.1	8.7	12.9	4.4	−15.9	15.3	0.1	6.5	5.5

[a] FAF = Financial Analysts' Forecasts of Earnings, MSM = Modified Submartingale, and IM = Index Model. Number of all cases given in parentheses.

[b] Simple average of the 11 years.

[c] See expression (2) in the text.

[d] See expression (3) in the text.

period t, α_i, and β_i are parameters and R_{mt} is the actual market rate of return for period t. The market rate of return is represented by the value-weighted rate of return of New York Stock Exchange stocks. Monthly abnormal returns were measured by the difference

$$\hat{\varepsilon}_{it\tau} = R_{it} - (\hat{\alpha} + \hat{\beta}_{it} R_{m\tau}) , \qquad (5)$$

where $\hat{\alpha}_i$ and $\hat{\beta}_i$ were estimated from the 48 months preceding the test period, t is the year index, and τ is the month index.

The average ß in the pooled sample (1247 observations) is 1.133. The slightly higher than one β's apparently reflect the simple averaging of β's which are computed from the value-weighted index.[10]

The test period for evaluating the models' predictions consisted of the 12-month period from April of year t ($\tau = 1$) to March of year $t + 1$ ($\tau = 12$) and was designed to cover the period of approximately 11 months preceding the release of the annual report and the month that follows it.

Cumulative abnormal returns were computed as

$$CAR_{it} = \sum_{t=1}^{12} \hat{\varepsilon}_{it\tau} , \qquad (6)$$

and the Abnormal Performance Index (*API*) was derived as

$$API_{it}^{k} = \text{sign}(e_{it}^{k}) \cdot CAR_{it} . \qquad (7)$$

2.3 Tests

The models will be tested according to the association of their errors with stock price movements. In examining prediction error and stock price behavior, the magnitude of the prediction error, in addition to its sign, will be considered. As shown by Beaver et al. (1979), the inclusion of the magnitude of the prediction error makes the association tests more powerful. In addition, using only the sign of the prediction error results in a serious

limitation of the tests since they rely exclusively on those cases where the models disagree as to the sign of the prediction error. Thus, the only relevant observations would belong to a group which might be a very small subset of the total sample. The following two tests, which incorporate the magnitude of the prediction error, alleviate this problem by exploiting the entire sample.

(a) *Correlation test:* The correlation between the magnitude of the prediction error (e_{it}^{k}) and the stock price movement (CAR_{it}) is computed. The model which yields the highest correlation is considered to be superior. This association test was employed recently by Beaver et al. (1979) in measuring the relationship between abnormal returns and prediction errors of earnings expectation models.

(b) *Weighted API test:* The second test (magnitude of API) involves the evaluation of an 'investment strategy' under which long or short positions in a portfolio are taken in accordance with the direction and magnitude of the prediction error produced by each model. Previous research which looked at the sign of the prediction error implicitly assumed that the same amount is invested (or disinvested) regardless of the magnitude of the error. It is plausible that the amount invested will be in direct proportion to the magnitude of the error. Indeed, if the 'unexpected' earnings (conveyed by the error) are expected to be permanent (consistent with the random-walk behavior of earnings over time) and the security risk is unaltered, the abnormal return will be proportional to the error. This test, therefore, evaluates an investment strategy under which the cross-sectional prediction errors of a given model k served each year to determine the weight of each security in that year's portfolio k. The *API* of the portfolio was computed as the weighted average across individual securities. Specifically, the weight assigned to each security i in year t of portfolio k is

$$a_{it}^{k} = |e_{it}^{k}| / \sum_{i} |e_{it}^{k}|, \qquad (8)$$

where e is the relative error from (1) and the portfolio's API is[11]

$$API_{k,t} = \sum_{i} a_{i,t}^{k} \cdot API_{k,t}. \qquad (9)$$

In designing the statistical tests, one should be aware of the potential existence of cross-sectional dependence between contemporaneous residuals (or abnormal returns). The dependence, which could stem from various sources (e.g., nonlinearity of the return generating function or the omission of common factors, such as industry, from the index model), makes it likely that the sample estimate of the variance of the residuals will be biased in an unknown manner. Cross-sectional dependence is likely to exist also between contemporaneous prediction errors due to the common factors underlying the generation of earnings (e.g., GNP; the use of the "index model" of earnings may have removed this source of dependence). For these reasons the t-tests to be reported here employ an estimate of the variance taken from a time-

series in which the serial correlation is no expected to be significantly different from zero. Specifically, the mean of the variable of interest was computed each year from the cross-section of observations. The 11 mean values were treated as a sample of independent observations. Similar procedures have been used by Beaver et al. (1979), Jaffe (1974), and Mandelker (1974).

2.4 Results and Discussion

Exhibit 2 presents the frequency of cases in which the signs of the prediction error and the price movement (measured by CAR) during the test period were consistent, that is, in the same direction. Overall, the models produced errors whose sign was consistent with the sign of CAR. Of the 1247 cases (company-years), the sign of the FAF prediction error was consistent with the sign of the CAR in 743 cases (60%). This is somewhat superior to the performance of the MSM and the index model which experienced prediction errors' signs that were consistent with that of the CAR in 670 cases (55%) and 679 cases (54%), respectively.

Exhibit 2 Frequency of Cases in which the Sign of the Prediction Error is Consistent with the Sign of the Corresponding Cumulative Abnormal Return (CAR)[a]

(a) *All cases*

CAR Realization	FAF Errors Consistent	FAF Errors Inconsistent	MSM Errors Consistent	MSM Errors Inconsistent	IM Errors Consistent	IM Errors Inconsistent
Positive	337	224	386	175	398	163
Negative	406	280	304	382	281	405
Total	743	504	690	557	679	568

(b) *Cases in which competing models disagree*

	FAF vs. MSM		FAF vs. IM		MSM vs. IM	
CAR Realization	FAF Errors Consistent	MSM Errors Consistent	FAF Errors Consistent	IM Errors Consistent	FAF Errors Consistent	MSM Errors Consistent
Positive	34	79	32	92	26	35
Negative	125	27	148	27	51	28
Total	159	106	180	119	77	73

[a] FAF = Financial Analysts' Forecasts of Earnings, MSM = Modified Submartingale, and IM = Index Model. Consistent sign is said to exist when the difference between the realized value and the predicted value $(A - P)$ has the same sign as the CAR.

A closer examination of the table reveals that FAF perform about equally well when the CAR is positive as when the CAR is negative (i.e., 337/561 ≈ 406/686 ≈ 743/1247 ≈ 60%). However, the time-series models do very well in times of positive CAR (MSM yields 69% and IM yields 71% consistent classifications), but rather poorly when the CAR is negative (MSM = 44%, IM = 41% consistent classifications).

The comparison between the models is more meaningful when only the disagreement cases are considered. Panel (b) of the table shows that FAF do poorer than the other models in periods of positive *CAR* (only 34/113 = 30% of the cases) but do extremely well in periods of negative *CAR* (125/152 = 82% of the cases).

The results of Exhibit 2 serve to highlight the limitation inherent in constructing *API* tests based on the sign (but not the magnitude) of the prediction errors. The difference between the *API*'s of two competing models, which is based on the sign of the prediction error, will reflect only those cases in which the models disagree with respect to the sign of the prediction error (in all other cases the models will produce the same *API*). These cases, however, represent only a small percentage of all cases. Indeed, as Exhibit 2 reveals, the proportion of disagreement cases in our sample is low (for instance, out of the 1247 predictions made by both models, FAF and MSM produced prediction errors of opposite signs in only 263, or 21%, of the cases). Results which utilize information on both the sign and magnitude of the prediction error (and therefore on the entire sample of 1247 observations) are presented in Exhibits 3 and 4.

Exhibit 3 presents the average cross-sectional correlation coefficients for all years, between the prediction error of each model and the corresponding CAR. The first three columns (under "All Cases") present the correlation coefficient calculated over the entire

Exhibit 3 Correlation Coefficients Between *CAR* and the Earnings Prediction Error[a]

	All Cases			Cases of Positive Errors			Cases of Negative Errors		
	FAF	MSM	IM	FAF	MSM	IM	FAF	MSM	IM
All Years[b]	0.33	0.27	0.27	0.23	0.18	0.18	0.17	0.18	0.17
1969	0.47	0.38	0.39	0.10	0.04	0.08	0.37	0.40	0.38
1970	0.41	0.33	0.31	−0.03	−0.02	0.09	0.37	0.32	0.43
1971	0.39	0.23	0.27	0.26	−0.02	0.02	0.38	0.36	0.32
1972	0.22	0.07	−0.01	−0.05	0.08	−0.13	0.08	0.08	−0.01
1973	0.35	0.46	0.44	0.43	0.45	0.47	0.19	0.21	0.15
1974	0.33	0.28	0.29	0.07	−0.02	0.00	0.30	0.23	0.30
1975	0.12	−0.20	−0.02	0.20	0.32	0.45	−0.04	−0.20	−0.20
1976	0.41	0.32	0.28	0.47	0.34	0.27	0.17	0.34	0.21
1977	0.37	0.43	0.36	0.33	0.19	0.17	0.24	0.21	0.26
1978	0.25	0.27	0.24	0.43	0.42	0.33	−0.17	−0.05	−0.07
1979	0.24	0.36	0.37	0.36	0.18	0.24	0.01	0.10	0.14

[a] FAF = Financial Analysts' Forecasts of Earnings, MSM = Modified Submartingale, and IM = Index Model. The critical value for the correlation coefficient at the 5% significance level for H_0:p = 0 and one-tail test using the z-statistic [see Freund (1962. pp. 310–311)] is 0.13 for most cells ($n \geq 40$) .

[b] Simple average of the 11 years.

Exhibit 4 Mean *API* over the Test Period of a Portfolio Weighted by the Magnitude of the Earnings Prediction Errors of its Members (Percentage)[a]

	All Cases			Cases of Positive Errors			Cases of Negative Errors		
	FAF	MSM	IM	FAF	MSM	IM	FAF	MSM	IM
All Years[b]	14.12	9.97	9.45	7.45	2.73	3.32	17.48	17.03	17.63
1969	22.67	19.06	19.02	10.76	3.72	5.08	24.11	25.63	27.53
1970	17.51	15.17	14.57	7.51	2.47	−0.47	17.92	16.52	16.59
1971	18.55	10.53	9.27	1.40	−7.33	−4.11	21.92	20.43	24.25
1972	9.96	−1.45	−4.26	−0.19	−4.68	−8.48	19.22	10.18	11.40
1973	16.98	18.26	16.90	16.64	17.49	16.25	17.67	21.74	20.15
1974	13.56	11.00	11.11	3.76	0.59	0.67	25.02	23.57	26.51
1975	7.33	−3.05	1.82	6.63	−2.61	9.68	7.50	−3.11	−0.60
1976	13.92	5.89	5.39	13.37	3.98	4.00	14.61	15.29	14.30
1977	16.90	17.85	14.09	10.92	9.18	6.13	18.84	23.71	22.12
1978	7.34	6.97	6.06	9.20	7.12	6.33	5.32	6.74	5.49
1979	10.63	9.47	9.99	1.93	0.06	1.41	20.14	26.58	26.23

[a] FAF = Financial Analysts' Forecasts of Earnings, MSM = Modified Submartingale, and IM = Index Model.
[b] Simple average of the 11 years.

sample for each of the models. The next six columns show the correlation coefficient calculated for each model separately for cases with positive prediction errors and cases with negative prediction errors. Generally, errors of all models show positive and, in most cases, significant correlation with *CAR*. Overall, FAF prediction errors are more strongly associated with *CAR* than the prediction errors of the other two models: the average coefficient of correlation over the 11 years between *CAR* and separately FAF, MSM and IM's errors are 0.33, 0.27 and 0.27, respectively. The *t*-test results for the differences between the correlations produced by FAF and the MSM and IM models are significant at the 10% and the 5% level, respectively. Looking at the positive error and negative error cases separately, the superiority of FAF is evident for positive error cases (0.23 > 0.18), but disappears for negative error cases.

Exhibit 4 provides *API* values [calculated using eqs. (8) and (9)] for a portfolio based on both sign and magnitude of the signal (prediction error). The exhibit reveals that FAF errors appear to be more strongly associated with stock price movement than the other models. All models yielded significant average *APIs* for all cases and for negative error cases (the *t*-test was used over the 11 years). However, only FAF produced significant *APIs* for the positive error cases. The *API* average yielded by FAF (14.12%) is higher than that produced by the MSM (9.97%) and the IM (9.45) models. For all cases FAF performed better than each of the other two models in nine of the 11 years. For positive error cases FAF performed better (i.e., the *API* was higher) than MSM in 10 years and better than IM in all 11 years. The corresponding differences between the *APIs* are significant (at the 5% significance level) for all cases and for the positive error cases. There is no significant difference between the models for the negative error cases.[12]

The foregoing results are consistent with the hypothesis that FAF, or information closely correlated with FAF, serve as an input to investment decisions by market participants. Furthermore, the findings suggest that FAF, or at least those outstanding in early April, might be more representative of market expectation of earnings than some time-series models widely used in the financial literature.

3. Causes of FAF Superiority

It can be argued that financial analysts' forecasts may have an edge over time-series prediction models for two main reasons:

(a) They use a broader information set which includes non-accounting information on the firm, its industry and the general economy.
(b) They have a timing advantage in that they are issued some time within the year being forecasted. As such, they can use more recent information about the firm's earnings which becomes available only after the end of the fiscal year.

In this study we provide an analysis of the contribution of each of the ingredients (broadness and timeliness of the information) to the performance of FAF.

3.1 Broadness of the Information Set

The FAF presumably utilize all publicly available (and occasionally unpublished) information while the time-series models examined rely exclusively on past earnings. There are several interesting questions in this context: the extent to which FAF are a product of a simple extrapolative procedure; the extent to which they incorporate other, autonomous information, unrelated to the time-series of earnings; and the degree to which they efficiently utilize all available extrapolative information.

In our analysis, the MSM and the index model of earnings serve as representatives of the family of extrapolative models.[13] The contribution of each component to the predictive power of FAF is measured by the partial correlation between actual earnings and FAF, given the time-series models prediction or $r_{AP.X}$, where A denotes the realized value, P is the FAF, and X is the prediction of the time-series model.[14] The extent to which FAF exploit the extrapolative potential of past earnings series (offered by the examined models) is measured by the partial correlation $r_{AX.P}$.

Values of $r_{AX.P} > 0$ suggest that FAF contain predictive power based not only on extrapolation, but also on an autonomous com-

Exhibit 5 Partial Correlations Between Realization and Predictions of Different Models[a]

	Correlation coefficient between realization and the prediction by:				
	FAF Given MSM	**FAF Given IM**	**FAF Given MSM and IM**	**MSM Given FAF**	**IM Given FAF**
	$(r_{AP.X_1})$	$(r_{AP.X_2})$	$(r_{AP.X_1X_2})$	$(r_{AX_1.P})$	$(r_{AX_2.P})$
All years[b]	0.55	0.56	0.51	−0.04	0.01
1969	0.43	0.45	0.43	−0.08	−0.07
1970	0.38	0.23	0.26	0.02	0.15
1971	0.53	0.80	0.53	0.06	−0.04
1972	0.63	0.60	0.55	0.00	0.13
1973	0.56	0.40	0.40	−0.12	0.01
1974	0.73	0.63	0.61	−0.38	−0.28
1975	0.63	0.64	0.60	0.01	−0.02
1976	0.67	0.79	0.67	0.10	−0.03
1977	0.50	0.52	0.56	−0.20	0.03
1978	0.53	0.59	0.53	0.09	0.08
1979	0.49	0.52	0.49	0.01	0.05

[a] FAF = Financial Analysts' Forecasts of Earnings, MSM = Modified Submartingale, and IM = Index Model.
[b] Simple average of the 11 years.

ponent. In addition, the magnitude of $r_{AX.P}$ indicates the extent of underutilization of available extrapolative information by FAF, since $r_{AX.P} > 0$ means that the time-series model contains some amount of predictive power that was not used in FAF.

The partial correlation results are presented in Exhibit 5. The average coefficient of the partial correlation between realization and FAF, given the time-series predictions, $r_{AP.X}$, is 0.55 and 0.56 for the comparison with MSM and IM, respectively. The values remain high, 0.51, when the correlation was conditional on the predictions of both of the other models. These values are significantly different from zero. Since $r_{AP.X}$ is a measure of the net contribution of the autonomous component, it appears that FAF utilize a considerable amount of information which is independent of the time series and cross-sectional properties of the series as captured by our extrapolative models.

The coefficients of the partial correlation between realization and time-series predictions, given FAF ($r_{AX.P}$), are generally very small and close to zero (the hypothesis that their mean is zero could not be rejected at the 5% significance level). This means that, in addition to the utilization of autonomous information, analysts also fully exploit the time-series and cross-sectional properties of the earnings series that are captured by the MSM and IM models of earnings.

The apparent reliance of FAF on extrapolations is also evident in the association between the performance of FAF and that of the other models: the mean error of each model in each of the 11 years (see Exhibit 1) was ranked (from 1 to 11); the Spearman coefficients of rank correlation between the mean error of FAF and those of MSM and IM are 0.77 and 0.85, respectively. Both values are significant at the 5% level. These results suggest that periods which are characterized by unusual deviations of earnings from their past pattern present forecasting difficulties not only to time-series models but also to FAF.

3.2 Timing of Information

Analysts presumably make use also of information that becomes available only after the end of the previous fiscal year. To gauge the effect of the use of more recent information by analysts, it would be desirable to compare the performance of forecasts released at different points of time. For this aim, we collected from the *Earnings Forecaster* the release month of each forecast; this information was not available for 1969, the first year in our sample.

The distribution of forecasts for the remaining 10 years was as follows: 253 issued before January, 435 in January, 1219 in February, 1988 in March and 1299 in early April. We expect forecasts with a later release date to incorporate more (accounting and non-accounting) information and therefore to be superior to earlier forecasts.

To examine whether this is so, we divided our sample into two groups of FAF: one, denoted as "early" forecasts, consists of forecasts released in January and February, and the other, denoted as "late" forecasts, consists of those released in March and early April. This particular grouping results in forecasts that were released on average, about six weeks apart. Only companies for which both early and late forecasts were available in a given year were considered.[15] The number of companies considered each year differs and varies from 56 (1979) to 111 (1973).[16]

The research design for this investigation is essentially the one described in section 2, except that we concentrate on comparing early with late FAF. Exhibit 6 shows the results of the *API* tests for the early and late FAF. The main findings are that a timing advantage does exist but has no significant impact on the comparative performance of the models considered. The average *API* over the 11 years is 12.78% and 13.15% for the early and late forecasts, respectively. The difference, although in the expected direction, when subjected to a *t*-test proved insignifi-

Exhibit 6 Mean API Over the Test Period of a Portfolio Weighted by the Magnitude of the Earnings Prediction Errors of its Members—All Cases (Percentages)[a]

	Early FAF	Late FAF	MSM[b]	IM[b]
All years	12.78	13.15	8.85	8.60
1970	16.92	18.29	15.42	15.00
1971	17.29	17.88	9.01	7.71
1972	11.78	9.09	0.97	−1.36
1973	17.80	17.05	18.45	17.35
1974	8.34	8.56	17.77	7.04
1975	6.95	9.67	−2.83	2.19
1976	14.15	16.88	7.93	7.75
1977	16.72	16.45	17.39	13.65
1978	7.01	7.00	6.88	6.48
1979	10.83	10.66	7.47	10.22

[a] FAF = Financial Analysts' Forecasts of Earnings, MSM = Modified Submartingale, and IM = Index Model. Averages calculated each year only for companies for which both early and late forecasts exist.

[b] The results for the MSM and IM do not correspond to those reported in Exhibit 4 since the sample now covers only the years 1970-1979 and consists of companies for which both early and late forecasts were available.

cant. The mean *APIs* for the time-series models computed over the same sample are lower than both FAF groups, 8.85% for the MSM and 8.60% for IM.

Exhibit 7 provides other summary statistics pertinent to the comparison between early and late forecasts (the mean API results re-

ported in Exhibit 6 are repeated here). The degree of correlation between the CAR and the earnings prediction error for the early forecasts is indistinguishable from that for the late forecasts (0.31 vs. 0.32).

The findings so far suggest that the timing advantage does not result in a significant improvement in the association of FAF with stock price movements. Another relevant consideration is the amount of information incorporated in the late vs. the early FAF. The partial correlation results reveal that late forecasts appear to rely somewhat less on extrapolation of past earnings data and more on autonomous information than early forecasts: the partial correlation between realization and prediction, given the predictions of both the MSM and IM is 0.46 and 0.51 for early and late forecasts, respectively. The timing advantage is more pronounced when we pit early and late forecasts against each other. While the partial correlation between realization and late forecasts, given the early forecasts is 0.26 (suggesting utilization of incremental information by late forecasts) the partial correlation between realization and early forecasts (not presented in the exhibit) was practically zero.

The findings indicate that the timing advantage of two months that late forecasts have over early forecasts affect their relative performance. Late forecasts employ a greater amount of autonomous information and their

Exhibit 7 Comparative Performance Results for Early and Late FAF (Over Years Averages)[a]

	Predictor			
Performance Measure	Early FAF	Late FAF	MSM	IM
Correlation of prediction error with *CAR*	0.31	0.34	0.25	0.26
Mean *API*, considering magnitude of error (%)	12.78	13.15	8.85	8.60
Partial correlation of realization and prediction, given both MSM and IM	0.46	0.51		
Partial correlation of realization and prediction, given early FAF		0.26	0.01	0.07
Partial correlation of realization and prediction, given early FAF, MSM, and IM		0.23		

[a] FAF = Financial Analysts' Forecasts of Earnings, MSM = Modified Submartingale, and IM = Index Model. The averages are calculated over the company-years for which both early and late FAF existed.

performance is somewhat better than that of early forecasts. Both early and late forecasts outperform the time-series models,[17] and it appears that the main factor behind the better performance of FAF is the broader information set used by them.

4. Concluding Remarks

The study provides evidence which indicates that, overall, analyst forecasts are a better surrogate for market expectation of earnings than time-series models customarily used in the literature. This finding does not invalidate the results of studies which use time-series models to find an association between unexpected earnings and share price changes. In fact, it reinforces the results by indicating that the association is even stronger. This paper's results provide added motivation for the study of other important properties of FAF such as time-series behavior and cross-sectional dispersion.

The study also analyzes the cause of the superior performance of FAF. The results point to the existence of some timing advantage to forecasts that are made well after the end of the fiscal year and which presumably incorporate more recent information. However, the main contributor to the better performance of FAF is their ability to utilize a much broader set of information than that used by the univariate time-series models. The findings further suggest that analysts efficiently exploit the extrapolative power of the earning series itself.

The findings of the study should be analyzed cautiously. Only two extrapolation models were considered—the submartingale (or MS) and the index model. It should be noted, however, that these models were found by previous research to perform well when compared to other, sometimes more complex, models.

The representative of FAF was the mean forecast. Even if FAF are associated with the true market expectations, the mean might not be the proper variable. A case can be made for other measures such as the median forecast. To the extent that the mean forecast is

Exhibit 8 Distribution of Company-Years by the Magnitude of Normalized First Differences of Earnings and the Corresponding Best Predictor

Normalized First Difference	This Sample		B & B Study[a]		Best Smoothing Model[b]	
	No. of Cases	% of Cases	No. of Cases	% of Cases	Order	Constant
9 < difference	16	1.3	89	0.8	1	0.90
6 < difference ≤ 9	28	2.2	205	1.9	1	1.00
4 < difference ≤ 6	77	6.2	466	4.4	1	1.00
2 < difference ≤ 4	294	23.6	1,781	16.7	1	1.00
1 < difference ≤ 2	256	20.5	2,136	20.0	1	1.00
0 ≤ difference ≤ 1	309	24.8	2,977	28.4	1	1.00
−1 ≤ difference < 0	122	9.8	1,531	14.3	1	1.00
−2 ≤ difference < −1	70	5.6	686	6.4	1	0.65
−4 ≤ difference < −2	60	4.8	478	4.4	1	0.45
−6 ≤ difference < −4	12	1.0	137	1.3	1	0.33
−9 ≤ difference < −6	3	0.2	81	0.8	1	0.1
difference > −9			52	0.5	2	0.2
	1,247	100.0	10,619	100.0		

[a] See Brooks and Buckmaster (1976, Table 3).

[b] The mean-absolute-error criterion is used.

ot the measure most strongly associated with market expectations, our results underestimate the superiority of FAF as an expectation surrogate.

Another potential source of bias, possibly against FAF, is the sample selection criterion whereby only firms with at least four contemporaneous forecasts were considered. The criterion, which was introduced to assure a meaningful measure of "consensus" forecast, led inevitably to the exclusion of many small firms that do not attract considerable attention by analysts.[18] If the remaining firms, which are larger, experience smaller earnings variability, the performance of the extrapolative models in the sample is expected to be better than the entire population.

Further research might address the interesting issue of the relationship between the independent, or autonomous, component in analysts' forecasts, which may serve as a measure of the research efforts, and possibly of their costs, and stock characteristics such as risk and marketability.

Appendix: Specification of the Exponential Smoothing Models and Their Application to the Sample

The selection of the order and coefficient of the exponential smoothing model was based on the findings of Brooks and Buckmaster (1976) hereafter referred to as B & B. The stratification was according to the normalized first difference, defined as

$$d_t = (A_t - A_{t-1}) / \sigma_{t-1} ,$$

where A_t is the EPS in year t and σ_{t-1} is the standard deviation of A over the available history of the company from 1959. Exhibit 8 presents the distribution of company-years in the sample according to d, the comparative distribution in the much larger sample used by B & B, and the order and coefficient of the best smoothing model using the minimization of the mean-absolute-error as the optimization criterion. The distribution of cases in our sample is essentially similar to that of B & B. However, our sample has a somewhat lower percentage of extreme observations. This might be due to the special care that was taken in verifying the correctness of apparent anomalous earnings changes in the data. This verification procedure was obviously infeasible in the large sample of B & B. Note that for almost 70% of the cases (company-years) in our sample, the martingale process is the best predictor.

The smoothing model for the nth order is

$$_n E (A_t) = \alpha A_{t-1} + (1 - \alpha)_n E (A_{t-1}) ,$$

where $_nE(A_t)$ is the smoothing function of the nth order model at time t (see endnote 6).

Endnotes

1. A short list of such studies, which is by no means exhaustive, includes Ball and Brown (1968), Barnea et al. (1976), Beaver and Dukes (1972), Brown and Kennelly (1972), Foster (1977), and Watts (1978).

2. This limitation was recognized in the literature [see, for example, Beaver and Dukes (1972) and Collins (1975)]. As Beaver and Dukes conclude: "... any inferences are conditioned upon the prediction models used to test the accounting measures tested ... any findings are the joint results of prediction models and accounting method and only appropriately specified joint statements are warranted" (p. 332).

3. See, for example, the report of the SEC Advisory Committee on Corporate Disclosure (1977).

4. These regression parameters were estimated over the first differences series of ΔA_t and ΔM_t.

5. The expectation is formed consistent with the model used to predict individual firm's earnings. We also used in all tests a version of the IM in which the *realized* market index is employed. The two versions yielded essentially the same results.

6. The smoothing parameter, α, used for each strata was the one found by B & B to be the best smoothing constant (see Exhibit 8).

7. Given the general increase over time in the EPS of all firms (the average annual increase in the average EPS, adjusted for capitalization, of S&P's 500 firms over the 20-year period, 1958 to 1977, was 12.4%), the upward bias in the prediction of earnings levels by FAF implies also an overestimation of the change in earnings. This finding contrasts with the observed tendency of economic

forecasters to underestimate changes in variables such as GNP and Personal Consumption [see Theil (1966, ch. V) and Mincer (1969, ch. 1)]. Two explanations might be offered for the finding: first, time-series behavior of earnings is apparently less regular and monotonic than that of economic variables leading to less reliance of earnings forecasts on past levels. Second, financial analysts who, as part of the "establishment" of the investor community and unlike most economic forecasters have a direct stake in the prosperity of the stock market, are perhaps more likely to issue an optimistic outlook than a dim one.

8. Since only aggregate results are produced, the findings are not comparable either to those reported by Brown and Rozeff (1979), which show that analysts predict in an adaptive manner—changing the forecasts in a direction opposite to last period's error—nor to those of Elton, Gruber and Gultekin (1981), which suggest persistence of error in consecutive years.

9. Whether users actually employ corrected forecasts depends on the cost of adjustment and on the degree of stationarity in the systematic behavior of the forecast.

10. For randomly selected securities, an unweighted average β greater than one would be expected if securities with low value weights have relatively high β's and vice versa. Higher β's for small firms is suggested by the results of Foster (1978) and Reinganum (1981).

11. The model assumes realistically that the proceeds from short sales are not collected at the time of sale and that, in addition, collateral in the amount of the sale is required. Other weighting schemes were also employed but led to essentially the same results.

12. We also derived *API* based only on the sign of the prediction error. The *API* based on FAF predictions calculated over the 11 years was on average 6.94%, while those based upon MSM and the IM yielded 3.79% and 3.42%, respectively. The difference between the FAF's *API* and the other model's *API* is significant at the 5% significance level.

The *API*s in this study are lower than those reported by Ball and Brown (1968). Note, however, that the survey periods are different. Also, the models are not exactly identical: we use a modified submartingale and an ex-ante index model. Finally, Ball and Brown averaged the *API*s cross-section-

ally and over years giving an equal weight to each company-year. In our analysis, we first find the simple average for each year and then the average across years, giving each year an equal weight. So for example, 1969, which has the highest average *API*, is given the same weight as any other year despite the fact that it is represented in the sample by the largest number of cases.

13. Other, more efficient extrapolative models probably exist. Thus, the conclusions from our analysis are expected to overstate the weight of the autonomous component and perhaps also the success of FAF in exploiting the available extrapolative information.

14. The notations A, P, and X, as well as the results presented, are stated in terms of earnings levels. Similar results were obtained for earnings changes.

15. We also used another version of the test under which this restriction was not imposed. Under this version, however, the composition of the company sample of the early forecasts was not identical to that of the company sample of the late forecasts. The results were essentially similar.

16. This particular definition of early and late forecasts allowed us to get a large sample size in each group. Looking at January's forecasts alone and comparing them to those made in March and April, which might theoretically accentuate the timing difference between the forecasts, resulted in a large drop in the sample size: in two of the years the number of available companies was less than six. The examination of the other eight years did not in fact show a larger difference between early and late FAF.

17. It should be noted that the comparison between the early FAF and the naive models is "unfair" to the former: naive models utilize the most recent earnings numbers and have an advantage over FAF that do not incorporate these yet undisclosed audited results for the year.

18. Indeed, size and earnings variability are negatively correlated: the cross-sectional correlation coefficient between the market value of the equity and the variance of the rate of growth of earnings of the sample firms, averaged over the 11 years, is −0.20 (significant at the 5% level). Plausibly, the correlation coefficient in the population (which is more diversified in terms of size) is even more negative.

References

Abdel-Khalik, Rashad and J. Espejo, 1978, "Expectations data and the predictive value of interim reporting." *Journal of Accounting Research*, Spring, 1-13.

Albrecht, Steve N., Larry L. Lookbill and James C. McKeown, 1976, "The time series properties of earnings," *Journal of Accounting Research*, Autumn, 226-244.

Ball, Ray and Philip Brown, 1968, "An empirical evaluation of accounting index numbers, *Journal of Accounting Research*, Autumn, 159-178.

Ball, Ray and Ross L. Watts, 1979, "Some additional evidence on survival biases," *Journal of Finance*, March, 197-206.

Barefield, R.M. and E. Comiskey, 1975, "The accuracy of analysts' forecasts of earnings per share," *Journal of Business Research*, July, 241-252.

Barnea, Amir, Joshua Ronen and Simcha Sadan, 1976, "Classificatory smoothing of income with extraordinary items," *The Accounting Review*, Jan., 110-122.

Beaver, William H. and R.E. Dukes, 1972, "Interperiod tax allocation, earnings expectations and the behavior of security prices," *The Accounting Review*, April, 320-332.

Beaver, William H., Roger Clark and William F. Wright, 1979, "The association between unsystematic security returns and the magnitude of earnings forecasts," *Journal of Accounting Research*, Autumn, 316-340.

Brooks, Leroy D. and Dale E. Buckmaster, 1976, "Further evidence of the time series properties of accounting income," *Journal of Finance*, Dec., 1359-1373.

Brown, Lawrence, D. and Michael S. Rozeff, 1978, "The superiority of analyst forecasts as measure of expectations: Evidence from earnings," *Journal of Finance*, March, 1-16.

Brown, Lawrence, D. and Michael S. Rozeff, 1979, "Adaptive expectation, time series models and analyst forecasts revision," *Journal of Accounting Research*, Autumn, 341-351.

Brown, Lawrence, D., John S. Hughes, Michael S. Rozeff and James H. Vanderweide, 1980, "Expectation data and the predictive value of interim reporting: A comment," *Journal of Accounting Research*, Spring, 278-288.

Brown, Philip and J. Kennelly, 1972, "The information content of quarterly earnings: An extension and some further evidence," *Journal of Business*, July, 403-415.

Collins, Daniel W., 1975, "SEC product line reporting and market efficiency," *Journal of Financial Economics*, June, 121-164.

Collins, William A. and William S. Hopewood, 1980, "A multiple analysis of annual earnings forecasts generated from quarterly forecasts of financial analysts and univariate time series models," *Journal of Accounting Research*, Autumn, 390-406.

Crichfield, Timothy, Thomas Dyckman and Josef Lakonishok, 1978, "An evaluation of security analysts' forecasts," *The Accounting Review*, July, 651-668.

Elton, Edwin J., Martin J. Gruber and Mustafa Gultekin, 1981, "Professional expectations: Accuracy and diagnosis of errors," Working paper, June (Graduate School of Business Administration, New York University, New York).

Foster, George, 1977, "Quarterly accounting data: Time series properties and predictive ability results," *The Accounting Review*, Jan., 1-21.

Foster, George, 1978, "Asset pricing models: Further tests," *Journal of Financial and Quantitative Analysis*, March, 39-53.

Freund, John E., 1962, *Mathematical statistics* (Prentice-Hall, Englewood Cliffs, NJ).

Givoly, Dan and Josef Lakonishok, 1979, "The information content of financial analysts' forecasts of earnings," *Journal of Accounting and Economics*, Winter, 1-21.

Givoly, Dan and Dan Palmon, 1981, "Timeliness of annual reports—Some empirical evidence," *The Accounting Review*, forthcoming.

Gonedes, N., 1973, "Properties of accounting numbers: Models and tests," *Journal of Accounting Research*, Autumn, 212-237.

Jaffe, Jeffrey F., 1976, "Insiders and market efficiency," *Journal of Finance*. Sept., 1141-1148.

Mandelker, Gershon, 1974, "The effect of mergers on the value of the firm," *Journal of Financial Economics*, Dec., 303-336.

McDonald, C., 1973, "An empirical examination of the reliability of published predictions of future earnings," *The Accounting Review*, July, 502-510.

Mincer, Jacob, ed., 1969, "Economic forecasts and expectations" (National Bureau of Economic Research, New York).

Patell, James M., 1976, "Corporate forecasts of earnings per share and stock price behavior: Empirical tests," *Journal of Accounting Research*, Autumn, 246-276.

Patell, James M., 1979, "The API and the design of experiments," *Journal of Accounting Research,* Autumn, 528-549.

Reinganum, Marc R., 1981, "Misspecification of capital asset pricing empirical anomalies based on earnings yields and market values," *Journal of Financial Economics* 9, 19-46.

Securities and Exchange Commission, 1977, "Report of the advisory committee on corporate disclosure" (S.E.C., Washington, DC).

Standard and Poor, 1967–1979, "Earnings Forecaster, Weekly" (S & P, New York).

Theil, Henry, 1966, *Applied economic forecasting* (North-Holland, Amsterdam).

Watts, Ross L., 1978, "Systematic abnormal returns after qurterly earnings announcements," *Journal of Financial Economics,* June-Sept. 127-150.

Watts, Ross L. and Richard W. Leftwich, 1977 "The time series of annual accounting earnings," *Journal of Accounting Research* Autumn, 253-271.

Chapter 13

When Forecasting Earnings, It Pays to Be Right!

Correct forecasts do earn significant excess returns

Robert C. Klemkosky, Ph.D.
Fred T. Greene Professor of Finance
Indiana University

William P. Miller
Portfolio Manager
IDS Financial Services

Security analysts spend a great deal of effort searching for any information that will help them make a more precise valuation of a security. Foremost in their search is an accurate forecast of earnings.[1] The earnings forecast is widely used in stock selection, because analysts have found that movements in stock price are closely linked to earnings changes.[2] Because evidence shows that earnings are not always fully and correctly reflected in stock prices,[3] it would appear that an accurate forecast of earnings should lead to superior stock selection performance.

What kinds of benefits can be expected to accrue from an accurate earnings forecast? One way of gaining insight into this question is by studying the relationship between forecast error (analysts' estimates compared to reported earnings per share) and stock price performance. In one of the earliest studies in this area, Niederhoffer and Regan analyzed the performance of the 50 best- and 50 worst-performing stocks on the New York Stock Exchange in 1970. They found stock performance to be closely related to the type of earnings forecast error. Those stocks whose earnings had been underestimated performed in a superior manner, while those whose earnings had been overestimated performed very poorly. These results demonstrate a basic relationship between forecast errors and stock price performance.

This study is different from Niederhoffer and Regan's, in that it analyzes a much larger sample of stocks, conducts a time-series analysis over a 10-year period, and utilizes a more advanced statistical methodology. The study also determines the relationship between the relative size and type of the forecast error and stock price performance. Fi-

Reprinted with permission from *The Journal of Portfolio Management,* Summer, 1984, pgs. 13–18.

nally, we also analyze the relationship between the size and type of forecast error and residual returns (total returns adjusted for market risk).

The empirical results generated by our study support Niederhoffer and Regan's earlier study; they indicate that underestimated earnings will result in superior stock price performance, while overestimated earnings will result in poor, below-average performance. This is true even after each stock's returns are adjusted for its market risk, implying that a more accurate forecast of earnings is a very valuable tool for stock selection. The results also provide some evidence as to what kind of performance we can expect from a stock, given the relative size of its earnings forecast error.

Data and Methodology

The Sample

We made a random selection of the 215 companies used in the study from a larger group, which consisted of all companies that satisfactorily met three criteria. First, each company must have been listed on the New York Stock Exchange during the period being studied (1972-1981). Second, each company must have had forecasts of earnings published in Standard & Poor's *Earnings Forecaster* during the period. Third, for validity of comparison, each firm was required to have a fiscal year ending on December 31. The sample included a wide variety of companies, representing many industries.

Earnings Forecasts

For each of these 215 companies, we collected earnings-per-share forecasts made 12 months, 6 months, and 3 months prior to the announcement of year-end earnings, as well as actual earnings, for each year 1972 through 1981. We took the 12-month prior forecasts from the February issue of Standard

& Poor's *Earnings Forecaster*, which included forecasts of earnings per share as reported by leading brokerage firms during January. The six-month prior forecasts were taken from the August issue each year, and the three-month prior forecasts from the November issue. The earnings predictions used were for primary earnings per share, with the proper adjustments made for all stock dividends and splits. In most cases, a company had several forecasts; in those cases, we used the arithmetic average (mean) of those forecasts to eliminate possible biases, although the correlation of forecasts by different institutions is very high.[4]

Actual Earnings

Actual primary earnings per share appear as reported, before extraordinary charges; they were properly adjusted for stock dividends or splits if necessary. These figures were also taken from the *Earnings Forecaster* with additional help from Standard & Poor's *Stock Guide*.

Forecast Errors

Using these forecasts and actual earnings figures, we calculated forecast errors for each company, for each forecast period, and for each of the 10 years. These errors were calculated in terms of both an absolute dollars-and-cents error and the percentage error based upon actual earnings for that period (relative error). The specific formulas we used were:

$$\text{Absolute Error} = \text{Forecasted Earnings} - \text{Actual Earnings} \quad (1)$$

$$\text{Relative Error} = \frac{\text{Forecasted Earnings} - \text{Actual Earnings}}{\text{Actual Earnings}} \quad (2)$$

There were, for any particular forecast period studied, a few companies that did not have any forecasts included in that issue of the *Earnings Forecaster*. In those cases, no figure as assumed or substituted, and we simply omitted those particular companies for that specific forecast period.

We then ranked the remaining forecast errors by magnitude, from the largest earnings overestimation to the largest underestimation for each year and period, separately for both the absolute and relative figures. Next, we divided this ranked list of errors into five groups, based upon the size and sign of the forecast error. For example, Portfolio #1 consisted of the group of largest overestimations, Portfolio #2 consisted of the group of the next largest overestimations, and so forth, until we reached Portfolio #5, which contained the firms with the most underestimated earnings per share. Thus, Portfolio #3 contained the group of stocks with the median forecast error, including firms with underestimated and overestimated earnings. Each group consisted of an approximately equal number of companies.

The purpose of grouping the firms into portfolios was to give the data some stationarity and stability. In some cases, however, a particular percentage error was so excessively large or small that it significantly altered the mean error of that portfolio. For instance, if a stock was forecast to have earnings of $7 per share, but actual earnings turned out to be .05, the relative error would be 13,900%. Distributed over the approximately 40 stocks in that portfolio, the average forecast error of the portfolio would be increased substantially. For this reason, we excluded any relative error greater than ± 1000% from that portfolio, and recomputed the average using the remaining forecasts in the portfolio. There were just a few of these "outliers"; only 30 of the approximately ,000 relative forecasts were eliminated this way. The portfolio forecast errors, absolute and relative, appear in Exhibit 1.

Total Returns

After computing the total returns for each company for each year and for each subpe-

riod, we compared them against the forecast errors previously calculated. Total return is the percentage change in stock price during a specific period. For the 12-month period, this would be the percentage change in price from December 31, 19A - December 31, 19B. The six-month return is calculated from June 30 - December 31, and the three-month return from September 30 - December 31.

These returns were calculated from the CRSP monthly returns file, using returns without dividends. The formulas used to calculate these period returns were:

$$12\text{–Month} = ((1 + r_{i1}) (1 + r_{i2}) \ldots (1 + r_{i12})) - 1 ;$$

$$6\text{–Month} = ((1 + r_{i7}) (1 + r_{i8}) \ldots (1 + r_{i12})) - 1 ;$$

$$3\text{–Month} = ((1 + r_{i10}) (1 + r_{i11}) (1 + r_{i12})) - 1 ;$$

where r_{it} is the monthly return for stock i, in month $t = 1, 2, \ldots, 12$.

We then calculated the returns for the five portfolios, assuming an equal weighting of each stock in the respective portfolio, followed by the average total return by forecast period for each portfolio over the 10 years.

Residual Returns

The total returns figures did not take into account any differences in risk for the companies in the sample. Consequently, we computed the residual return (total return adjusted for market risk) for each company, year, and period. The market model was used to adjust for risk:

$$\tilde{r}_{it} = \alpha + \beta \, \tilde{r}_{mt} + \tilde{e}_{it}$$

where r_{it} and r_{mt} are the security and market return, respectively, for month t; and are the regression coefficients; and e_{it} is the error term (residual return) for security i in month t. The monthly security returns were again taken from the CRSP monthly returns file without dividends, and the market returns from the CRSP Equally-Weighted Market Index without dividends.

Exhibit 1 Ten-Year Averages of Portfolio Forecast Errors, Returns, and Beta Coefficients

		Forecast Error	Total Return	Residual Return	Beta
12-Month Period					
Absolute Errors:	(1)	$2.03	−.073311	−.168237	.909968
	(2)	.41	−.014545	−.117269	.895295
	(3)	.02	.037692	−.063889	.834690
	(4)	−.31	.151370	.046843	.906199
	(5)	−1.40	.251914	.164205	.945807
Relative Errors:	(1)	.9526	−.056409	−.168572	.930949
	(2)	.1257	−.013888	−.124446	.842563
	(3)	.0073	.046291	−.059080	.821239
	(4)	−.1026	.156132	.048716	.885268
	(5)	−.4713	.220223	.153669	1.012242
6-Month Period					
Absolute Errors:	(1)	1.56	−.090428	−.090846	.936806
	(2)	.29	−.073665	−.036425	.919592
	(3)	.02	−.020563	−.024747	.825016
	(4)	−.18	.021536	.031882	.910985
	(5)	−.96	.063159	.078446	.952474
Relative Errors:	(1)	.7833	−.086169	−.081142	.948481
	(2)	.0840	−.055482	−.062166	.876252
	(3)	−.0011	−.021197	−.024747	.804628
	(4)	−.0606	.017625	.028269	.894164
	(5)	−.3929	.036786	.058254	1.026068
3-Month Period					
Absolute Errors:	(1)	1.23	−.044163	−.048719	.947390
	(2)	.18	−.026868	−.031515	.875558
	(3)	.02	.000004	−.000360	.872284
	(4)	−.12	.0277758	.020268	.897057
	(5)	−.67	.035429	.039813	.951303
Relative Errors:	(1)	.6216	−.040276	−.040944	.955883
	(2)	.0555	−.025201	−.032529	.863164
	(3)	.0027	.009928	.003700	.835687
	(4)	−.0390	.029070	.024493	.876561
	(5)	−.2682	.020213	.024665	1.011548

We performed a least-squares regression using the monthly returns for each stock and the monthly market index for the 60 months prior to the year being studied. We then applied the computed values for the alpha and beta coefficients to the returns for the period and the year being studied in order to compute monthly residual returns for each security. For example, to produce the 1972 residuals, the 1967-1971 values of r_{it} and r_{mt} were used to produce the coefficient values that were applied against the 1972 returns to produce monthly residual returns (e_{it}) for 1972.

The portfolios constructed using the residual returns figures were identical to those formed based upon the size of the forecast error. The average residual return for each portfolio was calculated for each period, assuming an equal amount invested in each security.

Results

Forecast Errors

The forecast error results have some interesting characteristics. For the 12-month period, 57% of all errors were underestimates. Over the six-month period, the number of overestimates and underestimates was approximately equal. On the other hand, over the three-month period, the trend had reversed: 54% of the errors were overestimates. Are analysts pessimistic or just prudent in the longer period? The historical estimation methods used, combined with the period's unanticipated inflation, may have caused the results. The switch to overestimation in the three-month forecast period may have been an attempt to overcompensate for the previous underestimation.

Also interesting is the large difference between the average sizes of the errors. Overestimates were almost always larger than underestimates. Over the 12-month period, the average absolute error of Portfolio #1 (the group of largest overestimates) was $2.03, or

95.26% greater than the actual earnings. The average error for Portfolio #5 (the group of largest underestimates) was −$1.40, or 47.13% of actual earnings. During the six-month and three-month periods, these differentials between average forecast errors of Portfolios #1 and #5 persisted, but narrowed substantially.

An expected trend in the forecast errors is that the size of both the over and underestimates would decrease as the fiscal year-end drew closer. The average overestimate in Portfolio #1 (largest overestimates) decreased 38% from January to October, while the average underestimate in Portfolio #5 decreased approximately 50%. This outcome was expected, given the substantial information content of announced quarterly earnings figures.[5] Nevertheless, it is still surprising that one-fifth of all the three-month-period forecast errors would have an average overestimation of over 62% as reported in the *Earnings Forecaster*.[6]

Overall, the consensus forecasts, even 12 months in advance, were within 12% of the actual reported earnings 60% of the time, even though the two extreme quintile groups exhibited large forecast errors both on an absolute and relative basis. The potential for improvement upon the earnings forecasts exists in these two groups of stocks. Whether this is possible or not is another question.

Total Returns

If we accept the premise that the market values a stock based upon earnings, and that unanticipated (misforecast) earnings cause a change in stock price, we expect the following: (1) if a stock's earnings have been overestimated (forecast greater than actual), we expect the market price, and thus the returns for that stock, to react in a negative fashion, and (2) if a stock's earnings have been underestimated (forecast less than actual), we expect the market price to react positively resulting in positive returns.

The evidence generated by this study fully supports the expectations outlined above. As shown in Exhibit 1, the portfolio of the most overestimated earnings showed, almost without exception, the poorest performance of the five portfolios. The second portfolio, consisting of the next-largest overestimated earnings companies, performed better than the first portfolio but worse than portfolios 3, 4, and 5, and so on, until Portfolio #5. Portfolio #5, consisting of these stocks with the most underestimated earnings had an average performance superior to all of the other portfolios. Only once, for the three-month period, is this trend broken.[7]

These results show that the relative performance of portfolios can be predicted if the portfolios are constructed based upon the size of the forecast error. If, over the 10-year period (1972-1981), Portfolio #5 had been held and reinvested each year in the new portfolio with the most underestimated earnings, the average annual return on that portfolio would have been over 25%. The 10-year appreciation to investors holding those portfolios would have been 770%—clearly superior performance by most standards. At the other extreme, if investors had invested in each year's most overestimated earnings portfolio, they could have expected an average annual return of –7.33%; over the 10-year period, they would have incurred a loss of 43%.

All stocks with misestimated earnings will not necessarily produce superior or inferior returns, as there is a great deal of variability within each portfolio. Furthermore, Portfolio #5 will only produce returns superior to the other portfolios comprised of stocks having smaller underestimates. In certain years, such as 1973 and 1974, even the portfolio with the most underestimated earnings produced negative returns, even though those returns were less negative than the returns produced by the other portfolios. The total return of a portfolio for any given year depended largely upon the market performance for that year.

A final note: There is little difference in the portfolios' total returns whether they are formed by absolute ($ and ¢) or relative forecast errors. There is just a slight difference, in that the averages based on relative errors have a little less dispersion.

Residual Returns

It is well-known that there is a relationship between a security's rate of return and its systematic risk.[8] We used the beta coefficient of the market model regression equation as an index of systematic risk, with stocks having a beta greater than one being more volatile than the market and stocks with betas less than one being less volatile than the market. The residual returns (the error terms of the regression equation) for each stock and each period were calculated as previously discussed and then formed into portfolios containing the same stocks as the forecast error portfolios. Exhibit 1 shows the average residual return for each portfolio over the 10-year period.

We can interpret these residual returns as the total returns adjusted for systematic risk. We can also view these returns as the result of influences other than market fluctuations, attributable to many unique industry and firm factors—including the forecast error of earnings. If this is true, even after each stocks return has been adjusted for its related systematic risk, the residual return should be related to the size of the earnings forecast error: (1) a stock with overestimated earnings should have a negative residual return, and (2) a stock with underestimated earnings should have a positive residual return.

The results of this study confirm those expectations. In almost every year and period, the size of the average residual return for a portfolio increased as the portfolio of forecast errors moved from the most overestimated stocks to the most underestimated stocks. As before, there is also a significant difference between the returns resulting from holding a

ortfolio of stocks with overestimated earn-
ngs and those resulting from holding a port-
olio of stocks with underestimated earnings.[9]
n this case, the average annual residual reurn for Portfolio #1 was –16.82%, while the
verage annual residual return for Portfolio
·5 was 16.42%. Again, there was little differ-
nce in results whether portfolios were
ormed by using either absolute or relative
orecast errors.

We can conclude from this evidence that
he size and sign of the forecast error of a
tock's earnings do have a relationship to the
narket risk-adjusted returns of that stock. This
neans that investors will be able to choose
tocks that will show superior performance for
hat period if they have the ability to forecast
arnings with greater accuracy than other ana-
ysts.[10] They should earn "excess" returns sig-
ificantly above those that would be expected
ased upon the market model.

Conclusions

he results of this study lead to the conclu-
ions that:

. There is a significant relationship between
the size and type of forecast error and total
returns, and
. There is a significant relationship between
the size and type of forecast error and residual returns.

The more underestimated a company's
arnings, the greater the expected total return
nd the greater the expected residual return.
)n the other hand, the more overestimated a
ompany's earnings, the lower the expected
otal return and the lower the expected resid-
al return.

So, it would appear that an investor with
he ability to forecast earnings with greater
ccuracy than most analysts could construct a
ortfolio that would produce abnormally high
eturns. This suggests that an accurate earn-
ngs forecast is of immense value for stock
election. Hence, expanded efforts aimed at

improving the accuracy of the earnings forecast may well be worthwhile.

Are some analysts able to consistently
forecast earnings with more accuracy than
other analysts? Past studies have provided
evidence that the correlation of forecasts by
different institutions and analysts is high, suggesting that the differences among the forecasts are not significant. On the other hand,
several studies have shown that analysts'
earnings forecasts are accurate relative to
time series models and management.[11] Given
that most analysts utilize the same information set, it may be impossible to improve
upon forecast accuracy, even for the stocks in
portfolios #1 and #5. Those with the ability to
do so, however, can achieve substantial excess returns.

Endnotes

1. The importance of earnings estimates to the
security analyst is pointed out by Elton and Gruber
[1978], who state: "Every brokerage house and financial intermediary approached for data during
the course of this study stated that they began the
stock evaluation process with an explicit forecast
of future earnings."

2. Several studies have shown that the ability to
predict reported earnings will enable the investor to
earn superior returns. Studies by Niederhoffer and
Regan [1972], Elton, Gruber, and Gultekin [1978],
and Brealey [1969] all found a significant relationship between reported earnings and stock returns.

3. An early study by Ball and Brown [1968] has
shown that stocks of companies reporting earnings
that differ significantly from those predicted by an
econometric model experience substantial price
changes. And Watts [1978], examining the abnormal (risk adjusted) returns following quarterly
earnings announcements, found that significant abnormal returns are observed after the earnings announcement. Several studies by Latane and Jones
[1977, 1979] and Rendleman, Jones, and Latane
[1982] have also found that investors could earn
excess holding-period returns subsequent to the announcements of unexpected quarterly earnings.
Their studies, based on a model called standardized
unexpected earnings (SUE), have been supported

by others, including Bidwell [1977] and Joy, Litzenberger, and McEnally [1977].

4. This was evident from the data in the *Earnings Forecaster* and also in a study by Cragg and Malkiel [1968]. They analyzed the earnings forecasts of the analysts of five firms and suggested that the high correlations among forecasts were the result of some common method of forecasting.

5. A study by Brown and Niederhoffer [1968] found that the information contained in quarterly earnings announcements allowed for more accurate annual earnings forecasts. As expected, they found that forecast accuracy improved over time, with the largest improvement coming form the third to the fourth quarter announcement.

6. The average overestimation and underestimation of portfolios #1 and #5 are somewhat overstated because of the skewness attributable to a few outliers. The extreme outliers were eliminated, but skewness still exists in the two portfolios.

7. One-way analysis of variance tests were used to test the null hypotheses of no significant difference in the mean total return among the five portfolios for each forecast period. The null hypotheses were rejected at the .01 level in each of the forecast periods, using both absolute and relative forecast errors.

8. A positive relationship between ex post systematic risk and return has been verified by, among others, Sharpe and Cooper [1972], Blume and Friend [1979], and Black, Jensen, and Scholes [1972]. In a recent article in this *Journal*, Arnott [1983] questions what type of risk investors are rewarded for bearing. He finds that one- and three-year stock returns are not significantly correlated with systematic risk (beta) or total risk (standard deviation). He does, however, find a significant relationship between returns and earnings-per-share uncertainty as well as several other firm variables.

9. These results confirm an earlier study by Bidwell [1977] in that stocks recommended by analysts do not, on average, perform better than the market on a risk-adjusted basis. A later study by Groth, Lewellen, Schlarbaum, and Lease [1978] also analyzed the risk-adjusted performance of stocks recommended by analysts, and concluded that consistently good research abilities do exist and distinctions can be drawn among analysts.

10. A survey article by Givoly and Lakonishok [1983] summarized all of the studies of analysts earnings forecasts. Most of these studies agree tha analysts produce earnings forecasts that are some what more accurate than those generated by naive models. Thus, analysts do provide an economic service that improves the efficiency of the stock market.

References

Arnott, Robert D. "What hath MPT wrought Which risks reap rewards?" *The Journal o Portfolio Management,* Fall 1983, pp. 5-11.

Ball, Ray, and Philip Brown. "An Empirical Evalu ation of Accounting Income Numbers." *Journa of Accounting Research,* Autumn 1968, pp 159-178.

Bidwell, Clinton. "How good is institutional bro kerage research?" *The Journal of Portfoli Management,* Winter 1977, pp. 26-31.

___. "A test of market efficiency: SUE/PE." *Th Journal of Portfolio Management,* Summe 1979, pp. 53-58.

Black, Fisher; Michael Jensen; and Myron Scholes "The Capital Asset Pricing Model: Some Em pirical Tests." In Michael A. Jensen (Ed.) *Stud ies in the Theory of Capital Markets.* Nev York: Praeger Publishers, 1972.

Blume, Marshall, and Irwin Friend. "Risk, Invest ment Strategy, and the Long-Run Rates of Re turn." *Review of Economics and Statistics,* Au gust 1979, pp. 259-289.

Brealey, Richard. *An Introduction to Risk and Re turn from Common Stocks.* Cambridge, Mass MIT Press, 1969.

Brown, Philip, and Victor Niederhoffer. "The Pre dictive Content of Quarterly Earnings." *Journc of Business,* October 1968, pp. 488-497.

Cragg, John G., and Burton G. Malkiel. "The Con sensus and Accuracy of Some Predictions of th Growth of Corporate Earnings." *The Journal Finance,* March 1968, pp. 67-84.

Elton, Edwin, and Martin Gruber. "Earnings Esti mation and the Accuracy of Expectation Data." *Management Science,* April 1972, pj 409-424.

Elton, Edwin, Martin Gruber, and M. Gultekir "The Usefulness of Analyst Estimates of Earn ings." Unpublished manuscript, 1978.

Givoly, Dan, and Josef Lakonishok. "Earnings Expectation and Properties of Earnings Forecast—A Review and Analysis of the Research." Working Paper, no. 778/83, Tel Aviv University, April 1983.

Groth, John; Wilbur Lewellen; Gary Schlarbaum; and Ronald Lease. "Security analysts: Some are more equal." *The Journal of Portfolio Management,* Spring 1978, pp. 43-48.

Joy, O. Maurice; Robert Litzenberger; and Richard McEnally. "The Adjustment of Stock Prices to Announcements of Unanticipated Changes in Quarterly Earnings." *Journal of Accounting Research,* Autumn 1977, pp. 207-225.

Latané, Henry, and Charles Jones. "Standardized Unexpected Earnings—A Progress Report." *The Journal of Finance,* December 1977, pp. 1457-1465.

___. "Standardized Unexpected Earnings–1971-77." *The Journal of Finance,* June 1979, pp. 717-724.

Niederhoffer, Victor, and Patrick Regan. "Earnings Changes, Analysts' Forecasts, and Stock Prices." *Financial Analysts Journal,* May-June 1972, pp. 65-71.

Rendleman, Richard, Jr.; Charles Jones; and Henry Latané. "Empirical Anomalies Based Upon Unexpected Earnings and the Importance of Risk Adjustments." *Journal of Financial Economics,* November 1982, pp. 269-287.

Sharpe, William, and Guy Cooper. "Risk-Return Classes of New York Stock Exchange Common Stocks, 1931-1967." *Financial Analysts Journal,* March-April 1972, pp. 46-54.

Watts, Ross. "Systematic Abnormal Returns after Quarterly Earnings Announcements." *Journal of Financial Economics,* June-September 1978, pp. 127-150.

Section 3:
Earnings Surprise

Chapter 14

Do Security Analysts Overreact?[*]

Werner F. M. De Bondt, Ph.D.
Frank Graner Professor of Investment Management
University of Wisconsin-Madison

Richard H. Thaler, Ph.D.
Henrietta Johnson Louis Professor of Economics
Cornell University

It has long been part of the conventional wisdom on Wall Street that financial markets "overreact." Both casual observation and academic research support this view. The October crashes of 1987 and 1989 reinforce the research by Robert Shiller and others that suggests that stock prices are too volatile. Also, Shiller's 1987 survey evidence reveals that investors were reacting to each other during these crashes, rather than to hard economic news. A similar conclusion is reached by Kenneth French and Richard Roll (1986) who find that prices are more volatile when markets are open than when they are closed.

Our own prior research (1985, 1987) argued that mean reversion in stock prices is evidence of overreaction. In our 1985 paper, we showed that stocks that were extreme "losers" over an initial three- to five-year period earned excess returns over the subsequent three to five years. In the 1987 paper, we showed that these excess returns cannot easily be attributed to changes in risk, tax effects, or the "small firm anomaly." Rather, we argued that the excess returns to losers might be explained by biased expectations of the future. We found that the earnings for losing firms had fallen precipitously during the formation period (while they were losing value), but then rebounded strongly over the next few years. Perhaps, we speculated, "the market" did not correctly anticipate this reversal in earnings. This hypothesis, of excessive pessimism about the future prospects of companies that had done poorly, was suggested by the work of Daniel Kahneman and Amos Tversky (1973). They found that people's intuitive forecasts have a tendency to over-

[*] We thank Dale Berman from Lynch, Jones & Ryan and Bart Wear from First Wisconsin Asset Management for providing the data used in this study. We also gratefully acknowledge financial support from the Research Foundation at the Institute of Chartered Financial Analysts (De Bondt) and the Russell Sage Foundation (Thaler). Helpful comments have been provided by Josef Lakonishok, John Elliott, and Andrew Lo, though, of course, errors are our own responsibility.

[†] Discussants: Andrew Lo, MIT; Andrei Shleifer, University of Chicago; Fischer Black, Goldman Sachs.

Reprinted with permission from *American Economic Review,* May, 1990, pgs. 52-57.

weight salient information such as recent news, and underweight less salient data such as long-term averages.

Of course, there are many reasons to be skeptical that actual investors (stock market professionals) are subject to the same biases as student subjects in laboratory experiments. Definitely, the market professionals are experts in their field, they have much at stake, and those who make systematic errors may be driven out of business. Therefore, we present here a study of the expectations of one important group of financial market professionals: security analysts who make periodic forecasts of individual company earnings. This is an interesting group to study on three counts. First, other investigators have repeatedly found that earnings forecasts (and forecast revisions) have an important influence on stock prices (Philip Brown et al., 1985). Second, past work suggests that analysts are rather good at what they do. For example, analyst forecasts often outperform time-series models (see Robert Conroy and Robert Harris, 1987). Finally, the precision of analyst expectations represents a natural upper bound to the quality of the earnings forecasts of less sophisticated agents. After all, most investors do not have the time or the skill to produce their own predictions and, accordingly, they buy (rather than sell) earnings forecasts. Thus, for all of the above reasons, it is particularly interesting to see whether market professionals display any of the biases discovered in studies of nonexpert judgment.

We specifically test for a type of generalized overreaction, the tendency to make forecasts that are too extreme, given the predictive value of the information available to the forecaster. This tendency is well illustrated by an experiment conducted by Kahneman and Tversky. Subjects were asked to predict the future grade point average (GPA) for each of ten students on the basis of a percentile score of some predictor. Three predictor variables were used: percentile scores for GPA, for a test of mental concentration, and for a test of

sense of humor. Obviously, a percentile measure of GPA is a much better predictor of actual GPA than is a measure of mental concentration which, in turn, is much more reliable than information on sense of humor. Therefore, subjects should give much more regressive forecasts in the latter two conditions, that is, the forecasts should be less variable. The results indicated that people were not nearly sensitive enough to this consideration. Subjects that were given a nearly useless predictor (the "sense of humor" condition) made predictions that were almost as extreme in variation as those given a nearly perfect predictor (the "percentile GPA" condition). This pattern leads to a systematic bias: forecasts that diverge the most from the mean will tend to be too extreme, implying that forecast errors are predictable.

This study asks whether security analysts display similar biases. Our focus is on forecasted changes in earnings per share (EPS) for one- and two-year time horizons. We study two questions. The first is whether forecast errors in EPS are systematically linked to forecasted changes. In particular, are the forecasts too extreme? Are most forecast revisions "up" ("down") if the analysts initially projected large declines (rises) in EPS? Clearly, under rationality, neither forecast errors nor forecast revisions should ever be predictable from forecasted changes. The second question is whether the bias in the forecasts gets stronger as uncertainty grows and less is (or objectively can be) known about the future.

Several of the regressions reported below are of the form $AC = \alpha + \beta\ FC$, where AC is the actual change and FC is the forecasted change. The null hypotheses of rational expectations is that $(\alpha, \beta) = (0,1)$. The two alternative behavioral hypotheses sketched above are:

H1. Forecasted changes are too extreme, so actual changes are less (in absolute value) than predicted: $\beta < 1$.

H2. The estimated β for the two-year forecasts is less than the β for the one-year forecasts.

The next two sections describe the data and the empirical results. We find considerable support for the behavioral view. We then briefly discuss the sources of the systematic forecast error.

I. Data

The analyst's earnings forecasts are taken from the Institutional-Brokers-Estimate-System tapes (IBES) produced by Lynch, Jones & Ryan, member of the New York Stock Exchange. We study forecasts between 1976 and 1984. Lynch, Jones & Ryan contacts individual analysts on a regular basis and computes summary data such as means, medians, or standard deviations. The summary data that we analyze are sold to institutional investors. Updates are available each month but here we only work with the April and December predictions of EPS for the current as well as the subsequent year. The April forecasts are approximately one- and two-year forecasts since we only consider companies with a fiscal year ending in December. For these firms, actually realized earnings are typically announced sometime during the first few months of the following calendar year.

We match the earnings forecasts for each company with stock returns and accounting numbers. The returns are provided by the Center for Research on Security Prices (CRSP) at the University of Chicago. The accounting data are listed on the annual industrial (main and delisted) COMPUSTAT files, sold by Standard & Poor's. Since all data sources contain full historical records, no survivorship biases affect the sample selection. Care is taken to adjust for stock splits and stock dividends so that all current and past returns, earnings figures, and forecasts are expressed on a comparable basis. When necessary, forecasts of fully diluted EPS are converted to forecasts of primary EPS (excluding extraordinary items).

While some IBES data are available for approximately 2300 to 2800 companies each year, our annual sample contains many fewer observations. For example, for the one-year forecasts, the number varies between 461 and 785. This follows from the data selection criteria that we use. Companies only qualify if they have 1) records on IBES, CRSP, and COMPUSTAT; 2) returns on CRSP for three years prior to the forecast month; 3) EPS numbers on COMPUSTAT for ten years prior to the forecast month; 4) a December fiscal year; 5) the data needed to compute the variables in the regressions described below. Despite the stringent data requirements, our sample (in firm-years) is the largest we know of that has been used to study the rationality of earnings forecasts (compare Edwin Elton et al., 1984).

II. Methods and Results

Much of the regression analysis is based on three sets of variables: forecasted changes in EPS ($FC1$, $FC2$, and $FC12$), actual changes in EPS ($AC1$, $AC2$, and $AC12$), and forecast revisions ($FR1$, $FR2$, and $FR12$). The "consensus" one and two-year forecasts of earnings per share ($FEPS(t)$ and $FEPS\ (t + 1)$) that we study are defined as the cross-sectional means or medians of analyst forecasts reported in April of year t ($t = 1976 \ldots 1984$). Forecasted changes are then computed as $FC1(t) = FEPS(t) - EPS\ (t - 1)$, $FC2(t) = FEPS(t + 1) - EPS(t - 1)$, and $FC12(t) = FEPS(t + 1) - FEPS(t)$, where $EPS(t)$ represents actually realized earnings per share. We compute actual earnings changes in a way that is similar to the forecasted changes. For example, $AC1(t) = EPS(t) - EPS(t - 1)$. Eight-month forecast revisions ($FR1$) subtract the April forecast of EPS(t) from the equivalent forecast in December. Twenty-month forecast revisions ($FR2$) are the difference between the December forecast in year $t + 1$ and

Exhibit 1 Tests for the Rationality of Earnings per Share Forecasts

Equation	Variables	Constant	Slope	Adj. R^2
1	AC1, FC1	−.094 (−3.7)	.648 (−21.7)	.217 [5736]
2	FR1, FC1	−1.20 (−6.7)	−.181 (−15.6)	.041 [5736]
3	AC2, FC2	−.137 (−2.3)	.459 (−19.5)	.071 [3539]
4	FR2, FC2	−.192 (−3.9)	−.381 (−16.8)	.074 [3538]
5	AC12, FC12	.153 (2.4)	−.042 (−16.9)	.000 [3520]
6	FR12, FC12	.348 (19.4)	−.439 (−25.3)	.153 [3562]

Note: All variables are as defined in the text. The dependent variable is listed first. T-values appear in parentheses beneath the regression coefficients and test whether they differ from zero. However, for the slopes of equations 1,3, and 5, the t-statistics test whether the coefficients differ from one. Note that the number of observations is given in brackets in the far right-hand column.

the April forecast of $EPS(t + 1)$. Similarly, $FR12$ subtracts the April $FC12(t)$ from the equivalent $FC12(t)$ in December of year t.

The regressions in Exhibit 1 use mean consensus forecasts. All variables are normalized by the standard deviation of earnings per share between years $t − 10$ and $t − 2$.[1] Even though we also ran the regressions year by year, the results in Exhibit 1 are based on the pooled samples. There are three main findings. Forecasts are too optimistic, too extreme, and even more extreme for two-year forecasts than for single-year predictions.

Equation 1 refers to the one-year forecasts. We regress the actual change in earnings on the April forecasted change. The intercept is significantly negative, indicating that the forecasts are too optimistic. This excessive optimism also appears in equation 3 for the two-year forecasts. The negative intercepts in equations 2 and 4 reveal that there is a general tendency for forecasts to be revised downwards between April and December.

The finding of unrealistic optimism seems consistent with the experimental research of Neil Weinstein (1980) and others who find such biases in the expectations of individuals in everyday life. However, we do not want to push this argument too far for two reasons. First, if we consider the nine individual year-by-year regressions, the intercepts are positive four times. Second, optimism bias also has a plausible agency interpretation. Many analysts work for brokerage houses that make money by encouraging trading. Since every customer is potentially interested in a buy recommendation, while only current stockholders (and a few willing to go short) are interested in sell recommendations, optimistic forecasts may be preferable. Indeed, it is well known that buy recommendations issued by brokerage houses greatly exceed sell recommendations.

All six regressions in Exhibit 1 present evidence supporting the hypothesis that forecasts are too extreme. Ignoring the constant term in equation 1, actual EPS changes average only 65 percent of the forecasted one-year changes. For the two-year forecasts (equation 3), this statistic falls to 46 percent.[2] In the year-by-year regressions equivalent to equations 1 and 3, the slope coefficients are less than one every single time.

Note that equations 1 and 3 could be rewritten with the forecast errors ($AC1 − FC1$ and $AC2 − FC2$) on the left-hand side and with the forecasted changes as the regressors. The new slope coefficients then equal the betas in Exhibit 1 minus one, while the t-statistics remain the same. The new slopes have a straightforward interpretation: The larger the forecasted changes, the larger is the forecast error in the opposite direction. The R^2s of these regressions are .076 and .097.

The previous findings all suggest that forecast revisions should also be predictable from forecasted changes, and indeed they are, as shown in equations 2 and 4. In these regressions, rationality implies that β should be equal to zero. In actuality, the slopes are significantly negative. By December, the average reversal of the one-year forecasts made in April equals 18 percent of the original predicted changes. For the two-year forecasts, the reversal amounts to 38 percent.

As expected, the results are stronger for the two-year and second year forecasts. The two-year results are clearly driven by the predicted changes for the second year (see equations 5 and 6). With the R^2 for equation 5 equal to zero, actual changes are simply unrelated to forecasted changes in EPS from year t to $t + 1$. On average, any non-zero prediction, either positive or negative, is pure error. By December, the analysts have reversed their April forecasted changes for the second year by 44 percent.

In sum, the above results are consistent with generalized overreaction. However, a different interpretation is based on the problem of errors in variables. If our measure of forecasted changes in earnings contains error, then the slope coefficients are biased downward. In evaluating this argument, one should consider the most likely sources of error. One possibility is IBES data entry errors. Following Patricia O'Brien (1988), we removed any data points for which the predicted change in EPS or the forecast revision was greater than $10. The results in Exhibit 1 reflect this error screen. In addition, we also recomputed regressions 1 and 3 using a smaller sample of firms for which the consensus forecast is based on the individual predictions of three analysts or more. For this subset, we then used the median forecasted earnings change as the regressor. The βs increased, but were still significantly less than one.

A second potential source of error stems from the fact that the forecasts on the IBES tape may be stale. In fact, O'Brien finds that the average forecast in the IBES sample is 34 days old. Stale forecasts are troublesome if the forecasters do not know the earnings for year $t - 1$ when they make their predictions

for year t. For example, a forecaster who thinks that year t earnings will remain unchanged from year $t - 1$ will appear to be predicting a change in earnings if his estimate of $t - 1$ earnings is wrong. We cannot completely rule out this interpretation of the results, but we selected April as the month to study with an eye toward minimizing the problem. We chose the longest possible forecast horizon where we could still be reasonably confident that the forecasters would know the previous year's earnings. The April forecasts are issued in the third week in April so that, by O'Brien's estimate, the average forecast was made in mid-March. At this point, the analysts should either know the past year's earnings exactly or have a very good estimate. Thus it seems unlikely that such a large bias could be produced by errors of this type.

Another reason for confidence in the results reported here is that others have obtained similar results in previous studies of professional forecasters, both security analysts and economists. Using just the 1976-78 years of the IBES data, Elton et al. estimated regressions similar to ours, and obtained slope coefficients less than one in each year. In a study of exchange rate expectations, Kenneth Froot and Jeffrey Frankel (1989) also found evidence consistent with overreaction or, what they call, "excessive speculation." Forecast errors are regressed on forecasted changes in exchange rates. The slope coefficients which, under rationality, should equal zero, are always significantly different from zero. When an instrumental variables technique is used to correct for errors-in-variables, the results do not change. Finally, David Ahlers and Josef Lakonishok (1983) study economists' forecasts of ten macroeconomic variables, using the Livingston data set. In regressions similar to our equation 1, they find slope coefficients significantly less than one for each of ten variables being forecast. In other words, predicted changes were more volatile than actual changes, consistent with overreaction.[3]

We have documented generalized overreaction. However, an interesting question remains: What causes excessive optimism or pessimism in earnings forecasts? We considered several variables that might explain EPS forecast errors. Two variables that are of interest in light of our previous work include a measure of market valuation, MV/BV, the ratio of the market value of a company's equity to its book value (at the end of year $t - 1$), and earnings trend (the growth rate of earnings over the years $t - 6$ to $t - 2$). Both variables were significantly related to forecast error in the expected direction, that is, excessive optimism for high MV/BV and high earnings growth firms, and excessive pessimism for firms low on these measures. Unfortunately, neither factor explained much of the variation in the forecast errors.

III. Conclusion

Formal economic models of financial markets typically assume that all agents in the economy are rational. While most economists recognize that, in fact, not everyone is fully rational, the existence of an irrational segment of the economy is often dismissed as irrelevant with the claim that there will be enough rational arbitrageurs to assure that rational equilibria will still obtain. Whatever the theoretical merits of this position (for a critique, see Bradford De Long et al., 1990; Thomas Russell and Thaler, 1985), an interesting empirical question is whether the presumed smart money segment actually can be identified. This paper investigates one possible source of rationality in financial markets, namely security analysts.

The conclusion we reach from our examination of analysts' forecasts is that they are decidedly human. The same pattern of overreaction found in the predictions of naive undergraduates is replicated in the predictions of stock market professionals. Forecasted changes are simply too extreme to be considered rational. The fact that the same pattern is observed in economists' forecasts of changes in exchange rates and macroeconomic variables adds force to the conclusion that generalized overreaction can pervade even the most professional of predictions.

The proper inference from this, we think, is to take seriously the behavioral explanations of anomalous financial market outcomes. When practitioners describe the recent October crashes as panics, produced by investor overreaction, perhaps they are right. After all, are not these practitioners the very same "smart money" that is supposed to keep markets rational?

Endnotes

1. We also tried other normalization procedures, such as dividing by company assets per share at the end of year $t - 1$, the stock price on the last trading day of year $t - 5$, or the standard deviation of EPS between $t - 5$ and $t - 2$. Results are qualitatively the same for all methods.

2. The two-year regressions are open to criticism because the sampling interval (one year) is shorter than the forecast interval (two years) creating a nonindependence across data points. To remove this problem, we break the sample in two, and replicate equation 3 using forecasts just from every other year, so that the time periods are non-overlapping. Results are comparable.

3. As mentioned above, analysts may have incentives to make biased forecasts in order to stimulate trading by customers. Our discussant, Andrew Lo, suggested that these agency problems could produce an over-reaction bias as well as an optimism bias. Whether or not this argument is plausible, the fact that the overreaction bias is observed for forecasters in domains in which the agency problem is not present suggests that the bias is produced by cognitive errors, rather than faulty incentives.

References

Ahlers, David and Lakonishok, Josef, "A Study of Economists' Consensus Forecasts." *Management Science*, October 1983, 29, 1113-25.

Brown, Philip, Foster, George and Noreen, Eric, *Security Analyst Multi-Year Earnings Forecasts and the Capital Market,* Sarasota: American Accounting Association, 1985.

Conroy, Robert and Harris, Robert, "Consensus Forecasts of Corporate Earnings: Analysts' Forecasts and Time Series Methods." *Management Science,* June 1987, 33, 725-38.

De Bondt, Werner F. M. and Thaler, Richard H., "Does the Stock Market Overreact?" *Journal of Finance,* July 1985, 40, 793-805.

_____ and _____, "Further Evidence on Investor Overreaction and Stock Market Seasonality." *Journal of Finance,* July 1987, 42, 557-81.

De Long, Bradford et al., "Noise Trader Risk in Financial Markets." *Journal of Political Economy,* forthcoming 1990.

Elton, Edwin J., Gruber, Martin J. and Gultekin, Mustafa N., "Professional Expectations: Accuracy and Diagnosis of Errors." *Journal of Financial and Quantitative Analysis,* December 1984, 19, 351-65.

French, Kenneth R. and Roll, Richard, "Stock Return Variances: The Arrival of Information and the Reaction of Traders." *Journal of Financial Economics,* September 1986, 17, 5-26.

Froot, Kenneth A. and Frankel, Jeffrey A., "Forward Discount Bias: Is It an Exchange Risk Premium?" *Quarterly Journal of Economics,* February 1989, 104, 139-61.

Kahneman, Daniel and Tversky, Amos, "On the Psychology of Prediction." *Psychological Review* 1973, 80, 237-51.

O'Brien, Patricia C., "Analysts' Forecasts as Earnings Expectations." *Journal of Accounting and Economics,* January 1988, 10, 53-83.

Russell, Thomas and Thaler, Richard H., "The Relevance of Quasi-Rationality in Competitive Markets," *American Economic Review,* December 1985, 75, 1071-82.

Shiller, Robert J., "Investor Behavior in the October 1987 Stock Market Crash: Survey Evidence," Working Paper, Cowles Foundation, Yale University, November 1987.

Weinstein, Neil, "Unrealistic Optimism about Future Life Events," *Journal of Personality and Social Psychology,* 1980, 806-20.

Chapter 15

Divergence of Earnings Expectations: The Effect on Market Response to Earnings Signals[*]

Dan Givoly, Ph.D.
Professor of Accounting Information Systems
J.L. Kellogg Graduate School of Management
Northwestern University

Josef Lakonishok, Ph.D.
William G. Karnes Professor of Finance
University of Illinois at Urbana-Champaign

Abstract

The paper examines the effect of earnings uncertainty on the information content of earnings. The uncertainty measures—dispersion of earnings expectations and earnings unpredictability—are derived from forecasts of financial analysts. The measures of uncertainty of individual companies are found to be quite stable over time, and positively related to other commonly employed risk variables. The measures appear to explain the intensity of market response to earnings signals. In particular, the higher are the values of these uncertainty measures, the weaker becomes the association between stock price movements and the earnings prediction error.

1. Introduction

The research on the information content of earnings stimulated by the seminal works of Ball and Brown (1968) and Beaver (1968), relied heavily on one signal emanating from the earnings report—the sign of the prediction error or the "unexpected" earnings. Empirically, unexpected earnings were defined as the difference between realized earnings and some point prediction produced by an assumed expectation model.

More recently, Beaver, Clark, and Wright (1979) have suggested another dimension to the earnings signal—the magnitude of the prediction error. They found a positive (although nonlinear) relationship between the

[*] We would like to thank Sudipto Bhattacharya, Bill Carleton, Nicholas Dopuch, Richard McEnally, George Oldfield and an anonymous referee for their helpful comments. The paper was presented at the 1982 Western Finance Association meetings and Financial Management Association meetings.

Reprinted with permission from *Stock Market Anomalies*, Elroy Dimson, editor, Cambridge University Press, 1988.

magnitude of unexpected earnings and stock market response to earnings disclosure. The use of the magnitude of the unexpected earnings is potentially rewarding: it enables researchers to better identify the information content of accounting numbers and to refine any analysis that is based on the association between stock price behavior and accounting signals (e.g., the comparison between accounting alternatives).

No theory exists at present that explains the exact mapping of unexpected earnings and price changes. Yet, it has been recognized that the stock price response to a given accounting signal may depend, among other things, on the characteristics of the reporting firm. Grant (1980), for instance, shows that stock price reaction to earnings disclosure is much more pronounced for small firms. His explanation rests with the relative unavailability of alternative information sources on the affairs of small firms which typically have thinly traded stock.

The extent, speed, and variability of market response to the disclosure of information are modeled in two interesting papers by Verrecchia (1980) and Holthausen and Verrecchia (1982). The model developed in the latter produces predictions which are consistent with Grant's findings. The model outlines factors which determine the magnitude of the unexpected price reaction to information releases. The model shows how market response to any given signal (e.g., the earnings announcement) depends on the precision of the signal relative to that of previous signals and, in general, relative to the precision of prior expectations of investors. An empirical examination of some of their predictions has been conducted by Pincus (1982) who operationalized the notion of precision. He found a relationship between the extent (and duration) of stock market reaction to earnings announcement and earnings predictability.

This paper represents another attempt to depart from sole reliance on mean unexpected earnings and to explore the relationship between other characteristics of the earnings numbers and stock price behavior. Unlike the works of Verrecchia (1980), Holthausen and Verrecchia (1982), and Pincus (1982), the focus here is on the information content of earnings rather than the price response to the earnings disclosure. Specifically, the paper is concerned about the relationship between the information content of earnings and the degree of uncertainty of earnings expectations. Similar to previous research, the information content is measured here as the abnormal return that could be obtained from a foreknowledge of the content of the earnings report, and is therefore measured over the period preceding and immediately following the earnings announcement. The uncertainty is measured by two alternative statistics: dispersion of earnings expectations and earnings unpredictability. Both measures are derived from earnings forecasts of financial analysts. The operationalization of earnings uncertainty will be discussed shortly.

An added incentive to investigate the relationship between the information content of earnings and the degree of uncertainty of earnings expectations is the wide dissemination of the uncertainty measures. Recently, practically all institutional investors, on a periodic basis, receive uncertainty measures for all the major U.S. corporations. The results of our study will shed some light on the value of such information.

It is important to clarify at the outset the expected relationship between uncertainty of earnings expectations and the information content of earnings. Uncertainty about future earnings stems from two sources: one is "real"—the difficulty of predicting future cash flows which are presumably mirrored by earnings. Another source of uncertainty is the noise created by the accounting system itself: reported earnings are subject to variability due to measurement errors, peculiarities of certain accounting methods, and management manipulations.

The direction of the association between earnings uncertainty and information content depends on the underlying cause of the uncertainty. Assume first that the accounting system is perceived by investors to be noiseless and the unpredictability of future earnings, therefore, stems exclusively from uncertainty surrounding future cash flows. Any resolution of this uncertainty by new information (accounting and non-accounting) is likely to generate market reaction in line with the news content. The greater is the uncertainty surrounding the initial expectations, the higher will be the first premium required by investors, and therefore, the lower will be the stock price.[1] The information content of earnings, measured over the period before and after the earnings release, will thus be greater, *ceteris paribus,* the greater is earnings uncertainty; for positive unexpected earnings a more favorable market response is expected and for negative unexpected earnings a less unfavorable response is expected. However, although perhaps less likely, new information which resolves the uncertainty of current earnings may increase the uncertainty about the future earnings and thus increase the risk premium. Obviously, a different market response will be predicted in such a case.

Consider now the case in which most or all uncertainty concerning future earnings is due to the noise of the reporting system rather than to unpredictability of cash flow. In this case, unexpected earnings—or the difference between realized and unexpected earnings—will be only loosely related to real economic developments and, therefore, weakly associated with stock price movements. We therefore expect that, *ceteris paribus,* the information content of earnings is greater, the less noisy is the earnings number, or high uncertainty will mitigate the impact of unexpected earnings. To better understand this case, let us take it to the extreme—there is no disagreement among analysts about the "real" future earnings, the only disagreement is about the reported earnings. If it is the case, we do not expect our uncertainty measures to be related to the market's response to earnings.

The two hypotheses suggested by us do not exhaust all the possibilities. We view our analysis as a preliminary one in which the empirical results will enhance our understanding about the uncertainty measures. Such an investigation can reveal that:

1. The uncertainty measures do not have any impact on the capital market's response to earnings.
2. The uncertainty measures are associated with the market's response to earnings. Based on our two hypotheses, the higher the earnings uncertainty, the milder should be the response to negative unexpected earnings. For positive unexpected earnings, the two hypotheses give opposite predictions. The truth is probably somewhere in between and the empirical results will indicate whether earnings uncertainty is due primarily to genuine uncertainty concerning future cash flows or to problems of measuring and reporting earnings. The uncertainty measures according to our hypotheses should provide a less ambiguous signal for negative unexpected earnings than for positive ones.

In the following section we describe the uncertainty measures. Section 3 describes the methodology and the data, and section 4 describes and analyzes the results. The final section contains concluding remarks.

2. Uncertainty Measures

To incorporate uncertainty into the analysis, a measure of uncertainty has to be defined. One alternative is earnings variability, which has long been employed by academicians and practitioners in their attempt to model investor behavior and evaluate stocks.[2]

The notion that past volatility of a variable is a good surrogate for its "unpredictability," or uncertainty, is deeply rooted in the economic thought: the variance of stock returns has been widely used to measure security risk; likewise, the variability of the rate of inflation and of the change in money supply have been considered as a measure of unpredictability (see, for example, Klein [1975]).

Past variability is a reasonable yardstick for unpredictability if the underlying stochastic structure of the series in question is assumed to be constant over time. However, past variability is of limited value in assessing the unpredictability of a process with nonstationary parameters. Moreover, market participants may consider other information, besides the variable's history, when forming economic expectations.

The idea that past volatility is only partially related to uncertainty surrounding future expectations has been recently developed by Cukierman and Wachtel [1982(a)], [1982(b)] and Cukierman and Givoly (1982). Cukierman and Wachtel prove in their papers that under plausible conditions, inflation uncertainty is not identical with, yet positively related to, both the variability of the inflation rate and the cross-sectional dispersion of the inflation forecasts. (Their model can be generalized to deal with variables other than inflation.) Cukierman and Givoly develop a model of earnings expectations whereby each forecaster, in making his prediction, employs both information common to all other forecasters (e.g., past earnings) and specific information. They show that under fairly general conditions (pertaining primarily to the stability of the variances of the series), the cross-sectional error in earnings forecasts is the correct empirical counterpart of uncertainty; that is, of the dispersion of the distribution of expected earnings. Their model also implies (and this implication is confirmed by empirical tests) that the cross-sectional error is positively associated with the dispersion of forecasts across forecasters.

With the enhanced availability of data on economic forecasts, the use of the dispersion of forecasts has increasingly attracted attention of researchers. Barnea, Dotan and Lak-onishok (1979), Bomberger and Williams (1981), and Levi and Makin (1979) all report an association between dispersion of inflation forecasts and interest rates; Friend, Westerfield and Granito (1978), Malkiel and Cragg (1980), and Friend and Westerfield (1981) use dispersion of earnings forecasts as an additional measure of risk, while Figlewski (1981) analyzes the implications of dispersion of forecasts for equilibrium prices. Dispersion of earnings forecasts and earnings unpredictability are apparently perceived by investors as valuable information, probably proxies for risk. *Value-Line* publishes regularly the unpredictability rating of companies' earnings; Standard and Poor's provides in its *Earnings Forecaster* publication a number of earnings forecasts for each of the about 1,500 companies listed in the publication, and a Wall Street firm, Lynch, Jones, and Ryan, supplies investors with such measures as range and standard deviation of a multitude of contemporaneous earnings forecasts made by different financial analysts.

This study presents evidence on incorporating the two uncertainty measures, dispersion of earnings expectations and earnings predictability, in testing the informational content of earnings.

3. Methodology and Data

Two alternative measures of earnings uncertainty are examined. One is the divergence of forecasts from the mean forecast and the other is the cross-sectional error of earnings forecasts. There is an intuitive appeal to both measures as surrogates of uncertainty, as is also evident from their use in empirical research (see the citations above). For a comprehensive discussion relating to these measures, see Cukierman and Givoly (1982).

The first measure (divergence of forecasts) is defined here as (the time subscripts will be omitted in the exposition for simplicity):

$$D_1^2 = \frac{1}{n-1} \sum_{i=1}^{n} [\ln(F_i) - \overline{\ln(F)}]^2 \tag{1}$$

where F_i is the forecast made by forecaster i and $\overline{\ln(F_i)}$ is the sample mean of $\ln(F)$ over n forecasters.

$$D_2^2 = \frac{1}{n-1} \sum_{i=1}^{n} [\ln(F_i) - \ln(A)]^2 \tag{2}$$

where A is the realization and the expression in parentheses corresponds to the percentage forecast error of forecaster i. Under the $\ln$ transformation, the magnitude of the earnings variable does not distort cross-sectional comparisons.[3] The two measures will be referred collectively as uncertainty measures. As indicated earlier, the second measure D^2, is, under fairly general conditions, the correct empirical counterpart of the ex-ante uncertainty surrounding earnings and it can be written as

$$D_2^2 = \frac{1}{n-1} \sum_{i=1}^{n} (\ln(F_i) - \overline{\ln(F)})^2$$

$$+ \frac{1}{n-1} - (\overline{\ln(F)} - \ln(A))^2 \tag{3}$$

Note that while the first term in the right-hand side of (3) is known to investors, who have access to analysts' forecasts, at the time of the forecast, the second (the bias) term is, obviously, unavailable at that time. This term has to be estimated and we estimate it from the most recent experience.

3.1 Tests

The research question to be addressed is whether the information content of earnings is associated with the degree of uncertainty of earnings expectation, and, if so, what is the direction of this association. To test this question, each year we partitioned the sample of stocks into portfolios, ranked first by the sign and magnitude of the earnings signal and then by the measure of uncertainty. The mean ab-

normal return, the mean prediction error, and the mean values of the uncertainty measures were computed for each of these portfolios. The prediction error was defined as

$$E \equiv \ln\left[\frac{A}{\overline{F}}\right] \text{ where } \overline{F} \equiv \frac{1}{n} \sum_{i=1}^{n} F_i$$

The very few cases (about 2% of all cases) in which the values of either A or F were negative were discarded.

The abnormal return for a given stock was defined by the use of the following time-series regression:

$$\tilde{R}_{it} - R_{ft} = \alpha_i + \beta_i (\tilde{R}_{mt} - R_{ft}) + \tilde{\varepsilon}_{it}, t = -48, ...,-1 \tag{4}$$

where $\tilde{R}_{it}$ is the return of stock i in month t, R_{ft} is the risk-free rate in month t measured by the yield on 30-day Treasury Bills and R_{mt} is the market return measured by the value-weighted index of the NYSE.[4]

The estimation period for a given year, for the α and β coefficients, was defined as the 48 months preceding the month of April of that year. April was defined as month 0 for companies for which the fiscal year ends in the following December (only December 31 companies were included in the sample) and the earnings were announced by the end of the following March (month 11).

The estimated residuals are derived as

$$\hat{\varepsilon}_{it} \equiv (R_{it} - R_{ft}) - [\hat{\alpha}_i + \hat{\beta}_i (R_{mt} - R_{ft})] \tag{5}$$

where $\hat{\alpha}_i$ and $\hat{\beta}_i$ are the estimated coefficients. The abnormal return was calculated as

$$CAR = \sum_{t=0}^{11} \hat{\varepsilon}_{it}$$

The stocks were ranked each year according to their prediction error (E) to form four groups. The stocks in each group were then ranked according to the uncertainty measure (D) (for each of the two Ds separately) to form four subgroups. The procedure yielded each year 16 subgroups (or portfolios).[5] To check the robustness of the results with respect to the grouping procedure, this procedure was repeated with stocks ordered first by D (for each of the two Ds separately) and then by E. By aggregating securities into portfolios, we reduce the measurement error inherent in the estimation of the beta and the uncertainty measures. For a detailed discussion of the grouping procedure, see Black and Sholes (1974).

Two cross-section regressions of the following form were estimated each year:

$$\text{CAR}_p = \alpha_j + \beta_{1j} E_p + \beta_{2j} D_{jp} + e_p \text{ for } j = 1,2 \quad (6)$$

where E_p is the mean prediction error of portfolio p, and D_{jp} is the average value of the uncertainty measure D_j in portfolio p.

Given the previous evidence on the association between the sign (and magnitude) of earnings prediction errors and price movement (see, for example, Ball and Brown [1968] and Beaver, Clark, and Wright [1979], we expect the coefficient β_1 to be positive. If uncertainty is important in explaining the association between stock price movements and the earnings signal, we expect β_2 to be significantly different from zero. If uncertainty matters (and regardless of its source), we expect a positive β_2 to be observed for negative prediction error cases. In other words, the greater is the earnings uncertainty, the higher (less negative) is the abnormal return expected to be associated with a negative prediction error (an "unfavorable surprise"). For positive prediction error cases, β_2 is expected to be negative if "noisiness" of the earnings number is the cause for its uncertainty, and positive if real factors are behind this uncertainty.

Since the hypothesized directional effect of uncertainty on abnormal returns may depend on the sign of the prediction error, the regression was estimated twice: once for 16 portfolios constructed by grouping cases with positive prediction errors and once for 16 portfolios formed by grouping cases with negative prediction errors (the number of companies with negative and positive prediction errors was very similar).

3.2 Data

Financial analysts' forecasts of earnings of a sample of companies were evaluated in each of the eleven years 1969 to 1979. The source of the forecasts was the S&P's *Earning, Forecaster.* A weekly publication that first appeared in 1967, the *Earnings Forecaster* lists in every second issue the outstanding EPS forecasts for about 1,500 companies. The forecasts are those made by S&P itself and by about 70 other security analysts and brokerage houses (the individuals making the forecast are not identified) who agreed to submit their forecasts, upon release, for the publication.

Strictly speaking, financial analysts' forecasts of earnings (hereafter FAF) reflect only the expectation of the respective analysts. Yet, their wide dissemination and the reliance of the public on the advice of financial analysts (see, for example, the report of the SEC Advisory Committee on Corporate Disclosure, [1977]) suggest that financial analysts' expectations may be shared by a wide group of investors. The notion that FAF might proxy for market expectations gains support from recent studies that show that FAF have a substantial influence on stock prices (see Elton, Gruber, and Gultekin [1981], Fried and Givoly [1982], and Givoly and Lakonishok [1979] and [1980]).

Considered each year were the FAF of that year's earnings as of the beginning of April. The time of the forecast is between the release of the annual report for the previous year (which is made on average, in early February—see Givoly and Palmon [1982]) and the release of the first quarterly actual earnings (typically late April).

Included in the sample each year were companies which satisfied these criteria:

(1) fiscal year ending December 31
(2) NYSE listing
(3) existence of at least four forecasts of the current year's earnings
(4) availability of monthly return data for

Exhibit 1 Mean and Standard Deviation of the Uncertainty and Error Measures, by Year

Year	D₁ Mean	D₁ s.d.	D₂ Mean	D₂ s.d.	|E| Mean	|E| s.d.
All years	0.050	0.045	0.190	0.202	0.163	0.215
1969	0.037	0.025	0.134	0.157	0.115	0.170
1970	0.046	0.030	0.240	0.240	0.212	0.248
1971	0.044	0.037	0.189	0.211	0.162	0.211
1972	0.046	0.037	0.128	0.140	0.098	0.126
1973	0.037	0.037	0.199	0.194	0.174	0.194
1974	0.061	0.049	0.257	0.221	0.216	0.200
1975	0.080	0.065	0.249	0.251	0.216	0.289
1976	0.064	0.056	0.165	0.151	0.130	0.172
1977	0.044	0.040	0.183	0.196	0.157	0.204
1978	0.047	0.048	0.183	0.218	0.167	0.258
1979	0.051	0.051	0.202	0.209	0.180	0.247

the forecast year, the following year, and the preceding four years.

The third criterion was introduced to allow the derivation of reliable measures for the average or "consensus" forecast and for the uncertainty measures. However, it apparently introduced a sample selection bias in favor of large and established companies which are more actively followed by investors (and hence forecasters). This criterion was responsible for eliminating most of the companies. The effect of the selection bias will be discussed in the next section.

All the contemporaneous company forecasts were for primary EPS before extraordinary items. When a forecast was for another defini-

tion and no conversion to a primary EPS number could be made, the observation was discarded. The number of such cases was negligible.

The final sample consists of 1,247 cases (company-years) with a total of 6,020 forecasts. The number of cases in each year differs and ranges from 95 (1972) to 173 (1969). This represents 424 distinct companies.

4. Results

Exhibits 1, 2, and 3 describe for the 11-year period the distribution of the two uncertainty

Exhibit 2 Relative Frequency Distribution of the Dispersion Measure (D₁)

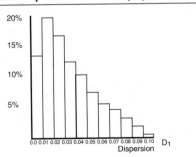

Exhibit 3 Relative Frequency Distribution of the Unpredictability Measure (D₂)

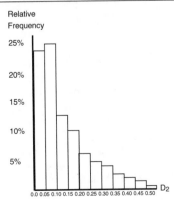

measures D_1 and D_2 (square roots of the measure in equations 1 and 2) and the error measure E. The average D_1 is 5% which is actually the standard deviation of the percentage deviation of forecasters from the mean forecast. The magnitude of the earnings unpredictability measure, D_2, is much larger (average of 19%) than that of D_1, suggests a strong commonality between the sign and the size of the errors of individual forecasters. One possible explanation for the high commonality has to do with agency considera-

tions; there may be a negative incentive to provide forecasts which differ substantially from the "normal" forecasts. Another possibility is that the various forecasts represent the unbiased opinion of the forecasters, and the high commonality is due to the process that generates the earning numbers.

Although the relative magnitude of the measures is stable over time, their magnitude is time-dependent. The mean absolute error measure (E) ranges over the years between 0.115 (in 1969) and 0.216 (in 1973 and

Exhibit 4 Rank Correlation of Portfolios Formed by D_j with D_j in Subsequent Years*

a. Results for the Dispersion Measure (D_1)

Portfolio Formation Year	Years Following the Portfolio Formation Year									
	1	2	3	4	5	6	7	8	9	10
1969	1.0	0.3	1.0	0.7	0.9	0.8	1.0	0.1	0.3	0.7
1970	0.8	1.0	0.5	0.1	0.9	1.9	−0.5	0.2	−0.1	
1971	0.7	0.7	−0.1	0.5	0.5	0.0	0.2	0.9		
1972	0.7	−0.3	0.3	0.5	0.1	0.0	0.8			
1973	0.4	0.8	0.7	0.5	0.1	0.8				
1974	0.9	0.8	0.8	0.8	0.7					
1975	1.0	0.7	0.4	0.2						
1976	0.6	0.9	0.7							
1977	1.0	0.7								
1978	−0.1									
	0.70	0.68	0.54	0.47	0.53	0.52	0.38	0.40	0.10	0.70

b. Results for the Unpredictability Measure (D_2)

Portfolio Formation Year	Years Following the Portfolio Formation Year									
	1	2	3	4	5	6	7	8	9	10
1969	1.0	0.2	1.0	0.3	0.6	0.7	0.9	−0.9	0.5	0.6
1970	0.8	0.7	0.8	0.6	0.9	1.0	0.3	0.1	−0.2	
1971	1.0	0.0	0.1	0.1	0.2	0.1	−0.4	0.6		
1972	0.1	0.4	0.5	0.6	0.0	−0.2	0.1			
1973	0.8	0.6	0.0	0.7	−0.3	0.7				
1974	0.9	0.7	0.3	0.9	0.9					
1975	0.9	−0.6	−0.3	−0.4						
1976	0.9	0.9	0.9							
1977	0.6	0.8								
1978	0.9									
	0.79	0.41	0.41	0.40	0.38	0.46	0.23	−0.06	0.15	0.60

* The Spearman rank correlation is used (see Conover (1971), pp. 245-249). All values of 0.80 and over are significant at the 5% level.

(974). Probably, there are years that are more difficult to predict than others. The potential cross-section dependence of prediction errors across firms suggests that observations taken from the same year might not be independent. Furthermore, the relationship between the variables might assume different forms in different years. These considerations led us to conduct the statistical tests on each of the 11 years separately rather than pooling all the observations together.

Exhibit 4 reports the rank correlation between the value of each uncertainty measure in one year and its value in subsequent years. For this purpose we ranked each year's firms according to the variable under examination and formed five equal size portfolios. (The investigation was conducted at the portfolio level to reduce the biases that arise from measurement errors in the explanatory variables.) We then followed these same portfolios in subsequent years and ranked them again according to the new average variable's value of their firm members. The first row of panel a in Exhibit 4 displays the rank correlations between the D_1s of portfolios formed in 1969 and the D_1s of the same portfolios in subsequent years. Similarly, the second row in that panel displays correlations between portfolios formed in 1970 and subsequent years.

The mean correlation of each column is reported at the bottom of each panel. The results suggest that there is a long-term persistency in the portfolio's D_1s and D_2s. The mean rank correlation between two adjacent years is 0.70 for D_1 and 0.79 for D_2. The rank correlation declines as the compared years are further apart; however, it remains fairly high for as long as seven years after the initial formation.[7] In other words, dispersion of earnings expectations and unpredictability of earnings have nontransient firm-unique components in addition to their time-dependent element (the latter is evident from the fluctuations of both D_1 and D_2 over the years, shown in Exhibit 1).

Exhibit 5 Mean Correlation Coefficients Between the Dispersion of Forecasts (D_1) Unpredictability of Earnings (D_2) and Selected Firms Characteristics*
(t values in parentheses**)

	D_1	D_2
β	0.19	0.15
	(4.50)	(4.97)
σ	0.20	0.18
	(5.10)	(6.63)
Marketability	0.21	0.23
	(4.09)	(8.47)
Size	−0.06	−0.05
	(−1.80)	(−0.83)
Earnings Growth	0.35	0.27
Variability	(10.55)	(8.95)
D_2	0.48	—
	(11.37)	

*The results in the table are based on individual cases.
**The t value is computed by dividing the table's value (the 11-year mean) by its standard deviation.

We now turn to the examination of the relationship between the uncertainty measures and other stock properties, particularly risk characteristics. Exhibit 5 presents the mean correlation (over the 11 yearly coefficients) between D_1 and D_2 and five other firms' variables: the beta, standard deviation of the residuals (both computed over the 48 months preceding the year for which the correlation is compared), marketability (shares traded during the year as a percentage of shares outstanding), firm's size (natural logarithm of the market value of the firm's equity at the end of the year), and earnings growth variability (measured as the standard deviation of the rate of growth in EPS over the years 1961-1980).

The table reveals a positive and significant association between D and the traditional market-based measures (β and α) and the accounting-based risk measure (earnings growth variability). There is a negative, although insignificant, correlation between size and D_1 and D_2. Both the dispersion and unpredictability measures tend to be greater for smaller companies. As will be discussed later, our sample consists mostly of large and estab-

Exhibit 6 Summary Results of the Regression of Cumulative Abnormal Return of the Earnings Prediction Error and Dispersion of Earnings Forecasts
(t values is parentheses)

| | a. Results for Dispersion | | | | | |
| | Cases of Positive Errors* | | | Cases of Negative Errors* | | |
Year	B_1	B_2	R^2 (%)	B_1	B_2	R^2 (%)
1969	0.53	−1.26	11.0	0.83	0.52	59.0
	(0.88)	(−0.97)		(3.65)	(0.34)	
1970	−0.17	1.15	4.2	0.30	2.09	44.0
	(−0.29)	(0.73)		(2.66)	(2.75)	
1971	0.35	−0.17	4.0	0.50	0.96	55.0
	(0.71)	(−0.11)		(3.90)	(1.18)	
1972	0.09	−1.35	12.5	−0.07	−0.43	0.5
	(0.22)	(−1.34)		(−0.19)	(−0.24)	
1973	0.78	2.38	73.9	0.55	1.48	24.6
	(4.49)	(2.19)		(1.44)	(0.77)	
1974	0.12	−1.07	8.6	0.69	1.82	27.4
	(0.59)	(−1.07)		(2.10)	(1.53)	
1975	0.28	1.51	23.8	0.10	2.13	43.4
	(0.42)	(1.50)		(0.67)	(2.82)	
1976	0.91	−0.48	63.5	0.37	0.84	11.8
	(4.35)	(−0.67)		(1.12)	(1.17)	
1977	0.81	−2.28	25.3	0.29	1.47	12.9
	(1.95)	(−1.62)		(1.33)	(1.20)	
1978	0.58	0.24	48.8	−0.02	−0.34	3.7
	(3.08)	(0.25)		(−0.14)	(−0.48)	
1979	0.55	−0.53	39.6	−0.24	−0.62	11.9
	(2.92)	(−0.69)		(−1.18)	(−0.61)	
Mean Over Years	0.44	−2.17	28.7	0.30	.90	26.3
Overall t***	(5.80)	(−0.53)		(4.64)	(3.12)	

(Continued)

lished companies. As a result, the sample is not rich in terms of cross-sectional variability of firm's size and the correlation is probably biased downward.

The relationship between marketability and D_1 and D_2 is positive. A plausible explanation of this association is that volume of trade is positively associated with divergent opinions with respect to the stock's future performance; greater marketability may in fact reflect a greater dispersion of forecasts. The table also shows that the two uncertainty measures are strongly correlated (correlation coefficient of 0.48). This is also expected from their functional relationship (see equation [3]). The somewhat low correlations in Exhibit 5 are probably

a result of the analysis being performed at the level of individual securities.

The association between the abnormal return, the prediction error and the uncertainty measures (results from the regressions in equation 6) are presented in Exhibit 6. The table shows the coefficients and the t values of the independent variables (prediction error and the uncertainty measures) and the R^2 of the regression for each year. The mean coefficients across the 11 years and the corresponding t statistic are shown at the bottom of each panel.

As expected, and in conformity with previous research, the t value of the coefficient of the prediction error is positive in almost all years. That is, the abnormal return is posi-

Exhibit 6 Summary Results of the Regression of Cumulative Abnormal Return of the Earnings Prediction Error and Dispersion of Earnings Forecasts (t values is parentheses) (continued)

| | b. Results for Unpredictability | | | | | |
| | Cases of Positive Errors* | | | Cases of Negative Errors* | | |
Year	B_1	B_2	R^2 (%)	B_1	B_2	R^2 (%)
1969						
1970	****	****	****	0.29	0.80	9.9
				(2.15)	(1.95)	
1971	0.51	0.00	4.8	0.36	0.17	23.4
	(0.92)	(−0.01)		(2.87)	0.64)	
1972	0.47	−0.79	17.8	0.25	−0.11	5.1
	(1.18)	(−2.43)		(0.74)	(−0.33)	
1973	0.61	0.21	13.5	0.36	0.45	12.0
	(2.23)	(0.47)		(1.02)	(0.65)	
1974	0.17	−0.28	8.1	0.63	−0.51	31.0
	(0.87)	(−1.58)		(2.40)	(−1.10)	
1975	1.22	0.69	47.7	−0.00	0.23	4.0
	(2.16)	(3.69)		(−0.00)	(1.18)	
1976	1.46	0.01	31.0	0.20	0.22	11.5
	(3.34)	(0.04)		(1.07)	(1.75)	
1977	0.70	0.04	15.9	0.07	−0.43	8.5
	(1.74)	(0.10)		(0.47)	(−1.73)	
1978	1.30	−0.24	43.0	0.01	0.03	0.1
	(4.91)	(−1.42)		(0.13)	(0.16)	
1979	0.79	−0.24	20.5	−0.05	0.26	11.5
	(3.13)	(−1.15)		(−0.38)	(1.46)	
Mean Over Years	0.72	−0.07	22.5	0.21	0.11	11.7
Overall t***	(6.84)	(−0.75)		(3.32)	(1.46)	

*The regression is specified in (4) and is estimated each year from a sample for 16 portfolios.
**The regression is specified in (4). However, the bias term of D_2 (see (3)) used in year 5 is that observed in year t-1. As a result, the regression could not be estimated for the first year, 1969. In some other years, there were too few observations for 16 portfolios. As a result, regressions based on individual cases were used.
***Derived by dividing the mean t value over the years, by its population standard deviation over the n years $(1/\sqrt{n})$.
****Insufficient number of observations (less than 10).

tively related to the sign and size of the prediction error. The mean coefficient, across the years, of the prediction error is positive and significant at the 1% level in both panels and for positive and negative error cases.[8]

To discuss the coefficients of the uncertainty measures, we will turn first to the cases with negative prediction errors of earnings. As stated earlier, in this case, if uncertainty matters, a positive coefficient is expected. Based on the result, in panel a (uncertainty defined in terms of dispersion) the mean β_2 is .90 and the t statistic is, 3.12 indicating that β_2 is highly significant. In addition to the statistical significance, β_2 has a substantial effect on abnormal returns. For example, a company whose dispersion measure is one standard deviation from the mean, (based on Exhibit 1, the standard deviation is .045) will have a return higher by 3.85% (.045 × .9) than a company with an average dispersion measure (assuming the same magnitude of unexpected earnings).

Looking at the individual years, the β_2 coefficient has the predicted sign in 8 out of the 11 years, and in 2 out of the 8 years the coefficient is statistically significant at the 1%

level. These results are similar to the results obtained for the β_1 coefficient which has the predicted sign also in 8 out of the 11 years and a statistically significant coefficient in 4 years. In general, the results for the individual years should not be given too much emphasis. When attempts are made to explain returns in a cross-sectional setting, results for short measuring intervals are in general weak and erratic. For example, over short measuring intervals no association was found between risk and return (see Fama and MacBeth [1973]). An examination of longer periods is necessary before significance of explanatory variables can be determined.

In panel b the results for the second uncertainty measure, earnings unpredictability, are presented. The overall mean of the β_2 coefficient is 0.11 and the t statistic is 1.46, which is associated with a significance level of 7.2%. Observing the results, for individual years, in 7 out of 10 years β_2 has the predicted sign, and in 2 out of the 7 years β_2 is statistically significant at the 5% level. The results for the unpredictability measure are not as strong as the results for the dispersion measure. We should not conclude from it that the dispersion measure is a better measure of uncertainty than the unpredictability measure. There are two good objective reasons for the relatively poor performance of the uncertainty measure. The first reason has to do with the fewer numbers of observations that were available to estimate the coefficient of the dispersion measure. (Only companies with two consecutive sets of earnings forecasts could be included.) The second reason is related to the first; because of the fewer number of observations, the coefficients were estimated using individual companies rather than portfolios. Therefore, the results for the unpredictability measure are subject to greater measurement errors and hence a more pronounced downward bias in the estimate of the coefficient. This leads to less significant results.

Overall, the results from negative earning prediction errors are consistent with the no tion that uncertainty has an effect on stoc price movement. A high uncertainty reduce the negative impact of unfavorable earnings.

Turning to the positive prediction errors we have two competing hypotheses. In gen eral, the mean coefficient of β_2 is negative ir panels a and b, but the results are not statisti cally significant. On a year-by-year basis, out of the 11 β_2 coefficients are negative ir panel a, and 5 out of 9 in panel b. Thes results are consistent with the two hypothese not being mutually exclusive and the "truth' lying somewhere in between.

The results presented so far about the un certainty measures appear to be promising and probably underestimate the importance o the uncertainty measures. There are at leas *two* elements unique to the setting of our ex periment that may result in an underestimatio of the importance of the uncertainty measures measurement errors in estimating the uncertainty variables and the sample composition that ma lead to an inefficient estimation.

The measurement error could stem from a least two sources. First, the uncertainty meas ures are estimated based on a relatively smal number of forecasts (typically five to seven) Yet, the true, unobserved dispersion or unpre dictability measures reflect the expectation o a great number of investors. Secondly, the ob served forecasts are, strictly speaking, no

Exhibit 7 Distribution of Observations by the Market Value of the Corresponding Firms

	(million dollars)	
	Our Sample*	ALL NYSE**
First Quartile	425	41
Median	864	144
Third Quartile	2,147	358

*Market values are averaged over the 11 years of the study (1969-1979).
**Estimated from Stoll and Whaley [Table 1, 1982]. Market values are averaged over the 20 years 1960-1979.

perfectly contemporaneous. There is a continuous process of forecast revision; since it takes S&P (our source of forecast data) a week or two to collect and publish new forecasts, any given issue of the *Earnings Forecaster* inevitably contains forecasts that are outdated to a varying degree. Both uncertainty measures would be contaminated by this publication lag.

In addition to the potential measurement error, the sample, by construction, might be poor in terms of the cross-section variability of the uncertainty measures. It is evident from Exhibit 7 that the sample companies are very large. The median firm has a market equity value of $864 million, compared to $149 million in the population of the New York Stock Exchange which itself consists of relatively large firms. The sample composition was dictated by the selection criterion whereby firms with less than four contemporaneous forecasts were excluded (due to the poor quality of the uncertainty measures estimates in these cases). The number of forecasts available at any given time probably mirrors the extent of interest of investors in the stock. We expect large companies to be watched closer by investors and therefore to be followed by more analysts. Exhibit 8 provides a strong support to this notion. The table presents the average number of earnings forecasts that are reported

by the Institutional Brokers Estimate System (IBES) for firms of different sizes. IBES is a publication of Lynch, Jones and Ryan, a Wall Street firm.[9] The table shows that the number of available forecasts increase with the size of the firm. In part, this is a reflection of the percentage of institutional holdings which is also shown by the table to be positively associated with size.

The deletion of small companies might eliminate companies with a high forecast dispersion or high earnings unpredictability. The resulting reduction in the cross-section variability of these measures in the sample might have led to less efficient estimates of their coefficients. In addition, it has been shown empirically that the stock market response to the release of earnings of small companies is much less intense than the response to earnings releases by large companies (see Grant [1980]). This phenomenon might also bias the results against the uncertainty measures.

5. Concluding Remarks

The paper introduces another element to the examination of the information content of earnings—the uncertainty of earnings expectations. Two measures of uncertainty are defined and tested in the paper. The first measure is based on dispersion of earnings forecasts among financial analysts, and the second measure is based on earnings unpredictability of financial analysts. The results suggest that there is an association between the uncertainty measures and stock price movement. In particular, for unfavorable earnings the evidence supports the notion that earnings uncertainty mollifies stock price response to earnings signals. The results are statistically significant and the impact of the uncertainty measures on returns is substantial. A company with a dispersion measure of one standard deviation above the mean would experience a return of 3.85% above the return of a company with an average dispersion measure. For favorable earnings, there is some in-

Exhibit 8 Number of Earnings Forecasts Available by IBES and Percentage of Institutional Holdings by Firm's Size

Size (Capitalization)	Average Number of Earnings Forecasts	Average of Percentage Institutional Holdings*
Below 100 M	6.7	26.4
100-200 M	8.4	35.5
200-400 M	9.8	38.1
401-1000 M	13.1	41.0
1001-5000 M	16.9	47.4
Over 5000 M	21.8	44.1

* Source: Computer Directions Advisors, Inc. [1981].

dication that earnings uncertainty tends to mollify stock price response to earnings. The results, however, are not statistically significant. The asymmetric response to favorable and unfavorable earnings is consistent with the two hypotheses presented in the paper.

The results with respect to the uncertainty measures are promising. The odds against finding significant results were quite substantial; the sample was comprised of large firms and the uncertainty measures are probably subject to severe measurement errors. A traditional call for further research in this area is probably appropriate at this point.

Endnotes

1. An assumption is made that earnings uncertainty is related to the systematic risk component, or to the unsystematic risk component if for some reason the market compensates for unsystematic risk. For a discussion of this topic, see Lakonishok and Shapiro (1982).

2. A number of stock valuation studies and related papers have employed earnings variability as a measure of risk. For example, Ahlers (1972), Beaver, Kettler, and Scholes (1970), and Litzenberger and Rao (1971). Financial services such as S&P and Value-Line report "safety" rating for stocks based on of earnings volatility.

3. The very few cases with negative or zero earnings were discarded.

4. The natural logarithms were used to measure the rate of returns.

5. The selection of the number of portfolios was made by weighting the need to have large enough portfolios so as to produce meaningful portfolios' averages against the wish to have as many portfolios (observations) as possible. The particular selection of 16 portfolios is, of course, arbitrary.

6. We could run one regression by creating dummy variables for the sign of unexpected earnings. But, such a procedure assumes that the distribution of the error term in equation 6 does not depend on the sign of the unexpected earnings. If this assumption does not hold, the significance tests will be biased.

7. The mean correlations for years 8, 9, and 10 after the portfolio formation year are not very

meaningful as they rely only on three, two, and one observations, respectively.

8. The results in panel a of Exhibit 6 are fo portfolios formed by ranking firms first according to their earnings predictions error (E) and the within each group according to their dispersion measure (D_1). The results for the reverse procedure were essentially similar.

9. IBES covers more companies and more fore casts per company than our sample, however, these data are available only for the last five years. Fur thermore, individual forecasts are not provided.

References

Ahlers, David M., 1972, "SEM: A Security Evaluation Model," reprinted in Elton and Gruber *Security Evaluation and Portfolio Analysis* (Prentice-Hall), pp. 227-44.

Ball, Ray and Philip Brown, 1968, "An Empirica Evaluating of Accounting Income Numbers," *Journal of Accounting Research,* Autumn, pp 159-178.

Barnea Amir, Amihud Dotan and Josef Lakon ishok, 1979, "The Effects of Price Level Uncertainty on the Determination of Nominal Interest Rates: Some Empirical Evidence," *Southern Economic Journal,* October, pp. 409-614

Beaver, William, Roger Clark and William F Wright, 1979, "The Association Between Unsystematic Security Returns and the Magnitude of Earnings Forecasts," *Journal of Accounting Research,* Autumn, pp. 316-340.

_____, 1968, "The Information Content of Annual Earnings' Announcements," *Empirical Research in Accounting,* Supplement to the *Journal of Accounting Research,* pp. 67-92.

_____, P. Kettler and M. Scholes, 1970, "The Association Between Market Determined and Accounting Determined Risk Measures," *The Accounting Review,* October, pp. 645-82.

Black, Fisher and Myron Scholes, 1974, "The Effects of Dividend Yield and Dividend Policy on Common Stock Prices and Returns," *Journal of Financial Economics,* March, pp.1-22.

Bomberger, William A., and William J. Frazer, Jr. 1981. "Interest Rates, Uncertainty and Livingston Data," *Journal of Finance,* June, pp. 661-675.

Computer Directions Advisors, Incorporated, 1981 *Spectrum* 1 and *Spectrum* 2 publications, June Maryland.

*nover, W.J., 1980, Practical Nonparametric Statistics, 2nd edition, John Wiley and Sons, Inc., New York.

*ockett, J. and Irwin Friend, 1974, "Stock Ownership in the United States, Characteristics and Trends," *Survey of Current Business,* November, pp. 16-40.

*kierman, Alex and Dan Givoly, 1982, "Heterogeneous Earnings Expectations and Earnings Uncertainty: Theory and Evidence," Working Papers, May, Carnegie-Mellon University.

____ , and Paul Wachtel, 1982a, "Relative Price Variability and Non-Uniform Inflationary Expectations," *Journal of Political Economy,* February, pp. 146-158.

____ and _____ , 1982b, "Inflationary Expectations: Reply and Further Thoughts on Inflation Uncertainty," *American Economic Review,* forthcoming.

*on, Edwin J., Martin J. Gruber, and Mustafa Gultekin, 1981, "Expectations and Share Prices," *Management Science,* September, pp. 975-987.

*ma, Eugene F. and James D. MacBth, 1973, "Risk, Return and Equilibrium: Empirical Tests," *Journal of Political Economy*, May, pp. 607-636.

*lewski, Stephen, 1981, "Capital Asset Pricing Under Heterogeneous Expectations and the Importance of Restrictions on Short Sales". *Journal of Financial and Quantitative Analysis,* November, pp. 463-476.

*ed, Dov and Dan Givoly, 1982, "Financial Analysts' Forecasts of Earnings: A Better Surrogate for Earnings Expectations," forthcoming, *Journal of Accounting and Economics.*

*iend, Irwin and Randolph Westerfield, 1981, "Risk and Asset Prices," *Journal of Banking and Finance,* September, pp. 291-315.

____ , and Michael Granito, 1978, "New Evidence on the Capital Asset Pricing Model," *Journal of Finance,* June, pp. 913-920.

*voly, Dan and Josef Lakonishok, 1979, "The Information Content of Financial Analysts' Forecasts of Earnings: Some Evidence on Semi-Strong Inefficiency," *Journal of Accounting and Economics,* Winter, pp. 165-185.

____ , 1980, "Financial Analysts' Forecast of Earnings: Their Value to Investors," *Journal of Banking and Finance,* September, pp. 221-223.

_____ and Dan Palmon, 1982, "Timeliness of Annual Reports—Some Empirical Evidence," *The Accounting Review,* forthcoming.

Grant, Edward B., 1980, "Market Implications of Differential Amounts of Interim Information," *Journal of Accounting Research,* Spring, pp. 255-268.

Holthausen, Robert W. and Robert E. Verrecchia, 1982. "The Change in Price Resulting from a Sequence of Information Releases," Working Paper No. 54, University of Chicago.

Klein, Benjamin, 1975, "Our New Monetary Standard: The Measurement and Effects of Price Uncertainty, 1880-1973," *Economic Inquiry,* December, pp. 1022-1027.

Lakonishok, Josef and Alan Shapiro, 1982, "Partial Diversification as an Explanation of the Small Firm Effect: An Empirical Analysis," Working Paper, September.

Levi, Maurice and M. Makin, 1980, "Inflation Uncertainty and the Phillips Curve: Some Empirical Evidence," *American Economic Review,* December, pp. 1022-1027.

Litzenberger, Robert H. and Cherukuri U. Rao, 1971, "Estimates of the Marginal Rate of Time Preference and Average Risk Aversion of Investors in Electric Utility Shares: 1960-66," *The Bell Journal of Economics and Management Science,* Spring, pp. 365-77.

Malkiel, Burton and John G. Cragg, 1980, "Expectations and the Valuation of Shares," Working Paper 471, April, National Bureau of Economics Research.

Pincus, Morton, 1982, "Information Characteristics of Earnings Announcements and Stock Market Behavior," Working Paper, Washington University (St. Louis).

Securities and Exchange Commission, 1977, Report of the Advisory Committee on Corporate Disclosure, Washington.

Stoll, Hans R. and Robert E. Whaley, 1982, "Transaction Costs and the Small Firm Effect," Vanderbilt University Working Paper, January.

Verrecchia, Robert E., 1980, "The Rapidity of Price Adjustments to Information," *Journal of Accounting and Economics,* March, pp. 63-92.

Chapter 16

Are Earnings Surprises Predictable?[*]

Donald J. Peters
Vice President
T. Rowe Price Associates

Researchers and investors have long known that earnings announcements that differ from market expectations have a material and positive relationship with equity returns (see, for example, Ball and Brown [1968]). In fact, earnings surprises—defined as (Actual earnings from operations − Expected earnings)/Absolute value of expected earnings—have been associated with some especially dramatic price movements, because the market's information set is updated by these announcements.

The importance of earnings surprises to investors is reflected by the fact that the information becomes available almost immediately after an announcement is made, and is updated and faxed several times a day to Zacks and IBES clients. The market's response to earnings surprises indicates that there are large rewards for those who can accurately predict earnings. Accordingly, money managers and investment banks devote significant resources to predicting earnings.

Research by Bernard and Thomas [1990] has extended our knowledge of earnings surprises. The authors use time series data to estimate earnings and conclude that the data exhibit serial correlation. That is, earnings surprises are to some extent predictable. My study differs by using analysts' consensus earnings estimates to provide further insight into the question of earnings surprise predictability.

Some studies have found that analysts' forecasts are superior to estimates provided by time series processes (Brown, Richardson, and Schwager [1987]). This result is intuitive and based on the resources allocated to research activities by market participants. Analysts also have a larger information set at their disposal when making their forecasts. They may receive guidance from insiders and consider current industry conditions along with a firm's previous operating history.

Because surprises have material effects on stock returns, publicly traded companies have

[*] The author wishes to thank Stephen Zimmerman and Zacks Investment Research for providing its historical earnings surprise database, Steven Handleman and John Petricelli for computational assistance, and Morris Hamburg for helpful comments.

Reprinted with permission from *The Journal of Investing,* Summer, 1993, pgs. 47-51.

strong incentives to monitor forecasts of their future earnings and ensure that these projections are reasonable. Although firms are extremely reluctant to provide a specific point estimate, many companies inform analysts whether they are comfortable with these forecasts.

General Approach

I use data supplied by Zacks Investment Research to capture the market's earnings expectation for a particular period before a firm announces its earnings. This database "freezes" its consensus estimates when a firm discloses its earnings. (Earnings reflect only income from continuing operations.) Accordingly, one can easily calculate earnings surprises for a broad universe of stocks. I use these data to consider whether, given today's information set, one can predict upcoming surprises.

I also consider a growth stock universe, or subset of the Zacks database. I make this segmentation because many investors follow a growth style, and the prices of growth stocks are more volatile. One factor explaining higher volatility is that growth stocks are more sensitive to revisions of expectations. These stocks have below-average yields, and their pricing largely reflects the market's consensus opinion of various possibilities coming to fruition.

The study considers over 22,000 observations for the general universe and over 10,000 ones for the growth universe from the quarter beginning July 1984 through June 1991. It focuses on median earnings surprises because the data have large outliers. Medians thus provide a better measure of centrality.

The economic information provided by these surprises is not especially sensitive to a specific number. That is, investors are interested first in whether a positive or a negative surprise has occurred and its magnitude. There is little economic significance between surprises of 11 percent, 13 percent, or 15 per-

cent, and likewise between –30 percent, –35 percent, or –40 percent.

One must also recognize that the earnings a firm reports are not the result of a process that is governed or constrained by the laws of nature. Companies have some discretion regarding the number they actually announce. Earnings are a product of many estimates and judgments; one should not underestimate the abilities of a pressured CFO.

Results

As many have long suspected, analysts are generally too optimistic. Exhibit 1 shows some summary statistics in which the median and average earnings surprises are negative for both universes. The Zacks Universe has a median earnings surprise of –1.9 percent and an average of –24.6 percent. Growth stocks have a similar median but a much smaller average of –7.5 percent.

The differences in the results of these universes may be influenced by my definition of a growth stock (see appendix), because it includes both financial quality and size screens. Nevertheless, it is noteworthy that the median numbers are close to zero.

The general universe has more outliers, as evidenced by its more negative average surprises, than the subset of growth stocks, and greater negative skewness. One explanation for the material differences between the median and mean of both universes is the "big bath" hypothesis. The argument goes that if one is going to miss analysts' projections one might as well recognize any budding problems. Management, therefore, has some in-

Exhibit 1 Earnings Surprise Summary Statistics

Zacks Universe:	Median	–0.019
	Average	–0.246
Growth Stocks:	Median	–0.014
	Average	–0.075

centive to manage its earnings number and hope for better-than-expectations announcements in the future. Alternatively, the market recognizes a large positive surprise as such, but probably perceives little economic difference between a 25 percent and 35 percent positive surprise.

Wall Street folklore argues that material negative earnings surprises do not occur just once; instead firms will have several sequential negative surprises. That is, companies have positively serially correlated earnings surprises.

Not surprisingly, because of the noisiness of the data, regression results regarding the predictability of subsequent earnings surprises did not yield statistically significant results. However, Spearman rank order correlations were significant at the 99 percent level. The correlation between Quarters 1 and 2 was 0.27 and 0.28 for Quarters 2 and 3. For growth stocks the correlation was 0.29 for the first two quarters and 0.3 for the last ones.

The rank order correlations lend support to the argument that earnings surprises are somewhat predictable. As surmised, investors are less concerned with a specific number than they are with the direction and magnitude of the surprise.

To test the hypothesis of serial correlation of earnings surprises further, I sort the universe into decile portfolios based on an initial period's earnings surprise and maintain the portfolios for two subsequent quarters. The periods analyzed start with the quarter beginning July 1984, the earliest period for which data are widely available, and extend through the quarter beginning April 1991. I follow this approach because I want to segregate those stocks with large positive and negative surprises.

Exhibits 2 and 3 show the median earnings surprises for holding the rank-ordered portfolios for the next two quarters. The data have a clear pattern: the portfolios with the worst initial surprises continue to have material negative surprises. The pattern and magnitude of

Exhibit 2 Median Earnings Surprise for Decile Portfolios After Initial Sorting on Previous Quarter's Surprise from October 1984 Through March 1991

1	−0.3428
2	−0.1491
3	−0.0841
4	−0.0554
5	−0.0305
6	−0.0124
7	0.0013
8	0.0108
9	0.0327
10	0.0627

Note: Portfolios with the worst initial surprises are listed first.

the surprises is dampened for the second holding period.

For example, the decile with the worst initial surprises has a median surprise of −34 percent the next quarter and −23 percent the following one. The decile with the next-worst initial surprises has median surprises of −15 percent and −11 percent for the next two respective quarters. It is noteworthy that the portfolios with the biggest initial negative surprises have the largest absolute median surprises the following periods.

Exhibit 3 Median Earnings Surprise for Decile Portfolios Second Quarter After Initial Sorting on Two Quarters' Ago Earnings Surprise from January 1985 Through June 1991

1	−0.2277
2	−0.1099
3	−0.0657
4	−0.0392
5	−0.0316
6	−0.0183
7	−0.0044
8	0.0043
9	0.0103
10	0.0057

Note: Portfolios with the worst initial surprises are listed first.

The data are also consistent. For both the decile with the worst initial surprises and that with the next-worst initial surprises, the median surprises are all negative the next quarter during the twenty-six periods analyzed. In the following quarter the worst decile has a negative surprise in twenty-five of the twenty-six periods and the next-worst in twenty-two of the twenty-six periods.

Moving from those deciles with the worst initial surprises to those with better initial surprises, the subsequent earnings surprises are generally better. Those stocks with the best initial surprises continue to have more favorable surprises. This portfolio has a positive surprise twenty-two times the following twenty-six quarters and twelve times in the subsequent one, and in seven other periods during this span the median surprise was 0. Thus, in nineteen of the twenty-six periods earnings were at least consistent with expectations.

Exhibits 4 and 5 present the data for growth stocks. The pattern is consistent with that found in the general universe. For both the subsequent quarter and the second quarter after the initial sorting, the worst portfolio has negative surprises twenty-five out of twenty-six periods. This portfolio has respective surprises of –24 percent and –18 percent for the

Exhibit 5 Median Earnings Surprise for Growth Decile Portfolios After Initial Sorting on Two Quarters' Ago Earnings Surprise from January 1985 Through June 1991

1	–0.1753
2	–0.0829
3	–0.0701
4	–0.0447
5	–0.0237
6	–0.0223
7	–0.0112
8	0.0058
9	0.0122
10	0.0217

Note: Portfolios with the worst initial surprises are listed first.

two following periods after the initial sorting. The next-worst decile has similar results to those found in the general universe.

The best decile, in contrast, has a positive surprise in twenty-two of the twenty-six periods the following quarter and sixteen times for the second reporting period after the initial sorting (in five periods the median surprise was 0). Its surprises for the respective periods are 6 percent and 2 percent. Like the general universe, the pattern and magnitude of the surprises remain generally consis

Exhibit 4 Median Earnings Surprise for Growth Decile Portfolios After Initial Sorting on Previous Quarter's Surprise from October 1984 Through March 1991

1	–0.2421
2	–0.1004
3	–0.0790
4	–0.0556
5	–0.0318
6	–0.0105
7	–0.0020
8	0.0076
9	0.0278
10	0.0621

Note: Portfolios with the worst initial surprises are listed first.

Exhibit 6 Decile Portfolios Excess Returns Quarter After Initial Sorting on Previous Quarter's Earnings Surprise from October 1984 Through March 1991

1	–0.0169
2	–0.0100
3	–0.0029
4	–0.0098
5	–0.0072
6	–0.0062
7	0.0153
8	0.0137
9	0.0113
10	0.0118

Note: Portfolios with the worst initial surprises are listed first.

Exhibit 7 Decile Portfolios Excess Returns Two Quarters After Initial Sorting on Two Quarters' Ago Earnings Surprise from January 1985 Through June 1991	
1	-0.0148
2	-0.0045
3	-0.0071
4	-0.0015
5	-0.0044
6	0.0025
7	0.0067
8	0.0026
9	0.0102
10	0.0095

Note: Portfolios with the worst initial surprises are listed first.

Exhibit 8 Growth Stock Decile Portfolios Excess Returns Quarter After Initial Sorting on Previous Quarter's Earnings Surprise from October 1984 Through March 1991	
1	-0.0209
2	-0.0145
3	-0.0045
4	-0.0131
5	-0.0144
6	0.0016
7	0.0160
8	0.0136
9	0.0170
10	0.0168

Note: Portfolios with the worst initial surprises are listed first.

nt but does decay as the holding period ngthens.

Exhibits 6 and 7 show the excess returns associated with holding these portfolios for two quarters after the initial surprise. There is positive relationship between market-adjusted returns and earnings surprises. The portfolio with the best initial surprises continues to have not only positive surprises but so good relative performance. Its excess returns are 118 basis points the quarter after the initial surprise and 95 the next.

The portfolio with the worst initial surprises trails the average stock's return by 169 basis points the subsequent quarter and 148 basis points the one after. In the quarter after the initial sorting, the portfolio with the worst initial surprises has positive excess returns in only eight out of the twenty-six periods, and the best initial portfolio has positive excess returns for seventeen periods. For the second quarter after the initial sorting the worst portfolio has positive returns ten periods, while the best one has them for nineteen out of the twenty-six quarters.

Exhibits 8 and 9 show how growth stock portfolios performed relative to the average growth stock's return. Their pattern is again similar to that found in the general universe,

but the magnitude of the excess returns is larger for the first quarter after the initial sorting. The portfolio with the worst initial surprises lags other growth stocks by 2 percent and 1.8 percent, respectively, in the two quarters following the initial sorting.

The decile with the best initial surprises, in contrast, has positive excess returns of 1.7 percent and 1.6 percent, respectively, in the next two quarters. These larger relative returns may reflect the fact that the pricing of growth stocks depends more on the market's

Exhibit 9 Growth Stock Decile Portfolios Excess Returns Two Quarters After Initial Sorting on Two Quarters' Ago Earnings Surprise from January 1985 Through June 1991	
1	-0.0181
2	-0.0049
3	-0.0024
4	-0.0087
5	-0.0071
6	0.0021
7	0.0096
8	0.0121
9	0.0036
10	0.0160

Note: Portfolios with the worst initial surprises are listed first.

opinion of future potential coming to fruition than it does for other stocks.

The portfolio with the worst initial surprises has positive excess returns eight out of the twenty-six periods in the quarter following the initial sorting and nine times in the subsequent quarter. The decile with the best initial surprises has positive excess returns in twenty-one of twenty-six quarters for the two quarters after the initial sorting.

Summary

This study shows that earnings surprises are to some extent predictable. Companies that are short analysts' estimates this quarter are likely to have negative earnings surprises subsequent quarters. The relative performance of these stocks is, as expected, negative.

I speculate that one of the reasons for these findings is that managements are well aware of the impact of earnings surprises. It follows that management has incentives, as well as the flexibility with generally accepted accounting principles to "bank" large positive surprises when they occur for future quarters. Firms try to meet analysts' expectations with their earnings announcements, and when they are unable to do so, they know the probable consequences.

It seems that once a company has a material shortfall, it has run out of reserves or buffers to smooth its reported income and is facing difficult operating conditions. The negative skewness of the data may reflect this assertion.

Appendix

This article's definition of a growth stock is identi cal to that found in Peters [1991]. Its goal is obtain a universe with several hundred grow stocks per quarter with high growth forecasts. also consider liquidity and financial quality.

The growth universe contains stocks that hav the following qualifications:

- Forecast mean long-term growth of great than or equal to 12 percent.
- At least two IBES growth forecasts.
- Sales of at least $50 million for the previo year.
- Positive earnings for the last four quarte (before extraordinary items and disconti ued operations).
- Pricing history for the period.

References

Ball, Ray, and Philip Brown. "An Empirical Eval ation of Accounting Income Numbers." *Journ of Accounting Research,* Autumn 1968, p 159-178.

Bernard, Victor L., and Jacob K. Thomas. "Ev dence that Stock Prices Do Not Fully Refle the Implications of Current Earnings for Futu Earnings." *Journal of Accounting and Econom ics,* 13 (1990), pp. 305-340.

Brown, Lawrence D., Gordon D. Richardson, an Steven J. Schwager. "An Information Interpre tation of Financial Analyst Superiority in For casting Earnings." *Journal of Accounting Re search,* Spring 1987, pp. 49-67.

Peters, Donald J. "Valuing a Growth Stock." *Jou nal of Portfolio Management,* Spring 1991, p 49-51.

Chapter 17

Valuing a Growth Stock[*]

Using PE/GROWTH ratios to develop a contrarian approach to growth stocks

Donald J. Peters
Vice President
T. Rowe Price Associates

Many researchers have discovered that low PE stocks earn superior returns relative to high PE stocks. The purpose of this article is to apply the basic concepts of the low PE studies to a growth stock universe in a systematic manner. Although many mutual funds and money managers follow a "growth" stock investment style, there is no generally accepted definition of a growth stock or much research directly addressing this area. I develop here a method of valuing a growth stock by using PE/GROWTH ratios.

The PE/GROWTH Ratio

Valuing a growth stock is not simple. The pricing of some stocks in this universe sometimes seems to defy rational thought. Traditional ratio measures such as PEs or price-to-cash flow are generally more applicable for mature companies, as these tools have limitations when used for growth stocks.

Consider an example. There are two companies in the same industry with $500 million in sales and $25 million in net income. They both pay no dividends and have identical capital structures, and all costs are variable. The only difference between them is that one is growing at 8% (assume that this is the same rate as the market), while the other is growing at 12%. In five years, the slower-growing one will have about $735 million in sales and earn $37 million. The faster-growing company will have $881 million in sales and $44 million in net income (19% more income than the other). If the slower-growing company is currently valued at the market PE multiple, what multiple should the faster-growing one have?

It is clear that the faster-growing one's PE multiple should be at least equal to the other's. In addition, one knows from the context of a dividend discount model that a stock's PE is a function of its growth rate.

The author thanks Bruce E. Terker and John J. Geewax for helpful comments and Steve Handleman, Tina Orr, and Joni Zee for computational assistance.

Reprinted with permission from *The Journal of Portfolio Management,* Spring 1991, pgs. 49-51.

Accordingly, our faster-growing company should have a PE greater than the slower-growing one. But how much of a premium is appropriate to value the company fairly?

PEs are a helpful and widely used tool in determining the relative valuation of stocks. The more homogeneous the stocks being analyzed, the easier it is to make comparisons using this ratio. However, our example shows one of the difficulties of using PEs in a heterogeneous situation.

One approach to this problem is the PE/GROWTH ratio: a stock's price to earnings ratio using trailing EPS divided by its mean long-term growth forecast. The PE/GROWTH ratio is used to get some measure of comparability for stocks growing at different rates. It is a valuation benchmark that puts a stock's PE in a per unit growth framework.

The ratio allows a comparison among growth stocks and the average growth stock. It helps analysts evaluate whether a stock is priced in accordance with others with similar characteristics. If the average growth stock has a PE/GROWTH ratio of 1, for example, the growth stocks in a particular industry have a ratio of 0.75, and a particular stock in this industry has a ratio of 1.5, one can conclude that the stock has a relatively high valuation, and much is expected of the company.

A Hypothesis Regarding Growth Stocks

I do not have an elegant answer to the difficult question of valuing growth stocks, but I do test a hypothesis about growth stocks using PE/GROWTH ratios. The hypothesis is that some growth stocks tend to get overvalued and subsequently underperform other growth stocks.

One way to view this assumption is in the context of a decision tree where several nodes reflect various future alternatives with their associated probabilities, and an estimated stock price is based on the events materializ-

ing. High-expectation growth stocks or those with high PE/GROWTH ratios seem to follow the upper path of the pricing tree. That is the pricing of these stocks reflects several o' many good alternatives coming to fruition Low PE/GROWTH stocks follow the lowe: paths, and their prices reflect that few goo alternatives occur.

Methodology

My study looks at a growth stock universe fo thirty quarterly periods. It starts with the quarter beginning 1 January 1982 and end: on 30 June 1989. This universe was selectee to address some real-world concerns regard ing implementation of a strategy to exploi any potential anomaly.

There are many ways to define a growth stock. This study defines one as a compan) that has long-term growth forecasts signifi cantly greater than the average growth ir nominal GNP for 1980-1989 (about 8%) Specifically, mean IBES long-term growth forecasts of 12% or more were used.

Liquidity was also considered by requiring at least $50 million in sales and coverage by at least two analysts. (The sales criterion wa: changed in 1984 to adjust for inflation.) A weak financial quality test (to screen ou bankruptcy candidates) was provided by re quiring companies to have positive trailing twelve-month earnings before extraordinar) items and discontinued operations. The back testing ended in 1981 because of limitation with IBES growth forecasts prior to that time

These screens resulted in several hundrec stocks per quarter in the universe. In sum mary, the growth stock universe include: stocks passing the following screen:

1. Forecasted growth of greater than or equa to 12%.

2. At least 2 growth forecasts.

3. Sales of at least $50 million for the pre vious year ($40 million beginning June 1984).

4. Positive earnings for the last four quarters.
5. Pricing history for the quarter.

The study avoids look-ahead bias by using only financial information that was publicly available at the beginning of the quarter. For example, in a quarter starting on 1 October, a company's earnings from the June quarter and the three previous quarters were used to compute its PE ratio. It also avoids survivorship bias; the backtesting reflects all companies that were public at the time for each respective period. Note that this work may not adequately reflect the impact of takeovers because it requires a pricing history for the entire quarter.

Tests and Results

Tests follow a naive strategy of sorting the growth universe into deciles according to PE/GROWTH ratios. A more sophisticated method for future studies may be to regress returns on forecasted growth, PEs, or other relevant factors.

Portfolios were equally weighted and rebalanced quarterly. The compounded returns of an invested $1 are displayed in Exhibit 1. (This study does not consider transaction costs.) The Exhibit segregates the final two and a half-year subperiod to determine whether this phenomenon was associated only with the early stages of the 1980s bull market.

There is a fairly direct relationship between portfolios with low PE/GROWTH ratios and higher relative returns. The portfolio with the lowest PE/GROWTH stocks materially outperforms an indexing strategy and the other deciles. The high PE/GROWTH portfolios substantially underperform both the S&P 500 and the average growth stock.

The difference in the compounded returns between the lowest and highest PE/GROWTH portfolios is striking. One dollar would have grown to $15.36 in the lowest expectation portfolio compared to $1.38 in the highest. These results are not attributable to the early stages of the 1980s bull market. The returns for the post-1987 period are similar; in the lowest portfolio a dollar grew to $1.59 compared to $1.14 for the highest portfolio.

The superior performance of the lowest PE/GROWTH portfolios is consistent. The low-

Exhibit 1 Effect of $1 Invested in PE/GROWTH Ratio Decile Portfolios

Decile	Compounded Returns (1982-June 1989)	Compounded Returns (1987-June 1989)
1	15.36	1.59
2	6.69	1.42
3	4.77	1.45
4	3.66	1.28
5	3.00	1.32
6	2.02	1.25
7	1.82	1.28
8	1.55	1.30
9	1.31	1.12
10	1.38	1.14
Average Growth Stock	3.04	1.31
S&P 500	3.56	1.43

Portfolios with the lowest PE/GROWTH ratios are listed first.

est expectation portfolio outperformed the average growth stock in twenty-six of the thirty quarters considered and outperformed the S&P twenty-one times. The portfolio with the next smallest ratio beat the average growth stock twenty-five times and the S&P twenty-two times.

The returns of the highest PE/GROWTH portfolios are dramatically different. The highest PE/GROWTH portfolio outperformed the average growth stock four times in the thirty quarters and the S&P 500 eight times. The next highest portfolio outperforms both the average and the S&P only four times.

Conclusion

The PE/GROWTH ratio is a valuable tool in the evaluation of growth stocks. It helps to gauge how much growth is already priced into a stock and is a benchmark for comparing stocks growing at different rates. Ease of use is an important positive factor with the PE/GROWTH ratio. The more easily one can calculate the ratio, the more likely it is to be used.

My results support a contrarian approach to growth stock investing: "Discounted" growth stocks outperform those with high expectations. The evidence implies that, on average, today's high fliers tend to crash and burn.

Chapter 18

An Evaluation of Alternative Proxies for the Market's Assessment of Unexpected Earnings*

Lawrence D. Brown, Ph.D.
Samuel P. Carpen Professor of Accounting
Jacobs Management Center, State University of New York at Buffalo

Robert L. Hagerman, Ph.D.
Professor of Accounting and Finance
State University of New York at Buffalo

Paul A. Griffin, Ph.D.
Professor of Accounting and Management
University of California-Davis

Mark E. Zmijewski, Ph.D.
Professor of Accounting
Graduate School of Business, University of Chicago

This study examines the association between abnormal returns and five alternative proxies for the market's assessment of unexpected quarterly earnings. We examine the role that measurement error potentially has in multiple regression tests of abnormal returns (occurring around the time of earnings announcements) on an unexpected earnings proxy and other non-earnings variables. The results indicate a potential measurement error interpretation of such multiple regression tests. We examine three procedures which reduce, to an unknown degree, the measurement error problem. Our procedures appear to be more (less) effective at reducing measurement error for small (large) firms and recent (non-recent) forecasts.

* The authors acknowledge comments on earlier versions from workshop participants at the University of California at Berkeley, University of Chicago, Columbia University, Duke University, University of Iowa, University of Michigan, New York University, University of North Carolina at Chapel Hill, Northwestern University, Purdue University, University of Rochester, State University of New York at Buffalo, and the University of Southern California. We extend special thanks to R. Castanias II, A. Christie, R. Holthausen, W. Landsman, R. Leftwich, T. Lys, P. O'Brien, R. Watts, and an anonymous reviewer for advice on various topics.

Reprinted with permission from *Journal of Accounting and Economics,* Vol. 9, 1987, pgs. 159-193.
© 1987, North-Holland Publishing Company

1. Introduction

Numerous studies have shown that stock market prices respond to the sign and magnitude of earnings that are unexpected by the market.[1] These studies use a proxy for the market's assessment of unexpected earnings ("market unexpected earnings") that is conditioned on a particular earnings forecast. If the unexpected earnings proxy measures the market's assessment with error, the results can, in certain experimental designs, lead to incorrect inferences. This issue is potentially important when the researcher attempts to hold constant the effects of unexpected earnings while testing hypotheses for other financial variables (e.g., accounting changes, non-earnings information). In tests of this type, any correlation between the measurement error in the unexpected earnings proxy and the other financial variables results in biased statistics.[2]

This study examines the association between abnormal (stock) returns and alternative proxies for market unexpected earnings and the significance of the measurement error in those unexpected earnings proxies. Three procedures are used to detect and reduce the measurement error effects. Daily security returns, assumed to impound the market's knowledge of earnings, are used to investigate unexpected earnings from five one-quarter-ahead expectation models. Four of the expectation models are based on the time series of quarterly earnings numbers; the fifth consists of quarterly earnings forecasts made by security analysts.[3]

The empirical analysis proceeds in five stages. First, we examine five alternative measures of unexpected earnings individually (i.e., five alternative unexpected earnings proxies). This allows us to link our findings with those of prior studies using a single proxy. Second, we assess the incremental explanatory power of a single unexpected earnings proxy vis-a-vis a combination of proxies that includes the single proxy; the emphasis is on combining alternative unexpected earn-

ings proxies to detect and reduce measurement error. Third, we examine factors that might explain differences in measurement error across firms. Fourth, we examine the effects of using the stock return prior to the abnormal return holding period to control for measurement error. Finally, we examine the effects of using instrumental variable procedures to reduce measurement error.

The results indicate that no single proxy consistently dominates in the simple association (e.g., regression) tests across the various abnormal return holding periods we examine. However, unexpected earnings that are based on financial analysts' earnings forecasts, in general, explain abnormal returns better than other proxies. Further, the results indicate a significant amount of measurement error in all earnings proxies and that our procedures may be useful for reducing (to an unknown degree) measurement error, especially for small firms and recent forecasts. Nevertheless, while our procedures do appear to mitigate the measurement error problem, we are unable to determine whether they produce reliable parameter estimates in a multiple regression research design (i.e., regressing abnormal returns on unexpected earnings and one or more additional non-earnings explanatory variables).

Overall, our results indicate that measurement error is a significant problem for the researcher using this multiple regression research design. Researchers must interpret the coefficients for the additional explanatory variables conditional on an assumed correlation between the additional variables and the measurement error in the unexpected earnings proxy variable. A non-zero correlation potentially results in a measurement error interpretation of the coefficients for the additional explanatory variables.

The paper is organized as follows. Section 2 describes the underlying empirical model and discusses the research design incorporating the potential effects of measurement error. The data, the forecasting models, and the variables for stock price adjustment and un-expected earnings are described and defined in Section 3. Section 4 presents and discusses the results. Section 5 contains a summary and conclusions.

2. The Underlying Model, Measurement Error, and Empirical Tests

2.1 The Model

The model below is used to show the effects of measurement error in a specific context. Although the model that underlies the empirical tests is consistent with models underlying many tests of association between stock price changes and unexpected earnings (as well as multiple regression models incorporating other financial variables), it is not the only specification. For alternative specifications, see Christie (1985), Miller and Rock (1985), and Watts and Zimmerman (1986). The model states

$$R_{it} = \alpha + \beta S_{it} + \mu_{it} , \qquad (1)$$

where

R_{it} = stock return resulting from the earnings announcement of firm i at time t,

S_{it} = the market unexpected earnings associated with the earnings announcement of firm i at time t,

μ_{it} = a random error term for firm i at time t with properties $\mu_{it} \sim N(0, \sigma^2 (\mu_{it}))$ and $\sigma(\mu_{it}, \mu_{j, t+k}) = 0$ for all k and $i \neq j$.

The parameters α and β are assumed to be identical across firms and stationary over time.[4] This assumption would be valid, for example, if S_{it} equals the change in the expectations of the appropriately discounted future cash flows available to equity holders when the conditioning signal for the change in expectations is the earnings announcement. In this case, $\alpha = 0$ and $\beta = 1$. However, due to

alternative specifications of eq. (1), including alternatives regarding the stochastic processes underlying S_{it}, we are unable to form definitive expectations on the magnitude of β, except that it is expected to be positive.

2.2 Measurement Error

Since S_{it} is unobservable, a proxy variable, $P_{it\lambda}$, must be used in the empirical tests. Let

$$P_{it\lambda} = S_{it} + \varepsilon_{it\lambda} \quad \text{for}$$

$$\lambda = 1,...., P \text{ models (proxies)} \qquad (2)$$

where $\varepsilon_{it\lambda}$ is a random error term for firm i at time t with properties

$\varepsilon_{it\lambda} \sim N(0, \sigma^2 (\varepsilon_{it\lambda}))$,

$\sigma(\varepsilon_{it\lambda}, \varepsilon_{it\lambda}) = 0$ for all $i \neq j$,

$\sigma(\varepsilon_{it\lambda}, R_{j,t+k}) = 0$ for all i, j, k ,

$\sigma(\varepsilon_{it\lambda}, S_{j,t+k}) = 0$ for all i, j, k ,

$\sigma(\varepsilon_{it\lambda}, \mu_{j,t+k}) = 0$ for all i, j, k ,

Substituting $P_{it\lambda}$ for S_{it} in eq. (1) yields

$$R_{it} = \alpha' + \beta' P_{it\lambda} + \mu'_{it} . \qquad (3)$$

It is well known that α' and β' are biased and inefficient estimates of α and β [Madalla (1977)]. In particular, the slope coefficient, β, is biased towards zero and the error variance is biased upwards. The direction of the bias in α depends on the signs of β and the mean of S_{it}. If β and the mean of S_{it} have identical signs, then the bias in α is positive; if they have opposite signs, the bias is negative; and if either is equal to zero, there is no bias in α. Researchers often assume that the measurement error in the proxy is small and can be ignored, especially in simple association tests, since the tests are biased against rejecting the null hypothesis of no association. Additionally, if it can be assumed that the dependent variable R_{it} is measured without error, a reverse regression can be conducted [see Beaver et al. (1987) for an example of this technique], resulting in unbiased estimates of α and β.

The impact of measurement error in the earnings proxy is less clear and more troublesome when using a multiple regression research design, i.e., using explanatory variables in addition to market unexpected earnings to explain R_{it}. To demonstrate this point, we add another independent variable to eq. (1), Z_{it}. We assume initially that this variable is uncorrelated with R_{it}, S_{it}, and μ_{it}. Let

$$R_{it} = \alpha + \beta S_{it} + \delta Z_{it} + \mu_{it} , \tag{4}$$

where, in addition to the above assumptions,

$\sigma(Z_{it}, R_{j, t+k}) = 0$ for all i, j, k ,

$\sigma(Z_{it}, S_{j, t+k}) = 0$ for all i, j, k ,

$\sigma(Z_{it}, \mu_{j, t+k}) = 0$ for all i, j, k ,

In this special case of eq. (4), that is, in the case where Z_{it} is uncorrelated with R_{it}, S_{it}, and, μ_{it}, $\delta = 0$, and the estimates of α and β are unbiased and efficient [Madalla (1977)].

Now, suppose eq. (4) can be estimated only by using proxies for S_{it}, namely, $P_{it\lambda}$, and assume that Z_{it} is perfectly correlated with the measurement error in $P_{it\lambda}$. In this extreme situation we have

$$R_{it} = \alpha'' + \beta'' P_{it\lambda} + \delta'' Z_{it} + \mu''_{it} , \tag{5}$$

where

$\sigma(Z_{it}) \sigma(\varepsilon_{it\lambda}) = |\sigma(Z_{it}, \varepsilon_{it\lambda})|$.

In this case, the estimates of α'' and δ'' are biased estimates of α and δ, respectively, and estimates of β'' and $\sigma(\mu''_{it})$ are unbiased estimates of β and $\sigma(\mu_{it})$. The sign of the bias in δ'' (and the sign of δ'', since $\delta = 0$) depends on the sign of β and the sign of the correlation between Z_{it} and, $\varepsilon_{it\lambda}, \rho(Z_{it}, \varepsilon_{it\lambda})$; $\delta'' > 0$ if β and $\rho(Z_{it}, \varepsilon_{it\lambda})$ have opposite signs; and $\delta'' < 0$ if β and $\rho(Z_{it}, \varepsilon_{it\lambda})$ have identical signs. However, Z_{it} does not have to be perfectly correlated with the measurement error

in $P_{it\lambda}$ to result in biased estimates of δ. Bias in δ, i.e., $\delta \neq 0$, results whenever Z_{it} has a non-zero correlation with the measurement error in $P_{it\lambda}$.

Additionally, the estimates of β'' and $\sigma(\mu''_{it})$ are unbiased estimates of β and $\sigma(\mu_{it})$ in this special case because Z_{it} is perfectly correlated with the measurement error in $P_{it\lambda}$. Since Z_{it} is not, most likely, perfectly correlated with the measurement error in $P_{it\lambda}$ [i.e., $0 < \rho(Z_{it}, \varepsilon_{it\lambda}) < 1$] , estimates of β'' *and* $\sigma(\mu''_{it})$ are biased estimates of β and $\sigma(\mu_{it})$. However, this bias decreases with increases in $|\rho(Z_{it}, \varepsilon_{it\lambda})|$.

If significant measurement error exists in the unexpected earnings proxies, studies using a multiple regression approach similar to eq. (5) may report estimates for the coefficients for the additional explanatory variables (e.g., δ'') that are significantly different from zero, not because there exists a relation between the additional explanatory variable (Z_{it}) and the dependent variable (R_{it}), conditional on market unexpected earnings (S_{it}), but because these coefficients may be picking up the measurement error in the unexpected earnings proxy variable.[5] The measurement error in an unexpected earnings proxy may be mitigated if another explanatory variable is added to eq. (3) that is highly correlated with the measurement error in $P_{it\lambda}$, yet uncorrelated with R_{it}, S_{it}, and μ_{it}. We use the above result in an attempt to reduce the measurement error in estimating eq. (3).[6]

2.3 Approaches to Assessing Measurement Error

(i) *Using two or more proxy variables:* Based on the preceding model, our first approach to document the existence of significant measurement error in alternative earnings proxies is to use jointly two or more proxies to estimate eq. (1). Consider a two proxy model of the form

$$R_{it} = \gamma_0 + \gamma_1 P_{it1} + \gamma_2 P_{it2} + \eta_{it}, \qquad (6)$$

where P_{it1} and P_{it2} are alternative unexpected earnings proxies as defined in eq. (2).

The sum of the coefficients of the unexpected earnings proxy variables (i.e., $\gamma_1 + \gamma_2$) is an estimate of the coefficient for unexpected earnings. If the sum of the proxy variable coefficients increases as the number of proxy variables in the regression increases, this suggests the existence of measurement error in the unexpected earnings proxy variables and a reduction in the bias of the estimates of β and σ (μ_{it}) in eq. (1). That is, for P_{it1} and P_{it2} less than perfectly correlated,

$$\beta - (\gamma_1 + \gamma_2) < \beta - \beta', $$

and

$$\sigma(\eta_{it}) - \sigma(\mu_{it}) < \sigma(\mu'_{it}) - \sigma(\mu_{it})$$

For the above specification of eq. (6), significant coefficients for both γ_1 and γ_2 indicate significant measurement error in both proxy variables P_{it1} and P_{it2}.[7] In order to examine the extent to which the use of multiple proxy variables may reduce measurement error, we examine the incremental explanatory power (i.e., the partial F-statistic) of adding an additional proxy variable to the (ex post) 'best' proxy variable among the alternative single proxy variable regressions, of adding an additional proxy variable to the 'best' set of two proxy variables among the alternative two proxy variable regressions, of adding an additional proxy variable to the 'best' set of three proxy variables among the alternative three proxy variable regressions, and of adding an additional proxy variable to the 'best' set of four proxy variables among the alternative four proxy variable regressions.[8]

(ii) *Using variables that are ex ante correlated with measurement error:* As a second approach for assessing measurement error, we incorporate potentially relevant stock return data as an additional explanatory variable in an attempt to control for the measurement er-

ror in the unexpected earnings proxies. We add the stock return from 100 trading days before the earnings announcement through the trading day before the dependent variable (abnormal return) is measured as an additional explanatory variable to eq. (3). Since the forecasts that are used to condition unexpected earnings are typically made prior to the period over which the abnormal return is calculated (in other words we use dated forecasts to condition unexpected earnings), we assume that the measurement error in the proxy for market unexpected earnings is positively correlated with this stock return.

We assume that $\beta > 0$, and hence, estimates of β are biased downward. Thus, an indication of the degree to which measurement error is reduced is given by the increase in the coefficient for unexpected earnings from estimating eq. (5) rather than eq. (3). Additionally, since we assume $\beta > 0$ and a positive correlation between the additional explanatory variable and the measurement error in the unexpected earnings proxy variable, the coefficient for the additional explanatory variable should be negative [see the discussion of eq. (5)].

(iii) *Using instrumental variables procedures:* Finally, as a third approach for assessing measurement error, we apply an instrumental variables technique. We follow the standard procedure [see Judge et al. (1984)]; namely, we (1) regress the earnings proxy, $P_{it\lambda}$, on K instruments, I_{ikt}, $k = 1, \ldots, K$, calculating a predicted value of the proxy, and (2) regress the original dependent variable, R_{it}, on the predicted proxy from the first regression. This two-stage procedure assumes that the instrument, I_{ikt}, is correlated with the true independent variable, S_{it}, and uncorrelated with (a) residuals from the stage 1 regression, (b) the eq. (1) residuals, μ_{it}, and (c) the measurement error in the proxy, $\varepsilon_{it\lambda}$. Unfortunately, we have no guidance as to the choice of instrumental variables and it is unlikely that the required assumptions hold literally for any set of instrumental variables we could choose.

For this reason, we examine four alternative sets of instrumental variables in an attempt to gain some insights on the usefulness of this approach. For a given proxy, the four sets of instrumental variables are (a) the four unexpected earnings proxy variables that are not the dependent variable in the stage 1 regression, (b) the signs of the five unexpected earnings proxy variables, (c) a stock return variable and the instrumental variables in (a), and (d) a stock return variable and the instrumental variables in (b). The stock return instrumental variable is the stock return from 100 days before the earnings announcement (day − 100) through the day before R_{jt} is measured (day $d − 1$).[9] However, the stock return variable most likely violates the assumption (c) above.

3. Sample and Variable Definitions

3.1 Sample

Two samples are obtained for this study. The first sample includes forecasts for the five-year period 1975-1979. The second sample is a subset of firms included in the first sample, with appropriate forecasts for the year 1980. All firms included in the first (second) sample satisfy three criteria:

(1) 1960-1979 (1960-1980) quarterly earnings per share available in *Moody's Handbook of Common Stocks,*
(2) the same fiscal year end between 1960 and 1979 (1960 and 1980),
(3) covered by *The Value Line Investment Survey* between 1975 through 1979 (1975 through 1980).

The number of firms satisfying these criteria is 233 for the first (1975-1979) sample and 212 for the second (1980) sample. We require additional data for the empirical tests and thus impose two more sample selection criteria:

(4) Sufficient data on the CRSP Daily Master file to deflate unexpected earnings by price and on the CRSP Daily return file to calculate abnormal returns,
(5) *Wall Street Journal Index* availability of the quarterly earnings announcement date.

The first criterion provides a source of quarterly earnings data that is used to generate time series forecasts based on the Box and Jenkins (1976) procedure. The second ensures that a firm's quarterly earnings reflects the same degree of seasonality each year. The third criterion is imposed because a source of analysts' forecasts of quarterly earnings is needed.[10] Criteria (4) and (5) are required for calculating the earnings proxy and stock return variables. Overall, there are at most 5,508 firm/year/quarter observations, but due to data requirements, the samples for various analyses range in size from 1,611 observations (for the longest abnormal return holding period) to 4,177 observations (for the shortest abnormal return holding period).[11] These criteria bias the sample toward larger firms.[12] Thus, the extent to which our results are generalizable to all firms is unknown. Nevertheless, our criteria are similar to the assumptions that have been made in previous research, so our results should be comparable to those of other studies.

3.2 Variable Definitions

We specify the proxy for market unexpected earnings for firm i in quarter t, conditional on forecasting model λ, as

$$UE_{it\lambda} = (E_{it} − F_{it\lambda}) / D_{it},\qquad(7)$$

where

E_{it} = earnings for firm i in quarter t,
$F_{it\lambda}$ = earnings forecast for firm i in quarter t by forecasting model,
D_{it} = stock price of firm i the day before the abnormal return holding period begins (i.e., the deflator for quarter t).[13]

We use five alternative forecasting models to generate $F_{it\lambda}$. The first is the seasonal random walk (SRW) model, defined as the most recently reported earnings number for the quarter whose earnings are being forecast. For example, the earnings forecast for the first quarter of 1979 conditional upon knowledge of the first, second, third, or fourth quarter of 1978 equals the earnings number reported for the first quarter of 1978. The second to fourth models, TS1, TS2, and TS3, respectively, are the forecasting models introduced by Brown and Rozeff (1979), Foster (1977), and Watts (1975)–Griffin (1977), respectively. The fifth model (VL) is the forecast reported in *The Value Line Investment Survey* after the quarter $t - 1$ earnings announcement, but before the quarter t earnings announcement. These models have commonly been used in the forecasting literature and performed well relative to other naive benchmarks over short horizons [Hopwood et al. (1982)]. The SRW and TS models use information up to and including the latest earnings number, and hence, assume approximately a ninety-day forecast horizon. Brown et al. (1987a) report that *Value Line* forecasts are made approximately thirty-nine calendar days before the earnings announcement.

We use four alternative holding periods to generate abnormal returns (CR): a short, two-day holding period, representing the day before and the day of the earnings announcement (−1,0); a long, forty-one-day holding period, representing a return cumulated from forty days before the earnings announcement through the day of the earnings announcement (−40,0); and two intermediate holding periods, (−10,0) and (−20,0). While the holding periods are admittedly ad hoc, they include those commonly used by researchers and they enable us to examine the sensitivity of the validity of our techniques to alternative holding periods.

Eq. (8) defines firm i's excess stock return for the holding period, trading day d through day 0, as

$$CR_{it}(d,0) = \sum_{t=d}^{0} (r_{it} - \hat{a}_0 - \hat{a}_1 r_{mt}) , \qquad (8)$$

where

$CR_{it}(d,0) =$ abnormal return for firm i, cumulated from day d ($d = -1, -10, -20, -40$) prior to the earnings announcement (i.e., day 0) through day 0,

$r_{it} =$ continuously compounded return on firms i's common stock on trading day t,

$r_{mt} =$ continuously compounded return on the CRSP value weighted market index on trading day t,

$\hat{a}_0, \hat{a}_1 =$ ordinary least squares regression parameters.[14]

4. Results

4.1 Comparison of Individual Proxies

Exhibit 1 presents individual analyses of the five unexpected earnings proxies, SRW, TS1, TS2, TS3, and VL. For each CR(d,0) calculation, the sample is constrained so that each company's *Value Line* report date occurs before the first day of the cumulation (day d) period. Thus, the longer the cumulation period, the fewer the number of observations in the sample. This constraint achieves a consistency between the holding period and the market's presumed knowledge of the *Value Line* forecast, and it enables researchers requiring measures of earnings expectations to ensure that the proxy variables they utilize are available to the market as of the start of the presumed holding period.

Panel A reports the weighted average excess (portfolio) returns (stated in percentages) from an investment strategy of (1) buying long (selling short) on the first day of the holding period (day d) common stock with positive (negative) unexpected earnings, $UE_{it\lambda}$, and (2) holding the portfolio of firms through the end of the earnings an-

Exhibit 1   Comparison of Individual Proxy Variables for Unexpected Earnings Based on Weighted Portfolio Excess Stock Returns and Correlations with Excess Stock Returns

Cumulative residuals[a]	Number of obs.[b]	Unexpected earnings $(UE_{it\lambda})$[c]				
		SRW	TS1	TS2	TS3	VL
Panel A. Weighted portfolio percentage abnormal returns[d]						
CR(−1,0)	4,177	1.174	1.470	1.422	1.478	1.666
CR(−10,0)	3,431	1.392	1.947	1.964	2.058	2.202
CR(−20,0)	2,931	1.334	1.669	2.027	2.122	2.006
CR(−40,0)	1,611	1.137	1.542	1.726	2.137	2.346
Panel B. Pearson correlations between CR_{it} (d,0) and $UE_{it\lambda}$						
CR(−1,0)	4,177	0.210	0.252	0.234	0.243	0.272
CR(−10,0)	3,431	0.136	0.180	0.177	0.182	0.198
CR(−20,0)	2,931	0.101	0.123	0.139	0.144	0.136
CR(−40,0)	1,611	0.076	0.093	0.093	0.110	0.117
Panel C. Rank correlations between CR_{it} (d,0) and $UE_{it\lambda}$						
CR(−1,0)	4,177	0.210	0.286	0.302	0.281	0.317
CR(−10,0)	3,431	0.144	0.202	0.234	0.207	0.227
CR(−20,0)	2,931	0.177	0.154	0.176	0.180	0.175
CR(−40,0)	1,611	0.097	0.124	0.155	0.149	0.137

[a] Cumulative residual, $CR(d,0)$, is the cumulated market model residual, cumulated from d days before the earnings announcement date through the earnings announcement date (day 0).

[b] Number of observations available for the test. The number of observations decreases as the cumulation period increases because an observation is constrained so that each observation's *Value Line* report date occurs before the first day of the cumulation period, d.

[c] Unexpected earnings for firm *i*, in quarter *t*, conditional on forecasting model λ is denoted as $UE_{it\lambda}$. There are five unexpected earnings proxy variables. SRW denotes the seasonal random walk forecasting model, TS1 the Brown and Rozeff (1979) model, TS2 the Foster (1977) model, TS3 the Watts (1975)–Griffin (1977) model, and VL the forecast in *The Value Line Investment Survey*.

[d] Weighted portfolio abnormal returns in percentages, conditional on forecasting model λ, are calculated as

$$\sum_{i=1}^{N} CR_{it}(d,0) \left[UE_{it\lambda} \Big/ \sum_{j=1}^{N} |UE_{jt\lambda}| \right]$$

where $CR_{it}(d,0)$ is the cumulative residual for firm *i* in quarter *t*, *N* the number of observations, and $|\cdot|$ the absolute value operator.

nouncement date (day 0). The weighted abnormal returns (for a sample of *N* observations) are calculated as follows:

$$\sum_{i=1}^{N} CR_{it}(d,0) \left[UE_{it\lambda} \Big/ \sum_{j=1}^{N} |UE_{jt\lambda}| \right],$$

where $|\cdot|$ is the absolute value operator.

The results in panel A indicate that SRW has the lowest abnormal return in every holding period. VL has the highest abnormal return for the (−1,0), (−10,0), and (−40,0) hold-

ing periods. However, TS2 and TS3 have slightly higher abnormal returns than VL for the (−20,0) holding period. Panels B and C, respectively, present pairwise Pearson and rank correlation coefficients between CR_{it} and $UE_{it\lambda}$. Consistent with panel A, VL has the highest correlation for the (−1,0) holding period.

In sum, proxies for unexpected earnings based on analysts' forecasts (VL) have the highest association with abnormal returns for one of the four holding periods. One of the time series models (SRW) is the worst proxy in that it consistently exhibits the poorest measure of association. Although not reported, weighted return measures which are based on the rank of the unexpected earnings measures are qualitatively identical. Also, tests based on unweighted abnormal returns display a similar pattern.[15]

4.2 Multiple Earnings Proxies

Exhibit 2 summarizes the results of using multiple unexpected earnings proxies in explaining abnormal returns for various holding periods. More specifically, it reports an adjusted R-square and the sum of cross-sectional regression coefficients (sum of $\gamma\lambda$) for the regression of abnomal returns on P $(P = 1, \ldots, 5)$ unexpected earnings proxy variable(s):

$$CR_{it}(d,0) = \gamma_0 + \sum_{\lambda=1}^{P} \gamma_\lambda \, UE_{it\lambda} + error. \qquad (9)$$

Because we estimate regression eq. (9) for all combinations of proxies, the results are presented in five panels. Panel A reports the regressions with one proxy variable in eq. (9) (five regressions for each of the four holding periods), panel B with two proxy variables (ten regressions for each of four holding periods), panel C with three proxy variables (ten regressions for each of the four holding periods), panel D with four proxy variables (five regressions for each of four holding periods), and panel E with five proxy variables (one regression for each of four holding periods). The principal findings from these analyses follow.

First, the $\gamma\lambda$ coefficient values for the single proxy variable forms of eq. (9), that is, the twenty regressions in panel A, are all highly significant with t-statistics significant at less than the 0.001 probability level. These results essentially confirm the results in Exhibit 1 and in the extant literature.

Second, the sum of coefficients tends to increase and the adjusted R-squares always decrease as the holding period for the regressions increases. These results are consistent

with the measurement error discussion in Section 2. The earnings forecasts we use are dated in that the forecast is made before the first day of the holding period and, as such, are not conditioned on the earnings related information that is released between the forecast date and the day before the holding period begins $(d + 1)$. Increasing the holding period reduces the datedness of the earnings forecast which should result in an increase in the estimate of β. Decreases in the adjusted R-squares over longer holding periods are consistent with the hypothesis that abnormal returns with longer holding periods contain more variation due to factors unrelated to the firm's earnings.[16]

Third, Exhibit 2 shows that the sum of $\gamma\lambda$ coefficients generally increases when additional proxies are added to regression eq. (9). While the increase in the sum of coefficients with respect to holding period is seldom monotonic, an examination of the table reveals that the sum of coefficients for the three longer holding periods (−10,0), (−20,0), and (−40,0) is always greater than it is for the shortest holding period (−1,0).

The following results pertain to the (−1,0) holding period. The highest sums of coefficients in panels A through E are 0.6985 (panel A, #5, VL), 0.7769 (panel B, #12, TS2, VL), 0.7868 (panel C, #24, TS2, VL, SRW), 0.7889 (panel D, #30, TS2, SRW, TS3, VL), and 0.7890 (panel E, #31, all five models), respectively; the lowest sum of coefficients in panels A through E are 0.3170 (panel A, #1, SRW), 0.4588 (panel B, #10, TS2, TS3), 0.4906 (panel C, #16, TS1, TS2, TS3), 0.5198 (panel D, #26, TS1, TS2, TS3, SRW), and 0.7890 (panel E, #31, all five models), respectively.

As discussed in Section 2.3, a finding that the sum of $\gamma\lambda$ coefficients increases when additional proxies are included in regression eq. (9) suggests that the proxy variables contain measurement error and the regressions with two or more proxy variables reduce (to an

Exhibit 2 Summary of Cross-Sectional Regressions Between Cumulative Residuals and One or More Unexpected Earnings Proxy Variable(s)

Regression: $CR_{it}(d,0) = \gamma_0 + \sum_{\lambda=1}^{P} \gamma_\lambda\, UE_{it\lambda} + error.$ [a]

	Dependent variable: Cumulative residual ($CR_{it}(d,0)$)							
	$CR_{it}(-1,0)$		$CR_{it}(-10,0)$		$CR_{it}(-20,0)$		$CR_{it}(-40,0)$	
Regression	4,177 Observations [b]		3,431 Observations		2,931 Observations		1,611 Observations	
Independent variable(s) [c]	Adjusted R-Square	Sum of Coeff. [d]	Adjusted R-Square	Sum of Coeff.	Adjusted R-Square	Sum of Coeff.	Adjusted R-Square	Sum of Coeff.
No.								
Panel A. Regression with one earnings proxy (P = 1)								
1. SRW	0.0437	0.3170	0.0182	0.3822	0.0099	0.3911	0.0044	0.3507
2. TS1	0.0631	0.4740	0.0321	0.6299	0.0149	0.6140	0.0081	0.6230
3. TS2	0.0547	0.3859	0.0311	0.5577	0.0189	0.6027	0.0080	0.5473
4. TS3	0.0590	0.4220	0.0329	0.5866	0.0205	0.6523	0.0115	0.6613
5. VL	0.0738	0.6985	0.0388	0.9335	0.0183	0.8927	0.0131	1.0096
Panel B. Regression with one earnings proxy (P = 2)								
6. TS1, TS2	0.0660	0.4871	0.0346	0.6565	0.0189	0.6505	0.0083	0.6444
7. TS1, TS3	0.0649	0.4809	0.0340	0.6372	0.0203	0.6279	0.0109	0.6433
8. TS1, SRW	0.0674	0.5029	0.0328	0.6555	0.0157	0.6531	0.0082	0.6715
9. TS1, VL	0.0886	0.7680	0.0445	0.9990	0.0208	0.9671	0.0133	1.0670
10. TS2, TS3	0.0644	0.4588	0.0360	0.6473	0.0223	0.7178	0.0112	0.7010
11. TS2, SRW	0.0675	0.4826	0.0341	0.6408	0.0203	0.6891	0.0089	0.6630
12. TS2, VL	0.0905	0.7769	0.0472	1.0239	0.0252	1.0185	0.0147	1.1259
13. TS3, SRW	0.0648	0.4662	0.0336	0.6200	0.0206	0.6828	0.0112	0.7067
14. TS3, VL	0.0891	0.7639	0.0463	0.9989	0.0251	0.9955	0.0156	1.1015
15. VL, SRW	0.0826	0.7335	0.0409	0.9666	0.0199	0.9383	0.0128	1.0294

(continued)

Panel C. Regressions with three earnings proxies (P= 3)

16.	TS1, TS2, TS3	0.0669	0.4906	0.0359	0.6599	0.0233	0.6585	0.0109	0.6615
17.	TS1, TS2, SRW	0.0709	0.5193	0.0354	0.6845	0.0199	0.6928	0.0085	0.7000
18.	TS1, TS2, VL	0.0918	0.7837	0.0470	1.0260	0.0251	1.0119	0.0142	1.1251
19.	TS1, TS3, SRW	0.0684	0.5058	0.0343	0.6568	0.0205	0.6535	0.0107	0.6809
20.	TS1, TS3, VL	0.0899	0.7715	0.0460	1.0005	0.0259	0.9722	0.0158	1.0718
21.	TS1, VL, SRW	0.0898	0.7718	0.0444	1.0032	0.0210	0.9770	0.0128	1.0713
22.	TS2, TS3, SRW	0.0702	0.5038	0.0366	0.6776	0.0223	0.7441	0.0109	0.7442
23.	TS2, TS3, VL	0.0924	0.7834	0.0480	1.0272	0.0262	1.0294	0.0152	1.1271
24.	TS2, VL, SRW	0.0933	0.7868	0.0472	1.0309	0.0252	1.0289	0.0142	1.1305
25.	TS3, VL, SRW	0.0903	0.7687	0.0461	1.0018	0.0248	0.9988	0.0150	1.1018

Panel D. Regressions with four earnings proxies (P = 4)

26.	TS1, TS2, TS3, SRW	0.0711	0.5198	0.0363	0.6827	0.0236	0.6884	0.0109	0.7055
27.	TS1, TS2, TS3, VL	0.0923	0.7845	0.0480	1.0246	0.0291	1.0111	0.0164	1.1243
28.	TS1, TS2, VL, SRW	0.0934	0.7888	0.0470	1.0311	0.0253	1.0232	0.0138	1.1316
29.	TS1, SRW, TS3, VL	0.0908	0.7743	0.0458	1.0027	0.0257	0.9772	0.0152	1.0737
30.	TS2, SRW, TS3, VL	0.0938	0.7889	0.0478	1.0299	0.0259	1.0321	0.0146	1.1274

Panel E. Regressions with five earnings proxies (TS1, TS2, TS3, SRW, VL) (P = 5)

31.	All Models	0.0936	0.7890	0.0478	1.0281	0.0290	1.0178	0.0158	1.1280

a $CR_{it}(d,0)$ is the cumulative residual for firm i in quarter t. It is calculated as the cumulated market model residual, cumulated from d days before the earnings announcement date through the earnings announcement date (day 0). UE_{itA} is the unexpected earnings proxy for firm i, in quarter t, conditional on forecasting model λ (see note c). γ_0 is the estimated regression intercept coefficient. $\gamma\lambda$ is the estimated regression coefficient for UE_{itA}.

b Number of observations available for the test. The number of observations decreases as the cumulation period increases because an observation is constrained so that each observation's Value Line report date occurs before the first day of the cumulation period, d.

c The independent variable(s) in the regressions are proxy variables for unexpected earnings. SRW indicates that the unexpected earnings proxy is calculated conditional on the seasonal random walk forecasting model, TS1 the Brown and Rozeff (1979) model, TS2 the Foster (1977) model, TS3 the Watts (1975)–Griffin (1977) model, and VL the forecast in The Value Line Investment Survey.

d Sum of coeff. is the sum of the coefficients for the proxy variables in the regression, i.e., the sum of $\gamma\lambda$. Since all independent variables are proxy variables for unexpected earnings, the sum of the coefficients represents the estimated coefficient for unexpected earnings. For the single proxy variable regressions (regressions 1 through 5), the sum of coefficients is the coefficient for the single proxy variable.

unknown degree) the measurement error. To examine the extent to which the use of multiple proxy variables reduces (ex post) measurement error, we examine the incremental explanatory power (i.e., the partial F-statistic) of adding an additional proxy variable to the (ex post) 'best' proxy variable among the alternative single proxy variable regressions, of adding an additional proxy variable to the 'best' set of two proxy variable regressions, and so on. Assuming that eq. (1) is the true model for R_{it}, a significant partial F-statistic suggests the existence of measurement error and that our procedure of combining earnings proxies reduces (to an unknown degree) measurement error.

Exhibit 3 presents a bar graph of the maximum adjusted R-squares from Exhibit 2 for a given number of proxy variables for each of the four holding periods. For example, for the $(-1,0)$ holding period, the proxy variables represented by the bar graph are regressions #5 (VL), #12 (TS2, VL), #24 (TS2, VL, SRW), #30 (TS2, SRW, TS3, VL), and #31 (all five models) for the regressions with one through five proxy variables, respectively. We first examine the t-statistic of TS2 in regression #12 to ascertain whether addition of a

second proxy variable significantly reduces measurement error. Finding a significant t-statistic, we conclude that a two proxy variable equation reduces measurement error in this case. Similarly, we examine the t-statistic of SRW in regression #24, of TS3 in regression #30, and of TS1 in regression #31, respectively, to ascertain whether addition of a third, fourth, and fifth explanatory variable to a set of two, three, and four explanatory variables significantly reduces measurement error. The incremental t-statistics of SRW and TS3 in regressions #24 and #30 were significant, but the t-statistic of TS1 in equation #31 was not significant.

The bar graph in Exhibit 3 representing the four proxy variable equation for the $(-1,0)$ holding period is designated by an asterisk to indicate that the four variable set appears to be (ex post) 'best' for this holding period. Similar analyses are conducted for the longest holding period $(-40,0)$ and the two intermediate holding periods $(-10,0)$ and $(-20,0)$. The 'best' set of proxy variable equations for these holding periods is also represented by an asterisk in Exhibit 3. Comparing the longest holding period $(-40,0)$ with the shortest holding period $(-1,0)$, it is evident that our procedure is more successful for reducing measurement error for the shortest holding period. More specifically, the 'best' set of proxy variable equations for the shortest holding period is represented by four proxy variables, while it is represented by two proxy variables for the longest holding period.

In summary, the results presented in Exhibits 2 and 3 suggest that our procedures are more effective for reducing measurement error for shorter abnormal return holding periods than they are for reducing measurement error for the longest $(-40,0)$ holding period. We cannot distinguish between the explanations that our procedure is not sufficiently powerful for detecting measurement error over the longest $(-40,0)$ holding period and that measurement error is not a significant problem in our sample for the longest holding

Exhibit 3 Maximum Adjusted *R*-squares Across Number of Proxy Variables— Exhibit 2 Regression

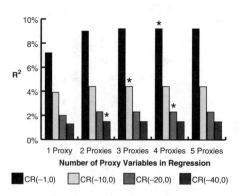

Number of Proxy Variables in Regression

■ CR(–1,0) ☐ CR(–10,0) ▨ CR(–20,0) ■ CR(–40,0)

period. However, for shorter holding periods, our results indicate that measurement error is a significant problem for the researcher using a multiple regression research design.

While we have demonstrated an increase in the explanatory power of the relation between CR_{it} and $UE_{it\lambda}$ by using multiple proxies for unexpected earnings—which we attribute in part to the reduction of the error in measuring the market's expectation of unexpected earnings—we realize that we do not purge all the error, and thus, the coefficient values that are estimated do not reveal the magnitude of the 'true' β implicit in eq. (1). Also, recall that the β coefficients are based on a cross-sectional estimation procedure, a technique that makes the simplifying assumption that the coefficient is cross-sectionally invariant.

4.3 Effects of Firm Size

Measurement error in unexpected earnings may differ on the basis of firm characteristics. Larger firms are subject to closer scrutiny by equity analysts [e.g., Advisory Committee on Corporate Disclosure (1977)] and earnings information of large firms generally is available earlier to the market. For large firms, the market obtains information from primary and secondary sources on a relatively continuous basis. On the other hand, for small firms, new information tends to be released less frequently, for example, at the time of earnings announcements.

In order to examine whether or not the results differ on the basis of firm size (i.e., the market value of equity measured two days before the earnings announcement), we segment our sample into four quartiles conditional on firm size, and present, in Exhibit 4, the results for the smallest and the largest quartiles for the shortest (−1,0) and longest (−40,0) holding periods. For the short holding period, (−1,0), small firms have equity with a market value of less than $274 million and large firms have equity with a market value of more than $1,269 million; for the long holding period, (−40,0), small firms have equity with a market value of less than $328 million and large firms have equity with a market value of more than $1,356 million. Consistent with the format of Exhibit 2, panel A of Exhibit 4 summarizes regressions with one proxy, panel B with two proxies, etc. In a manner similar to Exhibit 3, Exhibit 5 presents a bar graph of the maximum adjusted R-squares from Exhibit 4 for a given number of proxy variables (one to five) for the (−1,0) and (−40,0) holding period for the small and large firms. The principal results follow.

First, the γ_1 coefficient values for the single variable forms of eq. (9) are highly significant for the small firms for both the shortest and longest holding periods. However, they are not always significant for the large firms. The adjusted R-squares are actually negative in two instances for the large firms for the longest holding period. Second, the sum of the $\gamma\lambda$ coefficients always increases and the adjusted R-squares always decrease as the holding period increases for the small firms. Such is not the case, however, for the large firms. Third, the partitioning of the sample on firm size appears to have opposite effects for *Value Line* and the Box-Jenkins time series conditioned proxies. For the shortest (longest) holding period, the Box-Jenkins time series models (see regressions #2 through #4) are larger (smaller) for small firms than for large firms, while the opposite is observed for γ_1 (see regression #5). Fourth, the sum of the $\gamma\lambda$ coefficients generally increases when additional proxy variables are added to eq. (9), regardless of firm size or length of holding period.

Similar to Exhibit 3, the asterisks for Exhibit 5 designate the N proxy variable set that is (ex post) 'best' for the particular firm size/holding period. Exhibit 5 reveals that our procedures appear to be more effective at reducing measurement error for small than for large firms and for short than for long holding periods. More spe-

Exhibit 4 Summary of Cross-Sectional Regressions Between Cumulative Residuals and One or More Unexpected Earnings Proxy Variable(s), Comparison of Large and Small Firms

Regression: $CR_{it}(d,0) = \gamma_0 + \sum_{\lambda=1}^{P} \gamma_\lambda \, UE_{it\lambda} + error.$ [a]

Dependent variable: Cumulative residual ($CR_{it}(d,0)$)

| No. | Independent variable(s) [c] | $CR_{it}(-1,0)$ | | | | $CR_{it}(-40,0)$ | | | |
| | | 1,044 Small Firms | | 1,044 Large Firms | | 403 Small Firms | | 403 large firms | |
		Adjusted R-Square [b]	Sum of Coeff. [d]	Adjusted R-Square	Sum of Coeff.	Adjusted R-Square	Sum of Coeff.	Adjusted R-Square	Sum of Coeff.
		Panel A. Regression with one earnings proxy (P = 1)							
1.	SRW	0.0560	0.3220	0.0035	0.1393	0.0108	0.4464	-0.0025	-0.0449
2.	TS1	0.0810	0.4659	0.0146	0.3192	0.0108	0.6015	0.0054	1.1356
3.	TS2	0.0632	0.3583	0.0116	0.2527	0.0071	0.4325	0.0176	1.6575
4.	TS3	0.0880	0.4451	0.0146	0.3142	0.0218	0.7682	0.0049	1.0106
5.	VL	0.0945	0.6416	0.0383	0.7824	0.0252	1.0711	-0.0010	0.5796
		Panel B. Regression with one earnings proxy (P = 2)							
6.	TS1, TS2	0.0828	0.4789	0.0138	0.3205	0.0084	0.6052	0.0164	1.4482
7.	TS1, TS3	0.0904	0.4834	0.0144	0.3302	0.0215	0.6832	0.0031	1.1428
8.	TS1, SRW	0.0873	0.5055	0.0150	0.3079	0.0138	0.7411	0.0121	1.1704
9.	TS1, VL	0.1158	0.7391	0.0383	0.8036	0.0234	1.1166	0.0030	1.0511
10.	TS2, TS3	0.0894	0.4674	0.0139	0.3177	0.0194	0.7532	0.0156	1.5445
11.	TS2, SRW	0.0843	0.4840	0.0107	0.2568	0.0137	0.7127	0.0207	1.3563
12.	TS2, VL	0.1162	0.7468	0.0384	0.8043	0.0246	1.1711	0.0153	0.5051
13.	TS3, SRW	0.0938	0.4939	0.0151	0.3017	0.0230	0.8971	0.0093	0.9098
14.	TS3, VL	0.1239	0.7445	0.0389	0.8147	0.0290	1.2070	0.0024	0.9517
15.	VL, SRW	0.1071	0.6996	0.0376	0.7749	0.0258	1.1532	-0.0028	0.5279

(continued)

Panel C. Regressions with three earnings proxies (P = 3)

16.	TS1, TS2, TS3	0.0903	0.4897	0.0134	0.3303	0.0195	0.6936	0.0140	1.4522
17.	TS1, TS2, SRW	0.0901	0.5239	0.0141	0.3087	0.0119	0.7594	0.0186	1.4242
18.	TS1, TS2, VL	0.1187	0.7589	0.0376	0.8060	0.0224	1.1703	0.0140	1.4651
19.	TS1, TS3, SRW	0.0944	0.5148	0.0153	0.3208	0.0238	0.8114	0.0101	1.1835
20.	TS1, TS3, VL	0.1232	0.7475	0.0381	0.8157	0.0317	1.1512	0.0007	1.0446
21.	TS1, VL, SRW	0.1175	0.7495	0.0396	0.7986	0.0235	1.1698	0.0097	1.2494
22.	TS2, TS3, SRW	0.0955	0.5186	0.0142	0.3042	0.0206	0.8853	0.0188	1.4271
23.	TS2, TS3, VL	0.1248	0.7612	0.0380	0.8147	0.0266	1.1952	0.0132	1.4961
24.	TS2, VL, SRW	0.1210	0.7698	0.0387	0.7957	0.0247	1.2341	0.0185	1.5271
25.	TS3, VL, SRW	0.1246	0.7543	0.0411	0.8159	0.0280	1.2504	0.0070	1.0313

Panel D. Regressions with four earnings proxies (P = 4)

26.	TS1, TS2, TS3, SRW	0.0950	0.5260	0.0144	0.3203	0.0266	0.8406	0.0163	1.4311
27.	TS1, TS2, TS3, VL	0.1240	0.7602	0.0372	0.8161	0.0316	1.2195	0.0115	1.4597
28.	TS1, TS2, VL, SRW	0.1210	0.7725	0.0387	0.7996	0.0232	1.2428	0.0162	1.5486
29.	TS1, SRW, TS3, VL	0.1238	0.7550	0.0402	0.8159	0.0316	1.2011	0.0077	1.2426
30.	TS2, SRW, TS3, VL	0.1256	0.7722	0.0402	0.8158	0.0256	1.2408	0.0165	1.5405

Panel E. Regressions with five earnings proxies (TS1, TS2, TS3, SRW, VL) (P = 5)

31.	All Models	0.1251	0.7707	0.0393	0.8154	0.0322	1.2898	0.0140	1.5407

a $CR_{it}(d,0)$ is the cumulative residual for firm i in quarter t. It is calculated as the cumulated market model residual, cumulated from d days before the earnings announcement date through the earnings announcement date (day 0). $UE_{it\lambda}$ is the unexpected earnings proxy for firm i, in quarter t, conditional on forecasting model (see note c). γ_0 is the estimated regression intercept coefficient. P is the number of proxy variables for unexpected earnings in the regression, $P = 1, \ldots, 5$. $\gamma\lambda$ is the estimated regression coefficient for $UE_{it\lambda}$.

b Number of observations available for the test. The number of observations decreases as the cumulation period increases because an observation is constrained so that each observation's Value Line report date occurs before the first day of the cumulation period, d. The total number of observations for a particular cumulation period is partitioned into quartiles on the basis of size, then the upper quartile (large firms) is compared to the lower quartile (small firms) in the columns of the table. For CR_{it} (−1,0), small firms have equity with a market value of less than $274 million and large firms have equity with a market value of more than $1.269 million; for CR_{it} (−40,0) small firms have equity with a market value of less than $328 million and large firms have equity with a market value of more than $1.356 million.

c The independent variable(s) in the regressions are proxy variables for unexpected earnings. There are five unexpected earnings proxy variables. SRW indicates that the unexpected earnings proxy is calculated conditional on the seasonal random walk forecasting model, TS1 the Brown and Rozeff (1979) model, TS2 the Foster (1977) model, TS3 the Watts (1975)–Griffin (1977) model, and VL the forecast in The Value Line Investment Survey.

d Sum of coeff. is the sum of the coefficients for the proxy variables in the regression, i.e., the sum of $\gamma\lambda$. Since all independent variables are proxy variables for unexpected earnings, the sum of the coefficients represents the estimated coefficient for unexpected earnings. For the single proxy variable regressions (regressions 1 through 5), the sum of coefficients is the coefficient for the single proxy variable.

cifically, for the (–1,0) holding period, a four variable set appears to be 'best' for small firms, while a three variable set appears to be 'best' for large firms. For the (–40,0) holding period, a three variable set appears to be 'best' for small firms, while a two variable set appears to be ex post 'best' for large firms.

In sum, the results presented in Exhibits 4 and 5 again suggest the existence of measurement error in unexpected earnings proxies, that our procedures are more effective at reducing measurement error for the short holding period than they are for the long holding period, and that these results hold for both small and large firms. However, the results also suggest that the relation between abnormal returns and unexpected earnings is better specified for small than for large firms, and that our procedures are more effective at ameliorating measurement error for the small firms.

4.4 Effects of Forecast Timing

Another characteristic of our data is that all forecasts are not equally timely; some forecasts are more recent than others relative to the earnings announcement date. Time serie model forecasts have approximately a 90 da forecast horizon. However, security analyst make their forecasts with varying horizon [median forecast horizon (age) of 39 days]. I is possible that the older the forecast, the greater the measurement error, and hence the lower the estimated β coefficient. Exhibit examines this issue by presenting the adjuste R-squares and sum of $\gamma\lambda$ coefficients for recent and non-recent forecasts in a forma similar to Exhibits 2 and 4.

Firms with recent (non-recent) forecast are partitioned into the lowest (highest) quartile of days between the *Value Line* repor date and the earnings announcement date fo the entire sample. As a result, recent and non recent forecasts for the (–1,0) holding perioc are less than 21 days old and more than 6 days old, respectively, where 'days old' is de fined as the number of days the VL forecas precedes the earnings announcement day (da 0). Recent and non-recent forecasts for the (–40,0) holding period are less than 62 day old and more than 75 days old, respectively Exhibit 7 presents a bar graph of the maxi mum adjusted R-squares from Exhibit 6 for a given number of proxy variables for each o the two holding periods for both recent anc non-recent forecasts similar to Exhibit 3 anc 5. The principal results follow.

First, the γ_1 coefficient values for the sin gle firm variable forms of eq. (9) are highl significant for the recent forecasts for botl the shortest and longest holding periods However, they are not always significant fo the non-recent forecasts. The adjusted R square for TS2 in panel A is actually negative for the non-recent forecasts for the longes holding period. Second, with one exceptior (i.e., SRW in panel A), the sum of the $\gamma\lambda$ coefficients always increases and the adjustec R-squares always decrease as the holding pe riod increases for the recent forecasts. Simi larly, the sum of the $\gamma\lambda$ coefficients always increases and the adjusted R-squares always

Exhibit 5 Maximum Adjusted R-squares From Exhibit 4—Comparing Large Firms to Small Firms

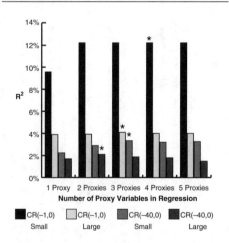

Number of Proxy Variables in Regression

■ CR(–1,0) Small □ CR(–1,0) Large ▨ CR(–40,0) Small ■ CR(–40,0) Large

ecrease for the non-recent forecasts. Third, or the short holding period, the sum of the $\gamma\lambda$ oefficients and the adjusted R-squares are always higher for the recent than for the non-recent forecasts. Similarly, for the long holding period, with the sole exception of SRW in anel A, the sum of the $\gamma\lambda$ coefficients and the adjusted R-squares for the recent forecasts re larger than those of firms with non-recent precasts. These results are consistent with the conjecture that unexpected earnings proxies that are conditioned on non-recent forecasts contain more measurement error than roxies that are conditioned on more recent precasts. Fourth, the sum of the $\gamma\lambda$ coefficients enerally increases when additional proxy variables are added to eq. (9), regardless of recency f forecast or length of holding period.

Similar to Exhibits 3 and 5, the asterisks in xhibit 7 designate the N proxy variable set aat is (ex post) 'best' for the particular recency of forecast/holding period. Exhibit 7 eveals that our procedures appear to be more ffective a reducing measurement error for recent than non-recent forecasts, and for short ather than long holding periods. More specifically, for the (–1,0) holding period, a three ariable set appears to be 'best' for the recent precasts, while a two proxy variable set appears to be 'best' for non-recent forecasts. For ae (–40,0) holding period, the multiple proxy ariable procedure is ineffectual in the sense that ae goodness of fit of the best two proxy variable quation is not significantly better than the goodess of fit of the 'best' single variable equation, egardless of the recency of the forecast.

In sum, the results in Exhibits 6 and 7 gain suggest the existence of measurement rror in unexpected earnings proxies and that ur procedures are more effective at reducing aeasurement error for the short abnormal reurn holding period than they are for the long olding period. However, the results suggest aat the relation between abnormal returns nd unexpected earnings is better specified or recent forecasts than for non-recent fore-

casts, and that our procedures are more effective at reducing measurement error for the recent forecasts.

4.5 Using Stock Returns to Control for Measurement Error

Given the model and underlying assumptions in Section 2, we show that including another independent variable in eq. (3) reduces the bias in estimating β in eq. (1) when the additional independent variable, Z_{it}, is correlated with the measurement error in the proxy, $\varepsilon_{it\lambda}$, and uncorrelated with the dependent variable, R_{it}, the independent variable, S_{it}, and the eq. (1) residuals, μ_{it}. For present purposes, we use as Z_{it} the firm's stock return from 100 days before the earnings announcement (day – 100) through the day before the cumulation period begins (day $d - 1$) and re-estimate eq. (9) with this additional variable. More formally, the model we estimate is

$$CR_{it}(d,0) = \gamma_0 + \sum_{\lambda=1}^{P} \gamma_\lambda \, UE_{it\lambda} + \omega \, R'_{jt} + \text{error} \; , \quad (10)$$

where R'_{jt} is our proxy for Z_{it}.

If earnings revisions and stock returns are positively correlated, then this additional stock return variable would be positively correlated with the measurement error in the (dated) unexpected earnings proxy variables. We assume that the stock return variable is positively correlated with the measurement error in the unexpected earnings proxy variables and uncorrelated with the dependent variable, the independent variable, and the residuals from the eq. (1) regression model. Since the additional return variable is assumed to be positively correlated with the measurement error in the unexpected earnings proxy variable, and β is assumed to be positive, we expect R'_{jt} to have a negative coefficient (i.e., $\omega < 0$).

Each of the regressions in Exhibit 2 [see eq. (9)] is re-estimated with inclusion of this

Exhibit 6 Summary of Cross-Sectional Regressions Between Cumulative Residuals and One or More Unexpected Earnings Proxy Variable(s), Comparison of Recent and Non-recent Forecasts

Regression: $CR_{it}(d,0) = \gamma_0 + \sum_{\lambda=1}^{p} \gamma_\lambda \cdot UE_{it\lambda} + error.^a$

Dependent variable: Cumulative residual ($CR_{it_b}(d,0)$)

	$CR_{it}(-1,0)$				$CR_{it}(-40,0)$			
Regression	1,056 recent[b]		1,095 non-recent		429 recent		409 non-recent	
No.	Independent variable(s)[c]	Adjusted R-Square	Sum of Coeff.[d]	Adjusted R-Square	Sum of Coeff.	Adjusted R-Square	Sum of Coeff.	Adjusted R-Square	Sum of Coeff.

No.	Independent variable(s)	Adjusted R-Square	Sum of Coeff.	Adjusted R-Square	Sum of Coeff.	Adjusted R-Square	Sum of Coeff.	Adjusted R-Square	Sum of Coeff.
	Panel A. Regression with one earnings proxy (P = 1)								
1.	SRW	0.0640	0.3536	0.0173	0.1852	0.0005	0.2795	0.0057	0.4041
2.	TS1	0.0746	0.4458	0.0359	0.3684	0.0169	0.8631	0.0013	0.4197
3.	TS2	0.0672	0.3762	0.0226	0.2561	0.0358	1.0467	-0.0001	0.3139
4.	TS3	0.0676	0.4032	0.0387	0.3711	0.0197	0.7269	0.0036	0.5185
5.	VL	0.0860	0.7544	0.0526	0.5572	0.0118	1.1926	0.0037	0.6183
	Panel B. Regression with two earnings proxies (P = 2)								
6.	TS1, TS2	0.0784	0.4619	0.0350	0.3681	0.0356	0.9039	-0.0010	0.4091
7.	TS1, TS3	0.0756	0.4562	0.0386	0.3871	0.0180	0.8230	0.0024	0.4596
8.	TS1, SRW	0.0820	0.4795	0.0370	0.3892	0.0147	0.8324	0.0038	0.5277
9.	TS1, VL	0.1096	0.8318	0.0565	0.6005	0.0169	1.2389	0.0014	0.6317
10.	TS2, TS3	0.0746	0.4360	0.0383	0.3825	0.0337	1.0325	0.0021	0.4704
11.	TS2, SRW	0.0889	0.4972	0.0289	0.3257	0.0338	0.9845	0.0035	0.4834
12.	TS2, VL	0.1134	0.8513	0.0560	0.6073	0.0344	1.2993	0.0013	0.6241
13.	TS3, SRW	0.0788	0.4581	0.0394	0.3914	0.0176	0.6775	0.0050	0.6199
14.	TS3, VL	0.1088	0.8358	0.0588	0.6096	0.0204	1.1990	0.0024	0.6846
15.	VL, SRW	0.1037	0.7890	0.0524	0.5628	0.0096	1.2044	0.0047	0.6492

(continued)

Panel C. Regressions with three earnings proxies ($P = 3$)

16.	TS1, TS2, TS3	0.0781	0.4662	0.0378	0.3887	0.0334	0.8950	0.0001	0.4500
17.	TS1, TS2, SRW	0.0887	0.5069	0.0361	0.3898	0.0333	0.8940	0.0014	0.5195
18.	TS1, TS2,VL	0.1144	0.8547	0.0560	0.6093	0.0358	1.2984	-0.0010	0.6259
19.	TS1, TS3, SRW	0.0819	0.4851	0.0391	0.4030	0.0161	0.7701	0.0043	0.5573
20.	TS1, TS3, VL	0.1103	0.8399	0.0579	0.6087	0.0181	1.2035	0.0022	0.6639
21.	TS1, VL, SRW	0.1115	0.8288	0.0557	0.6007	0.0150	1.2113	0.0022	0.6498
22.	TS2, TS3, SRW	0.0882	0.5009	0.0390	0.4019	0.0317	0.9851	0.0035	0.5716
23.	TS2, TS3, VL	0.1142	0.8572	0.0582	0.6181	0.0326	1.3132	0.011	0.6446
24.	TS2, VL, SRW	0.1189	0.8548	0.0553	0.6080	0.0328	1.2630	0.0022	0.6406
25.	TS3, VL, SRW	0.1113	0.8321	0.0579	0.6095	0.0188	1.1571	0.0028	0.6949

Panel D. Regressions with four earnings proxies ($P = 4$)

26.	TS1, TS2, TS3, SRW	0.0878	0.5069	0.0383	0.4054	0.0312	0.8797	0.0019	0.5500
27.	TS1, TS2, TS3, VL	0.1138	0.8569	0.0577	0.6204	0.0337	1.2897	-0.0002	0.6542
28.	TS1, TS2, VL, SRW	0.1180	0.8548	0.0552	0.6095	0.0337	1.2810	-0.0002	0.6412
29.	TS1, SRW, TS3, VL	0.1116	0.8358	0.0571	0.6087	0.0165	1.1625	0.0026	0.6741
30.	TS2, SRW, TS3, VL	0.1181	0.8551	0.0574	0.6181	0.0308	1.2784	0.0014	0.6564

Panel E. Regressions with five earnings proxies (TS1, TS2, TS3, SRW, VL) ($P = 5$)

31.	All Models	0.1172	0.8552	0.0568	0.6204	0.0316	1.2677	0.0002	0.6666

a $CR_{it}(d,0)$ is the cumulative residual for firm i in quarter t. It is calculated as the cumulated market model residual, cumulated from d days before the earnings announcement date through the earnings announcement date (day 0). UE_{it} is the unexpected earnings proxy for firm i, conditional on forecasting model (see note c). γ_0 is the estimated regression intercept coefficient. P is the number of proxy variables for unexpected earnings in the regression, $P = 1, \ldots, 5$. $\gamma\lambda$ is the estimated regression coefficient for UE_{it}.

b Number of observations available for the test. The number of observations decreases as the cumulation period increases because an observation is constrained so that each observation's *Value Line* report date occurs before the first day of the cumulation period, d. The total number of observations for the particular cumulation period is partitioned into quartiles on the basis of the age of the forecast, then the upper quartile (non-recent forecasts) is compared to the lower quartile (recent forecsts) in the columns of the table. For $CR_{it}(-1,0)$, the recent forecasts are less than 21 days old and the non-recent forecasts are more than 67 days old; for $CR_{it}(-40,0)$ the recent forecasts are less than 62 days old and the non-recent forecasts are more than 75 days old.

c The independent variable(s) in the regressions are proxy variables for unexpected earnings. There are five unexpected earnings proxy variables. SRW indicates that the unexpected earnings proxy is calculated conditional on the seasonal random walk forecasting model, TS1 the Brown and Rozeff (1979) model, TS2 the Foster (1977) model, TS3 the Watts (1975)–Griffin (1977) model, and VL the forecast in *The Value Line Investment Survey*.

d Sum of coeff. is the sum of the coefficients for the proxy variables in the regression, i.e., the sum of $\gamma\lambda$. Since all independent variables are proxy variables for unexpected earnings, the sum of the coefficients represents the estimated coefficient for unexpected earnings. For the single proxy variable regressions (regressions 1 through 5), the sum of coefficients is the coefficient for the single proxy variable.

Exhibit 7 Maximum Adjusted R-squares from Exhibit 6—Comparing Recent to Non-Recent Forecasts

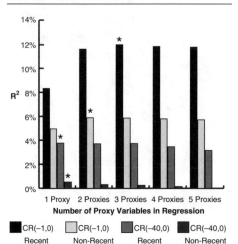

Number of Proxy Variables in Regression

■ CR(–1,0) Recent □ CR(–1,0) Non-Recent ▨ CR(–40,0) Recent □ CR(–40,0) Non-Recent

additional stock return variable [see eq. (10)]. The percentage increase in the sum of the co-efficients resulting from the addition of this additional variable is reported in Exhibit 8 for each of the 124 regressions in Exhibit 2. The coefficients for ω (not reported in the table) are, as expected, negative and have t-statistics which reject the null hypothesis that ω is greater than or equal to 0 at less than the 0.01 probability level for every proxy variable combination and for every holding period (i.e., for all 124 regressions).

Further, with the sole exception of regression #1 (SRW) for the (–2,0) holding period, the percentage change in the sum of the $\gamma\lambda$ coefficients is positive; that is, the sum of the $\gamma\lambda$ coefficients increases with the addition of the return variable for 123 of the 124 regressions. However, the percentage increases are small, the 124 regressions are not independent tests, and we do not conduct statistical tests for the significance of the increases. For the (–1,0) holding period, the percentage increases range from 0.36 percent to 2.65 percent. The amount of the increase does not generally appear to be affected by the number of proxy variables in the regression. The in-crease in the percentage change increases as the holding period increases from (–1,0) to (–10,0) and from (–10,0) to (–40,0). The percentage increase is greatest for the (–40,0) hold-ing period, ranging from 3.50 to 12.33 percent.

In sum, the results from the addition of the stock return variable to the multiple proxy vari-able regression [eq. (9)] are consistent with the discussion of the measurement error problem above. These results indicate the existence of measurement error for long as well as short ab-normal return holding periods. Further, the use of a multiple proxy variable research design does not appear to be a substitute for the addi-tion of the stock return variable in that the addi-tion of the stock return variable to a multiple proxy regression research design appears to re-duce additional measurement error.

4.6 Instrumental Variables

As discussed in Section 2.2, an instrumental variables procedure regresses a proxy vari-able on a set of instrumental variables; the predictions from this regression are then used in a second regression of $CR(d,0)$ on the pre-dicted variable. More specifically, the follow-ing two regressions are estimated:

$$UE_{it\lambda} = \delta_0 + \sum_{k=1}^{K} \delta_k I_{ikt} + \text{error}_1 , \quad (11)$$

$$CR_{it}(d,0) = \beta_0 + \beta_1 \left[\hat{\delta}_0 + \sum_{k=1}^{K} \hat{\delta}_k I_{ikt} \right] + \text{error}_2 , (12)$$

where

δ_0, β_0 = regression intercept coefficients for eqs. (11) and (12), respectively,

I_{ikt} = instrumental variable k for firm i, in quarter t; k is the number of instru-mental variables that are used in eq. (a) in Exhibit 9, $k = 4$, 5, or 6,

δ_k = regression coefficient for I_{ikt}

β_1 = slope coefficient in eq. (12).

Since it is unlikely that any variable exists that precisely meets the instrumental variable requirements discussed in Section 2.2, we examine four alternative sets of instrumental variables which are based on earnings and stock returns. The four sets of instrumental variables are: (i) the four unexpected earnings proxy variables that are not the dependent variable in eq. (11), (ii) the 6 signs of the five unexpected earnings proxy variables, (iii) a stock return variable and the instrumental variables in (i), and (iv) a stock return variable and the instrumental variables in (ii). The stock return instrumental variable is the stock return from 100 trading days before the earnings announcement through the day before the abnormal return holding period.

Panels A through D of Exhibit 9 summarize the tests examining four alternative sets of instrumental variables for each of the five proxy variables. The Exhibit 9 results suggest that the instrumental variables technique has the desired effect of reducing measurement error. The β coefficient estimates are higher than in any of the regression estimates (based on the sum of the γ_λ coefficients) reported earlier in Exhibit 2. For example, the highest coefficient estimates in Exhibit 2 are 0.7890, 1.0311, 1.0321, and 1.1316 for the (–1,0), (–10,0), (–20,0), and (–40,0) holding periods, respectively. These estimates are dominated by the highest coefficient estimates based on the instrumental variables approach in Exhibit 9 for these same holding periods: 1.7908, 2.0073, 2.5671, and 3.4194, respectively.

These results reveal the importance of using analysts' forecasts in conjunction with non-VL proxies as measures of unexpected earnings. The magnitudes of the β coefficients are generally highest in regressions #5, #10, #15, and #20; that is, where the instrumental variable technique uses non-VL proxies to purge error from the VL proxy. Moreover, relative to using the VL proxy without attempting to purge error, the magnitude of the coefficient increases considerably (more than 100 percent in some cases, e.g., compare regression #5, Exhibit 2, with regressions #5,

#10, #15, and #20, Exhibit 9, for the various holding periods).[17]

In sum, relative to the multiple regression approach with and without the inclusion of prior stock return data, and despite possible violations of the underlying assumptions, the instrumental variables approach apparently improves the estimation of the β coefficient. The effects of the instrumental variable procedure are most evident when the technique is used to purge error from an unexpected earnings proxy derived from *Value Line* analysts' forecasts.

5. Summary and Conclusions

This study compares and evaluates five alternative proxy variables for the market's assessment of unexpected earnings for four alternative abnormal return holding periods. Since such proxy variables measure the markets assessment of unexpected earnings with error, we examine procedures to detect and potentially reduce the measurement error in these proxy variables. The procedures we examine are (i) the use of multiple unexpected earnings proxy variables in a regression of abnormal returns on unexpected earnings (multiple proxy procedure), (ii) the addition of an explanatory variable that is, ex ante, uncorrelated with the abnormal return (dependent) variable and correlated with the measurement error in the unexpected earnings proxies (additional explanatory variable procedure), and (iii) the use of an instrumental variables procedure (instrumental variable procedure). Additionally, we examine the relation of abnormal returns and unexpected earnings conditional on the size of the firm and on the age of the financial analysts' forecast. The major results follow.

For short holding periods, the results consistently indicate significant measurement error in all five unexpected earnings proxy variables and the reduction (to an unknown degree) in measurement error using any of the

Exhibit 8 Summary of Cross-Sectional Regressions Between Cumulative Residuals and One or More Unexpected Earnings Proxy Variable(s) Using Stock Return to Control for Measurement Error in Unexpected Earnings

Regression: $CR_{it}(d,0) = \gamma_0 + \sum_{\lambda=1}^{P} \gamma_\lambda UE_{i\lambda} + \omega R'_{it} + error.$ [a]

			Dependent variable: Cumulative residual ($CR_{it}(d,0)$)					
Regression		$CR_{it}(-1,0)$ 4,177 observations [b]		$CR_{it}(-10,0)$ 3,431 observations		$CR_{it}(-20,0)$ 2,931 observations		$CR_{it}(-40,0)$ 1,611 observations
No.	Independent variable(s) [c]	Sum of Coeff. [d]	Exhibit 2 Change	Sum of Coeff.	Exhibit 2 Change	Sum of Coeff.	Exhibit 2 Change	Sum of Coeff.	Exhibit 2 Change
Panel A. Regression with one earnings proxy (P = 1)									
1.	SRW	0.3182	0.36%	0.3829	0.20%	0.3882	-0.73%	0.3630	3.50%
2.	TS1	0.4788	1.01%	0.6434	2.15%	0.6198	0.95%	0.6550	5.15%
3.	TS2	0.3910	1.33%	0.5790	3.83%	0.6180	1.35%	0.5814	6.23%
4.	TS3	0.4273	1.26%	0.6048	3.10%	0.6587	0.99%	0.6887	4.15%
5.	VL	0.7163	2.54%	0.9728	4.21%	0.9198	3.03%	1.1341	12.33%
Panel B. Regression with two earnings proxies (P = 2)									
6.	TS1, TS2	0.4927	1.14%	0.6736	2.61%	0.6575	1.07%	0.6790	5.38%
7.	TS1, TS3	0.4861	1.10%	0.6520	2.32%	0.6340	0.98%	0.6757	5.04%
8.	TS1, SRW	0.5073	0.88%	0.6667	1.71%	0.6566	0.54%	0.7038	4.80%
9.	TS1, VL	0.7860	2.35%	1.0375	3.85%	0.9917	2.54%	1.1827	10.84%
10.	TS2, TS3	0.4652	1.39%	0.6700	3.51%	0.7260	1.16%	0.7364	5.05%
11.	TS2, SRW	0.4875	1.01%	0.6567	2.48%	0.6928	0.54%	0.6984	5.34%
12.	TS2, VL	0.7975	2.65%	1.0688	4.38%	1.0461	2.71%	1.2507	11.08%
13.	TS3, SRW	0.4708	1.00%	0.6338	2.22%	0.6859	0.46%	0.7350	4.00%
14.	TS3, VL	0.7834	2.55%	1.0405	4.17%	1.0212	2.58%	1.2194	10.70%
15.	VL, SRW	0.7498	2.22%	1.0023	3.69%	0.9607	2.38%	1.1487	11.58%

(continued)

Panel C. Regressions with three earnings proxies (P = 3)

16.	TS1, TS2, TS3	0.4965	1.20%	0.6779	2.72%	0.6657	1.09%	0.6964	5.27%
17.	TS1, TS2, SRW	0.5246	1.01%	0.6993	2.16%	0.6973	0.65%	0.7354	5.06%
18.	TS1, TS2, VL	0.8035	2.53%	1.0697	4.26%	1.0398	2.67%	1.2502	11.13%
19.	TS1, TS3, SRW	0.5105	0.94%	0.6686	1.80%	0.6572	0.56%	0.7134	4.77%
20.	TS1, TS3, VL	0.7903	2.43%	1.0403	3.98%	0.9975	2.60%	1.1876	10.80%
21.	TS1, VL, SRW	0.7892	2.25%	1.0402	3.68%	0.9998	2.32%	1.1853	10.64%
22.	TS2, TS3, SRW	0.5095	1.12%	0.6956	2.66%	0.7491	0.67%	0.7802	4.85%
23.	TS2, TS3, VL	0.8040	2.63%	1.0719	4.35%	1.0562	2.60%	1.2509	10.98%
24.	TS2, VL, SRW	0.8062	2.46%	1.0732	4.10%	1.0538	2.43%	1.2526	10.80%
25.	TS3, VL, SRW	0.7873	2.41%	1.0413	3.94%	1.0226	2.38%	1.2177	10.51%

Panel D. Regressions with four earnings proxies (P = 4)

26.	TS1, TS2, TS3, SRW	0.5252	1.04%	0.6977	2.20%	0.6929	0.67%	0.7410	5.03%
27.	TS1, TS2, TS3, VL	0.8047	2.57%	1.0690	4.34%	1.0386	2.71%	1.2494	11.13%
28.	TS1, TS2, VL, SRW	0.8079	2.42%	1.0732	4.08%	1.0481	2.44%	1.2549	10.90%
29.	TS1, SRW, TS3, VL	0.7924	2.34%	1.0410	3.81%	1.0008	2.42%	1.1879	10.64%
30.	TS2, SRW, TS3, VL	0.8085	2.48%	1.0724	4.12%	1.0572	2.43%	1.2491	10.80%

Panel E. Regressions with five earnings proxies (TS1, TS2, TS3, SRW, VL) (P = 5)

31.	All Models	0.8084	2.46%	1.0707	4.15%	1.0433	2.51%	1.2513	10.94%

[a] CR_{it} (d,0) is the cumulative residual for firm i in quarter t. It is calculated as the cumulative market model residual, cumulated from d days before the earnings announcement date through the earnings announcement day (day 0). $UE_{it\lambda}$ is the unexpected earnings proxy for firm i, in quarter t, conditional on the forecasting model λ (see note c). γ_0 is the estimated regression intercept coefficient. P is the number of proxy variables for unexpected earnings in the regression, $P = 1, \ldots, 5$. $\gamma\lambda$ is the estimated regression coefficient for $UE_{it\lambda}$. ω is the coefficient for R'_{ij} which is firm's stock return from day -100 through the day before the cumulation period begins (day $d - 1$).

[b] Number of observations available for the test. The number of observations decreases as the cumulation period increases because an observation is constrained so that each observations *Value Line* report date occurs before the first day of the cumulation period, d.

[c] There are five unexpected earnings proxy variables. SRW indicates that the unexpected earnings proxy is calculated conditional on the seasonal random walk forecasting model, TS1 the Brown and Rozeff (1979) model, TS2 the Foster (1977) model, TS3 the Watts (1975)–Griffin (1977) model, and VL the forecast in *The Value Line Investment Survey*.

[d] Sum of coeff. is the sum of the coefficients for the proxy variables in the regression, i.e., the sum of $\gamma\lambda$, estimated via eq. (10). Exhibit 4 change is the percentage change in the sum of the coefficients from Exhibit 4 [estimated via eq. (9)] to Exhibit 8 [estimated via eq. (10)]. Since all independent variables are proxy variables for unexpected earnings, the sum of the coefficients represents the estimated coefficient for the unexpected earnings. For the single proxy variable regressions (regressions 1 through 5), the sum of coefficients is the coefficient for the single proxy variable. To the extent R'_{ij} is correlated with the measurement error in the proxy variable, the sum of the coefficients should increase.

Exhibit 9 Summary of Cross-Sectional Regressions Between Cumulative Residuals and Instrumental Variables for Unexpected Earnings

Regression: (a) $UE_{it\Lambda} = \delta_0 + \sum_{k=1}^{K} \delta_k I_{ikt} + error_1$, (b) $CR_{it}(d,0) = \beta_0 + \beta_1 \left[\hat{\delta}_0 + \sum_{k=1}^{K} \hat{\delta}_k I_{ikt} \right] + error_2$. [a]

Dependent variable: Cumulative residual ($CR_{it}(d,0)$)

| | | $CR_{it}(-1,0)$ | | $CR_{it}(-10,0)$ | | $CR_{it}(-20,0)$ | | $CR_{it}(-40,0)$ | |
| | | 4,177 observations [b] | | 3,431 observations | | 2,931 observations | | 1,611 observations | |
No.	Initial Proxy [c]	Adjusted R-Square	β_1 Coeff.	Adjusted R-Square	β_1 Coeff.	Adjusted R-Square	β_1 Coeff.	Adjusted R-Square	β_1 Coeff.
Panel A. Instrumental variables are the four unexpected earnings proxies not used as the initial unexpected earnings proxy variable (K = 4)									
1.	TS1	0.0753	0.5663	0.0402	0.7600	0.0246	0.8500	0.0135	0.8618
2.	TS2	0.0618	0.5049	0.0331	0.7005	0.0160	0.6833	0.0072	0.6317
3.	TS3	0.0686	0.5096	0.0342	0.6612	0.0165	0.6552	0.0088	0.6652
4.	SRW	0.0750	0.6307	0.0393	0.8686	0.0207	0.9035	0.0131	1.0450
5.	VL	0.0675	1.1734	0.0333	1.4175	0.0157	1.3759	0.0082	1.2856
Panel B. Instrumental variables are the signs of the five unexpected earnings proxy variables (K = 5)									
6.	TS1	0.0838	0.8590	0.0396	1.1239	0.0346	1.4667	0.0307	1.9088
7.	TS2	0.0844	0.9504	0.0329	1.1243	0.0255	1.3849	0.0235	1.8538
8.	TS3	0.0818	0.9982	0.0343	1.2280	0.0329	1.6828	0.0286	2.1560
9.	SRW	0.0818	0.9982	0.0343	1.2280	0.0329	1.6828	0.0286	2.1560
10.	VL	0.0743	1.7908	0.0290	2.0073	0.0247	2.5671	0.0230	3.4194

(continued)

Panel C. Instrumental variables are the four unexpected earnings proxies not used as the initial unexpected earnings proxy variable and the stock return variable (K = 5)

11.	TS1	0.0757	0.5679	0.0411	0.7681	0.0247	0.8531	0.0140	0.8752
12.	TS2	0.0611	0.5017	0.0317	0.6848	0.0157	0.6772	0.0066	0.6064
13.	TS3	0.0681	0.5077	0.0334	0.6529	0.0164	0.6525	0.0088	0.6648
14.	SRW	0.0762	0.6349	0.0414	0.8904	0.0217	0.9229	0.0141	1.0834
15.	VL	0.0627	1.1149	0.0296	1.3280	0.0141	1.2993	0.0051	1.0301

Panel D. Instrumental variables are the signs of the five unexpected earnings proxy variables and the stock return variable (K = 6)

16.	TS1	0.0871	0.9990	0.0395	1.2701	0.0368	1.7160	0.0342	2.2544
17.	TS2	0.0751	0.9374	0.0267	1.0559	0.0258	1.4571	0.0215	1.8788
18.	TS3	0.0817	0.9324	0.0305	1.0801	0.0253	1.3782	0.0234	1.8509
19.	SRW	0.0822	1.0009	0.0365	1.2632	0.0348	1.7190	0.0305	2.2240
20.	VL	0.0644	1.6118	0.0234	1.7749	0.0216	2.3701	0.0143	2.6530

[a] UE_{itt} is the unexpected earnings proxy for firm i, in quarter t, conditional on forecasting model λ (see note c). δ_0 and β_0 are the regression intercept coefficients for eqs. (a) and (b), respectively. I_{ikt} is instrumental variable k for firm i, in quarter t. K is the number of instrumental variables that are used in eq. (a), $k = 4,5,5,6$. The instrumental variables are (i) the four unexpected earnings proxy variables that are not the dependent variable in eq. (a), see note c, (ii) the signs of the five unexpected earnings proxy variables, (iii) a stock return variable and the instrumental variables in (i), and (iv) a stock return variable and the instrumental variables in (ii). The stock return instrumental variable is the stock return from day -100 through the day before the cumulation period (day $d + 1$). δ_k is the regression coefficient for I_{ikt}. $CR_{itt}(d,0)$ is the cumulative residual for firm i in quarter t. It is calculated as the cumulated market model residual, cumulated from d days before the earnings announcement date through the earnings announcement date (day 0). β_1 is the slope coefficient in eq. (b) and it is denoted as β_1 coeff. in the table.

[b] Number of observations available for the test. The number of observations decreases as the cumulation period increases because an observation is constrained so that each observation's *Value Line* report date occurs before the first day of the cumulation period, d.

[c] The initial proxy variable in the regressions are proxy variables for unexpected earnings. There are five unexpected earnings proxy variables. SRW indicates that the unexpected earnings proxy is calculated conditional on the seasonal random walk forecasting model, TS1 the Brown and Rozeff (1979) model, TS2 the Foster (1977) model, TS3 the Watts (1975)–Griffin (1977) model, and VL the forecast in *The Value Line Investment Survey*.

three procedures we examine. For the longest holding period, the results are mixed. The multiple proxy procedure is less effective for reducing measurement error for the longest holding period than for the shorter holding periods. However, the additional explanatory variable procedure and the instrumental variables procedure detect and appear to reduce measurement error for all holding periods.

The multiple proxy procedure is used to examine the sensitivity of our results to firm size and forecast age. This procedure appears to be more effective at detecting and/or reducing measurement error for the shortest holding period than for the longest holding period, regardless of firm size or forecast age. The relation between abnormal returns and unexpected earnings appears to be better specified for small firms and firms with more recent forecasts than for large firms and firms with non-recent forecasts. Moreover, our procedures appear to be more effective at reducing measurement error for small firms and firms with more recent forecasts than for large firms and firms with non-recent forecasts.

The more critical caveat to this study concerns the unknown effects of misspecifying the underlying relation between abnormal returns and unexpected earnings. For instance, our evidence suggests that earnings variables explain only a small portion of the market's response at the time of an earnings announcement (e.g., our largest adjusted R-square equals 0.1256). Future research may consider additional variables in conjunction with earnings surprise (e.g., extent of analyst coverage, stochastic nature of the process generating cash flows or earnings, confounding events) for the purpose of detecting measurement error and controlling for omitted variables. Also, we may have misspecified the properties of the error in measuring unexpected earnings. The sensitivity of our results to the unbiasedness property of earnings measurement error may be evaluated. In addition, we examine only two factors that potentially explain measurement error firm size and age of forecast. Future research could consider other potential explanatory factors.[1]

Overall, our results indicate that measurement error is a significant problem for the researcher using a multiple regression research design; that is, regressing abnormal returns (capturing the information content of accounting earnings) on an unexpected earnings proxy variable and additional non-earnings explanatory variable(s). For expositional purposes, assume a researcher is regressing abnormal returns on an unexpected earnings proxy variable and one additional non-earnings explanatory variable. Our results indicate that the researcher must interpret the coefficient for the additional non-earnings explanatory variable conditional on an assumed correlation between the additional variable and the measurement error in the unexpected earnings proxy variable. A non-zero correlation potentially results in a measurement error interpretation of the coefficient for the additional non-earnings explanatory variable.

The procedures we examine to reduce measurement error, while reducing the measurement error problem to some extent, do not eliminate the problem. Our results indicate that it may be useful to use multiple unexpected earnings proxy variables and a stock return variable (observed before the abnormal return holding period) in a multiple regression research design. If inclusion of multiple unexpected earnings proxy variables or the stock return variable alters the estimates of the coefficient of the additional non-earnings explanatory variable, then a measurement error interpretation of this variable is likely. Unfortunately, if inclusion of the additional unexpected earnings proxy variables and the stock return variable does not alter the estimate of the coefficient of the additional non-earnings explanatory variable, our results do not imply that a measurement error interpretation of the additional non-earnings explanatory variable is invalid.

Endnotes

1. See Foster (1986, ch. 11), Watts and Zimmerman (1986, ch. 3), or Brown (1987, ch. 2) for a review of this literature.

2. The effects of measurement error are of less concern in studies of the relation between stock price changes and unexpected earnings when the null hypothesis of no relation is rejected, see Beaver et al. (1987) and Collins et al. (1987).

3. The proxy variables are conditioned on a seasonal random walk model, three Box and Jenkins (1976) models, and forecasts from *The Value Line Investment Survey*.

4. For evidence on the cross-sectional variation in β, see Easton and Zmijewski (1987).

5. An alternative explanation for observing that $\delta \neq 0$ is that the additional independent variable(s) 'pick up' misspecification of the basic model (e.g., cross-sectional variation in β). We assume throughout the paper that eq. (1) is the true model (i.e., we do not have an omitted variables problem) and that R_{it} is measured without error.

6. See also Lys and Sivaramakrishnan (1986).

7. Non-zero coefficients may also indicate misspecification of the underlying model of the form of the measurement error in the proxies. See section 2.1 for the required assumptions of the underlying model.

8. 'Best' is determined on the basis of adjusted R-squares. The model with the highest adjusted R-square is deemed the 'best' of a particular set of proxy variable alternatives. It is most likely (but not necessary) that the 'best' $N + 1$ variable model includes all the variables in the 'best' N variable model.

9. Given the instrumental variables we examine, this approach is similar to estimating a cross-sectional ex post composite forecast from alternative forecasting models.

10. *The Value Line Investment Survey* is the only publicly available source of quarterly analysts' forecasts for the period under study.

11. The maximum number of firm/year/quarter observations of 5,508 is calculated as (223 firms × 5 years × 4 quarters) + (212 firms × 4 quarters).

12. An examination of the percentage of sample firms contained in each size decile of all American and New York Stock Exchange firms (based on market value of common equity) revealed that over half the firms are in the largest size decile, and over 85 percent of the firms are in the largest four size deciles in every year under study.

13. While a common stock price deflator for earnings forecast errors has not been widely used in the literature, Christie (1985), Easton and Zmijewski (1987), and others have argued that such a deflator is appropriate. We use the stock price the day before the period over which the abnormal return is measured (day $d + 1$). An earlier version of this paper reported results using three alternative deflators: actual earnings, forecasted earnings, and the mean and standard deviation of earnings. Those results are similar to the results presented here, except that the use of actual earnings as a deflator appears to increase measurement error.

14. For all holding periods (the period from day d through day 0), the regression parameters are estimated using returns from day −361 to day −61, where day 0 is the earnings announcement date. We require a minimum of 100 daily returns over the estimation period and all returns over the holding period for an observation to be included in a particular test.

15. Additional results indicate: (1) The five $UE_{it\lambda}$ proxy variables have identical signs in approximately 48 percent of the cases, (2) four of the five $UE_{it\lambda}$ variables have identical signs for approximately 78 percent of the cases, and (3) when the proxies disagree in the sign of $UE_{it\lambda}$, the magnitudes of the $UE_{it\lambda}$'s are closer to zero than they are when the proxies agree in sign. The latter finding suggests that grouping on the basis of consistency of sign of $UE_{it\lambda}$ is positively correlated with grouping on the basis of magnitude of $UE_{it\lambda}$.

16. The actual timing of the analysts forecast is also critical here. We would expect, for instance, that if all analyst's forecasts are made just before earnings announcements, the coefficient for the (-1,0) holding period would be higher. Unfortunately, we cannot examine this issue with our analyst data, as the average forecast in our sample is made approximately 39 days prior to the earnings announcement date (our day 0).

17. We do not claim that the reported coefficient estimates are close to what they would be if all variables are measured without error. Such predictions depend on a particular model of the earnings change versus price change relation. These models make numerous simplifying assumptions

about earnings behavior, the relation of earnings to cash flow, and the mapping of earnings or cash flows into prices. The models, however, generally predict that the β coefficient should be positive. Recent examples of models linking earnings to prices include Miller and Rock (1985) and Watts and Zimmerman (1986).

18. One possibility would be to consider the firms information environment. Brown et al. (1987b) show that analyst superiority in predicting firms earnings relative to time series model forecasts is positively related to firm size and the extent of analyst agreement regarding their ex ante earnings predictions. Our finding that it is easier to reduce measurement error for small firms than for large firms is consistent with Brown et al. (1987b). Future research may examine whether it is easier to reduce measurement error in earnings proxies for firms for which analyst have heterogeneous rather than homogeneous ex ante earnings expectations.

References

Advisory Committee on Corporate Disclosure, 1977, Report of the advisory committee on corporate disclosures to the securities and exchange commission (U.S. Government Printing Office, Washington, DC).

Beaver, W.H., R.A. Lambert and S. Ryan, 1987, The information content of security prices: A second look, *Journal of Accounting and Economics* 9, this issue.

Box, G.E. and G.M. Jenkins, 1976, Time series models: Forecasting and control (Holden Day, San Francisco, CA).

Brown, L.D., 1987, The modern theory of financial reporting (Business Publications, Inc., Plano, TX).

Brown, L.D., P.A. Griffin, R.L. Hagerman and M.E. Zmijewski, 1987a, Security analyst superiority relative to univariate time-series models in forecasting quarterly earnings, *Journal of Accounting and Economics* 9, 61-87.

Brown, L.D., G.D. Richardson and S.A. Schwager, 1987b, An information interpretation of financial analyst superiority in forecasting earnings, *Journal of Accounting Research* 25, 49-67.

Brown, L.D. and M.S. Rozeff, 1979, Univariate time-series models of quarterly accounting earnings per share: A proposed model, *Journal of Accounting Research* 17, 179-189.

Christie, A.A., 1985, On cross-sectional analysis in accounting research, Unpublished working paper (University of Southern California, Los Angeles, CA).

Collins, D.W., S.P. Kothari and J.D. Rayburn, 1987, Firm size and the information content of prices with respect to earnings, *Journal of Accounting and Economics* 9, this issue.

Easton, P.E. and M.E. Zmijewski, 1987, Cross-sectional variation in the stock markets response to corporate earnings, Unpublished paper (University of Chicago, Chicago, IL).

Foster, G., 1977, Quarterly accounting data: Time-series properties and predictive-ability results, *The Accounting Review* 52, 1-21.

Foster, G., 1986, *Financial statement analysis* (Prentice-Hall, Englewood Cliffs, NJ).

Griffin, P.A., 1977, The time-series behavior of quarterly earnings: Preliminary evidence, *Journal of Accounting Research* 15, 71-83.

Hopwood, W.S., J.C. McKeown and P.A. Newbold, 1982, The additional information content of quarterly earnings reports: Intertemporal disaggregation, *Journal of Accounting Research* 20, 343-349.

Judge, G., R. Hill, W. Griffiths, H. Lutkepohl and T. Lee, 1984, *Introduction to the theory and practice of econometrics* (Wiley, New York).

Kross, W. and D. Shroeder, 1985, Firm prominence and the differential information content of quarterly earnings announcements, Unpublished working paper (Purdue University, West Lafayette IN).

Lys, T. and S. Sivaramakrishnan, 1986, Earnings expectations and capital restructuring: The case of equity-for-debt swaps, Unpublished paper (Northwestern University, Evanston, IL).

Madalla, G.S., 1977, Econometrics (McGraw Hill, New York).

Miller, M.H. and K. Rock, 1985, Dividend policy under asymmetric information, *Journal of Finance* 40, 1031-1051.

Watts, R.L., 1975, The time series behavior of quarterly earnings, Unpublished paper (University of Newcastle, Newcastle, New South Wales).

Watts, R.L. and J.L. Zimmerman, 1986, *Positive Accounting Theory* (Prentice-Hall, Englewood Cliffs, NJ).

Section 4:
Related Research

Chapter 19

Risk and Return: A New Look[*]

Burton G. Malkiel, Ph.D.
Chemical Bank Chairman's Professor of Economics
Princeton University

One of the best-documented propositions in the field of finance is that, on average, investors have received higher rates of return on investment securities for bearing greater risk. This chapter looks at the historical evidence regarding risk and return, explains the fundamentals of portfolio and asset-pricing theory, and then goes on to take a new look at the relationship between risk and return using some unexplored risk measures that seem to capture quite closely the actual risks being valued in the market.

2.1 Some Historical Evidence

Risk is a most slippery and elusive concept. It is hard for investors—let alone economists—to agree on a precise definition. The dictionary defines risk as the possibility of suffering harm or loss. If I buy one-year Treasury bills to yield, say, 10 percent and hold them until they mature, I am virtually certain of earning a 10 percent monetary return before income taxes. The possibility of loss is so small as to be considered nonexistent. But if I hold common stock in my local power and light company for one year on the basis of an anticipated 12.5 percent dividend return, the possibility of loss increases. The dividend of the company might be cut and, more important, the market price at the end of the year could be much lower, so that I might suffer a serious net loss. Risk is the chance that expected security returns will not materialize

* The research reported in this chapter has been supported by the National Bureau of Economic Research, the Institute for Quantitative Research in Finance, the John Weinberg Foundation, and the Princeton Financial Research Center. As indicated in note 3, the empirical tests reported at the end of the chapter are taken from a joint study with John G. Cragg of NBER and the University of British Columbia.

The National Bureau of Economic Research is a private, nonprofit, nonpartisan organization engaged in quantitative analysis of the American economy. NBER reprints are intended for educational and research purposes. They have not been reviewed by the Board of Directors of the NBER and are not official NBER publications.

The research reported here is part of the NBER research project on the Changing Role of Debt and Equity Finances in the United States, which is being financed by a grant from the American Council of Life Insurance.

An earlier version of this paper appeared as NBER Working Paper No. 700. It is reprinted with permission from The University of Chicago Press, publisher, from *The Changing Roles of Debt and Equity in Financing U.S. Capital Formation,* edited by Benjamin M. Friedman (1982), pages 27-45. Copyright © 1982 by the National Bureau of Economic Research. All rights reserved.

and, in particular, that the securities I hold will fall in price.

Once academics had accepted the idea that risk for investors is related to the chance of disappointment in achieving expected security returns, a natural measure suggested itself—the probable variability or dispersion of future returns. Thus, financial risk has generally been defined as the variance or standard deviation of returns.[1]

Empirical studies of broad classes of securities confirm the general relationship between risk and return. The most thorough recent study has been done by Ibbotson and Sinquefield (1979). Their data covered the period 1926 through 1978. The results are shown in Exhibit 1.

A quick glance shows that, over long periods of time, common stocks have, on average, provided relatively generous total rates of return. These returns, including dividends and capital gains, have exceeded by a substantial margin the returns from long-term corporate bonds and U.S. Treasury bills. The stock returns have also tended to be well in excess of the inflation rate as measured by the annual rate of increase in consumer prices. The data show, however, that common stock returns are highly variable as measured by the standard deviation and the range of annual returns shown in the last three columns of the table. Returns from equities have ranged from

a gain of over 50 percent (in 1933) to a loss of almost the same magnitude (in 1931). Clearly, the extra returns that have been available to investors from stocks have come at the expense of assuming considerably higher risk.

The patterns evident in Ibbotson and Sinquefield's chart also appear when the returns and risks of individual stock portfolios are compared. Indeed, most of the differences that exist in the returns from different mutual funds can be explained by differences in the risk they have assumed. However, there are ways in which investors can reduce the risks they take. This brings us to the subject of modern portfolio theory.

2.2 Reducing Risk: Modern Portfolio Theory

Portfolio theory begins with the premise that all investors are risk averse. They want high returns and guaranteed outcomes. The theory tells investors how to combine stocks in their portfolios to give them the least risk possible, consistent with the return they seek. It also gives a rigorous mathematical justification for the time-honored investment maxim that diversification is a sensible strategy for individuals who like to reduce their risks. The basic idea was that a portfolio of risky (volatile) stocks can be put together in such a way

Exhibit 1 Selected Performance Statistics, 1926-1978

	Annual (Geometric) Mean Rate of Return	Number of Years Returns Are Positive	Number of Years Returns Are Negative	Highest Annual Return (and Year)	Lowest Annual Return (and Year)	Standard Deviation of Annual Returns
Common Stocks	8.9	35	18	54.0% (1933)	−43.3 (1931)	22.4
Long-term corporate bonds	4.0	43	10	18.4 (1970)	−8.1 (1969)	5.8
U.S. Treasury bills	2.5	52	1	8.0 (1974)	−0.0 (1940)	2.1
Consumer Price Index	2.5	43	10	18.2 (1946)	−10.3 (1932)	4.7

Source: Ibbotson and Sinquefield (1979).

as to be less risky than any one of the individual stocks in it. A simple illustration will make the whole game clear.

Let us suppose we have an island economy with only two businesses. The first is a large resort with beaches, tennis courts, a golf course, and the like. The second is a manufacturer of umbrellas. Weather affects the fortunes of both. During sunny seasons the resort does a booming business and umbrella sales plummet. During rainy seasons the resort owner does very poorly, while the umbrella manufacturer enjoys high sales and large profits. Exhibit 2 shows some hypothetical earnings for the two businesses during the different seasons. I assume that all earnings are paid out as dividends, so these are also the returns paid out to investors.

Suppose that, on average, one-half the seasons are sunny and one-half are rainy (i.e., the probability of a sunny or rainy season is one-half). An investor who bought stock in the umbrella manufacturer would find that half the time he earned a 50 percent return and half the time he lost 25 percent of his investment. On average, he would earn a return of 12.5 percent. This is what we call the investor's *expected return*. Similarly, investment in the resort would produce the same results. Investing in either one of these businesses would be fairly risky, however, because the results are quite variable, and there could be several sunny or rainy seasons in a row.

Suppose, however, that instead of buying only one security an investor with two dollars diversified and put half his money in the umbrella manufacturer's and half in the resort owner's business. In sunny seasons, a one-dollar investment in the resort would produce a fifty-cent return, while a one-dollar investment in the umbrella manufacturer would

lose twenty-five cents. The investors total return would be twenty-five cents, which is 12.5 percent of his total investment of two dollars.

Note that during rainy seasons exactly the same thing happens—only the names are changed. Investment in the umbrella manufacturer produces a good 50 percent return while the investment in the resort loses 25 percent. Again, however, the diversized investor makes a 12.5 percent return on his total investment.

This simple illustration points out the basic advantage of diversification. Whatever happens to the weather, and thus to the island economy, by diversifying investments over both of the firms an investor is sure of making a 12.5 percent return each year. The trick that made the game work was that while both companies were risky (returns were variable from year to year), the companies were affected differently by weather conditions. As long as there is some lack of parallelism in the fortunes of the individual companies in the economy, diversification will always reduce risk. In the present case, where there is a perfect negative relationship between the companies' fortunes (one always does well when the other does poorly), diversification can totally eliminate risk.

Of course, there is always a rub, and the rub in this case is that the fortunes of most companies move pretty much in tandem. When there is a recession and people are unemployed, they may buy neither summer vacations nor umbrellas. Therefore, one should not expect in practice to get the neat total risk elimination just shown. Nevertheless, since company fortunes do not always move completely in parallel, investment in a diversified portfolio of stocks is likely to be less risky than investment in one or two single securities. While a portfolio of General Motors and its major steel and tire supplier would not reduce risk much, if at all, a portfolio of GM and a defense contractor in a depressed area might reduce risk substantially.

Exhibit 2 An Example of Diversification

	Umbrella Manufacturer	Resort Owner
Rainy season	50%	−25%
Sunny season	−25%	50%

The example may seem a bit strained, and most investors will realize that when the market gets clobbered just about all stocks go down. Still, at least at certain times, some stocks do move against the market. Gold stocks are often given as an example of securities that do not typically move in the same direction as the general market. Similarly, international diversification can reduce risk. The point to realize in setting up a portfolio is that true diversification of a portfolio depends on having stocks that are not all dependent on the same economic variables (total spending in the economy, inflation rates, etc.). Wise investors will diversify their portfolios not by names or industries but by the determinants that influence the fluctuations of various securities.

2.3 Modeling Risk: The Capital-Asset Pricing Model (CAPM)

Portfolio theory has important implications for how stocks are actually valued. If investors seek to reduce risk in anything like the manner described by portfolio theorists, the stock market will tend to reflect these risk-reducing activities. This brings us to what is called the "Capital-Asset Pricing Model."

I have mentioned that the reason diversification cannot usually produce the miracle of risk elimination is that usually stocks tend to move up and down together. Still, diversification is worthwhile—it can eliminate some risks. What the CAPM did was to focus directly on what part of a security's risk could be eliminated by diversification and what part could not.

The theory begins by classifying the sources of the variability of an individual stock. Part of total risk or variability may be called the security's *systematic risk,* arising from the basic variability of stock prices in general and the tendency for all stocks to go along with the general market, at least to some extent. The remaining variability in a stock's returns is called *unsystematic risk* and results from factors peculiar to that particular

company, for example, a strike, the discovery of a new product, and so on.

Systematic risk, also called market risk, captures the reaction of individual stocks (or portfolios) to general market swings. Some stocks and portfolios tend to be very sensitive to market movements. Others are more stable. This relative volatility or sensitivity to market moves can be estimated on the basis of the past record, and is popularly known as the beta calculation. This calculation is essentially a comparison between the movements of an individual stock (or portfolio) and the movements of the market as a whole. It is a numerical description of systematic risk.

The calculation begins by assigning a beta of 1 to a broad market index, such as the NYSE index or the S&P 500. If a stock has a beta of 2, then on average it swings twice as far as the market. If the market goes up 10 percent, the stock rises 20 percent. If a stock has a beta of 0.5, it tends to be more stable than the market (it will go up or down 5 percent when the market rises or declines 10 percent). Professionals often call high-beta stocks aggressive investments and label low-beta stocks as defensive.

Now the important thing to realize is that *sytematic risk cannot be eliminated by diversification.* It is precisely because all stocks move more or less in tandem (a large share of their variability is systematic) that even diversified stock portfolios are risky. Indeed, if I diversified extremely broadly by buying a share in the S&P index (which by definition has a beta of 1), I would still have quite variable (risky) returns because the market as a whole fluctuates widely.

Unsystematic risk is the variability in stock prices (and, therefore, in returns from stocks) that results from factors peculiar to an individual company. Receipt of a large new contract, discovery of mineral resources on the company's property, labor difficulties, the revelation that the corporation's treasurer has had his hand in the company till—all can make a stock's price move independently of the market. The risk associated with such variability is precisely the kind that diversification can reduce. The whole point of portfolio theory was that, to the extent that stocks do not move in tandem all the time, variations in the returns from any one security will tend to be washed away or smoothed out by complementary variation in the returns from other securities.

Exhibit 3 illustrates the important relationship between diversification and total risk. Suppose we randomly selected securities for our portfolio that tended on average to be just as volatile as the market. (The average betas for the securities in our portfolio will always be equal to 1.) Exhibit 3 shows that as we add more securities, the total risk of our portfolio declines, especially at the start.

When ten securities are selected for our portfolio, a good deal of the unsystematic risk is eliminated, and additional diversification yields little further risk reduction. By the time twenty securities are in the portfolio, the unsystematic part of risk is substantially eliminated, and our portfolio (with a beta of 1) will tend to move up and down essentially in tandem with the market.

Now comes the key step in the argument. Both financial theorists and practitioners had agreed for years that investors should be compensated for taking on more risk by receiving

a higher expected return. Stock prices must therefore adjust to offer higher returns where more risk is perceived, to ensure that all securities are held by someone. What is different about the new theory is the definition and measurement of risk. Before the advent of the CAPM, it was often suggested that the return on each security would be related to the total risk inherent in that security. It was believed that the return from holding a security would vary with the instability of that security's particular performance, that is, with the variability or standard deviation of the returns it produced. The new theory says that the *total* risk of each individual security is irrelevant. Only the systematic component of that total instability is relevant for valuation. Because stocks can be combined in portfolios to eliminate specific risk (see Exhibit 3), only the undiversifiable or systematic part of the risk will command a risk premium (i.e., an extra return over and above that obtainable from a riskless asset). Investors will not get paid for bearing risks that can be diversified away. The only part of total risk that investors will get paid for bearing is systematic risk, the risk that diversification cannot eliminate. This is the basic logic behind the CAPM.

If investors did get an extra return (a risk premium) for bearing unsystematic risk, diversified portfolios made up of stocks with large amounts of unsystematic risk would give larger returns than equally risky portfolios of stocks with less unsystematic risk. Investors would snap at these higher returns by bidding up the prices of stocks with large unsystematic risk and selling stocks with equivalent betas but lower unsystematic risk. This would continue until the prospective returns of stocks with the same betas were equalized and no risk premium could be obtained for bearing unsystematic risk. Thus, the CAPM says that returns for any stock (or portfolio) will be related to beta, the systematic risk that cannot be diversified away. Any other results would be inconsistent with the existence of efficient markets.

Exhibit 3 How Diversification Reduces Risk

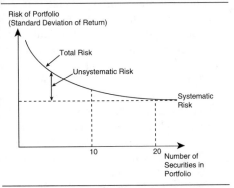

From Franco Modigliani and Gerald A. Pogue, "An Introduction to Risk and Return," *The Financial Analyst Journal*, March-April 1974.

The key relationship of the theoy is shown in Exhibit 4. (For the moment, ignore the dashed line in the diagram.) As the systematic risk (beta) of an individual stock (or portfolio) increases, so does the return an investor should expect. If an investor's portfolio has a beta of zero, as might be the case if all his funds were invested in a very short-term Treasury bill (beta would be zero since the returns from the certificate would not vary at all with swings in the stock market), the investor would receive some modest rate of return, which is generally called the risk-free rate of interest.[2] As the individual takes on more risk, however, the return should increase. If the investor holds a portfolio with a beta of 1 (for example, one share in one of the broad stock market averages), his return will equal the general return from common stocks. This return has over long periods of time exceeded the risk-free rate of interest, but the investment is a risky one. In certain periods the return is much less than the risk-free rate and involves taking substantial losses. This, as we have said, is precisely what is meant by risk.

Exhibit 4 Risk and Return According to the Capital-Asset Pricing Model

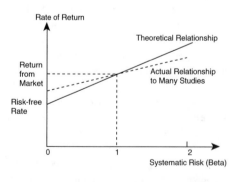

Rate of return = risk-free rate + beta × (return from market – risk-free rate). In other words, the return you get on any stock or portfolio increases directly with the beta value you assume. From *A Random Walk down Wall Street,* 2nd college ed. © 1981 by Burton G. Malkiel. Used with permission of the publishers, W.W. Norton & Company, Inc.

Exhibit 4 shows that a number of different expected returns are possible simply by adjusting the beta of the portfolio. For example, suppose an investor put half of her money in a T-bill and half in a share of the market averages. In this case she would receive a return midway between the risk-free return and the return from the market, and her portfolio would have an average beta of 0.5. The theory then asserts very simply that to get a higher average long-run rate of return, one must simply increase the beta of the portfolio. An investor can get a portfolio with a beta larger than 1 either by buying high-beta stocks or by purchasing a portfolio with average volatility on margin.

2.4 Tests of the CAPM Model

Tests of the CAPM have tried to ascertain if security returns are in fact directly related to beta, as the theory asserts. The early evidence seemed to support the theory. The relationship between the performance of a large number of professionally managed funds and the beta measure of relative volatility was generally consistent with the theory. The portfolio returns have varied positively with beta in roughly a straight-line manner, as is shown in Exhibit 5, so that over the long pull, high-beta portfolios have provided larger total returns than low-risk ones.

Unfortunately, however, as more evidence accumulated, a number of disquieting results came to light. First, the measured actual risk-return relationships found in the market appear to be much flatter than those implied by the theory. In Exhibit 4, for example, the actual measured relationships have usually looked more like the dashed line than the solid line, which represents the theoretical relationship. There seems to be a phenomenon much like that found at the racetrack, in that low-risk stocks earn higher returns and high-risk stocks earn lower returns than the theory predicts. (At the racetrack, long shots seem to go off at much lower odds than their true

Exhibit 5 Average Annual Return versus Risk: Selected Institutional Investors, 1965-1978

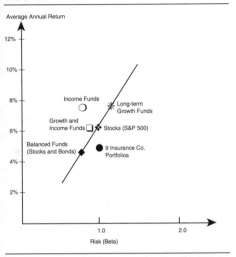

Source: Buck Consultants, Inc. From *The Inflation Beater's Investment Guide: Winning Strategies for the 1980s.* © 1980 by Burton G. Malkiel. Used with permission of the publishers, W.W. Norton & Company, Inc.

probability of winning would indicate, whereas favorites go off at higher odds than is consistent with their winning percentages.)

The divergence of theory from evidence is even more striking in the short run. For some short periods, it may happen that risk and return are *negatively* related. In 1972, for example, which was an up-market year, it turned out that safer (lower-beta) stocks went up more than did more volatile securities. *Fortune* magazine commented dryly on this well-publicized failure: "The results defied the textbooks." What happened was that in 1972, styles changed in Wall Street, as institutional investors eschewed younger, more speculative companies, the "faded ladies" of the late 1960s, and became much more enamored of the highest quality, most stable leading corporations in the so-called first tier of stocks. It became clear that beta could not be used to guarantee investors a predictable performance over periods of a few months or even a year. And even over some longer periods of time—

when the market has produced a positive rate of return—investors have actually been penalized for taking on more risk.

Another problem the theory encounters is the instability of measured betas. The beta of a stock is measured on the basis of historical relationships between returns for that stock and the returns from the market. It turns out that these past betas for individual stocks are relatively poor predictors of future betas. While the problem is less severe for portfolios, which are averages of many stocks, it is clear that past betas are quite imperfect estimates of future volatility numbers. Moreover, as Roll (1977) has pointed out, it is impossible to observe the market's return against which we measure beta. In principle, the market includes *all* stocks, a variety of other financial instruments, and even nonmarketable assets. The Standard and Poor's Index (or any other index) is a very imperfect market proxy at best. And, when we measure "market risk" using imperfect proxies, we may obtain quite imperfect estimates of market sensitivity. Roll (1977) showed that by changing the market index against which betas are measured, one can obtain quite different measures of the risk level of individual stocks or portfolios and thus quite different predictions of future returns. It is clear, then, that in judging risk, beta cannot be a substitute for brains.

2.5 Toward a Broader Method of Risk Measurement

To understand the logic of the risk measurement system proposed here, it is important to remember the correct insight underlying the CAPM. The only risk that investors should be compensated for bearing is the risk that cannot be diversified away. Only systematic risk will command a risk premium in the market. But, the systematic elements of risk in particular stocks and portfolios may be far more complicated than can be captured by a beta measure—the tendency of stocks to move more or less than any particular stock index.

Let us take a look at several other potential systematic risk elements. Changes in National Income, for example, may affect returns from individual stocks in a systematic way. This was mentioned earlier in the illustration of a simple island economy. During a recession, consumers might buy neither vacations nor umbrellas. Changes in National Income also mirror the changes in the personal income available to individuals, and so the systematic relationship between security returns and salary income can be expected to be important elements in individual behavior. For example, the worker in a Ford plant will find that a holding of Ford common stock is particularly risky since job layoffs and poor returns from Ford stock are likely to occur at the same time. Changes in National Income may also reflect changes in other forms of property income and may therefore be relevant for institutional portfolio managers as well.

Changes in interest rates also systematically affect the returns from individual stocks and are important nondiversifiable risk elements. To the extent that stocks tend to suffer as interest rates go up, equities are a risky investment, and those stocks that are particularly vulnerable to increases in the general level of interest rates are especially risky. Since fixed-income securities are included in the portfolios of many institutional investors, this systematic risk factor is particularly important for some of the largest investors in the market. Clearly, then, investors who think of risk in its broadest and most meaningful sense will be sensitive to the tendency of stocks to be affected by changes in interest rates.

Changes in the rate of inflation will similarly tend to have systematic influences on the returns from common stocks. This is so for at least two reasons. First, an increase in the rate of inflation tends to increase interest rates and thus may lead to the lower prices of equities just discussed. Second, increases in inflation may squeeze profit margins for certain groups of companies such as public utilities, which often find that rate increases lag behind increases in their costs. On the other

hand, inflation may benefit the prices of some common stocks, such as those in natural resource industries. Thus, again there are important systematic relationships between stock returns and economic variables that may not be captured adequately by a simple beta measure of risk.

The final new risk variable introduced is a measure of the dispersion among Wall Street security analysts concerning the future earnings and dividend growth of the company. If analysts differ greatly in their growth forecasts for a company, we shall consider the stock to be relatively risky. At first glance, this forecast dispersion variable may seem like a measure of total variability for a company—precisely the kind of measure that was used before the advent of the Capital-Asset Pricing Model. While such an interpretation is possible, the dispersion of analysts' forecasts may actually serve as a particularly useful proxy for a variety of systematic risks. The following illustration will explain why.

Suppose we had two companies, one a steel company that is extremely sensitive to systematic influences in the economy, the other a pharmaceutical firm that is quite insensitive to economic conditions. It may be that Wall Street analysts agree completely on how economic conditions will affect the two companies, but still differ greatly on their economic forecasts. If this were so, there could be a big dispersion in earnings forecasts for the steel company (because of the differences in economic forecasts and the sensitivity of the company to economic conditions), and very small differences in forecasts in the drug company (because economic conditions have little effect on that company).

Exhibit 6 illustrates the situation. Analyst 1 is optimistic about real growth and convinced that inflation and interest rates will fall. Analyst 2 predicts sluggish real growth but believes that inflation and interest rates will remain high. The analysts may agree completely on how economic conditions affect the two companies. Nevertheless, they

Exhibit 6 How Economic Forecasts Affect Earnings Forecasts

	Economic Forecast	Steel Company Forecast	Drug Company Forecast
Analyst 1	GNP: up sharply Inflation: down Interest rates: down	Sales up Raw material prices steady Borrowing costs down	Sales up whatever happens to GNP Uses few raw materials—no effect No borrowing—no effect
		Strong earnings growth	Strong earnings growth
Analyst 2	GNP: no growth Inflation: remains high Interest rates: remain high	Sales flat Raw material prices up Borrowing costs up	Sales up whatever happens to GNP Uses few raw materials—no effect No borrowing—no effect
		Weak earnings growth	Strong earnings growth

can differ in their earnings forecasts, because their economic forecasts differ and the two companies are not equally sensitive to these economic conditions. The steel company is very sensitive to GNP growth because it affects sales, to inflation because it affects raw material prices, and to interest rates because they affect borrowing costs. Thus, analyst 1 sees strong earnings growth for the steel company while analyst 2 predicts a very weak performance. As for the drug company, since, by assumption, it is relatively unaffected by economic conditions, the analysts agree on their earnings forecasts despite differences in their economic forecasts. The important point to note about this illustration is that the company for which the forecasts differed was the company most sensitive to systematic risk factors, i.e., the company with the greatest systematic sensitivity to economic conditions. Hence, differences in analysts' forecasts may be a most useful proxy for systematic risk in the broadest sense of the term.

2.6 Some Statistical Tests

It is possible to test statistically the influence of variable risk factors on anticipated rates of return for different common stocks. We hypothesize that stocks with larger systematic risks ought to promise investors a higher expected rate of return—the bigger the risk, the larger should be the reward.[3] Several alternative measures of systematic risk were used in the analysis.

1. Market Risk: Market risk is measured by beta, the historical sensitivity of the stock to swings in the overall market index. Stocks very sensitive to fluctuations in the overall market are riskier and therefore should provide higher anticipated rates of return.

2. Economic Activity Risk: This risk measures the sensitivity of an individual stock to movements in the level of National Income. It is estimated on the basis of past sensitivity of a security's return to changes in National Income. Stocks that are more sensitive to fluctuations in economic activity will have more systematic risk and hence ought to offer a larger rate of return.

3. Inflation Risk: Stocks which tend systematically to produce very poor returns when inflation accelerates are considered to have large systematic risk with respect to inflation. Hence, stocks with greater inflation risk should offer a higher anticipated rate of return.

4. Interest Rate Risk: Stocks which are extremely sensitive to interest rates also contain greater systematic risk. Alternatively, stocks that do well when interest rates rise would be particularly valuable in portfolios which contain both stocks and bonds. Thus, stocks that are particularly sensitive to change in market interest rates should be considered riskier and hence command a larger prospective rate of return.

5. Dispersion of Analysts' Forecasts: As indicated above, this risk variable may serve as a good proxy for a variety of systematic risk. The larger the dispersion of forecasts, the larger the anticipated return ought to be to the holder of securities.

The hypothesis to be tested is that expected returns on individual stocks should be related to a variety of risk variables. In order to perform the test, however, we need some way of measuring expected returns on individual stocks. We also need expectational data on the forecasts of security analysts from which we can measure the forecast dispersion mentioned above. Fortunately, a long-standing study done at Princeton's Financial Research Center has provided the expectational data we need. For each year during the 1960s, data were collected from a number of leading investment houses on forecasts of the long-run growth of dividends and earnings for a substantial sample of investment-grade issues. We also obtained similar data for the end of 1980 from the Institutional Brokerage Estimate System (IBES) of the investment firm of Lynch, Jones, and Ryan. The IBES provided estimates of long-run earnings growth as well as the dispersion of forecasts.

Anticipated rates of return on individual common stocks were derived from the standard dividend discount valuation model. According to that model the worth of a common stock is equal to the present value of the future stream of dividends an investor can expect to receive from that stock. It turns out that this model has a very simple implication. The expected rate of return on any stock can be derived by summing the dividend yield of the stock and the long-run expected growth rate of the earnings and dividends per share. An example will make the calculations clear. Say that American Telephone and Telegraph is selling at a dividend yield of approximately 10.5 percent. Say the average Wall Street forecast for the long-run expected growth rate of dividends is 6 percent. It will then turn out that a long-run holder of AT&T common stock can expect a 16.5 percent rate of return from holding AT&T stock. This is made up of a 10.5 percent dividend yield plus a 6 percent growth rate.[4]

We have now discussed the measurement of all the variables used in the study as well as the hypothesis to be tested. We turn next to the results of the analysis. Exhibit 7 shows the statistical relationship between expected rates of return for a sample of individual

Exhibit 7 Association of Risk Measures and Expected Returns
(Correlation Coefficients and T-Values of Regression Coefficients)

	Market Risk (Beta)		Economy Risk		Inflation Risk		Interest Rate Risk		Dispersion of Analysis Forecasts	
	Corr. Coef.	T-Value	Corr. Coef.	T-Value	Corr. Coef.	T-Value	Corr. Coef.	T-Value	Corr. Coef.	T-Value
1961	.32	3.65	.32	3.98	.11	1.31	.03	0.36	.25	2.57
1962	.26	3.32	.29	3.84	.08	1.03	.07	0.93	.44	6.30
1963	.04	0.55	.21	2.70	.10	1.29	.10	1.22	.28	3.74
1964	.13	1.65	.22	2.87	.18	2.24	.22	2.89	.42	5.95
1965	.29	3.79	.26	3.42	.24	3.17	.25	3.31	.47	6.97
1966	.39	5.35	.25	3.27	.40	5.40	.37	4.90	.22	2.79
1967	.31	3.49	.30	3.85	.47	6.59	.43	5.74	.20	2.54
1968	.27	3.35	.32	3.91	.49	6.50	.39	4.97	.74	12.86
1980	.27	4.56	.21	3.24	.16	2.56	.05	0.78	.31	5.29

stocks and the five risk measures listed above. While the pairwise correlation coefficients are not terribly high they are statistically significant in most instances. Thus, the results indicate that each of these risk variables does seem to be important in explaining the structure of anticipated returns. The t-statistics also support this conclusion. A handy rough rule is that any t-statistic larger than 2 indicates a statistically significant relationship.

While the traditional beta measure of risk does seem to be related to expected returns in the manner described by the theory, it appears that there are a variety of systematic risk influences on individual stocks and portfolios. Systematic susceptibility to economic conditions as measured by National Income, interest rates, and the rate of inflation also seems to play an important role in explaining differences in expected returns. This can be seen by looking at the correlation coefficients relating each risk measure to expected returns and by examining the t-values. The fact that so many of the t-values are statistically significant in the table suggests that several systematic risk influences clearly influence expected returns. Moreover, when several of these systematic risk influences are used together, a far better explanation of differences in expected returns is found than can be obtained using any single measure alone. This can be seen by comparing the multiple correlation coefficients in Exhibit 8 with the single-variable correlations shown in Exhibit 7.[5] Although this is not shown in the table, it should be noted that several of the risk variables were statistically significant in each year. This indicates that several systematic risk elements influence expected security returns.

If, however, we wanted for simplicity to select the one risk measure that is most closely related to expected returns, the traditional beta measure would probably not be our first choice. The best single risk proxy appears to be the dispersion of analysts' forecasts. This risk measure generally produced the highest correlations with expected returns

Exhibit 8 Multiple Correlation Coefficients Using All Five Risk Variables Together

Year	Multiple Correlation Coefficient
1961	.44
1962	.49
1963	.37
1964	.52
1965	.48
1966	.45
1967	.54
1968	.80
1980	.38

and the highest t-values in Exhibit 7. Companies for which there is a broad consensus with respect to future earnings and dividends seem to be less risky (and hence have lower expected returns) than companies for which there is little agreement among security analysts. It is possible to interpret this result as contradicting modern asset-pricing theory, which suggests that total variability per se will not be relevant for valuation. As we have shown, however, this dispersion of forecasts could well result if different companies were particularly susceptible to systematic risk elements, and thus our dispersion measure may be the best individual proxy available to capture the variety of systematic risk elements to which securities are subject.

2.7 Implications of the Analysis

The quest for better risk measures is not simply an amusing exercise that accomplishes only the satisfaction of permitting academics to play with their computers. It has important implications for protecting investors. A good illustration of how a better understanding of the many facets of risk can aid investors is provided by the recent fascination with so-called yield-tilted index funds, which had gained a considerable following in the investment community by the 1980s. Yield-tilted index funds tried to match closely the general composition of one of the broad stock indices such as the S&P 500 stock index, but their portfolios were tilted toward relatively high yield stocks. Such funds were being especially recommended for tax-exempt investors.

The reasoning behind the yield-tilted index fund seemed appealingly plausible. Since dividends are generally taxed more highly than capital gains, and since the market equilibrium is presumably achieved on the basis of after-tax returns, the equilibrium pretax returns for stocks that pay high dividends ought to be higher than for securities which produce lower dividends and correspondingly higher capital gains. Hence, the tax-exempt investor should specialize in buying high-dividend-paying stocks. In order to avoid the assumption of any greater risk than is involved in buying the market index, however, this tax-exempt investor was advised to purchase a yield-tilted *index* fund, that is, a very broadly diversified portfolio of high-dividend paying stocks that mirrored the market index in the sense that it had a beta coefficient precisely equal to one.

Even on a priori grounds one might question the logic of the yield-tilted index fund. Many of the largest investors in the market are tax-exempt (such as pension and endowment funds), and other investors (such as corporations) actually pay a higher tax on capital gains than on dividend income.[6] Thus, it is far from clear that many of the most important investors in the stock market prefer to receive income through capital gains rather than through dividend payments. But apart from these a priori arguments, the statistical results just reviewed can be interpreted as providing another argument against the yield-tilted index fund.

If the traditional beta calculation does not provide a full description of systematic risk, the yield-tilted index fund may well fail to mirror the market index. Specifically, during the periods when inflation and interest rates rise, high-dividend stocks may be particularly vulnerable. Public utility common stocks are a good example. Although they are known as low-beta stocks, they are likely to have high systematic risk with respect to interest rates and inflation. This is so not only because they are good substitutes for fixed-income securities, but also because public utilities are vulnerable to a profits squeeze during periods of rising inflation because of regulatory lags and increased borrowing costs. Hence, the yield-tilted index fund with beta equal to one may not mirror the market index when inflation accelerates.

The actual experience of yield-tilted index funds during the 1979-80 period was far from reassuring. The performance of these funds was significantly worse than that of the market. Of course, we should not reject a model simply because of its failure over any specific short-term period. Nevertheless, I believe that an understanding of the wider aspects of systematic risk, such as provided here, would have helped prevent what turned out to be (at least over the short term) some serious investment errors.

Conclusion

I have argued here that no single measure is likely to capture adequately the variety of systematic risk influences on individual stocks and portfolios. Returns are sensitive to general market swings, to changes in interest rates and in the rate of inflation, to changes in National Income and, undoubtedly, to other economic factors as well. Moreover, if one were to select the best individual risk estimate, the traditional beta measure would probably not be our first choice. The dispersion of analysts' forecasts seems to have a closer relationship with expected returns and may be the best single measure of systematic risk available.

Endnotes

1. Variance is defined as the average squared deviation of the (periodic) investment returns from their average. The square root of the variance is the standard deviation and is also often used to measure variability and, thus, risk. While it is true that only downward surprises constitute risk, as long as the distribution of returns is symmetric, a variance measure will serve as a good proxy for the chance of disappointment.

2. Of course, the yield from a Treasury bill is risk free only in a nominal sense. An investor will be guaranteed a certain money rate of return from the investment but his/her real rate of return will be uncertain. The risk-return relationships described here concern relationships between nominal returns before inflation and before taxes.

3. A formal theoretical justification for the hypothesis tested can be found in Malkiel and Cragg (1980). See also Ross (1976).

4. If we assume that the price-earnings multiple and dividend yield do not change, even a short-run holder can expect the same 16.5 percent rate of return. This is so because by assumption the stock's value will grow at 6.0 percent because of the increase in dividends and earnings. Hence, an individual selling AT&T stock after a year would realize 6.0 percent appreciation as well as a 10.5 percent dividend return. Although the results are not reported here, anticipated rates of return were also derived from a somewhat different version of

the standard valuation model that allowed for variable long-term growth rates. The results were quite similar to those obtained from the simple model, and only the results from the standard model are reported here.

5. In general, the correlations are not as close for 1980. 1980 used a different data set and is therefore not directly comparable. The general findings for 1980 are similar, however.

6. For corporate investors, 85 percent of dividend income is excluded from taxable income while capital gains are taxed at normal gains rates.

References

Ibbotson, Roger G., and Sinquefield, Rex A. 1979. Stocks, Bonds, Bills, and Inflation: Historical Returns (1926-1978). Financial Analysts Research Foundation, University of Virginia, Charlottesville.

Malkiel, Burton G., and Cragg, John G. 1980. Expectations and the Valuation of Shares. NBER Working Paper No. 471, Cambridge, MA. April.

Roll, Richard. 1977. A Critique of the Asset Pricing Theory's Tests. Part I: On Past and Potential Testability of the Theory. *Journal of Financial Economics* 4 (March): 129-76.

Ross, Stephen. 1976. The Arbitrage Theory of Capital Asset Pricing. *Journal of Economic Theory* 13 (December): 341-60.

Chapter 20

The Significance of P/Es for Portfolio Returns

After controlling for firm size, industry effects, and infrequent trading, low P/E stocks provide clearly superior risk-adjusted returns

John W. Peavy III, Ph.D.
Chairman
Founders Trust Company

David A. Goodman

The one-period Capital Asset Pricing Model (CAPM) developed by Sharpe [1964] and elaborated by Lintner [1965] and Black [1972] asserts that, in equilibrium, the expected return on any asset equals the risk-free rate plus a risk premium based on the asset's riskiness relative to the market. A substantial amount of empirical research substantiates the CAPM's assertion of market efficiency, i.e. abnormal returns cannot be obtained after adjusting for risk (see Fama [1970] for a review of many of these studies).

Yet other studies challenge the validity of the efficient market hypothesis. One such group contends that low price-earnings (P/E) ratio securities tend to outperform high P/E stocks. Nicholson [1960, 1968] showed that low P/E stocks consistently achieved higher returns than high P/E issues. McWilliams [1966] and Miller and Widmann [1966] confirmed Nicholson's findings. Breen [1968] also detected higher-than-market returns on low P/E stocks. In his study he pointed out a potential industry effect due to the tendency for low P/E securities to cluster in certain industry groups.

Nevertheless, none of these pioneering studies formally threatened the CAPM's validity, because they neglected to adjust returns for risk. Since the CAPM asserts that higher risk warrants higher return, the findings that low P/E stocks generate higher-than-market returns is not surprising if one believes that low P/E stocks are riskier than their high P/E counterparts.

Basu [1977] mounted a more robust challenge to the CAPM by demonstrating that low P/E portfolios, on average, earned higher rates of return even after adjusting for risk. The contention that returns on low P/E securities are higher than suggested by the underlying risk violates the foundation of the CAPM—thus implying that the CAPM may be misspecified or even false.

Reprinted with permission from *The Journal of Portfolio Management,* Winter 1983, pgs. 43-47.

Additional research, however, contends that these abnormal returns may be attributable to some non-P/E consideration. The purpose of this study is to determine whether, for a sample of common stocks, an investor can achieve excess risk-adjusted rates of return by acquiring portfolios of low P/E stocks while controlling for those non-P/E-related effects that otherwise might account for any abnormal returns. These non-P/E effects are: (1) the small firm effect, (2) the infrequent trading effect, and (3) the industry effect. The following section describes these effects and the manners in which they are controlled.

Effects of Non-P/E Factors on Security Returns

Reinganum [1980] illustrated that the returns generated by small firms' stocks systematically exceeded those indicated by the CAPM. He also detected a significant correlation between the P/E and firm size—the larger the firm, typically, the higher the P/E. Banz [1981] and Reinganum [1981] also observed that small firms' stocks yield excess returns. Since firm size and P/E are closely related, any abnormal return associated with a low P/E might really be more attributable to the small firm size than to the low ratio. To eliminate the possible bias created by small firm size, the selected sample for this study includes only those companies whose year-end 1980 common shares outstanding had a market value exceeding $100 million. This filter is designed to screen out small capitalization firms; thus, the low P/Es reported in this study will not merely be proxies for small firm size.

Dimson [1979] delved farther into the small firm effect and showed that infrequent trading of a security creates a bias in its risk parameter, beta. When infrequent trading exists, positive serial correlation is induced into the calculated returns and beta, the estimated risk coefficient, is biased downward. Roll [1981] connected the findings of the above-

mentioned studies by revealing that the abnormal returns of small firms could be caused by a significant bias in the measurement of their betas, which in turn was the result of infrequent trading. After adjusting for beta bias, abnormal returns no longer existed for infrequently traded stocks.

Smith [1978] found that risk underestimation was particularly acute when analysts used small trading intervals, such as daily, but as the trading interval was lengthened, the beta bias tended to disappear. For this study, we used quarterly trading intervals to overcome the intervaling problem. Also, we limited our sample to stocks with an average monthly trading volume exceeding 25,000 shares, and no selected stock experienced less than 10,000 shares traded in any single month during the observed time period. The combined effects of the lengthening of the trading interval, the deletion of small firms, and the elimination of infrequently traded securities compensates for any downward beta bias that might otherwise exist.

A final consideration pertains to the effect of industry bias. Some industries, such as food, characteristically show a preponderance of low P/E ratio securities. Thus, any broad grouping of stocks in rank order of P/E ratio would most likely enter proportionately more securities from characteristically low ratio industries into the lowest P/E category, while virtually ignoring stocks from high P/E industries. In this manner, most food company stocks, for example, would be classified into the lowest P/E groups, whereas most electronics stocks, which sport high P/Es, would be included in the highest ratio categories. Consequently, any detected return differences among groups might be caused by variances in industry performance rather than the P/E level.

We eliminated potential bias by analyzing stocks by industry classification. In this study, securities from the electronics, paper/container, and food industries are alternatively analyzed. We selected these industries to provide samples of stocks with higher-than-average (electronics), average (paper/container), and lower-than-average (food) market price volatility. The stocks of firms from each individual industry are grouped into P/E quintiles, so that all quintiles consist entirely of stocks from a single industry. Such a grouping permits us to compare the returns experienced by low ratio food stocks, for instance, to those achieved by high P/E food stocks. Since, for analysis purposes, all stocks belong to the same industry, any potential industry bias is eliminated.

The Data

The data for this study are retrieved from the COMPUSTAT data tapes. We selected 40 firms from each of the electronics, paper/container, and food industries, subject to the following constraints: (i) the fiscal year-end of the firm is December 31 or quarterly intervals thereof; (ii) the firm's stock traded continuously from December 31, 1969 to June 30, 1980; (iii) average monthly trading volume for each stock exceeded 25,000 shares; (iv) the firm's common stock had a 1980 total market value of at least $100 million, and (v) the relevant return, risk, and accounting data were available. This brought our sample to a total of 120 firms. We used Standard & Poor's 400 Index (S&P 400) and the 91-day Treasury bill interest rate as surrogates for the market and the risk-free rate, respectively.

Methodology

The P/E ratio of each sample security was computed quarterly from the beginning of 1970 to mid-year 1980, a total of 42 consecutive quarters. The numerator of the ratio is the closing market price per share at the end of the quarter and the denominator is the sum of the four most recent quarterly earnings per common share, fully diluted before extraordinary items. For purposes of this study, we assumed that investors have already anticipated that quarter's earnings per share and have correspondingly acted upon that information

when determining a stock's price at quarter-end. This assumption is substantiated by the findings of Ball and Brown [1968].

The stocks in each industry sample were ranked by P/E magnitude and grouped into portfolio quintiles. We then calculated the quarterly returns on each of these quintiles, assuming equal initial investment in each stock, as follows:

$$R_q = (P_q - P_{q-1} + D_q) / P_{q-1}$$

where:

R_q = the quarterly return (percentage) in quarter q,

P_q = the market price per share at the end of quarter q, and

D_q = the cash dividend paid per common share during quarter q.

This procedure was repeated at the end of each quarter of the selected time period from the start of 1970 to mid-year 1980, thus providing 42 quarters of return data for each of the five P/E portfolios. The composition of each portfolio was adjusted quarterly to reflect shifts in P/E rankings. Thus, if a stock's P/E increased beyond the boundaries of its P/E group, that stock would be "sold" at quarter-end and replaced in the portfolio with the lowest P/E issue from the next highest category. The "sold" stock would then advance to a higher P/E group and be "bought" for that portfolio.

The above return calculation formula does not compensate for risk. The CAPM postulates that, if capital markets are in equilibrium, returns incorporate a risk premium. When the assumptions of the CAPM are met, a security's risk premium, i.e., its expected return less the risk-free rate of interest, is proportional to the risk premium of the overall market and is expressed as follows:

$$E(R_i) - R_f = \beta_i [E(R_m) - R_f] ,$$

where:

$E(R_i)$ = the equilibrium expected return on asset i;

R_f = the risk-free rate of interest;
$E(R_m)$ = the expected return on the market portfolio, and
β_i = the risk of asset i relative to the market portfolio (the "beta" coefficient).

The beta coefficient is the crucial risk gauge, measuring an asset's covariance with the market as a whole. It is expressed as follows:

$$\beta_1 = \sigma_{mj, R_m} / \sigma_m^2$$

In other words, the CAPM implies that a particular asset will generate a higher than market return only if that asset has a higher than market beta (1.0). Consequently, a low P/E portfolio should outperform the market only if it has a higher than market beta.

Treynor's return-to-volatility measure was used to adjust security returns for beta risk. This procedure converts a security's expected return, $E(R_I)$, to a risk-adjusted expected return, $E(R_I)$, in the following manner:

$$E(R_i)' = R_f + [E(R_i) - R_f] / \beta_i$$

We then calculated the mean, risk-adjusted quarterly return of each P/E quintile for the 42 quarters. We used a geometric progression to incorporate the effect of compounding, expressed as follows:

$$1 + \overline{R}_q = \prod_{q=1}^{n} (1 + R_q)^{1/n}$$

where:

$\overline{R}_q$ = the geometric mean quarterly return,
R_q = the percentage return for quarter q, and
n = the number of quarters in the compounding period.

The resultant mean quarterly returns for each quintile are observed to determine whether significant return differences do exist among the various P/E portfolios. The results are presented and explained in the next section.

Empirical Results

Exhibit 1 summarizes the mean quarterly return and risk data for the three test industries over the experimental period of 42 quarters from January 1970 to July 1980. The data are arranged into five P/E portfolios (1 = lowest P/E, 2, 3, 4, 5 = highest P/E).

Several observations on the data in Exhibit 1 are pertinent. First, the mean industry betas, based on the pooled 1970-1980 quarterly data, differ considerably among the three industries. The electronics industry's average beta of 1.18 exceeded the paper/container and food industries' mean betas of 1.02 and 0.87, respectively. These average betas are compatible with the assumption that the three industries are representative of stocks with greater-than (electronics), similar (paper/container), and lower-than (food) market price variability. On the other hand, in most cases the mean beta did not differ significantly among the P/E quintiles for a given industry. For both the paper/container and food industries, for example, the mean beta was identical for the lowest and highest P/E groups; this implies that neither quintile possessed more systematic risk than the other. The high P/E electronics group, however, did exhibit greater systematic risk ($\beta = 1.29$) than did the low P/E quintile ($\beta = 1.15$). Overall, the mean betas reveal that low P/Es are not associated with more systematic risk than are high P/Es. In fact, just the opposite conclusion emerges for electronics stocks.

The second observation focuses on the mean quarterly P/E ratios. In each industry the mean P/E differs significantly across the portfolio quintiles. The greatest dispersion in P/Es appears in the electronics industry and the lowest shows up in the food industry. Thus, a trend emerges: the higher the systematic risk of an industry's stocks, the greater the variability in those stocks underlying P/E ratios.

Finally, Exhibit 1 reveals important trends in quarterly returns across the P/E portfolios. For all industries, the low P/E portfolio substantially

Exhibit 1 Summary of Results: January 1970 - July 1980

	Quintile					
Industry	1	2	3	4	5	Industry Mean
Electronics						
Number of Stocks	8.	8.	8.	8.	8.	40.
Mean Quarterly Return	9.24	5.45	5.11	2.96	2.21	5.05
Mean Quarterly Return*	8.53	4.71	4.34	2.53	1.86	4.51
Mean P/E Ratio	7.1	10.3	13.4	17.4	25.5	14.7
Mean Beta	1.15	1.12	1.13	1.19	1.29	1.18
Paper/Container						
Number of Stocks	8.	8.	8.	8.	8.	40.
Mean Quarterly Return	5.37	3.40	3.99	2.38	0.94	3.41
Mean Quarterly Return*	5.26	3.29	4.21	2.21	0.83	3.28
Mean P/E Ratio	6.7	8.5	10.2	12.4	20.2	11.6
Mean Beta	1.02	1.02	1.00	1.03	1.02	1.02
Food						
Number of Stocks	8.	8.	8.	8.	8.	40.
Mean Quarterly Return	5.53	3.79	2.70	0.81	0.65	2.83
Mean Quarterly Return*	5.97	4.12	2.97	0.89	0.71	3.04
Mean P/E Ratio	7.2	9.5	11.1	12.8	16.8	11.5
Mean Beta	0.90	0.85	0.86	0.86	0.90	0.87

* Risk-adjusted.

outperformed the high ratio portfolio. In fact, with only one exception (quintile 2 in the paper/container industry), the returns decline monotonically as the portfolio mean ratio increases. Despite this—and contrary to the CAPM—the higher returns experienced by the low P/E portfolio were not characterized by higher levels of systematic risk. Consequently, after we adjusted the returns for systematic risk by Treynor's return-to-volatility measure, the same trend persisted, i.e. low P/E portfolios outperformed high P/E portfolios.

We conducted a series of tests to assess the statistical significance of the portfolio return

**Exhibit 2 Results of Two Sample Tests
Quintile 1 Versus Quintile 5**

Industry	Z Value	Level of Significance
Electronics	4.0	.01
Paper/Container	3.2	.01
Food	3.8	.01

differentials. The initial test was designed to measure the significance of the difference between the risk-adjusted returns of quintile 1 (low P/Es) and quintile 5 (high P/Es). For each of the industries, a Z value was calculated, measuring the extent to which returns differ in quintile 1 versus quintile 5. Exhibit 2 presents the Z value and the corresponding level of significance for each industry. In each case, the difference of returns between the two P/E portfolios is significant at the .01 level, thus substantiating the contention that returns on low P/E stocks in the electronics, paper/container, and food industries exceed the returns of high ratio securities.

We then performed tests to gauge the difference between each industry's mean return versus the industry's low and high P/E quintiles, respectively. Exhibit 3 reveals that quintile 1 returns are higher than their industry mean at an .02 significance level or better. On the other hand, the returns of quintile 5 were significantly (.02 level or better) lower than

Exhibit 3 Results of One Sample Test Selected Quintiles Versus Industry Mean

Industry	Quintile 1		Quintile 5	
	2	Significance	2	Significance
Electronics	2.4	.01	3.6	.01
Paper/Container	2.4	.01	2.1	.02
Food	2.3	.02	3.0	.01

the respective industry mean returns. These results suggest that, for the selected industry samples, high ratio stocks not only significantly underperform their low P/E counterparts, but they also perform poorly when compared to the industry average return. At the same time, low P/E portfolios appear to generate higher returns than either high P/E or industry average portfolios.

The final set of tests was designed to examine the significance of the quintile classification scheme as a whole. First, a nonparametric chi-square test for K independent samples was used. The calculated chi-square statistic for each industry indicates that the mean quarterly returns differ significantly (.02 level or better) among the P/E quintiles. Exhibit 4 displays these results.

Also, a parametric one-way analysis of variance test is used to check the significance of the return differences for each of the three industries. The calculated F-statistic and corresponding significance level shown in Exhibit 5 confirm the findings of the chi-square test that significant return differences (.01 level) prevail among the quintiles for each in-

dustry. These statistical results reinforce the contention that portfolio returns vary inversely with the magnitude of the portfolio's average P/E ratio.

Conclusions

The purpose of this study was to test the validity of the P/E ratio as a predictor of risk-adjusted security returns. An attempt was made to control for three potential sources of return bias: small firm size, infrequent trading, and industry effect. The results of every statistical test performed indicated that the P/E ratio is, in fact, a significant factor related to security returns. Low P/E industry portfolios tend to outperform high ratio portfolios as well as the industry mean, both before and after adjustment for beta. Furthermore, as the ratio increases, both sets of returns decrease monotonically. The results of the study suggest that excess industry returns can be achieved by adhering to a low P/E strategy. If so, the one-period CAPM may be an inadequate description of the behavior of capital markets.

Exhibit 4 Results of Chi-Square Test for K Independent Samples Quintiles 1-5

Industry	x^2	Significance
Electronics	30.0	.02
Paper/Container	37.0	.01
Food	39.3	.01

Exhibit 5 Results of One-Way Analysis of Variance Quintiles 1-5

Industry	F Value	Significance
Electronics	5.9	.01
Paper/Container	3.7	.01
Food	4.8	.01

References

Rolf W. Banz. "The Relationship Between Return and Market Value of Common Stocks." *Journal of Financial Economics,* 9, 1981, pp. 3-18.

S. Basu. "Investment Performance of Common Stocks in Relation to Their Price-Earnings Ratios: A Test of the Efficient Market Hypothesis." *Journal of Finance,* June 1977, pp. 663-682.

S. Basu. "The Information Content of Price-Earning Ratios." *Financial Management,* Summer 1975, pp. 53-64.

Fischer Black. "Capital Market Equilibrium with Restricted Borrowing." *Journal of Business,* July 1972, pp. 444-455.

William Breen. "Low Price-Earnings Ratios and Industry Relatives." *Financial Analysts Journal,* July-August 1968, pp. 125-127.

William Breen and Eugene Lerner. "Corporate Financial Strategies and Market Measures of Risk and Return." *Journal of Finance,* June 1976, pp. 339-351.

Elroy Dimson. "Risk Measurement When Shares Are Subject to Infrequent Trading." *Journal of Financial Economics,* 7, 1979, pp. 197-226.

Eugene F. Fama. "Efficient Capital Markets: A Review of Theory and Empirical Work." *Journal of Finance,* May 1970, pp. 383-417.

John Lintner. "The Valuation of Risky Assets and the Selection of Risky Investments in Stock Portfolios and Capital Budgets." *Review of Economics and Statistics,* February 1965, pp. 13-37.

James D. McWilliams. "Prices, Earnings, and P-E Ratios." *Financial Analysts Journal,* May-June 1966, pp. 137-142.

Paul F. Miller and Ernest R. Widmann. "Price Performance Outlook for High and Low P-E Stocks." *1966 Stock and Bond Issue, Commercial and Financial Chronicle,* September 29, 1966, pp. 26-28.

Nicholas Molodovsky. "Building A Stock Market Measure—A Case Study." *Financial Analysts Journal,* May-June 1967, pp. 43-46.

Francis Nicholson. "Price Ratios in Relation to Investment Results." *Financial Analysts Journal,* January-February 1968, pp. 105-109.

Francis Nicholson. "Price-Earnings Ratios." *Financial Analysts Journal,* July-August 1960, pp. 43-45.

Marc R. Reinganum. "Misspecification of Capital Asset Pricing." *Journal of Financial Economics,* 9, 1981, pp. 19-46.

Marc R. Reinganum. "Abnormal Returns in Small Firm Portfolios." *Financial Analysts Journal,* March-April 1981, pp. 52-56.

Richard Roll. "A Possible Explanation of the Small Firm Effect." *Journal of Finance,* September 1981, pp. 879-888.

William F. Sharpe. "Capital Asset Prices: A Theory of Market Equilibrium Under Conditions of Risk." *Journal of Finance,* September 1964.

K. V. Smith. "The Effect of Intervaling on Estimating Parameters of the Capital Asset Pricing Model." *Journal of Financial and Quantitative Analysis,* 1978, pp. 313-332.

Chapter 21

Risk Perceptions of Institutional Investors[*]

Subjective elements are at least as important as ex post statistical measures like beta and total variance

Gail E. Farrelly, Ph.D.
Associate Professor of Accounting
Faculty of Management, Rutgers University

William R. Reichenstein, Ph.D.
The Pat and Thomas R. Powers Chair in Investment Management
Baylor University

Over the past 30 years, mathematical modeling has proven to be a powerful methodology in financial research. Much of it has focused on the use of objective measures of market-wide risk,[1] especially ex post beta. Risk, however, is such an elusive concept that it cannot be handled easily with mathematical precision. The disenchantment with beta by theoreticians and practitioners alike (Roll [1977] and Wallace [1980]), has led to a shift to a study of risk perception at the individual level in some of the recent literature.

Our study takes this "nontraditional" approach, in that it begins with risk ratings provided by portfolio managers and security analysts and then analyzes which of the publicly available measures of risk (some based entirely on past data and others based at least in part on subjective input) best "explain" the perceived risk. The publicly available measures of risk that we analyze are the dispersion of analysts' forecasts, plus the following measures of risk published by Value Line: beta, safety, timeliness, price stability, earnings predictability, and growth persistence. We then regress a measure of expected return on the risk measures to examine which measure of risk the market seems to be pricing.

Studying risk at a market-wide level is not the only, and perhaps not even the best, method of studying risk. Attempts to learn more about the factors affecting individuals' risk perceptions may be worthwhile, because they may lead to more relevant direction to

[*] The authors thank John L. Dugan and Eugene E. Hawkins. They are also grateful to the Institutional Brokers Estimate System (of Lynch, Jones & Ryan) for providing data for this study as well as Dovalee Dorsett, now at Baylor University, for her assistance in analyzing data. They are also grateful for the funds provided by the subject area of accounting and by the research and development office at Southern Methodist University.

Reprinted with permission from *The Journal of Portfolio Management,* Summer 1984, pgs. 5-12.

investors and security analysts engaged in risk assessment as well as to improved measures of risk. This is an especially desirable goal. As Malkiel (1982) recently commented: "The quest for better risk measures is not simply an amusing exercise that accomplishes only the satisfaction of permitting academics to play with their computers. It has important implications for protecting investors."

This paper is divided into several sections. The first section discusses the theoretical background of risk perception. This is followed by a consideration of research design. We then provide empirical analysis, along with suggestions for future research and some concluding remarks.

Background

Mathematical modeling, in conjunction with computers, has led a generation of financial researchers to concentrate on finding and applying market-wide risk surrogates. Rubenstein (1972) provides a summary of mean-variance models that have been used with some success by theoreticians and practitioners. The resulting models generally use objective measures of risk.

Nevertheless, treatment of risk by these models seems inadequate and leaves much to be desired. Even ex post measures of beta, popularized by both theoreticians and practitioners, seem substantially incomplete. Today it is deemed necessary to "adjust" historic beta for factors such as industry, dividend yield, and financial ratios to obtain better predictors of future risk (see Sharp [1981, pp. 345-346]). Despite these adjustments, the resulting risk proxies, which are still objective measures, seem substantially incomplete to all concerned.

On the other hand, efforts to measure risk through market-wide proxies based on past data continue to dominate the literature, despite the difficulties encountered along the way. There is, however, growing recognition of another type of financial research dealing

with risk. This research emphasizes the perception of risk on an individual, rather than a market-wide basis. This is a promising line of inquiry, since it is individuals' perception of and ultimately their reaction to, risk that affects stock price.[1]

For example, Filer, Maital, and Simon (1979) and Gooding (1975) challenge the notion of using only historical data to derive measures of ex ante risk. The former authors find that people who believe in their own ability to control events and outcomes (as measured by a 29-item scale devised by social psychologist Julian Rotter) choose riskier portfolios than those who do not hold such a belief. That is, despite the "riskiness" of the portfolio, the *perception* of its riskiness will depend on the personality of the individual making risk assessments.

Cooley (1977) used multidimensional scaling techniques to examine perceptions of risk as reflected by return-distribution moments. As expected, nearly all of the institutional investors who served as subjects viewed variance, the second moment, as an important part of risk. In addition, however, about half of the investors exhibited a negative association between skewness and risk. This evidence is consistent with a number of other studies that indicate the importance of higher order moments in investor decision making—see, for example, Coombs and Pruitt (1960) and Alderfer and Bierman (1970).

Furthermore, Crum, Laughhunn, and Payne (1981) find individual investment behavior depends upon whether expected returns are below or above a target return level. Such evidence suggests a complex utility function not adequately represented merely by expected return and variance, an assumption of the mean-variance asset pricing theory. Bart (1978) quantified the price expectations of actual market participants and found that the assumption of a simplistic utility function may not be warranted. For example, he found that buyers introducing a stock into their portfolios were generally more myopic and optimistic about the future rate of price change than buyers adding to their position in a stock. This optimism, however, was accompanied by the perception of greater total variability and downside potential.

In short, these studies portray risk perception as a complicated psychological process. The amount of risk perceived and investment behavior vary from individual to individual and can depend upon such conditions as how much the particular investor feels that he controls his environment, the prior existence of a specific stock in the investor's portfolio at time of purchase, and the relationship of expected return to the investor's determined target.

The present research study builds upon the work of McDonald and Stehle (1975). Probing the risk perceptions of individuals, they used a questionnaire approach to directly examine security risk as perceived by a sample of investment professionals. They asked respondents to supply risk ratings (the definition of risk was intentionally left to the individual) for each of 25 stocks, and these ratings were regressed on publicly available data (beta, non-market risk, etc.). McDonald and Stehle found that over 80 percent of the variation in the perceived risk of individual stocks could be "explained" by beta (15 percent) and non-market risk (69 percent).

The work of McDonald and Stehle is interesting, because it provides direct evidence that mathematical measures of risk presently in use are significant and important. We believe this work is worth further study for two reasons:

1. Its failure to specify the setting (individual or portfolio basis) in which the stock's risk should be assessed raises critical questions concerning the proper interpretation of the analysts' responses.
2. The risk perceptions could be regressed against data sets other than those considered by McDonald and Stehle. For example, Malkiel and Cragg (1980) recently provided a theoretical justification

for another risk measure that can be interpreted as a measure of systematic risk—the dispersion of analysts' forecasts of earnings. Malkiel, in a separate paper in which he drew heavily from the first (1982), reported tests on several alternative measures of systematic risk, including the dispersion of forecasts and beta. He concluded that, "The dispersion of analysts' forecasts seems to have a closer relationship with expected returns and may be the best single measure of systematic risk available."

Practitioners and academicians have long accepted the hypothesis that risk is used in pricing securities, resulting in a positive relationship between perceived risk and expected return. Malkiel and Cragg (1980) used this hypothesized relationship to examine various measures of systematic risk. They devised measures of the market's expected rate of return on securities and regressed these on their risk measures. In doing so they performed a joint test of four hypotheses:

1. A positive relationship exists between expected return and risk.
2. They are accurately measuring expected return.
3. Markets consider only systematic risk.
4. Their risk measures reflect ex ante systematic risk.

Not surprisingly, the authors' results are relatively weak. Their risk measures seldom explain more than 25 percent of the variation in their measures of expected return. The authors suspect "that a major part of the difficulty stems from error-in-variables problems," measuring expected return and perceived risk. As researchers often discover, there can be many a slip 'twixt cup and lip.

In an effort to reduce this slippage, we limit our analysis in the first part of our study to a search for a better measure of perceived risk; this part of the study can best be viewed as an extension of the work of McDonald and Stehle. The general acceptance of the first hypothesis mentioned above—that investors price risk to offer a higher expected return—reduces the need to demonstrate its existence and allows us to avoid the inherently difficult task of measuring the market's expected rate of return on securities. There is another difference between Malkiel and Cragg's study and ours. They limit their analysis to measures of systematic risk, although they admit that one of the risk measures examined—the dispersion of analysts' earnings forecast—could be interpreted as a measure of total risk. In contrast, we do not make this a priori assumption.

Thus, in the first part of our study, we focus more narrowly than Malkiel and Cragg, in an effort to avoid some of the problems they encountered. Nevertheless, in the spirit of Malkiel and Cragg, we also attempt the more difficult task of estimating the market's expected return and regressing these values on various risk measures. The specifics of the research design for both parts of the study follow.

Research Design

We utilized a modified version of the McDonald and Stehle (1975) research design to obtain direct market estimates of securities' risk. We sent a questionnaire to 500 portfolio managers and financial analysts from the membership lists of the Financial Analysts Federation in May 1982. The respondents were provided with a list of 25 well-known and widely followed stocks and asked to assess the risk of each on a scale of one (low) to nine (high) (see Appendix A). One stock, E. F. Hutton, was eliminated from the study because a measure of the dispersion of analysts' forecasts was not available. Unlike McDonald and Stehle, who purposely left the definition of risk up to the individual respondent, we explicitly asked the respondents to estimate the risk of each stock as if it were to be added to a diversified portfolio (see Appendix B):

Interpretation of the risk ratings requires establishment of the setting in which the stock's risk should be assessed. Two hundred and nine usable responses were received within two weeks for a response rate of 42 percent.

The risk ratings of respondents were regressed on several publicly available measures of risk. These measures and their definitions include the following:

Dispersion 1982 (Disp. '82)—the coefficient of variation of analysts' 1982 EPS forecasts, available from the Institutional Brokers Estimate System (IBES);

Dispersion 1983 (Disp. '83)—the IBES coefficient of variation of analysts' 1983 EPS forecasts. (The Disp. '82 observation for International Harvester was used for the missing Disp. '83 value. The high correlation, .84, between Disp. '82 and Disp. '83, suggests that this interpolation is reasonable);

Beta—a Value Line measure derived from a regression analysis of weekly data for the past five years using the NYSE Composite Index. The betas are adjusted for the tendency of high beta stocks to become lower beta stocks and vice versa;

Price Stability—a Value Line index of total risk, or market plus company specific risk—of a stock. The index is based on the standard deviation of the weekly percentage changes in the price of a stock over the last five years;

Safety—a Value Line measure of total risk. Price stability accounts for about 80 percent of safety with the remaining 20 percent being a *subjective* consideration of "any important, very recent changes in the company's business or the quality of its earnings";

Earnings Predictability—a Value Line measure of the reliability of an earnings forecast. The earnings stability is based upon the standard deviation of percent changes in quarterly earnings over a five-year period. Special adjustments are made for comparisons around zero and from plus to minus;

Growth Persistence—a Value Line index designed to measure the historic consistency of the stock's price growth relative to the general market; and

Timeliness—a Value Line measure of expected performance during the next 12 months.

Three of the risk proxies (Disp. '82, Disp. '83, and beta) are measures of systematic risk, while the other five proxies are designed to be more inclusive than systematic risk. Of the eight proxies:

- four (beta, price stability, earnings predictability, and growth persistence) are entirely objective, that is, formulated from past data only.
- four (Disp. '82, Disp. '83, safety, and timeliness) are based, at least in part, on subjective input.

Exhibit 1 Summary of Risk Perceptions

Name of Stock	Average Perceived Risk (1 = low, 9 = high)	Rank of Average Perceived Risk (1 = low, 24 = high)
American Telephone	1.89	1
Procter & Gamble	2.36	2
IBM	2.39	3
General Electric	2.69	4
Exxon	2.7	5
Commonwealth Edison	3.2	6
Dow Jones & Co.	3.57	7
McDonalds	3.87	8
Sears Roebuck	3.91	9
Du Pont	4.11	10
Safeway	4.28	11
Citicorp	4.3	12
Dr Pepper	4.32	13
General Motors	4.59	14
Xerox	4.69	15
American Broadcasting	4.9	16
Holiday Inns	5.13	17
Tandy	5.54	18
Litton Industries	5.66	19
RCA	5.67	20
Georgia-Pacific	5.88	21
Emery Air Freight	5.92	22
U.S. Homes	7.23	23
International Harvester	8.78	24

Empirical Analysis

We examine three questions, using two methodologies.

In the first methodology, the average risk rating for each stock is calculated (see Exhibit 1). These 24 average risk ratings serve as the observations on the dependent variable. Simple regressions are run on each of the eight prospective proxies.

In the second methodology, the midpoint of Value Line's three-to-five year projected annual total return is used as a proxy for the market's expected return. These 24 observations serve as the dependent variable and are regressed on each of the eight risk proxies.

There is some question whether the above measure of expected return reflects the market's expectations as opposed to Value Line's. The popularity of the Value Line Investment Survey suggests that its projections are not wholly unrepresentative of market expectations. Nevertheless, due to the inherent difficulty of measuring market expectations, appropriate caution is warranted in interpreting the expected return results.

Our calculations show that all of the proxies except growth persistence are correctly signed and significant at the 5 percent level or better in the risk perception regressions (see Exhibit 2). Growth persistence is thus removed from further consideration. The perceived risk of International Harvester, however, even in a portfolio sense, is so great (8.78 on a 9 point scale) that we examined the regressions with and without International Harvester (IH).

We use the above methodologies to examine the following three issues:

1. Whether the dispersion of analysts' forecasts is a better measure of systematic risk than ex post beta;
2. Whether analysts' risk perceptions and securities' expected returns are most highly correlated with measures of sys-

Exhibit 2 Perceived Risk as Explained by Selected Risk Measures

Dependent Variables = Average Risk Perceptions

	A (With Inter. Harvester)		B (Without Inter. Harvester)	
Independent Variable	R^2	Rank	R^2	Rank
Beta	.36	7	.55	3
Disp. '82	.61	3	.43	4
Disp. '83	.59	4	.39	5
Safety	.86	1	.81	1
Price Stability	.65	2	.67	2
Earn. Predictability	.49	5	.39	5
Timeliness	.47	6	.37	7

R^2 indicates the percent of variation in the dependent variable explained by the independent variable. For example, the first row of the table indicates that beta alone explains 36 percent of the variation in risk perception in the sample of 24 stocks (IH included) and 55 percent of the variation in risk perception in the sample of 23 stocks (IH excluded).

All variables are significant at the 5 percent level or better.

The top three rankings are not sensitive to the removal of additional firms besides International Harvester. The R-squares of the others are usually closely bunched.

tematic risk or with more inclusive measures of risk; and

3. Whether objective measures of risk conform more closely to analysts' risk perceptions and securities' expected return than do subjective measures.

Systematic Risk—Beta Versus Dispersion of Analysts' Forecasts

The first issue is whether we can accept Malkiel's hypothesis that the dispersion of analysts' forecasts represents a better method of measuring systematic risk than beta. The results from the risk perception regressions in Exhibit 2 are mixed. The dispersion of forecasts for 1982 and the dispersion for 1983 explain a higher percentage of the variation in analysts' risk perceptions (R-squares of .61 and .59) than beta (.36) when the sample includes International Harvester. On the other hand, beta (.55) outperforms both dispersion measures (.43 and .39) when IH is removed from the sample.

The expected return regressions in Exhibit 3 strongly support the dispersion of earnings for 1982 as the best measure of systematic risk. Disp. '82 consistently outperforms beta and Disp. '83. It even performs slightly better than the average of analysts' risk perceptions (not shown). In contrast, beta never exhibits statistical significance at the usual levels in any expected return regression examined. It appears to be only marginally related to expected return. These results corroborate Malkiel and Cragg's finding that the dispersion of forecasts appears to be more highly correlated with expected return than with beta.

Exhibit 3 Expected Return as Explained by Selected Risk Measures

Dependent Variables – Expected Return

	(With Inter. Harvester)		(Without Inter. Harvester)	
Independent Variable	R^2	Rank	R^2	Rank
Publicly Available Risk Measures				
Beta	.04	7	.10	5
Disp. '82	.58*	1	.29*	1
Disp. '83	.44*	2	.08	6
Safety	.40*	3	.19*	3
Price Stability	.19*	6	.12	4
Earn. Predictability	.20*	5	.06	7
Timeliness	.35*	4	.22*	2
Nonpublicly Available Risk Measure				
Risk Perception	.50*		.28*	

R^2 indicates the percent of variation in the dependent variable explained by the independent variable.

* Indicates significance at the 5 percent level or better.

The first five rankings are not sensitive to the removal of additional firms besides International Harvester.

In both methodologies, the coefficient of determination, R^2, decreases for beta and increases for the other risk proxies when IH is included in the sample. This is important, because it means that beta apparently fails to reflect significant aspects of risk that are better reflected by the dispersion measures. One may argue that beta is the preferred measure of systematic risk, although it is inappropriate for use in evaluating an endangered company like International Harvester. This argument advocates the selective use of beta. Such a use of beta would no longer be objective, however: It would be subjective.

Systematic Versus Total Risk

We can use the average risk ratings to examine the hypothesis based on modern portfolio theory that the market values only systematic risk. We find that, despite the implications of modern portfolio theory, analysts' perceptions are most highly correlated with measures of total risk. Exhibit 2 indicates that safety and stock price stability (measures specifically formulated by Value Line as proxies for total, rather than systematic, risk) are the most highly correlated risk measures, whether or not International Harvester is included in the sample.

Disp. '82 is the clear winner in the expected return regressions, with two measures of total risk—safety and timeliness—also turning in consistently significant results. The performance of Disp. '82 is even more remarkable when one considers that it beat Value Line's risk measures against Value Line's own expected return forecasts!

Malkiel and Cragg emphasize throughout their study that the dispersion measures could easily be interpreted as measures of total risk, despite their preference of interpreting them as proxies for systematic risk. Considering this interpretation difficulty with beta's failure to demonstrate significance, the results raise serious questions concerning the validity of CAPM's assumption that the market prices only systematic risk.

Objective Versus Subjective Measures of Risk

The third issue concerns the importance of subjective factors in the formation and pricing of risk perceptions. This issue is examined in part by comparing the relative performance of totally objective measures of risk with those measures which are at least partially subjective. Beta, price stability, earnings predictability, and growth persistence are in the former category, while Disp. '82, Disp. '83, safety, and timeliness are in the latter.

In the risk perception regressions, the subjective measures tend to outperform objective measures. As we can see in Exhibit 2, whether or not IH is included in the sample, a *subjective* measure (namely, safety) tops the list in explaining the variations in average risk perceptions. Price stability (an objective measure) comes in second, but it is a distant second, explaining much less of the variation than safety—21 percent less with IH and 14 percent less without IH. Moving beyond the top two performers, we find that the remaining results shown in Exhibit 2 are somewhat mixed regarding the performance of objective versus subjective measures.

It is interesting to compare the performance of safety with that of price stability. As previously indicated, safety is formulated by adjusting price stability for subjective factors such as the quality of earnings. The importance of subjective factors in the formulation of risk perceptions is demonstrated by safety's superior performance. This tells us that the subjective adjustments made by Value Line are in close agreement with the subject considerations of the institutional investors.

The expected return regressions also support the importance of subjective factors in risk measures. The top three performers in each set of regressions are subjective measures of risk.

The subjective–objective issue is further illuminated by regressing the average risk ratings on two major objective measures of risk and comparing the results to a regression on two major subjective measures. The best objective measures of systematic and total risk—beta and price stability—account for 68 percent of the variation in perceived risk, while the corresponding subjective measures, Disp. '82 and safety, account for 91 percent of the variation in perceived risk. These results indicate, once again, the contribution of subjective considerations to the formation of risk perceptions.

We do not suggest that objective measures are necessarily poor measures of risk. After all, price stability performs consistently well. The regressions do, however, indicate that objective measures, based as they are entirely on past data, will be incomplete measures of risk because of their failure to consider important subjective risk considerations.

Exhibit 4 presents further evidence on the subjective versus objective issues. This table shows the regression residuals on 10 stocks— the 5 perceived as least risky and the 5 perceived as most risky. Safety (the best subjective measure) outperforms price stability (the best objective measure) for 9 of these 10 stocks.

The residual patterns in Exhibit 4 bear closer scrutiny. In general, the six risk measures overpredict (negative residuals) the average risk ratings of the five stocks with the lowest-perceived risk and underpredict (positive residuals) the risk ratings on the stocks with the highest-perceived risk. These residual patterns are consistent with the hypothesis that the risk proxies fail to consider important aspects of risk. A misspecified relationship where one or more important variables are left out of the regression, yields biased results.

Exhibit 4 Regression Residuals* on Stocks** with Low and High Risk Perceptions

	Regression Residuals					
	Objective Risk Measures			Subjective Risk Measures		
Low Risk Perception Stocks	Beta	Price Stability	Earnings Predictability	Safety	Disp. '82	Disp. '83
AT&T	−1.10	−1.03	−1.30	−0.64	−1.76	−1.69
Procter & Gamble	−1.03	−0.57	−0.84	−0.17	−1.10	−1.46
IBM	−1.80	−0.81	−1.98	−0.14	−1.27	−1.25
GE	−1.50	−0.51	−0.69	0.16	−0.72	−0.83
Exxon	−1.09	−0.23	−1.76	0.17	−1.55	−1.61
Mean Error	−1.30	−0.63	−1.11	−0.12	−1.28	−1.37
High Risk Perception Stocks						
Int. Harvester	4.39	2.58	2.15	0.57	0.26	−0.16
US Homes	0.65	−0.05	1.33	0.45	1.37	0.48
Emery Air Fr.	1.73	0.81	2.00	0.55	−0.72	2.15
Georgia Pacific	1.09	1.59	1.42	0.51	−0.39	0.24
RCA	1.08	1.11	−0.24	0.30	0.64	1.11
Mean Error	1.79	1.21	1.33	0.48	0.23	0.76

* Residual = Average Risk Perception - Fitted Value
   A negative residual implies perceived risk is lower than fitted value. A positive residual implies perceived risk is higher than fitted value.
** n = 24
   Similar residual patterns are found on the regressions that exclude International Harvester (that is, n = 23).
   Note: Growth persistence and timeliness, the worst performers in the risk perception regressions, are omitted from this analysis.

The error patterns exhibited in Exhibit 4 are thus consistent with the hypothesis that the risk proxies fail to reflect important factors affecting risk perceptions. That is, to a large extent, market-wide measures of risk (at least the ones that we have selected for use in this study) leave much to be desired in terms of their ability to explain risk perception and, presumably, the pricing of risk in financial markets. We simply do not know enough about what makes investors perceive and react to risk.

A closer analysis of these residual patterns reveals that the dispersion measures perform markedly better for stocks of high, rather than low, risk. This suggests that other factors besides the uncertainty of future earnings can partially account for these low risk ratings. Firm size may be another one of the missing factors. Reinganum (1981a, 1981b) and Banz (1981) present evidence consistent with this hypothesis. They find that, after adjusting for other factors, larger firms have higher P/E ratios, which could be a reflection of lower perceived risk. Thus, the negative residuals on the low risk stocks may be due to the failure of the risk proxies to appropriately consider the impact of a firm's size on perceived risk. The expected return residuals (not shown) are also generally supportive of this hypothesis; the larger the firm, the lower the risk, and the lower is the expected return.

One particularly important finding is that the residual patterns on the dispersion measures suggest that some risk measures are more relevant for some stocks than for others. Consequently, no one measure or group of measures will prove to be best for all stocks. In addition to improving the market-wide risk measures now in use, we may wish to expand our research endeavors toward the finding of risk measures that are particularly well-suited to an analysis of a limited set of stocks. For example, we may be able to find a risk measure that reflects the key risk dimensions that are especially relevant to the analysis of firms in a specific industry. Such research has important practical implications for analysts who specialize in one type of stock and have need for risk measures designed for their corner of the market.

Conclusion

This study provides evidence that:

1. As suggested by Malkiel, the dispersion of analysts' earnings forecasts appears to be a better risk proxy than beta. It may be the best measure of systematic risk. A clearer determination of this issue is clouded by the problems surrounding the proper interpretation of the dispersion of forecasts as a measure of systematic risk.

2. Despite the implications of modern portfolio theory, the best risk proxies appear to be measures that are more inclusive than systematic risk. Safety and price stability, measures specifically designed by Value Line to reflect a security's total risk, are most closely correlated with analysts' risk perceptions. The dispersion of forecasts, which could be interpreted as a measure of total risk, is most closely related to securities' expected return.

3. Subjective measures of risk appear to conform more closely to analysts' risk perceptions and securities' expected return than do objective measures. This suggests that, in the process of risk perception, there is a component of subjective input that bears further attention.

We regard these conclusions as interesting but tentative. Thus, the study lends itself to a variety of extensions. The stocks and risk measures were limited in number, and institutional rather than individual investors were used as subjects. It would be interesting to observe whether the same results would hold with a different set of stocks and risk measures and with individual rather than institutional investors.

Although it is informative to look to how investors rate the risk of a variety of stocks, we realize that providing an undimensional scale of one to nine for this rating may be simplistic. It does, however, provide some preliminary insight into the complicated process of risk perception. Probing more deeply into this process appears warranted. Through interviews and/or intensive survey techniques, we may be able to learn more about how investors perceive and price risk. Such knowledge may ultimately lead to better quantitative measures of risk to be used in mathematical modeling, more relevant direction for investors engaged in risk assessment, and better guidance for managers making decisions about risk tolerance and risk disclosure.

Appendix A

Risk Questionnaire

Stock	Risk Rating from 1 to 9 (1 = low risk, 9 = high risk)
1. U.S. Homes	1. _____
2. Georgia-Pacific	2. _____
3. Procter & Gamble	3. _____
4. General Electric	4. _____
5. RCA Corporation	5. _____
6. IBM	6. _____
7. Xerox Corpoation	7. _____
8. E. F. Hutton	8. _____
9. DuPont	9. _____
10. Litton Industries	10. _____
11. International Harvester	11. _____
12. Safeway Stores	12. _____
13. Dr Pepper Company	13. _____
14. Sears Roebuck	14. _____
15. Tandy Corporation	15. _____
16. Holiday Inns	16. _____
17. Dow Jones & Co.	17. _____
18. Citicorp	18. _____
19. American Broadcasting	19. _____
20. American Telephone	20. _____
21. Commonwealth Edison	21. _____
22. General Motors	22. _____
23. Emery Air Freight	23. _____
24. McDonalds	24. _____
25. Exxon	25. _____

____ Check here if you wish to receive a copy of the research paper upon completion.

_____

Name (Please print)

_____

Firm

Appendix B

Dear_____

Since risk is a basic determinant of stock price knowing more about how investors perceive risk is important to both theoreticians and practitioners. We are interested in learning more about risk perception and request that you help us in this learning process by completing the attached one-page questionnaire and returning it in the enclosed envelope.

Please consider the riskiness, over the next year of each stock listed on the next page. Assume that each stock is being added to a diversified portfolio. Assign a risk rating from 1 (low risk) to 9 (high risk) to each stock on the list. You may not be as familiar with some stocks as you are with others but we ask that you do not omit any ratings.

We are grateful for your participation and will be glad to share the results of our research upon completion.

Thank you,

Dr. Gail Farrelly
Assistant Professor of Accounting

Dr. William Reichenstein
Visiting Professor of Finance

GF/WR:ps

Enclosure

Endnotes

1. In this article, an objective measure is one based entirely on past data. A subjective measure is based, at least in part, on subjective input. By market-wide measures, we mean those that assess a security's risk as measured or reflected by "the market." Such measures are aggregate or macro measures as opposed to micro measures of risk which assess the risk perceptions of individuals.

2. Howe and Beedles (1984) point that three, rather than two, attributes of security returns (return, risk, skewness) are valued by the market. They suggest a security selection rule especially designed for defensive investors who are willing to give up positive skewness to obtain higher returns or lower risk.

References

Alderfer, Clayton P., and Harold Bierman. 1970. "Choice with Risk: Beyond the Mean and Variance." *Journal of Business* (July).

Arrow, Kenneth J. 1982. "Risk Perception in Psychology and Economics." *Economic Inquiry* (January).

Banz, Rolf W. Barry. 1981."The Relationship between Return and Market Value of Common Stocks." *Journal of Financial Economics* (March).

Bart, John T. 1978."The Nature of the Conflict between Transactors' Expectations of Capital Gain." *Journal of Finance* (September).

Blume, M. W. 1971. "On the Assessment of Risk." *Journal of Finance* (March).

Blustein, Paul. 1980. "Money Managers' Bedrock Theory of Investing Comes under Attack." *The Wall Street Journal*, 8 September.

Cooley, Philip L. 1977. "A Multidimensional Analysis of Institutional Investor Perception of Risk." *Journal of Finance* (March).

Coombs, C. H., and D. G. Pruitt. 1960. "Components of Risk in Decision Making; Probability and Variance Preference." *Journal of Experimental Psychology* (November).

Crum, Roy L.; Dan J. Laughhunn; and John W. Payne. 1981. "Risk-Seeking Behavior and Its Implications for Financial Models." *Financial Management*. (Winter).

Farrelly, Gail. 1980 "A Behavioral Science Approach to Financial Research." *Financial Management* (Autumn).

Filer, Randall, Shlomo Maital, and Julian Simon. 1979. "Risk-Taking and Risk Aversion: A Game-Simulation of Stock Market Behavior." Unpublished paper read at the Spring meeting of the Eastern Finance Association, April 21, Washington, D.C.

Gooding, Arthur E. 1975. "Quanitifcation of Investors' Perceptions of Common Stocks; Risk and Return Dimension." *Journal of Finance* (December).

Howe, John S., and William L. Beedles. 1984. "Defensive Investing Using Fundamental Data." *Journal of Portfolio Management* (Winter).

Malkiel, Burton G. 1982. "Risk and Return: A New Look," in *The Changing Role of Debt and Equity in Financing U.S. Capital Formation*, ed. Benjamin M. Friedman. University of Chicago Press, 27–45.

Malkiel, Burton G., and John C. Cragg. 1980. "Expectations and the Valuation of Shares." National Bureau of Economic Research Working Paper no. 471. Cambridge, Mass. (April).

McDonald, John G., and Richard E. Stehle. 1975. "How Do Institutional Investors Perceive Risk?" *Journal of Portfolio Management* (Fall).

Reinganum, Marc R. 1981a. "Misspecification of Capital Asset Pricing." *Journal of Financial Economics* (March).

———— 1981b. "Abnormal Returns in Small Firm Portfolios." *Financial Analysis Journal* (March-April).

Roll, Richard. 1977. "A Critique of the Asset Pricing Theory's Tests; Part 1: On Past and Potential Testability of the Theory." *Journal of Financial Economics* (March).

Rubenstein, Marck I. 1972. "A Mean-Variance Synthesis of Corporate Financial Theory." *Journal of Finance* (September).

Sharpe, William F. 1981. *Investments*, 2d ed., Englewood Cliffs, NJ. Prentice-Hall.

Wallace, Anise. 1980. "Is Beta Dead?" *Institutional Investors* (July).

Chapter 22

Security Analyst Superiority Relative to Univariate Time-Series Models in Forecasting Quarterly Earnings[*]

Lawrence D. Brown, Ph.D.
Samuel P. Carpen Professor of Accounting
Jacobs Management Center, State University of New York at Buffalo

Robert L. Hagerman, Ph.D.
Professor of Accounting and Finance
State University of New York at Buffalo

Paul A. Griffin, Ph.D.
Professor of Accounting and Management
University of California–Davis

Mark E. Zmijewski, Ph.D.
Professor of Accounting
Graduate School of Business, University of Chicago

This paper provides evidence of security analyst (SA) superiority relative to univariate time-series (TS) models in predicting firms quarterly earnings numbers and shows that SA forecast superiority in our sample is attributable to: (1) better utilization of information existing on the date that TS model forecasts can be initiated, a contemporaneous advantage; and (2) use of information acquired between the date of initiation of TS model forecasts and the date when SA forecasts are published, a timing advantage.

[*] The authors are grateful for the research assistance of G. Chae, P. Jablin, J. Jang, P. McCourt, K. Ravindran, P. Shah, and S. Swaminathan. The helpful comments of the workshop participants at the University of Chicago, University of Massachusetts, McMaster University, New York University, University of Rochester, University of Southern California, and University of Buffalo are gratefully acknowledged. The authors are, of course, responsible for any remaining errors.

Reprinted with permission from *Journal of Accounting and Economics,* Vol. 9, 1987, pgs. 61-87. © 1987, North-Holland Publishing Company.

1. Introduction

Academic researchers require accurate measures of the market's expectation of firms' future earnings to conduct various types of empirical research studies. The investment community requires earnings forecasts to evaluate firms and make portfolio decisions. When academic researchers require expectations of a firm's earnings, they typically utilize estimates derived from time-series (TS) models. The investment community, on the other hand, relies on earnings forecasts generated by security analysts (SA).[1]

Several studies compare the predictive ability of SA with TS model forecasts. Some studies conclude that SA forecasts significantly outpredict TS model forecasts [Brown and Rozeff (1978), Collins and Hopwood (1980)], while others contend that SA earnings forecasts are not significantly more accurate than TS model forecasts [Cragg and Malkiel (1968), Elton and Gruber (1972), Imhoff and Pare (1982)]. These conflicting findings have led some researchers to conclude that the evidence in favor of comparative SA forecast accuracy may have been overstated [Griffin (1982)], and others to attribute SA superiority to an artifact of certain experimental design issues.

As examples of experimental design issues, Abdel-khalik and Thompson (1977-78) and Collins, Hopwood and McKeown (1984), respectively, assert that SA superiority pertains only to particular years or fiscal quarter reporting periods; Imhoff and Pare (1982) maintain that SA superiority disappears over longer forecast horizons. SA forecast superiority could also be an artifact of other experimental design issues, such as definition of forecast error, identification and/or treatment of outliers, the fiscal quarter upon which the forecasts are conditioned, and/or the statistical test statistic on which inferences are drawn.

Past research has generally focused on the issue of SA forecast superiority per se, and has not examined whether SA forecast superiority is due to: (1) SA utilization of information existing

at the TS model forecast initiation date (i.e., SA possess a "contemporaneous advantage"), and (2) SA utilization of information acquired after the TS model forecast initiation date but before the SA forecast initiation date (i.e., SA possess a "timing advantage").[2] Watts and Zimmerman (1986) argue that SA forecast superiority may be due to the fact that the SA forecast initiation date follows the TS model forecast initiation date. Thus, Watts and Zimmerman suggest that SA superiority may only possess a timing advantage.

The purposes of this paper are twofold. First, we re-evaluate the issue of comparative forecast superiority of SA versus TS models by addressing the experimental design issues that are discussed above. After demonstrating that for our sample SA are superior forecasters of quarterly earnings, we examine whether that forecasting superiority is due to SA's contemporaneous advantage, their timing advantage, or both.

We focus on the quarterly reporting interval and, as such, evaluate forecasts for relatively short horizons. Based on measures of forecast error, we show that for our sample SA forecast superiority is *not* an artifact of: (1) chronological subperiods—the evidence is consistent across six years, (2) forecast horizon (up to three-quarter forecast horizons)—the evidence exists for one-through three-quarter forecast horizons, (3) forecast error definition or treatment of outliers—the results hold for the 16 error metric/outlier treatment combinations that are examined, (4) conditioning quarter—the findings pertain to all four fiscal quarters on which a forecast is conditioned (specifically, the most recent quarter of the earnings time-series), or (5) the statistical test statistic on which inferences are drawn—the results are consistent using both parametric and non-parametric tests as well as after making adjustments for extreme cross-sectional correlation. The evidence indicates that SA forecast superiority is due to better utilization of information existing at the forecast initiation date for the TS models, a contemporaneous advantage, and acquisition and use of information after the TS model's forecast initiation date, a timing advantage.

Our purpose is not to resolve unambiguously the conflicting findings of the extant literature, not is it to ascertain the specific attributes of the SA information set that potentially allow for SA superiority. Resolution of the conflicting findings of the extant literature would require a consideration of all analysts, firms, time periods, and methodologies used in the extant literature. A determination of the specific attributes of the SA information set that allow for SA superiority would require an examination of such factors as SA knowledge of the process generating share prices, reported earnings, and cash dividends.

Our goals are more modest. We re-evaluate the issue of SA versus TS model forecast superiority by conducting individual analyses of chronological subperiods, forecast horizons, forecast error definitions, treatments of outliers, and fiscal quarters of forecast initiation. Moreover, we examine whether analysts possess a contemporaneous and/or a timing advantage. However, we consider only one analyst firm (Value Line), a six-year period (24 quarters), and a limited sample size (212-233 firms).

Moreover, we use a rather weak benchmark for evaluating analysts (forecasts by univariate TS models). As such, our findings may not pertain to stronger benchmarks, such as composite forecasts. Nevertheless, examination of SA's ability to predict is an interesting issue, and evidence obtained by using a weak benchmark can provide information on this issue.

The paper proceeds as follows. Section 2 discusses methodological issues. The comparative forecast superiority of SA versus TS model forecasts is investigated in Section 3. Section 4 examines potential sources of SA forecast superiority. The paper is summarized in Section 5.

2. Methodological Issues

2.1 Database

Two samples are obtained for this study. The first sample includes SA and TS model fore-

casts for the five-year period, 1975-1979. The second sample is a subset of those firms included in the first sample, that has available SA and TS model forecasts for the year 1980.

All firms included in the first (second) sample satisfy three criteria:

1) 1960 through 1979 (1960 through 1980) quarterly earnings per share available in *Moody's Handbook of Common Stocks,*
2) no change in fiscal year end between 1960 and 1979 (1960 and 1980), and
3) coverage by *The Value Line Investment Survey* from 1975 through 1979 (1975-1980).

The number of firms satisfying these criteria is 233 for the first (1975-1979) sample and 212 for the second (1980) sample.

The *Moody's* data are used to generate TS model forecasts. The estimation procedure we adopt is the Box and Jenkins (1976) ARIMA method, a modeling method requiring a large number of observations for obtaining efficient parameter estimates. The change in fiscal year criterion is adopted to avoid any "shifts" which may have occurred in the seasonal component of the TS models. *Value Line* data are employed because *Value Line* was the only publicly available source of SA quarterly earnings forecasts during our study period.[3]

2.2 Models

Four alternative earnings forecasts of one-, two-, and three-quarter forecast horizons are obtained for each conditioning quarter (forecast initiation): three univariate Box and Jenkins (1976) TS model forecasts and the SA forecasts contained in *Value Line*. Expressing the TS models in $(p,d,q)(P,D,Q)$ notation, the four models are:[4]

1) TS1: $(1,0,0)(0,1,1)$, examined by Brown and Rozeff (1979),
2) TS2: $(1,0,0)(0,1,0)$ plus a constant, analyzed by Foster (1977),
3) TS3: $(0,1,1)(0,1,1)$, investigated by Watts (1975) and Griffin (1977), and
4) SA: security analysts' earnings forecasts published by *Value Line*.

To attain maximum utilization of the data, each set of TS model forecasts is conditioned on the entire past history of quarterly reports in the database. For example, the first set of TS model forecasts, 1Q-1975, is conditioned on the 60 quarters 1Q-1960 to 4Q-1974; the second set of forecasts, 2Q-1975, on the 61 quarters 1Q-1960 to 1Q-1975; . . . ; and the 23rd (last) set of forecasts, 4Q-1980, on the 83 quarters 1Q-1960 to 3Q-1980.[5] SA earnings forecasts of one-, two-, and three-quarter horizons have been collected for this study and are compared to TS model forecasts of one-, two-, and three-quarter horizons have been collected for this study and are compared to TS model forecasts of one-, two-, and three-quarter horizons.

2.3 Forecast Error Specification

The primary variable of interest in this study is the unsigned forecast error of a firm's quarterly earnings per share divided by the actual earnings number being forecast. More particularly, we examine the ex post percentage error in forecasting the quarterly earnings number, Q_{ijt}, where the subscripts refer to the earnings of firm i in quarter j for year t. All forecasts of Q_{ijt} are conditioned upon a given sequence of quarterly reports, with no missing observations.[6]

The unsigned forecast error in forecasting Q_{ijt} by model m is defined as follows:

$$\text{Unsigned forecast error} = E_{mijt(h)} = \left| \frac{Q_{ijt} - F_{mijt(h)}}{Q_{ijt}} \right|$$

where

$E_{mijt(h)} =$ error by model m (m = TS1, TS2, TS3, SA) in forecasting earnings for firm i ($i = 1, \ldots, 233$), in quarter j ($j = 1, \ldots, 4$), for year t ($t = 1975, \ldots, 1980$), where the forecast is made h quarters ($h = 1, 2, 3$) in advance,

$Q_{ijt} =$ actual earnings for firm i, in quarter j, for year t,

$F_{mijt(h)} =$ forecast by model m of Q_{ijt}, made h quarters in advance of Q_{ijt}, and

$|.| =$ the absolute value operator.[7]

It is common in the forecasting literature to "pull in" or "truncate" outliers. We adopt the "truncation rule" of setting all errors greater than 100 percent exactly equal to 100 percent [used by Brown and Rozeff (1978, 1979) and Foster (1977)]. The effect of the truncation rule is discussed in the next section of the paper.

To ensure that the results are not due to the specific deflator/truncation choice, we examine three additional specifications of the deflator and three additional truncation rules. The three additional deflators are the earnings number forecast (F_{mijt}), the mean of the quarterly earnings series up to and including the conditioning quarter, and the standard deviation of the quarterly earnings series. The three additional truncation rules are no truncation, truncate at 300 percent, and truncate at three (cross-sectional) standard deviations. Results qualitatively equivalent to the results presented in this paper are obtained across all 16 possible deflator/truncation combinations.

2.4 Distributional Properties of Unsigned Forecast Errors

Exhibit 1 presents summary statistics (means) of the unsigned forecast errors as defined by $E_{mijt(h)}$. The results are segmented by model, conditioning quarter, year, and forecast horizon. For example, the mean absolute error for one-quarter ahead TS1 forecasts conditioned on 1Q-1976 is 20.196 percent.

Two features of the exhibit merit discussion. First, for a given model and conditioning quarter, the unsigned errors are generally an increasing function of the forecast horizon. For example, for SA, the two-quarter ahead forecast is less accurate than the one-quarter ahead forecast in 22 of 23 cases, and the three-quarter ahead forecast is less accurate than the two-quarter ahead forecast in 17 of 22 cases.

Exhibit 1 Mean (Unsigned) Percentage Forecast Errors by Conditioning Quarter and Year[ab]

Conditioning Quarter	Year	No. Obs.	One-Quarter Ahead Forecast			
			TS1	TS2	TS3	SA
First Quarter	1975	200	30.351	35.207	34.364	23.418
	1976	199	20.196	27.678	23.060	15.448
	1977	200	21.341	18.625	19.030	13.223
	1978	203	22.720	19.185	20.566	13.542
	1979	201	21.200	22.568	22.175	17.137
	1980	191	34.987	37.455	35.881	26.213
Second Quarter	1975	201	28.245	33.333	33.258	23.519
	1976	203	20.784	22.709	22.936	19.078
	1977	204	20.199	21.562	19.628	19.479
	1978	199	22.094	22.132	21.523	17.783
	1979	203	25.405	25.294	25.734	23.331
	1980	181	34.723	37.637	34.537	26.555
Third Quarter	1975	202	33.648	39.076	33.330	24.611
	1976	201	31.147	32.484	31.062	25.568
	1977	204	26.539	24.821	25.721	19.469
	1978	203	25.736	25.016	22.770	17.810
	1979	200	28.327	28.983	27.796	20.349
	1980	192	30.573	30.786	32.308	24.604
Fourth Quarter	1974	162	39.512	42.212	42.858	28.426
	1975	171	31.741	41.026	33.116	19.987
	1976	170	26.136	26.246	27.747	18.441
	1977	170	25.612	26.474	25.667	20.125
	1978	170	24.465	28.289	24.247	18.136
	1979	161	30.147	28.721	30.941	22.113
Statistics across 24 quarters/years						
Mean		191	27.337	29.063	27.927	20.682
Std. Dev.		15	5.215	6.740	6.034	3.926
Minimum		161	20.196	18.625	19.030	13.223
Maximum		204	39.512	42.212	42.858	28.426
No. of Quarters Model has the Lowest Mean			0	0	0	24

Continued on next page

Exhibit 1 Mean (Unsigned) Percentage Forecast Errors by Conditioning Quarter and Year[a][b] (continued)

Conditioning Quarter	Year	No. Obs.	Two-Quarters Ahead Forecast			
			TS1	TS2	TS3	SA
First Quarter	1975	230	35.331	40.337	39.271	30.966
	1976	229	24.179	29.220	27.142	24.628
	1977	228	26.478	24.266	24.132	24.925
	1978	230	27.764	24.832	25.066	20.881
	1979	231	20.361	29.724	28.342	25.786
	1980	211	39.551	42.083	40.490	33.360
Second Quarter	1975	232	38.562	43.872	41.154	31.615
	1976	232	34.217	36.229	35.419	33.413
	1977	233	29.367	28.429	26.943	25.616
	1978	229	26.916	26.905	24.696	21.159
	1979	230	29.105	29.089	29.900	24.865
	1980	199	32.290	31.252	33.149	27.765
Third Quarter	1975	225	32.344	42.627	32.812	24.985
	1976	228	29.220	29.662	29.979	26.537
	1977	231	28.040	26.656	25.823	25.489
	1978	231	27.717	30.438	26.841	24.578
	1979	208	31.852	33.025	34.707	29.395
Fourth Quarter	1974	187	40.970	45.197	43.583	31.921
	1975	193	30.064	36.772	31.460	22.391
	1976	194	25.287	22.941	22.960	18.594
	1977	195	24.027	22.556	22.206	17.385
	1978	194	26.200	26.108	24.893	22.729
	1979	179	36.552	38.789	37.406	35.371
Statistics across 24 quarters/years						
Mean		216	30.713	32.218	30.799	26.276
Std. Dev.		18	4.758	6.916	6.212	4.716
Minimum		179	24.027	22.556	22.206	17.385
Maximum		233	40.970	45.197	43.583	35.371
No. of Quarters Model has the Lowest Mean			1	0	1	21

Continued on next page

Exhibit 1 Mean (Unsigned) Percentage Forecast Errors by Conditioning Quarter and Year[ab] (continued)

Conditioning Quarter	Year	No. Obs.	Three-Quarters Ahead Forecast			
			TS1	TS2	TS3	SA
First Quarter	1975	231	40.340	43.216	42.408	32.882
	1976	229	35.116	36.717	35.838	34.388
	1977	228	32.444	29.174	29.961	29.136
	1978	231	33.359	29.232	28.633	21.968
	1979	230	29.791	29.311	28.965	25.774
	1980	209	33.005	32.661	32.969	29.825
Second Quarter	1975	55	41.942	55.529	46.293	32.277
	1976	202	32.620	30.526	33.056	30.753
	1977	206	29.539	27.579	28.243	27.957
	1978	201	30.208	31.735	27.765	26.723
	1979	185	32.687	31.778	34.305	32.990
Third Quarter	1975	225	32.545	39.643	33.094	25.519
	1976	228	27.120	24.004	25.507	20.511
	1977	231	25.524	22.773	22.845	19.232
	1978	231	28.204	25.687	25.752	25.436
	1979	209	37.615	39.602	39.711	34.981
Fourth Quarter	1974	187	38.920	45.776	47.501	34.334
	1975	194	32.034	35.358	35.829	26.172
	1976	195	29.310	26.219	27.182	29.198
	1977	195	29.282	26.734	26.553	22.675
	1978	194	33.487	32.030	31.954	29.970
	1979	179	42.596	44.235	43.719	37.954
Statistics across 24 quarters/years						
Mean		203	33.077	33.615	33.095	28.666
Std. Dev.		37	4.571	7.996	6.862	4.880
Minimum		55	25.524	22.773	22.845	19.232
Maximum		231	42.596	55.529	47.501	37.954
No. of Quarters Model has the Lowest Mean			0	4	0	18

[a] The unsigned percentage forecast error is calculated as the absolute value of actual earnings minus the earnings forecast, both divided by actual earnings and multiplied by 100 percent. Errors in excess of 100 percent are set equal to 100 percent.

[b] TS1 = Box-Jenkins model attributed to Brown and Rozeff (1979),
TS2 = Box-Jenkins model attributed to Foster (1977),
TS3 = Box-Jenkins model attributed to Watts (1975) and Griffin (1977),
SA = security analysts' earnings forecasts published by the *Value Line Investment Survey*,
No. obs. = number of observations in the subsample.

Second, based on means, the SA earnings forecasts are more accurate than the TS model forecasts. The mean across the 24 quarter/year means (see the bottom of Exhibit 1) of SA vs. the best TS model (i.e., the TS model with the lowest mean unsigned percentage forecast error) are 20.682 vs. 27.337 percent for the one-quarter horizon, 26.276 vs. 30.713 percent for the two-quarter horizon, and 28.666 vs. 33.077 percent for the three-quarter horizon. The number of quarter/years for which SA forecast accuracy is greater (i.e., the mean unsigned percentage forecast error is smaller) than all of the TS models is 24 for the 24 one-quarter horizon comparisons, 21 for the 23 two-quarter horizon comparisons, and 18 for the 22 three-quarter horizon comparisons.

The preceding summary results are silent on other characteristics of the forecast error distributions. Exhibits 2 through 5 present a forecast percentage error histogram for each forecast model for the one-quarter ahead forecasts. (Similar figures for the two- and three-quarter ahead forecasts are available on request.) Errors are truncated at 200 percent to show the effect of outliers. While all models involve limited and skewed truncation (slightly more observations are truncated at the left tail), the SA histogram (Exhibit 5) clearly shows the least amount of truncation relative to TS model errors, though the number of errors truncated for any model is small.[8] The SA forecast error distribution is also tighter (i.e., has the smallest standard deviation) than the three TS models. On the other hand, the SA distribution is more skewed than the three TS models; it appears that SA forecasts tend to be more optimistic.

The next two sections present the results of statistical tests applied to the data. Since the *unsigned* percentage forecast error ($E_{mijt\,(h)}$) distributions are not normally distributed, the succeeding sections focus the discussion on non-parametric test procedures. In fact, Kolmogorov-Smirnov tests for normality of the *signed* forecast error distributions indicate rejection of the null hypothesis (of a normal distribution). Nevertheless, both non-parametric (i.e., Friedman) and parametric (i.e., Hotelling's T^2) tests of the *unsigned* percentage forecast errors result in identical statistical inferences. That is, the choice of statistical tests does not affect our results presented in Exhibits 6 and 8.

3. Comparative Forecast Superiority

This section presents the results of two types of statistical tests applied to the unsigned forecast errors. The first test examines the effect of the forecast model (SA and the three TS models) on forecast accuracy. The statistical procedure chosen for this purpose, the non-parametric ANOVA or Friedman test [Hollander and Wolfe (1973)], has been utilized regularly in the forecasting literature [Brown and Rozeff (1978, 1979), Collins, Hopwood and McKeown (1984), Foster (1977), Imhoff and Pare (1982)] and is appropriate for our purposes.[9] The null hypothesis of the Friedman test as used in this study is that there is no forecast model (i.e., treatment) effect on forecast accuracy. If the Friedman test rejects the null hypothesis of no forecast model effect, a second test can be conducted to determine if the mean absolute SA forecast error is less than the best (most accurate) TS model error. The null hypothesis of this test, the multiple comparison test [Hollander and Wolfe (1973)], is that the SA forecast accuracy is less than or equal to the forecast accuracy of the "best" TS model.

Exhibit 6 presents the Friedman and multiple comparison *t*-test results across 24 quarter/year means.[10] These tests address the potential cross-sectional dependence of the observations by assuming that extreme cross-sectional dependence exists such that each quarter/year represents only one independent observation. Thus, observations are grouped by each of the 24 quarter/years and the mean absolute error for each quarter/year is used as one observation in the test [see O'Brien (1985) for a discussion of this procedure].[11]

Exhibit 2 Histogram of Percentage Errors of One-Quarter Ahead Forecasts: TS1

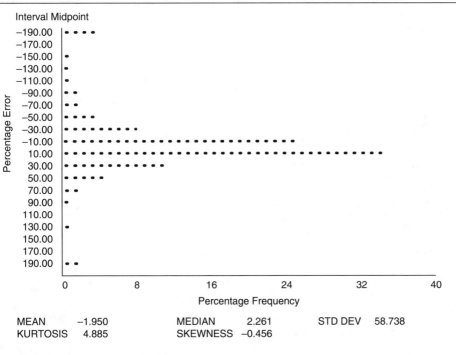

| MEAN | −1.950 | MEDIAN | 2.261 | STD DEV | 58.738 |
| KURTOSIS | 4.885 | SKEWNESS | −0.456 | | |

Exhibit 3 Histogram of Percentage Errors of One-Quarter Ahead Forecasts: TS2

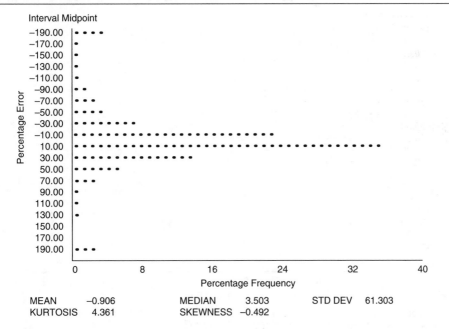

| MEAN | −0.906 | MEDIAN | 3.503 | STD DEV | 61.303 |
| KURTOSIS | 4.361 | SKEWNESS | −0.492 | | |

Exhibit 4 Histogram of Percentage Errors of One-Quarter Ahead Forecasts: TS3

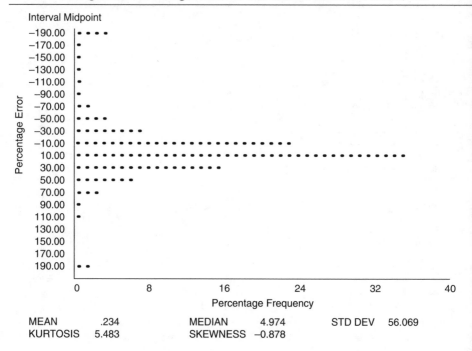

MEAN	.234	MEDIAN	4.974	STD DEV	56.069
KURTOSIS	5.483	SKEWNESS	−0.878		

Exhibit 5 Histogram of Percentage Errors of One-Quarter Ahead Forecasts: SA

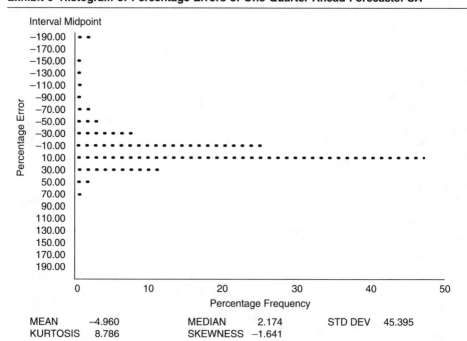

MEAN	−4.960	MEDIAN	2.174	STD DEV	45.395
KURTOSIS	8.786	SKEWNESS	−1.641		

Exhibit 6 **Friedman and Multiple Comparison *t*-Tests Across 24 Quarter/Year Means** [a,b]

	One-Quarter Ahead Forecast				Two-Quarters Ahead Forecast				Three-Quarters Ahead Forecast			
	TS1	TS2	TS3	SA	TS1	TS2	TS3	SA	TS1	TS2	TS3	SA
Friedman tests (based on ranks)												
No. of Observations		24				23				22		
Chi-Square Statistic (DF)		46.550[e]		(3)		35.974[e]		(3)		27.655[e]		(3)
F-Statistic (df/df)[c]		42.069[e]	(3/69)			23.964[e]	(3/66)			15.145[e]	(3/63)	
Mean Rank	2.708	3.375	2.917	1.000	2.870	3.217	2.783	1.130	3.091	2.682	2.955	1.273
Multiple comparison t-tests (based on ranks)[d]												
TS1	0.00	2.95[e]	0.92	-7.55[e]	0.00	1.29	-0.32	-6.46[e]	0.00	-1.35	-0.45	-5.99[e]
TS2		0.00	-2.03[f]	-10.49[e]		0.00	-1.61	-7.75[e]		0.00	0.90	-4.64[e]
TS3			0.00	-8.47[e]			0.00	-6.14[e]			0.00	-5.54[e]
SA				0.00				0.00				0.00

[a] The results reported in this table are based on the mean quarter/year absolute percentage errors reported in Exhibit 1. Each quarter/year subperiod is treated as an independent observation.

[b] TS1 = Box-Jenkins model attributed to Brown and Rozeff (1979).
TS2 = Box-Jenkins model attributed to Foster (1977).
TS3 = Box-Jenkins model attributed to Watts (1975) and Griffin (1977).
SA = Security analysts' earnings forecasts published by *The Value Line Investment Survey*.

[c] The Friedman *F*-statistic (*F*-stat) has 3 degrees of freedom for the numerator and N degrees of freedom for the denominator, where *N* is equal to the number of observations multiplied by 3, minus 3.

[d] The multiple comparison t-tests (based on ranks) compare the mean rank of the row model to the mean rank of the column model (row minus column). A positive (negative) *t*-statistics indicates that the row model has a smaller (larger) mean rank than the column model.

[e] Significant at the 0.01 level of significance (two-tailed test for multiple comparison *t*-statistics).

[f] Significant at the 0.05 level of significance (two-tailed test for multiple comparison *t*-statistics).

The chi-square and *F*-statistics from the Friedman test reveal that the null hypothesis of no forecast model effect can be rejected in favor of its alternative (at least one forecast model is different) at the 1 percent level or less for each of the three forecast horizons. The multiple comparison *t*-statistics comparing the mean (Friedman) rank of SA with the mean rank of each of the three TS models show that the SA model has the lowest mean rank in all nine model/horizon comparisons. Moreover, SA superiority is demonstrated at the 1 percent level or less in every test. More specifically, the multiple comparison *t*-tests comparing SA to TS1, TS2, and TS3 are 7.55, 10.49, and 8.47 for the one-quarter horizon comparisons, respectively; 6.46, 7.75, and 6.14 for the two-quarter horizon comparisons, respectively; 5.99, 4.64, and 5.54 for the three-quarter horizon comparisons, respectively. These results indicate that SA forecasts are significantly more accurate than those of TS models.

Similar tests using individual firm observations (which assume no cross-sectional correlation) within each year, conditioning quarter, and forecast horizon combination were also conducted, and are available from the authors upon request. The chi-square and *F*-statistics from the Friedman test reveal that the null hypothesis of no forecast model effect can be rejected in favor of its alternative at the 10 percent level or less in 60 of 69 tests. The multiple comparison *t*-statistics comparing the mean (Friedman) rank of SA with the mean rank of the "best" TS model (i.e., that TS model having the lowest mean rank of the three TS models) show that the SA forecast error has the lowest mean rank 61 of 69 times, with significance in 47 of these cases. Furthermore, the eight cases in which the SA do not possess the lowest mean rank forecast error are not distinguished by any pattern (i.e., they are not confined to particular years, conditioning quarters, or forecast horizons), and the differences are never statistically significant in favor of any TS model.

4. Potential Sources of Analyst Forecast Superiority

4.1 Preliminary Discussion

TS model forecasts conditional upon *j* quarterly reports can be generated on the date that the firms *j*th quarterly report becomes available. This date, the TS model forecast initiation date, is assumed to be the date the *j*th qurterly report is announced in the *Wall Street Journal* (WSJ). SA model forecasts, on the other hand, are published sometime later; that is, the SA forecast initiation date follows the TS model forecast initiation date. Hence, SA possess a timing advantage over TS model forecasts. Letting *d* designate the SA timing advantage in days, the median *d* in our sample is 39 days.

A finding that SA outperform TS models when the SA and TS forecast initiation dates are contemporaneous suggests that SA better utilize information available at the contemporaneous forecast initiation date and, hence, possess a "contemporaneous advantage" in forecasting earnings. A finding that SA forecast superiority vis-a-vis TS models increases with the SA timing advantage (*d*) suggests that SA acquire and utilize information that becomes available after the TS forecast initiation date but before the SA forecast initiation date and, hence, possess a "timing advantage" in forecasting earnings.

By construction, the information available to TS models is confined to a sequence of past reported earnings; SA, on the other hand, have available past reported earnings along with a variety of other information. It is beyond the scope of this inquiry to ascertain which particular facets of the SA's information set result in SA forecast superiority. Thus, a finding that SA outperform TS models on the date the *j*th quarterly report becomes available may indicate that SA utilize information contained in the time series of past quarterly earnings numbers better than do TS models and/or that SA utilize information unavailable to TS models, such as earnings reports of other firms [Foster (1981)] or strikes in progress [Brown and Zmijewski (1987)].[12] Similarly, a finding that SA forecast superiority increases as d increases is consistent with the statement that SA benefit from information released after the most recent earnings announcement, but it reveals nothing regarding the nature of that information.

4.2 Tests of Contemporaneous Advantage

Ideally, to investigate whether SA possess a contemporaneous advantage, SA forecasts should be compared with TS model forecasts which have contemporaneous forecast initiation dates. In other words, an ideal test would set the SA timing advantage (d) equal to zero. However, as SA do not normally initiate their forecasts on the TS model forecast initiation date, we undertake two alternative tests which have the effect of approximating the removal of the SA timing advantage. In the first test, the SA forecast initiation date follows the TS model forecast initiation date by ten days or less so that both the SA and TS model forecasts are conditional upon the same number of quarterly reports. In this test, SA possess a small timing advantage relative to TS models. In the second test, the SA forecasts are conditional upon one less quarterly report than the TS model forecasts. More specifically, the SA forecast initiation date *precedes* the TS model forecast initiation date by ten days or less. In these tests, the SA two- and three- quarter ahead forecasts are compared to the TS model one- and two- quarter ahead forecasts, and hence, SA possess a small timing *disadvantage* relative to TS models.

Both tests utilize a subsample of the observations that are used to calculate the 24 quarter/year means that are reported in Exhibit 1. In the first test, the data are ordered by the SA timing advantage and tests are conducted across the 24 quarter/year means on the Exhibit 1 subsample where the SA forecast initiation date follows the most recent quarterly

earnings announcement by ten days or less. In the context of Exhibit 1, a subsample of SA observations with a one-quarter horizon is compared to a subsample of TS observations with a one-quarter horizon. Similarly, SA observations with two- and three-quarter horizons are compared to TS observations with two- and three-quarter horizons.

In the second test, the data are ordered by the SA timing disadvantage and tests are conducted on the Exhibit 1 subsample where the SA forecast initiation date precedes the TS model initiation date by ten days or less. For example, a SA timing advantage of ten days indicates that the SA two-quarter ahead forecast of quarter j was initiated ten days before the TS model one-quarter ahead forecast of qurter j. Thus, in the context of Exhibit 1, a subsample of SA observations with a two-quarter horizon is compared to a subsample of TS observations with a one-quarter horizon. Similarly, a subsample of SA observations with a three-quarter horizon is compared to a subsample of TS observations with a two-quarter horizon.

The 24 quarter/year means calculated for the two tests are summarized in panels A and B of Exhibit 7, respectively. The mean percentage forecast errors across the 24 quarter/year means of SA vs. the "best" TS model for the first test are 18.470 vs. 21.524 percent for the one-quarter horizon, 21.153 vs. 23.481 percent for the two-quarter horizon, and 23.307 vs. 25.439 percent for the three-quarter horizon. The number of quarters for which SA forecast accuracy is greater than all of the TS models is 15 for the 23 one-quarter horizon comparisons, 12 for the 22 two-quarter horizon comparisons, and 10 for the 21 three-quarter comparisons. The means across the 24 quarter/year means of SA vs. the "best" TS model for the second test are 22.637 vs. 24.880 percent for the SA two-quarter horizon vs. the TS one-quarter horizon, and 25.376 vs. 26.871 percent for the SA three-quarter horizon vs. the TS two-quarter horizon. The number of quarters for which SA

Exhibit 7 Mean (Unsigned) Percentage Forecast Errors for the 24 Quarter/Year Means [a,b]

Panel A—Security analyst forecast follows most recent earnings announcement by ten days or less

Summary 24 Qtr./Yr.	One-Quarter Ahead Forecast				No. Obs.	Two-Quarters Ahead Forecast				No. Obs.	Three-Quarters Ahead Forecast				No. Obs.
	TS1	TS2	TS3	SA		TS1	TS2	TS3	SA		TS1	TS2	TS3	SA	
Mean	21.524	22.664	22.320	18.470	19	23.481	24.812	24.729	21.153	22	25.439	25.706	26.038	23.307	22
Std. Dev.	6.047	7.813	5.957	7.557	6	6.272	7.318	8.081	6.388	6	7.987	7.986	8.626	6.968	7
Minimum	14.398	12.905	15.479	8.051	4	11.220	12.284	11.340	13.630	9	3.321	12.064	9.214	11.111	1
Maximum	40.320	45.647	39.060	38.425	26	39.225	41.628	42.575	41.614	29	40.010	44.165	43.640	41.042	29
No. of Qtrs. Model Has the Lowest Mean	3	3	2	15		6	1	3	12		2	5	4	10	

Panel B—Security analyst forecast precedes next earnings announcement by ten days or less

Summary 24 Qtr./Yr.	SA 2 Qtr. vs. TSi 1 Qtr. Forecast [c]				No. Obs.	SA 3 QTR. vs. TSi 2 Qtr. Forecast [c]				No. Obs.
	TS1	TS2	TS3	SA		TS1	TS2	TS3	SA	
Mean	24.880	27.640	25.301	22.637	15	28.778	30.203	26.871	25.376	18
Std. Dev.	7.315	9.280	7.708	7.045	4	6.981	10.224	7.749	7.742	5
Minimum	12.056	13.563	13.380	14.540	7	15.287	14.715	13.712	13.238	10
Maximum	38.039	47.517	37.730	40.365	20	41.179	50.674	39.722	40.537	27
No. of Qtrs. Model Has the Lowest Mean	6	4	4	9		1	3	5	13	

[a] The unsigned percentage forecast error is calculated as the absolute value of actual earnings minus the earnings forecast both divided by actual earnings and multiplied by 100 percent. Errors in excess of 100 percent are set equal to 100 percent.

[b]
TS1 = Box-Jenkins model attributed to Brown and Rozeff (1979),
TS2 = Box-Jenkins model attributed to Foster (1977),
TS3 = Box-Jenkins model attributed to Watts (1975) and Griffin (1977),
SA = Security analysts' earnings forecasts published by The Value Line Investment Survey,
No. Obs. = Number of observations in the subsample.

[c] SA 2 (3) qtr. versus TSi 1 (2) qtr. indicates that SA two-(three)-quarter ahead forecasts are compared to TSi one-(two) quarter ahead forecasts for observations for which the SA forecast date precedes the next WSJ earnings announcement by ten days or less.

Exhibit 8 Friedman and Multiple Comparison *t*-Tests Across 24 Quarter/Year Means; Contemporaneous Advantage [a,b]

Panel A—Security analyst forecast follows most recent earnings announcement by ten days of less

	One-Quarter Ahead Forecast				Two-Quarters Ahead Forecast				Three-Quarters Ahead Forecast			
	TS1	TS2	TS3	SA	TS1	TS2	TS3	SA	TS1	TS2	TS3	SA
Friedman tests (based on ranks)												
No. of Observations		23				22				21		
Chi-Square Statistic (df)		9.626[g]	(3)			7.909[g]	(3)			4.371	(3)	
F-Statistic (df/df)[c]		3.567[g]	(3/66)			2.859[g]	(3/63)			1.491	(3/60)	
Mean Rank	2.696	2.696	2.826	1.783	2.409	2.909	2.773	1.909	2.857	2.286	2.714	2.143
Multiple comparison t-tests (based on ranks)[d]												
TS1	0.00	0.00	0.36	-2.53[g]	0.00	1.34	0.97	-1.34	0.00	-1.45	-0.36	-1.81
TS2		0.00	0.36	-2.53[g]		0.00	-0.36	-2.68[f]		0.00	1.09	-0.36
TS3			0.00	-2.89[f]			0.00	-2.31[g]			0.00	-1.45
SA				0.00				0.00				0.00

Continued on next page

Exhibit 8 Friedman and Multiple Comparison t-Tests Across 24 Quarter/Year Means; Contemporaneous Advantage [a,b] (continued)

Panel B—Security analyst forecast precedes next earnings announcement by ten days or less

	SA 2 Quarter vs. TSi Quarter Forecast[c]				SA 3 Quarter vs. TSi 2 Quarter Forecast[c]			
	TS1	TS2	TS3	SA	TS1	TS2	TS3	SA
Friedman tests (based on ranks)								
No. of Observations		23				22		
Chi-Square Statistic (df)		3.887	(3)			12.055	(3)	
F-Statistic (df/df)[c]		1.313	(3/66)			4.693	(3/63)	
Mean Rank	2.435	2.913	2.478	2.174	3.000	2.955	2.046	2.000
Multiple comparison t-tests (based on ranks)[d]								
TS1	0.00				0.00			
TS2	1.26	0.00			-0.13	0.00		
TS3	0.12	-1.15	0.00		-2.65f	-2.52g	0.00	
SA	-0.69	-1.95	-0.80	0.00	-2.78f	2.65f	-0.13	0.00

[a] The results reported in this table are based on the mean quarter/year absolute percentage errors summarized in Exhibit 7. Each quarter/year subperiod is treated as an independent observation.

[b] TS1 = Box-Jenkins model attributed to Brown and Rozeff (1979).
  TS2 = Box-Jenkins model attributed to Foster (1977).
  TS3 = Box-Jenkins model attributed to Watts (1975) and Griffin (1977).
  SA = Security analysts' earnings forecasts published by *The Value Line Investment Survey.*

[c] The Friedman F-statistic (F-stat) has 3 degrees of freedom for the numerator and N degrees of freedom for the denominator, where N is equal to the number of observations multiplied by 3, minus 3.

[d] The multiple comparison t-tests (based on ranks) compare the mean rank of the row model to the mean rank of the column model (row minus column). A positive (negative) t-statistic indicates that the row model has a smaller (larger) mean rank than the column model.

[e] SA 2 (3) qtr. versus TSi 1 (2) qtr. indicates that SA two-(three) quarter ahead forecasts are compared to TSi one-(two) quarter ahead forecasts for observations for which the SA forecast date precedes the next WSJ earnings announcement by ten days or less.

[f] Significant at the 0.01 level of significance (two-tailed test for multiple comparison t-statistics).

[g] Significant at the 0.05 level of significance (two-tailed test for multiple comparison t-statistics).

forecast accuracy is greater than all of the TS models is 9 for the 23 SA two-quarter horizon vs. TS one-quarter horizon comparisons, and 13 for the 22 SA three-quarter horizon vs. TS two-quarter horizon comparisons. The evidence presented in Exhibit 7, while not as convincing as the results reported in Exhibit 1, is consistent with the hypothesis that SA make better use of information existing at the TS model forecast initiation date; that is, SA possess a contemporaneous advantage.

The results of the two tests of the SA contemporaneous advantage are reported in panels A and B of Exhibit 8, respectively.[13] For the tests that are conducted on the subsample of observations for which the SA have a ten-day or less timing advantage (panel A), the chi-square and F-statistics from the Friedman test indicate that the null hypothesis of no forecast model effect can be rejected in favor of its alternative (at least one forecast model is different) at the 5 percent level or less for the one- and two-quarter horizon forecasts, but not for the three-quarter horizon forecasts.[14] The multiple comparison t-statistics reveal that SA superiority is demonstrated at the 5 percent level or less for all three tests for the one-quarter ahead forecasts, and in two of three tests for the two-quarter ahead forecasts. More specifically, the multiple comparison t-tests comparing SA to TS1, TS2, and TS3 are 2.53, 2.53, and 2.89 for the one-quarter horizon comparisons, respectively, and 1.34, 2.68, and 2.31 for the two-quarter horizon comparisons, respectively. For the tests that are conducted on the subsample of observations for which the SA have a ten-day or less timing disadvantage (panel B), the chi-square and F-statistics from the Friedman test indicate that the null hypothesis of no forecast model effect can be rejected in favor of its alternative at the 1 percent level or less for the SA three-quarter horizon vs. the TS two-quarter horizon, but not for the SA two-quarter horizon vs. the TS one-quarter horizon.[15] The multiple comparison t-statistics show that SA superiority is demonstrated at the 1 percent level or less in two of three tests for the SA three-quarter hori-

zon vs. the TS two-quarter horizon. More specifically, the multiple comparison t-tests comparing SA to TS1, TS2, and TS3 for the SA three-quarter horizon versus the TS two-quarter horizon are 2.78, 2.65, and 0.13, respectively.

Thus, assuming that our test procedures effectively eliminate any SA timing advantage, our results indicate that the SA superiority demonstrated in Section 3 is attributable, in part, to possession by SA of a contemporaneous advantage in forecasting earnings. This evidence is consistent with the statement that SA make better use of information existing at the TS forecast initiation date.

4.3 Tests of Timing Advantage

Next, the SA acquisition and use of information arriving after the TS model forecast initiation date but before the SA forecast initiation is examined. We examine this issue indirectly by making the following assumption. If SA acquire and use information arriving after the TS model forecast initiation date, we would expect SA comparative forecast superiority (relative to a particular TS model) to increase as the number of days the SA forecast initiation date follows the TS model forecast initiation date increases (i.e., SA timing advantage increases). More specifically, we would expect to observe a positive association between SA comparative forecast superiority and SA timing advantage. Conversely, a negative association is expected when tests are designed so that SA have a timing disadvantage; that is, we would expect SA comparative forecast superiority to decrease as the SA timing disadvantage increases.

SA comparative forecast superiority, $CFS_{(m)ijt(h)}$ relative to TS model m, firm i, quarter j, for year t, and horizon h is defined as

$$CFS_{(m)ijt(h)} = E_{(m)ijt(h)} - E_{(SA)ijt(h)}$$

where

$E_{(m)ijt(h)}$ = error by TS model m (m = TS1, TS2, or TS3) in forecasting earn-

Exhibit 9 Association of Security Analyst Forecast Superiority with Security Analyst Timing Advantage [a,b]

Portfolio[c]	SA Timing Advantage Mean No. of Days	One-Quarter Ahead Forecast Mean Percentage Error Difference			Two-Quarter Ahead Forecast Mean Percentage Error Difference			Three-Quarter Ahead Forecast Mean Percentage Error Difference		
		TS1-SA	TS2-SA	TS3-SA	TS1-SA	TS2-SA	TS3-SA	TS1-SA	TS2-SA	TS1-SA
1	5.26	2.17	2.24	2.93	3.67	4.65	4.62	4.25	2.48	5.30
2	8.50	3.06	3.16	3.54	0.21	1.02	0.52	0.89	-0.35	0.39
3	10.14	6.98	8.34	5.16	5.66	5.67	4.64	3.80	4.70	2.32
4	14.93	4.20	5.91	5.39	0.76	2.64	1.27	1.93	1.23	1.62
5	19.12	3.44	7.80	4.48	2.36	5.10	3.37	1.87	3.69	2.49
6	22.00	9.06	9.66	7.78	2.47	4.75	2.87	5.26	6.95	5.84
7	23.45	1.83	6.09	2.99	3.17	6.22	5.14	0.42	0.40	1.39
8	27.21	1.96	2.25	2.41	3.39	1.74	1.58	2.96	1.42	0.18
9	29.45	5.46	8.49	7.16	2.48	7.95	3.24	4.93	5.99	5.46
10	31.32	2.43	4.04	3.68	2.47	3.70	2.17	2.68	4.19	2.64
11	35.47	5.46	6.26	5.44	2.89	4.89	1.78	3.58	3.74	2.53
12	37.00	4.10	9.50	8.88	4.14	9.75	5.41	5.13	10.45	6.58
13	40.25	5.82	5.25	7.14	3.59	4.52	5.06	0.26	2.21	0.77
14	43.93	8.70	13.63	11.44	7.92	8.94	7.16	3.69	3.95	4.25
15	48.87	4.36	8.16	5.58	4.49	6.14	4.61	3.92	4.33	3.16
16	53.20	6.72	8.01	6.61	4.63	5.20	4.73	4.00	6.36	5.08
17	59.71	9.32	10.78	9.62	6.08	7.11	5.94	3.99	2.13	3.29
18	64.85	4.68	5.85	5.68	3.34	5.04	5.31	6.27	0.77	3.82
19	70.09	7.74	9.97	8.76	4.51	5.69	3.37	7.33	6.22	5.08
20	74.35	10.99	10.83	10.24	3.04	4.87	4.66	6.06	4.81	6.02
21	78.00	11.36	11.16	10.26	6.19	5.34	5.58	7.40	5.64	5.39
22	79.45	9.26	8.68	6.11	10.01	8.66	7.59	9.25	7.71	6.72
23	84.17	10.38	12.50	9.04	6.32	9.32	3.76	6.36	7.43	4.88
24	86.38	5.88	8.68	6.67	7.40	7.91	5.79	9.10	6.11	4.26
25	91.93	12.02	13.35	11.50	6.40	5.77	6.03	7.86	6.64	6.22

Continued on next page

Exhibit 9 Association of Security Analyst Forecast Superiority with Security Analyst Timing Advantage [a,b] (continued)

Statistics across 25 portfolios

Mean	45.56	6.30	8.02	6.74	4.30	5.70	4.25	4.53	4.37	3.86
Std. Dev.	26.47	3.08	3.13	2.64	2.22	2.17	1.78	2.46	2.59	1.98
Minimum	5.26	1.83	2.24	2.41	0.21	1.02	0.52	0.26	−0.35	0.18
Maximum	91.93	12.02	13.63	11.50	10.01	9.75	7.59	9.25	10.45	6.72

Rank order correlations (mean SA timing advantage with mean error difference in column)

Correlations	0.705	0.656	0.703	0.692	0.519	0.623	0.732	0.526	0.540	
Significance Level	0.000	0.000	0.000	0.000	0.004	0.000	0.000	0.003	0.003	

Pearson correlations (mean SA timing advantage with mean error difference in column)

Correlations	0.715	0.646	0.661	0.666	0.472	0.559	0.780	0.465	0.552	
Significance Level	0.000	0.000	0.000	0.000	0.005	0.001	0.000	0.005	0.001	

[a] This table reports the association between SA forecast superiority and SA timing advantage. SA forecast superiority is calculated as the mean percentage error difference between a TS model and SA (TS model portfolio mean absolute percentage error minus SA model portfolio mean absolute percentage error). SA timing advantage is calculated as the number of days the SA forecast follows the most recent earnings announcement. The association between the mean SA timing advantage and the mean percentage error difference is measured (across the 25 portfolios) by the rank order and Pearson correlations that are reported at the bottom of the table.

[b] TS1 = Box-Jenkins model attributed to Brown and Rozeff (1979),
  TS2 = Box-Jenkins model attributed to Foster (1977),
  TS3 = Box-Jenkins model attributed to Watts (1975) and Griffin (1977),
  SA   = Security analysts' earnings forecasts published by *The Value Line Investment Survey.*

[c] The portfolios are formed by ranking all observations on SA timing advantage and partitioning the sample into 25 portfolios of equal size.

Exhibit 10 Association of Security Analyst Forecast Superiority with Security Analyst Timing Disadvantage[a, b]

Portfolio[c]	SA Timing Disadvantage Mean No. of Days	SA 2 Qtr. vs. TS1 Qtr. Forecast Mean Percentage Error Difference			SA 3 Qtr. vs. TS2 Forecast Mean Percentage Error Difference		
		TS1-SA	TS2-SA	TS3-SA	TS1-SA	TS2-SA	TS3-SA
1	5.16	3.92	5.78	4.14	3.40	3.68	1.36
2	7.80	−0.11	3.89	1.37	2.21	5.38	0.70
3	12.25	2.99	3.09	1.89	7.01	7.57	6.28
4	14.00	−1.93	0.09	−0.18	5.45	3.21	3.97
5	18.28	0.09	3.78	−0.02	2.98	3.80	3.40
6	20.53	0.51	2.85	−0.05	2.75	1.90	0.72
7	25.91	2.93	4.41	4.31	−1.47	1.30	0.36
8	31.24	3.28	4.56	3.00	2.99	4.94	4.46
9	37.57	3.12	4.42	2.45	5.22	6.61	4.27
10	41.62	0.45	1.91	0.51	0.62	1.56	0.09
11	46.81	2.65	5.02	4.56	4.92	8.07	5.43
12	49.56	−2.37	2.14	0.40	−1.53	−1.26	−2.78
13	54.20	−1.93	0.88	−0.36	0.62	2.41	0.83
14	56.00	0.92	−0.97	2.04	1.93	1.65	−0.34
15	59.67	0.03	3.27	1.35	−0.68	1.42	0.65
16	61.55	−0.27	4.13	1.38	−0.75	1.79	−0.45
17	63.00	1.44	0.80	1.42	2.08	2.96	0.91
18	67.22	−1.44	0.40	0.37	−1.25	0.73	−0.76
19	69.00	4.76	7.77	3.86	1.84	3.64	0.62
20	71.89	−0.78	1.19	−2.95	0.54	4.38	0.67
21	75.53	1.29	1.14	0.48	5.68	6.94	5.57
22	79.35	−0.84	1.86	−0.21	−1.39	2.19	−1.39
23	82.51	0.82	0.05	−0.06	0.46	−0.03	−0.10
24	84.00	1.79	1.17	2.36	3.66	3.08	3.37
25	89.67	−4.61	−1.76	−1.44	−0.37	2.57	1.29
Statistics across 25 portfolios							
Mean	48.98	0.67	2.47	3.22	1.88	3.22	1.57
Std. Dev.	25.62	2.18	2.21	1.81	2.46	2.30	2.31
Minimum	5.16	−4.61	−1.76	−2.95	−1.53	−1.26	−2.78
Maximum	89.67	4.76	7.77	4.56	7.01	8.07	6.28
Rank order correlations (mean SA timing advantage with mean error difference in column)							
Correlations		−0.245	−0.501	−0.330	−0.392	−0.284	~0.32
Significance Level		0.119	0.006	0.054	0.026	0.085	0.060
Pearson correlations (mean SA timing advantage with mean error difference in column)							
Correlations		−0.303	−0.452	−0.331	−0.418	−0.280	−0.291
Significance Level		0.071	0.012	0.053	0.019	0.087	0.079

Continued on next page

Exhibit 10 **Association of Security Analyst Forecast Superiority with Security Analyst Timing Disadvantage[a,b] (continued)**

[a] This table reports the association between SA forecast superiority and SA timing disadvantage. SA forecast superiority is calculated as the mean percentage error difference between a TS model and SA (TS model portfolio mean absolute percentage error minus SA model portfolio mean absolute percentage error). SA timing disadvantage is calculated as the number of days the SA forecast precedes the next earnings announcement. SA two-(three) quarter ahead forecasts are compared to TS model one-(two) quarter ahead forecasts. The association between the mean SA timing disadvantage and the mean percentage error difference is measured (across the 25 portfolios) by the rank order and Pearson correlations that are reported at the bottom of the table.

[b] TS1 = Box-Jenkins model attributed to Brown and Rozeff (1979),
TS2 = Box-Jenkins model attributed to Foster (1977),
TS3 = Box-Jenkins model attributed to Watts (1975) and Griffin (1977),
SA = Security analysts' earnings forecasts published by the *Value Line Investment Survey.*

[c] The portfolios are formed by ranking all observations on SA timing disadvantage and partitioning the sample into 25 portfolios of equal size.

ings for firm i, in quarter j, for year t, where the forecast is made h quarters in advance, and

$\varepsilon_{(SA)ijt(h)}$ = error by SA in forecasting earnings for firm i, in quarter j, for year t, where the forecast is made h quarters in advance.

For the SA timing advantage tests, all observations are ranked on the SA timing advantage (the number of days the SA forecast initiation date follows the TS model initiation date). Next, the observations are partitioned into 25 equally-sized portfolios and the mean timing advantage and the mean $CFS_{(m)ijt(h)}$ (for m = TS1,TS2,TS3, and h = 1,2,3) are calculated for each portfolio. These means are reported in Exhibit 9 for all nine comparisons (three TS models times three forecast horizon comparisons). The measure of association between the SA comparative forecast superiority and SA timing advantage is measured by rank order and Pearson correlations between the mean portfolio SA comparative forecast superiority and the mean portfolio SA timing advantage. The results of the nine association tests are reported at the bottom of Exhibit 9. The rank order correlations range from 0.519 to 0.732 and all are statistically significant at the 0.004 level or less. The Pearson correlations range from 0.465 to

0.780 and are all statistically significant at the 0.005 level or less.

For the SA timing disadvantage tests, all observations are ranked on the SA timing disadvantage (the number of days the SA forecast initiation date precedes the next earnings announcement).[16] Next, the observations are partitioned into 25 equally-sized portfolios and the mean timing disadvantage and the $CFS_{(m)ijt(h)}$ (for m = TS1,TS2,TS3, and h = 1,2 for the TS models, and h = 2,3 for the SA) are calculated for each portfolio. These means are reported in Exhibit 10 for all six comparisons (three TS models times two forecast horizon comparisons). The degree of association between SA comparative forecast superiority and SA timing disadvantage is measured by rank order and Pearson correlations between the mean portfolio SA comparative forecast superiority and the mean portfolio SA timing disadvantage. The results of the six association tests are reported at the bottom of Exhibit 10. The rank order correlations range from −0.245 to −0.501 and all are statistically significant at the 0.119 level or less. The Pearson correlations range from −0.280 to −0.452 and are statistically significant at the 0.087 level or less.

Thus, both tests indicate that SA comparative forecast superiority (relative to a particular TS model) increases as the SA timing advantage increases (or the SA timing disadvantage decreases). This evidence is consistent with the statement that SA acquire and use information arriving after the TS model forecast initiation date.

5. Summary

The results of tests applied to 233 firms over 24 quarters suggest that SA are superior earnings forecasters relative to the three univariate TS models often represented in the literature as generating firms' quarterly earnings numbers. We also examined whether the SA model's advantage is due to: (1) better utilization of information existing on the date that TS models are able to initiate forecasts—a contemporaneous advantage, and (2) acquisition of information between the date of initiation of TS model forecasts and the date when SA forecasts are published—a timing advantage. Although our evidence suggests that SA superiority is attributable to both of these factors, we do not assess the relative importance of these factors, nor do we identify the specific attributes of the SAs information set that result in SA forecast superiority.

Several important caveats pertain to this study. First, our results are applicable in the strictest sense only to our source of analysts, sample firms, time periods, and benchmak TS models. As such, they may not be generalizable to all analysts, firms, time periods, and models. Second, our study does not resolve the ambiguity of the extant literature which compares the predictive accuracy of SA and TS models. Resolution of the conflicting findings of the extant literature would require a consideration of all analysts, firms, time periods, and methodologies used in the extant literature. Third, we do not consider the magnitude of the costs and benefits of using SA vs. TS model forecasts. Among other factors, future research should consider the relative cost of obtaining SA forecasts vs. TS model forecasts, the sensitivity of results of prior information content studies using SA

forecasts vs. TS model forecasts, and the potential circumstances when TS model forecasts are more accurate than those of the SA.

Finally, we limited our focus to the predictive accuracy of SA vs. TS model forecasts. Our findings that SA out-predict TS models may not be very surprising considering that SA have available past earnings data as well as information that is unavailable to TS models (e.g., earnings reports of other firms, management forecasts, new contracts). Moreover, our findings that SA out-predict TS model forecasts do not imply that SA forecasts are superior measures of expectations to be used in "event" or information content studies. The relevant criterion for evaluating expectation models for these studies is unexpected returns, associated with information arrival, not predictive ability. Further research should use broader-based forecasts as benchmarks, by supplementing past earnings with such information as share prices [Beaver, Lambert and Morse (1980)], macroeconomic data [Hopwood and McKeown (1981)], firm-specific financial statement data [Freeman, Ohlson and Penman (1982)], and analyst forecasts [Brown, Griffin, Hagerman and Zmijewski (1987)], and it should use the unexpected return criterion rather than the predictive ability one.

Endnotes

1. Recent studies using TS models to proxy for firms' earnings estimates include Foster, Olsen and Shevlin (1984), Penman (1983), Rendleman, Jones and Latane (1982), and Watts (1978). Sources of analysts' forecasts used by the investment community include *The Value Line Investment Survey*, *S&P Earnings Forecaster*, *ICARUS*, and *Institutional Brokers Estimate System* (IBES). For reasons why academic researchers select TS models rather than SA forecasts, see Brown and Griffin (1983).

2. The forecast initiation date for a one-quarter ahead forecast horizon is the date when a one-quarter ahead forecast for quarter t is (can be) available. The TS model forecast initiation date is presumed to be the date that the previous (i.e., $t-1$) quarterly

earnings number is announced in *The Wall Street Journal.* The SA forecast initiation date is the *Value Line Investment Survey*'s publication date following the announcement of the previous (i.e., $t-1$) quarterly earnings number. The median number of days the SA forecast initiation date follows the TS model forecast initiation date is 39 in the sample that is analyzed in this study. This time period is called the SA timing advantage and is denoted as d in Section 4.1.

3. Two other sources of SA quarterly forecasts have since become available—IBES by Lynch, Jones & Ryan and ICARUS by Zacks Investment Research. IBES and ICARUS are consensus forecasts collected from as many as 1,800 analysts and 100 brokerage firms. Value Line, Inc. is an investment advisory service employing more than 50 analysts whose forecasts for a particular firm are generally the product of one or two individuals. One other publicly available source of consensus analysts' forecasts exists, the *S & P Earnings Forecaster*, but these forecasts are annual, not quarterly.

4. The three BJ models are used as benchmark forecasts because they have been shown to generate more accurate forecasts than both naive TS models (martingale with drift) and individually identified BJ models. [See Bao et al. (1983) for a discussion of these issues.]

5. The restatement and updating procedure is often utilized in the forecasting literature [e.g., Collins and Hopwood (1980), Collins, Hopwood and McKeown (1984), and Foster (1977)]. Each firm's TS model parameters were re-estimated 24 times, the number of firms in the sample was 233 from 1975 to 1979 and 212 in 1980, and there were three TS models. Thus, 16,524 separate BJ estimations were conducted. For each firm with complete data, the ex-post accuracy of SA forecasts was compared with that of the three TS models in 24 one-quarter ahead comparisons (i.e., forecasts of 1Q-1975 to 4Q-1980), 23 two-quarter ahead comparisons (i.e., forecasts of 2Q-1975 to 4Q-1980), and 22 three-quarter ahead comparisons (i.e., forecasts of 3Q-1975 to 4Q-1980).

6. The data collection procedure insures that the SA did not have available any reported (i.e., publicly available) quarterly earnings numbers which were unavailable to TS models. That is, the SA forecast initiation date always precedes *The Wall Street Journal* announcement date of the quarterly earnings to be forecast. Nevertheless, analysts may possess advance knowledge of earnings numbers soon to be released.

7. Selection of the unsigned forecast error as a metric is consistent with the assumption that financial statement users act as if they possess linear, symmetric loss functions. Our approach is consistent with that of past research [e.g., Foster (1977), Fried and Givoly (1982)]. However, as little is known about the characteristics of investors' and creditors' loss functions, this assumption may be inappropriate.

8. The 100 percent truncation rule for our data pulled in more TS model forecast errors than SA forecast errors. More particularly, conditional upon the first-, second-, third-, and fourth-quarter reports, respectively (for a one-quarter ahead forecast horizon), the (100 percent truncation) procedure pulled in 4.0, 6.4, 6.7, and 5.7 percent of the SA errors. In contrast, the procedure pulled in 6.0, 7.8, 9.4, and 9.7 percent of the errors for the TS1 model; 8.3, 9.4, 10.8, and 11.3 for the TS2 model; and 7.6, 8.6, 9.3, and 10.6 for the TS3 model. By pulling in more outliers for the TS models than for SA, the procedure does not induce any unintentional bias in favor of SA. In contrast, both the 300 percent and three standard deviation procedures pulled in fewer outliers for all forecasts, and the gap between the percent of errors pulled in by the TS models and the SA was reduced considerably. In fact, the three standard deviation procedure caused slightly more SA errors than TS model errors to be pulled in.

9. The Friedman test assumes that forecast errors are composed of an unknown mean effect, an unknown firm effect, an unknown treatment (forecast model) effect, and mutually independent and continuously distributed error terms. The null hypothesis is that the treatment (forecast model) effect is equal across the four forecast models. The alternative hypothesis is that at least one treatment effect is different than at least one other.

10. Hotelling's t-squared and multiple comparison t-tests (based on magnitudes) were also conducted and the results were qualitatively equivalent to the Friedman and multiple comparison t-tests (based on ranks).

11. The mean (unsigned) percentage forecast errors for the 24 quarter/years used in this test are presented in Exhibit 1.

12. The TS model forecast initiation date (i.e., the WSJ earnings announcement date) occurs dur-

ing the next fiscal quarter. [Chambers and Penman (1984) state that the median reporting lag for the first three fiscal quarters is 25 days, and for the fourth quarter 44 days.] Thus, when SA make their one-quarter ahead forecasts for quarter t on the WSJ date (i.e., when $d = 0$ so that they do not have a timing advantage), they do have access to information regarding events that have already occurred during quarter t.

13. The results presented in the table are Friedman and multiple comparison t-tests (based on ranks) across 24 quarter/year means. Hotelling's t-squared and multiple comparison t-tests (based on magnitudes) were also conducted and the results are qualitatively equivalent to the Friedman and multiple comparison t-tests (based on ranks).

14. As no significant results are obtained for the three-quarter horizon forecasts, the multiple comparison test results reported in panel A are not discussed.

15. As no significant results are obtained for the SA two-quarter vs. the TS one-quarter horizon forecasts, the multiple comparison test results reported in panel B are not discussed.

16. See Section 4.2 for discussion of the measurement of SA forecast timing disadvantage.

References

Abdel-khalik, A.R. and R.B. Thompson, 1977-78, Research on earnings forecasts: The state of the art, *Accounting Journal*, 1, 180-209.

Bao, D.H., M.T. Lewis, W.T. Lin and J.G. Manegold, 1983, Applications of time-series analysis in accounting: A review, *Journal of Forecasting* 2, 405-424.

Beaver, W.H., R.A. Lambert and D. Morse, 1980, The information content of security prices, Journal of Accounting and Economics 2, 3-28.

Box, G.E.P. and G.M. Jenkins, 1976, Time series analysis: Forecasting and control (Holden-Day, San Francisco, CA).

Brown, L.D. and P.A. Griffin, 1983, Perspectives on forecasting research in accounting and finance, *Journal of Forecasting* 2, 325-330.

Brown, L.D. and M.S. Rozeff, 1978, The superiority of analyst forecasts as measures of expectations: Evidence from earnings, *Journal of Finance* 33, 1-16.

Brown, L.D. and M.S. Rozeff, 1979, Univariate time-series models of quarterly accounting

earnings per share: A proposed model, *Journal of Accounting Research* 17, 179-189.

Brown, L.D. and M.E. Zmijewski, 1987, The effect of labor strikes on security analysts' forecast superiority and on the association between risk-adjusted stock returns and unexpected earnings, *Contemporary Accounting Research* 3, forthcoming.

Brown, L.D., P.A. Griffin, R.L. Hagerman and M.E. Zmijewski, 1987, An evaluation of alternative proxies for the market's expectation of earnings, *Journal of Accounting and Economics* 9, forthcoming.

Chambers, A.E. and S.H. Penman, 1984, Timeliness of reporting and the stock price reaction to earnings announcements, *Journal of Accounting Research* 22, 21-47.

Collins, W.A. and W.S. Hopwood, 1980, A multivariate analysis of annual earnings generated from quarterly forecasts of financial analysts and univariate time-series models, *Journal of Accounting Research* 18, 390-406.

Collins, W.A., W.S. Hopwood and J.C. McKeown, 1984, The predictability of interim earnings over alternative quarters, *Journal of Accounting Research* 22, 467-479.

Cragg, J.G. and B.G. Malkiel, 1968, The consensus and accuracy of some predictions of the growth of corporate earnings, *Journal of Finance* 23, 67-84.

Elton, E.J. and M.J. Gruber, 1972, Earnings estimates and the accuracy of expectational data, *Management Science* 18, 409-424.

Foster, G., 1977, Quarterly accounting data: Time-series properties an predictive ability results, *Accounting Review* 52, 1-21.

Foster, G., 1981, Intra-industry information transfers associated with earnings releases, *Journal of Accounting and Economics* 3, 201-232.

Foster, G., C. Olsen and T. Shevlin, 1984, Earnings releases, anomalies, and the behavior of securities returns, *Accounting Review* 59, 574-603.

Freeman, R.N., J.A. Ohlson and S.H. Penman, 1982, Book rate-of-return and prediction of earnings changes: An empirical investigation, *Journal of Accounting Research* 20, 639-653.

Fried, D. and D. Givoly, 1982, Financial analysts' forecasts of earnings: A better surrogate for market expectations, *Journal of Accounting and Economics* 4, 85-107.

Griffin, P.A., 1977, Time series behavior of quarterly earnings: Preliminary evidence, *Journal of Accounting Research* 15, 71-83.

Griffin, P.A., 1982, The usefulness to investors and creditors of information provided by financial reporting: A review of empirical research (Financial Accounting Standards Board, Stamford, CT).

Hollander, M. and D.A. Wolfe, 1973, *Nonparametric statistical methods* (Wiley, New York).

Hopwood, W.S. and J.C. McKeown, 1981, An evaluation of univariate time-series earnings models and their generalization to a single input transfer function, *Journal of Accounting Research* 19, 313-322.

Imhoff, E.A., Jr. and P.V. Pare, 1982, Analysis and comparison of earnings forecast agents, *Journal of Accounting Research* 20, 429-439.

O'Brien, P., 1985, An empirical analysis of forecasts of earnings per share. Unpublished dissertation (University of Chicago, IL).

Penman, S.H., 1983, The predictive content of earnings forecasts and dividends, *Journal of Finance* 38, 1181-1199.

Rendleman, R.J., C.P. Jones and H.A. Latane, 1982, Empirical anomalies based on unexpected earnings and the importance of risk adjustments, *Journal of Financial Economics* 10, 269-287.

Watts, R.L., 1975, The time series behavior of quarterly earnings, Working paper (University of Newcastle, Newcastle-upon-Tyne).

Watts, R.L., 1978, Systematic abnormal returns after quarterly earnings announcements, *Journal of Financial Economics* 6, 127-150.

Watts, R.L. and J.L. Zimmerman, 1986, *Positive accounting theory* (Prentice-Hall, Englewood Cliffs, NJ).

Chapter 23

Analyst Judgment: The Efficient Market Hypothesis versus a Psychological Theory of Human Judgment[*]

John E. Hunter, Ph.D.
Distinguished Professor of Industrial Psychology
Michigan State University

T. Daniel Coggin, Ph.D.
Director of Research
Virginia Retirement System

This paper considers the psychological processes used by financial analysts in making earnings forecasts by pitting two models against each other: the efficient market hypothesis, an economic model which asserts that the stock market virtually instantaneously and perfectly assimilates all available investment information; and personal construct theory, a psychological model of human judgment which emphasizes the fact that human decision making is based on formal and informal models of the phenomenon under consideration. Path models derived from personal construct theory fit data for 1963 gathered by Cragg and Malkiel and data for 1979-1983 gathered for this study. The efficient market hypothesis was not supported in any test on either data set.

Most studies of financial analysts' forecasts of earnings growth have considered the forecast as an independent variable. The dependent variable in these studies is usually forecast accuracy (e.g., Brown & Rozeff, 1978; Coggin & Hunter, 1982-1983; Elton, Gruber, & Gultekin, 1984), investment return (e.g., Bjerring, Lakonishok, & Vermaelen, 1983; Elton, Gruber, & Gultekin, 1981; Malkiel & Cragg, 1970), or both forecast accuracy and investment return (Coggin & Hunter, 1987). An excellent summary of this literature is given in Brown, Foster, and Noreen (1985). To focus on accuracy and return is consistent with viewing the analyst as an instrument which translates information for the stock market. The *efficient market hypothesis* (hereafter denoted EMH) from finan-

* We thank Michael S. Rozeff and two anonymous referees for helpful comments on an earlier version of this paper. Requests for reprints should be sent to John E. Hunter, Department of Psychology, Snyder Hall, Michigan State University, East Lansing, MI 48824.

cial economics asserts that the market virtually instantaneously and correctly assimilates all current information and any new information about the economy and individual firms.[1] However, many studies of human judgment have revealed gross distortions and often a high degree of oversimplification in judgment. It would not be surprising then to find that the EMH does not fit the actual behavior of financial analysts.

Criticism of the EMH and the global rationality assumption of economic theory is not new (e.g., Simon 1947, 1979). Nonetheless, financial theorists have been reluctant to drop this model without a concrete alternative. This study seeks to test an alternative model derived from the last 30 years of work in the psychology of human decision making. The specific model is Kelly's (1963) *personal construct theory* (hereafter denoted PCT) which emphasizes the role that formal and informal theories play in human judgment. This model can be formalized as a path model and will be pitted against the EMH in two data sets: data from 1963 gathered by Cragg and Malkiel (1982) and data for the years 1979-1983 gathered for this study.

Kelly's theory was originally developed as a theory of personality. As such, it can be applied to all "market participants" (i.e., investors and analysts). The large overshoots in stock prices observed by Shiller (1984) could be explained if there were a great many investors who held the same theory about when to buy and sell, but who did not know how to factor each other into their individual calculations. Roll (1986) has recently suggested that corporate takeover activity reveals striking departures from conventional models of economic behavior. However, in this study, we do not have data on investor behavior and hence cannot test his hypothesis. The data used in this study are professional financial analysts' forecasts of company-level earnings in 1963 and 1979-1983. In applying Kelly's theory to these data, we have assumed that most analysts accept the existing financial theories of their time. Thus the *consensus analyst* earnings forecast should be greatly influenced by the dominant financial theory for the period in question.

It is important to study what financial analysts actually consider in making earning forecasts. A major step in this regard was taken by Cragg and Malkiel (1982) in an extensive update and reanalysis of Cragg and Malkiel (1968) and Malkiel and Cragg (1970). They provide data relating analysts' earnings forecasts to short-term and long-term historical earnings growth rates which we reanalyze below. Our conclusions for the Cragg and Malkiel data differ considerably from theirs. This result is partly due to the fact that they focused almost entirely on analyst forecast accuracy while we focus on data relating the analyst forecast to historical earnings growth rates. However, we have also done an extensive reanalysis of their data and offer results that Cragg and Malkiel (1982) did not report. Our reanalysis of their 1963 data shows that, in forecasting long-term earnings growth, the consensus analyst forecast was virtually identical to the long-term historical earnings growth rate ($r = .91$). In fact, as predicted by PCT, the partial correlation between analyst forecast and actual earnings growth drops to zero once the historical earnings growth rate is controlled.

The data analyzed by Cragg and Malkiel (1982) were gathered during the 1960s. Thus their sample of analysts had not been fully exposed to the Sharpe-Lintner capital asset pricing model (CAPM), which was first proposed and expanded during the middle and late 1960s. It seems reasonable to hypothesize that analyst behavior would be quite different if they espoused the CAPM. In particular, PCT predicts that analysts in the 1980s would deemphasize historical earnings growth rates and rely instead on the CAPM beta which measures the market's expectation for the covariance of the return on a financial asset with the return on the overall market (Sharpe, 1985, Chap. 7). Our analysis of data for 1979-1983 shows this prediction to be correct. We begin with a discussion of the two models of analyst judgment.

Two Competing Models of Analyst Judgment

Our approach to the study of analyst judgment is theoretical. We have attempted to use the results of psychological studies of human judgment to understand analysts' forecasts of earnings growth. The findings of psychologists are very much in disagreement with the writings of those who espouse the notion of an efficient market. Psychologists have found that judges rarely use as much information as scientists studying the same phenomenon, and they use the same information less effectively.

An important theory in the psychological study of judgment is Kelly's PCT. Kelly noted that the theories of human information processing used in studying the behavior of scientists (as in the philosophy, history, and sociology of science) are radically different from the theories of judgment implicit in the study of ordinary people (as in personality theory). Throughout the first half of this century, psychologists and other students of human behavior (including sociologists and psychoanalysts) tended to view human judgment as being qualitatively different from scientific reasoning; always stressing the irrational aspects of judgment. Kelly argued that these theories are basically wrong. He argued that people in all contexts act as scientists—that the basic processes of judgment involve the formation of theories and the gathering of data to test those theories. He argued that many of the "irrationalities" in human judgment stem from the application of false premises and from the use of inadequate rules for drawing inferences from data—problems which also afflict scientific reasoning, though to a lesser degree. The hundreds of empirical studies of human judgment which followed have largely confirmed Kelly's basic hypothesis. In all areas—including person perception, moral judgment, and politics—judges start from personal theories of the phenomenon they are perceiving and code information according to those theories.

It follows from Kelly's theory that lay judges thinking about a given topic will usually be less sophisticated than scientific thinking about the same topic. The reason for this is that scientists are usually familiar with all the theories in a given area and will be aware of the fact that data disconfirm many of those theories. Thus scientists will not use the more implausible theories that captivate many lay judges. This prediction has been borne out in many subsequent studies of judgment. Studies typically find that judges tend to be very selective; they pick out only a few things to look at and tend to rely too much on indicators with limited validity (e.g., Kahneman, Slovic, & Tversky, 1982; Kahneman & Tversky, 1973). Some of the most interesting work in this area has stemmed from Meehl's (1954) classic work comparing clinical prediction to statistical prediction in making judgments about personality and behavior (e.g., Dawes, 1979; Slovic, 1972; Tversky & Kahneman, 1971). Meehl found that once information is coded, statistical formulae make much better predictions than do even trained clinical psychologists using the same information.

In the investment area, Kelly's theory predicts that financial analysts will be influenced by the financial theories they espouse. Analysts will be sensitive only to those pieces of information which their theories imply to be relevant. Moreover, analysts would be expected to make less effective use of that information compared to scientific analyses of the same data. The dominant theories of investment analysis during the 1950s and early 1960s were time series theories (see Malkiel, 1963 and Cottle, 1965, for a discussion)—meaning theories that make extensive use of extrapolation from historical data. Thus one would expect the analysts of that era to be strongly influenced by historical earnings growth data in predicting future earnings growth. On the other hand, Kelly's theory also predicts that analysts would do a poorer job of using that information than scientific procedures such as regression analysis. We will show that the Cragg and Malkiel data for 1963 support both hypotheses.

A contrast in theories of human information processing can also be found in the minds of financial theorists: a contrast between "ordinary people" and "investors." When thinking about ordinary people, most financial writers—like most people in general—view their friends and officemates as subject to significant irrationality and often make light of their "foolish errors." Yet when switching from "people" to "investors," financial theorists experience a massive transformation in thought. According to the semistrong form of the EMH, investors make virtually instant, correct interpretations of any information about firms which becomes "publicly available." This is a feat far beyond the achievements of the current scientific work in finance. Yet, the EMH implies that analysts rarely give undue weight to imperfect data and are sensitive to information that is beyond the reckoning of mere academic students of finance. Hence, the semistrong form of the EMH asserts that market participants are, in general, a breed apart—perfectly efficient information processors. This assertion is not a "straw man." It is fundamental to the equilibrium theory of rational asset pricing in a competitive market (Sharpe, 1985, Chap. 3).

Formalizing the Models as Path Models

Kelly's PCT and the EMH make very different predictions about analysts' forecasts. Slovic, Fleissner, and Bauman (1972) have argued that investment decisions can be formalized using linear statistical models. In our case, the differences between the two theories are formalized using a multiple regression model known as a path model. A path model (sometimes called a structural equation model or a causal model) is a way of organizing a

set of hypotheses about the causal relations among the variables in a particular domain. The hypotheses are coded into a path diagram by drawing a straight arrow from one variable to another if the first variable is thought to have a causal impact on the second. The numerical strength of each causal impact is estimated using linear regression. Specifically path analysis (the statistical analysis of a path model) allows one to test sets of hypotheses about relationships among variables simultaneously rather than one at a time. Once a particular path model is specified, it is tested by attempting to reproduce the observed correlations among the variables using the direct and indirect links between them. Path models are then evaluated on the basis of the magnitude of the errors in reproducing the observed correlations. For an expanded discussion, see Godberger and Duncan (1973), Duncan (1975), Kenny (1979), and Hunter and Gerbing (1982).

The competing path models relevant to the Cragg and Malkiel data are shown in Exhibit 1. The EMH argues that historical growth data are just one piece of data available to analysts. They will use those data only in so far as they are deemed relevant to actual performance. Thus historical growth data will have a causal impact on analyst forecast, but

Exhibit 1 Contrasting Path Models Relating Analyst Forecast to Actual Growth

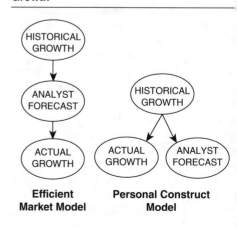

Efficient
Market Model

Personal Construct
Model

will make to direct contribution to actual growth. That is, since analysts already make perfect use of the information in historical growth rates, historical growth taken separately should not be a predictor of actual growth. This argument follows from the weak form of the EMH, which asserts that all available historical information about firms is fully assimilated by market participants.

Since the dominant theory in the financial literature of the early 1960s was time series extrapolation, Kelly's theory predicts that analysts' forecasts of long-term earnings growth would tend to rely almost entirely on long-term historical earnings growth data. Similarly, analysts' predictions of short-term earnings growth would tend to rely on short-term historical earnings growth data. However, Kelly's theory would also predict that analysts are likely to overuse what they perceive to be relevant information, and introduce noise into their predictions due to imperfect use of the quantitative information. Thus analysts' judgments using historical growth data are likely to be less accurate than simple extrapolation from the historical data alone. The corresponding path model predicts that historical growth data have an impact on analyst forecast, but that analyst forecast would be valid only to the extent that it is correlated with historical data. That is, Kelly's PCT predicts no causal arrow from analyst forecast to actual growth.

It is possible to state the difference between the path models for PCT and the EMH more generally. The EMH predicts that any relationship between historical variables and actual earnings growth is mediated by analyst judgment; i.e., analysts' forecasts make use of any information available in historical data. On the other hand, PCT predicts that analysts' forecasts are only "spuriously" related to actual earnings growth; i.e., analysts do not make full and correct use of historical information, and analysts only use information that prior theories have shown to be relevant.

Kelly's PCT would also predict a change in the nature of the path model for analysts of the 1970-1980s. In the early 1960s, the dominant investment model was time series extrapolation. However, despite its well known problems and criticisms (e.g., Roll, 1977), the 1970-1980s is the era of the CAPM in financial theory (McDonald & Stehle, 1975). Thus PCT predicts that analysts of the 1970-1980s would use a statistic from the CAPM called "beta." The basic idea is that, over the period from 1970-1980, financial theory generally rejected the notion that historical earnings are useful in predicting future earnings. Hence, while there might still be some impact of historical growth on analyst forecast, it would be weaker. The path models for analyst judgment in the 1970-1980s are shown in Exhibit 2.

Since the determinants of historical earnings growth and historical beta are outside the scope of PCT, the arrow between them is curved denoting no causal inference. Since we see no reason to believe that the relationship between historical earnings growth and actual earnings growth has changed over time, the arrow from historical growth to actual growth is carried over from Exhibit 1. The relationship between historical beta and actual earnings growth is also outside the scope of PCT. However, previous studies summarized in Elton and Gruber (1987, Chap. 13) have suggested that there may be at least a weak relationship between beta and investment return. Thus a dotted arrow from beta to actual growth was added to the path model. The path models in Exhibit 2 will be tested later in the section dealing with analyst judgment in the 1980s. We now begin the presentation of our results with a reanalysis of the Cragg and Malkiel data for 1963.

Results

Reanalysis of Cragg and Malkiel: Long-term Growth Forecasts

Cragg and Malkiel (1982) provide data relevant to the theoretical issue of this study. They present data on six variables: long-term historical earnings growth, short-term histori-

Exhibit 2 Path Models for Analyst Forecast Behavior in Two Different Time Settings as Derived from Kelly's (1963) Personal Construct Theory

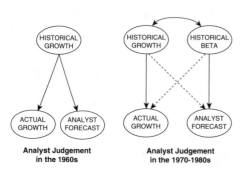

Analyst Judgement in the 1960s

Analyst Judgement in the 1970-1980s

cal earnings growth, analyst forecast of long-term earnings growth, analyst forecast of short-term earnings growth, actual long-term earnings growth, and actual short-term earnings growth, gathered from a sample of 19 investment firms over the period 1961-1969.[2] However, it is not possible to develop a path model of all six variables, because some firms asked analysts to forecast long-term growth while other firms asked analysts to forecast short-term growth. Cragg and Malkiel were unable to obtain data relating the forecasts for the two time horizons. Other data suggest that the two forecasts are quite different. This section will consider the data for long-term growth which was defined in the Cragg and Malkiel study as the 5-year earnings growth rate. Cragg and Malkiel did not have our path analysis in mind. They focused on analyst forecast accuracy and presented complete data on accuracy. Moreover, other correlations did not appear relevant to them and were presented only on a sporadic basis. Some correlations we could reconstruct, while others we could not. This limited the extent of our reanalysis. In particular, we were able to analyze only the data for 1963, though Cragg and Malkiel presented data for several other years.

Analysts' forecasts can be analyzed on two levels: forecasts by single analysts and the forecast of the consensus analyst. We considered each source of forecast data (i.e., each investment firm) in the Cragg and Malkiel study as one "analyst." We defined the consensus analyst to be the average of all analysts.[3] The two correlation matrices are presented in Exhibit 3, with the data for single analysts given in Exhibit 3a and the data for the consensus analyst given in Exhibit 3b.

The three variables most directly relevant to testing the EMH against the PCT are long-term historical earnings growth, analyst forecast of long-term earnings growth, and actual long-term earnings growth. Consider the data for *long-term single analyst forecast.* According to the EMH, the partial correlation between historical earnings growth and actual earnings growth should drop to zero if analyst forecast is held constant. In fact, the observed partial correlation is .30. Since our reported correlations are averages of correlations with a total sample size of 638 stocks, the observed partial correlation of .30 is far greater than would be expected on the basis of chance ($t = 7.93$). According to the PCT, the partial correlation between analyst forecast and actual earnings growth should drop to zero if historical growth is held constant. The observed partial correlation is .0021. Thus the PCT fits the data for the long-term single analyst forecast while the EMH does not.

Consider the data for *long-term consensus analyst forecast.* According to the EMH, the partial correlation between historical earnings growth and actual earnings growth should drop to zero if consensus analyst forecast is held constant. The observed partial correlation is .21, which is too large to be a chance departure ($t = 5.42$). According to the PCT, the partial correlation between consensus analyst forecast and actual earnings growth should drop to zero if historical growth is held constant. The observed partial correlation is -.0011. Thus the PCT fits the data for the long-term consensus analyst forecast while the EMH does not.

Exhibit 3 A Reanalysis of the Cragg and Malkiel (1982) Data for 1963 on Long-Term Growth (N = 638 Stocks)

a. Average correlations for single analyst forecast of long-term growth, decimals omitted.

		LHG	SAF	ALG	SHG
Long-term historical growth	LHG	100	77	44	52
Single analyst forecast	SAF	77	100	34	52
Actual long-term growth	ALG	44	34	100	47
Short-term historical growth	SHG	52	52	47	100

b. Average correlations for consensus analyst forecast of long-term growth, decimals omitted.

		LHG	CAF	ALG	SHG
Long-term historical growth	LHG	100	91	44	52
Consensus analyst forecast	CAF	91	100	40	61
Actual long-term growth	ALG	44	40	100	47
Short-term historical growth	SHG	52	61	47	100

There are other correlations in Exhibit 3 that are relevant to a comparison of the two models. Both models assume that historical earnings growth will influence analyst judgment. The observed correlation between long-term historical earnings growth and analyst forecast is .77 for single analysts and .91 for the consensus analyst. Thus individual analysts are affected by idiosyncratic factors in making forecasts. On the other hand, the average correlation between analyst forecast and actual long-term earnings growth is .34 for single analysts and .40 for the consensus analyst. Thus the idiosyncratic factors considered by single analysts act like random error. This would be predicted by the PCT but not by the EMH. According to the strong form of the EMH, all market participants are perfectly efficient and so there should be no "inside information" gained by asking more than one analyst.[4]

Cragg and Malkiel also present data for short-term historical earnings growth (i.e., prior 1-year growth). Although short-term historical earnings growth is less highly correlated with the consensus analyst forecast than long-term historical earnings growth (.61 versus .91), regression analysis suggests that short-term historical earnings growth does play a role in analysts' forecasts. A multiple

regression of the long-term consensus analyst forecast onto long-term and short-term historical earnings growth produced standardized regression weights of .19 for short-term growth and .81 for long-term growth. The multiple correlation is .92, which is only slightly larger than .91 for long-term historical earnings growth alone. Furthermore, short-term historical earnings growth is relevant to the prediction of actual long-term earnings growth. In fact, actual long-term earnings growth is slightly more highly correlated with short-term historical earnings growth than with long-term historical earnings growth (.47 versus .44), and the standardized regression weights are .33 for short-term and .27 for long-term historical earnings growth. The multiple correlation is .52. The correspondingly modified path model is presented in Exhibit 4c.

Exhibit 4 presents three path models derived from PCT which fit the Cragg and Malkiel data. Exhibit 4a presents the path model relating long-term historical earnings growth to forecasts by single analysts. Exhibit 4b presents the path model relating long-term historical earnings growth to the consensus analyst forecast. Exhibit 4c presents the modified path model incorporating short-term historical earnings growth.

Exhibit 4   Three Path Models Which Fit the Cragg and Malkiel (1982) Data for 1963

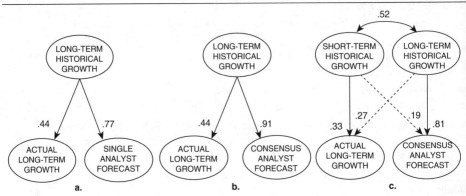

a.   b.   c.

The estimation of the standardized path coefficients in Exhibit 4c leaves only one correlation free to test: the correlation between the consensus analyst forecast and actual long-term earnings growth. The observed correlation is .40, while the predicted correlation is .45. The difference is small enough that it could be considered sampling error. Even if it were not sampling error, the difference is in the wrong direction for the EMH. According to the EMH, the correlation between analyst forecast and actual earnings growth should be larger than can be accounted for by historical earnings growth. In this case, the observed correlation is smaller than the predicted correlation. Thus, if this difference were real, it would mean that analysts are less accurate than would be predicted on the basis of how they use historical information. PCT fits these data while the EMH does not.

Reanalysis of Cragg and Malkiel: Short-Term Growth Forecasts

The correlation matrices for single analyst and consensus analyst forecasts of short-term (1-year) earnings growth are presented in Exhibit 5. Exhibit 5a is the correlation matrix for the single analyst and Exhibit 5b is the correlation matrix for the consensus analyst. One correlation could not be retrieved from Cragg and Malkiel (1982), the correlation between

short-term historical earnings growth and actual short-term earnings growth. Alas, this correlation turns out to be important. Thus our reanalysis of short-term growth is less satisfactory than our reanalysis of long-term growth.

The accepted financial theory of the early 1960s was time series extrapolation. Thus PCT predicts that the analysts of the early 1960s would tend to rely on short-term historical earnings growth to predict short-term earnings growth. The data confirm this prediction. The correlation between short-term consensus analyst forecast (CAF) and short-term historical earnings growth is .68, while the correlation for long-term historical earnings growth is .54. Standardized multiple regression reveals a dramatic contrast (*t*-statistics in parentheses, R = adjusted multiple correlation coefficient):

$$\text{long}-\text{term} \, CAF = .19 \, SHG + .81 \, LHG \, , \quad R = .92$$

$$(9.50) \quad (40.50)$$

$$\text{short}-\text{term} \, CAF = .55 \, SHG + .26 \, LHG \, , \quad R = .71.$$

$$(18.33) \quad (8.67)$$

During the early 1960s, analysts making long-term earnings growth forecasts tended to rely on long-term historical earnings growth while analysts making short-term earnings growth forecasts tended to rely on short-term historical earnings growth. This result is consistent with PCT.

Exhibit 5 A Reanalysis of the Cragg and Malkiel (1982) Data for 1963 on Short-Term Growth (N = 779 Stocks)

a. Average correlations for single analyst forecast of short-term (1-year) growth, decimals omitted.

		SHG	SAF	ASG	LHG
Short-term historical growth	SHG	100	54	NA	52
Single analyst forecast	SAF	54	100	24	36
Actual short-term growth	ASG	NA	24	100	26
Long-term historical growth	LHG	52	36	26	100

b. Average correlations for consensus analyst forecast of short-term growth, decimals omitted.

		SHG	CAF	ASG	LHG
Short-term historical growth	SHG	100	68	NA	52
Consensus analyst forecast	CAF	68	100	30	54
Actual short-term growth	ASG	NA	30	100	26
Long-term historical growth	LHG	52	54	26	100

Note: "na" denotes the correlation between SHG and ASG was not available in the Cragg and Malkiel (1982) data.

Since analysts making short-term earnings forecasts tended to rely on short-term historical earnings growth, the three relevant variables for the key path model are short-term historical earnings growth, short-term analyst forecast, and actual short-term earnings growth. Because the correlation between short-term historical earnings growth and actual short-term earnings growth is missing, this path analysis cannot be done. Thus a powerful test pitting the EMH against the PCT cannot be performed on these data.

PCT predicts that long-term forecasts will rely heavily on long-term historical growth while short-term forecasts will rely largely on short-term historical growth. However, it may

be possible to produce arguments that a perfectly efficient information processor might also make different predictions for the short-term than for the long-term. If so, this finding would be consistent with the EMH as well.

Analyst Judgment in the 1980s: An Update of Cragg and Malkiel

The structure of our 1980s database was set by the availability of analyst forecast data. We obtained analyst estimate data from the ICARUS file of analysts' forecasts maintained by Zacks & Company (Chicago, IL). This commercial service regularly obtains analysts' estimates from participating New

Exhibit 6 Variable Definitions for the 1979-1983 Data

SHG	=	Short-term (1-year) historical earnings growth rate.
LHG	=	Long-term (5-year) historical earnings growth rate (annualized).
HB	=	Historical beta from the Value Line Investment survey. Like fundamental beta described below, this number is an estimate of the market's expectation for the covariance of the return on an asset with the return on the overall market portfolio.
FB	=	Fundamental beta from Wilshire Associates. Fundamental beta is a multi-factor risk index described in Rosenberg and Guy (1976a, 1976b).
CAF	=	Consensus analyst forecast of long-term (5-year) earnings growth rate taken from the ICARUS file of Zacks & Company. This number is the mean of the analysts' forecasts for a company and is based on an average of 7.0 forecasts per company. Single analyst forecast data were not available in this file.
ASG	=	Actual short-term (1-year) earnings growth rate.

Exhibit 7 Average Correlations Between the Variables in the 1979-1983 Data, Decimals Omitted (N = 499 Stocks)

		SHG	LHG	HB	FB	CAF	ASG
Short-term historical growth	SHG	100	12	−06	01	10	−15
Long-term historical growrth	LHG	12	100	22	07	26	−19
Historical beta	HB	−06	22	100	53	46	−10
Fundamental beta	FB	01	07	53	100	45	−10
Consensus analyst forecast	CAF	10	26	46	45	100	00
Actual short-term growth	ASG	−15	−19	−10	−10	00	100

York and regional brokerage houses. Means and standard deviations of the analysts' company-level earnings forecasts are available in this file. Unlike the Cragg and Malkiel data for 1963, single analyst forecasts were not available in this file. The companies included in our sample were taken from intersection of the ICARUS file with the set of companies followed by the bank trust investment department where one of the authors was employed, and represent relatively large capitalization, institutional quality firms with December fiscal years. Our sample is broadly diversified across all major industry categories.

The time period for this part of our study is the five 1-year periods from 1979 to 1983. The variables used are defined in Exhibit 6. All variables were measured as of the beginning of each year except ASG, which was measured as of the end of each year. The number of stocks for each time period is 42, 84, 124, 123, and 126, respectively (total n = 499). Our sample of companies increased as the coverage of the Zacks database increased over the 5 years. A correlation matrix was computed for each time period separately. These correlation matrices were then averaged across time by weighting each matrix by

Exhibit 8 A Path Model Which Fits the Data for 1979-1983

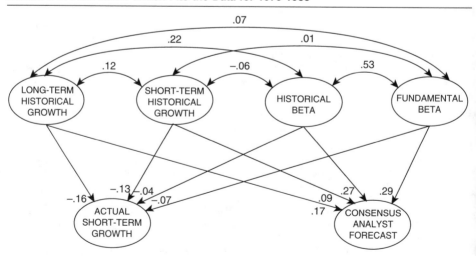

the number of stocks in the sample for that time period. The weighted-average correlation matrix is presented in Exhibit 7.

The values in Exhibit 7 can be compared to the values in Exhibit 3b for 1963. In 1963, the correlation between long-term historical earnings growth and consensus analyst forecast was .91. By 1979-1983, this correlation had dropped to .26. The correlation between short-term historical earnings growth and consensus analyst forecast dropped from .61 in 1963 to .10 in 1979-1983. On the other hand, the correlations between consensus analyst forecast and historical and fundamental beta from the CAPM are .46 and .45, respectively. Thus, by 1979-1983, analysts had shifted their emphasis from the time series extrapolation model of the 1960s toward the new theory—the CAPM. This contrast is also seen in the two standardized multiple regression equations:

$$1963: \text{CAF} = .19 \text{ SHG} + .81 \text{ LHG} , \quad R = .92$$
$$(9.50) \qquad (40.50)$$

$$1979-1983: \text{CAF} = .09 \text{ SHG} + .17 \text{ LHG}$$
$$(2.25) \qquad (4.25)$$

$$+ .27 \text{ HB} + .29 \text{ FB} ,$$
$$(6.75) \qquad (7.25)$$

$$R = .55 .$$

These regressions for long-term consensus analyst forecast support the predictions of PCT for the two periods.

The relationship between historical earnings growth and future earnings growth also changed dramatically between 1963 and 1979-1983. In 1963 (Exhibit 5b), there was a correlation of .26 between long-term historical earnings growth and actual short-term earnings growth. For 1979-1983, this correlation is −.19. That is, the correlation changed from positive to negative.

According to the EMH, historical data are completely taken into account by market participants. Thus historical data should add nothing to prediction once analysts' forecasts are included. This hypothesis can be tested with standardized multiple regression:

$$\text{ASG} = -.13 \text{ SHG} - .16 \text{ LHG} - .04 \text{ HB} - .07 \text{ FB} ,$$
$$(-3.25) \qquad (-4.00) \qquad (-.80) \qquad (-1.40)$$

$$R = .23$$

$$\text{ASG} = -.15 \text{ SHG} - .19 \text{ LHG} - .08 \text{ HB} - .11 \text{ FB}$$
$$(-3.25) \qquad (-4.25) \qquad (-1.60) \qquad (-2.20)$$

$$+ .15 \text{ CAF} ,$$
$$(3.00)$$

$$R = .26 .$$

The regressions for actual short-term earnings growth for 1979-1983 disconfirm the EMH. The regression weights for SHG, LHG, HB, and FB should all be zero once CAF is added to the regression. Instead, the standardized regression weights for the historical variables actually increase in magnitude (i.e., become more negative) when consensus analyst forecast is added to the regression equation. Moreover, the simple correlation of ASG with CAF is .00, whereas the multiple correlation is .26.

Exhibit 8 presents the path model derived from PCT for the 1979-1983 data. In substantive terms, the original path model of Exhibit 2 is invalidated by the negative correlations between the historical data and subsequent earnings growth. The paths in Exhibit 2 are implicitly positive and reflect the assumption that earnings growth has momentum. However, the formal path model with the negative correlations can still be applied to test the fundamental hypothesis from PCT—that the predictive power of analyst forecast is mediated by the variables required by the financial theory used by the analysts.

For the path model in Exhibit 8, there is only one observed correlation which is not predetermined by the estimation procedure: the correlation between consensus analyst forecast and actual short-term earnings growth. The correlation implied by the path model is $-.10$, while the observed correlation is $.00$. This discrepancy is not statistically significant, hence the PCT path model in Exhibit 8 fits the 1979-1983 data.

Summary and Conclusion

Analyst Judgment

PCT asserts that human judgments are based on personal theories of the phenomenon under consideration. Hence PCT predicts that, during the time series era of the early 1960s, financial analysts based their forecasts on the most directly relevant historical data. However, by 1979-1983, analysts would be expected to have deemphasized time series extrapolation in favor of the CAPM. Thus, in forecasting earnings, analysts would be expected to base their judgments more on CAPM beta than on historical earnings growth.

The results presented here conform to the predictions of PCT. In 1963, the correlation between the consensus analyst forecast of long-term earnings growth and long-term historical earnings growth was almost perfect, $r = .91$. By 1979-1983, the importance of long-term historical earnings growth had dropped sharply ($r = .91$ to $r = .26$), while the importance of both historical beta ($t = 6.75$) and fundamental beta ($t = 7.25$) from the CAPM is clear.

The Efficient Market Hypothesis

According to the EMH, market participants have access to and perfectly absorb *all available investment information*. If all historical information were properly absorbed by financial analysts, then historical information should predict future values only indirectly through analyst judgment. To illustrate, suppose that the only information contained in long-term historical earnings growth (LHG) as a predictor of actual long-term earnings growth (ALG) were represented by the regression equation:

$$ALG = .44 \text{ LHG}, \quad R = .44.$$

The EMH holds that analysts would know this equation and would weigh LHG accordingly in making earnings forecasts. If multiple regression were done with both consensus analyst forecast and LHG as predictors, there should be no new information in LHG and it should have a regression weight of zero. That is, LHG can add to the predictions of analysts only if the analysts do not make proper use of the information contained in LHG. This hypothesis is disconfirmed in the Cragg and Malkiel data for 1963:

$$ALG = .44 \text{ LHG} + .00 \text{ CAF}, \quad R=.44.$$
$$(5.50) \quad\quad (.00)$$

When consensus analyst forecast and historical data are considered together as predictors of actual long-term earnings growth, it is the regression weight for the consensus analyst forecast (CAF) that vanishes rather than the regression weight for long-term historical earnings growth.

The EMH is also disconfirmed by the results for 1979-1983. The correlation between consensus analyst forecast and actual short-term earnings growth is actually $.00$, which implies that analysts do not forecast earnings growth at all. On the other hand, the multiple correlation for the historical variables is $R = .23$. That is, historical variables predict earnings growth while consensus analyst forecast does not. When consensus analyst forecast and historical variables are considered together, the regression weights for the historical variables actually become larger in magnitude rather than vanish as the EMH predicts. In statistical language, this means that consensus analyst forecast acts like a "suppressor variable" (Darlington, 1968) for the historical variables.

The EMH asserts that all market participants make full use of all available investment information. If this were true, then each individual analyst would predict as well as any other analyst and there would be no gain from considering more than one analysts' judgment. One challenge to this hypothesis can be drawn from a comparison of the predictive power of the consensus analyst. For 1963, in predicting actual short-term earnings growth, the correlation for single analysts was .24, while the correlation for the consensus analyst was .30. In predicting actual long-term earnings growth, the correlation for single analysts was .34, while the correlation for the consensus analyst was .40. In both cases, the increase is significant. Thus single analysts are less accurate than the consensus analyst. This means that single analysts are subject to idiosyncratic error; idiosyncracy which should not exist according to the strong form of the EMH. Moreover Slovic, Fleissner, and Bauman (1972) and Ebert and Kruse (1978) detected significant idiosyncracy in experiments where analysts were asked to evaluate hypothetical companies and were given exactly the same data to analyze on each company. We were unable to test this hypothesis in the 1979-1983 sample because we had no single analyst forecast data.

The efficient market hypothesis was not supported in two data sets: the Cragg and Malkiel (1982) data for 1963 and more recent data collected for 1979-1983. One model which does fit both data sets is Kelly's (1963) personal construct theory.

Endnotes

1. The EMH is a rather complex hypothesis which comes in three forms: the *weak form,* the *semistrong form,* and the *strong form.* These three forms are described in detail in Fama (1970). We shall introduce each form where applicable as our discussion continues.

2 The data we took from Cragg and Malkiel (1982) were presented in their Exhibits 2.1, 2.2, 2.11, 2.13, 2.14, 2.16, and 2.23. The accuracy of forecasts varied dramatically as a function of the number of stocks followed by each participating firm. Cragg and Malkiel explained this by noting that all firms followed the three "outliers": IBM, Xerox, and Polaroid. The impact of these three companies was larger when embedded in a small number of stocks than when embedded in a large number of stocks. An examination of the data showed that the essential number of stocks required to eliminate the bias is 100. Thus we only averaged across firms that covered more than 100 stocks. These averages yielded an effective sample size of 638 stocks for the long-term earnings forecast data and 779 for the short-term earnings forecast data. Cragg and Malkiel make several references to "mechanical" historical data (i.e., log-linear trends), though they present little data for those models. Instead they present a number of historical trend estimates provided by two firms, which they treat as perceptions of historical earnings growth. The sum of these two indicators ($g_{p2} + g_{p4}$) correlates .96 with the mechanical indicator g_{c4} (see their Exhibit 2.11). Thus we used that sum as the measure of long-term historical earnings growth. The only measure of short-term historical earnings growth offered was that provided by a single firm (i.e., g_{p3}). We assume that firms are at least as accurate in their assessment of short-term historical growth as of long-term historical growth, so we used that indicator for short-term historical earnings growth.

3. The covariance of the consensus analyst forecast with another variable is the average of the covariances of the individual analysts with that other variable. For an infinite number of analysts, the variance of the consensus analyst is the average of the correlations between analysts. Thus the correlation between the consensus analyst and another variable is estimated by the ratio of the average individual analyst correlation with that variable divided by the square-root of the average inter-analyst correlation.

4. Shiller (1984, fn. 37) has noted that there is disagreement in the literature of financial economics concerning the precise definition of the EMH. A recent special issue of *The Journal of Business* (Vol. 59, Oct. 1986) was devoted entirely to papers debating the status of behavioral rationality in economics. Roll (1986, p. 214) cites one writer who criticized his "hubris hypothesis of corporate takeovers" because it alleges to be consistent with strong form market effciency while allowing systematic errors on the part of "one set of" market participants. Roll's view (1986, p. 199) is that such errors can exist since they will "cancel out" in the aggregate market. Our view is that the strong form of the EMH requires homogeneous expectations on the part of all market participants, and thus implies that there should be nothing gained by seeking information from more than one financial analyst.

References

Bjerring, J. H., Lakonishok, J., & Vermaelen, T. (1983). Stock prices and financial analysts' recommendations. *Journal of Finance, 38,* 187-204.

Brown, L. D., & Rozeff, M. S. (1978). The superiority of analyst forecasts as measures of expectations: Evidence from earnings. *Journal of Finance, 33,* 1-16.

Brown, P., Foster, G., & Noreen, E. (1985). Security analyst multi-year earnings forecasts and the capital market (Studies in Accounting Research No. 21). Sarasota, FL: American Accounting Association.

Coggin, T. D., & Hunter, J. E. (1982-1983). Analysts' forecasts nearer actual than statistical models. *Journal of Business Forecasting,* 1, 20-23.

Coggin, T. D., & Hunter, J. E. (1987). Analysts' forecasts for EPS and EPS growth: Decomposition of error, relative accuracy and relation to return. Working Paper, Virginia Retirement System, Richmond, VA.

Cottle, S. (1965). Corporate earnings: A record of contrast and change. *Financial Analysts Journal,* 21, November-December, 67-81.

Cragg, J. G., & Malkiel, B. G. (1968). The consensus and accuracy of some predictions of the growth of corporate earnings. *Journal of Finance,* 23, 67-84.

Cragg, J. G., & Malkiel, B. G. (1982). *Expectations and the structure of share prices.* Chicago, IL: Univ. of Chicago Press.

Darlington, R. B. (1968). Multiple regression in psychological research and practice. *Psychological Bulletin,* 69, 161-182.

Dawes, R. M. (1979). The robust beauty of improper linear models in decision making. *American Psychologist,* 34, 571-582.

Duncan, O. D. (1975). *Structural equation models.* New York: Academic Press.

Ebert, R. J., & Kruse, T. E. (1978). Bootstrapping the security analyst. *Journal of Applied Psychology,* 63, 110-119.

Elton, E. J., & Gruber, M. J. (1987). *Modern portfolio theory and investment analysis* (3rd ed.). New York: Wiley.

Elton, E. J., Gruber, M. J., & Gultekin, M. N. (1981). Expectations and share prices. *Management Science,* 27, 975-987.

Elton, E. J., Gruber, M. J., & Gultekin, M. N. (1984). Professional expectations: Accuracy and diagnosis of errors. *Journal of Financial and Quantitative Analysis,* 19, 351-363.

Fama, E. F. (1970). Efficient capital markets: A review of theory and empirical work. *Journal of Finance,* 25, 383-417.

Goldberger, A. S., & Duncan, O. D. (Eds.). (1973). *Structural equation models in the social sciences.* New York: Seminar Press.

Hunter, J. E., & Gerbing, D. W. (1982). Unidimensional measurement, second-order factor analysis and causal models. In B. M. Staw & L. L. Cummings (Eds.), *Research in organizational psychology* (Vol. 4, pp. 267-320). Greenwich, NJ: JAI Press.

Kahneman, D., Slovic, P., & Tversky, A. (Eds.). (1982). *Judgment under uncertainty: Heuristics and biases.* New York: Cambridge Univ. Press.

Kahneman, D., & Tversky, A. (1973). On the psychology of prediction. *Psychological Review,* 80, 237-251.

Kelly, George A. (1963). *A theory of personality.* New York: Norton.

Kenny, D. A. (1979). *Correlation and causality.* New York: Wiley.

Malkiel, B. G. (1963). Equity yields, growth and the structure of share prices. *American Economic Review,* 53, 1004-1031.

Malkiel, B. G., & Cragg, J. G. (1970). Expectations and the structure of share prices. *American Economic Review,* 60, 601-617.

McDonald, J. G., & Stehle, R. E. (1975). How do institutional investors perceive risk? *Journal of Portfolio Management,* 2, 11-16.

Meehl, P. E. (1954). *Clinical versus statistical prediction.* Minneapolis, MN: Univ. of Minnesota Press.

Roll, R. (1977). A critique of the asset pricing theorys tests, part I: On past and potential testability of the theory. *Journal of Financial Economics,* 4, 129-176.

Roll, R. (1986). The hubris hypothesis of corporate takeovers. *Journal of Business,* 59 (2, Pt. 1), 197-216.

Rosenberg, B., & Guy, J. (1976a). Prediction of beta from investment fundamentals, part one. *Financial Analysts Journal,* 32, May/June, 3-15.

Rosenberg, B., & Guy, J. (1976b). Prediction of beta from investment fundamentals, part two. *Financial Analysts Journal,* 32, July/August, 3-11.

Sharpe, W. F. (1985). *Investments (3rd ed.)*. Englewood Cliffs, NJ: Prentice-Hall.

Shiller, R. J. (1984). Stock prices and social dynamics. *Brookings Papers on Economic Activity, 2*, 457-510.

Simon, H. A. (1947). *Administrative behavior.* New York: Macmillan Co.

Simon, H. A. (1979). Rational decision making in business organizations. *American Economic Review, 69*, 493-513.

Slovic, P. (1972). Psychological study of human judgment: Implications for investment decision making. *Journal of Finance, 27*, 779-799.

Slovic, P., Fleissner, D., & Bauman, W. S. (1972). Analyzing the use of information in investment decision making: A methodological proposal. *Journal of Business, 45*, 283-301.

Tversky, A., & Kahneman, D. (1971). Belief in the 'law of small numbers,' *Psychological Bulletin, 76*, 105-110.

Chapter 24

Earnings Expectations and Security Prices

Eugene H. Hawkins
President
Investment Analytics

Stanley C. Chamberlin
Chairman
Chamberlin and Pearson Research Associates, Inc.

Wayne E. Daniel
President
Daniel Consulting

Can generally available information about consensus earnings expectations be used to generate risk-adjusted excess returns? If the market is truly efficient, such information should be discounted instantaneously and offer no profit opportunity. If the market is inefficient, however, and discounts new information only gradually, then it should be possible to demonstrate a relation between current consensus forecasts and subsequent stock price behavior.

Using a data base that contained earnings estimates for over 2,400 stocks made by more than 70 brokerage firms, the authors examined month-to-month percentage changes in consensus estimates to determine whether large positive revisions in earnings expecta-

tions can predict changes in stock prices. Their findings indicate that this information can be used to achieve returns significantly above the market's return. Furthermore, the returns remain superior after risk adjustment and after transaction costs.

For each of the 24 quarters from March 1975 through December 1980, the authors initiated a portfolio consisting of the 20 stocks with the largest one-month increase in their mean, or consensus, earnings estimate. Not only did these test portfolios achieve a 12-month alpha of 14.2 percent versus the S&P 500, but 66 percent of the stocks selected outperformed the S&P 500 on an absolute basis, assuming a six-month holding period. The performance of the selected portfolios also proved superior when compared with the returns on portfolios of similar risk chosen randomly from the same universe.

"The moves of the market are based, not on current reality, but on investors' views of the future. To rewrite Heraclitus, the Greek philosopher, investors never swim in an actual river even once; they always bathe in a stream of expectations."

—*Leonard Silk*
The New York Times

Both informed intuition and empirical evidence have led many investors to accept the view that expectations—more specifically, earnings expectations—are a significant determinant of common stock prices. Utilizing this premise, several studies have demonstrated that, because consensus earnings expectations are reflected in stock prices, an investor who correctly identifies errors in consensus forecasts and acts accordingly can earn risk-adjusted excess returns.

An investor taking such an approach is, in effect, "arguing with the consensus," his objective being to identify situations in which he believes his estimates are better than the consensus. Of course, a prerequisite to such an approach is a research capability that produces superior estimates. Alternatively, an investor might choose to "go along with the consensus," in the belief that certain consensus data contain information that has not yet been fully discounted in market prices. This approach requires the ability to discern such significant information, rather than the ability to make superior forecasts.

In a recent study, Elton, Gruber, and Gultiken offer comfort to practitioners using both approaches.[1] First, they demonstrated the efficacy of superior earnings forecasts for producing worthwhile excess returns. They then showed that even greater excess returns can be earned when one is able to predict changes in the consensus estimate (as opposed to more accurate earnings predictions *per se*).

These results suggest that, in an inefficient market that discounts new information only gradually, revisions in consensus earnings estimates could be used to predict changes in stock prices. This article examines this proposition.

"The most important single factor determining a stock's value is now held to be the indicated average future earnings power, i.e., the estimated average earnings for a future span of years."

—*Graham, Dodd, and Cottle*
Security Analysis

The Study

We based our study on earnings per share expectations collected by the Institutional Brokers Estimate System (I/B/E/S).[2] I/B/E/S produces data that allow investors to evaluate the earnings expectations for over 3,000 companies, including the level of current expectations in comparison with each company's historical record and with the expectations for other companies, and the degree of uniformity or "confidence" with which knowledgeable analysts hold expectations.

A regular monthly feature of I/B/E/S is a screen that lists those stocks followed by three or more analysts that have shown the greatest increase in their mean earnings forecasts since the prior month (I/B/E/S Screen #1).[3] In order to ascertain whether knowledge of these changes might be useful for predicting future stock price performance, we selected from these screens the 20 stocks with the largest increase in their mean estimates and constructed a set of equally weighted portfolios initiated at quarterly intervals between March 1975 and December 1980.[4]

Although the screened lists were available at mid-month, we measured each portfolio's performance assuming purchase at month-end. To measure investment return, we used cumulative monthly total returns (price change plus reinvested dividends), linking total monthly return data for each stock (sup-

Exhibit 1 12-Month Holding Period Returns

	Screen #1	I/B/E/S	S&P 500
March 1975	51.6%	33.3%	28.1%
June 1975	26.5	13.2	13.9
Sept. 1975	31.5	33.0	30.2
Dec. 1975	52.5	30.4	23.8
March 1976	8.1	3.3	−0.1
June 1976	14.0	7.2	0.7
Sept. 1976	2.8	3.1	−3.9
Dec. 1976	3.5	0.1	−7.1
March 1977	15.7	4.5	−4.7
June 1977	25.0	10.2	0.1
Sept. 1977	48.0	25.4	11.4
Dec. 1977	19.0	10.4	6.3
March 1978	23.3	22.6	19.5
June 1978	30.2	16.0	13.0
Sept. 1978	9.9	15.2	12.1
Dec. 1978	66.9	32.0	18.1
March 1979	19.2	5.8	6.0
June 1979	30.7	18.5	17.1
Sept. 1979	65.6	25.1	20.8
Dec. 1979	53.1	31.5	32.1
March 1980	79.3	59.9	39.5
June 1980	26.2	38.0	20.5
Sept. 1980	−12.6	3.1	−3.8
Dec. 1980	8.7	6.2	−6.1
Mean	29.1	18.7	12.0

plied by the Interactive Data Corporation) to compute the cumulative holding period return for each security and finding the portfolios' rates of return by averaging the cumulative rates of return for each stock. We used the same approach to compute total return for the I/B/E/S universe, the Standard & Poor's (S&P) 500, and 24,000 random portfolios that were generated to assess the role chance might have played in obtaining Screen #1's results.

Performance Before Risk Adjustment

Exhibits 1 through 9 present total return data for the 24 Screen #1 portfolios, the I/B/E/S universe, and the S&P 500 over the 6 3/4-year test period ending December 31, 1981. As Exhibit 1 indicates, the average 12-month return for the Screen #1 portfolios was 29.1 percent, versus 18.7 percent for the I/B/E/S universe and 12.0 percent for the S&P 500. The Screen #1 portfolios outperformed the I/B/E/S universe in 19 of the 24 holding periods and did better than the S&P 500 in all but two periods. Exhibits 3 and 4 plot the excess returns of the Screen #1 portfolios (in ascending order of relative performance) versus the I/B/E/S universe and the S&P 500, respectively.

Exhibit 5 compares graphically the average cumulative total returns for holding periods of one to 12 months for the 24 Screen #1 portfolios, the I/B/E/S universe, and the S&P 500. Average returns for the 24 portfolios always exceeded those for the I/B/E/S universe, which in turn always outperformed the S&P 500 on a cumulative total return basis. Exhibit 2 gives the values used to plot Exhibit 5.

Exhibit 6 presents the average monthly returns for the 24 Screen #1 portfolios, the I/B/E/S universe, and the S&P 500, as well as differences between various sets of these returns. On a monthly basis, the Screen #1 portfolios outperformed both the selection universe and the S&P 500 in all but the ninth month. The maximum one-month return advantage occurred in the second month.

Exhibit 2 Average Total Returns (Cumulative)

	Month 1	Month 2	Month 3	Month 4	Month 5	Month 6	Month 7	Month 8	Month 9	Month 10	Month 11	Month 12
Screen #1	2.0%	5.6%	8.4%	10.6%	13.9%	16.4%	17.2%	20.5%	21.9%	23.1%	25.8%	29.1%
I/B/E/S	1.1	3.2	5.2	5.9	8.0	9.6	10.4	12.4	14.0	14.9	16.9	18.7
S&P 500	0.5	1.3	3.5	3.6	4.2	6.3	6.6	7.2	9.1	9.5	10.0	12.0

Exhibit 3 12-Month Excess Return, Screen #1 Portfolio Minus I/B/E/S Universe

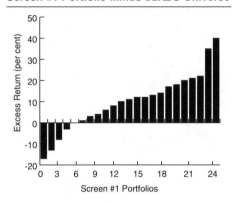

Screen #1 Portfolios

Exhibit 5 Cumulative Total Monthly Returns

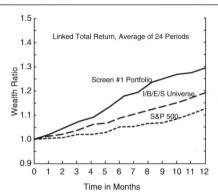

Time in Months

Long-Term Results

Exhibit 7 shows the returns that would have resulted if Screen #1 portfolios had been held for varying periods—i.e., three, six, nine and 12 months—and then rolled into the next available portfolio. These returns are compared with returns from simultaneous buy-and-hold investments made in the two benchmark portfolios.

Exhibit 8 illustrates the method used to obtain these results. The six-year gain of 468 percent for a six-month rollover strategy with Screen #1, for example, is the average of out-

Exhibit 4 12-Month Excess Return, Screen #1 Portfolio Minus S&P 500

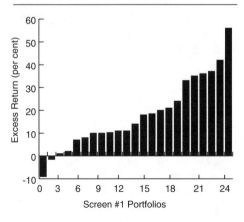

Screen #1 Portfolios

comes for Columns (B) and (C) in Exhibit 8, using linked six-month returns for the indicated periods. Note that each Screen #1 portfolio was included once, and only once, to obtain the six-year results. Thus the returns in Exhibit 7 represent averages for strategies that did not require *simultaneous* investment in a number of portfolios.

Exhibit 7 shows that the three-month returns gave the highest long-run results (at least for tax-exempt investors). The "hidden" long-term results of compounding periodic rates are also evident in Exhibit 7. Using a six-month rollover strategy, for example, the six-year gain of 468 percent for Screen #1 is 4.7 times as great as the S&P's return of 99 percent, whereas the annual rate of 34 percent is "only" 2.8 times as great as the S&P's 12 percent.

Exhibit 9 reports the results obtained when a 0.7 percent trading expense is deducted for each buy or sell transaction (1.4 percent round trip).[5] On an after-expense basis, it is the six-month rollover strategy that offers the highest returns.

Levering the Market

According to the Capital Asset Pricing Model (CAPM), only by assuming higher levels of systematic, or market-related, risk can an investor expect to earn a premium for risk-tak-

Exhibit 6 Average Monthly Returns for 24 Portfolios

	Monthly Total returns			Differences in Monthly Total Returns		
Month	Screen #1	I/B/E/S	S&P 500	Screen #1 - S&P 500	Screen #1 - I/B/E/S	I/B/E/S - S&P 500
1	2.0%	1.1%	0.5%	1.5%	0.9%	0.6%
2	3.5	2.1	0.8	2.8	1.4	1.3
3	2.7	1.9	2.2	0.5	0.8	−0.3
4	2.0	0.7	0.1	1.9	1.3	0.6
5	3.0	2.0	0.6	2.4	1.0	1.4
6	2.2	1.5	2.0	0.2	0.7	−0.5
7	0.7	0.7	0.2	0.5	0.0	0.5
8	2.8	1.8	0.6	2.2	1.0	1.2
9	1.2	1.4	1.9	−0.7	−0.2	−0.5
10	1.0	0.8	0.3	0.7	0.2	0.5
11	2.2	1.7	0.5	0.2	0.5	1.2
12	2.6	1.5	1.8	0.8	1.1	−0.3
Mean	2.2	1.4	1.0	1.1	0.7	0.5

Exhibit 7 Six-Year Returns for Linked Portfolios (Before Trading Expenses)

Number of Linked Portfolios	Linked Holding Periods	Total Six-Year Returns			Annual Rate of Return		
		Screen #1	I/B/E/S	S&P 500	Screen #1	I/B/E/S	S&P 500
24	3 mos.	505%	205%	115%	35.0%	20.4%	13.6%
12	6 mos.	468	181	99	33.6	18.7	12.3
8	9 mos.	362	172	98	29.1	18.1	12.1
6	12 mos.	332	168	90	27.6	17.9	11.3

ing over and above that paid on the overall market portfolio. The CAPM defines systematic risk as the covariance of an asset's returns with the market, which is normally measured by the beta coefficient of regression. In theory, however, there is no distinction between a 1.50 beta portfolio and investing, say, $150 in the market portfolio using $50 of debt and $100 of equity—if the cost of debt equals the risk-free rate. Under these conditions, the levered investment will have perfect covariance with the market and a beta (on invested equity) equal to 1.00 plus the dollar amount borrowed divided by the dollar amount of equity.

What level of borrowing, combined with the market portfolio, would have been necessary to match the results of the Screen #1 portfolios given in Exhibit 9? It is possible to

show that a tax-exempt investor who levered the S&P 500 would have needed $437 of debt for every $100 of invested equity in order to match the six-year linked return of 335 percent (after trading expenses) on Screen #1 using a three-month rollover strategy. Exhibit 10 gives the data to support this conclusion.[6]

Below, we use conventional regression analysis to show that returns on the Screen #1 portfolios would have been poorly predicted by the CAPM's expected return equation, given prior knowledge of the market's return and the actual covariance (average beta of 1.39) for the portfolios. Exhibit 10 already indicates, however, that the amount of debt, combined with the market portfolio, needed to match Screen #1's results goes far beyond what most investors (not to mention lending institutions) would find acceptable.

Exhibit 8 Turnover Dates for Linked Portfolios*

Date of Purchase	3 months (A)	6 months (B)	(C)	9 months (D)	(E)	(F)	12 months (G)	(H)	(I)	(J)
March 1975	x	x		x			x			
June 1975	x		x		x			x		
Sept. 1975	x	x				x			x	
Dec. 1975	x		x	x						x
March 1976	x	x			x		x			
June 1976	x		x			x		x		
Sept. 1976	x	x		x					x	
Dec. 1976	x		x		x					x
March 1977	x	x				x	x			
June 1977	x		x	x				x		
Sept. 1977	x	x			x				x	
Dec. 1977	x		x			x				x
March 1978	x	x		x			x			
June 1978	x		x		x			x		
Sept. 1978	x	x				x			x	
Dec. 1978	x		x	x						x
March 1979	x	x			x		x			
June 1979	x		x			x		x		
Sept 1979	x	x		x					x	
Dec. 1979	x		x		x					x
March 1980	x	x				x	x			
June 1980	x		x	x				x		
Sept 1980	x	x			x				x	
Dec. 1980	x		x			x				x
Last Sale Month (1981)	3	3	6	3	6	9	3	6	9	12
Years Invested	6	6	6	6	6	6	6	6	6	6

* Each "x" indicates a turnover date for one of the linked portfolios.

Exhibit 9 Six-Year Returns for Linked Portfolios (After Trading Expenses)

Number of Linked Portfolios	Linked Holding Periods	Total Six-Year Returns			Annual Rate of Return		
		Screen #1	I/B/E/S	S&P 500	Screen #1	I/B/E/S	S&P 500
24	3 mos.	335%	200%	112%	27.7%	20.1%	13.3%
12	6 mos.	383	175	97	30.0	18.4	12.0
8	9 mos.	312	167	96	26.6	17.8	11.9
6	12 mos.	298	165	87	25.9	17.6	11.0

Exhibit 10 Levering the S&P 500 to Match Screen #1 Results*

	Equity Capital	$100.00
+	Borrowed Capital	437.30
=	Total Invested Capital	537.30
+	S&P 500 Return at 112%	601.78
=	Terminal Portfolio Value	1,139.00
–	Borrowed Capital	(437.30)
–	Interest on Borrowings	(266.75)
–	Equity Capital	(100.00)
=	Required Return of 335%	335.03

* Based on 90-day Commercial Paper rate. Contrary to the CAPM's assumption, investors clearly cannot borrow at the risk-free Treasury bill rate.

Risk-Adjusted Performance

Exhibit 1 indicated that the I/B/E/S universe systematically outperformed the S&P 500. The combined effects of investment in small firms and use of equally weighted portfolios are no doubt factors in this result. To the extent that both absolute and risk-adjusted returns for small firms have consistently exceeded those of large companies over the past 15 years or so, the inclusion of a number of small capitalization firms in the selection universe, together with the equal weighting of portfolio positions, may have systematically enhanced Screen #1's performance versus the

Exhibit 11 Screen #1 Portfolios vs. S&P 500*

		Annual Alpha	Std. Error of Annual Alpha	Monthly Alpha	Std. Error of Annual Alpha	Beta	Std. Error of Beta	R^2
March	1975	18.365%	3.969	1.414%	1.146	1.059	0.227	0.685
June	1975	11.275	2.784	0.893	0.804	1.043	0.168	0.793
Sept.	1975	–6.347	2.477	–0.545	0.715	1.371	0.169	0.869
Dec.	1975	21.945	2.911	1.667	0.840	1.114	0.195	0.766
March	1976	7.953	1.856	0.640	0.535	0.971	0.173	0.758
June	1976	12.666	2.378	0.999	0.687	0.854	0.213	0.616
Sept.	1976	4.702	2.427	0.384	0.701	0.953	0.223	0.647
Dec.	1976	11.232	2.456	0.891	0.709	0.983	0.233	0.640
March	1977	27.760	0.821	2.063	0.237	1.458	0.070	0.977
June	1977	24.773	2.255	1.862	0.651	0.970	0.174	0.755
Sept.	1977	32.138	2.710	2.350	0.782	1.366	0.201	0.822
Dec.	1977	15.875	2.333	1.235	0.673	1.813	0.146	0.938
March	1978	–2.314	4.359	–0.195	1.258	1.903	0.272	0.830
June	1978	15.288	4.091	1.193	1.181	1.907	0.273	0.830
Sept.	1978	–1.512	3.709	–0.127	1.071	1.595	0.250	0.803
Dec.	1978	36.391	3.382	2.620	0.976	1.903	0.242	0.860
March	1979	21.970	3.912	1.669	1.129	1.944	0.245	0.863
June	1979	10.300	3.468	0.820	1.001	1.883	0.215	0.884
Sept	1979	32.923	3.924	2.400	1.133	1.852	0.235	0.862
Dec.	1979	6.929	2.389	0.560	0.690	1.634	0.139	0.932
March	1980	22.517	5.385	1.707	1.555	1.330	0.366	0.569
June	1980	4.837	2.851	0.394	0.823	1.111	0.205	0.746
Sept.	1980	–4.750	3.787	–0.405	1.093	1.209	0.239	0.720
Dec.	1980	16.825	5.047	1.304	1.457	1.003	0.375	0.417
Mean		14.238	3.153	1.075	0.910	1.385	0.219	0.774

* Based on regressions of total return minus the risk-free rate.

Exhibit 12 Screen #1 Portfolios vs. the I/B/E/S Universe*

		Annual Alpha	Std. Error of Annual Alpha	Monthly Alpha	Std. Error of Monthly Alpha	Beta	Std. Error of Beta	R^2
March	1975	15.813%	3.279	1.231%	0.947	0.946	0.156	0.786
June	1975	12.533	2.107	0.988	0.608	0.935	0.109	0.880
Sept.	1975	−5.820	1.578	−0.498	0.455	1.208	0.092	0.946
Dec.	1975	16.656	2.067	1.292	0.597	1.043	0.118	0.886
March	1976	4.962	1.083	0.404	0.313	1.044	0.099	0.917
June	1976	6.226	1.831	0.505	0.528	0.981	0.169	0.772
Sept.	1976	0.106	1.666	0.009	0.481	1.074	0.154	0.829
Dec.	1976	3.435	1.900	0.282	0.548	1.018	0.180	0.761
March	1977	11.709	1.763	0.927	0.509	1.350	0.150	0.890
June	1977	13.445	1.179	1.057	0.340	1.004	0.085	0.933
Sept.	1977	12.874	1.892	1.014	0.546	1.322	0.122	0.922
Dec.	1977	8.183	1.669	0.658	0.482	1.413	0.080	0.969
March	1978	−2.828	3.083	−0.239	0.890	1.470	0.142	0.915
June	1978	11.368	2.372	0.901	0.685	1.485	0.115	0.943
Sept.	1978	−4.959	2.354	−0.423	0.679	1.213	0.112	0.921
Dec.	1978	17.531	2.237	1.355	0.934	1.532	0.178	0.881
March	1979	18.663	3.506	1.436	1.012	1.489	0.166	0.889
June	1979	10.212	3.450	0.814	0.996	1.335	0.152	0.886
Sept.	1979	31.437	4.065	2.304	1.174	1.293	0.170	0.852
Dec.	1979	12.572	1.550	0.992	0.447	1.315	0.072	0.971
March	1980	−5.766	4.777	−0.494	1.379	1.536	0.284	0.745
June	1980	−11.874	2.797	−1.048	0.808	1.222	0.198	0.791
Sept.	1980	−9.560	2.249	−0.834	0.649	1.483	0.160	0.896
Dec.	1980	4.425	2.564	0.361	0.740	1.193	0.176	0.821
Mean		7.139	2.417	0.541	0.698	1.246	0.143	0.875

* Based on regressions of total return minus the risk-free rate.

S&P 500 as well. To "compensate" for these effects (but not to remove the enigmas they pose for advocates of market efficiency), we calculated risk-adjusted perormance data using the equal-weighted I/B/E/S universe as well as the capitalization-weighted S&P 500 as benchmarks for measuring portfolio covariances. Exhibits 11, 12 and 13 show the results of regressing monthly portfolio returns minus the risk-free rate (the three-month Treasury bill rate) on the capitalization-weighted S&P 500 and the equally weighted I/B/E/S universe.

Exhibit 11 gives the annual and monthly alphas and betas, their associated standard er-

rors, and the coefficient of determination (R^2) statistic that result when each of the Screen #1 portfolios is regressed against the capitalization-weighted S&P. An average monthly alpha of 1.08 percent for the Screen #1 portfolios resulted in an annual risk-adjusted excess return, or alpha, of 14.24 percent for the 24 Screen #1 portfolios. These portfolios had positive alphas in 20 of the 24 holding periods. Their betas ranged from 0.85 to 1.94 and averaged 1.39.

Exhibit 12 shows comparable data for the equally weighted Screen #1 portfolios regressed against the equally weighted I/B/E/S universe. The portfolios had an average

Exhibit 13 The I/B/E/S Universe vs. the S&P 500*

		Annual Alpha	Std. Error of Annual Alpha	Monthly Alpha	Std. Error of Monthly Alpha	Beta	Std. Error of Beta	R^2
March	1975	1.656%	1.839	0.137%	0.531	1.152	0.105	0.923
June	1975	−1.345	1.694	−0.113	0.489	1.130	0.102	0.924
Sept.	1975	−0.134	1.783	−0.011	0.515	1.123	0.121	0.895
Dec.	1975	4.362	1.973	0.356	0.569	1.070	0.132	0.868
March	1976	2.911	1.089	0.239	0.314	0.970	0.102	0.901
June	1976	6.417	1.076	0.520	0.311	0.925	0.096	0.902
Sept.	1976	4.544	1.321	0.371	0.381	0.929	0.121	0.855
Dec.	1976	7.687	1.233	0.619	0.356	0.986	0.117	0.876
March	1977	9.491	1.184	0.758	0.342	0.980	0.101	0.905
June	1977	10.322	1.456	0.822	0.420	1.012	0.113	0.890
Sept.	1977	12.901	1.690	1.016	0.488	1.020	0.125	0.869
Dec.	1977	5.019	2.183	0.409	0.630	1.230	0.137	0.890
March	1978	0.312	2.027	0.026	0.585	1.299	0.127	0.913
June	1978	2.234	1.814	0.184	0.524	1.315	0.121	0.922
Sept.	1978	2.863	1.960	0.236	0.566	1.345	0.132	0.912
Dec.	1978	10.594	1.409	0.843	0.407	1.216	0.101	0.935
March	1979	1.811	1.643	0.150	0.474	1.285	0.103	0.940
June	1979	0.252	1.519	0.021	0.439	1.380	0.094	0.955
Sept.	1979	1.307	1.690	0.108	0.487	1.388	0.101	0.950
Dec.	1979	−2.916	2.431	−0.246	0.702	1.186	0.142	0.875
March	1980	18.702	2.270	1.439	0.655	0.862	0.154	0.758
June	1980	15.873	2.163	1.235	0.624	0.796	0.156	0.724
Sept.	1980	3.278	2.158	0.269	0.623	0.801	0.136	0.777
Dec.	1980	14.509	2.262	1.135	0.653	1.053	0.168	0.797
Mean		5.527	1.744	0.438	0.504	1.102	0.121	0.882

* Based on regressions of total return minus the risk-free rate.

monthly alpha of 0.54 percent (7.14 percent annualized) and had positive alphas in 18 of the 24 periods. Their betas, versus the universe from which they were drawn, ranged from 0.94 to 1.54 and averaged 1.25.

Exhibit 13 gives the results of regressing the equally weighted I/B/E/S universe against the capitalization-weighted S&P 500. The I/B/E/S universe had a monthly alpha of 0.44 percent (5.53 percent annualized) and had positive alphas in 21 of the 24 periods. The beta of the selection universe ranged from 0.80 to 1.39 and averaged 1.10.

The finding of risk-adjusted (non-market-related) returns of the magnitude reported in Exhibits 11, 12 and 13 is inconsistent with the tenets of either the CAPM or market efficiency. Other studies that have obtained excess risk-adjusted returns using systematic decision rules have asserted that the CAPM's equations, not to mention its underlying assumptions and imputed causal relations, are misspecified.

In our (perhaps unsolicited) view, the CAPM is an eloquent specification of the market conditions that ought to produce "equilibrium" pricing (or at least nondiscernible mispricing). However, many of these

Exhibit 14 Percentage Mean Absolute Deviation (%MAD)

		Screen #1	I/B/E/S	1,000 Random Portfolios	S&P 500
March	1975	6.929	5.781	5.924	5.781
June	1975	6.540	6.073	6.414	4.960
Sept.	1975	8.950	8.513	8.520	6.603
Dec.	1975	10.044	6.061	6.104	5.039
March	1976	2.492	2.015	2.576	2.392
June	1976	2.189	2.214	2.682	2.193
Sept.	1976	2.849	1.610	2.293	2.095
Dec.	1976	2.339	2.339	4.134	3.980
March	1977	4.448	2.411	2.775	2.376
June	1977	5.980	4.966	5.064	4.505
Sept.	1977	4.567	3.614	4.060	4.282
Dec.	1977	9.865	6.759	6.832	4.000
March	1978	12.388	7.235	7.369	4.836
June	1978	7.393	4.728	5.074	3.119
Sept.	1978	8.129	6.932	6.989	4.585
Dec.	1978	5.800	4.632	4.860	2.666
March	1979	9.557	9.014	9.185	4.877
June	1979	8.289	5.354	5.584	3.399
Sept.	1979	8.624	5.892	6.274	3.859
Dec.	1979	6.776	5.082	5.619	3.448
March	1980	15.076	10.067	10.218	7.467
June	1980	9.661	7.854	8.010	7.184
Sept.	1980	13.715	9.317	9.389	8.878
Dec.	1980	9.788	5.012	5.533	2.376
Mean		7.600	5.561	5.895	4.371

conditions simply do not pertain in the real world, and it would probably help little if they did, given the frequently irrational and impulse-driven behavior of investors. Thus we doubt that the "Markowitz revolution," elevating expected security returns, variances, covariances and weightings to the mathematical equivalent of quantum mechanics, has significantly changed the way investors behave. Specifically, we believe investors continue to base their decisions mostly on earnings expectations (not the mean and variance of return!) for individual stocks (not portfolios!) and have little patience for dividend estimates and associated prediction risks stretching 40 to 60 years into the future, on

which the value of a stock today theoretically depends.

In Comparison with Random Portfolios

As an alternative approach to performance evaluation, we compared the risk and return characteristics of randomly selected portfolios with those of the Screen #1 portfolios.[7] For this approach, we used monthly geometric average returns as the return measure and percentage mean absolute deviation (%MAD) as the risk measure. The %MAD measures the deviation, plus or minus, from the compound interest line fitted through the begin-

Exhibit 15 Monthly Geometric Return per Unit of %MAD

		Screen #1	I/B/E/S	1,000 Random Portfolios	S&P 500
March	1975	0.509	0.419	0.409	0.360
June	1975	0.303	0.171	0.161	0.220
Sept.	1975	0.258	0.283	0.279	0.336
Dec.	1975	0.356	0.367	0.365	0.357
March	1976	0.261	0.134	0.097	0.000
June	1976	0.503	0.262	0.220	0.027
Sept.	1976	0.081	0.155	0.105	−0.158
Dec.	1976	0.124	0.004	0.002	−0.156
March	1977	0.274	0.153	0.137	−0.168
June	1977	0.313	0.163	0.160	0.002
Sept.	1977	0.727	0.526	0.461	0.215
Dec.	1977	0.148	0.123	0.120	0.128
March	1978	0.142	0.236	0.232	0.310
June	1978	0.300	0.262	0.238	0.327
Sept.	1978	0.097	0.172	0.172	0.209
Dec.	1978	0.752	0.505	0.481	0.525
March	1979	0.154	0.052	0.047	0.100
June	1979	0.273	0.265	0.249	0.388
Sept.	1979	0.497	0.319	0.298	0.412
Dec.	1979	0.533	0.455	0.411	0.682
March	1980	0.331	0.396	0.389	0.378
June	1980	0.203	0.346	0.338	0.219
Sept.	1980	−0.081	0.035	0.022	−0.036
Dec.	1980	0.071	0.101	0.090	−0.211
Mean		0.297	0.246	0.228	0.186

ning and ending portfolio dollar values. These dollar deviations are converted into a percentage measure by dividing each deviation by the fitted value at that point, and the %MAD is the absolute mean of the N-1 intraperiod percentage deviations.[8]

Exhibit 14 gives the value of the %MAD measure of monthly interim variability over all 12-month holding periods for the 24 Screen #1 portfolios, the two benchmark portfolios, and the sample of 1,000 random portfolios. Exhibit 15 gives the results obtained when each portfolio's monthly geometric return is divided by its risk, as measured by %MAD. On average, return per unit of risk was highest for the 24 Screen #1 portfolios

(0.30) and positive in 23 of 24 periods. This measure was always positive for the I/B/E/S universe (with an average value of 0.25), as well as for the 1,000 random portfolios (average value, 0.23). The S&P 500 came in at 0.19 on return per unit of risk, with positive values in 19 of the 24 periods.

To "scale" the risk and return characteristics of the Screen #1 portfolios, we located each portfolio's rank within the 1,000 random portfolios by both holding period return and %MAD. (The rank position of 1,000 was assigned to both the highest return portfolio and to the highest %MAD portfolio.) Thus, for each period, we first sorted the 12-month holding period returns for each of the

Exhibit 16 Rank of Screen #1 Portfolios within the 1,000 Random Portfolios

		Total Return Rank	% MAD Rank	Return/ Unit % MAD Rank
March	1975	977	893	858
June	1975	970	594	950
Sept.	1975	463	593	360
Dec.	1975	999	982	436
March	1976	854	517	869
June	1976	885	222	914
Sept.	1976	927	856	445
Dec.	1976	752	65	866
March	1977	973	983	809
June	1977	995	791	915
Sept.	1977	992	780	969
Dec.	1977	927	988	700
March	1978	572	1,000	35
June	1978	977	992	763
Sept.	1978	183	795	133
Dec.	1978	1,000	770	866
March	1979	945	622	946
June	1979	931	990	615
Sept.	1979	1,000	957	938
Dec.	1979	973	899	825
March	1980	953	984	210
June	1980	80	742	38
Sept.	1980	8	978	39
Dec.	1980	463	998	433
Mean		783	791	622

Exhibit 17 Rank of Screen #1 Portfolios on Total Return within 1,000 Random Portfolios

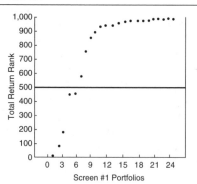

Screen #1 Portfolios

Exhibit 18 Rank of Screen #1 Portfolios Within the 100 Random Portfolios of Similar Risk

		Total Return Rank	% MAD Rank	Return/ Unit % MAD Rank
March	1975	98	50	98
June	1975	97	50	97
Sept.	1975	44	50	44
Dec.	1975	99	82	97
March	1976	83	50	83
June	1976	84	50	84
Sept.	1976	38	50	38
Dec.	1976	77	50	77
March	1977	94	83	89
June	1977	98	50	98
Sept.	1977	100	50	100
Dec.	1977	84	88	76
March	1978	34	100	6
June	1978	95	92	91
Sept.	1978	17	50	17
Dec.	1978	100	50	100
March	1979	94	50	94
June	1979	74	90	63
Sept.	1979	100	57	100
Dec.	1979	94	50	94
March	1980	87	84	71
June	1980	4	50	4
Sept.	1980	2	78	2
Dec.	1980	35	98	26
Mean		72	65	69

1,000 random portfolios from highest to lowest, and then found the position of the Screen #1 portfolio within this sort. Exhibit 16 shows the results, together with the ranks by %MAD and return per unit of risk.

The table indicates that, when performance is assessed on the basis of total return, the Screen #1 portfolios attained an average rank position of 783 within the 1,000 random portfolios selected over comparable time periods. Exhibit 17 provides a clear picture of these results, plotting in ascending order the rank position according to total return of each of the 24 Screen #1 portfolios. These results are even more im-

Exhibit 19 Rank of Screen #1 Portfolios on Return Per Unit of Risk within 1,000 Random Portfolios

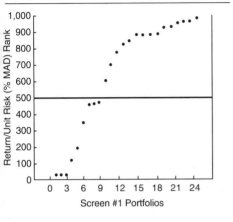

Exhibit 20 Rank of Screen #1 Portfolios on Return Per Unit of Risk within 100 Random Portfolios

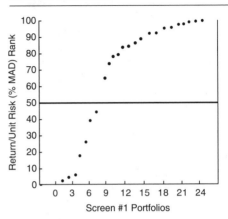

pressive when one considers that a naive investor selecting at random from the 1,000 control portfolios available in each of the 24 periods had one chance in five million of obtaining an average rank score higher than 783.[9]

The Screen #1 portfolios also ranked high in terms of interim variability, as shown by their average position of 791 among the control portfolios ranked by mean absolute deviation of monthly returns. Combining the two measures of total return and monthly %MAD to obtain return per unit of interim variability, we find the Screen #1 portfolios had an average rank position of 622 among the 1,000 control portfolios selected for each 12-month period. The probability of beating these results merely by chance is one in 57.

This evidence strongly suggests to us that the Screen #1 portfolios were superior investments. Moreover, the return per unit of %MAD measure reveals that 15 of the 24 portfolios (63 percent) were above the median of the 1,000 random portfolios drawn for the comparable holding period. Exhibit 19 shows these results by plotting rank of return per unit of risk for each Screen #1 portfolio.

Returns on Portfolios of Similar Risk

In order to compare the return characteristics of the test portfolios with returns on portfolios of similar risk, we identified 100 of the 1,000 random portfolios with a %MAD most like that of each Screen #1 portfolio. Whenever possible, we used the nearest 50 portfolios above and 50 portfolios below the Screen #1 portfolio. We were able to do this for 14 of the 24 periods; in the other 10 periods, the 100 highest-risk portfolios were used. Exhibit 18 gives the results.

In 17 (or 71 percent) of the 24 periods, Screen #1's *return* ranked in the top half of the distribution of 100 similar-risk portfolios. In 16 (or 67 percent) of the periods, the Screen #1 portfolio was in the top quartile of similar-risk portfolios. For 11 of the periods (46 percent), return was in the top decile.

Exhibit 20 plots the rank position among the 100 similar-risk portfolios of each Screen #1 portfolio's *return per unit of risk*. This fell in the top half of the distribution 71 percent of the time (17 of 24 periods), in the top quartile 63 percent of the time (15 periods), and in the top decile 42 percent of the time (10 periods).

The problems associated with selecting a single "benchmark" portfolio are not a factor in these results. The results are, moreover, not dependent on various disputed assumptions about the return-generating process under conditions of market efficiency, inasmuch as beta has been replaced by return per unit of interim variability within a large sample of random portfolios having identical characteristics (number of holdings and equal weighting) as well as similar risk. There remains, of course, enormous latitude for judgment about the interpretation and relevance of *ex post* return per unit of interim variability as a measure of investment performance. Still, the Screen #1 portfolios, in our opinion, proved superior when measured by this standard, and it is likely the same conclusion would emerge from a direct comparison of Screen #1 portfolios with actively managed portfolios, inasmuch as several studies have shown that cross-sectional return distributions for randomly selected portfolios have characteristics very similar to those of actively managed portfolios.

In summary, we believe that the evidence strongly suggests that revisions in consensus earnings estimates can be used to predict subsequent stock price performance, and that the market is not efficient in processing such information. For the 1975–81 period, at least, we have found strong support for the "sociology of information recognition" thesis described by Arthur Zeikel:

"Most professionals still accept what can be considered the 'sociology of information recognition.' This is the belief that the recognition of new information and its proper interpretation flow from the intelligent, well-informed and understanding, sophisticated segments of the market, who do tend to act quickly, to the lesser-informed, slower-moving elements at the other end of the spectrum. This, in turn, is believed to cause the development of

a sequence of interim stock price movements, which reflects the accompanying gradual discounting of new information as it moves through the investor system." [10]

Endnotes

1. Elton, Edwin J., Martin J. Gruber and Mustafa Gultiken, "Expectations and Share Prices," *Management Science,* September 1981.

2. The Institutional Brokers Estimate System (I/B/E/S) is a service of Lynch, Jones & Ryan, members of the New York Stock Exchange, which monitors earnings estimates for over 3,000 companies that are produced by more than 1,800 analysts in the research departments of 90 leading Wall Street and regional brokerage firms. The database contains about 40,000 individual estimates for the current year, the following year, and long-term earnings growth. These forecasts are continually updated and made available to institutional subscribers on a weekly basis.

3. The number of estimates making up each mean can vary from three to about 30, depending on the number of analysts following each company.

4. As might be expected, there was some overlap between the stocks included in the portfolios. The 24 quarterly portfolios contained a total of 333 stocks (out of a possible 480). Of these, 244 were included in only one portfolio. Among the remaining 89, there were 43 instances of "runs"—i.e., cases where the same stock appeared in two or more successive portfolios—and 123 instances of nonsuccessive appearances. The appearances broke down as follows:

No. of Appearances	No. of Companies
1	244
2	55
3	20
4	11
5	2
6	2

5. These costs conform to those that Beebower and Priest found in their definitive study of institutional trading expenses. See Gilbert Beebower and William Priest, "The Tricks of the Trade: How Much Does Trading Really Cost?" *The Journal of Portfolio Management,* Winter 1980.

6. The equation for finding required borrowings of $437.30 in Exhibit 9 is given by:

X = 100(A-B)/(C-D),

where:

X = dollar borrowings to be invested in market index,

A = dollar holding period return for Screen #1 per $100 invested,

B = dollar holding period return for S&P 500 per $100 invested,

C = percentage holding period return for S&P 500, and

D = percentage holding period cost of debt.

7. One thousand portfolios containing 20 stocks each were drawn at random from the I/B/E/S universe for each of the 24 holding periods.

8. The mean absolute deviation for the December 1978 portfolio, for example, was calculated as follows. The 12-month holding period gain on the portfolio was 66.9 percent, which is equivalent to an average monthly compound rate of return of 4.36 percent. Thus, given an initial investment of $100, the portfolio's trendline value would be $104.36 after one month and $108.91 after two months. The actual value of the portfolio after one month, however, was $110.50, or 5.9 percent above trendline. After two months the actual value was $106.90, or 1.9 percent below trendline. Based on returns over a 12-month period, one can obtain 11 monthly observations of this type, because the beginning and ending values of the portfolio are coincident with the beginning and ending values on the trendline as we have defined it. The mean absolute deviation over a one-year period is then found by calculating the absolute average of the 11 interim-monthly deviations derived in the above manner.

9. Based on a simulation involving 35.2 million trials in which there were only seven occasions where the mean of 24 drawings (from 24 sampling populations that contained the numbers one through 1,000) was greater than 783. The highest sample mean was 802.

10. From the Fall 1974 issue of *The Journal of Portfolio Management.*

Chapter 25

Valuation Factors Across Countries[*]

William E. Jacques
Partner and Chief Investment Officer
Martingale Asset Management

Dan Rie
Senior Vice President
Colonial Management Assoc.

Summary

This paper examines whether it is appropriate to use the same stock valuation model across all countries, or whether it may be better to build individual valuation models for each country.

Theory tells us that if international capital markets were completely integrated, then an equilibrium model, such as a dividend discount model, would be suitable.[1] However, if markets were completely segregated, a different model for each country would be better.

Prior studies[2] are inconclusive as to whether the international markets are integrated or segregated. The presence of foreign exchange and political risks, accounting differences, taxes, high transactions costs, trade restrictions, information costs, and local tastes and preferences, argue for segmented markets. However, increasing flows of capital across borders argue for more integrated markets.

Both schools of thought claim the bragging rights as the model of choice. The two camps are reminiscent of the chants from adjoining sections at sporting events, the "Tastes Great" section and the "Less Filling" section. We inspect the empirical data to determine whether investors across countries are relatively homogeneous in their preferences, or whether local preferences dominate.

We observe how investors value fundamental factors from country to country. We specifically measure the valuation of dividends, current earnings, future earnings, risk, assets, and sales for the United States, Japan and the United Kingdom. Cross sectional results are examined to determine whether dividends are as important to investors in Japan as they are to investors in the U.K. or the U.S. (and hence, the relevance of applying dividend discount models abroad), or whether

---

[*] The authors would like to thank Lynch, Jones and Ryan for supplying their I/B/E/S International Edition data. They would also like to thank Richard Grinold and Ron Lanstein for their insights.

what is important to investors in one country may be irrelevant to investors in another country.

We also investigate both pre- and post-October 19, 1987 to determine whether investor preferences have changed significantly since the world market collapse.

Review of Past Work

The theory is straightforward. If investors are homogeneous, if there are no friction costs, and if all goods across all countries are "traded" goods, then the global capital markets will be perfectly integrated.[3] However, the world does not always conform to the theory.

If global markets are integrated, then an international CAPM would explain country returns reasonably well. If the markets are segregated, then the total variability of each country will better explain country returns. Empirical studies reveal[4] that historical returns correlate to global betas and total variability equally well. Neither the hypothesis that the markets are integrated, nor the hypothesis that the markets are segregated could be rejected. We are still in limbo.

Another way to look at the question is to see if a stock's return is more closely related to its own stock market, or its worldwide industry. If the return is more related to its own stock market, then the segmented approach looks better, and vice-versa. Returns do seem more closely related to local stock markets than global industry returns.[5]

Multinational corporations offer a good test of the degree of market integration. If capital markets were integrated, one would expect to gain the same diversification benefits from investing in multinational companies as investing in multiple countries. The benefits of a globally diversified book of business should flow through to the investor. However, studies conclude that investing in multinationals is a poor substitute for true global diversification.[6]

On the risk side, there has been extensive research done to explore the importance of factors to explain stock price movement within different local stock markets.[7] This research indicates that factors that are important in one country also appear to be important in other countries. However, the rank ordering of these factors within each country can vary dramatically. For instance, a company's size is very important in explaining stock risk in Japan, but not nearly as important in the U.S. or the U.K.

Past work indicates that the world's capital markets are not perfectly integrated. Most of us believe that the markets will be more integrated as more capital flows freely around the world seeking the highest possible return per unit of risk. However, for now, we believe it is more productive to understand the differences and deal with them than to wait for these differences to disappear. It could be a long wait.

Our Data

Our study examined the relative importance of company fundamental data to stock price formation in Japan, the United Kingdom (UK), and the United States (US). We related stock prices (PRICE) to current earnings per share (MSE), current dividends per share (DIVPS), current sales per share (SLSPS), current book value per share (BVPS), growth rate in earnings per share (EFRO), company size (SIZE), and the beta of the company versus its local market index (BETA).[8]

International data tends to be less "clean" than the sometimes dirty domestic data that most of us are used to. For example, I/B/E/S has documented instances where the normally simple task of trying to determine last year's reported earnings per share is a chore. The value of last year's earnings per share often depends on who you ask, a range of possibilities rather than a point estimate results. Therefore, filter rules must be used that will trap most of the unclean data. However, one must also be careful to avoid throwing out potentially valid data. Therefore, human intervention (and even looking up some data by hand) does enter into the filtering process during the data cleanup, turning it into a labor intensive job.

We observed both pre-crash (September 30, 1987) and post-crash (December 31, 1987) periods to determine how the crash affected differential valuations across countries.

Our Model

We used a form of cross sectional regression to identify which company fundamentals were important in determining stock prices within each country. Since our model is based on actual relationships between prices and underlying company fundamentals, we have called it the *Empirical Pricing Model.*[9]

To establish how important current earnings per share were to investors in a country, at a particular point in time, we ran the following regression:

$$PRICE_{ict} = \alpha_{ct} \, MSE_{ict}$$

where i,c,t = company i in country c for time period t

For example, using least squares, we looked at the relationship between share price and earnings per share in the UK on September 30, 1987:

$$PRICE_{iuk} = 15.8 \times MSE_{iuk} + \varepsilon_i \quad {}^{10}$$

(42.3)

The simple model relating stock prices to current earnings works fairly well in the UK for this time period. This model actually assumes that all companies in the UK have the same p/e ratio of 15.8. The t-statistic on this constant p/e ratio is 42.3; hence, current earnings do seem to matter. However, an examination of the error terms reveals problems. Below we plot the error term versus stock price and find that the variance of the error terms are related to stock price. This problem is solved by using generalized least squares.

The General Form

The actual model that we used is a more general form of equation (1), and is given below:

$$PRICE_{ict} = \alpha_{1ct} \, VAR1_{ict} + \alpha_{2ct} \, VAR2_{ict} + ... + \alpha_{nct} \, VARN_{ict}$$

where

$VARN = Fundamental\ Variable\ N\ (e.g.EPSOorDPSO)$

$\alpha_{nct} = $ Coefficient on Variable N for Country c and time period t

$PRICE_{ict} = $ Price of stock i in county c at time period t

Features of the Model

This model has several interesting features. It allows us to determine which company fundamentals are important to investors in each country. We will use the t-statistic as the measure of the relative importance of each company fundamental, as it puts all variables on the same basis. Thus, by rank ordering the t-statistics of variables within each country, and comparing the rank ordering across countries, we can determine whether investor preferences differ across countries.[11]

Our cross sectional model is also very responsive to changes in investor preferences across time. The change in coefficients on the fundamental variables will be a measure of shifting preferences.

It turns out the the dividend discount model is a special case of our general *Empiri-*

Exhibit 1 Importance of Current Earnings Price = MSE

	Japan	UK	US
Sept. 1987			
Coefficient	32.4	14.5	12.8
T-Stat	19.5	22.8	17.6
R^2	.61	.75	.50
Dec. 1987			
Coefficient	31.6	9.6	9.9
T-Stat	24.9	23.6	21.4
R^2	.71	.76	.57

cal Pricing Model. To get there, the stream of future dividend payments is used as the independent variables on the right hand side of our equation, e.g.:

$$PRICE_{ict} = \alpha_{ict}\,DIV1 + \alpha_{2ct}DIV2 \ldots$$

$$+ \alpha_{nct}\,DIVN \quad ^{12}$$

The dividend discount model, being a normative model, requires that α_{1ct} equal $1/(1 + ddr)$, $\alpha_{2ct} = 1/(1 + ddr)^2$,etc. [13] Hence, it would be a mere coincidence if the market based discount rates (our), actually equalled those implied by the dividend discount model. This highlights one of the restrictive assumptions of the dividend discount model.

Our Conclusions

Exhibit 1 shows that current earnings are important to investors around the world. In all cases current earnings became more important after the October crash than before.

Exhibit 2 highlights the relative importance of current earnings versus current dividends. Investors around the world seem to place more importance on earnings than dividends. This is particularly true in the U.S. Dividends seem to matter the most to the U.K. investors.

Exhibit 3 examines the relative importance of Morgan Stanley current earnings versus I/B/E/S expected earnings. Across the board, I/B/E/S earnings are more closely related to stock prices. This is most noticable in the U.S.

Exhibit 4 shows the results of our multiple factor valuation model. Current earnings (MSE) are universally important. Company size (MVD) is quite significant to stock prices in the U.S. and Japan. Future earnings growth (IBE/MSE) is important to U.K. investors and not so important to U.S. and Japanese investors.

Hence, it appears that different valuation factors seem to be important in each country. There appear to be enough differences for us to throw our hat in the segmented markets ring, and *viva la difference.*

Exhibit 2 Current Earnings vs. Dividends
Price = MSE; Price = DIVPS

	Japan		UK		US	
	E	D	E	D	E	D
Sept. 1987						
Coefficient	32.4	110.5	14.5	23.8	12.8	14.0
T-Stat	19.5	11.2	22.8	17.5	17.6	5.3
R^2	.61	.33	.75	.65	.50	.08
Dec. 1987						
Coefficient	31.6	122.9	9.6	17.2	9.9	12.2
T-Stat	24.9	14.7	23.6	22.0	21.4	7.2
R^2	.71	.45	.76	.74	.57	.13

Exhibit 3 MSCIP vs. I/B/E/S
Price = MSE; Price = IBE

	Japan		UK		US	
	M	**I**	**M**	**I**	**M**	**I**
Sept. 1987						
Coefficient	32.4	31.2	14.5	11.5	12.8	13.0
T-Stat	19.5	25.5	22.8	25.1	17.6	28.3
R²	.61	.72	.75	.79	.50	.72
Dec. 1987						
Coefficient	31.6	29.9	9.6	8.5	9.9	11.0
T-Stat	24.9	31.5	23.6	27.6	21.4	36.5
R²	.71	.79	.76	.82	.57	.79

Exhibit 4 Valuation Factors Ranked by Country

	Japan		UK		US	
	9/87	**12/87**	**9/87**	**12/87**	**9/87**	**12/87**
MSE	1	1	1	1	2	2
DIVPS	5–	6–	3	2	4–	5
EGRO	4	4	2	3	6	6
BETA	6	5	6–	5–	5–	4–
BV	2	3	5–	6–	3	3
MVD	3	2	4	4	1	1

Endnotes

1. Terminology borrowed from Sharpe, William F., *Investments*, Prentice Hall, 1985, pp. 719-721.

2. See Donald R. Lessard, "World, Country and Industry Relationships in Equity Returns: Implications for Risk Reduction Through International Diversification," *Financial Analysts Journal,* 32, no. 1 (January-February 1976), 32-38, and Roger G. Ibbotson, Richard C. Carr, and Anthony W. Robinson, "International Equity and Bond Returns," *Financial Analysts Journal,* July-August, 1982.

3 See F. L. A. Grauer, R. H. Litzenberger, and R. F. Stehle, "Sharing Rules and Equilibrium in an International Capital Market," *Journal of Financial Economics,* June, 1976 for a detailed analysis.

4. Ibbotson, et al, op. cit.

5. Lessard, op. cit.

6. Bertrand Jacquillat and Bruno Solnick, "Multinationals Are Poor Tools for Diversification," *Journal of Portfolio Management,* Winter, 1978.

7. See BARRA, seminar notes.

8. All data, except for EPSGROW, obtained from Morgan Stanley Capital International Perspective PC database, EPSGROW, is derived from Lynch, Jones and Ryan's I/B/E/S International Edition.

9. Statistically relating stock prices to earnings and dividends has a long history. This was particularly popular in the 1940 to 1965 period. Samples of this work include H. Pastoriza, "Valuing Utility Earnings, Distributed and Retained," *The Analysts Journal,* July, 1945, pp. 11-15; M. Gordon, "Dividends, Earnings and Stock Prices," *Review of Economics and Statistics,* May, 1959, pp. 99-105; B. Graham and D. L. Dodd, *Security Analysis: Principles and Techniques,* 4th edition (New York: McGraw-Hill, 1962), p. 486. See J. Hoffmeister, Dividends and Share Value: Graham and Dodd Revisited, *Financial Analyst Journal,* May-June, 1985, pp. 77-78 for additional references.

10. The intercept term is set to zero to give the equation more economic meaning. If there were an intercept above zero, this would imply a positive share price for no earnings.

11. One must be careful in the interpretation of the *t*-statistics. For instance, current earnings may prove to be statistically significant in one country and not another. Investors may truly value the economic earnings in the second country, however, the accounting earnings that are reported in MSCIP for that country may be randomly related to economic earnings. For now, we will assume that the accountants are equally skillful in each country.

12. This is the same method used to predict forward rates from bond coupon payments.

13. *ddr* equals the dividend discount rate.

Price Per Share in Local Currency

Price   Summary of Variable Over Period: September 1987

		Mean	Std. Dev.	NOBS
Global Summary	**All Sectors**	688.905	1437.579	762
United States	All Sectors	54.199	39.550	348
United Kingdom	All Sectors	4.675	2.876	165
Japan	All Sectors	2029.370	1911.048	249

Price   Summary of Variable Over Period: September 1987

		Mean	Std. Dev.	NOBS
Global Summary	**All Sectors**	688.905	1437.579	762
Global Summary	Cons. Goods	944.739	1530.381	171
Global Summary	Capital Equip.	889.784	1454.457	169
Global Summary	Finance	437.275	846.877	40
Global Summary	Materials	396.004	645.552	101
Global Summary	Multi-Industry	42.848	68.013	30
Global Summary	Energy	422.204	1025.878	77
Global Summary	Service	699.651	1883.975	174

Price   Summary of Variable Over Period: September 1987

		Mean	Std. Dev.	NOBS
Global Summary	**All Sectors**	688.905	1437.579	762
United States	Cons. Goods	56.979	29.639	67
United States	Capital Equip.	54.617	26.922	60
United States	Finance	50.419	21.858	20
United States	Materials	55.858	26.228	44
United States	Multi-Industry	76.398	79.113	16
United States	Energy	37.250	16.748	55
United States	Service	58.483	55.028	86
United Kingdom	Finance	7.510	3.805	11
United Kingdom	Materials	5.209	3.217	27
United Kingdom	Cons. Goods	4.904	3.156	34
United Kingdom	Capital Equip.	3.455	1.548	32
United Kingdom	Service	4.173	2.379	39
United Kingdom	Multi-Industry	4.506	1.675	14
United Kingdom	Energy	5.615	3.313	8
Japan	Capital Equip.	1908.909	1653.428	77
Japan	Materials	1246.600	609.379	30
Japan	Cons. Goods	2250.943	1682.544	70
Japan	Service	2378.510	2945.077	49
Japan	Finance	1822.222	842.665	9
Japan	Energy	2172.572	1429.024	14

Price Per Share in Local Currency

Price	Summary of Variable Over Period: December 1987			
		Mean	Std. Dev.	NOBS
Global Summary	**All Sectors**	611.041	1441.903	790
United States	All Sectors	40.427	30.567	351
United Kingdom	All Sectors	3.298	1.942	172
Japan	All Sectors	1752.678	2044.765	267
Price	**Summary of Variable Over Period: December 1987**			
		Mean	Std. Dev.	NOBS
Global Summary	**All Sectors**	611.041	1441.903	790
Global Summary	Cons. Goods	767.432	1211.073	174
Global Summary	Capital Equip.	705.628	1150.264	177
Global Summary	Finance	332.212	648.850	40
Global Summary	Materials	386.956	760.180	110
Global Summary	Multi-Industry	29.472	53.277	32
Global Summary	Energy	377.991	854.589	77
Global Summary	Service	768.838	2336.176	180
Price	**Summary of Variable Over Period: December 1987**			
		Mean	Std. Dev.	NOBS
Global Summary	**All Sectors**	611.041	1441.903	790
United States	Cons. Goods	42.575	23.447	68
United States	Capital Equip.	38.852	18.080	60
United States	Finance	40.575	19.819	20
United States	Materials	41.793	21.469	46
United States	Multi-Industry	52.507	64.881	17
United States	Energy	31.935	13.818	54
United States	Service	42.007	42.164	86
United Kingdom	Finance	5.635	2.687	11
United Kingdom	Materials	3.402	1.794	29
United Kingdom	Cons. Goods	3.619	2.053	34
United Kingdom	Capital Equip.	2.404	1.121	37
United Kingdom	Service	3.005	1.695	39
United Kingdom	Multi-Industry	3.365	1.262	15
United Kingdom	Energy	3.835	2.699	7
Japan	Capital Equip.	1530.950	1297.618	80
Japan	Materials	1158.400	970.550	35
Japan	Cons. Goods	1812.708	1296.021	72
Japan	Service	2448.382	3714.303	55
Japan	Finance	1379.444	673.945	9
Japan	Energy	1709.625	1129.320	16

Earnings Report Date (MS-CIP)

EDATE	Summary of Variable Over Period: September 1987			
		Mean	Std. Dev.	NOBS
Global Summary	All Sectors	7.371	0.200	762
United States	All Sectors	7.511	0.043	348
United Kingdom	All Sectors	7.358	0.167	165
Japan	All Sectors	7.183	0.197	249

EDATE	Summary of Variable Over Period: September 1987			
		Mean	Std. Dev.	NOBS
Global Summary	All Sectors	7.371	0.200	762
Global Summary	Cons. Goods	7.335	0.223	171
Global Summary	Capital Equip.	7.346	0.189	169
Global Summary	Finance	7.419	0.141	40
Global Summary	Materials	7.368	0.188	101
Global Summary	Multi-Industry	7.442	0.120	30
Global Summary	Energy	7.448	0.127	77
Global Summary	Service	7.374	0.227	174

EDATE	Summary of Variable Over Period: September 1987			
		Mean	Std. Dev.	NOBS
Global Summary	All Sectors	7.371	0.200	762
United States	Cons. Goods	7.512	0.044	67
United States	Capital Equip.	7.511	0.039	60
United States	Finance	7.500	0.000	20
United States	Materials	7.502	0.022	44
United States	Multi-Industry	7.516	0.044	16
United States	Energy	7.509	0.034	55
United States	Service	7.518	0.060	86
United Kingdom	Finance	7.409	0.193	11
United Kingdom	Materials	7.364	0.165	27
United Kingdom	Cons. Goods	7.338	0.160	34
United Kingdom	Capital Equip.	7.357	0.181	32
United Kingdom	Service	7.348	0.161	39
United Kingdom	Multi-Industry	7.357	0.124	14
United Kingdom	Energy	7.406	0.174	8
Japan	Capital Equip.	7.213	0.157	77
Japan	Materials	7.175	0.175	30
Japan	Cons. Goods	7.164	0.220	70
Japan	Service	7.141	0.254	49
Japan	Finance	7.250	0.000	9
Japan	Energy	7.232	0.064	14

Earnings Report Date (MS-CIP)

EDATE	Summary of Variable Over Period: December 1987			
		Mean	Std. Dev.	NOBS
Global Summary	**All Sectors**	7.563	0.260	790
United States	All Sectors	7.758	0.039	351
United Kingdom	All Sectors	7.576	0.167	172
Japan	All Sectors	7.300	0.245	267
EDATE	Summary of Variable Over Period: December 1987			
		Mean	Std. Dev.	NOBS
Global Summary	**All Sectors**	7.563	0.260	790
Global Summary	Cons. Goods	7.545	0.293	174
Global Summary	Capital Equip.	7.513	0.260	177
Global Summary	Finance	7.575	0.238	40
Global Summary	Materials	7.558	0.243	110
Global Summary	Multi-Industry	7.630	0.194	32
Global Summary	Energy	7.661	0.206	77
Global Summary	Service	7.577	0.254	180
EDATE	Summary of Variable Over Period: December 1987			
		Mean	Std. Dev.	NOBS
Global Summary	**All Sectors**	7.563	0.260	790
United States	Cons. Goods	7.765	0.045	68
United States	Capital Equip.	7.757	0.035	60
United States	Finance	7.750	0.000	20
United States	Materials	7.752	0.021	46
United States	Multi-Industry	7.730	0.045	17
United States	Energy	7.758	0.033	54
United States	Service	7.763	0.047	86
United Kingdom	Finance	7.477	0.249	11
United Kingdom	Materials	7.606	0.122	29
United Kingdom	Cons. Goods	7.652	0.115	34
United Kingdom	Capital Equip.	7.507	0.157	37
United Kingdom	Service	7.592	0.146	39
United Kingdom	Multi-Industry	7.517	0.232	15
United Kingdom	Energy	7.643	0.124	7
Japan	Capital Equip.	7.333	0.247	80
Japan	Materials	7.264	0.187	35
Japan	Cons. Goods	7.286	0.286	72
Japan	Service	7.277	0.220	55
Japan	Finance	7.306	0.157	9
Japan	Energy	7.344	0.248	16

Historic E/P Ratio

MSEPR   Summary of Variable Over Period: September 1987

		Mean	Std. Dev.	NOBS
Global Summary	**All Sectors**	0.047	0.031	762
United States	All Sectors	0.062	0.031	341
United Kingdom	All Sectors	0.059	0.016	165
Japan	All Sectors	0.019	0.012	249

MSEPR   Summary of Variable Over Period: September 1987

		Mean	Std. Dev.	NOBS
Global Summary	**All Sectors**	0.047	0.031	762
Global Summary	Cons. Goods	0.042	0.025	171
Global Summary	Capital Equip.	0.037	0.026	169
Global Summary	Finance	0.070	0.044	40
Global Summary	Materials	0.049	0.027	101
Global Summary	Multi-Industry	0.064	0.019	30
Global Summary	Energy	0.072	0.043	77
Global Summary	Service	0.042	0.022	174

MSEPR   Summary of Variable Over Period: September 1987

		Mean	Std. Dev.	NOBS
Global Summary	**All Sectors**	0.047	0.031	762
United States	Cons. Goods	0.055	0.022	67
United States	Capital Equip.	0.049	0.023	60
United States	Finance	0.104	0.031	20
United States	Materials	0.061	0.025	44
United States	Multi-Industry	0.065	0.022	16
United States	Energy	0.084	0.044	55
United States	Service	0.051	0.020	86
United Kingdom	Finance	0.054	0.022	11
United Kingdom	Materials	0.062	0.011	27
United Kingdom	Cons. Goods	0.061	0.017	34
United Kingdom	Capital Equip.	0.065	0.014	32
United Kingdom	Service	0.053	0.014	39
United Kingdom	Multi-Industry	0.062	0.014	14
United Kingdom	Energy	0.053	0.014	8
Japan	Capital Equip.	0.016	0.009	77
Japan	Materials	0.017	0.009	30
Japan	Cons. Goods	0.021	0.013	70
Japan	Service	0.019	0.011	49
Japan	Finance	0.016	0.004	9
Japan	Energy	0.035	0.017	14

Historic E/P Ratio

MSEPR Summary of Variable Over Period: December 1987

		Mean	Std. Dev.	NOBS
Global Summary	**All Sectors**	0.063	0.042	790
United States	All Sectors	0.084	0.040	35
United Kingdom	All Sectors	0.085	0.024	172
Japan	All Sectors	0.023	0.014	262

MSEPR Summary of Variable Over Period: December 1987

		Mean	Std. Dev.	NOBS
Global Summary	**All Sectors**	0.063	0.042	790
Global Summary	Cons. Goods	0.057	0.037	174
Global Summary	Capital Equip.	0.051	0.037	177
Global Summary	Finance	0.093	0.057	40
Global Summary	Materials	0.067	0.042	110
Global Summary	Multi-Industry	0.090	0.033	32
Global Summary	Energy	0.086	0.048	77
Global Summary	Service	0.058	0.034	180

MSEPR Summary of Variable Over Period: December 1987

		Mean	Std. Dev.	NOBS
Global Summary	**All Sectors**	0.063	0.042	790
United States	Cons. Goods	0.077	0.036	68
United States	Capital Equip.	0.066	0.032	60
United States	Finance	0.136	0.037	20
United States	Materials	0.087	0.038	46
United States	Multi-Industry	0.092	0.042	17
United States	Energy	0.101	0.048	54
United States	Service	0.076	0.026	86
United Kingdom	Finance	0.074	0.033	11
United Kingdom	Materials	0.092	0.020	29
United Kingdom	Cons. Goods	0.084	0.022	34
United Kingdom	Capital Equip.	0.093	0.023	37
United Kingdom	Service	0.075	0.022	39
United Kingdom	Multi-Industry	0.086	0.018	15
United Kingdom	Energy	0.078	0.021	7
Japan	Capital Equip.	0.020	0.010	80
Japan	Materials	0.021	0.009	35
Japan	Cons. Goods	0.026	0.016	72
Japan	Service	0.020	0.011	55
Japan	Finance	0.021	0.005	9
Japan	Energy	0.042	0.020	16

E/P Ratio—Forecasted E.P.S.

IBEPR   **Summary of Variable Over Period: September 1987**

		Mean	Std. Dev.	NOBS
Global Summary	**All Sectors**	0.058	0.032	762
United States	All Sectors	0.077	0.025	348
United Kingdom	All Sectors	0.076	0.017	165
Japan	All Sectors	0.021	0.010	249

IBEPR   **Summary of Variable Over Period: September 1987**

		Mean	Std. Dev.	NOBS
Global Summary	**All Sectors**	0.058	0.032	762
Global Summary	Cons. Goods	0.052	0.030	171
Global Summary	Capital Equip.	0.051	0.032	169
Global Summary	Finance	0.080	0.043	40
Global Summary	Materials	0.059	0.028	101
Global Summary	Multi-Industry	0.077	0.016	30
Global Summary	Energy	0.079	0.036	77
Global Summary	Service	0.055	0.027	174

IBEPR   **Summary of Variable Over Period: September 1987**

		Mean	Std. Dev.	NOBS
Global Summary	**All Sectors**	0.058	0.032	762
United States	Cons. Goods	0.070	0.021	67
United States	Capital Equip.	0.072	0.022	60
United States	Finance	0.112	0.025	20
United States	Materials	0.071	0.016	44
United States	Multi-Industry	0.076	0.019	16
United States	Energy	0.094	0.027	55
United States	Service	0.069	0.018	86
United Kingdom	Finance	0.072	0.028	11
United Kingdom	Materials	0.081	0.011	27
United Kingdom	Cons. Goods	0.076	0.017	34
United Kingdom	Capital Equip.	0.084	0.014	32
United Kingdom	Service	0.068	0.015	39
United Kingdom	Multi-Industry	0.078	0.011	14
United Kingdom	Energy	0.071	0.014	8
Japan	Capital Equip.	0.020	0.008	77
Japan	Materials	0.021	0.009	30
Japan	Cons. Goods	0.021	0.011	70
Japan	Service	0.021	0.011	49
Japan	Finance	0.019	0.006	9
Japan	Energy	0.026	0.010	14

E/P Ratio—Forecasted E.P.S.

IBEPR	Summary of Variable Over Period: December 1987			
		Mean	Std. Dev.	NOBS
Global Summary	**All Sectors**	0.074	0.042	790
United States	All Sectors	0.097	0.029	351
United Kingdom	All Sectors	0.105	0.025	172
Japan	All Sectors	0.025	0.012	267

IBEPR	Summary of Variable Over Period: December 1987			
		Mean	Std. Dev.	NOBS
Global Summary	**All Sectors**	0.074	0.042	790
Global Summary	Cons. Goods	0.067	0.039	174
Global Summary	Capital Equip.	0.068	0.046	177
Global Summary	Finance	0.097	0.051	40
Global Summary	Materials	0.077	0.040	110
Global Summary	Multi-Industry	0.103	0.021	32
Global Summary	Energy	0.090	0.040	77
Global Summary	Service	0.071	0.038	180

IBEPR	Summary of Variable Over Period: December 1987			
		Mean	Std. Dev.	NOBS
Global Summary	**All Sectors**	0.074	0.042	790
United States	Cons. Goods	0.091	0.026	68
United States	Capital Equip.	0.094	0.030	60
United States	Finance	0.132	0.028	20
United States	Materials	0.093	0.024	46
United States	Multi-Industry	0.101	0.024	17
United States	Energy	0.106	0.030	54
United States	Service	0.091	0.025	86
United Kingdom	Finance	0.092	0.037	11
United Kingdom	Materials	0.112	0.013	29
United Kingdom	Cons. Goods	0.102	0.020	34
United Kingdom	Capital Equip.	0.120	0.025	37
United Kingdom	Service	0.094	0.021	39
United Kingdom	Multi-Industry	0.105	0.016	15
United Kingdom	Energy	0.101	0.037	7
Japan	Capital Equip.	0.024	0.009	80
Japan	Materials	0.025	0.009	35
Japan	Cons. Goods	0.027	0.014	72
Japan	Service	0.022	0.012	55
Japan	Finance	0.025	0.007	9
Japan	Energy	0.033	0.012	16

Sales to Price Ratio

SLSPR	Summary of Variable Over Period: September 1987	Mean	Std. Dev.	NOBS
Global Summary	**All Sectors**	1.429	2.365	762
United States	All Sectors	1.379	1.061	348
United Kingdom	All Sectors	1.393	1.403	165
Japan	All Sectors	1.522	3.772	249

SLSPR	Summary of Variable Over Period: September 1987	Mean	Std. Dev.	NOBS
Global Summary	**All Sectors**	1.429	2.365	762
Global Summary	Cons. Goods	1.140	1.357	17
Global Summary	Capital Equip.	1.274	0.901	169
Global Summary	Finance	1.147	0.853	40
Global Summary	Materials	1.149	0.604	101
Global Summary	Multi-Industry	1.607	1.360	30
Global Summary	Energy	1.353	0.962	77
Global Summary	Service	2.152	4.478	174

SLSPR	Summary of Variable Over Period: September 1987	Mean	Std. Dev.	NOBS
Global Summary	**All Sectors**	1.429	2.365	762
United States	Cons. Goods	1.144	0.896	67
United States	Capital Equip.	1.669	1.076	60
United States	Finance	1.451	0.808	20
United States	Materials	1.133	0.713	44
United States	Multi-Industry	1.642	1.651	16
United States	Energy	1.397	0.948	55
United States	Service	1.409	1.218	86
United Kingdom	Finance	1.173	0.908	11
United Kingdom	Materials	1.206	0.581	27
United Kingdom	Cons. Goods	1.635	2.493	34
United Kingdom	Capital Equip.	1.480	0.903	32
United Kingdom	Service	1.243	1.007	39
United Kingdom	Multi-Industry	1.567	0.902	14
United Kingdom	Energy	1.385	1.250	8
Japan	Capital Equip.	0.880	0.494	77
Japan	Materials	0.783	0.276	30
Japan	Cons. Goods	0.896	0.731	70
Japan	Service	4.178	7.878	49
Japan	Finance	0.438	0.264	9
Japan	Energy	1.163	0.785	14

Sales to Price Ratio

SLSPR	Summary of Variable Over Period: December 1987	Mean	Std. Dev.	NOBS
Global Summary	All Sectors	1.582	2.669	790
United States	All Sectors	1.556	1.253	351
United Kingdom	All Sectors	1.443	0.989	172
Japan	All Sectors	1.706	4.285	267

SLSPR	Summary of Variable Over Period: December 1987	Mean	Std. Dev.	NOBS
Global Summary	All Sectors	1.582	2.669	790
Global Summary	Cons. Goods	1.230	1.025	174
Global Summary	Capital Equip.	1.447	1.053	177
Global Summary	Finance	1.238	0.980	40
Global Summary	Materials	1.127	0.497	110
Global Summary	Multi-Industry	1.775	1.132	32
Global Summary	Energy	1.463	1.011	77
Global Summary	Service	2.424	5.208	180

SLSPR	Summary of Variable Over Period: December 1987	Mean	Std. Dev.	NOBS
Global Summary	All Sectors	1.582	2.669	790
United States	Cons. Goods	1.256	1.007	68
United States	Capital Equip.	1.895	1.290	60
United States	Finance	1.651	1.149	20
United States	Materials	1.187	0.585	46
United States	Multi-Industry	1.865	1.270	17
United States	Energy	1.481	0.988	54
United States	Service	1.718	1.660	86
United Kingdom	Finance	1.081	0.528	11
United Kingdom	Materials	1.252	0.469	29
United Kingdom	Cons. Goods	1.527	1.244	34
United Kingdom	Capital Equip.	1.696	1.060	37
United Kingdom	Service	1.265	0.944	39
United Kingdom	Multi-Industry	1.673	0.942	15
United Kingdom	Energy	1.552	1.160	7
Japan	Capital Equip.	0.997	0.552	80
Japan	Materials	0.946	0.308	35
Japan	Cons. Goods	1.067	0.884	72
Japan	Service	4.351	8.854	55
Japan	Finance	0.513	0.244	9
Japan	Energy	1.360	1.013	16

Book Value to Price Ratio

BVPR	Summary of Variable Over Period: September 1987			
		Mean	**Std. Dev.**	**NOBS**
Global Summary	**All Sectors**	0.386	0.221	762
United States	All Sectors	0.470	0.244	348
United Kingdom	All Sectors	0.367	0.182	165
Japan	All Sectors	0.280	0.152	249
BVPR	Summary of Variable Over Period: September 1987			
		Mean	**Std. Dev.**	**NOBS**
Global Summary	**All Sectors**	0.386	0.221	762
Global Summary	Cons. Goods	0.328	0.196	171
Global Summary	Capital Equip.	0.376	0.173	169
Global Summary	Finance	0.496	0.305	40
Global Summary	Materials	0.351	0.166	101
Global Summary	Multi-Industry	0.427	0.176	30
Global Summary	Energy	0.619	0.271	77
Global Summary	Service	0.336	0.196	174
BVPR	Summary of Variable Over Period: September 1987			
		Mean	**Std. Dev.**	**NOBS**
Global Summary	**All Sectors**	0.386	0.221	762
United States	Cons. Goods	0.329	0.210	67
United States	Capital Equip.	0.454	0.189	60
United States	Finance	0.648	0.209	20
United States	Materials	0.437	0.170	44
United States	Multi-Industry	0.491	0.187	16
United States	Energy	0.720	0.228	55
United States	Service	0.402	0.221	86
United Kingdom	Finance	0.404	0.342	11
United Kingdom	Materials	0.371	0.114	27
United Kingdom	Cons. Goods	0.369	0.213	34
United Kingdom	Capital Equip.	0.410	0.177	32
United Kingdom	Service	0.310	0.135	39
United Kingdom	Multi-Industry	0.353	0.127	14
United Kingdom	Energy	0.418	0.115	8
Japan	Capital Equip.	0.301	0.117	77
Japan	Materials	0.208	0.081	30
Japan	Cons. Goods	0.306	0.169	70
Japan	Service	0.240	0.136	49
Japan	Finance	0.270	0.249	9
Japan	Energy	0.339	0.221	14

Book Value to Price Ratio

BVPR   Summary of Variable Over Period: December 1987

		Mean	Std. Dev.	NOBS
Global Summary	**All Sectors**	0.495	0.289	790
United States	All Sectors	0.612	0.315	315
United Kingdom	All Sectors	0.506	0.247	172
Japan	All Sectors	0.335	0.185	267

BVPR   Summary of Variable Over Period: December 1987

		Mean	Std. Dev.	NOBS
Global Summary	**All Sectors**	0.495	0.289	790
Global Summary	Cons. Goods	0.425	0.266	174
Global Summary	Capital Equip.	0.494	0.252	177
Global Summary	Finance	0.641	0.405	40
Global Summary	Materials	0.464	0.239	110
Global Summary	Multi-Industry	0.599	0.264	32
Global Summary	Energy	0.728	0.302	77
Global Summary	Service	0.433	0.273	180

BVPR   Summary of Variable Over Period: December 1987

		Mean	Std. Dev.	NOBS
Global Summary	**All Sectors**	0.495	0.289	790
United States	Cons. Goods	0.440	0.306	68
United States	Capital Equip.	0.621	0.277	60
United States	Finance	0.826	0.296	20
United States	Materials	0.596	0.257	46
United States	Multi-Industry	0.699	0.281	17
United States	Energy	0.830	0.257	54
United States	Service	0.548	0.306	86
United Kingdom	Finance	0.539	0.463	11
United Kingdom	Materials	0.512	0.134	29
United Kingdom	Cons. Goods	0.487	0.271	34
United Kingdom	Capital Equip.	0.577	0.258	37
United Kingdom	Service	0.425	0.185	39
United Kingdom	Multi-Industry	0.486	0.187	15
United Kingdom	Energy	0.639	0.174	7
Japan	Capital Equip.	0.360	0.136	80
Japan	Materials	0.253	0.091	35
Japan	Cons. Goods	0.383	0.210	72
Japan	Service	0.258	0.152	55
Japan	Finance	0.353	0.314	9
Japan	Energy	0.424	0.271	16

Return on Equity

ROE   Summary of Variable Over Period: September 1987

		Mean	Std. Dev.	NOBS
Global Summary	**All Sectors**	14.078	10.941	762
United States	All Sectors	15.453	7.888	348
United Kingdom	All Sectors	20.873	16.569	165
Japan	All Sectors	7.653	4.784	249

ROE   Summary of Variable Over Period: September 1987

		Mean	Std. Dev.	NOBS
Global Summary	**All Sectors**	14.078	10.941	762
Global Summary	Cons. Goods	15.066	9.512	171
Global Summary	Capital Equip.	10.709	9.808	169
Global Summary	Finance	21.708	26.516	40
Global Summary	Materials	14.180	6.631	101
Global Summary	Multi-Industry	16.882	7.325	30
Global Summary	Energy	11.746	4.669	77
Global Summary	Service	15.114	10.275	174

ROE   Summary of Variable Over Period: September 1987

		Mean	Std. Dev.	NOBS
Global Summary	**All Sectors**	14.078	10.941	762
United States	Cons. Goods	20.710	9.415	67
United States	Capital Equip.	12.421	6.238	60
United States	Finance	17.216	6.455	20
United States	Materials	15.108	5.421	44
United States	Multi-Industry	14.219	4.183	16
United States	Energy	11.450	4.352	55
United States	Service	16.031	8.712	86
United Kingdom	Finance	41.155	43.652	11
United Kingdom	Materials	17.977	4.606	27
United Kingdom	Cons. Goods	19.319	7.040	34
United Kingdom	Capital Equip.	19.691	16.441	32
United Kingdom	Service	21.323	13.227	39
United Kingdom	Multi-Industry	19.926	8.809	14
United Kingdom	Energy	13.552	4.925	8
Japan	Capital Equip.	5.643	2.647	77
Japan	Materials	9.400	6.983	30
Japan	Cons. Goods	7.599	4.132	70
Japan	Service	8.561	5.227	49
Japan	Finance	7.922	2.499	9
Japan	Energy	11.879	5.421	14

Return on Equity

ROE   Summary of Variable Over Period: December 1987

		Mean	Std. Dev.	NOBS
Global Summary	**All Sectors**	14.506	11.241	790
United States	All Sectors	16.330	8.320	351
United Kingdom	All Sectors	21.298	16.690	172
Japan	All Sectors	7.733	4.841	267

ROE   Summary of Variable Over Period: December 1987

		Mean	Std. Dev.	NOBS
Global Summary	**All Sectors**	14.506	11.241	790
Global Summary	Cons. Goods	15.760	10.448	174
Global Summary	Capital Equip.	11.047	9.867	177
Global Summary	Finance	22.131	26.448	40
Global Summary	Materials	14.553	6.988	110
Global Summary	Multi-Industry	16.988	6.877	32
Global Summary	Energy	12.038	4.486	77
Global Summary	Service	15.587	10.949	180

ROE   Summary of Variable Over Period: December 1987

		Mean	Std. Dev.	NOBS
Global Summary	**All Sectors**	14.506	11.241	790
United States	Cons. Goods	22.155	10.451	68
United States	Capital Equip.	12.685	6.929	60
United States	Finance	17.840	5.979	20
United States	Materials	15.684	5.617	46
United States	Multi-Industry	14.294	4.883	17
United States	Energy	12.152	4.193	54
United States	Service	17.289	8.496	86
United Kingdom	Finance	41.580	43.544	11
United Kingdom	Materials	18.978	5.518	29
United Kingdom	Cons. Goods	20.075	7.262	34
United Kingdom	Capital Equip.	19.759	15.283	37
United Kingdom	Service	21.804	15.508	39
United Kingdom	Multi-Industry	20.042	7.504	15
United Kingdom	Energy	12.990	5.010	7
Japan	Capital Equip.	5.789	2.574	80
Japan	Materials	9.400	6.506	35
Japan	Cons. Goods	7.684	4.811	72
Japan	Service	8.517	5.200	55
Japan	Finance	7.895	2.456	9
Japan	Energy	11.253	5.045	16

Index